FIRMS, ORGANIZATIONS AND CONTRACTS

A Reader in Industrial Organization

Edited by

Peter J. Buckley
Jonathan Michie

OXFORD UNIVERSITY PRESS

OXFORD
UNIVERSITY PRESS

Great Clarendon Street, Oxford OX2 6DP

Oxford University Press is a department of the University of Oxford.
It furthers the University's objective of excellence in research, scholarship,
and education by publishing worldwide in

Oxford New York

Athens Auckland Bangkok Bogotá Buenos Aires Calcutta
Cape Town Chennai Dar es Salaam Delhi Florence Hong Kong Istanbul
Karachi Kuala Lumpur Madrid Melbourne Mexico City Mumbai
Nairobi Paris São Paulo Singapore Taipei Tokyo Toronto Warsaw

with associated companies in Berlin Ibadan

Oxford is a registered trade mark of Oxford University Press
in the UK and in certain other countries

Published in the United States
by Oxford University Press Inc., New York

Introduction and compilation
© Peter Buckley and Jonathan Michie 1996

First published 1996
Paperback edition reprinted 1997, 1999

3 2280 00705 4380

British Library Cataloguing in Publication Data

Data available

Library of Congress Cataloging in Publication Data

Data available

ISBN 0-19-877435-4
ISBN 0-19-877436-2 (Pbk)

Printed in Great Britain
on acid-free paper by
Biddles Ltd., Guildford and King's Lynn

Preface and Acknowledgements

The benefits of having the present collection of articles brought together in one volume had been clear to both editors for some time as a result of our having taught courses whose reading lists have consisted largely of the articles reproduced here. There is of course a huge saving of time and effort on everyone's part in being able to refer students to a single volume rather than to a reading list of individual articles, some of which are often surprisingly difficult to aquire. But the benefit of having these readings brought together is far more than simply convenience. The exercise helps focus attention on the contribution which this whole literature on the economics of contracts and industrial organization has made, of which the articles reproduced here are of course merely a selected few. Seeing the articles together dramatizes the links, the common themes, the differences, and the remaining gaps. We are therefore grateful for discussions on this material to our past students, especially those from the Management Studies Tripos and Management Studies Diploma at Cambridge, and MBA and Doctoral students from the University of Bradford Management Centre and the University of Leeds.

While for some time, therefore, we have thought that it would be useful if someone were to publish a collection such as this, the impetus for the two of us to do it came from our collaboration on the Economic and Social Research Council's 1992-97 research programme on Contracts and Competition, of which Michie was Director and Buckley an award holder. We are therefore also grateful to our colleagues on this programme for many illuminating discussions, as well as to the ESRC. While in no way wishing to implicate them in our choice of readings or introductory remarks, we are particularly grateful to Martin Cave, Malcolm Chapman, Simon Deakin, Alan Hughes, Peter Nolan, John Vickers, David Vines and Frank Wilkinson. Ronald Coase has shown a continuing interest in the work of the Contracts and Competition research programme; we are grateful to him for this and also for kindly contributing the Foreword to this volume.

If these were the 'pull' factors that lead us to undertake the job of bringing this collection together, the 'push' factor was undoubtedly David Musson, Oxford University Press's commissioning editor for management and business, who offered thoughtful and helpful comment and advice throughout. We are grateful to him and also to Donald Strachan and Jenni Scott who admirably oversaw much of the work at OUP.

Preface and Acknowledgements

We are of course indebted to a large number of other colleagues and friends for discussions in seminars, conferences and in other settings over the years, and in particular to our colleagues at our respective academic institutions.

Finally, it is appropriate that the importance of learning as an activity within firms does emerge from the literature which this volume reports as a vital element missing in much of economics. We have both learned a lot as a result of OUP suggesting that we edit this collection, and not just about the academic subject but also about the amount of editorial work involved in producing a Reader. The task would appear a simple one, of choosing the readings and writing an introduction. Appearances can be deceptive. Personally we have enjoyed the hours spent reading and re-reading dozens of possible articles, although inevitably this is the sort of work which gets pushed into evenings and weekends, so we should thank our families for their patience: in the case of Buckley, Ann, eleven-year-old Alice, and seven-year-old Thomas; and in the case of Michie, Carolyn, plus six-year-old Alex, and nought-year-old Duncan.

Peter J. Buckley
Jonathan Michie
December 1995

....

Acknowledgements

Nicholas Kaldor, 'The Equilibrium of the Firm', *Economic Journal* 44 (1934), pp. 60–76. Reprinted with the permission of Blackwell Publishers.

Ronald Coase, 'The Nature of the Firm', *Economica* 4 (1937), pp. 386–405. Reprinted with the permission of Blackwell Publishers.

George Richardson, 'The Organization of Industry', *Economic Journal* (1972), pp. 883–96. Reprinted with the permission of Blackwell Publishers.

A. A. Alchian and H. Demsetz, 'Production, Information and Economic Organization', *American Economic Review* Vol. 62, (1972), pp. 777–95. Reprinted with permission of the American Economic Association.

M. C. Jensen, W. H. Meckling, 'The Theory of the Firm: Managerial Behaviour, Agency Costs and Ownership Structure' in *Journal of Financial*

Economics (1976), pp. 305–360. Reprinted with permission of Elsevier Science S.A., Switzerland.

Oliver E. Williamson, 'Transaction-Cost Economics: The Governance of Contractual Relations', *Journal of Law and Economics* XXII, No. 2, (1979), pp. 233–61. Reprinted with permission. Copyright © 1979 by the University of Chicago.

Oliver Hart, 'An Economist's Perspective on the Theory of the Firm' originally appeared at 89 *Columbia Law Review* 1757 (1989). Reprinted by permission.

David M. Kreps, 'Corporate Culture and Economic Theory', in *Technological Innovation and Business Strategy* (1986) ed. by M. Tsuchiya. Reprinted with the permission of Nihon Keizai Shimbun, Inc.

P. Mariti and R. H. Smiley, 'Cooperative Agreements and the Organization of Industry', *Journal of Industrial Economics* 31 (1983), pp. 437–51. Reprinted with the permission of Blackwell Publishers.

K. Imai and H. Itami, 'Interpretation of Firm and Market'. Reprinted from *International Journal of Industrial Organization*, pp. 285–310 (1984) with the kind permission of Elsevier Science B.V., Amsterdam, The Netherlands.

Keith Blois, 'Vertical Quasi-Integration', *Journal of Industrial Economics* 20 (1972), pp. 253–72. Reprinted with the permission of Blackwell Publishers.

Stewart Macaulay, 'Non-Contractual Relations in Business: A Preliminary Study'. Material in public domain.

Ronald Dore, 'Goodwill and the Spirit of Market Capitalism', *British Journal of Sociology*, Vol. 34, No. 4, pp. 459–82. Reprinted with permission of Routledge.

Reprinted from 'Joint Ventures and Interorganizational Interdependence' by Jeffrey Pfeffer and Phillip Nowak published in *Administrative Science Quarterly* Vol. 21, No. 3 (September 1976) by permission of *Administrative Science Quarterly*. Copyright © 1976 by Cornell University.

Peter J. Buckley and Mark Casson, 'Joint Ventures'. Reprinted from *Enterprise and Competitiveness* by Mark Casson (1990) by permission of Oxford University Press.

Raymond E. Miles and Charles C. Snow, 'Organizations: New Concepts for New Forms'. Copyright 1986 by The Regents of the University of California. Reprinted from the *California Management Review*, Vol. 28, No. 3. By permission of The Regents.

William G. Ouchi, 'Markets, Bureaucracies, and Clans'. Reprinted from *Administrative Science Quarterly* Vol. 25, No. 1 (March 1980) by permission of *Administrative Science Quarterly*. Copyright © 1980 by Cornell University.

Paul Milgrom and John Roberts, 'Economic Theories of the Firm: Past, Present and Future', *Canadian Journal of Economics*, Vol. 21 (1988), pp. 444–58. Reprinted by permission of the *Canadian Journal of Economics*.

Contents

Contents

List of Contributors

Armen A. Alchian	Professor of Economics, University of California, Los Angeles
K. J. Blois	Fellow of Templeton College, Oxford
Peter Buckley	Professor of International Business, University of Leeds
Mark Casson	Professor of Economics, University of Reading
R. H. Coase	Professor in the Law School, University of Chicago
Harold Demsetz	Professor of Economics, University of California, Los Angeles
Ronald Dore	Research Fellow at the Centre for Economic Performance, London School of Economics and Adjunct Professor, Department of Political Science, Massachusetts Institute of Technology
Oliver Hart	Professor of Economics, Harvard University
Ken-ichi Imai	Professor in the Graduate School of Commerce, Hitotsubashi University
Hiroyuki Itami	Professor in the Graduate School of Commerce, Hitotsubashi University
Michael C. Jensen	Professor of Economics, Harvard Business School
Nicholas Kaldor	Former Professor of Economics, University of Cambridge
David M. Kreps	Professor of Economics at the Graduate School of Business, Stanford University
Stewart Macauley	Law School, University of Wisconsin
P. Mariti	Faculty of Political Science, University of Pisa
William H. Meckling	Dean Emeritus, Simon Graduate School of Business Administration, University of Rochester
Raymond E. Miles	Former Dean at the Haas School of Business, University of California, Berkeley
Paul Milgrom	Professor of Economics, Stanford University
Phillip Nowak	Planning Economist, Contra Costa County
William G. Ouchi	Professor, Anderson Graduate School of Management, University of California, Los Angeles
Jeffrey Pfeffer	Professor, Graduate School of Business, Stanford University
G. B. Richardson	Former Warden of Keble College and former Secretary to the Delegates, Oxford University Press

List of Contributors

John Roberts	Lovelace Professor of Economics, Graduate School of Business, Stanford University
R. H. Smiley	Dean of the Graduate School of Management, University of California at Davis
Charles C. Snow	Pennsylvania State University
Oliver E. Williamson	Professor of Economics, Business and Law at the University of California, Berkeley

Foreword

The editors of *The Economics of Contracts and Industrial Organization* have put us in their debt by compiling an extremely valuable collection of articles on a subject the importance of which has only recently been recognized. However, work on it is now going on apace in many countries and the issue of this book of readings is therefore timely.

What is this new subject? Williamson called it 'the new institutional economics' or 'transaction cost economics' and its scope is well described by the title of this book. The articles in Part I, 'The Theory of the Firm', tell us about the origin and development of the ideas that were to produce 'transaction cost economics'. In my article 'The Nature of the Firm' (published in 1937) I introduced the concept of transaction costs and the dichotomy of co-ordination through the market and within the firm. For reasons that are not altogether clear to me, it was not until the 1970s and 1980s that the subject came alive again. What followed in those years was the very influential series of articles reprinted in Part I that carried the analysis well beyond my earlier formulation. Ambiguities were removed, errors corrected, new concepts introduced. The articles in Part II, Markets and Industrial Organization, and III, Joint Ventures, Networks, Clans and Alliances, carried the story forward. In them the focus is expanded and new questions are raised. The importance of such factors as reputation, the organization form, relationships outside contract and inter-firm agreements of various kinds, is demonstrated. These articles make clear that we have travelled far from a simple choice between the firm and the market, and that what we have to understand is the functioning of an intricate interrelated institutional structure about which we are extremely ignorant. Dispelling this ignorance will be an immense task, but, in carrying it out, the guidance provided by the articles in this book of readings will be of the greatest help.

Ronald Coase

Introduction and Overview

....

Peter Buckley and Jonathan Michie

The literature contained and reviewed in this volume represents a strand of intellectual endeavour that has a broad relevance. The concepts it raises have widespread applications, particularly to business behaviour and the planning of corporate strategy. The practical scope of its application covers:

- the 'make or buy' decision of firms,
- vertical links between firms,
- horizontal integration and internalization decisions,
- the use of subcontracting and co-operative forms of doing business,
- alternative governance structures in firms,
- foreign market servicing and sourcing decisions in the internationalization of firms,
- the internal management processes of firms (including teamwork and business process re-engineering),
- the organizational architecture adopted by companies, and
- accounting practice and cost control.

Each of these applications is briefly treated below.

This extensive list suggests that this volume should be of interest not only to those academics, practitioners, and students who define themselves as economists, but also to those involved with corporate planning, business strategy, international business, organizational behaviour, human resource management, finance, and accountancy. Many of these readings are suitable for MBA courses and modules for which students need to display a fundamental grasp of key concepts. The study of industrial organization in its modern form has transcended its former attachment to 'structure–conduct–performance' models; it now demonstrates a rather more eclectic choice of method (including, importantly, game-theoretic approaches) and scope. The introduction of institutionalist, evolutionary, and critical perspectives makes this field an important linchpin of management studies in their most rigorous form. The following section illustrates these points by touching on some applications of the basic concepts.

....

Applications

The 'make or buy' decision is fundamental to business planning, since the overall composition of all such decisions determines **the scope of the firm**. The boundary of the firm is set by the point at which organizing a transaction internally is marginally more costly than buying in the necessary good or service. The scope of the firm is thus set by the costs of contracting. This fundamental insight was articulated by Ronald Coase in 1937 (Chapter 2 below). Coase's insight also has ramifications for other managerial concerns, from accounting to internal organizational architecture and governance structures, as we shall see.

An important development from Coase's seminal article is represented by Richardson's (1972) article on 'The Organisation of Industry' (Chapter 3). Richardson cogently and persuasively made the point that 'market' and 'firm' are not opposing terms but extreme points on a continuum running from 'pure market' to 'pure firm' with many intermediate states in between—firm-like markets or market-like firms. This analysis was taken up by Imai and Itami in 1984 (Chapter 10 below). These intermediate states represent an important challenge for analysis; they encompass most of the observable, empirical world.

The changes in state that we observe in the business world—from firm to market or from market to firm—are a major component of **business strategy.** The direction in which a firm grows—by absorbing markets (internalization) or by subcontracting out business (externalization)—is of great interest to business strategists; so, too, are the essential concepts of horizontal integration (doing more of the same), vertical integration (adding a stage in the manufacturing process, either backward, towards raw materials, or forward, towards the market) and conglomerate diversification (controlling an unrelated business). Indeed, modern business strategy research developed, in large part, from studies in American business history propelled by the pioneering research of Alfred Chandler. The readings in this volume provide analytical approaches and empirical detail which are of great relevance to business strategy and business history.

It is not only the relationship between the firm and the market that this volume illuminates. The internal organization of the firm is also very much grist to our mill. Two issues right at the forefront of current debate are analysed here: the governance of the firm and the organization of business processes.

Corporate governance is of central concern in international and national business. Who makes the strategic decisions in firms, how they are made, and who is responsible for their consequences are key problems facing not only firms but also interest groups and government bodies. As well as the external consequences of corporate decision making, managers, in particular, are directly concerned with the implementation of their decisions. Once we move beyond a single-person firm, the business of monitoring workers and making sure that corporate policy is followed become key issues for top management. These issues have been analysed in two important streams of literature. One is principal–agent theory, which concerns the problem of ensuring that subordinates follow the objectives of the organization as a whole, rather than their own divergent objectives (see Chapter 5). The second is the whole issue of the 'costs of governance', which links directly with the literature of transaction costs (Chapter 6).

A further concern in business circles is the **optimum organization** of linked activities within the firm, as the current vogue for 'business process re-engineering' demonstrates. The internal organizational architecture of the firm relies on linking processes that might otherwise remain separated by internal organizational walls. This approach is dependent on building teams, which means that the economic theory of teams is highly relevant. So, too, is the economics of information, since organizational structure depends in large measure on how information is disseminated and used in the organization. Alchian and Demsetz (Chapter 4) and Hart (Chapter 7) tackle these issues in ways that shed a great deal of light on the re-engineering debate.

Students in **international business** will also find much of interest in this volume. The economics of contracts and industrial organization, for example, is crucial to the analysis of the foreign market servicing strategies of companies. These strategies concern the choice of method of reaching foreign purchasers; broadly, they cover exporting, licensing, and foreign direct investment. Such decisions will be determined in part by the location of value added (home or abroad), but the choice of internal transfer (exports and foreign direct investment) or external transfer (licensing and other contractual methods) is central to international business strategy. Right at the forefront of international business theory currently is the explication of international joint ventures and alliances. These intermediate forms of activity are analysed in Part III by authors who have interestingly different perspectives on what constitutes the correct form of analysis and explanation.

There are exciting developments still to come in the conctractual explanation of international alliances.

The analysis of **alliances between companies** draws directly on the literature of non-contractual relationships between economic agents. It has long been realized that 'simple' market dealings are in fact socially embedded relationships. The pieces by Macaulay and Dore (Chapters 12 and 13) are starting-points on the long road to a full exploration and analytically manageable understanding of these relationships. The notions of goodwill, trust, commitment, and reputation are building-blocks for a fuller and richer analysis of economic and business relationships. The complete story of the balance between co-operation and competition in economic and social activity is beginning to emerge.

A further set of applications arises for **accounting.** Many of the pieces included here address the problem of information within the company. Information is crucial to the 'make or buy' decision, to problems of monitoring effort, to setting strategy, and to the control of costs. The 'correct' interpretation of strategic information for managers, via management accounts, is an essential function of practising accountants. Attempts to characterize the true situation of the firm more accurately have led to activity-based costing and efforts to replicate Japanese practices. The theory of the firm and of industrial organization provides an important framework for the discussion of more exact and useful information presentation.

....

The Readings

Part I: Theory of the Firm

Kaldor's 1934 article on 'The Equilibrium of the Firm' (Chapter 1) called into question the received theory of the firm. No doubt there are some people who would say that any shortcomings in the theory *circa* 1934 have long since been overcome by the advance of economic theory. Nevertheless, Kaldor's dissatisfaction with the tendency of theorists to assume equilibrium conditions is echoed by many of the authors whose readings from the 1980s are contained in this volume. The fact that these authors wrote largely from outside what would strictly be seen as 'economics' may be of significance. Currently, much of the interesting work on the economics of industrial organization is being done outside the discipline of economics, or mainstream economics at any rate.

Kaldor pointed out that the most fundamental building-block of economics, the supply curve, is dependent on a number of assumptions which, he argued, are simply not valid. Certainly, in re-reading this piece, one of the present writers was reminded of his Sixth-Form College teacher's presentation of the idea of the supply curve (back in 1973). The teacher had explained the idea of the demand curve without any problem. He then drew the supply curve, explained its meaning (that higher output would be supplied at a higher price), acknowledged that he did not necessarily expect anyone in the class to believe this, since we would no doubt think that higher output could be supplied at a lower price with the spreading of overheads and so forth, but stated that we would in any case just have to accept it. Without this assumption none of the rest of the course, he explained, would make sense.

The assumption that firms face declining marginal productivity and rising marginal costs as they expand output—and hence the assumption of rising supply curves at the aggregate level—has been subject to a variety of critiques over the years. For example:

The chief obstacle against which they have to contend when they want gradually to increase their production does not lie in the cost of production—which, indeed, generally favours them in that direction—but in the difficulty of selling the larger output of goods without reducing the price, or without having to face increased marketing expenses. This necessity of reducing prices in order to sell a larger quantity of one's own product is only an aspect of the usual descending demand curve, with the difference that instead of concerning the whole of a commodity, whatever its origin, it relates only to the goods produced by a particular firm . . .

This method of regarding the matter appears the most natural and that which adheres to the reality of things. (Sraffa 1926: 543; discussed in Michie 1987)

And this was backed up empirically by the findings of Coutts, Godley, and Nordhaus (1978) on mark-up pricing over what would be broadly horizontal cost curves (were that work to be cast in those terms).

This discussion is relevant to the issue raised by Coase in 1937 (Chapter 2 below): why firms are the size they are. The fact that firms exist must mean that there are advantages to be had by performing functions within the boundaries of a firm rather than through market contracting. Thus the question arises, what is it that prevents the market becoming subsumed within one giant, global firm? The assumption in the literature, even before Coase's article, was that indivisibilities, causing rising costs, explain the limitations on the size of the firm; but even in 1934 Kaldor had disputed the logic of this argument, since such indivisibilities would only cause rising costs over certain ranges and 'thus do not explain the limitation upon the size of the firm so long as *all* factors are freely available and all prices are constant'.[1] After dismissing other possible explanations for the existence of a limit on firm size, Kaldor suggested that the one aspect of the received theory which could offer an explanation was the existence of a relatively 'fixed' factor, namely entrepreneurship.

Again, Kaldor's idea of the role played by entrepreneurship in the theory of the firm has reappeared in the subsequent literature in a number of ways (see Prendergast 1996). Kaldor distinguished different meanings within the term 'entrepreneurial function': first, risk or uncertainty bearing, and secondly, management, which itself consists of two things—supervision and co-ordination. The importance of the supervisory role made a massive comeback in the literature with the publication in 1976 of Jensen and Meckling's article on 'The Theory of the Firm' (Chapter 5 below). However, Kaldor doubted that this supervisory role alone could explain the limit on firm size, since there is no necessary reason why there should be diminishing returns to this activity. He suggested that it is the co-ordinating function which could be said to be in relatively fixed supply; but he argued that, since this is 'an *essentially dynamic function*', it is a feature of disequilibrium rather than equilibrium. Thus, far from providing support for the usual representation of an individual firm's cost curve, it renders the cost-function of the individual firm indeterminate, since there can be no equilibrium position which the firm is continually tending to approach.

Coase opened his 1937 article by stating that the necessity for economists to give a clear definition of the word 'firm' follows from the fact pointed out in Kaldor's article that economic theory tends to start with the individual firm rather than with the industry. (Kaldor was also objecting to the tendency to draw conclusions about the industry first and then assume that the individual firm was whatever would be required to produce those conclusions.) Coase set out to deal with Kaldor's more general complaint by stating from the outset that the definition of the firm given in his paper was both realistic and tractable for economists. It was this combination which led to Williamson picking up Coase's analysis and developing from it what is now a huge and growing body of work on transaction-cost analysis (see Chapter 6).

Coase began by pointing out that there is planning within firms: 'If a workman moves from department Y to department X, he does not go because of a change in relative prices, but because he is ordered to do so.' So what determines when market mechanisms will be used and when direct planning? Coase's discussion was set out very much as a logical answer to the question; almost as a hypothesis to be tested against empirical evidence. And in a sense it is this testing which has been undertaken by Williamson and others. Thus Coase pointed out that it is not a simple case of 'either/or': 'Of course, the degree to which the price mechanism is superseded varies greatly.

. . . In the Lancashire cotton industry, a weaver can rent power and shop-room and can obtain looms and yarn on credit.' Of course, historically, matters were not left like this. The bringing together within factories of labourers who were still left largely to their own devices, as in Coase's example, led to a second stage in the development of the factory system. In this stage the labourers' work itself—its direction and pace—was increasingly brought under the control of the capitalist (and/or manager), with as many aspects as possible of the labourer's control over the labour process being consciously stamped out (see Marx 1867 [1995]). This point is an important one, since it suggests that questions such as 'why do firms exist?' can be answered in very different ways from those evident in this collection, despite the diversity that this collection itself contains. Thus a rather different starting-point would be to look historically at how and why firms come into being. This is not to play down the importance or validity of the rather different approaches included here; it is vital to insist on what Coase described as the 'comparatively simple' task of 'definition and clarification'. As argued above, provided the hypotheses put forward appear logical, the task is then to test them against the evidence. This should include a re-reading of existing material in light of the new conceptual framework being suggested, to evaluate the extent to which new insights can be gleaned from existing evidence analysed from new angles. This task should also include the collection of evidence specifically designed to test the new theory.

The point made above, that it is not in reality a simple 'either/or' distinction between firm and market was picked up by Richardson in 1972 (Chapter 3 below). Richardson pointed out that even supposedly 'market' relations will often involve close co-operation and other forms of non-price relations, including legal relations such as shareholdings and long-term contracts. He thus disputed the idea that there are just two ways in which economic activity can be co-ordinated, 'the one, conscious planning, holding sway within firms, the other, the price mechanism, operating spontaneously on the relations between firms and between firms and their customers'. He went on to argue that while he imagined that 'this account of things might be acceptable, as a harmless first approximation, to a large number of economists', it was an incorrect picture of how firms actually operate in 'the market': 'What I have in mind is the dense network of co-operation and affiliation by which firms are inter-related.' Now, Richardson recognized that 'Theories necessarily abstract and it is always easy to point to things they leave out of account', but, he argued, 'I hope to show that the excluded phenomena in this case are of importance and that by looking at industrial reality in terms of a sharp dichotomy between firm and market we obtain a distorted view of how the system works'. If we relate Richardson's approach to Coase's, Richardson explicitly distinguished between two phenomena subsumed within Coase's category 'market': on the one hand, what might be thought of as 'genuinely' market transactions and, on the other hand, a rather different mode of co-ordination, namely, inter-firm cooperation.

Alchian and Demsetz (1972, Chapter 4 below) also saw their work as an extension of Coase's, in this case by adding considerations of team production, team organization, the difficulties of metering outputs, and the problem of shirking as explanations for the existence of the firm.

Alchian and Demsetz's paper is widely known in terms of its discussion of the grocer. 'Telling an employee to type this letter rather than to file that document is like my telling a grocer to sell me this brand of tuna rather than that brand of bread. I have no contract to continue to purchase from the grocer and neither the employer nor the employee is bound by any contractual obligations to continue their relationship.' Now this might suggest that neither Alchian nor Demsetz enjoyed much by way of tenure while they were writing their article, because of course many workers do have various degrees of contractual obligation to continue their relationship with their employer. They may be required to give a certain period of notice, and may possibly even have signed a so-called 'garden leaves' clause whereby, if they do leave their employer, they are then prevented from working for any competitor.[2] Likewise, employers may have various contractual obligations to their employees—to continue their employment, for example, or to make redundancy payments—unless, of course, the employee has been refusing to carry out reasonable instructions at work: hence, indeed, the authority which the employer has in the workplace. It is this authority that Alchian and Demsetz denied: 'It is common to see the firm characterized by the power to settle issues by fiat, by authority, or by disciplinary action superior to that available in the conventional market. This is a delusion. . . . It has no power of fiat, no authority, no disciplinary action any different in the slightest degree from ordinary market contracting between any two people.' They recognized that the firm can fire an employee, but argued that this is analogous to anyone being able to fire their grocer by ceasing to purchase from that shop. But the two processes are, of course, vastly different, as indicated, for example, by studies demonstrating the effects of redundancy on the individual, which often include mental and physical ill-health, or even suicide (Burchell 1992).

The point here is not to dramatize or be emotive, but to give substance to what for most people is the authority which their firm or their manager has. Certainly, if enough people decided to 'sack' their grocer then the grocer might go out of business and might even suffer the same personal consequences as workers who have been sacked. But this does not suggest that the relationship between the market customer and the grocer is the same as that between an employer and an employee. Rather, it suggests that the power which an employer (or a firm) has is not unique: others can also try to play that game. If a grocer's customers group together to bring pressure to bear then this might indeed have an effect. In the case of the self-employed grocer it could force them into bankruptcy; in the case where the grocer's shop is part of a large chain, the pressure which the customers bring to bear, proxying the power of an employer over an employee, will in fact take precisely this form, with the parent company sacking that grocer—due to the poor business being done—and replacing them with someone else.

Alchian and Demsetz's point in making these assertions was to suggest a rationale for the existence of the firm other than that it gives power over employees. For them, the key point about a firm was that it involves a team productive process with a centralized contractual agent. This gives a framework within which the concepts of shirking and metering become key. Certainly these issues are important one. In fact, they have been analysed by a number of writers, often using different terms but with the same central question: how is activity within the firm so organized as to maximize productivity? However, by appearing to dismiss the role played by authority, the discussion of how the process of organizing production actually takes place comes to appear rather artificial, as if nothing is ever done unless it is— and is believed subjectively by everyone involved to be—in the best interest of all individuals concerned.[3] Alchian and Demsetz's story was that bringing workers together in teams within a firm gives the potential to raise productive efficiency, thus making everyone better off, but that the extent to which this potential is realized in practice depends on the degree to which rewards can be linked to output, thus encouraging productivity. Thus they dismissed the textbook view that workers are paid according to their marginal productivity, on the grounds that this simply assumes the existence of mechanisms both to measure this productivity and then to actually make such an allocation. They denied that such mechanisms will necessarily be in place, and argued that a key task for firms is to try to introduce such mechanisms, since this will lead to increased productivity as workers seek to gain the resulting rewards. They thus asserted that the direction of causation is from rewards to productivity, rather than vice versa as in the textbooks. Note, though, that their argument is quite different from an efficiency wage one, where increased wages may lead to increased productivity without formally being tied to such a result. Indeed, it may be that by forcing through an increase in wages, workers oblige the firm to increase productivity, whether by improved management practices or by upgrading their productive processes. For Alchian and Demsetz, workers will only increase productivity if they see that this will bring a reward in terms of higher wages. In reality, productivity may be increased by improved management practices or by increased investment in the latest machinery, regardless of the views of the workers. But there may still be a link between rewards and productivity, since an increase in wages may have forced management to achieve an increase in productivity somehow.

While we have suggested that Alchian and Demsetz may have been too sweeping in their denial of the role of authority within real firms, their assumption is nevertheless helpful in thinking through some rather different questions: on the one hand, why do firms exist and how do they behave, and on the other hand, why should firms exist and how should they behave? While their assumption does not accord with the actual historical develop-ment and behaviour of firms—our first set of questions above—it does highlight the following question: leaving aside the historical and institutional context within which firms actually came to dominate society's productive activities, and leaving aside the fact that firms may not in practice operate with the sole goal of exploiting the opportunities which firm organization offers for the mutual benefit of all concerned, what are those opportunities? Do they give a convincing explanation of why organizing in firms would be a good idea even if it were not at present being done? And how could these opportunities best be realized? Alchian and Demsetz's article is a classic discussion of these questions (even if it is not quite phrased in this way).

In practice, though, there may be a variety of ways in which firms' revenues are divided and the various work tasks shared out, each of which may represent different relative benefits for owners, managers, and workers (as well as for different divisions within these three categories). The solution which provides the 'general' maximization of incomes may not be the same as that which maximizes the outcome for any one of these three groups. Thus the split of the revenues, once other costs have been covered, between owners, managers, and workers might, under four different scenarios, be, respectively: 5, 3, 3; 3, 5, 3; 3, 3, 5; or 4, 4, 4. The last of these would maximize the joint revenues, but is the only one of the four outcomes which no one will seek to pursue: the owners will seek the first, the managers the second, and the workers the third. Of course, it is possible to construct a scenario in which one or more of these groups would decide that the risk of ending up with a '3' was not worth taking, and might seek the fourth option, offering to compensate the group that might otherwise have got a '5'. Equally, however, it is possible to imagine that no such scenario would emerge. Whether or not the generally preferred solution will be achieved will depend on the political and institutional environment and arrangements.

The split between owners and managers was analysed by Jensen and Meckling in 1976 (Chapter 5 below). They discussed agency costs and focused on the behavioural implications of the property rights specified in the contracts between the owners and managers of the firm. They began by pointing out that

While the literature of economics is replete with references to the 'theory of the firm', the material generally subsumed under that heading is not a theory of the firm but actually a theory of markets in which firms are important actors. The firm is a 'black box' operated so as to meet the relevant marginal conditions with respect to inputs and outputs, thereby maximizing profits, or more accurately, present value.

Jensen and Meckling explicitly situated their discussion of agency costs and the importance of these to the theory of the firm as bearing a close relationship to the problems of shirking and monitoring of team production discussed by Alchian and Demsetz. However, they played down the importance of team production and emphasized instead the essential nature of contractual relations, which they defined as 'simply one form of legal fiction which serves as a nexus for contracting relationships'. Whether there is really no more to the 'black box' that is the firm than a nexus of contracts is called into question by almost all the readings reproduced in Parts II and III of this volume.

While the last three readings discussed all cited Coase and to some extent positioned their contributions in relation to Coase's 1937 article, it was Williamson (1975, 1979 [Chaper 6 below], 1985) who really set about trying to put meat on the bones of Coase's transaction costs. Williamson (Chapter 6) acknowledged that there is some scepticism about the use of transaction cost analysis, citing as typical Fischer's (1977) comment that 'Transaction costs have a well-deserved bad name as a theoretical device . . . [partly] because there is a suspicion that almost anything can be rationalized by invoking suitably specified transaction costs.' However, Williamson considered that a 'general consensus' appeared to be developing on the following four general propositions: first, that opportunism (which he defined as 'self-interest seeking with guile') is a central concept in the study of transaction costs; secondly, that opportunism is especially important for economic activity that involves transaction-specific investments in human and physical capital; thirdly, that the efficient processing of information is an important and related concept; and fourthly, that the assessment of transaction costs is a comparative institutional undertaking.

Hart's 1989 discussion of the theory of the firm (Chapter 7 below) echoed many of the above authors by stating that

most formal models of the firm are extremely rudimentary, capable only of portraying hypothetical firms that bear little relation to the complex organizations we see in the world. Furthermore, theories that attempt to incorporate real world features of corporations, partnerships and the like often lack precision and rigor, and have therefore failed, by and large, to be accepted by the theoretical mainstream.

Kaldor and Coase were making such complaints in the 1930s; Richardson in the 1970s; Hart in 1989. Hart's particular offering was a property rights-based theory of the firm, an approach he explicitly chose in contrast to Jensen and Meckling. He saw this approach as being very much in the spirit of the transaction cost literature associated with Coase (and Williamson), but differed by focusing on the role of physical, i.e. nonhuman, assets in the contractual relationship. He also saw it as representing an advance on what he termed 'neoclassical' theory (by which he meant neoclassical theory before the various theoretical developments of the 1970s on, discussed above). Thus:

> We now have the basic ingredients of a theory of the firm. In a world of transaction costs and incomplete contracts, ex post residual rights of control will be important because, through their influence on asset usage, they will affect ex post bargaining power and the division of ex post surplus in a relationship. . . . Hence, when contracts are incomplete, the boundaries of firms matter in that these boundaries determine who owns and controls which assets.

The advantage to a firm of producing in-house rather than buying through the market is that in-house it can control production and, for example, increase the supply of components if demand rises without having to renegotiate a contract with a supplier. This, then, represents an incentive to expand the size of the firm, possibly, for example, by buying-up component suppliers. Hart concluded with the hope that over the coming years the best aspects of all the above-discussed approaches would be drawn on to develop a more comprehensive and realistic theory of the firm.

Part II: Markets and Industrial Organization

In 1990, Kreps wrote that until recently 'economists had very little to say of any substance concerning the role of organizations' (Chapter 8 below). However, following on from the literature on the theory of the firm collected in Part I of this volume, Kreps's paper aims to give a definite role to organization and to culture within the organization, defining a firm as 'an intangible asset carrying a reputation that is beneficial for efficient transactions, conferring that reputation upon whoever currently owns the asset'. Kreps distinguishes between two types of transaction—hierarchical and specified. In a specified transaction all terms are spelled out in advance. In a hierarchical transaction 'certain terms are left unspecified; what is specified is that one of the two parties has, within broad limits, the contractual right to specify how the contract will be fulfilled'. Note the analogy with the argument that a firm gives the manager the right (within broad limits) to direct workers to undertake tasks, even though these specific tasks will not have been agreed beforehand in a contract. But what Kreps goes on to stress is the authority that derives not from ownership, but from reputation. Herein lies the importance of corporate culture: the firm becomes the reputation-bearer, and in some cases reputation may be the only way to effect a transaction.

Mariti and Smiley also situated their 1983 analysis of industrial organization within the framework of Coase's distinction between organizing economic activity internally or externally, as well as of Williamson's distinction between interactions within the marketplace and mergers (Chapter 9 below). Against either of the alternatives posed by these authors, Mariti and Smiley investigated 'an intermediate form of interrelationship between firms, which provides yet another way of organizing economic activity, the co-operative agreement'. By a co-operative agreement they meant any long-term, explicit agreement between two or more firms. While acknowledging the contributions of Richardson and of Blois (1972, see Chapter 11 and the following discussion) they argued that this third option had received almost no attention in the academic literature, and it was this deficiency which their paper was intended to correct.

The existence of a strict dichotomy between markets and organization was also called into question by Imai and Itami in 1984 (Chapter 10 below). They did not discuss the third option of co-operation, but rather analysed the way in which the two alternatives[4] interpenetrate each other in practice, with market principles penetrating into the firm's resource allocation, and organization principles creeping into market allocations. They found that such interpenetration patterns are different in the two countries they analysed—the USA and Japan—due to institutional, economic, and societal differences. Broadly, US organizations have more market-like elements, while Japanese market allocation has more organization-like elements. These differences in turn affect corporate behaviour in the two countries in terms of diversification strategy, corporate financing, and innovation. However, even Imai and Itami distinguished the framework of co-operative relationships among firms in Japan—Mariti and Smiley's third way—from 'pure' market transactions. Indeed, they referred to such co-operative relationships as leading to 'intermediate organization'. However, on this theme of the firm/market dichotomy, and whether a third way needs to be included in our conceptualization, Imai and Itami would draw different conclusions for each country, seeing US industrial organization as relatively bipolarized, and intermediate organizations playing a more significant role in Japan than in the USA.

The concept of vertical co-operation, discussed by Imai and Itami, was analysed in more detail in 1972 by Blois (Chapter 11 below). Blois discussed the conditions under which a supplier can become dependent on a single customer, and the ways in which a large customer is able to assert its influence over a supplier. In particular, such a large customer will consider the possibility of gaining the advantages of vertical integration—a situation that Blois characterized in the title of his paper 'vertical quasi-integration'.

However, even within this single example of a firm's relations with a supplier, the analytical framework which has emerged repeatedly in this Introduction is of relevance. On the one hand, we have a market/firm dichotomy posed by the choice to 'make or buy' and, on the other hand, we find co-operative relations developing between the customer and the supplier (a 'third way'). Echoing Imai and Itami's paper, the degree to which, in practice, customer–supplier relations are 'hands on' rather than 'arms length' will vary between countries. Britain, for example, is usually characterized as relying on arms-length relations, while German companies are said to have closer working relations with their suppliers.

The theme of the nature and use of contracts runs throughout this volume, from the definition of what a firm is, through the question of when to contract out and when to keep in-house, to the nature of any contractual relations entered into. This theme is the explicit focus of Macaulay's 1963 article (Chapter 12 below), which investigated when the gains to firms from using contracts outweigh the costs, and hence analysed the circumstances under which business relations will be contractual or non-contractual. He found that relatively non-contractual practices are common, since in most situations contracts are not needed; it is when there is a likelihood that significant problems will arise that contracts tend to be used.

The last paper in Part II is Dore's 1983 discussion of the phenomenon of 'obligated relational contracting' found between Japanese firms (Chapter 13 below). This involves long-term trading relations in which goodwill (with 'give-and-take') is expected to temper the pursuit of self-interest, although this and other labour market practices have since come under strain, especially following the relatively slow economic growth of the early and mid-1980s. Dore argued that such relations are more common in Western economies than is generally recognized. While it may be objected that relational contracts lead to price-distortions and hence to a loss of allocative efficiency, they do lead to high levels of other kinds of efficiency. Specifically, 'the relative security of such relations encourages investment in supplying firms', 'the relationships of trust and mutual dependency make for a more rapid flow of information', and 'a by-product of the system is a general emphasis on quality'. This discussion links back to a number of the other papers, including Richardson in Part I and Mariti and Smiley in Part II. Dore cites Macaulay's paper as demonstrating that relational contracting is indeed valued by firms in the USA as well as in Japan. The circumstances for, and consequences of the development of such long-term relations into actual joint ventures, networks, and clans are analysed in the papers reproduced in Part III of this volume.

Part III: Joint Ventures, Networks, Clans and Alliances

In 1976, Pfeffer and Nowak (Chapter 14 below) noted the variety of inter-organizational linkages, including the forms of contractual and non-contractual relations analysed by Macaulay (whom they cite). In an attempt to understand such phenomena, they chose to analyse one particular type of interorganizational linkage, namely joint ventures among domestic corporations. (Co-operation in international business is analysed explicitly in the following paper, by Buckley and Casson.) Pfeffer and Nowack found that organizations will establish joint ventures in an attempt to reduce the uncertainty that is otherwise created by the competitive and symbiotic interdependence of firms operating in the same environment—when there is resource interdependence, for example.

Buckley and Casson (Chapter 15 below) asked to what extent co-operative ventures really are co-operative, and what 'exactly is meant by *co-operation* in this context?' Their definition of co-operation is 'co-ordination effected through mutual forbearance'. In the context of the present volume, this may be a useful way of thinking about the various contributions on the themes of both co-ordination and co-operation. One method of co-ordination is via the hidden hand of co-ordination through the market; the alternative is to co-operate. As has been demonstrated above, this can be done by bringing the activity within the firm but need not take this route. It may be *interfirm* rather than *intrafirm*: there are the various half-way houses, which we have characterized above as collectively constituting a 'third way'. The specific third way analysed by Buckley and Casson is the 50:50 equity joint venture. One important methodological point that emerges from their discussion is that the conventional assumption that a party's objectives are unchanged by involvement in a co-ordinating venture needs to be relaxed when the concept of commitment is introduced; preferences prove to be endogenous. If nothing succeeds like success, so nothing promotes successful co-operation—and the subjective preference for pursuing co-operative relations further—like successful co-operation.

In 1986 the increased use of joint ventures, subcontracting, and licensing activities across international borders was taken by Miles and Snow (Chapter 16 below) as evidence of the emergence of a new organizational form in industry in response to the new competitive environment of the 1980s. They characterized this new organizational form as 'the dynamic network', 'to suggest that its major components can be assembled and reassembled in order to meet complex and changing competitive conditions'. So once again, the alternative to producing in-house need not necessarily be to buy through the market. Instead there is a third way when faced with the 'make or buy' decision, namely to contract out the work but to create a network to include supplier firms—as well as others, such as distributors.

Our third category in Part III—the clan—was discussed in 1980 by Ouchi (Chapter 17 below), who again saw a third way of mediating and controlling. Building explicitly on the ideas of Coase and Williamson, Ouchi discussed the various costs involved in organizing activities either internally, within a firm, or externally, through the market. If the costs of market transactions are too high then firms will internalize, and if markets are more efficient, then firms will externalize. But if both alternatives—market or firm (or in Ouchi's terminology, 'bureaucracies')—are more costly than a third option, in this case the clan,[5] then this provides an economic case for organizing activities neither through the market nor through the firm, but rather through the clan.

Finally, in 1988 Milgrom and Roberts (Chapter 18 below) discussed the development of the theory of the firm and pointed to what they saw as promising avenues for continuing research. After surveying much of the work discussed above (and referring to many of the papers reproduced in this volume), Milgrom and Roberts argued that 'the incentive-based transaction costs theory has been made to carry too much of the weight of explanation in the theory of organizations'; they expected 'competing and complementary theories to emerge—theories that are founded on economizing on bounded rationality and that pay more attention to changing technology or to evolutionary considerations'.

The papers included in this volume that are not referred to by Milgrom and Roberts would tend to support such a conclusion: the more the firm/market dichotomy is unpicked, or the 'make or buy' decision analysed, the clearer it becomes that the 'market', or the decision to 'buy', are far from simple categories. And one reason for this is that the information collection and processing requirements which would be necessary for them to work in terms of the simple textbook categories are often beyond the limits set in practice by bounded rationality. So the alternative to internalizing is often found to be some 'third way'. However, as demonstrated above, once this 'third way' is investigated it turns out itself to embrace a multitude of phenomena—concepts such as trust and reputation, at one level, which work themselves through at the institutional level to constructs such as joint ventures, networks, or clans.

Conclusions

There are of course a huge number of pieces which we would have liked to have included but which, given space constraints, had to be left out. Faced with the need to select, we decided to start from the 1930s, leaving out Smith, Marx, Marshall, Knight, and others. Even so, there are many writers from our chosen period, including such as Penrose, Chandler, and Simon, who could have been included (and would have been, had space allowed). And then there are whole other literatures that could have constituted additional Parts in such a volume, such as managerial theories of the firm (e.g. Berle and Means, and Marris), work on evolutionary theories of the firm (e.g. Nelson and Winter, Teece, Loasby, and Metcalfe), or work on the internationalization of the firm (e.g. Dunning and Cantwell, and Pavitt and Patel).[6]

One conclusion that does come through clearly from the present collection is the need for an interdisciplinary approach to analysing these issues of industrial organization and explaining the various concepts and practices, from the nature of contracts and contracting to the development of trust and reputation. These issues constitute active research fields within economics, sociology, management studies, law[7] and other disciplines.[8] So the subject is multidisciplinary in a formal sense; the key to taking this research agenda forward may lie in the extent to which it can become multidisciplinary in a more active sense, with individual researchers from different disciplinary backgrounds able to contribute to a common research effort. That of course requires, at a minimum, that we speak to each other, rather than to ourselves, or at others; and this in turn requires a common language. We think that the work included in this volume demonstrates that this can be done.

What also comes across strongly is the range of research methods that has been used to make progress on these issues, both theoretical and empirical (case study and survey work, statistical analysis, and so on). The need for this mix of approaches is well illustrated by Ronald Coase's comments on the papers given at a symposium held on contract economics, when he complained that:

We have tried to discuss contracts in a realistic way, but . . . I couldn't easily discern the relationship between the different chapters . . . we need to have more cross-fertilization, but as was evident from the comments this will not be an easy process. If you look at the various chapters and ask, 'why was it that I couldn't relate what was said in one chapter to what was said in others?' the tentative conclusion I have come to is that most of them were lacking in any empirical content. It was hard to pin down what we were discussing. In fact people from time to time would say 'what are contracts?' and so on, and it was often very hard to know what in practice the concepts that were being employed really meant. (Coase 1992: 333)

Coase goes on to call for more empirical work, including the collection of contracts, 'so that in future we do not have to pretend to know their characteristics and therefore devote ourselves to studying imaginary contracts rather than real ones'. But Coase is certainly not calling for some simple empiricism; he also makes a methodological point about theoretical modelling which, although he doesn't say so himself, would undermine much of the work on economic theory done in this area to date:

I also want to say something else about modelling . . . I think you can be too precise too soon and that this is a situation you are liable to be in when you are very ignorant. And I think that we are very ignorant in this field . . . To have a model that simply incorporates what you know (or think you know) at an early stage may, in fact, by producing results that are very misleading, prevent useful research from taking place . . . I fear that we might be in this sort of condition now where people will produce models in which we ignore what subsequently are discovered to be important aspects of the problem, but which, in the meantime, put us off doing the research necessary to find them. (Coase 1992: 335–6)[9]

Examples of such important aspects might include the concepts of 'knowledge', 'trust', and 'power'. These are surely central to an understanding of contracts and their use, the firm and its operation, and industrial organization more generally, when firms go out into the 'market', but rarely as passive price-takers. Instead we see co-operation, collusion, and various other relationships, including the development of joint ventures, networks, and clans.

Notes

1. Coase additionally argues that since a firm may produce more than one product, there would in any case be no reason for rising cost curves to limit the size of the firm (Coase, 1937, p. 402; this volume, p. 51).
2. The 'garden leaves' clause is so called because if an employee quits, he or she is obliged to spend the next two years (or whatever the specified period) sitting at home watching the garden leaves.
3. In the library copy of Alchian and Demsetz's article used for reference in writing this Introduction, alongside their question 'How can the members of a team be rewarded and induced to work efficiently?', someone had written 'stop exploiting them!!'. Now of course there is not, in fact, any exploitation in the Alchian and Demsetz story—even if output levels from a given group of workers has increased, this can only have happened, in Alchian and Demsetz's world, because it is good for the workers concerned. But this last point is perhaps what provoked

the comment to be added in the margin, since there appears to be no place within this world for issues such as exploitation even to be considered.

4. While the title of Imai and Itami's paper is 'Interpenetration of *Organization* and *Market*' (emphasis added), they make clear that by 'organization' they mean the firm.

5. To describe what he means by a 'clan', Ouchi quotes Durkheim (1933: 365):

> For organic solidarity to exist, it is not enough that there be a system of organs necessary to one another, which in a general way feel solidarity, but it is also necessary that the way in which they should come together, if not in every kind of meeting, at least in circumstances which most frequently occur, be predetermined. . . . Otherwise, at every moment new conflicts would have to be equilibrated. . . . It will be said that there are contracts. But, first of all, social relations are not capable of assuming this juridical form. . . . A contract is not self-sufficient, but supposes a regulation which is as extensive and complicated as contractual life itself. . . . A contract is only a truce, and very precarious, it suspends hostilities only for a time.

> Ouchi goes on to argue that this solidarity to which Durkheim refers 'contemplates the union of objectives between individuals which stems from their necessary dependence upon one another. In this sense, any occupational group which has organic solidarity may be considered a clan. Thus, a profession, a labor union, or a corporation may be a clan . . . '.

6. See Buckley and Ghauri (1993). See also the various contributions to the February 1995 Special Issue of the *Cambridge Journal of Economics*, and in particular those by Cantwell, Fransman and Patel. On the immense contribution to this field by Dunning, see Buckley and Casson (1992).

7. Coase concludes thus on the legal system: 'it is not at all easy to say what the legal system is actually doing. Some of the things it does will lower transaction costs, some of them will raise transaction costs, and the only generalization one can make is that if a change is made it will increase the income of lawyers' (Coase, 1992, p. 33).

8. Williamson (Chapter 6) describes transaction cost economics itself as an interdisciplinary undertaking that 'joins economics with aspects of organization theory and overlaps extensively with contract law'. The 'other disciplines' referred to in the text would include both international business and international management; on the former, see Buckley (1992), and on the relation between these two disciplines, see Buckley (1994).

9. On the legacy of Coase for economic analysis, see Medema (1995).

References

Buckley, P. (ed.) (1992), *New Directions in International Business: Research Priorities for the 1990s*, Aldershot: Edward Elgar.

—— (1994). 'International Business Versus International Management? International Strategic Management from the Viewpoint of Internalisation Theory', *Journal of the Economics of Business*, 1(1): 95–104.

—— and Casson, M. (eds.) (1992), *Multinational Enterprises in the World Economy: Essays in Honour of John Dunning*, Aldershot: Edward Elgar.

—— and Ghauri, P. (eds.) (1993), *The Internationalization of the Firm*, London: Academic Press.

Burchell, B. (1992), 'Changes in the Labour Market and the Psychological Health of the Nation', in J. Michie (ed.), *The Economic Legacy: 1979–1992*, London: Academic Press.

Coase, R. (1992), 'Remarks for a Panel Discussion', in L. Werin and H. Wijkander (eds), *Contract Economics*, Oxford: Blackwell.

Coutts, K., Godley, W., and Nordhaus, W. (1978), *Industrial Pricing in the United Kingdom*, Cambridge: Cambridge University Press.

Durkheim, E. (1933), *The Division of Labor in Society*, (G. Simpson, trans.), New York: Free Press.

Fischer, S. (1977), 'Long-term Contracting, Sticky Prices, and Monetary Policy: Comment', *Journal of Monetary Economics*, 3: 322.

Iwaki, H. (1996), 'Labour Market Mechanisms in Japan', in J. Michie and J. Grieve Smith (eds.), *Creating Industrial Capacity: Towards Full Employment*, Oxford: Oxford University Press.

Marx, K. (1867), *Capital, Volume 1*, London: Lawrence and Wishart (various editions); and Oxford: Oxford University Press, 1995, for an abridged edition.

Medema, S. (1995), *The Legacy of Ronald Coase in Economic Analysis*, 2 vols., Aldershot: Edward Elgar.

Michie, J. (1987), *Wages in the Business Cycle: An Empirical and Methodological Analysis*, London : Frances Pinter.

—— (1994), 'Managing the Public Sector', (review article of P. Taylor-Gooby and R. Lawson, *Markets and Managers: New Issues in the Delivery of Welfare*), *International Review of Applied Economics*, 8(3): 333–5.

—— (1995), 'Institutional Aspects of Regulating the Private Sector', in J. Groenewegen, C. Pitelis, and S.-E. Sjöstrand (eds.), *On Economic Institutions: Theory and Applications*, Aldershot: Edward Elgar.

—— (1996), 'Privatisation and Regulation', in M. Warner (ed.), *International Encyclopedia of Business and Management*, London: Routledge.

Prendergast, R. (1996), 'The Environment for Entrepreneurship', in R. Auty and J. Toye (eds.), *Challenging the Orthodoxies*, Macmillan.

Sraffa, P. (1926), 'The Laws of Returns under Competitive Conditions', *The Economic Journal*, 26(144): 535–50.

Werin, L. and Wijkander, H. (eds.) (1992), *Contract Economics*, Oxford: Blackwell.

Williamson, O. E. (1975), *Markets and Hierarchies*, New York: The Free Press.

—— (1985), *The Economic Institutions of Capitalism*, New York: The Free Press.

I. THEORY OF THE FIRM

Why do we need a theory of the firm? There are various possible answers which are not necessarily mutually exclusive, or even contradictory; the question as to why we need a theory of the firm might be seeking the answer to several different puzzles, each one of which needs to be answered differently. Perhaps the starting point should be to consider how the economic system in which we live can best be analysed, understood and explained. One simple-minded approach would be to start with individuals as rational agents who consume and who may take part in some productive activity, with the behaviour of actual economies then being determined by the sum of the actions of these individuals. This of course begs all sorts of questions regarding aggregation problems and externalities—whereby the outcomes for any one individual will not be determined solely by their choices regarding either consumption or production but will instead be influenced by the actions of other individuals and by the outcome at the 'macro' level of all individual decisions. But these complications need not concern us unduly here. Instead, let us focus on the single idea that the level of output for the economy—the national income—derives from the decisions of individuals to produce. How does this production take place? The answer is that it takes place largely within firms and other organizations. This latter distinction—between firms on the one hand and other organizations on the other—is explored in Sections II and III of this book. This opening Section leaves this distinction largely to one side and focuses instead on the question of the firm itself. If production takes place by individuals deciding to take part in such activity, and if this productive activity takes place largely within things called firms, then what is this thing, the 'firm'? The answer, as the collection of readings in this Section illustrates, is that the term covers a multitude of concepts. Indeed, in one of the seminal works in this area, *The Theory of the Growth of the Firm* (Oxford University

Section I

Press, 1959; third edition, 1995), Edith Penrose described the problem in terms reminiscent of Humpty Dumpty's claim that his words could mean just what he wanted them to, neither more nor less; thus:

A 'firm' is by no means an unambiguous clear-cut entity; it is not an observable object physically separable from other objects, and it is difficult to define except with reference to what it does or what is done within it. Hence each analyst is free to choose any characteristics of firms that he is interested in, to define firms in terms of those characteristics, and to proceed thereafter to call the construction so defined a 'firm'. Herein lies a potential source of confusion . . . (p. 10)

Attempting to define a firm in terms of determinate cost functions is simply inadequate, as pointed out in the first article, from Kaldor, and elaborated on in the piece from Richardson. Of course, simplifying assumptions are necessary for any theorizing to proceed; the mistake in economics is to then make predictions about the output or pricing behaviour of firms on the basis of a model in which everything that is distinctive about a firm has been assumed away. The theory of the firm outlined in the article reproduced from Coase, and taken further by Williamson (including in the piece reproduced in this Section from him), is based on the idea that combining together in firms rather than acting individually will reduce transactions costs.

The role played by information runs as a theme through this Section on the theory of the firm: thus Fransman ('Information, Knowledge, Vision and Theories of the Firm', *Industrial and Corporate Change*, Vol. 3, No. 3, pp. 713–757) shows that the Alchian and Demsetz theory of the firm as joint team production, and the Jensen and Meckling theory of the firm as a nexus of contracts between principals and agents, are derived from the definition of information as data relating to states of the world and the state-contingent consequences that follow from events in the world, plus the assumption that information is unevenly distributed among agents (that is, there is asymmetric information). Fransman also shows that Coase's approach to the firm is essentially an approach based on information-related problems, while Williamson instead sees opportunism as the problem, otherwise the information could just be shared; the point is, though, that unless the information was asymmetric in the first place, the opportunity for withholding or distorting it would not arise. How the theory of the firm has responded to these developments in the literature is surveyed in the Section's concluding piece, by Hart.

1 The Equilibrium of the Firm

Nicholas Kaldor

I

The exploration of the conditions of equilibrium of the individual firm has in recent times occupied to an increasing degree the attention of economists. This, as should be evident, was a necessary development of the so-called 'particular equilibrium' method of analysis developed by Marshall and especially of the conception of the 'supply-curve': the postulation of a definite functional relationship between price and rate of supply in the various industries. The latter, though an integral part of the Marshallian system, was by no means such a straightforward self-evident conception as its counterpart, the demand curve. The reasons for this asymmetry are not far to seek. The assumption that buyers respond to price stimuli in a definite and unequivocal manner (which is all that the demand curve implies) can be deduced from the general proposition that they have a definite system of wants and act in accordance with it; that is to say, it can be directly derived from the general postulates of the subjective theory of value. But the assumption that sellers do the same is a much more complex affair—at any rate in a world where production is carried on on a co-operative basis. It implies that there exists a mechanism which translates technical and psychological resistances into cost computations in such a way that a definite amount of a commodity will be offered by each producing unit in response to any price. It implies, therefore, that there is a definite relationship between the costs incurred and the amount produced for each individual source of supply and between price and the number of such producing units; and finally between price and some derivative of the cost function of the individual producing unit. Briefly then, it assumes two things: perfect competition[1] and the existence of a definite cost function for each firm. (The assumption of perfect competition is, of course, also necessary in the case of the demand curve. But on the demand side this can more or less be treated as a 'datum'—at least in so far as the demand for consumers' goods is concerned[2]—for it follows from the facts that in buying individuals act alone[3] and that the contribution of a single individual to the social income and, thus, his individual spending power, is relatively small. But the nature of the conditions of competition on the supply side, as is now increasingly realized, is itself something to be explained.) In order to arrive at the supply curve for an industry, therefore, it must be shown that corresponding to each price there will be a definite number of firms in the industry and a definite amount produced by each *when all firms are in equilibrium.*[4]

Moreover, the importance attached to the nature of the supply-function in post-Marshallian economics, the division of industries into those of 'increasing,' 'constant' and 'diminishing supply price', and the distinction between 'external' and 'internal' economies, which postulated different cost functions for individual firms and for the aggregate of firms composing the industry, made it more than ever necessary to analyse the conditions of equilibrium for the individual firms *before* any postulates were made about the supply-function of an industry. For only when the necessary functions are found which determine the behaviour of individual firms and some formal conclusions have been arrived at about the forms which these functions can actually take and when the inter-relations of these cost-functions have been analysed, only then can we derive those supply-curves of various shapes which the simple two-dimensional diagram at once suggests to the mind.[5]

II

Marshall realized that it was necessary to describe the mechanism with the aid of which the reactions which the supply-curve exhibits actually come about; and this, I believe, was the reason which led him to the conception of the 'representative firm'. His purpose was therefore not the establishment of a concept which has analytical significance as such, but rather the construction of a mental tool with the aid of which the reaction-mechanism postulated by the supply-curve can be, if not analysed, at least rendered plausible. The 'representative firm' was therefore meant to be no more than a firm which answers the requirements expected from it by the supply-curve. In the words of Mr D. H. Robertson: 'In my view it is not necessary . . . to regard it (i.e. the representative firm) as anything other than a small-scale replica of the supply-curve of the industry as a whole.'[6] In this sentence, I believe, Mr Robertson has admirably summarized the real weakness of the Marshallian concept; perhaps more so than he would himself care to admit. It is just because the 'representative firm' was meant to be nothing more than a small-scale replica of the industry's supply-curve that it is unsuitable for the purpose it has been called into being. Instead of analysing at first the conditions of equilibrium for individual 'firms' and then deriving from them, as far as possible, the conditions of equilibrium for an 'industry', Marshall first postulated the latter and then created a *Hilfskonstruktion* which answered its requirements.

Professor Robbins has shown[7] that Marshall's conception of the representative firm (apart from the defect that it is nowhere in the *Principles* adequately defined) is open to the prima facie objection that it introduces elements which are not consistent with the general assumptions upon which economic theory is based. We are here asked to concentrate our attention upon a particular firm, which, whether it is conceived as one selected from a large number of actual firms or merely some sort of average of all existing firms, is supposed to fulfil a special rôle in the determination of equilibrium in a way which other firms do not. 'There is no more need for us to assume a representative firm or a representative producer than there is for us to assume a representative piece of land, a representative machine or a representative worker.'[8] Professor Robbins' criticism only affects Marshall's particular solution, however; and shows that the kind of short-cut Marshall attempted will not do. It enhances rather than obviates the necessity for analysing the conditions of firm-equilibrium as such.

Since Marshall's time the analysis of the equilibrium of the firm has been carried to a much higher stage of refinement. In one respect, however, later constructions suffer from the same deficiency as Marshall's. They also assume cost-conditions for the individual firms which *fit in* with the postulates made about equilibrium rather than prove how the cost functions of individual sources of supply make possible, under a given system of prices, a determinate equilibrium for the industry. Explicitly or implicitly, the equilibrium of the 'firm' is made dependent upon the equilibrium of the 'industry' rather than the other way round.[9] And although, in this particular branch of economics, attention has more and more concentrated upon the equilibrium of the individual firm,[10] it has never been called into question, so far as the present writer is aware, whether the assumption of a determinate cost-schedule (upon which the whole theory of supply rests) can be derived from the premises upon which static analysis, in general, is based. It is the purpose of the present paper to show that the conception of such a determinate cost-function, obvious and elementary as it may seem, involves unforeseen difficulties as soon as an attempt is made to analyse the factors which actually determine it.

....

III

We propose to start in a roundabout way, by postulating at first the two assumptions on which the Marshallian supply-curve is based: namely, perfect competition[11] and the existence of a definite functional relationship between the costs incurred and the amount produced by the individual firm;[12] and then to examine whether it is possible to find a form for this cost-function which will make these two assumptions compatible with each other. We shall see that an analysis of the factors which determine the form of this cost-curve will lead us to doubt the legitimacy of the concept itself. We shall also see later on that our results retain some interest even after the assumption of perfect competition is dropped.

As is well known, the requirement of the firm's cost-curve under perfect competition is that it must slope upwards after a certain amount is produced[13]—an amount which is small enough to leave a sufficiently large number of firms in the field (for any given total output of the industry) for the conditions of perfect competition to be preserved. For the short-run analysis this presents no difficulties. In the short-run (by definition) the supply of some factors is assumed to be fixed, and as the price of the other (freely variable) factors is given, costs per unit[14] must necessarily rise after a certain point.[15] (This follows simply from the assumption, frequently styled 'the law of non-proportional returns', that the degree of variability of the technical coefficients is less than infinite—which is just another way of saying that there are different kinds of factors.) But such a short-run curve will be hardly sufficient for our purpose. Unless we can assume that the 'fixed factors' are fixed by Nature and not as a result of a previous act of choice (and it is hardly legitimate to make such an assumption in the case of an individual firm), we must again inquire why the 'fixed factors' came to be of such a magnitude as they actually are. The problem of equilibrium again presents itself.

We must start, therefore, at the beginning, i.e. the problem is essentially one of long-run equilibrium. All factors which the firm employs are therefore assumed to be freely variable in supply and all prices to be given. What will be the shape of the cost-curve? Will costs per unit vary with output, and if so, how?

(i) If the assumption of complete divisibility of all factors is dropped we know that cost per unit, for some length at any rate, must necessarily fall. This is due to the fact that with increasing output more and more 'indivisibilities' (actual and potential) are overcome, i.e. *either* the efficiency of the actually employed factors increases *or* more efficient factors are employed whose employment was not remunerative at a smaller output.[16] Given the state of knowledge, however, a point must be reached where all technical economies are realized and costs of production therefore reach a minimum. Beyond this point costs may rise over a certain range, but (if, in accordance with our assumptions, factors continue to be obtainable at constant prices) afterwards they must again fall until they once more reach their minimum at the same level as before. The optimum point can then only be reached for certain outputs, but there is no reason why the successive optimum points should not be on the same level of average costs. Indivisibilities, causing rising costs over certain ranges, thus do not explain the limitation upon the size of the firm so long as *all* factors are freely variable and all prices are constant.

(ii) It has been suggested, alternatively, that there are 'external diseconomies' under which (as pecuniary diseconomies are ruled out by definition) must be meant the limitation upon the supply of such factors as the firm does not directly employ but only indirectly uses. (Cf. Pareto's example of the rising costs to transport agencies owing to traffic congestion.) But such external diseconomies (assuming that they exist) are again not sufficient for our purpose. By definition, they affect all firms equally,[17] and therefore do not explain why the output of the individual firm remains relatively small (the number of firms in the industry relatively large), as they only give a reason why the costs of the industry should be rising, but not why the costs of the individual firm should be rising *relatively to the costs of the industry*. The diseconomies, therefore—in order that they should account for the limitation upon the size of the firm—must be *internal*.

(iii) It follows clearly from these considerations that (as diminishing returns to *all* factors together are not conceivable) the technically optimum size of a productive combination cannot be determined if only the prices of the factors and the production-function of the commodity are known. Knowledge of these only enables us to determine the optimum proportions in which to combine the factors but not the optimum amounts of these factors. In order to determine, therefore, the optimum size of the combination it is necessary to assume that the supply of at least one of the factors figuring in the production-function should be fixed—in which case the 'optimum size' (or at any rate the maximum amount of the product which can be produced at minimum costs) becomes determinate as a result of the operation of the law of non-proportional returns.[18]

Moreover, it is necessary that the factor whose supply is 'fixed' for the firm should at the same time have a flexible supply for the 'industry'—otherwise the industry would have to consist of one firm or at least a fixed number of firms. It is not the case, therefore, of a factor which is rent-yielding for an 'industry' (a special kind of land, for example, which, though its supply for the industry is fixed, must have under the assumption of perfect competition a definite supply-price for the individual firm!), but rather the reverse: a factor which *is* rent-yielding (price-determined) for the firm but has a definite supply-price for the industry. In this case, therefore, the fixity of supply must arise, not from a natural limitation of the amount available, but from a special peculiarity of the firm's production-function; that is to say, there must be *a* factor, of which the firm cannot have 'two' units—just because *only one unit* can do the job.

It has been suggested that there is such a 'fixed factor' for the individual firm even under long-run assumptions—namely, the factor alternatively termed 'management' or 'entrepreneurship'. As it follows from the nature of the entrepreneurial function that a firm cannot have two entrepreneurs, and as the ability of any one entrepreneur is limited, the costs of the individual firm must be rising owing to the diminishing returns to the other factors when applied in increasing amounts to the same unit of entrepreneurial ability. The fact that the firm is a productive combination under a single unit of control explains, therefore, by itself why it cannot expand beyond a certain limit without encountering increasing costs. The rest of this paper will be taken up by a discussion of the problems arising out of this suggestion: what is meant by entrepreneurship as a factor of production? Is its supply really fixed in the long run? And finally, does it justify the construction of a determinate long-run cost-curve of the required form?

....

IV

The term 'entrepreneurship' as a factor of production is somewhat ambiguous—or rather more than ambiguous, possessing as it does at least three distinct meanings. What is generally called the 'entrepreneurial function' can be either (1) risk—or rather uncertainty-bearing; or (2) management, which consists of two things; (a) supervision, (b) co-ordination. The latter two are not generally kept separate, although, in the writer's view, to distinguish between them is essential to an understanding of the problem. 'Supervision' is necessary in the case of co-operative production (where several individuals work together for a common result) in order to ensure that everybody should do the job expected of him—in other words, to see that contracts already entered into should, in fact, be carried out. 'Co-ordination', on the other hand, is that part of the managerial function which determines what sort of contracts should be entered into: which carries out the adjustments to the given constellation of 'data'. Which of these three functions can be considered as having a 'fixed supply' in the long run?

The first of these functions—uncertainty-bearing—can be dismissed offhand, from our point of view. Because whatever measure of uncertainty-bearing it will ultimately be found most convenient to adopt—the theory of risks and expectations is as yet too undeveloped for us to talk about a 'unit' of uncertainty-bearing—it is highly unlikely that it will be found to have a fixed supply for the individual firm. The mere fact that with the rise of joint-stock companies it was possible to spread the bearing of uncertainty over a great number of individuals and to raise capital for an individual firm far beyond the limits of an individual's own possession, excludes that possibility.

Nor is it likely that 'management' possesses these unique characteristics—in so far as this term refers to the function of supervision. Supervising may require a special kind of ability, and it is probable that it is a relatively indivisible factor. It may not pay to employ a 'foreman' for less than fifty men and it may be most economic to employ one for every seventy-five; but is there any reason why it should not be possible to double output by doubling both, foremen and men? An army of supervisors may be just as efficient (provided it consists of men of equal ability) as one supervisor alone.

This is not true, however, with regard to the co-ordinating factor: that essential part of the function of management which is concerned with the allocation of resources along the various lines of investment, with the adjustment of the productive concern to the continuous changes of economic data. You cannot increase the supply of co-ordinating ability available to an enterprise alongside an increase in the supply of other factors, as it is the essence of co-ordination that every single decision should be made on a comparison with all other decisions already made or likely to be made; it must therefore pass through a single brain. This does not imply, of course, that the task of co-ordination must necessarily fall upon a single individual; in a modern business organization it may be jointly undertaken by a whole Board of Directors. But then it still remains true that all the members of that Board will, in all important decisions, have to keep all the alternatives in their minds—in regard to this most essential mental process there will be no division of labour between them—and that it will not be possible, at any rate beyond a certain point, to increase the supply of co-ordinating ability available to that enterprise merely by enlarging the Board of Directors.[19, 20] The efficiency of the supply of co-ordinating ability can be increased by the introduction of new technical devices, e.g. by a better system of accounting; but given the state of technical knowledge and given the co-ordinating ability represented by that enterprise, the amount of 'other factors' which can be most advantageously employed by that enterprise will be limited, i.e. the supply of 'co-ordinating ability' *for the individual firm* is 'fixed'.

It follows from these considerations that for theoretical purposes the most satisfactory definition of a firm is that of a 'productive combination possessing a given unit of co-ordinating ability' which marks it off from 'productive combinations' (such as an 'industry') not possessing this distinguishing peculiarity. It is the one factor which in the long run is 'rigidly attached to the firm', which, so to speak, lives and dies with it; whose remuneration, therefore, is always price-determined.[21, 22] On this definition, firms whose co-ordinating ability changes, while preserving their legal identity, would not remain the same firms; but then all the theoretically relevant characteristics of a firm change with changes in co-ordinating ability. It might as well be treated, therefore, as a different firm.

V

We have found, therefore, that the firm's long-run cost-curve is determined by the fixity of supply of the co-ordinating ability represented by it. Further considerations, however, so far from lending support to the usual representation of this cost-function and the supply-function which is based upon it, lead to the conclusion that this very fact renders the cost-function of the individual firm indeterminate. For the function which lends uniqueness and determinateness to the firm—the ability to adjust, to co-ordinate—is an *essentially dynamic function*; it is only required so long as adjustments are required; and the extent to which it is required (which, as its supply is 'fixed', governs the amount of other factors which can be most advantageously combined with it) depends on the frequency and the magnitude of the adjustments to be undertaken. It is essentially a feature not of 'equilibrium' but of 'disequilibrium'; it is needed only so long as, and in so far as, the actual situation in which the firm finds itself deviates from the equilibrium situation. With every successive adjustment to a given constellation of data, the number of 'co-ordinating' tasks still remaining becomes less and the 'volume of business' which a given unit of co-ordinating ability can most successfully manage becomes greater; until finally, in a full long-period equilibrium (in Marshall's stationary state), the task of management is reduced to pure 'supervision', 'co-ordinating ability' becomes a free good and the technically optimum size of the individual firm becomes infinite (or indeterminate). There is thus no determinate ideal or 'equilibrium' position which a firm is continuously tending to approach, because every approximation to that situation also changes the ideal position to which it tends to approximate. It is not possible, therefore, to derive the firm's cost-function from the economic data: namely, from a given system of prices and a given production-function: because the nature of that production-function, or, rather, the relative position which the factor 'co-ordinating ability' occupies in that production-function, is not given independently of equilibrium, but it is part of the problem of equilibrium itself.[23]

It is possible, of course, that if the frequency and the magnitude of the adjustments to be undertaken remain the same (in other words, the degree to which economic data are changing per unit of time is constant), the theoretically optimum size of the individual firm might remain constant. But even if it were possible to formulate a kind of theory of static-dynamics where, having once found a suitable measure of 'economic change' (a kind of compound variable made up of the degree of variation of all the different data and weighted according to some arbitrary standard), the magnitude of the latter could be assumed to remain constant, the above conclusion by no means follows necessarily. For the 'optimum size' would still be dependent upon the nature of the change and upon the degree to which adjustments to each given constellation of data can be made in a given time (in other words, the degree to which the path actually followed deviates from the 'equilibrium path').[24] Thus the mere introduction of dynamic change does not render the situation any more determinate than it was without it. It might mean, however, that in the actual world, the average size of individual firms will remain more or less the same because the inherent tendency of the size of the firm to expand will be continuously defeated by the spontaneous 'changes of data' which check it.

VI

What conclusions follow, from a theoretical point of view, from these considerations? It follows, first, that under static assumptions[25] (i.e. a given constellation of economic data) there will be a continuous tendency for the size of the firm to grow and therefore *long-period static equilibrium and perfect competition are incompatible assumptions.* Even if conditions of perfect competition obtain in any given situation, that situation cannot become one of equilibrium so long as the conditions of perfect competition remain preserved. It follows, secondly, that the existing organization of the economic system, the division of the productive organization into a great number of independent units under a single control, is essentially one adapted to the existence of dynamic change and imperfect foresight; and therefore the institutional pattern borrowed from a dynamic world cannot readily be applied to a theoretical static society where every kind of dynamic change is absent. It follows, lastly, that all conceptions which are derived from the twin assumptions of a determinate static equilibrium and perfect competition (such as that of a determinate, 'reversible' supply-function) are open to the prima facie objection that they are derived from assumptions which are mutually inconsistent. In fact, the idea of a determinate equilibrium corresponding to each given constellation of 'tastes' and 'obstacles' becomes questionable in a world where the existence of indivisibilities offers advantages for co-operative production.[26]

VII

We started off by inquiring into the cause which makes the cost curve of the individual firm rise relatively to the costs of the industry and thus makes a determinate equilibrium under perfect competition possible. We came to the conclusion that there is no such thing. We now have to drop the assumption of perfect competition and assume, in accordance with the conditions in the real world, that a firm can, at any rate beyond a certain point, influence by its own action the prices of the goods it is buying and selling. The limitation upon the size of the firm no longer presents any problem. It is sufficiently accounted for by the supply and demand curves with which it is confronted. But the element of indeterminateness, which the isolating assumption of perfect competition enabled us to detect, still continues in force when the basic assumption is removed. In so far as the relative place of 'co-ordinating ability' is still not 'given' by the production-function, but depends on, and changes with, the relation of the actual situation to the equilibrium situation, it still remains true that the cost-curve of the individual firm, and consequently its position of equilibrium in relation to a given system of supply and demand curves, is indeterminate.

On closer scrutiny, however, there appears a line of escape for those who believe that the position of equilibrium under imperfect competition is otherwise determinate. 'Co-ordinating ability' may be regarded as a 'fixed' factor, but it is not, or at least it need not be, regarded as an 'indivisible' factor.[27] Although it is not possible to increase the amount of factors applied to a unit of co-ordinating ability beyond a certain limit without loss of efficiency, there is no ground for assuming that there will be 'increasing returns' to the other factors if they are applied in less than a certain amount to a unit of co-ordinating ability.[28] A certain business manager may not be able to manage more than a certain volume of business, in a certain situation, with undiminished efficiency, but why should he not be able to manage *less* equally well?[29] Thus the indeterminateness in the amount of co-ordinating ability required per unit of product does not affect the downwards sloping portion of the cost-curve, it merely affects the upwards sloping portion. Now, under conditions of imperfect competition, only the downward-sloping section of the firm's cost-curve is relevant from the point of view of the determination of equilibrium, as in equilibrium the firm's average cost-curve must be falling.[30]

On further consideration, however, this point turns out *not* to be very serious. The costs which, in equilibrium, must be falling are average total costs, including the remuneration of uncertainty and co-ordinating ability (including, therefore, all profits which cannot be eliminated by the forces of competition); it is not a condition of equilibrium that marginal costs or even average costs, in our definition of the term,[31] should be falling[32] while those sections of the cost-curve, where these are rising, will be indeterminate. Moreover, it is possible to argue that changes in the amount of co-ordinating ability required per unit of product will affect 'normal profits' in Mrs Robinson's definition[33] (i.e. the amount of profits necessary to induce new firms to come into the industry), and thus change the position of the demand-curves with which existing firms are confronted. In case this is true, not only the equilibrium amount produced by a given firm will be indeterminate, but also the number of firms in the industry, given the conditions of the demand for goods and the supply of factors.

....

VIII

There remains, finally, to answer a more practical question: *what is the effect of the elements of indeterminateness above analysed on the actual world? How can their influence be evaluated in terms of what some writers call 'the instability of capitalism'?* And here we can conclude our investigation with a more reassuring note.

In relatively 'quiet' times, that is in times when tastes and the rate of saving are steady, technical innovations rare and changes in the population small, we may expect the actual size of 'representative firms' to expand. If the system is one in growth (i.e. if capital and population are increasing), this will probably take place without a diminution in the number of existing firms. It is in any case questionable how far this tendency for the individual firms to expand can actually lead to a diminution in the number of firms. Although if 'relatively static conditions' prevail long enough the number of firms existing must fall, and fall rapidly, it is very questionable whether in any actual case the process could be carried far. In the first place, the fall in the scarcity of co-ordinating ability represents, from the point of view of society as a whole, a reduction in real costs. It implies an increase in the 'bundle of utilities' which can be produced out of a given amount of resources. It is quite possible, therefore, that the increase in the amount produced by the 'representative firm' should run *pari passu* with an increase in the social product and should not necessitate any diminution of production elsewhere. In the second place (and this seems more important), the growth in the size of some firms, due to the fact that they periodically revise their ideas of their own cost-curves (which is what the change in co-ordinating ability comes to), throws new 'co-ordinating tasks' upon other firms (to whom this must appear as a 'change of data'), and even if it does not oblige them to reduce their output, at least it will check their growth. For this reason alone it is not to be expected that the process of expansion will be smooth and continuous, even under purely static conditions.

The reverse is true in times of 'disquietude', when changes of data become more frequent and more far-reaching. But while the tendency to expand in quiet times mainly acts in the 'long run' through changing the supply of the long-period variable factors (because so long as plant, machinery, etc., are given, the tendency to expand is effectively blocked by the limitation upon the amount of other factors which can be combined with them[34]), the tendency to contraction may affect short-period output, by raising the prime costs (marginal costs) curve.

All this must in no way be construed as an attempt by the present writer to put forward yet another theory of the Trade Cycle. Although if all major causes of fluctuations were absent there would exist a certain range of fluctuations due to the causes above analysed, in the author's view these are completely covered up in the real world by the more violent fluctuations which emanate from other causes—just as the ripples on the sea which emanate from the movement of ships (and which would make their effect felt over wide ranges if the sea were absolutely quiet) are fully absorbed by the more powerful waves which are due to the winds and the movements of the moon. When compared with the instabilties due to the monetary system, the rigidities of certain prices and the uncertainty of international trading conditions, the instability caused by the vagaries of the factor 'co-ordinating ability' must appear insignificant.

Notes

1. Under 'perfect competition', here and in the following, we simply mean a state of affairs where all prices are given to the individual firm, independently of the actions of that firm.

2. The demand for producers' goods (derived demand functions), on the other hand, are more like supply-functions in this and the following respects.

3. This is not to be interpreted as saying that 'co-operative buying' is not feasible. But the advantages of buyers' co-operation consist solely in marketing advantages (in 'exploiting' sellers), while the advantages of sellers' (producers') co-operation follow from the principle of the division of labour and exist independently of any additional marketing advantage which can thereby be gained.

4. Both Marshall and Professor Pigou appear to argue that an 'industry' can be in equilibrium without all the firms composing it being simultaneously in equilibrium. This is true in one sense but not in another. If it is assumed that firms have a finite life like individuals, that they gradually reach their prime and then decline, it is, of course, not necessary that all the firms' outputs should be constant when the industry's output is constant. But if the growing output of young firms is to cancel out the declining output of old ones on account of something more than a lucky coincidence, it is necessary to assume that all firms are in equilibrium, i.e. that they produce the output appropriate to the ruling prices, to their costs and *to their age*. The introduction of a third type of 'variable' (i.e. the firm's age) merely implies that equilibrium must also be established with respect to this; it certainly does not imply that equilibrium need not be established with respect to the other variables.

5. With the growing realisation of the difficulties confronting any attempt at a workable definition of the concept 'commodity', doubts arose concerning the legitimacy of the concept of a single 'industry' which are probably more

important and fundamental than the objections raised in the present article. But as the results of our investigation do not depend upon the validity of this concept, while its use considerably simplifies the analysis, we shall assume for the purposes of the present article that production can be divided up between a definite number of 'standardized' commodities, each of which is sufficiently unlike the other to justify the use of the word 'industry' applied to it.

6. 'Increasing Returns and the Representative Firm', *Economic Journal*, March 1930, 89.

7. 'The Representative Firm', *Economic Journal*, September 1928.

8. Ibid. 393.

9. Cf. especially the definition of the 'equilibrium firm' by Professor Pigou: ' . . . whenever the industry as a whole is in equilibrium in the sense that it is producing a regular output y in response to a normal supply price p, [it] will itself also be individually in equilibrium with a regular output x_r' (*Economics of Welfare*, 3rd ed., 788). Professor Pigou does not, however, make clear whether (*a*) the conception of the 'equilibrium of the industry' necessarily involves the conception of the 'equilibrium firm' (he merely says that 'the conditions of the industry are compatible with the existence of such a firm'), and (*b*) whether the existence of an 'equilibrium firm' is a sufficient condition for the equilibrium of the industry. In our view, the conception of an 'equilibrium of the industry' has no meaning except as the simultaneous equilibrium of a number of firms; and consequently the conditions of the latter must be analysed before the concept of the 'equilibrium of the industry' and the categories of industries of increasing, constant and diminishing supply-price can be established.

10. Cf. especially the writings of Professor Pigou, Mr Shove, Mr Harrod, Mr and Mrs Robinson in England, Professor Viner, Professor Yntema, and Professor Chamberlin in the United States, Dr Schneider and Dr von Stackelberg in Germany, Professor Amoroso in Italy.

11. If competition is imperfect, only the amount produced *under given conditions of demand* can be determined, but there is no definite relation between *price* and supply. Mrs Joan Robinson employs the concept of the supply-curve even under conditions of imperfect competition (*The Economics of Imperfect Competition*, ch. VI), but a perusal of her book shows that she merely retains the name of the latter for an analysis of the former.

12. We ought to start, in an analysis of this sort, by attempting to define a 'firm'. This, however, would render the treatment unnecessarily complicated, and as will be seen later on, a definition, sufficient for the purpose, emerges by itself in the course of the analysis (see below).

13. This was first pointed out by Cournot (*Researches*, 91). Marshall's remarks in a footnote (*Principles*, 8th ed., 459) concerning Cournot's alleged error on this point were wholly unjustified. I am indebted to Dr J. R. Hicks for this point.

14. Under 'costs' here and in the following we include only such payments for the factors which are necessary in order to retain those factors in their actual employment, at a given efficiency. The remuneration of 'fixed' factors (i.e. factors which are rigidly attached to the firm) form, therefore, no part of

costs. (Fixity of supply implies both (*a*) that the factor is available to the firm irrespective of its remuneration, and (*b*) that its efficiency is not a function of its remuneration.)

15. They must also necessarily fall up to a certain point if the fixed factors are also indivisible. Indivisibility and fixity of supply are, however, two entirely distinct properties which are frequently not kept apart, as both give rise to 'fixed' costs, i.e. costs which do not vary with output. But on our definition of costs, only the remuneration of indivisible factors whose supply is not fixed enters into costs; while indivisible factors of fixed supply, although no part of costs, influence costs (through changing the physical productivity of the other factors) in a manner in which factors of fixed supply which are not indivisible do not. (Factors of the latter category can only influence costs *upwards*, not *downwards*.) The relevance of this distinction in connection with the present paper will become clear later on (see Sect. VII below).

16. It appears methodologically convenient to treat all cases of large-scale economies under the heading 'indivisibility'. This introduces a certain unity into analysis and makes possible at the same time a clarification of the relationship between the different kinds of economies. Even those cases of increasing returns where a more-than-proportionate increase in output occurs merely on account of an increase in the amounts of the factors used, without any change in the proportions of the factors, are due to indivisibilities; only in this case it is not so much the 'original factors', but the specialised functions of those factors, which are indivisible.

17. If external diseconomies affect different firms unequally, this merely explains why some firms should expand relatively to others, but not why their size should be limited. (Similarly to the case where different firms have different access to external economies.)

18. It would be sufficient for the determination of the 'optimum size' if one of the factors had a rising supply-curve to the firm. This, however, is not compatible with the assumption of perfect competition.

19. The essential difference between supervising and co-ordinating ability is that in the case of the former, the principle of the division of labour works smoothly: each supervisor can limit his activities to a particular department, or a particular sub-department, and so forth. In the case of a Board of Co-ordinators, each member of that Board will have to go through the same mental processes, and the advantages of co-operation will consist solely in the checking and counter-checking of each other's judgments. If the Board consists of men of equal ability, this will not materially improve the quality of their decisions: while if the abilities of the different members are markedly unequal, the supply of co-ordinating ability could probably be enlarged by dismissing the Board and leaving the single most efficient individual in control. In practice, of course, a certain amount of co-ordinating activity will be undertaken by Departmental Managers alone in large businesses, but this will always refer to such 'infra-marginal' cases where the weighing of *all* alternatives is manifestly superfluous. Only such decisions, however, which affect the 'margins' fall under the heading

Co-ordination, properly defined. (Cf. Professor Knight's distinction between the 'important decisions' always reserved for the entrepreneur, and the 'routine work' of management. *Risk, Uncertainty and Profit*, ch. X *passim*. For a fuller treatment of 'marginal' and 'infra-marginal' acts of choice, cf. Rosenstein-Rodan, art. 'Grenznutzen', *Handwörterbuch der Staatswissenschaften*, 4th ed., vol. IV, 1198 ff.)

20. Cf. the analysis on the problem of Co-ordination in E. A. G. Robinson, *The Structure of Competitive Industry*, 44 ff.

21. The case of the Salaried General Manager of modern joint-stock companies presents difficulties which the present writer by no means professes to have solved. Professor Knight, *Risk, Uncertainty and Profit*, seems to take the extreme view that control always rests with those who bear the ultimate risks; while the salaried managers are only concerned with 'routine work'. This is manifestly untrue in certain cases, if 'control' is to be interpreted as the 'making of important decisions'. Also, we have to take into account the possibility that the efficiency of a given unit of co-ordinating ability should vary with the amount of profits it receives—though just in the case of the entrepreneur this is very unlikely. In so far as it does, however, the supply of co-ordinating ability will be variable and the entrepreneur's remuneration (or rather that proportion of it which is necessary to maintain him in a given degree of efficiency) will enter into costs. All these, however, though they put difficulties in the way of the definition we have chosen, do not affect the rest of the argument.

22. Which does not imply, of course, that 'co-ordinating ability' is rigidly attached to an industry—as a given unit of co-ordinating ability (and thus a 'firm') can always leave one industry and turn to another. Similarly, there are factors which are 'rigidly attached to the industry', but not to the firm: specialised kinds of machinery, for example, which can only be used by the industry in question, but which a firm will not continue to employ if they yield a greater product in combination with a different unit of co-ordinating ability than they do for the firm which originally possesses them.

23. Similar ideas are expressed by Professor Chamberlin concerning his curve of selling costs (*The Theory of Monopolistic Competition*, 137). Professor Chamberlin, however, does not draw the consequences which, in our view, follow from these in regard to his own analysis.

24. Only if all future changes, and the consequences of these changes, are completely foreseen by everybody, will the situation be different; but then it will be analogous to a continuous long-run equilibrium and co-ordinating ability will be unnecessary. For the conception of a dynamic equilibrium with complete foresight see Hicks, 'Gloichgewicht und Konjunktur', *Zeitschrift für Nationalökonomie*, vol. IV, no. 4.

25. The sole significance of static assumptions in this connection is that in this case the tendency to equilibrium is not dependent on the degree of foresight. All our conclusions also apply to a dynamic world with complete foresight. (Cf. also Knight, *Risk, Uncertainty and Profit*, 287: 'To imagine that one man could

adequately manage a business enterprise of indefinite size and complexity is to imagine a situation in which effective uncertainty is entirely absent.')

26. It is at least questionable whether the same conclusions would hold in a world of 'perfect divisibility' where *all* economies of scale are absent; and it is to be remembered that it was under this assumption that the conception of equilibrium of the Lausanne School was elaborated. We have seen that the extent to which 'co-ordination' is needed, in any given situation, depends on the 'volume of business' (i.e. the scale of operations of the individual producing unit); and in a world where the scale of operations offers no *technical* advantages, 'economies' could be gained by reducing that scale further and further until the need for 'co-ordination' (i.e. the need for a specialised function of control, of decision-making) was completely eliminated. (This is not to be interpreted as saying that each 'infinitesimal' unit would not have to co-ordinate its own activities—in the sense of 'equalising its alternatives on the margin'—but these would be completely similar to the 'co-ordinating activities' undertaken by each individual on the side of consumption. There would be no need for 'co-ordinators', i.e. factors of production specialised in the function of co-ordination. It was with this idea in mind that we found it legitimate to assume earlier in this article [cf. n. 3] that in buying, individuals act alone and thus treat perfect competition on the demand side as a 'datum'. In such a world, therefore, there would be no organization of production into 'firms', or anything comparable to it; and 'perfect competition' would establish itself merely as a result of the 'free play of economic forces'.

27. Cf. n. 16 for the distinction between 'fixed' and 'indivisible' factors.

28. There might be 'increasing returns for other reasons (if the factors themselves are indivisible), but this does not concern us here.

29. 'Co-ordinating ability' can also be assumed to be an indivisible factor if the type of decisions which entrepreneurs have to make varies in accordance with the volume of business and if an individual entrepreneur is better fitted for the making of some kinds of decisions than other kinds. In case this assumption is preferred, the rest of the argument in the present paragraph becomes irrelevant.

30. Cf. Chamberlin, *The Theory of Monopolistic Competition*, ch. V, and Joan Robinson, *The Economics of Imperfect Competition*, ch. VII.

31. Cf. n. 14. The importance of choosing this definition lies in the fact that it draws attention to the purely tautological nature of the conclusions arrived at by including 'price-determined' remunerations under the cost-items.

32. On this point cf. Mr Harrod's note on 'Decreasing Costs' (*Economic Journal*, June 1933).

33. *The Economics of Imperfect Competition*, 92.

34. Save in the case where the long-period factors are divisible, i.e. consist of small units, and where, therefore, their supply can be expanded, though not contracted, within a short period. For example, in a factory which uses a great number of highly durable machines it is always possible to increase their number in a short period, but it may not be possible to diminish it until some of them wear out.

2 The Nature of the Firm

R. H. Coase

Economic theory has suffered in the past from a failure to state clearly its assumptions. Economists in building up a theory have often omitted to examine the foundations on which it was erected. This examination is, however, essential not only to prevent the misunderstanding and needless controversy which arise from a lack of knowledge of the assumptions on which a theory is based, but also because of the extreme importance for economics of good judgment in choosing between rival sets of assumptions. For instance, it is suggested that the use of the word 'firm' in economics may be different from the use of the term by the 'plain man'.[1] Since there is apparently a trend in economic theory towards starting analysis with the individual firm and not with the industry,[2] it is all the more necessary not only that a clear definition of the word 'firm' should be given but that its difference from a firm in the 'real world', if it exists, should be made clear. Mrs Robinson has said that 'the two questions to be asked of a set of assumptions in economics are: Are they tractable? and: Do they correspond with the real world?'[3] Though, as Mrs Robinson points out, 'more often one set will be manageable and the other realistic,' yet there may well be branches of theory where assumptions may be both manageable and realistic. It is hoped to show in the following paper that a definition of a firm may be obtained which is not only realistic in that it corresponds to what is meant by a firm in the real world, but is tractable by two of the most powerful instruments of economic analysis developed by Marshall, the idea of the margin and that of substitution, together giving the idea of substitution at the margin.[4] Our definition must, of course, 'relate to formal relations which are capable of being *conceived* exactly.'[5]

I

It is convenient if, in searching for a definition of a firm, we first consider the economic system as it is normally treated by the economist. Let us consider the description of the economic system given by Sir Arthur Salter.[6] 'The normal economic system works itself. For its current operation it is under no central control, it needs no central survey. Over the whole range of human activity and human need, supply is adjusted to demand, and production to consumption, by a process that is automatic, elastic and responsive.' An economist thinks of the economic system as being co-ordinated by the price mechanism and society becomes not an organization but an organism.[7] The economic system 'works itself'. This does not mean that there is no planning by individuals. These exercise foresight and choose between alternatives. This is necessarily so if there is to be order in the system. But this theory assumes that the direction of resources is dependent directly on the price mechanism. Indeed, it is often considered to be an objection to economic planning that it merely tries to do what is already done by the price mechanism.[8] Sir Arthur Salter's description, however, gives a very incomplete picture of our economic system. Within a firm, the description does not fit at all. For instance, in economic theory we find that the allocation of factors of production between different uses is determined by the price mechanism. The price of factor A becomes higher in X than in Y. As a result, A moves from Y to X until the difference between the prices in X and Y, except in so far as it compensates for other differential advantages, disappears. Yet in the real world, we find that there are many areas where this does not apply. If a workman moves from department Y to department X, he does not go because of a change in relative prices, but because he is ordered to do so. Those who object to economic planning on the grounds that the problem is solved by price movements can be answered by pointing out that there is planning within our economic system which is quite different from the individual planning mentioned above and which is akin to what is normally called economic planning. The example given above is typical of a large sphere in our modern economic system. Of course, this fact has not been ignored by economists. Marshall introduces organization as a fourth factor of production; J. B. Clark gives the co-ordinating function to the entrepreneur; Professor A. Knight introduces managers who co-ordinate. As D. H. Robertson points out, we find 'islands of conscious power in this ocean of unconscious co-operation like lumps of butter coagulating in a pail of buttermilk.'[9] But in view of the fact that it is usually argued that co-ordination will be done by the price mechanism, why is such organization necessary? Why are there these 'islands of conscious power'? Outside the firm, price movements direct production, which is co-ordinated through a series of exchange transactions on the market. Within a firm, these market transactions are eliminated and in place of the complicated market structure with exchange transactions is substituted the entrepreneur-co-ordinator, who directs production.[10] It is clear that these are alternative methods of co-ordinating production. Yet, having regard to the fact that if production is regulated by price movements, production could be carried on without any organization at all, well might we ask, why is there any organization?

Of course, the degree to which the price mechanism is superseded varies greatly. In a department store, the allocation of the different sections to the various locations in the building may be done by the controlling authority or it may be the result of competitive price bidding for space. In the Lancashire cotton industry, a weaver can rent power and shop-room and can obtain looms and yarn on credit.[11] This co-ordination of the various factors of production is, however, normally carried out without the intervention of the price mechanism. As is evident, the amount of 'vertical' integration, involving as it does the suspension of the price mechanism, varies greatly from industry to industry and from firm to firm.

It can, I think, be assumed that the distinguishing mark of the firm is the supersession of the price mechanism. It is, of course, as Professor Robbins points out, 'related to an outside network of relative prices and costs',[12] but it is important to discover the exact nature of this relationship. This distinction between the allocation of resources in a firm and the allocation in the economic system has been very vividly described by Mr Maurice Dobb when discussing Adam Smith's conception of the capitalist: 'It began to be seen that there was something more important than the relations inside each factory or unit captained by an undertaker; there were the relations of the undertaker with the rest of the economic world outside his immediate sphere . . . the undertaker busies himself with the division of labour inside each firm and he plans and organizes consciously,' but 'he is related to the much larger economic specialization, of which he himself is merely one specialized unit. Here, he plays his part as a single cell in a larger organism, mainly unconscious of the wider rôle he fills.'[13]

In view of the fact that while economists treat the price mechanism as a co-ordinating instrument, they also admit the co-ordinating function of the 'entrepreneur', it is surely important to enquire why co-ordination is the work of the price mechanism in one case and of the entrepreneur in another.

The purpose of this paper is to bridge what appears to be a gap in economic theory between the assumption (made for some purposes) that resources are allocated by means of the price mechanism and the assumption (made for other purposes) that this allocation is dependent on the entrepreneur-co-ordinator. We have to explain the basis on which, in practice, this choice between alternatives is effected.[14]

....

II

Our task is to attempt to discover why a firm emerges at all in a specialized exchange economy. The price mechanism (considered purely from the side of the direction of resources) might be superseded if the relationship which replaced it was desired for its own sake. This would be the case, for example, if some people preferred to work under the direction of some other person. Such individuals would accept less in order to work under someone, and firms would arise naturally from this. But it would appear that this cannot be a very important reason, for it would rather seem that the opposite tendency is operating if one judges from the stress normally laid on the advantage of 'being one's own master'.[15] Of course, if the desire was not to be controlled but to control, to exercise power over others, then people might be willing to give up something in order to direct others; that is, they would be willing to pay others more than they could get under the price mechanism in order to be able to direct them. But this implies that those who direct pay in order to be able to do this and are not paid to direct, which is clearly not true in the majority of cases.[16] Firms might also exist if purchasers preferred commodities which are produced by firms to those not so produced; but even in spheres where one would expect such preferences (if they exist) to be of negligible importance, firms are to be found in the real world.[17] Therefore there must be other elements involved.

The main reason why it is profitable to establish a firm would seem to be that there is a cost of using the price mechanism. The most obvious cost of 'organizing' production through the price mechanism is that of discovering what the relevant prices are.[18] This cost may be reduced but it will not be eliminated by the emergence of specialists who will sell this information. The costs of negotiating and concluding a separate contract for each exchange transaction which takes place on a market must also be taken into account.[19] Again, in certain markets, e.g. produce exchanges, a technique is devised for minimizing these contract costs; but they are not eliminated. It is true that contracts are not eliminated when there is a firm but they are greatly reduced. A factor of production (or the owner thereof) does not have to make a series of contracts with the factors with whom he is co-operating within the firm, as would be necessary, of course, if this co-operation were as a direct result of the working of the price mechanism. For this series of contracts is substituted one. At this stage, it is important to note the character of the contract into which a factor enters that is employed within a firm. The contract is one whereby the factor, for a certain remuneration (which may be fixed or fluctuating), agrees to obey the directions of an entrepreneur *within certain limits*.[20] The essence of the contract is that it should only state the limits to the powers of the entrepreneur. Within these limits, he can therefore direct the other factors of production.

There are, however, other disadvantages—or costs—of using the price mechanism. It may be desired to make a long-term contract for the supply of some article or service. This may be due to the fact that if one contract is made for a longer period, instead of several shorter ones, then certain costs of making each contract will be avoided. Or, owing to the risk attitude of the people concerned, they may prefer to make a long rather than a short-term contract. Now, owing to the difficulty of forecasting, the longer the period of the contract is for the supply of the commodity or service, the less possible, and indeed, the less desirable it is for the person purchasing to specify what the other contracting party is expected to do. It may well be a matter of indifference to the person supplying the service or commodity which of several courses of action is taken, but not to the purchaser of that service or commodity. But the purchaser will not know which of these several courses he will want the supplier to take. Therefore, the service which is being provided is expressed in general terms, the exact details being left until a later date. All that is stated in the contract is the limits to what the persons supplying the commodity or service is expected to do. The details of what the supplier is expected to do is not stated in the contract but is decided later by the purchaser. When the direction of resources (within the limits of the contract) becomes dependent on the buyer in this way, that relationship which I term a 'firm' may be obtained. A firm is likely therefore to emerge in those cases where a very short term contract would be unsatisfactory. It is obviously of more importance in the case of services—labour—than it is in the case of the buying of commodities. In the case of commodities, the main items can be stated in advance and the details which will be decided later will be of minor significance.

We may sum up this section of the argument by saying that the operation of a market costs something and by forming an organization and allowing some authority (an 'entrepreneur') to direct the resources, certain marketing costs are saved. The entrepreneur has to carry out his function at less cost, taking into account the fact that he may get factors of production at a lower price than the market transactions which he supersedes, because it is always possible to revert to the open market if he fails to do this.

The question of uncertainty is one which is often considered to be very relevant to the study of the equilibrium of the firm. It seems improbable that a firm would emerge without the existence of uncertainty. But those, for instance, Professor Knight, who make the *mode of payment* the distinguishing mark of the firm—fixed incomes being guaranteed to some of those engaged in production by a person who takes the residual, and fluctuating, income— would appear to be introducing a point which is irrelevant to the problem we are considering. One entrepreneur may sell his services to another for a certain sum of money, while the payment to his employees may be mainly or wholly a share in profits.[22] The significant question would appear to be why the allocation of resources is not done directly by the price mechanism.

Another factor that should be noted is that exchange transactions on a market and the same transactions organized within a firm are often treated differently by Governments or other bodies with regulatory powers. If we consider the operation of a sales tax, it is clear that it is a tax on market transactions and not on the same transactions organized within the firm. Now since these are alternative methods of 'organization'—by the price mechanism or by the entrepreneur—such a regulation would bring into existence firms which otherwise would have no *raison d'être*. It would furnish a reason for the emergence of a firm in a specialized exchange economy. Of course, to the extent that firms already exist, such a measure as a sales tax would merely tend to make them larger than they would otherwise be. Similarly, quota schemes, and methods of price control which imply that there is rationing, and which do not apply to firms producing such products for themselves, by allowing advantages to those who organize within the firm and not through the market, necessarily encourage the growth of firms. But it is difficult to believe that it is measures such as have been mentioned in this paragraph which have brought firms into existence. Such measures would, however, tend to have this result if they did not exist for other reasons.

These, then, are the reasons why organizations such as firms exist in a specialized exchange economy in which it is generally assumed that the distribution of resources is 'organized' by the price mechanism. A firm, therefore, consists of the system of relationships which comes into existence when the direction of resources is dependent on an entrepreneur.

The approach which has just been sketched would appear to offer an advantage in that it is possible to give a scientific meaning to what is meant by saying that a firm gets larger or smaller. A firm becomes larger as additional transactions (which could be exchange transactions co-ordinated through the price mechanism) are organized by the entrepreneur and becomes smaller as he abandons the organization of such transactions. The question which arises is whether it is possible to study the forces which determine the size of the firm. Why does the entrepreneur not organize one less transaction or one more? It is interesting to note that Professor Knight considers that:

the relation between efficiency and size is one of the most serious problems of theory, being, in contrast with the relation for a plant, largely a matter of personality and historical accident rather than of intelligible general principles. But the question is peculiarly vital because the possibility of monopoly gain offers a powerful incentive to *continuous and unlimited* expansion of the firm, which force must be offset by some equally powerful one making for decreased efficiency (in the production of money income) with growth in size, if even boundary competition is to exist.[23]

Professor Knight would appear to consider that it is impossible to treat scientifically the determinants of the size of the firm. On the basis of the concept of the firm developed above, this task will now be attempted.

It was suggested that the introduction of the firm was due primarily to the existence of marketing costs. A pertinent question to ask would appear to be (quite apart from the monopoly considerations raised by Professor Knight), why, if by organizing one can eliminate certain costs and in fact reduce the cost of production, are there any market transactions at all?[24] Why is not all production carried on by one big firm? There would appear to be certain possible explanations.

First, as a firm gets larger, there may be decreasing returns to the entrepreneur function, that is, the costs of organizing additional transactions within the firm may rise.[25] Naturally, a point must be reached where the costs of organizing an extra transaction within the firm are equal to the costs involved in carrying out the transaction in the open market, or, to the costs of organizing by another entrepreneur. Secondly, it may be that as the transactions which are organized increase, the entrepreneur fails to place the factors of production in the uses where their value is greatest, that is, fails to make the best use of the factors of production. Again, a point must be reached where the loss through the waste of resources is equal to the marketing costs of the exchange transaction in the open market or to the loss if the transaction was organized by another entrepreneur. Finally, the supply price of one or more of the factors of production may rise, because the 'other advantages' of a small firm are greater than those of a large firm.[26] Of course, the actual point where the expansion of the firm ceases might be determined by a combination of the factors mentioned above. The first two reasons given most probably correspond to the economists' phrase of 'diminishing returns to management'.[27]

The point has been made in the previous paragraph that a firm will tend to expand until the costs of organizing an extra transaction within the firm become equal to the costs of carrying out the same transaction by means of an exchange on the open market or the costs of organizing in another firm. But if the firm stops its expansion at a point below the costs of marketing in the open market and at a point equal to the costs of organizing in another firm, in most cases (excluding the case of 'combination'[28]), this will imply that there is a market transaction between these two producers, each of whom could organize it at less than the actual marketing costs. How is the paradox to be resolved? If we consider an example the reason for this will become clear. Suppose A is buying a product from B and that both A and B could organize this marketing transaction at less than its present cost. B, we can assume, is not organizing one process or stage of production, but several. If A therefore wishes to avoid a market transaction, he will have to take over all the processes of production controlled by B. Unless A takes over all the processes of production, a market transaction will still remain, although it is a different product that is bought. But we have previously assumed that as each producer expands he becomes less efficient; the additional costs of organizing extra transactions increase. It is probable that A's cost of organizing the transactions previously organized by B will be greater than B's cost of doing the same thing. A therefore will take over the whole of B's organization only if his cost of organizing B's work is not greater than B's cost by an amount equal to the costs of carrying out an exchange transaction on the open market. But once it becomes economical to have a market transaction, it also pays to divide production in such a way that the cost of organizing an extra transaction in each firm is the same.

Up to now it has been assumed that the exchange transactions which take place through the price mechanism are homogeneous. In fact, nothing could be more diverse than the actual transactions which take place in our modern world. This would seem to imply that the costs of carrying out exchange transactions through the price mechanism will vary considerably as will also the costs of organizing these transactions within the firm. It seems therefore possible that quite apart from the question of diminishing returns the costs of organizing certain transactions within the firm may be greater than the costs of carrying out the exchange transactions in the open market. This would necessarily imply that there were exchange transactions carried out through the price mechanism, but would it mean that there would have to be more than one firm? Clearly not, for all those areas in the economic system where the direction of resources was not dependent directly on the price mechanism could be organized within one firm. The factors which were discussed earlier would seem to be the important ones, though it is difficult to say whether 'diminishing returns to management' or the rising supply price of factors is likely to be the more important.

Other things being equal, therefore, a firm will tend to be larger:

(a) the less the costs of organizing and the slower these costs rise with an increase in the transactions organized.

(b) the less likely the entrepreneur is to make mistakes and the smaller the increase in mistakes with an increase in the transactions organized.

(c) the greater the lowering (or the less the rise) in the supply price of factors of production to firms of larger size.

Apart from variations in the supply price of factors of production to firms of different sizes, it would appear that the costs of organizing and the losses through mistakes will increase with an increase in the spatial distribution of the transactions organized, in the dissimilarity of the transactions, and in the probability of changes in the relevant prices.[29] As more transactions are organized by an entrepreneur, it would appear that the transactions would tend to be either different in kind or in different places. This furnishes an additional reason why efficiency will tend to decrease as the firm gets larger. Inventions which tend to bring factors of production nearer together, by lessening spatial distribution, tend to increase the size of the firm.[30] Changes like the telephone and the telegraph which tend to reduce the cost of organizing spatially will tend to increase the size of the firm. All changes which improve managerial technique will tend to increase the size of the firm.[31-2]

It should be noted that the definition of a firm which was given above can be used to give more precise meanings to the terms 'combination' and 'integration'.[33] There is a combination when transactions which were previously organized by two or more entrepreneurs become organized by one. This becomes integration when it involves the organization of transactions which were previously carried out between the entrepreneurs on a market. A firm can expand in either or both of these two ways. The whole of the 'structure of competitive industry' becomes tractable by the ordinary technique of economic analysis.

....

III

The problem which has been investigated in the previous section has not been entirely neglected by economists and it is now necessary to consider why the reasons given above for the emergence of a firm in a specialized exchange economy are to be preferred to the other explanations which have been offered.

It is sometimes said that the reason for the existence of a firm is to be found in the division of labour. This is the view of Professor Usher, a view which has been adopted and expanded by Mr Maurice Dobb. The firm becomes 'the result of an increasing complexity of the division of labour . . . The growth of this economic differentiation creates the need for some integrating force without which differentiation would collapse into chaos; and it is as the integrating force in a differentiated economy that industrial forms are chiefly significant.'[34] The answer to this argument is an obvious one. The 'integrating force in a differentiated economy' already exists in the form of the price mechanism. It is perhaps the main achievement of economic science that it has shown that there is no reason to suppose that specialization must lead to chaos.[35] The reason given by Mr Maurice Dobb is therefore inadmissible. What has to be explained is why one integrating force (the entrepreneur) should be substituted for another integrating force (the price mechanism).

The most interesting reasons (and probably the most widely accepted) which have been given to explain this fact are those to be found in Professor Knight's *Risk, Uncertainty and Profit*. His views will be examined in some detail.

Professor Knight starts with a system in which there is no uncertainty:

acting as individuals under absolute freedom but without collusion men are supposed to have organised economic life with the primary and secondary division of labour, the use of capital, etc., developed to the point familiar in present-day America. The principal fact which calls for the exercise of the imagination is the internal organisation of the productive groups or establishments. With uncertainty entirely absent, every individual being in possession of perfect knowledge of the situation, there would be no occasion for anything of the nature of responsible management or control of productive activity. Even marketing transactions in any realistic sense would not be found. The flow of raw materials and productive services to the consumer would be entirely automatic.[36]

Professor Knight says that we can imagine this adjustment as being 'the result of a long process of experimentation worked out by trial-and-error methods alone', while it is not necessary 'to imagine every worker doing exactly the right thing at the right time in a sort of "pre-established harmony" with the work of others. There might be managers, superintendents, etc., for the purpose of co-ordinating the activities of individuals', though these managers would be performing a purely routine function, 'without responsibility of any sort'.[37]

Professor Knight then continues:

With the introduction of uncertainty—the fact of ignorance and the necessity of acting upon opinion rather than knowledge—into this Eden-like situation, its character is entirely changed . . . With uncertainty present doing things, the actual execution of activity, becomes in a real sense a secondary part of life; the primary problem or function is deciding what to do and how to do it.[38]

This fact of uncertainty brings about the two most important characteristics of social organization.

In the first place, goods are produced for a market, on the basis of entirely impersonal prediction of wants, not for the satisfaction of the wants of the producers themselves. The producer takes the responsibility of forecasting the consumers' wants. In the second place, the work of forecasting and at the same time a large part of the technological direction and control of production are still further concentrated upon a very narrow class of the producers, and we meet with a new economic functionary, the entrepreneur. . . . When uncertainty is present and the task of deciding what to do and how to do it takes the ascendancy over that of execution the internal organisation of the productive groups is no longer a matter of indifference or a mechanical detail. Centralisation of this deciding and controlling function is imperative, a process of 'cephalisation' is inevitable.[39]

The most fundamental change is:

the system under which the confident and venturesome assume the risk or insure the doubtful and timid by guaranteeing to the latter a specified income in return for an assignment of the actual results. . . . With human nature as we know it it would be impracticable or very unusual for one man to guarantee to another a definite result of the latter's actions without being given power to direct his work. And on the other hand the second party would not place himself under the direction of the first without such a guarantee. . . . The result of this manifold specialisation of function is the enterprise and wage system of industry. Its existence in the world is the direct result of the fact of uncertainty.[40]

These quotations give the essence of Professor Knight's theory. The fact of uncertainty means that people have to forecast future wants. Therefore, you get a special class springing up who direct the activities of others to whom they give guaranteed wages. It acts because good judgment is generally associated with confidence in one's judgment.[41]

Professor Knight would appear to leave himself open to criticism on several grounds. First of all, as he himself points out, the fact that certain people have better judgment or better knowledge does not mean that they can only get an income from it by themselves actively taking part in production. They can sell advice or knowledge. Every business buys the services of a host of advisers. We can imagine a system where all advice or knowledge was bought as required. Again, it is possible to get a reward from better knowledge or judgment not by actively taking part in production but by making contracts with people who are producing. A merchant buying for future delivery represents an example of this. But this merely illustrates the point that it is quite possible to give a guaranteed reward providing that certain acts are performed without directing the performance of those acts. Professor Knight says that 'with human nature as we know it it would be impracticable or very unusual for one man to guarantee to another a definite result of the latter's actions without being given power to direct his work.' This is surely incorrect. A large proportion of jobs are done to contract, that is, the contractor is guaranteed a certain sum providing he performs certain acts. But this does not involve any direction. It does mean, however, that the system of relative prices has been changed and that there will be a new arrangement of the factors of production.[42] The fact that Professor Knight mentions that the 'second party would not place himself under the direction of the first without such a guarantee' is irrelevant to the problem we are considering. Finally, it seems important to notice that even in the case of an economic system where there is no uncertainty Professor Knight considers that there would be co-ordinators, though they would perform only a routine function. He immediately adds that they would be 'without responsibility of any sort', which raises the question by whom are they paid and why? It seems that nowhere does Professor Knight give a reason why the price mechanism should be superseded.

....

IV

It would seem important to examine one further point and that is to consider the relevance of this discussion to the general question of the 'cost-curve of the firm'.

It has sometimes been assumed that a firm is limited in size under perfect competition if its cost curve slopes upward,[43] while under imperfect competition, it is limited in size because it will not pay to produce more than the output at which marginal cost is equal to marginal revenue.[44] But it is clear that a firm may produce more than one product and, therefore, there appears to be no *prima facie* reason why this upward slope of the cost curve in the case of perfect competition or the fact that marginal cost will not always be below marginal revenue in the case of imperfect competition should limit the size of the firm.[45] Mrs Robinson[46] makes the simplifying assumption that only one product is being produced. But it is clearly important to investigate how the number of products produced by a firm is determined, while no theory which assumes that only one product is in fact produced can have very great practical significance.

It might be replied that under perfect competition, since everything that is produced can be sold at the prevailing price, then there is no need for any other product to be produced. But this argument ignores the fact that there may be a point where it is less costly to organize the exchange transactions of a new product than to organize further exchange transactions of the old product. This point can be illustrated in the following way. Imagine, following von Thunen, that there is a town, the consuming centre, and that industries are located around this central point in rings. These conditions are illustrated in the following diagram in which A, B and C represent different industries. Imagine an entrepreneur who starts controlling exchange transactions from x. Now as he extends his activities in the same product (B), the cost of organizing increases until at some point it becomes equal to that of a dissimilar product which is nearer. As the firm expands, it will therefore from this point include more than one product (A and C). This treatment of the problem is obviously incomplete,[47] but it is necessary to show that merely proving that the cost curve turns upwards does not give a limitation to the size of the firm. So far we have only considered the case of perfect competition; the case of imperfect competition would appear to be obvious.

To determine the size of the firm, we have to consider the marketing costs (that is, the costs of using the price mechanism), and the costs of organizing of different entrepreneurs and then we can determine how many products

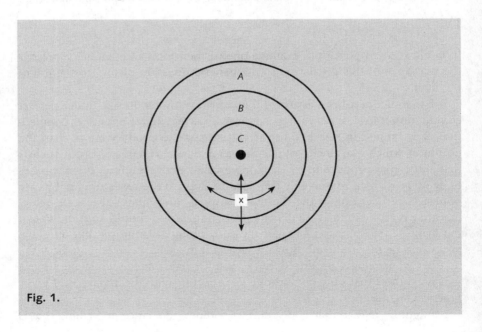

Fig. 1.

will be produced by each firm and how much of each it will produce. It would, therefore, appear that Mr Shove[48] in his article on 'Imperfect Competition' was asking questions which Mrs Robinson's cost curve apparatus cannot answer. The factors mentioned above would seem to be the relevant ones.

....

V

Only one task now remains; and that is, to see whether the concept of a firm which has been developed fits in with that existing in the real world. We can best approach the question of what constitutes a firm in practice by considering the legal relationship normally called that of 'master and servant' or 'employer and employee'.[49] The essentials of this relationship have been given as follows:

(1) the servant must be under the duty of rendering personal service to the master or to others on behalf of the master, otherwise the contract is a contract for sale of goods or the like.

(2) The master must have the right to control the servant's work, either personally or by another servant or agent. It is this right of control or interference, of being entitled to tell the servant when to work (within the hours of service) and when not to work, and what work to do and how to do it (within the terms of such service) which is the dominant characteristic in this relation and marks off the servant from an independent contractor, or from one employed merely to give to his employer the fruits of his labour. In the latter case, the contractor or performer is not under the employer's control in doing the work or effecting the service; he has to shape and manage his work so as to give the result he has contracted to effect.[50]

We thus see that it is the fact of direction which is the essence of the legal concept of 'employer and employee', just as it was in the economic concept which was developed above. It is interesting to note that Professor Batt says further:

That which distinguishes an agent from a servant is not the absence or presence of a fixed wage or the payment only of commission on business done, but rather the freedom with which an agent may carry out his employment.'[51]

We can therefore conclude that the definition we have given is one which approximates closely to the firm as it is considered in the real world.

Our definition is, therefore, realistic. Is it manageable? This ought to be clear. When we are considering how large a firm will be the principle of marginalism works smoothly. The question always is, will it pay to bring an extra exchange transaction under the organizing authority? At the margin, the costs of organizing within the firm will be equal either to the costs of organizing in another firm or to the costs involved in leaving the transaction to be 'organized' by the price mechanism. Business men will be constantly experimenting, controlling more or less, and in this way, equilibrium will be maintained. This gives the position of equilibrium for static analysis. But it is clear that the dynamic factors are also of considerable importance, and an investigation of the effect changes have on the cost of organizing within the firm and on marketing costs generally will enable one to explain why firms get larger and smaller. We thus have a theory of moving equilibrium. The above analysis would also appear to have clarified the relationship between initiative or enterprise and management. Initiative means forecasting and operates through the price mechanism by the making of new contracts. Management proper merely reacts to price changes, rearranging the factors of production under its control. That the business man normally combines both functions is an obvious result of the marketing costs which were discussed above. Finally, this analysis enables us to state more exactly what is meant by the 'marginal product' of the entrepreneur. But an elaboration of this point would take us far from our comparatively simple task of definition and clarification.

Notes

1. Joan Robinson, *Economics is a Serious Subject*, 12.
2. See N. Kaldor, 'The Equilibrium of the Firm', *Economic Journal*, March, 1934.
3. *Economics is a Serious Subject*, 6.
4. J. M. Keynes, *Essays in Biography*, 223–4.
5. L. Robbins, *Nature and Significance of Economic Science*, 63.
6. This description is quoted with approval by D. H. Robertson, *Control of Industry*, 85, and by Professor Arnold Plant, 'Trends in Business Administration', *Economica*, February, 1932. It appears in *Allied Shipping Control*, 16–17.
7. See F. A. Hayek, 'The Trend of Economic Thinking', *Economica*, May, 1933.
8. See F. A. Hayek, ibid.
9. Robertson, *Control of Industry*, 85.
10. In the rest of this paper I shall use the term entrepreneur to refer to the person or persons who, in a competitive system, take the place of the price mechanism in the direction of resources.
11. *Survey of Textile Industries*, 26.
12. Robbins, *Nature and Significance*, 71.

13. *Capitalist Enterprise and Social Progress*, 20. Cf., also, Henderson, *Supply and Demand*, 3–5.

14. It is easy to see when the State takes over the direction of an industry that, in planning it, it is doing something which was previously done by the price mechanism. What is usually not realised is that any business man in organizing the relations between his departments is also doing something which could be organized through the price mechanism. There is therefore point in Mr Durbin's answer to those who emphasise the problems involved in economic planning that the same problems have to be solved by business men in the competitive system. (See 'Economic Calculus in a Planned Economy', *Economic Journal*, December, 1936.) The important difference between these two cases is that economic planning is imposed on industry while firms arise voluntarily because they represent a more efficient method of organizing production. In a competitive system, there is an 'optimum' amount of planning!

15. Cf. Harry Dawes, 'Labour Mobility in the Steel Industry', *Economic Journal*, March, 1934, who instances 'the trek to retail shopkeeping and insurance work by the better paid of skilled men due to the desire (often the main aim in life of a worker) to be independent' (p. 86).

16. None the less, this is not altogether fanciful. Some small shopkeepers are said to earn less than their assistants.

17. G. F. Shove, 'The Imperfection of the Market: a Further Note', *Economic Journal*, March, 1933, 116, n. 1, points out that such preferences may exist, although the example he gives is almost the reverse of the instance given in the text.

18. According to N. Kaldor, 'A Classificatory Note of the Determinateness of Equilibrium', *Review of Economic Studies*, February, 1934, it is one of the assumptions of static theory that 'All the relevant prices are known to all individuals.' But this is clearly not true of the real world.

19. This influence was noted by Professor Usher when discussing the development of capitalism. He says: 'The successive buying and selling of partly finished products were sheer waste of energy.' (*Introduction to the Industrial History of England*, 13). But he does not develop the idea nor consider why it is that buying and selling operations still exist.

20. It would be possible for no limits to the powers of the entrepreneur to be fixed. This would be voluntary slavery. According to Professor Batt, *The Law of Master and Servant*, 18, such a contract would be void and unenforceable.

21. Of course, it is not possible to draw a hard and fast line which determines whether there is a firm or not. There may be more or less direction. It is similar to the legal question of whether there is the relationship of master and servant or principal and agent. See the discussion of this problem below.

22. The views of Professor Knight are examined below in more detail.

23. *Risk, Uncertainty and Profit*, Preface to the Re-issue, London School of Economics Series of Reprints, no. 16, 1933.

24. There are certain marketing costs which could only be eliminated by the abolition of 'consumer's choice' and these are the costs of retailing. It is conceivable that these costs might be so high that people would be willing to

R. H. Coase

accept rations because the extra product obtained was worth the loss of their choice.

25. This argument assumes that exchange transactions on a market can be considered as homogeneous; which is clearly untrue in fact. This complication is taken into account below.

26. For a discussion of the variation of the supply price of factors of production to firms of varying size, see E. A. G. Robinson, *The Structure of Competitive Industry*. It is sometimes said that the supply price of organizing ability increases as the size of the firm increases because men prefer to be the heads of small independent businesses rather than the heads of departments in a large business. See Jones, *The Trust Problem*, 531, and Macgregor, *Industrial Combination*, 63. This is a common argument of those who advocate Rationalization. It is said that larger units would be more efficient, but owing to the individualistic spirit of the smaller entrepreneurs, they prefer to remain independent, apparently in spite of the higher income which their increased efficiency under Rationalization makes possible.

27. This discussion is, of course, brief and incomplete. For a more thorough discussion of this particular problem, see N. Kaldor, 'The Equilibrium of the Firm', *Economic Journal*, March, 1934, and E. A. G. Robinson, 'The Problem of Management and the Size of the Firm', *Economic Journal*, June, 1934.

28. A definition of this term is given below.

29. This aspect of the problem is emphasised by N. Kaldor, 'Equilibrium of the Firm'. Its importance in this connection had been previously noted by E. A. G. Robinson, *The Structure of Competitive Industry*, 83–106. This assumes that an increase in the probability of price movements increases the costs of organizing within a firm more than it increases the cost of carrying out an exchange transaction on the market—which is probable.

30. This would appear to be the importance of the treatment of the technical unit by E. A. G. Robinson, *Structure of Competitive Industry*, 27–33. The larger the technical unit, the greater the concentration of factors and therefore the firm is likely to be larger.

31. It should be noted that most inventions will change both the costs of organizing and the costs of using the price mechanism. In such cases, whether the invention tends to make firms larger or smaller will depend on the relative effect on these two sets of costs. For instance, if the telephone reduces the costs of using the price mechanism more than it reduces the costs of organizing, then it will have the effect of reducing the size of the firm.

32. An illustration of these dynamic forces is furnished by Maurice Dobb, *Russian Economic Development*, 68. 'With the passing of bonded labour the factory, as an establishment where work was organized under the whip of the overseer, lost its *raison d'être* until this was restored to it with the introduction of power machinery after 1846.' It seems important to realise that the passage from the domestic system to the factory system is not a mere historical accident, but is conditioned by economic forces. This is shown by the fact that it is possible to move from the factory system to the domestic system, as in the Russian

example, as well as *vice versa*. It is the essence of serfdom that the price mechanism is not allowed to operate. Therefore, there has to be direction from some organizer. When, however, serfdom passed, the price mechanism was allowed to operate. It was not until machinery drew workers into one locality that it paid to supersede the price mechanism and the firm again emerged.

33. This is often called 'vertical integration', combination being termed 'lateral integration'.

34. Dobb, *Russian Economic Development*, 10. Professor Usher's views are to be found in his *Introduction to the Industrial History of England*, 1–18.

35. Cf. J. B. Clark, *Distribution of Wealth*, 19, who speaks of the theory of exchange as being the 'theory of the organization of industrial society'.

36. *Risk, Uncertainty and Profit*, 267.

37. Ibid. 267–8.

38. Ibid. 268.

39. Ibid. 268–95.

40. Ibid. 269–70.

41. Ibid. 270.

42. This shows that it is possible to have a private enterprise system without the existence of firms. Though, in practice, the two functions of enterprise, which actually influences the system of relative prices by forecasting wants and acting in accordance with such forecasts, and management, which accepts the system of relative prices as being given, are normally carried out by the same persons, yet it seems important to keep them separate in theory. This point is further discussed below.

43. See Kaldor, 'Equilibrium of the Firm', and Robinson, *Problem of Management*.

44. Mr Robinson calls this the Imperfect Competition solution for the survival of the small firm.

45. Mr Robinson's conclusion, 'Problem of Management' 249, n. 1, would appear to be definitely wrong. He is followed by Horace J. White, Jr., 'Monopolistic and Perfect Competition', *American Economic Review*, December, 1936, 645, n. 27. Mr White states 'It is obvious that the size of the firm is limited in conditions of monopolistic competition'.

46. *Economics of Imperfect Competition*.

47. As has been shown above, location is only one of the factors influencing the cost of organizing.

48. G. F. Shove, 'The Imperfection of the Market', *Economic Journal*, March, 1933, 115. In connection with an increase in demand in the suburbs and the effect on the price charged by suppliers, Mr Shove asks ' . . . why do not the old firms open branches in the suburbs?' If the argument in the text is correct, this is a question which Mrs Robinson's apparatus cannot answer.

49. The legal concept of 'employer and employee' and the economic concept of a firm are not identical, in that the firm may imply control over another person's property as well as over their labour. But the identity of these two concepts is

sufficiently close for an examination of the legal concept to be of value in appraising the worth of the economic concept.

50. Batt, *The Law of Master and Servant*, 6.
51. Ibid. 7.

3 The Organization of Industry

G. B. Richardson

I

I was once in the habit of telling pupils that firms might be envisaged as islands of planned co-ordination in a sea of market relations. This now seems to me a highly misleading account of the way in which industry is in fact organized. The underlying idea, of course, was of the existence of two ways in which economic activity could be co-ordinated, the one, conscious planning, holding sway within firms, the other, the price mechanism, operating spontaneously on the relations between firms and between firms and their customers. The theory of the firm, I argued, had as its central core an elaboration of the logic of this conscious planning; the theory of markets analysed the working of the price mechanism under a variety of alternative structural arrangements.

I imagine that this account of things might be acceptable, as a harmless first approximation, to a large number of economists. And yet there are two aspects of it that should trouble us. In the first place it raise a question, properly central to any theory of economic organization, which it does not answer; and secondly, it ignores the existence of a whole species of industrial activity which, on the face of it, is relevant to the manner in which co-ordination is achieved. Let us deal with each of these matters in turn.

Our simple picture of the capitalist economy was in terms of a division of labour between the firm and the market, between co-ordination that is planned and co-ordination that is spontaneous. But what then is the principle

I am grateful to Mr J. F. Wright, Mr L. Hannah and Mr J. A. Kay, each of whom gave helpful comments on a draft of this article.

of this division? What kinds of co-ordination have to be secured through conscious direction within firms and what can be left to the working of the invisible hand? One might reasonably maintain that this was a key question— perhaps the key question—in the theory of industrial organization, the most important matter that the Divine Maker of market economies on the first day of creation would have to decide. And yet, as I hope soon to show, it is a matter upon which our standard theories, which merely assume but do not explain a division between firm and market, throw little light.

Let me now turn to the species of industrial activity that our simple story, based as it is on a dichotomy between firm and market, leaves out of account. What I have in mind is the dense network of co-operation and affiliation by which firms are inter-related. Our theoretical firms are indeed islands, being characteristically well-defined autonomous units buying and selling at arms' length in markets. Such co-operation as takes place between them is normally studied as a manifestation of the desire to restrict competition and features in chapters about price agreements and market sharing. But if the student closes his textbook and takes up a business history, or the financial pages of a newspaper, or a report of the Monopolies Commission, he will be presented with a very different picture. Firm A, he may find, is a joint subsidiary of firms B and C, has technical agreements with D and E, sub-contracts work to F, is in marketing association with G—and so on. So complex and ramified are these arrangements, indeed, that the skills of a genealogist rather than an economist might often seem appropriate for their disentanglement.[1] But does all this matter? Theories necessarily abstract and it is always easy to point to things they leave out of account. I hope to show that the excluded phenomena in this case are of importance and that by looking at industrial reality in terms of a sharp dichotomy between firm and market we obtain a distorted view of how the system works. Before doing so, however, I wish to dwell a little longer on the several forms that co-operation and affiliation may take; although the arrangements to be described are no doubt well known to the reader, explicit mention may nevertheless help to draw attention to their variety and extent.

II

Perhaps the simplest form of inter-firm co-operation is that of a trading relationship between two or more parties which is stable enough to make demand expectations more reliable and thereby to facilitate production planning. The relationship may acquire its stability merely from goodwill or from more formal arrangements such as long-term contracts or shareholding. Thus, for example, the Metal Box Company used to obtain a discount from its tin plate suppliers in return for undertaking to buy a certain proportion of its requirements from them, and the same company owned 25% of the share capital of the firm supplying it with paints and lacquers. In the same way Imperial Tobacco owned shares in British Sidac, which made cellophane wrapping, and in Bunzl, which supplied filter tips. Occasionally shareholdings of this kind may be simply investments held for their direct financial yield, but more generally they give stability to relationships through which the activities of the parties are co-ordinated both quantitatively and qualitatively. Not only is it made easier to adjust the quantity of, say, lacquer to the quantity of cans which it is used to coat but the specification and development of the lacquers can be made appropriate to the use to be made of them. And in the synthetic fibre industry likewise, linkages between firms at the various stages—polymer manufacture, yarn spinning and finishing, textile weaving—help bring about the co-ordinated development of products and processes. The habit of working with models which assume a fixed list of goods may have the unfortunate result of causing us to think of co-ordination merely in terms of the balancing of quantities of inputs and outputs and thus leave the need for qualitative co-ordination out of account.

Co-operation may frequently take place within the framework provided by sub-contracting. An indication of the importance of this arrangement is provided by the fact that about a quarter of the output of the Swedish engineering industry is made up of sub-contracted components, while for Japan the corresponding figure is about a third and in that country's automobile industry almost a half. Sub-contracting on an international basis, moreover, is said to be becoming more widespread and now a dense network of arrangements links the industries of different countries.[2] Now the fact that work has been sub-contracted does not by itself imply the existence of much co-operation between the parties to the arrangement. The plumbing work on a building contract may be sub-contracted on the basis of competitive tenders for the individual job. Frequently, however, the relationship between the parties acquires a degree of stability which is important for two reasons. It is necessary, in the first place, to induce sub-contractors to assume the risks inherent in a rather narrow specialisation in skills and equipment; and, secondly, it permits continuing co-operation between those concerned in the development of specifications, processes and designs.

Co-operation also takes place between firms that rely on each other for manufacture or marketing and its fullest manifestation is perhaps to be found in the operations of companies such as Marks and Spencer and British Home Stores. Nominally, these firms would be classified as retail chains, but in reality they are the engineers or architects of complex and extended patterns of co-ordinated activity. Not only do Marks and Spencer tell their suppliers how much they wish to buy from them, and thus promote a quantitative adjustment of supply to demand, they concern themselves equally with the specification and development of both processes and products. They decide, for example, the design of a garment, specify the cloth to be used and control the processes even to laying down the types of needles to be used in knitting and sewing. In the same way they co-operate with Ranks and Spillers in order to work out the best kind of flour for their cakes and do not neglect to specify the number of cherries and walnuts to go into them. Marks and Spencer have laboratories in which, for example, there is development work on uses of nylon, polyester and acrylic fibres. Yet all this orchestration of development, manufacture and marketing takes place without any shareholding by Marks and Spencer in its suppliers and without even long-term contracts.

Mention should be made, finally, of co-operative arrangements specifically contrived to pool or to transfer technology. Surely the field of technical agreements between enterprises is one of the under-developed areas of economics. These agreements are commonly based on the licensing or pooling of patents but they provide in a quite general manner for the provision or exchange of know-how through the transfer of information, drawings, tools and personnel. At the same time they are often associated with the acceptance by the parties to them of a variety of restrictions on their commercial freedom—that is to say with price agreements, market sharing and the like.

This brief description of the varieties of inter-firm co-operation purports to do no more than exemplify the phenomenon. But how is such co-operation to be defined? And how in particular are we to distinguish between co-operation on the one hand and market transactions on the other? The essence of co-operative arrangements such as those we have reviewed would seem to be the fact that the parties to them accept some degree of obligation—and therefore give some degree of assurance—with respect to their future conduct. But there is certainly room for infinite variation in the scope of such assurances and in the degree of formality with which they are expressed. The blanket manufacturer who takes a large order from Marks and Spencer commits himself by taking the appropriate investment and organizational decisions; and he does so in the expectation that this company will continue to put business his way. In this instance, the purchasing company gives no formal assurance but its past behaviour provides suppliers with reason to expect that they can normally rely on getting further orders on acceptable terms. The qualification 'normally' is, of course, important, and the supplier is aware that the continuation of orders is conditional on a sustained demand for blankets, satisfaction with the quality of his manufacture and so on. In a case such as this any formal specification of the terms and conditions of the assurance given by the supplier would scarcely be practicable and the function of goodwill and reputation is to render it unnecessary.

Where buyer and seller accept no obligation with respect to their future conduct, however loose and implicit the obligation might be, then co-operation does not take place and we can refer to a pure market transaction. Here there is no continuing association, no give and take, but an isolated act of purchase and sale such, for example, as takes place on an organized market for financial securities. The pure market transaction is therefore a limiting case, the ingredient of co-operation being very commonly present, in some degree, in the relationship between buyer and seller. Thus although I shall have occasion to refer to co-operation and market transactions as distinct and alternative modes of co-ordinating economic activity, we must not imagine that reality exhibits a sharp line of distinction; what confronts us is a continuum passing from transactions, such as those on organized commodity markets, where the co-operative element is minimal, through intermediate areas in which there are linkages of traditional connection and goodwill, and finally to those complex and interlocking clusters, groups and alliances which represent co-operation fully and formally developed. And just as the presence of co-operation is a matter of degree, so also is the sovereignty that any nominally independent firm is able to exercise on a *de facto* basis, for the substance of autonomy may often have been given up to a customer or a licensor. A good alliance, Bismarck affirmed, should have a horse and a rider, and, whether or not one agrees with him, there is little doubt that in the relations between firms as well as nation states, the condition is often met.

III

It is time to revert to the main line of our argument. I had suggested that theories of the firm and of markets normally provide no explanation of the principle of the division of labour between firms and markets and of the roles within a capitalist economy of planned and spontaneous co-ordination. And I also maintained that these theories did not account for the existence of inter-firm co-operation and affiliation. It is upon the first of these two deficiencies that I now wish to concentrate.

Probably the simplest answer to the question as to the division of labour between firm and market would be to say that firms make products and market forces determine how much of each product is made. But such an answer is quite useless. If 'products' are thought of as items of final expenditure such as cars or socks, then it is clear that very many different firms are concerned with the various stages of their production, not only in the sense that firms buy in components and semi-manufactures from other firms but also in that there may be a separation of manufacture and marketing (as in the case of Marks and Spencer and its suppliers) or of development and manufacture (as in the case of licensors and licencees). If, alternatively, we simply define 'products' as what firms do, then the statement that firms make products is a tautology which, however convenient, cannot be the basis of any account of the division of labour between firm and market.

It is worth observing that we learn nothing about this division of labour from the formal theory of the firm. And this is perhaps not surprising as the theory, in its bare bones, is little more than an application of the logic of choice to a particular set of problems. It may be that the theory indeed makes it more difficult to answer our question in that, in order the better to exhibit this logic of choice, it is formulated on the assumption of 'given production functions' which represent the maximum output obtainable from different input combinations. However useful this representation of productive possibilities, it leaves one important class of ingredients out of account. It abstracts totally from the roles of organization, knowledge, experience and skills, and thereby makes it the more difficult to bring these back into the theoretical foreground in the way needed to construct a theory of industrial organization. Of course I realise that production functions presume a certain level of managerial and material technology. The point is not that production is thus dependent on the state of the arts but that it has to be undertaken (as Mrs Penrose has so very well explained)[3] by human organizations embodying specifically appropriate experience and skill. It is this circumstance that formal production theory tends to put out of focus, and justifiably, no doubt, given the character of the optimisation problems that it is designed to handle; nevertheless, it seems to me that we cannot hope to construct an adequate theory of industrial organization and in particular to answer our question about the division of labour between firm and market, unless the elements of organization, knowledge, experience and skills are brought back to the foreground of our vision.

It is convenient to think of industry as carrying out an indefinitely large number of *activities*, activities related to the discovery and estimation of future wants, to research, development and design, to the execution and co-ordination of processes of physical transformation, the marketing of goods and so on. And we have to recognize that these activities have to be carried out by organizations with appropriate *capabilities*, or, in other words, with appropriate knowledge, experience and skills. The capability of an organization may depend upon command of some particular material technology, such as cellulose chemistry, electronics or civil engineering, or may derive from skills in marketing or knowledge of and reputation in a particular market. Activities which require the same capability for their undertaking I shall call *similar activities*. The notion of capability is no doubt somewhat vague, but no more so perhaps than that of, say, liquidity and, I believe, no less useful. What concerns us here is the fact that organizations will tend to specialize in activities for which their capabilities offer some comparative advantage; these activities will, in other words, generally be similar in the sense in which I have defined the term although they may nevertheless lead the firm into a variety of markets and a variety of product lines. Under capitalism, this degree of specialisation will come about through competition but it seems to me likely to be adopted under any alternative system for reasons of manifest convenience. Mrs Penrose has provided us with excellent accounts of how companies grow in directions set by their capabilities and how these capabilities themselves slowly expand and alter.[4] Dupont, for example, moved from a basis in nitro-cellulose explosives to cellulose lacquers, artificial leather, plastics, rayon and cellophane and from a basis in coal tar dyestuffs into a wide range of synthetic organic chemicals, nylon and synthetic rubber. Similarly, Marks and Spencer, having acquired marketing and organizational techniques in relation to clothing were led to apply them to foodstuffs.

There is therefore a strong tendency for the activities grouped within a firm to be similar, but this need not always be so. In the history of any business random factors will have left an influence, and the incentive to take up a particular activity will sometimes be provided, not by the prior possession of an appropriate capability, but by the opportunity of a cheap acquisition, through a family or business connection or because of management's belief that the profitability of investment in some direction was being generally under-estimated. There is no need to deny, moreover, that a variety of potential gains are provided by grouping activities irrespective of their character; risks can be spread, the general managerial capability of the firm can be kept fully employed and the allocation of finance can be planned from the centre. None of this is in contradiction with the principle that it will pay most firms for most of the time to expand into areas of activity for which their particular capabilities lend them comparative advantage. A firm's activities may also, on occasions, be more similar than they superficially appear. If a firm acquired companies irrespective of the character of their activities we should term it conglomerate; but if the motive for the purchases were the belief that the companies were being badly managed, the hope being to restore them to health before re-selling them at a profit, the management would be exercising a particular capability.

....

IV

I have argued that organizations tend to specialize in activities which, in our special sense of the term, are similar. But the organization of industry has also to adapt itself to the fact that activities may be *complementary*. I shall say that activities are complementary when they represent different phases of a process of production and require in some way or another to be co-ordinated. But it is important that this notion of complementarity be understood to describe, for instance, not only the relationship between the manufacture of cars and their components, but also the relationship of each of these to the corresponding activities of research and development and of marketing. Now it is clear that similarity and complementarity, as I have defined them, are quite distinct; clutch linings are complementary to clutches and to cars but, in that they are best made by firms with a capability in asbestos fabrication, they are similar to drain-pipes and heat-proof suits. Similarly, the production of porcelain insulators is complementary to that of electrical switchgear but similar to other ceramic manufacture. And while the activity of retailing toothbrushes is complementary to their manufacture, it is similar to the activity of retailing soap. This notion of complementarity will require closer definition at a later stage, but it will be convenient first to introduce one further (and final) set of conceptual distinctions.

It is clear that complementary activities have to be co-ordinated both quantitatively and qualitatively. Polymer production has to be matched, for example, with spinning capacity, both in terms of output volume and product characteristics, and investment in heavy electrical equipment has likewise to be appropriate, in scale and type, to the planned construction of power stations. Now this co-ordination can be effected in three ways; by *direction*, by *co-operation* or through *market transactions*. Direction is employed when the activities are subject to a single control and fitted into one coherent plan. Thus where activities are to be co-ordinated by direction it is appropriate that they be *consolidated* in the sense of being undertaken jointly by one organization. Co-ordination is achieved through co-operation when two or more independent organizations agree to match their related plans in advance. The institutional counterparts to this form of co-ordination are the complex patterns of co-operation and affiliation which theoretical formulations too often tend to ignore. And, finally, co-ordination may come about spontaneously through market transactions, without benefit of either direction or co-operation or indeed any purposeful intent, as an indirect consequence of successive interacting decisions taken in response to changing profit opportunities. Let us now make use of this somewhat crude categorisation to re-interpret the questions with which we started.

....

V

What is the appropriate division of labour, we should now ask, between consolidation, co-operation and market transactions?

If we were able to assume that the scale on which an activity was undertaken did not affect its efficiency, and further that no special capabilities were ever required by the firm undertaking it, then there would be no limit to the extent to which co-ordination could be affected by direction within one organization. If production could be set up according to 'given' production functions with constant returns, no firm need ever buy from, or sell to, or co-operate with any other. Each of them would merely buy inputs, such as land and labour, and sell directly to consumers—which, indeed, is what in our model-building they are very often assumed to do. But, of course, activities do exhibit scale economies and do require specialized organizational capabilities for their undertaking, the result being that self-sufficiency of this kind is unattainable. The scope for co-ordination by direction within firms is narrowly circumscribed, in other words, by the existence of scale economies and the fact that complementary activities need not be similar. The larger the organization the greater the number of capabilities with which one may conceive it to be endowed and the greater the number of complementary activities that can, in principle, be made subject to co-ordination through direction; but even if a national economy were to be run as a single business, it would prove expedient to trade with the rest of the world. Some co-ordination, that is to say, must be left either to co-operation or to market transactions and it is to the respective roles of each of these that our attention must now turn.

Building and brick-making are dissimilar activities and each is undertaken by large numbers of enterprises. Ideally, the output of bricks ought to be matched to the volume of complementary construction that makes use of them and it is through market transactions that we expect this to come about. Brickmakers, in taking investment and output decisions, estimate future market trends; and errors in these estimates are registered in stock movements and price changes which can lead to corrective actions. As we all know, these adjustments may work imperfectly and I have myself argued elsewhere[5] that the model which we often use to represent this type of market is unsatisfactory. But this is a matter with which we cannot now concern ourselves. What is important, for our present purposes, is to note that impersonal co-ordination through market forces is relied upon where there is reason to expect aggregate demands to be more stable (and hence predictable) than their component elements. If co-ordination were to be sought through co-operation, then individual brick-makers would seek to match their investment and output plans *ex ante* with individual builders. Broadly speaking, this does not happen, although traditional links between buyers and sellers, such as are found in most markets, do introduce an element of this kind. Individual brick manufacturers rely, for the most part, on having enough customers to ensure some cancelling out of random fluctuations in their several demands. And where sales to final consumers are concerned, this reliance on the law of large numbers becomes all but universal. Thus we rely on markets when there is no attempt to match complementary activities *ex ante* by deliberately co-ordinating the corresponding plans; salvation is then sought, not through reciprocal undertakings, but on that stability with which aggregates, by the law of large numbers, are providentially endowed.

Let us now consider the need to co-ordinate the production of cans with tin plate or lacquers, of a particular car with a particular brake and a particular brake lining, of a type of glucose with the particular beer in which it is to be used, or a cigarette with the appropriate filter tip. Here we require to match not the aggregate output of a general-purpose input with the aggregate output for which it is needed, but of particular activities which, for want of a better word, we might call *closely complementary*. The co-ordination, both quantitative and qualitative, needed in these cases requires the co-operation of those concerned; and it is for this reason that the motor car companies are in intimate association with component makers, that Metal Box interests itself in its lacquer suppliers, Imperial Tobacco with Bunzl and so on. Co-ordination in these cases has to be promoted either through the consolidation of the activities within organizations with the necessary spread of capabilities, or through close co-operation, or by means of institutional arrangements which, by virtue of limited shareholdings and other forms of affiliation, come somewhere in between.

Here then we have the prime reason for the existence of the complex networks of co-operation and association the existence of which we noted earlier. They exist because of the need to co-ordinate closely complementary but dissimilar activities. This co-ordination cannot be left entirely to direction within firms because the activities are dissimilar, and cannot be left to market forces in that it requires not the balancing of the aggregate supply of something with the aggregate demand for it but rather the matching, both qualitative and quantitative, of individual enterprise plans.

VI

It is perhaps easiest to envisage co-ordination in terms of the matching, in quantity and specification, of intermediate output with final output, but I have chosen to refer to activities rather than goods in order to show that the scope is wider. The co-operation between Marks and Spencer and its suppliers is based most obviously on a division of labour between production and marketing; but we have seen that it amounts to much more than this in that Marks and Spencer performs a variety of services in the field of product development, product specification and process control that may be beyond the capability of the supplying firms. And one may observe that inter-firm co-operation is concerned very often with the transfer, exchange or pooling of technology. Thus a sub-contractor commonly complements his own capabilities with assistance and advice from the firm he supplies. New products also frequently require the co-operation of firms with different capabilities, and it was for this reason that ICI originally co-operated with Courtaulds in the development of nylon spinning and now co-operates with British Sidac in developing polypropylene film.

It is indeed appropriate to observe that the organization of industry has to adapt itself to the need for co-ordination of a rather special kind, for co-ordination, that is to say, between the development of technology and its exploitation. A full analysis of this important subject cannot be attempted here but it is relevant to consider those aspects of it that relate to our principal themes. What then are the respective roles, in relation to this kind of co-ordination, of direction, co-operation and market transactions? Obviously there are reasons why it may be convenient to co-ordinate the activities of development and manufacture through their consolidation within a single organization. Manufacturing activity is technology-producing as well as technology-dependent; in the process of building aircraft or turbo-alternators difficulties are encountered and overcome and the stock of knowledge and experience is thereby increased. But there are also good reasons why a firm might not be content to seek the full exploitation of its development work through its own manufacturing activity. The company that develops a new product may itself lack sufficient capacity to manufacture it on the scale needed to meet the demand and may not have time enough to build up the required additional organization and material facilities. It could, of course, seek to acquire appropriate capacity by buying firms that already possessed it, but this policy might prove unattractive if it entailed taking over all the other interests to which these firms were committed. The innovating firm might judge that its comparative advantage lay in developing new products and be reluctant therefore to employ its best managerial talents in increasing the output of old ones. It would be aware, moreover, that not only manufacturing but marketing capability would be needed and might properly consider that it neither possessed nor could readily acquire this, especially in foreign countries. All these considerations may lead firms to seek some indirect exploitation of a product development. And, in the case of the new process, the incentive might be a wide variety of fields of production in which the process could be used.

The indirect exploitation of new technology could be sought, in terms of our nomenclature, either through market transactions or through co-operation with other firms. But technology is a very special commodity and the market for it a very special market. It is not always easy, in the first place, to stop knowledge becoming a free good. The required scarcity may have to be created artificially through a legal device, the patent system, which establishes exclusive rights in the use or the disposal of new knowledge. Markets may then develop in licences of right. But these are very special markets in that the commercial freedom of those operating within them is necessarily restricted. For suppose that A were to sell to B for a fixed sum a licence to make a new product, but at the same time retained the unfettered right to continue to produce and sell the product himself. In this case the long- and short-run marginal costs of production of the good would, for both parties, be below unit costs (because of the fixed cost incurred by A in the development work and B as a lump sum paid for the licence) so that unrestrained competition would drive prices to unremunerative levels. It might at first seem that this danger could be avoided if licences were charged for as a royalty on sales, which, unlike a fixed sum, would enter into variable costs. But the licensee might still require assurance that the licensor, unburdened by this cost element, would not subsequently set a price disadvantageous to him or even license to others on more favourable terms. These dangers could be avoided if the parties were to bind themselves by price or market-sharing agreements or simply by the prudent adoption of the policy of live and let live. But, in one way or another, it seems likely that competition would in some degree have been diminished.[6]

It would appear, therefore, on the basis of these considerations, that where the creation and exploitation of technology is co-ordinated through market transactions—transactions in licences—there will already be some measure of co-operation between the parties. The co-operation may, of course, amount to little more than is required not to rock, or at any rate not to sink, the boat. But there are reasons why it will generally go beyond this. Technology cannot always be transferred simply by selling the right to use a process. It is rarely reducible to mere information to be passed on but consists also of experience and skills. In terms of Professor Ryle's celebrated distinction, much of it is 'knowledge how' rather than 'knowledge that'. Thus when one firm agrees to provide technology to another it will, in the general case, supply not only licences but also continuing technical assistance, drawings, designs and tools. At this stage the relation between the firms becomes clearly co-operative and although, at its inception, there may be a giver and a receiver, subsequent development may lead to a more equal exchange of assistance and the pooling of patents. Arrangements of this kind form an important part of the networks of co-operation and affiliation to which I have made such frequent reference.

VII

This article began by referring to a vision of the economy in which firms featured as islands of planned co-ordination in a sea of market relations. The deficiencies of this representation of things will by now be clear. Firms are not islands but are linked together in patterns of co-operation and affiliation. Planned co-ordination does not stop at the frontiers of the individual firm but can be effected through co-operation between firms. The dichotomy between firm and market, between directed and spontaneous co-ordination, is misleading; it ignores the institutional fact of inter-firm co-operation and assumes away the distinct method of co-ordination that this can provide.

The analysis I presented made use of the notion of activities, these being understood to denote not only manufacturing processes but to relate equally to research, development and marketing. We noted that activities had to be undertaken by organizations with appropriate capabilities. Activities that made demands on the same capabilities were said to be similar; those that had to be matched, in level or specification, were said to be complementary. Firms would find it expedient, for the most part, to concentrate on similar activities. Where activities were both similar and complementary they could be co-ordinated by direction within an individual business. Generally, however, this would not be the case and the activities to be co-ordinated, being dissimilar, would be the responsibility of different firms. Co-ordination would then have to be brought about either through co-operation, firms agreeing to match their plans *ex ante*, or through the processes of adjustment set in train by the market mechanism. And the circumstances appropriate to each of these alternatives were briefly discussed.

Let me end with two further observations. I have sought to stress the co-operative element in business relations but by no means take the view that where there is co-operation, competition is no more. Marks and Spencer can drop a supplier; a sub-contractor can seek another principal; technical agreements have a stated term and the conditions on which they may be re-negotiated will depend on how the strengths of the parties change and develop; the licensee of today may become (as the Americans have found in Japan) the competitor of tomorrow. Firms form partners for the dance but, when the music stops, they can change them. In these circumstances competition is still at work even if it has changed its mode of operation.

Theories of industrial organization, it seems to me, should not try to do too much. Arguments designed to prove the inevitability of this or that particular form of organization are hard to reconcile, not only with the differences between the capitalist and socialist worlds, but also with the differences that exist within each of these. We do not find the same organization of industry in Jugoslavia and the Soviet Union, or in the United States and Japan. We ought to think in terms of the substitutability of industrial structures in the same way as Professor Gerschenkron has suggested in relation to the prerequisites for economic development. It will be clear, in some situations, that co-ordination has to be accomplished by direction, by co-operation or through market transactions, but there will be many others in which the choice will be difficult but not very important. In Great Britain, for example, the artificial textile industry is vertically integrated and the manufacturers maintain that this facilitates co-ordination of production and development. In the United States, on the other hand, antitrust legislation has checked vertical integration, but the same co-ordination is achieved through close co-operation between individual firms at each stage. It is important, moreover, not to draw too sharp lines of distinction between the techniques of co-ordination themselves. Co-operation may come close to direction when one of the parties is clearly predominant; and some degree of *ex ante* matching of plans is to be found in all markets in which firms place orders in advance. This points, however, not to the invalidity of our triple distinction but merely to the need to apply it with discretion.[7]

Notes

1. The sceptical reader might care to look up a few cases in the reports of the Monopolies Commission. The following example is found in the report on cigarette filter tips. Cigarette Components Ltd. made filter tips for Imperial Tobacco and Gallaher using machines hired from these companies. It has foreign subsidiaries, some wholly and some partially owned. It was both licensee and

licensor of various patents one of which was held by the Celfil Trust, registered in Liechtenstein, with regard to the ultimate control of which Cigarette Components told the Monopolies Commission they could only surmise. Nevertheless, this patent was of key importance in that the Celfil licensees, of which Cigarette Components was only one, were bound by price and market sharing arrangement. Cigarette Components was itself owned by Bunzl Ltd., in which Imperial Tobacco had a small shareholding. The raw material for the tips is cellulose acetate tow which was made by Ectona Fibres Ltd., a company in which Bunzl had a 40% interest and a subsidiary of Eastman Kodak 60%. Agreements had been made providing that, should Bunzl lose control of Cigarette Components, then Eastman could buy out their shares in Ectona . . . etc., etc.

2. See the *Economic Bulletin for Europe*, vol. 21, no. 1.
3. E. T. Penrose, *The Theory of the Growth of the Firm* (Oxford University Press, 1959).
4. E. T. Penrose, ibid.
5. In *Information and Investment* (Oxford University Press, 1961).
6. Professor Arrow reaches a different conclusion. The matter is considered in his article 'Economic Welfare and the Allocation of Resources for Invention' published in *The Rate and Direction of Inventive Activity*, (edited by National Bureau of Economic Research, Princeton University Press, 1952). Professor Arrow maintains that 'an incentive to invent can exist even under perfect competition in the produce markets though not, of course, in the "market" for the information containing the invention' and that 'provided only that suitable royalty payments can be demanded, an inventor can profit without disturbing the competitive nature of the industry.'

The issue is simplest in the case of a cost-saving invention. Professor Arrow considers a product made under constant costs both before and after the invention and shows how the inventor can charge a royalty that makes it just worth while for firms making the product to acquire a licence. On the face of it one might then conclude that the licensor would have no need to bind himself not to reduce price below the level that provided licensees with a normal profit or to re-license for a lesser royalty, for, if he were to do either of these things, existing licensees would make losses, stop producing and therefore discontinue royalty payments. But this conclusion is valid only under the highly special assumption of there being no fixed costs. For firms will in general continue in production so long as price does not fall below variable costs. Thus the licensor could find it in his interest, having sold as many licences as he could at the higher royalty, to license others at a lower royalty, or to enter the market himself. He would thus extend the market for the product and increase his earning provided, of course, that price were kept above variable costs and therefore high enough to induce the original (and by then no doubt aggrieved) licensees to stay in business. It is true, of course, that *in the long run* fixed plant would wear out and firms deprived of their quasi-rents would cease producing, but the fact that an opportunity for exploitation is merely temporary does not warrant our assuming that it will not be seized. In general the licensor would stand to gain by 'cheating' the licensees in the manner described and the latter would therefore want some measure of assurance (which need not be formal) that he would not do so. There would be a market for licences, that is to say, only if the commercial freedom of the licensor were in this way reduced.

It may be that Professor Arrow would not consider this to represent a significant restriction of competition; and indeed the important practical issue concerns the manner and degree in which the parties accept limitations on their freedom of action. I have suggested that the licensor would be in a position, having licensed other firms, subsequently to deprive them of expected profits. A firm will therefore seek a licence only if it believes that this will not happen, but it may consider that sufficient assurance is provided by the fact that the licensor, in his own long-run interest, will not wish to acquire the reputation for such sharp practice. Much the same situation obtains in the context of the relationship between a large purchaser and a small supplier. Marks and Spencer, having offered attractive enough terms to induce the blanket manufacturer to devote a large proportion of his capacity to meet its needs, might subsequently press for a price reduction that left him with a poor return. The hapless supplier, in the short run at any rate, might have no option but to give way. But although the purchaser could thus act, it could scarcely be in his own long-run interest to acquire the reputation for doing so.

The upshot would therefore seem to be this. A market for licences can function only if the parties to the transactions accept some restraints, but, in certain circumstances, no more restraint might be required than enlightened self-interest could be depended upon by itself to ensure. In practice, of course, licensing arrangements are commonly associated with much more—and often more for-mal—restraint of trade, the extent of which may or may not be greater than is necessary for the transfer of technology to take place.

7. In his article, 'The Nature of the Firm', _Economica_, 1937, 386–405, R. H. Coase explains the boundary between firm and market in terms of the relative cost, at the margin, of the kinds of co-ordination they respectively provide. The explana-tion that I have provided is not inconsistent with his but might be taken as giving content to the notion of this relative cost by specifying the factors that affect it. My own approach differs also in that I distinguish explicitly between inter-firm co-operation and market transactions as modes of co-ordination.

4 Production, Information Costs, and Economic Organization

Armen A. Alchian and Harold Demsetz

The mark of a capitalistic society is that resources are owned and allocated by such nongovernmental organizations as firms, households, and markets. Resource owners increase productivity through cooperative specialization and this leads to the demand for economic organizations which facilitate co-operation. When a lumber mill employs a cabinetmaker, co-operation between specialists is achieved within a firm, and when a cabinetmaker purchases wood from a lumberman, the co-operation takes place across markets (or between firms). Two important problems face a theory of economic organization—to explain the conditions that determine whether the gains from specialization and cooperative production can better be obtained within an organization like the firm, or across markets, and to explain the structure of the organization.

It is common to see the firm characterized by the power to settle issues by fiat, by authority, or by disciplinary action superior to that available in the conventional market. This is delusion. The firm does not own all its inputs. It has no power of fiat, no authority, no disciplinary action any different in the slightest degree from ordinary market contracting between any two people. I can 'punish' you only by withholding future business or by seeking redress in the courts for any failure to honor our exchange agreement. That is exactly all that any employer can do. He can fire or sue, just as I can fire my grocer by stopping purchases from him or sue him for delivering faulty products. What then is the content of the presumed power to manage and assign workers to various tasks? Exactly the same as one little consumer's power to

Acknowledgment is made for financial aid from the E. Lilly Endowment, Inc. grant to UCLA for research in the behavioural effects of property rights.

manage and assign his grocer to various tasks. The single consumer can assign his grocer to the task of obtaining whatever the customer can induce the grocer to provide at a price acceptable to both parties. That is precisely all that an employer can do to an employee. To speak of managing, directing, or assigning workers to various tasks is a deceptive way of noting that the employer continually is involved in renegotiation of contracts on terms that must be acceptable to both parties. Telling an employee to type this letter rather than to file that document is like my telling a grocer to sell me this brand of tuna rather than that brand of bread. I have no contract to continue to purchase from the grocer and neither the employer nor the employee is bound by any contractual obligations to continue their relationship. Long-term contracts between employer and employee are not the essence of the organization we call a firm. My grocer can count on my returning day after day and purchasing his services and goods even with the prices not always marked on the goods—because I know what they are—and he adapts his activity to conform to my directions to him as to what I want each day . . . he is not my employee.

Wherein then is the relationship between a grocer and his employee different from that between a grocer and his customers? It is in a *team* use of inputs and a centralized position of some party in the contractual arrangements of *all* other inputs. It is the *centralized contractual agent in a team productive process*—not some superior authoritarian directive or disciplinary power. Exactly what is a team process and why does it induce the contractual form, called the firm? These problems motivate the inquiry of this paper.

1. The Metering Problem

The economic organization through which input owners cooperate will make better use of their comparative advantages to the extent that it facilitates the payment of rewards in accord with productivity. If rewards were random, and without regard to productive effort, no incentive to productive effort would be provided by the organization; and if rewards were negatively correlated with productivity the organization would be subject to sabotage. Two key demands are placed on an economic organization—metering input productivity and metering rewards.[1]

Metering problems sometimes can be resolved well through the exchange of products across competitive markets, because in many situations markets yield a high correlation between rewards and productivity. If a farmer increases his output of wheat by 10 per cent at the prevailing market price, his receipts also increase by 10 per cent. This method of organizing economic activity meters the *output directly*, reveals the marginal product and apportions the *rewards* to resource owners in accord with that direct measurement of their outputs. The success of this decentralized, market exchange in promoting productive specialization requires that changes in market rewards fall on those responsible for changes in *output*.[2]

The classic relationship in economics that runs from marginal productivity to the distribution of income implicitly *assumes* the existence of an organization, be it the market or the firm, that allocates rewards to resources in accord with their productivity. The problem of economic organization, the economical means of metering productivity and rewards, is not confronted directly in the classical analysis of production and distribution. Instead, that analysis tends to assume sufficiently economic—or zero cost—means, as if productivity automatically created its reward. We conjecture the direction of causation is the reverse—the specific system of rewarding which is relied upon stimulates a particular productivity response. If the economic organization meters poorly, with rewards and productivity only loosely correlated, then productivity will be smaller; but if the economic organization meters well productivity will be greater. What makes metering difficult and hence induces means of economising on metering costs?

....

2. Team Production

Two men jointly lift heavy cargo into trucks. Solely by observing the total weight loaded per day, it is impossible to determine each person's marginal productivity. With team production it is difficult, solely by observing total output, to either define or determine *each* individual's contribution to this output of the cooperating inputs. The output is yielded by a team, by definition, and it is not a *sum* of separable outputs of each of its members. Team production of Z involves at least two inputs, X_i, and X_j, with $\partial^2 Z / \partial X_i \partial X_j \neq 0$.[3] The production function is *not* separable into two functions each involving only inputs X_i or only inputs X_j. Consequently there is no *sum* of Z of two separable functions to treat as the Z of the team production function. (An example of a *separable* case is $Z = aX_i^2 + bX_j^2$, *which is separable into* $Z_i = aX_i^2$, and $Z_j = bX_j^2$, and $Z = Z_i + Z_j$. This is not team production.) There exist production techniques in which the Z obtained is greater than if

X_i and X_j had produced separable Z. Team production will be used if it yields an output enough larger than the sum of separable production of Z to cover the costs of organizing and disciplining team members—the topics of this paper.[4]

Usual explanations of the gains from cooperative behavior rely on exchange and production in accord with the comparative advantage specialization principle with separable additive production. However, as suggested above there is a source of gain from cooperative activity involving working as a *team*, wherein individual cooperating inputs do not yield identifiable, separate products which can be *summed* to measure the total output. For this cooperative productive activity, here called 'team' production, measuring *marginal* productivity and making payments in accord therewith is more expensive by an order of magnitude than for separable production functions.

Team production, to repeat, is production in which 1) several types of resources are used and 2) the product is not a sum of separable outputs of each cooperating resource. An additional factor creates a team organization problem—3) not all resources used in team production belong to one person.

We do not inquire into why all the jointly used resources are not owned by one person, but instead into the types of organization, contracts, and informational and payment procedures used among owners of teamed inputs. With respect to the one-owner case, perhaps it is sufficient merely to note that (a) slavery is prohibited, (b) one might assume risk aversion as a reason for one person's not borrowing enough to purchase all the assets or sources of services rather than renting them, and (c) the purchase-resale spread may be so large that costs of short-term ownership exceed rental costs. Our problem is viewed basically as one of organization among different people, not of the physical goods or services, however much there must be selection and choice of combination of the latter.

How can the members of a team be rewarded and induced to work efficiently? In team production, marginal products of cooperative team members are not so directly and separably (i.e. cheaply) observable. What a team offers to the market can be taken as the marginal product of the team but not of the team members. The costs of metering or ascertaining the marginal products of the team's members is what calls forth new organizations and procedures. Clues to each input's productivity can be secured by observing *behavior* of individual inputs. When lifting cargo into the truck, how rapidly does a man move to the next piece to be loaded, how many cigarette breaks does he take, does the item being lifted tilt downward toward his side?

If detecting such behavior were costless, neither party would have an incentive to shirk, because neither could impose the cost of his shirking on the other (if their co-operation was agreed to voluntarily). But since costs must be incurred to monitor each other, each input owner will have more incentive to shirk when he works as part of a team, than if his performance could be monitored easily or if he did not work as a team. If there is a net increase in productivity available by team production, net of the metering cost associated with disciplining the team, then team production will be relied upon rather than a multitude of bilateral exchange of separable individual outputs.

Both leisure and higher income enter a person's utility function.[5] Hence, each person should adjust his work and realized reward so as to equate the marginal rate of substitution between leisure and production of real output to his marginal rate of substitution in consumption. That is, he would adjust his rate of work to bring his demand prices of leisure and output to equality with their true costs. However, with detection, policing, monitoring, measuring or metering costs, each person will be induced to take more leisure, because the effect of relaxing on *his realized* (reward) rate of substitution between output and leisure will be less than the effect on the *true* rate of substitution. His realized cost of leisure will fall more than the true cost of leisure, so he 'buys' more leisure (i.e. more nonpecuniary reward).

If his relaxation cannot be detected perfectly at zero cost, part of its effects will be borne by others in the team, thus making *his* realized cost of relaxation less than the true total cost to the team. The difficulty of detecting such actions permits the private costs of his actions to be less than their full costs. Since each person responds to his private realisable rate of substitution (in production) rather than the true total (i.e. social) rate, and so long as there are costs for other people to detect his shift toward relaxation, it will not pay (them) to force him to readjust completely by making him realize the true cost. Only enough efforts will be made to equate the marginal gains of detection activity with the marginal costs of detection; and that implies a lower rate of productive effort and more shirking than in a costless monitoring, or measuring, world.

In a university, the faculty use office telephones, paper, and mail for personal uses beyond strict university productivity. The university administrators could stop such practices by identifying *the* responsible person in each case, but they can do so only at higher costs than administrators are willing to incur. The extra costs of identifying each party (rather than merely identifying the presence of such activity) would exceed the savings from diminished faculty 'turpitudinal peccadilloes'. So the faculty is allowed some degree of 'privileges, perquisites, or fringe-benefits.' And the total of the pecuniary wages paid is lower because of this irreducible (at acceptable costs) degree of amenity-seizing activity. Pay is lower in pecuniary terms and higher in leisure, conveniences, and ease of work. But still every person would prefer to see detection made more effective (if it were somehow possible to monitor costlessly) so that he, as part of the now more effectively producing team, could thereby realize a higher pecuniary pay and less leisure. If everyone could, at zero cost, have his reward-realized rate brought to the true production possibility real rate, all could achieve a more preferred position. But detection of the responsible parties is costly; that cost acts like a tax on work rewards.[6] Viable shirking is the result.

What forms of organizing team production will lower the cost of detecting 'performance' (i.e. marginal productivity) and bring personally realized rates of substitution closer to true rates of substitution? Market competition, in principle, could monitor some team production. (It already *organizes* teams.) Input owners who are not team members can offer, in return for a smaller share of the team's rewards, to replace excessively (i.e. overpaid) shirking members. Market competition among potential team members would determine team membership and individual rewards. There would be no team leader, manager, organizer, owner, or employer. For such decentralized organizational control to work, outsiders, possibly after observing each team's total output, can speculate about their capabilities as team members and, by a market competitive process, revised teams with greater productive ability will be formed and sustained. Incumbent members will be constrained by threats of replacement by outsiders offering services for lower reward shares or offering greater rewards to the other members of the team. Any team member who shirked in the expectation that the reduced output effect would not be attributed to him will be displaced if his activity is detected. Teams of productive inputs, like business units, would evolve in apparent spontaneity in the market—without any central organizing agent, team manager, or boss.

But completely effective control cannot be expected from individualized market competition for two reasons. First, for this competition to be completely effective, new challengers for team membership must know where, and to what extent, shirking is a serious problem, i.e. know they can increase net output as compared with the inputs they replace. To the extent that this is true it is probably possible for existing fellow team members to recognize the shirking. But, by definition, the detection of shirking by observing team output is costly for team production. Secondly, assume the presence of detection costs, and assume that in order to secure a place on the team a new input owner must accept a smaller share of rewards (or a promise to produce more). Then his incentive to shirk would still be at least as great as the incentives of the inputs replaced, because he still bears less than the entire reduction in team output for which he is responsible.

3. The Classical Firm

One method of reducing shirking is for someone to specialize as a monitor to check the input performance of team members.[7] But who will monitor the monitor? One constraint on the monitor is the aforesaid market competition offered by other monitors, but for reasons already given, that is not perfectly effective. Another constraint can be imposed on the monitor: give him title to the net earnings of the team, net of payments to other inputs. If owners of co-operating inputs agree with the monitor that he is to receive any residual product above prescribed amounts (hopefully, the marginal value products of the other inputs), the monitor will have an added incentive not to shirk as a monitor. Specialization in monitoring plus reliance on a residual claimant status will reduce shirking; but additional links are needed to forge the firm of classical economic theory. How will the residual claimant monitor the other inputs?

We use the term monitor to connote several activities in addition to its disciplinary connotation. It connotes measuring output performance, apportioning rewards, observing the input behavior of inputs as means of detecting or estimating their marginal productivity and giving assignments or instructions in what to do and how to do it. (It also includes, as we shall show later, authority to terminate or revise contracts.) Perhaps the contrast between a football coach and team captain is helpful. The coach selects strategies and tactics and sends in instructions about what plays to utilize. The captain is essentially an observer and reporter of the performance at close hand of the members. The latter is an inspector-steward and the former a supervisor manager. For the present all these activities are included in the rubric 'monitoring'. All these tasks are, in principle, negotiable across markets, but we are presuming that such market measurement of marginal productivities and job reassignments are not so cheaply performed for team production. And in particular our analysis suggests that it is not so much the costs of spontaneously negotiating contracts in the markets among groups for team production as it is the detection of the performance of individual members of the team that calls for the organization noted here.

The specialist *who receives the residual rewards* will be the monitor of the members of the team (i.e. will manage the use of co-operative inputs). The monitor earns his residual through the reduction in shirking that he brings about, not only by the prices that he agrees to pay the owners of the inputs, but also by observing and directing the actions or uses of these inputs. *Managing or examining the ways to which inputs are used in team production is a method of metering the marginal productivity of individual inputs to the team's output.*

To discipline team members and reduce shirking, the residual claimant must have power to revise the contract terms and incentives of *individual* members without having to terminate or alter every other input's contract. Hence, team members who seek to increase their productivity will assign to the monitor not only the residual claimant right but also the right to alter individual membership and performance on the team. Each team member, of course, can terminate his own membership (i.e. quit the team), but only the monitor may unilaterally terminate the membership of any of the other members without necessarily terminating the team itself or his association with the team; and he alone can expand or reduce membership, alter the mix of membership, or sell the right to be the residual claimant-monitor of the team. It is this entire bundle of rights: 1) to be a residual claimant; 2) to observe input behavior; 3) to be the central party common to all contracts with inputs; 4) to alter the membership of the team; and 5) to sell these rights, that defines the *ownership* (or the employer) of the *classical* (capitalist, free-enterprise) firm. The coalescing of these rights has arisen, our analysis asserts, because it resolves the shirking-information problem of team production better than does the noncentralized contractual arrangement.

The relationship of each team member to the *owner* of the firm (i.e. the party common to all input contracts *and* the residual claimant) is simply a 'quid pro quo' contract. Each makes a purchase and sale. The employee 'orders' the owner of the team to pay him money in the same sense that the employer directs the team member to perform certain acts. The employee can terminate the contract as readily as can the employer, and long-term contracts, therefore, are not an essential attribute of the firm. Nor are 'authoritarian', 'dictational', or 'fiat' attributes relevant to the conception of the firm or its efficiency.

In summary, two necessary conditions exist for the emergence of the firm on the prior assumption that more than pecuniary wealth enter utility functions: 1) It is possible to increase productivity through team-oriented production, a production technique for which it is costly to directly measure the marginal outputs of the co-operating inputs. This makes it more difficult to restrict shirking through simple market exchange between co-operating inputs. 2) It is economical to estimate marginal productivity by observing or specifying input behavior. The simultaneous occurrence of both these preconditions leads to the contractual organization of inputs, known as the *classical capitalist firms* with (a) joint input production, (b) several input owners, (c) one party who is common to all the contracts of the joint inputs, (d) who has rights to renegotiate any input's contract independently of contracts with other input owners, (e) who holds the residual claim, and (f) who has the right to sell his central contractual residual status.[8]

3.1. *Other Theories of the Firm*

At this juncture, as an aside, we briefly place this theory of the firm in the contexts of those offered by Ronald Coase and Frank Knight.[9] Our view of the firm is not necessarily inconsistent with Coase's: we attempt to go further and identify refutable implications. Coase's penetrating insight is to make more of the fact that markets do not operate costlessly, and he relies on the cost of using markets to *form* contracts as his basic explanation for the existence of firms. We do not disagree with the proposition that, *celeris paribus*, the higher is the cost of transacting across markets the greater will be the comparative advantage of organizing resources within the firm; it is a difficult proposition to disagree with or to refute. We could with equal ease subscribe to a theory of the firm based on the cost of managing, for surely it is true that, *celeris paribus*, the lower is the cost of managing the greater will be the comparative advantage of organizing resources within the firm. To move the theory forward, it is necessary to know what is meant by a firm and to explain the circumstances under which the cost of 'managing' resources is low relative to the cost of allocating resources through market transaction. The conception of and rationale for the classical firm that we propose takes a step down the path pointed out by Coase toward that goal. Consideration of team production, team organisation, difficulty in metering outputs, and the problem of shirking are important to our explanation but, so far as we can ascertain, not in Coase's. Coase's analysis insofar as it had heretofore been developed would suggest open-ended contracts but does not appear to imply anything more—neither the residual claimant status nor the distinction between employee and subcontractor status (nor any of the implications indicated below). And it is not true that employees are generally employed on the basis of long-term contractual arrangements any more than on a series of short-term or indefinite length contracts.

The importance of our proposed additional elements is revealed, for example, by the explanation of why the person to whom the control monitor is responsible receives the residual, and also by our later discussion of the implications about the corporation, partnerships, and profit sharing. These alternative forms for organization of the firm are difficult to resolve on the basis of market transaction costs only. Our exposition also suggests a definition of the classical firm—something crucial that was heretofore absent.

In addition, sometimes a technological development will lower the cost of market transactions while, at the same time, it expands the role of the firm. When the 'putting out' system was used for weaving, inputs were organized largely through market negotiations. With the development of efficient central sources of power, it became economical to perform weaving in proximity to the power source and to engage in team production. The bringing in of weavers surely must have resulted in a reduction in the cost of negotiating (forming) contracts. Yet, what we observe is the beginning of the factory system in which inputs are organized within a firm. Why? The weavers did not simply move to a common source of power that they could tap like an electric line, purchasing power while they used their own equipment. Now team production in the joint use of equipment became more important. The measurement of marginal productivity, which now involved interactions between workers, especially through their joint use of machines, became more difficult though contract negotiating cost was reduced, while managing the *behavior* of inputs became easier because of the increased centralization of activity. The firm as an organization expanded even though the cost of transactions was reduced by the advent of centralized power. The same could be said for modern assembly lines. Hence the emergence of central power sources expanded the scope of productive activity in which the firm enjoyed a comparative advantage as an organizational form.

Some economists, following Knight, have identified the bearing of risks of wealth changes with the director or central employer without explaining why that is a viable arrangement. Presumably, the more risk-averse inputs become employees rather than owners of the classical firm. Risk averseness and uncertainty *with regard to the firm's fortunes* have little, if anything, to do with our explanation although it helps to explain why all resources in a team are not owned by one person. That is, the role of risk taken in the sense of absorbing the windfalls that buffet the firm because of unforeseen competition, technological change, or fluctuations in demand are not central to our theory, although it is true that imperfect knowledge and, therefore, risk, in *this* sense of risk, underlie the problem of monitoring team behavior. We deduce the system of paying the manager with a residual claim (the equity) from the desire to have efficient means to reduce shirking so as to make team production economical and not from the smaller aversion to the risks of enterprise in a dynamic economy. We conjecture that 'distribution-of-risk' is not a valid rationale for the *existence* and organization of the *classical* firm.

Although we have emphasized team production as creating a costly metering task and have treated team production as an essential (necessary?) condition for the firm, would not other obstacles to cheap metering also call forth the same kind of contractual arrangement here denoted as a firm? For example, suppose a farmer produces wheat in an easily ascertained quantity but with subtle and difficult to detect quality variations determined by how the farmer grew the wheat. A vertical integration could allow a purchaser to control the farmer's behavior in order to more economically estimate productivity. But this is not a case of joint or team production, unless 'information' can be considered part of the product. (While a good case could be made for that broader conception of production, we shall ignore it here.) Instead of forming a firm, a buyer can contract to have his inspector on the site of production, just as home builders contract with architects to supervise building contracts; that arrangement is not a firm. Still, a firm might be organized in the production of many products wherein no team production or jointness of use of separately owned resources is involved.

This possibility rather clearly indicates a broader, or complementary, approach to that which we have chosen. 1) As we do in this paper, it can be argued that the firm is the particular policing device utilized when joint team production is present. If other sources of high policing costs arise, as in the wheat case just indicated, some other form of contractual arrangement will be used. Thus to each source of informational cost there may be a different type of policing and contractual arrangement. 2) On the other hand, one can say that where policing is difficult across markets, various forms of contractual arrangements are devised, but there is no reason for that known as the firm to be uniquely related or even highly correlated with team production, as defined here. It might be used equally probably and viably for other sources of high policing cost. We have not intensively analyzed other sources, and we can only note that our current and readily revisable conjecture is that 1) is valid, and has motivated us in our current endeavour. In any event, the test of the theory advanced here is to see whether the conditions we have identified are necessary for firms to have long-run viability rather than merely births with high infant mortality. Conglomerate firms or collections of separate production agencies into one owning organization can be interpreted as an investment trust or investment diversification device—probably along the lines that motivated Knight's interpretation. A holding company can be called a firm, because of the common association of the word firm with any ownership unit that owns income sources. The term firm as commonly used is so turgid of meaning that we can not hope to explain every entity to which the name is attached in common or even technical literature. Instead, we seek to identify and explain a particular contractual arrangement induced by the cost of information factors analyzed in this paper.

4. Types of Firms

4.1. Profit-Sharing Firms

Explicit in our explanation of the capitalist firm is the assumption that the cost of *managing* the team's inputs by a central monitor, who disciplines himself because he is a residual claimant, is low relative to the cost of metering the marginal outputs of team members.

If we look within a firm to see who monitors—hires, fires, changes, promotes, and renegotiates—we should find him being a residual claimant or, at least, one whose pay or reward is more than any others correlated with fluctuations in the residual value of the firm. They more likely will have options or rights or bonuses than will inputs with other tasks.

An implicit 'auxiliary' assumption of our explanation of the firm is that the cost of team production is increased if the residual claim is not held entirely by the central monitor. That is, we assume that if profit sharing had to be relied upon for *all* team members, losses from the resulting increase in central monitoring shirking would exceed the output gains from the increased incentives of other team members not to shirk. If the optimal team size is only two owners of inputs, then an equal division of profits and losses between them will leave each with stronger incentives to reduce shirking than if the optimal team size is large, for in the latter case only a smaller percentage of the losses occasioned by the shirker will be borne by him. Incentives to shirk are positively related to the optimal size of the team under an equal profit-sharing scheme.[10]

The preceding does not imply that profit sharing is never viable. Profit sharing to encourage self-policing is more appropriate for small teams. And, indeed, where input owners are free to make whatever contractual arrangements suit them, as generally is true in capitalist economies, profit sharing seems largely limited to partnerships with a relatively small number of *active*[11] partners. Another advantage of such arrangements for smaller teams is that it permits more effective reciprocal monitoring among inputs. Monitoring need not be entirely specialized.

Profit sharing is more viable if small team size is associated with situations where the cost of specialized management of inputs is large relative to the increased productivity potential in team effort. We conjecture that the cost of managing team inputs increases if the productivity of a team member is difficult to correlate with his behavior. In 'artistic' or 'professional' work, watching a man's activities is not a good clue to what he is actually thinking or doing with his mind. While it is relatively easy to manage or direct the loading of trucks by a team of dock workers where input activity is so highly related in an obvious way to output, it is more difficult to manage and direct a lawyer in the preparation and presentation of a case. Dock workers can be directed in detail without the monitor himself loading the truck, and assembly line workers can be monitored by varying the speed of the assembly line, but detailed direction in the preparation of a law case would require in much greater degree that the monitor prepare the case himself. As a result, artistic or professional inputs, such as lawyers, advertising specialists, and doctors, will be given relatively freer reign with regard to individual behavior. If the management of inputs is relatively costly, or ineffective, as it would seem to be in these cases, but, nonetheless if team effort is more productive than separable production with exchange across markets, then there will develop a tendency to use profit-sharing schemes to provide incentives to avoid shirking.[12]

4.2. *Socialist Firms*

We have analyzed the classical proprietorship and the profit-sharing firms in the context of free association and choice of economic organization. Such organizations need not be the most viable when political constraints limit the forms of organization that can be chosen. It is one thing to have profit sharing when professional or artistic talents are used by small teams. But if political or tax or subsidy considerations induce profit-sharing techniques when these are not otherwise economically justified, then additional management techniques will be developed to help reduce the degree of shirking.

For example, most, if not all, firms in Jugoslavia are owned by the employees in the restricted sense that all share in the residual. This is true for large firms and for firms which employ nonartistic, or nonprofessional, workers as well. With a decay of political constraints, most of these firms could be expected to rely on paid wages rather than shares in the residual. This rests on our auxiliary assumption that general sharing in the residual results in losses from enhanced shirking by the monitor that exceed the gains from reduced shirking by residual-sharing employees. If this were not so, profit sharing with employees should have occurred more frequently in Western societies where such organizations are neither banned nor preferred politically. Where residual sharing by employees is politically imposed, as in Jugoslavia, we are led to expect that some management technique will arise to reduce the shirking by the central monitor, a technique that will not be found frequently in Western societies since the monitor retains all (or much) of the residual in the West and profit sharing is largely confined to small, professional-artistic team production situations. We do find in the larger scale residual-sharing firms in Jugoslavia that there are employee committees that can recommend (to the state) the termination of a manager's contract (veto his continuance) with the enterprise. We conjecture that the workers' committee is given the right to recommend the termination of the manager's contract precisely because the general sharing of the residual increases 'excessively' the manager's incentive to shirk.[13]

4.3. The Corporation

All firms must initially acquire command over some resources. The corporation does so primarily by selling promises of future returns to those who (as creditors or owners) provide financial capital. In some situations resources can be acquired in advance from consumers by promises of future delivery (for example, advance sale of a proposed book). Or where the firm is a few artistic or professional persons, each can 'chip in' with time and talent until the sale of services brings in revenues. For the most part, capital can be acquired more cheaply if many (risk-averse) investors contribute small portions to a large investment. The economies of raising large sums of equity capital in this way suggest that modifications in the relationship among corporate inputs are required to cope with the shirking problem that arises with profit sharing among large numbers of corporate stockholders. One modification is limited liability, especially for firms that are large relative to a stockholder's wealth. It serves to protect stockholders from large losses no matter how they are caused.

If every stock owner participated in each decision in a corporation, not only would large bureaucratic costs be incurred, but many would shirk the task of becoming well informed on the issue to be decided, since the losses associated with unexpectedly bad decisions will be borne in large part by the many other corporate shareholders. More effective control of corporate activity is achieved for most purposes by transferring decision authority to a smaller group, whose main function is to negotiate with and manage (renegotiate with) the other inputs of the team. The corporate stockholders retain the authority to revise the membership of the management group and over major decisions that affect the structure of the corporation or its dissolution.

As a result a new modification of partnerships is induced—the right to sale of corporate shares without approval of any other stockholders. Any shareholder can remove his wealth from control by those with whom he has differences of opinion. Rather than try to control the decisions of the management, which is harder to do with many stockholders than with only a few, unrestricted salability provides a more acceptable escape to each stockholder from continued policies with which he disagrees.

Indeed, the policing of managerial shirking relies on across-market competition from new groups of would-be managers as well as competition from members within the firm who seek to displace existing management. In addition to competition from outside and inside managers, control is facilitated by the temporary congealing of share votes into voting blocs owned by one or a few contenders. Proxy battles or stock-purchases concentrate the votes required to displace the existing management or modify managerial policies. But it is more than a change in policy that is sought by the newly formed financial interests, whether of new stockholders or not. It is the capitalization of expected future benefits into stock prices that concentrates on the innovators the wealth gains of their actions if they own large numbers of shares. Without capitalization of future benefits, there would be less incentive to incur the costs required to exert informed decisive influence on the corporation's policies and managing personnel. Temporarily, the structure of ownership is reformed, moving away from diffused ownership into decisive power blocs, and this is a transient resurgence of the classical firm with power again concentrated in those who have title to the residual.

In assessing the significance of stockholders' power it is not the usual diffusion of voting power that is significant but instead the frequency with which voting congeals into decisive changes. Even a one-man owned company may have a long term with just one manager—continuously being approved by the owner. Similarly a dispersed voting power corporation may be also characterized by a long-lived management. The question is the probability of replacement of the management if it behaves in ways not acceptable to a majority of the stockholders. The unrestricted salability of stock and the transfer of proxies enhances the probability of decisive action in the event current stockholders or any outsider believes that management is not doing a good job with the corporation. We are not comparing the corporate responsiveness to that of a single proprietorship; instead, we are indicating features of the corporate structure that are induced by the problem of delegated authority to manager-monitors.[14]

4.4. Mutual and Nonprofit Firms

The benefits obtained by the new management are greater if the stock can be purchased and sold, because this enables *capitalization* of anticipated future improvements into present *wealth* of new managers who bought stock and created a larger capital by their management changes. But in nonprofit corporations, colleges, churches, country clubs, mutual savings banks, mutual insurance companies, and 'coops', the future consequences of improved management are not capitalized into present wealth of stock-holders. (As if to make more difficult that competition by new would-be monitors, multiple shares of ownership in those enterprises cannot be bought by one person.) One should, therefore, find greater shirking in nonprofit, mutually owned enterprises. (This suggests that nonprofit enterprises are especially appropriate in realms of endeavour where more shirking is desired and where redirected uses of the enterprise in response to market-revealed values is less desired.)

4.5. Partnerships

Team production in artistic or professional intellectual skills will more likely be by partnerships than other types of team production. This amounts to market-organized team activity and to a non-employer status. Self-monitoring partnerships, therefore, will be used rather than employer-employee contracts, and these organizations will be small to prevent an excessive dilution of efforts through shirking. Also, partnerships are more likely to occur among relatives or long-standing acquaintances, not necessarily because they share a common utility function, but also because each knows better the other's work characteristics and tendencies to shirk.

4.6. Employee Unions

Employee unions, whatever else they do, perform as monitors for employees. Employers monitor employees and similarly employees monitor an employer's performance. Are correct wages paid on time and in good currency? Usually, this is extremely easy to check. But some forms of employer performance are less easy to meter and are more subject to employer shirking. Fringe benefits often are in non-pecuniary, contingent form; medical, hospital, and accident insurance, and retirement pensions are contingent payments or performances partly in *kind* by employers to employees. Each employee cannot judge the character of such payments as easily as money wages. Insurance is a contingent payment—what the employee will get upon the contingent event may come as a disappointment. If he could easily determine what other employees had gotten upon such contingent events he could judge more accurately the performance by the employer. He could 'trust' the employer not to shirk in such fringe contingent payments, but he would prefer an effective and economic monitor of those payments. We see a specialist monitor—the union employees' agent—hired by them and monitoring those aspects of employer payment most difficult for the employees to monitor. Employees should be willing to employ a specialist monitor to administer such hard-to-detect employer performance, even though their monitor has incentives to use pension and retirement funds not entirely for the benefit of employees.

5. Team Spirit and Loyalty

Every team member would prefer a team in which no one, not even himself, shirked. Then the true marginal costs and values could be equated to achieve more preferred positions. If one could enhance a common interest in nonshirking in the guise of a team loyalty or team spirit, the team would be more efficient. In those sports where team activity is most clearly exemplified, the sense of loyalty and team spirit is most strongly urged. Obviously the team is better, with team spirit and loyalty, because of the reduced shirking—not because of some other feature inherent in loyalty or spirit as such.[15]

Corporations and business firms try to instill a spirit of loyalty. This should not be viewed simply as a device to increase profits by over-working or misleading the employees, nor as an adolescent urge for belonging. It promotes a closer approximation to the employees' potentially available true rates of substitution between production and leisure and enables each team member to achieve a more preferred situation. The difficulty, of course, is to create economically that team spirit and loyalty. It can be preached with an aura of moral code of conduct—a morality with literally the same basis as the ten commandments—to restrict our conduct toward what we would choose if we bore our full costs.

6. Kinds of Inputs Owned by the Firm

To this point the discussion has examined why firms, as we have defined them, exist? That is, why is there an owner-employer who is the common party to contracts with other owners of inputs in team activity? The answer to that question should also indicate the kind of the jointly used resources likely to be owned by the central-owner-monitor and the kind likely to be hired from people who are not team-owners. Can we identify characteristics or features of various inputs that lead to their being hired or to their being owned by the firm?

How can residual-claimant, central-employer-owner demonstrate ability to pay the other hired inputs the promised amount in the event of a loss? He can pay in advance or he can commit wealth sufficient to cover negative residuals. The latter will take the form of machines, land, buildings, or raw materials committed to the firm. Commitments of labor-wealth (i.e. human wealth) given the property rights in people, is less feasible. These considerations suggest that residual claimants—owners of the firm—will be investors of resalable capital equipment in the firm. The goods or inputs more likely to be invested, than rented, by the owners of the enterprise, will have higher resale values relative to the initial cost and will have longer expected use in a firm relative to the economic life of the good.

But beyond these factors are those developed above to explain the existence of the institution known as the firm—the costs of detecting output performance. When a durable resource is used it will have a marginal product and a depreciation. Its use requires payment to cover at least use-induced depreciation; unless that user cost is specifically detectable, payment for it will be demanded in accord with *expected* depreciation. And we can ascertain circumstances for each. An indestructible hammer with a readily detectable marginal product has zero user cost. But suppose the hammer were destructible and that careless (which is easier than careful) use is more abusive and causes greater depreciation of the hammer. Suppose in addition the abuse is easier to detect by observing the way it is used than by observing only the hammer after its use, or by measuring the output scored from a hammer by a laborer. If the hammer were rented and used in the absence of the owner, the depreciation would be greater than if the use were observed by the owner and the user charged in accord with the imposed depreciation. (Careless use is more likely than careful use—if one does not pay for the greater depreciation.) An absentee owner would therefore ask for a higher rental price because of the higher *expected* user cost than if the item were used by the owner. The expectation is higher because of the greater difficulty of observing specific user cost, by inspection of the hammer after use. Renting is therefore in this case more costly than owner use. This is the valid content of the misleading expressions about ownership being more economical than renting—ignoring all other factors that may work in the opposite direction, like tax provision, short-term occupancy and capital risk avoidance.

Better examples are tools of the trade. Watch repairers, engineers, and carpenters tend to own their own tools especially if they are portable. Trucks are more likely to be employee owned rather than other equally expensive team inputs because it is relatively cheap for the driver to police the care taken in using a truck. Policing the use of trucks by a nondriver owner is more likely to occur for trucks that are not specialized to one driver, like public transit buses.

The factor with which we are concerned here is one related to the costs of monitoring not only the gross product performance of an input but also the abuse or depreciation inflicted on the input in the course of its use. If depreciation or user cost is more cheaply detected when the owner can see its use than by only seeing the input before and after, there is a force toward owner use rather than renting. Resources whose user cost is harder to detect when used by someone else, tend on this count to be owner-used. Absentee ownership, in the lay language, will be less likely. Assume momentarily that labor service cannot be performed in the absence of its owner. The labor owner can more cheaply monitor any abuse of himself than if somehow labor-services could be provided without the labor owner observing its mode of use or knowing what was happening. Also his incentive to abuse himself is increased if he does not own himself.[16]

The similarity between the preceding analysis and the question of absentee landlordism and of sharecropping arrangements is no accident. The same factors which explain the contractual arrangements known as a firm help to explain the incidence of tenancy, labor hiring or sharecropping.[17]

....

7. Firms as a Specialized Market Institution for Collecting, Collating, and Selling Input Information

The firm serves as a highly specialized surrogate market. Any person contemplating a joint-input activity must search and detect the qualities of available joint inputs. He could contact an employment agency, but that

Armen A. Alchian and Harold Demsetz

agency in a small town would have little advantage over a large firm with many inputs. The employer, by virtue of monitoring many inputs, acquires special superior information about their productive talents. This aids his *directive* (i.e. market hiring) efficiency. He 'sells' his information to employee-inputs as he aids them in ascertaining good input combinations for team activity. Those who work as employees or who rent services to him are using him to discern superior combinations of inputs. Not only does the director-employer 'decide' what each input will produce, he also estimates which heterogeneous inputs will work together jointly more efficiently, and he does this in the context of a privately owned market for forming teams. The department store is a firm and is a superior private market. People who shop and work in one town can as well shop and work in a privately owned firm.

This marketing function is obscured in the theoretical literature by the assumption of homogeneous factors. Or it is tacitly left for individuals to do themselves via personal market search, much as if a person had to search without benefit of specialist retailers. Whether or not the firm arose because of this efficient information service, it gives the director-employer more knowledge about the productive talents of the team's inputs, and a basis for superior decisions about efficient or profitable combinations of those heterogeneous resources.

In other words, opportunities for profitable team production by inputs already within the firm may be ascertained more economically and accurately than for resources outside the firm. Superior combinations of inputs can be more economically identified and formed from resources already used in the organization than by obtaining new resources (and knowledge of them) from the outside. Promotion and revision of employee assignments (contracts) will be preferred by a firm to the hiring of new inputs. To the extent that this occurs there is reason to expect the firm to be able to operate as a conglomerate rather than persist in producing a single product. Efficient production with heterogeneous resources is a result not of having *better* resources but in *knowing more accurately* the relative productive performances of those resources. Poorer resources can be paid less in accord with their inferiority; greater accuracy of knowledge of the potential and actual productive actions of inputs rather than having high productivity resources makes a firm (or an assignment of inputs) profitable.[18]

8. Summary

While ordinary contracts facilitate efficient specialization according to comparative advantage, a special class of contracts among a group of joint inputs to a team production process is commonly used for team production. Instead of multilateral contracts among all the joint inputs' owners, a central common party to a set of bilateral contracts facilitates efficient organization of the joint inputs in team production. The terms of the contracts form the basis of the entity called the firm—especially appropriate for organizing team production processes.

Team productive activity is that in which a union, or joint use, of inputs yields a larger output than the sum of the products of the separately used inputs. This team production requires—like all other production processes—an assessment of marginal productivities if efficient production is to be achieved. Nonseparability of the products of several differently owned joint inputs raises the cost of assessing the marginal productivities of those resources or services of each input owner. Monitoring or metering the productivities to match marginal productivities to costs of inputs and thereby to reduce shirking can be achieved more economically (than by across market bilateral negotiations among inputs) in a firm.

The essence of the classical firm is identified here as a contractual structure with: 1) joint input production; 2) several input owners; 3) one party who is common to all the contracts of the joint inputs; 4) who has rights to renegotiate any input's contract independently of contracts with other input owners; 5) who holds the residual claim; and 6) who has the right to sell his central contractual residual status. The central agent is called the firm's owner and the employer. No authoritarian control is involved; the arrangement is simply a contractual structure subject to continuous renegotiation with the central agent. The contractual structure arises as a means of enhancing efficient organization of team production. In particular, the ability to detect shirking among owners of jointly used inputs in team production is enhanced (detection costs are reduced) by this arrangement and the discipline (by revision of contracts) of input owners is made more economic.

Testable implications are suggested by the analysis of different types of organizations—nonprofit, proprietary for profit, unions, cooperatives, partnerships, and by the kinds of inputs that tend to be owned by the firm in contrast to those employed by the firm.

We conclude with a highly conjectural but possibly significant interpretation. As a consequence of the flow of information to the central party (employer), the firm takes on the characteristic of an efficient market in that information about the productive characteristics of a large set of specific inputs is now more cheaply available. Better recombinations or new uses of resources can be more efficiently ascertained than by the conventional search through the general market. In this sense inputs compete with each other within and via a firm rather than solely across markets as conventionally conceived. Emphasis on interfirm competition obscures intrafirm competition among inputs. Conceiving competition as the *revelation and exchange* of knowledge or information about qualities, potential uses of different inputs in different potential applications indicates that the firm is a device for enhancing competition among sets of input resources as well as a device for more efficiently rewarding the inputs. In contrast to markets and cities which can be viewed as publicly or nonowned market places, the firm can be considered a privately owned market; if so, we could consider the firm and the ordinary market as competing types of markets, competition between private proprietary markets and public or communal markets. Could it be that the market suffers from the defects of communal property rights in organizing and influencing uses of valuable resources?

Notes

1. Meter means to measure and also to apportion. One can meter (measure) output and one can also meter (control) the output. We use the word to denote both; the context should indicate which.

2. A producer's wealth would be reduced by the present capitalized value of the future income lost by loss of reputation. Reputation, i.e. credibility, is an asset, which is another way of saying that reliable information about expected performance is both a costly and a valuable good. For acts of God that interfere with contract performance, both parties have incentives to reach a settlement akin to that which would have been reached if such events had been covered by specific contingency clauses. The reason, again, is that a reputation for 'honest' dealings—i.e. for actions similar to those that would probably have been reached had the contract provided this contingency—is wealth.

   Almost every contract is open-ended in that many contingencies are uncovered. For example, if a fire delays production of a promised product by A to B, and if B contends that A had not fulfilled the contract, how is the dispute settled and what recompense, if any, does A grant to B? A person uninitiated in such questions may be surprised by the extent to which contracts permit either party to escape performance or to nullify the contract. In fact, it is hard to imagine any contract, which, when taken solely in terms of its stipulations, could not be evaded by one of the parties. Yet that is the ruling, viable type of contract. Why? Undoubtedly the best discussion that we have seen on this question is by Stewart Macaulay.

There are means not only of detecting or preventing cheating, but also for deciding how to allocate the losses or gains of unpredictable events or quality of items exchanged. Sales contracts contain warranties, guarantees, collateral, return privileges and penalty clauses for specific nonperformance. These are means of assignment of *risks* of losses of cheating. A lower price without warranty—an 'as is' purchase—places more of the risk on the buyer while the seller buys insurance against losses of his 'cheating.' On the other hand, a warranty or return privilege or service contract places more risk on the seller with insurance being bought by the buyer.

3. The function is separable into additive functions if the cross partial derivative is zero, i.e. if $\partial^2 Z / \partial X_i \partial X_j = 0$.

4. With sufficient generality of notation and conception this team production function could be formulated as a case of the generalised production function interpretation given by our colleague, E. A. Thompson.

5. More precisely: 'if anything other than pecuniary income enters his utility function.' Leisure stands for all nonpecuniary income for simplicity of exposition.

6. Do not assume that the sole result of the cost of detecting shirking is one form of payment (more leisure and less take home money). With several members of the team, each has an incentive to cheat against each other by engaging in more than the average amount of such leisure if the employer can not tell at zero cost which employee is taking more than the average. As a result the total productivity of the team is lowered. Shirking detection costs thus change the form of payment and also result in lower total rewards. Because the cross partial derivatives are positive, shirking reduces other people's marginal products.

7. What is meant by performance? Input energy, initiative, work attitude, perspiration, rate of exhaustion? Or output? It is the latter that is sought—the *effect* or output. But performance is nicely ambiguous because it suggests both input and output. It is *nicely* ambiguous because as we shall see, sometimes by inspecting a team member's input activity we can better judge his output effect, perhaps not with complete accuracy but better than by watching the output of the *team*. It is not always the case that watching input activity is the only or best means of detecting, measuring or monitoring output effects of each team member, but in some cases it is a useful way. For the moment the word performance glosses over these aspects and facilitates concentration on other issues.

8. Removal of (b) converts a capitalist proprietary firm to a socialist firm.

9. Recognition must also be made to the seminal inquiries by Morris Silver and Richard Auster, and by H. B. Malmgren.

10. While the degree to which residual claims are centralized will affect the size of the team, this will be only one of many factors that determine team size, so as an approximation, we can treat team size as exogenously determined. Under certain assumptions about the shape of the 'typical' utility function, the incentive to

avoid shirking with unequal profit-sharing can be measured by the Herfindahl index.

11. The use of the word active will be clarified in our discussion of the corporation, which follows below.

12. Some sharing contracts, like crop sharing, or rental payments based on gross sales in retail stores, come close to profit sharing. However, it is gross output sharing rather than profit sharing. We are unable to specify the implications of the difference. We refer the reader to S. N. Cheung.

13. Incidentally, investment activity will be changed. The inability to capitalize the investment value as 'take-home' proviate property *wealth* of the members of the firm means that the benefits of the investment must be taken as annual income by those who are employed at the time of the income. Investment will be confined more to those with shorter life and with higher rates or pay-offs if the alternative of investing is paying out the firm's income to its employees to take home and use as private property. For a development of this proposition, see the papers by Eirik Furobotn and Svetozar Pejovich, and by Pejovich.

14. Instead of thinking of shareholders as joint *owners*, we can think of them as investors, like bondholders, except that the stockholders are more optimistic than bondholders about the enterprise prospects. Instead of buying bonds in the corporation, thus enjoying smaller risks, shareholders prefer to invest funds with a greater realizable return if the firm prospers as expected, but with smaller (possibly negative) returns if the firm performs in a manner closer to that expected by the more pessimistic investors. The pessimistic investors, in turn, regard only the bonds as likely to pay off.

   If the entrepreneur-organizer is to raise capital on the best terms to him, it is to his advantage, as well as that of prospective investors, to recognize these differences in expectations. The residual claim on earnings enjoyed by share-holders does not serve the function of enhancing their efficiency as monitors in the general situation. The stockholders are 'merely' the less risk-averse or the more optimistic member of the group that finances the firm. Being more optimistic than the average and seeing a higher mean value future return, they are willing to pay more for a certificate that allows them to realize gain on their expectations. One method of doing so is to buy claims to the distribution of returns that 'they see' while bondholders, who are more pessimistic, purchase a claim to the distribution that they see as more likely to emerge. Stockholders are then comparable to warrant holders. They care not about the voting rights (usually not attached to warrants); they are in the same position in so far as voting rights are concerned as are bondholders. The only difference is in the probability distribution of rewards and the terms on which they can place their bets.

   If we treat bondholders, preferred and convertible preferred stockholders, and common stockholders and warrant holders as simply different classes of inves-tors—differing not only in their risk averseness but in their beliefs about the probability distribution of the firm's future earnings, why should stockholders be regarded as 'owners' in any sense distinct from the other financial investors?

The entrepreneur-organizer, who let us assume is the chief operating officer and sole repository of control of the corporation, does not find his authority residing in common stockholders (except in the case of a take over). Does this type of control make any difference in the way the firm is conducted? Would it make any difference in the way the firm is conducted? Would it make any difference in the kinds of behavior that would be tolerated by competing managers and investors (and we here deliberately refrain from thinking of them as owner-stockholders in the traditional sense)?

Investment old timers recall a significant incidence of nonvoting common stock, now prohibited in corporations whose stock is traded on listed exchanges. (Why prohibited?) The entrepreneur in those days could hold voting shares while investors held nonvoting shares, which in every other respect were identical. Nonvoting shareholders were simply investors devoid of ownership connotations. The control and behavior of inside owners in such corporations has never, so far as we have ascertained, been carefully studied. For example, at the simplest level of interest, does the evidence indicate that nonvoting shareholders fared any worse because of not having voting rights? Did owners permit the nonvoting holders the normal return available to voting shareholders? Though evidence is prohibitively expensive to obtain, it is remarkable that voting and nonvoting shares sold for essentially identical prices, even during some proxy battles. However, our casual evidence deserves no more than interest-initiating weight.

One more point. The facade is deceptive. Instead of nonvoting shares, today we have warrants, convertible preferred stocks all of which are solely or partly 'equity' claims without voting rights, though they could be converted into voting shares.

In sum, is it the case that the stockholder-investor relationship is one emanating from the *division of ownership* among several people, or is it that the collection of investment funds from people of varying anticipations is the underlying factor? If the latter, why should any of them be thought of as the owners in whom voting rights, whatever they may signify or however exercisable, should reside in order to enhance efficiency? Why voting rights in any of the outside, participating investors?

Our initial perception of this possibly significant difference in interpretation was precipitated by Henry Manne. A reading of his paper makes it clear that it is hard to understand why an investor who wishes to back and 'share' in the consequences of some new business should necessarily have to acquire voting power (i.e. power to change the manager-operator) in order to invest in the venture. In fact, we invest in some ventures in the hope that no other stockholders will be so 'foolish' as to try to toss out the incumbent management. We want him to have the power to stay in office, and for the prospect of sharing in his fortunes we buy nonvoting common stock. Our willingness to invest is enhanced by the knowledge that we can act legally via fraud, embezzlement and other laws to help assure that we outside investors will not be 'milked' beyond our initial discounted anticipations.

15. *Sports Leagues*: Professional sports contests among teams is typically conducted by a *league* of teams. We assume that sports consumers are interested not only in absolute sporting skill but also in skills *relative* to other teams. Being slightly better than opposing teams enables one to claim a major portion of the receipts; the inferior team does not release resources and reduce costs, since they were expected in the play of contest. Hence, absolute skill is developed beyond the equality of marginal investment in sporting skill with its true social marginal value product. It follows there will be a tendency to overinvest in training athletes and developing teams. 'Reverse shirking' arises, as budding players are induced to overpractice hyperactively relative to the social marginal value of their enhanced skills. To prevent overinvestment, the teams seek an agreement with each other to restrict practice, size of teams, and even pay of the team members (which reduces incentives of young people to overinvest in developing skills). Ideally, if all the contestant teams were owned by one owner, overinvestment in sports would be avoided, much as ownership of common fisheries or underground oil or water reserve would prevent overinvestment. This hyperactivity (to suggest the opposite of shirking) is controlled by the league of teams, wherein the league adopts a common set of constraints on each team's behavior. In effect, the teams are no longer really owned by the team owners but are supervized by them, much as the franchisers of some product. They are not full-fledged owners of their business, including the brand name, and can not 'do what they wish' as franchises. Comparable to the franchiser, is the league commissioner or conference president, who seeks to restrain hyperactivity, as individual team supervisors compete with each other and cause external diseconomies. Such restraints are usually regarded as anticompetitive, anti-social, collusive-cartel devices to restrain free open competition, and reduce players' salaries. However, the interpretation presented here is premised on an attempt to avoid hyperinvestment in team sports production. Of course, the team operators have an incentive, once the league is formed and restraints are placed on hyper-investment activity, to go further and obtain the private benefits of monopoly restriction. To what extent overinvestment is replaced by monopoly restriction is not yet determinable; nor have we seen an empirical test of these two competing, but mutually consistent interpretations. (This interpretation of league-sports activity was proposed by Earl Thompson and formulated by Michael Canes.) Again, athletic teams clearly exemplify the specialization of monitoring with captains and coaches; a captain detects shirkers while the coach trains and selects strategies and tactics. Both functions may be centralized in one person.

16. Professional athletes in baseball, football, and basketball, where athletes having sold their source of service to the team owners upon entering into sports activity, are owned by team owners. Here the team owners must monitor the athletes' physical condition and behavior to protect the team owners' wealth. The athlete has *less* (not, *no*) incentive to protect or enhance his athletic prowess since capital value changes have less impact on his own wealth and more on the team owners. Thus, some athletes sign up for big initial bonuses (representing

present capital value of future services). Future salaries are lower by the annuity value of the prepaid 'bonus' and hence the athlete has *less* to lose by subsequent abuse of his athletic prowess. Any decline in his subsequent service value would in part be borne by the team owner who owns the players' future service. This does not say these losses of future salaries have no effect on preservation of athletic talent (we are not making a 'sunk cost' error). Instead, we assert that the preservation is reduced, not eliminated, because the amount of loss of wealth suffered is smaller. The athlete will spend less to maintain or enhance his prowess thereafter. The effect of this revised incentive system is evidenced in comparisons of the kinds of attention and care imposed on the athletes at the 'expense of the team owner' in the case where athletes' future services are owned by the team owner with that where future labor service values are owned by the athlete himself. Why athletes' future athletic services are owned by the team owners rather than being hired is a question we should be able to answer. One presumption is cartelization and monopsony gains to team owners. Another is exactly the theory being expounded in this paper—costs of monitoring production of athletes; we know not on which to rely.

17. The analysis used by Cheung in explaining the prevalence of sharecropping and land tenancy arrangements is built squarely on the same factors—the costs of detecting output performance of jointly used inputs in team production and the costs of detecting user costs imposed on the various inputs if owner used or if rented.

18. According to our interpretation, the firm is a specialized surrogate for a market for team use of inputs; it provides superior (i.e. cheaper) collection and collation of knowledge about heterogeneous resources. The greater the set of inputs about which knowledge of performance is being collated within a firm the greater are the present costs of the collation activity. Then, the larger the firm (market) the greater the attenuation of monitor control. To counter this force, the firm will be divisionalized in ways that economise on those costs—just as will the market be specialized. So far as we can ascertain, other theories of the reasons for firms have no such implications.

In Japan, employees by custom work nearly their entire lives with one firm, and the firm agrees to that expectation. Firms will tend to be large and conglomerate to enable a broader scope of input revision. Each firm is, in effect, a small economy engaging in 'intranational and international' trade. Analogously, Americans expect to spend their whole lives in the United States, and the bigger the country, in terms of variety of resources, the easier it is to adjust to changing tastes and circumstances. Japan, with its lifetime employees, should be characterized more by large, conglomerate firms. Presumably, at some size of the firm, specialized knowledge about inputs becomes as expensive to transmit across divisions of the firms as it does across markets to other firms.

....

References

M. Canes, 'A Model of a Sports League', unpublished doctoral dissertation, UCLA 1970.

S. N. Cheung, *The Theory of Share Tenancy* (Chicago, 1969).

R. H. Coase, 'The Nature of the Firm', *Economica*, Nov. 1937, 4, 386–405; reprinted in G. J. Stigler and K. Boulding (eds). *Readings in Price Theory* (Homewood 1952), 331–51.

E. Furobotn and S. Pejovich, 'Property Rights and the Behavior of the Firm in a Socialist State', *Zeitschrift für Nationalökonomic*, 1970, 30: 431–54.

F. H. Knight, *Risk, Uncertainty and Profit* (New York, 1965).

S. Macaulay, 'Non-Contractual Relations in Business: A Preliminary Study', *Amer. Sociological Rev.*, 1968, 28: 55–69.

H. B. Malmgren, 'Information, Expectations and the Theory of the Firm', *Quart. J. Econ.*, Aug. 1961, 75: 399–421.

H. Manne, 'Our Two Corporation Systems: Law and Economics', *Virginia Law Rev.*, Mar. 1967, 53: no. 2, 259–84.

S. Pejovich, 'The Firm, Monetary Policy and Property Rights in a Planned Economy', *Western Econ. J.*, Sept. 1969, 7: 193–200.

M. Silver and R. Auster, 'Entrepreneurship, Profit, and the Limits on Firm Size', *J. Bus. Univ. Chicago*, Apr. 1969, 42: 277–81.

E. A. Thompson, 'Nonpecuniary Rewards and the Aggregate Production Function', *Rev. Econ. Statist.*, Nov. 1970, 52: 395–404.

5 Theory of the Firm: Managerial Behavior, Agency Costs, and Ownership Structure

Michael C. Jensen and William H. Meckling

This paper integrates elements from the theory of agency, the theory of property rights and the theory of finance to develop a theory of the owner-ship structure of the firm. We define the concept of agency costs, show its relationship to the 'separation and control' issue, investigate the nature of the agency costs generated by the existence of debt and outside equity, demon-strate who bears these costs and why, and investigate the Pareto optimality of their existence. We also provide a new definition of the firm, and show how our analysis of the factors influencing the creation and issuance of debt and equity claims is a special case of the supply side of the completeness of markets problem.

The directors of such [joint-stock] companies, however, being the managers rather of other people's money than of their own, it cannot well be expected, that they should watch over it with the same anxious vigilance with which the partners in a private copartnery frequently watch over their own. Like the stewards of a rich man, they are apt to consider attention to small matters as not for their master's honour, and

At the time of writing, Michael C. Jensen and William H. Meckling were Associated Professor and Dean, respectively, Graduate School of Management, University of Rochester. An earlier version of this paper was presented at the Conference on Analysis and Ideology, Interlaken, Switzerland, June 1974, sponsored by the Center for Research in Government Policy and Business at the University of Rochester, Graduate School of Management. We are indebted to F. Black, E. Fama, R. Ibbotson, W. Klein, M. Rozeff, R. Weil, O. Williamson, an anonymous referee, and to our colleagues and members of the Finance Workshop at the University of Rochester for their comments and criticisms, in particular G. Benston, M. Canes, D. Henderson, K. Leffler, J. Long, C. Smith, R. Thompson, R. Watts and J. Zimmerman.

103

very easily give themselves a dispensation from having it. Negligence and profusion, therefore, must always prevail, more or less, in the management of the affairs of such a company.

Adam Smith, *The Wealth of Nations*, 1776, Cannan Edition
(Modern Library, New York, 1937) 700.

1. Introduction and Summary

1.1. *Motivation of the Paper*

In this paper we draw on recent progress in the theory of (1) property rights, (2) agency, and (3) finance to develop a theory of ownership structure[1] for the firm. In addition to tying together elements of the theory of each of these three areas, our analysis casts new light on and has implications for a variety of issues in the professional and popular literature such as the definition of the firm, the 'separation of ownership and control', the 'social responsibility' of business, the definition of a 'corporate objective function', the determination of an optimal capital structure, the specification of the content of credit agreements, the theory of organizations, and the supply side of the completeness of markets problem.

Our theory helps explain:

(1) why an entrepreneur or manager in a firm which has a mixed financial structure (containing both debt and outside equity claims) will choose a set of activities for the firm such that the total value of the firm is *less* than it would be if he were the sole owner and why this result is independent of whether the firm operates in monopolistic or competitive product or factor markets;

(2) why his failure to maximize the value of the firm is perfectly consistent with efficiency;

(3) why the sale of common stock is a viable source of capital even though managers do not liberally maximize the value of the firm;

(4) why debt was relied upon as a source of capital before debt financing offered any tax advantage relative to equity;

(5) why preferred stock would be issued;

(6) why accounting reports would be provided voluntarily to creditors and stockholders, and why independent auditors would be engaged by management to testify to the accuracy and correctness of such reports;

(7) why lenders often place restrictions on the activities of firms to whom they lend, and why firms would themselves be led to suggest the imposition of such restrictions;

(8) why some industries are characterized by owner-operated firms whose sole outside source of capital is borrowing;

(9) why highly regulated industries such as public utilities or banks will have higher debt equity ratios for equivalent levels of risk than the average non-regulated firm;

(10) why security analysis can be socially productive even if it does not increase portfolio returns to investors.

1.2. Theory of the Firm: An Empty Box?

While the literature of economics is replete with references to the 'theory of the firm', the material generally subsumed under that heading is not a theory of the firm but actually a theory of markets in which firms are important actors. The firm is a 'black box' operated so as to meet the relevant marginal conditions with respect to inputs and outputs, thereby maximizing profits, or more accurately, present value. Except for a few recent and tentative steps, however, we have no theory which explains how the conflicting objectives of the individual participants are brought into equilibrium so as to yield this result. The limitations of this black box view of the firm have been cited by Adam Smith and Alfred Marshall, among others. More recently, popular and professional debates over the 'social responsibility' of corporations, the separation of ownership and control, and the rash of reviews of the literature on the 'theory of the firm' have evidenced continuing concern with these issues.[2]

A number of major attempts have been made during recent years to construct a theory of the firm by substituting other models for profit or value maximization; each attempt motivated by a conviction that the latter is inadequate to explain managerial behavior in large corporations.[3] Some of these reformulation attempts have rejected the fundamental principle of maximizing behavior as well as rejecting the more specific profit maximizing model. We retain the notion of maximizing behavior on the part of all individuals in the analysis to follow.[4]

1.3. Property Rights

An independent stream of research with important implications for the theory of the firm has been stimulated by the pioneering work of Coase, and extended by Alchian, Demsetz and others.[5] A comprehensive survey of this literature is given by Furobotn and Pejovich (1972). While the focus of this research has been 'property rights',[6] the subject matter encompassed is far broader than that term suggests. What is important for the problems addressed here is that specification of individual rights determines how costs and rewards will be allocated among the participants in any organization. Since the specification of rights is generally effected through contracting (implicit as well as explicit), individual behavior in organizations, including the behavior of managers, will depend upon the nature of these contracts. We focus in this paper on the behavioral implications of the property rights specified in the contracts between the owners and managers of the firm.

1.4. Agency Costs

Many problems associated with the inadequacy of the current theory of the firm can also be viewed as special cases of the theory of agency relationships in which there is a growing literature.[7] This literature has developed independently of the property rights literature even though the problems with which it is concerned are similar; the approaches are in fact highly complementary to each other.

We define an agency relationship as a contract under which one or more persons (the principal(s)) engage another person (the agent) to perform some service on their behalf which involves delegating some decision making authority to the agent. If both parties to the relationship are utility maximizers there is good reason to believe that the agent will not always act in the best interests of the principal. The *principal* can limit divergences from his interest by establishing appropriate incentives for the agent and by incurring monitoring costs designed to limit the aberrant activities of the agent. In addition in some situations it will pay the *agent* to expend resources (bonding costs) to guarantee that he will not take certain actions which would harm the principal or to ensure that the principal will be compensated if he does take such actions. However, it is generally impossible for the principal or the agent at zero cost to ensure that the agent will make optimal decisions from the principal's viewpoint. In most agency relationships the principal and the agent will incur positive monitoring and bonding costs (non-pecuniary as well as pecuniary), and in addition there will be some divergence between the agent's decisions[8] and those decisions which would maximize the welfare of the principal. The dollar equivalent of the reduction in welfare experienced by the principal due to this divergence is also a cost of the agency relationship, and we refer to this latter cost as the 'residual loss'. We define *agency costs* as the sum of:

1. the monitoring expenditures by the principal,[9]
2. the bonding expenditures by the agent,
3. the residual loss.

Note also that agency costs arise in any situation involving cooperative effort (such as the co-authoring of this paper) by two or more people even though there is no clear cut principal–agent relationship. Viewed in this light it is clear that our definition of agency costs and their importance to the theory of the firm bears a close relationship to the problem of shirking and monitoring of team production which Alchian and Demsetz (1972) raise in their paper on the theory of the firm.

Since the relationship between the stockholders and manager of a corporation fit the definition of a pure agency relationship it should be no surprise to discover that the issues associated with the 'separation of ownership and control' in the modern diffuse ownership corporation are intimately associated with the general problem of agency. We show below that an explanation of why and how the agency costs generated by the corporate form are born leads to a theory of the ownership (or capital) structure of the firm.

Before moving on, however, it is worthwhile to point out the generality of the agency problems. The problem of inducing an 'agent' to behave as if he were maximizing the 'principal's' welfare is quite general. It exists in all organizations and in all cooperative efforts—at every level of management in firms,[10] in universities, in mutual companies, in cooperatives, in governmental authorities and bureaus, in unions, and in relationships normally classified as agency relationships such as are common in the performing arts and the market for real estate. The development of theories to explain the form which agency costs take in each of these situations (where the contractual relations differ significantly), and how and why they are born will lead to a rich theory of organizations which is now lacking in economics and the social sciences generally. We confine our attention in this paper to only a small part of this general problem—the analysis of agency costs generated by the contractual arrangement between the owners and top management of the corporation.

Our approach to the agency problem here differs fundamentally from most of the existing literature. That literature focuses almost exclusively on the normative aspects of the agency relationship; that is how to structure the contractual relation (including compensation incentives) between the principal and agent to provide appropriate incentives for the agent to make choices which will maximize the principal's welfare given that uncertainty and imperfect monitoring exist. We focus almost entirely on the positive aspects of the theory. That is, we assume individuals solve these normative problems and given that only stocks and bonds can be issued as claims, we investigate the incentives faced by each of the parties and the elements entering into the determination of the equilibrium contractual form characterizing the relationship between the manager (i.e. agent) of the firm and the outside equity and debt holders (i.e. principals).

1.5. *Some General Comments on the Definition of the Firm*

Ronald Coase (1937) in his seminal paper on 'The Nature of the Firm' pointed out that economics had no positive theory to determine the bounds of the firm. He characterized the bounds of the firm as that range of exchanges over which the market system was suppressed and resource allocation was accomplished instead by authority and direction. He focused on the cost of using markets to effect contracts and exchanges and argued that activities would be included within the firm whenever the costs of using markets were greater than the costs of using direct authority. Alchian and Demsetz (1972) object to the notion that activities within the firm are governed by authority, and correctly emphasize the role of contracts as a vehicle for voluntary exchange. They emphasize the role of monitoring in situations in which there is joint input or team production.[11] We sympathize with the importance they attach to monitoring, but we believe the emphasis which Alchian–Demsetz place on joint input production is too narrow and therefore misleading. Contractual relations are the essence of the firm, not only with employees but with suppliers, customers, creditors, etc. The problem of agency costs and monitoring exists for all of these contracts, independent of whether there is joint production in their sense; i.e. joint production can explain only a small fraction of the behavior of individuals associated with a firm. A detailed examination of these issues is left to another paper.

It is important to recognize that most organizations are simply *legal fictions*[12] *which serve as a nexus for a set of contracting relationships among individuals.* This includes firms, non-profit institutions such as universities, hospitals and foundations, mutual organizations such as mutual savings banks and insurance companies and cooperatives, some private clubs, and even governmental bodies such as cities, states and the Federal government, government enterprises such as TVA, the Post Office, transit systems, etc.

The private corporation or firm is simply one form of *legal fiction which serves as a nexus for contracting relationships and which is also characterized by the existence of divisible residual claims on the assets and cash flows of the organization which can generally be sold without permission of the other contracting individuals.*

While this definition of the firm has little substantive content, emphasizing the essential contractual nature of firms and other organizations focuses attention on a crucial set of questions—why particular sets of contractual relations arise for various types of organizations, what the consequences of these contractual relations are, and how they are affected by changes exogenous to the organization. Viewed this way, it makes little or no sense to try to distinguish those things which are 'inside' the firm (or any other organization) from those things that are 'outside' of it. There is in a very real sense only a multitude of complex relationships (i.e. contracts) between the legal fiction (the firm) and the owners of labor, material and capital inputs and the consumers of output.[13]

Viewing the firm as the nexus of a set of contracting relationships among individuals also serves to make it clear that the personalization of the firm implied by asking questions such as 'what should be the objective function of the firm', or 'does the firm have a social responsibility' is seriously misleading. *The firm is not an individual.* It is a legal fiction which serves as a focus for a complex process in which the conflicting objectives of individuals (some of whom may 'represent' other organizations) are brought into equilibrium within a framework of contractual relations. In this sense the 'behavior' of the firm is like the behavior of a market; i.e. the outcome of a complex equilibrium process. We seldom fall into the trap of characterizing the wheat or stock market as an individual, but we often make this error by thinking about organizations as if they were persons with motivations and intentions.[14]

1.6. An Overview of the Paper

We develop the theory in stages. Sections 2 and 4 provide analyses of the agency costs of equity and debt respectively. These form the major foundation of the theory. Section 3 poses some unanswered questions regarding the existence of the corporate form of organization and examines the role of limited liability. Section 5 provides a synthesis of the basic concepts derived in Sections 2–4 into a theory of the corporate ownership structure which takes account of the tradeoffs available to the entrepreneur-manager between inside and outside equity and debt. Some qualifications and extensions of the analysis are discussed in Section 6, and Section 7 contains a brief summary and conclusions.

2. The Agency Costs of Outside Equity

2.1. Overview

In this section we analyze the effect of outside equity on agency costs by comparing the behavior of a manager when he owns 100 per cent of the residual claims on a firm to his behavior when he sells off a portion of those claims to outsiders. If a wholly owned firm is managed by the owner, he will make operating decisions which maximize his utility. These decisions will involve not only the benefits he derives from pecuniary returns but also the utility generated by various non-pecuniary aspects of his entrepreneurial activities such as the physical appointments of the office, the attractiveness of the secretarial staff, the level of employee discipline, the kind and amount of charitable contributions, personal relations ('love', 'respect', etc.) with employees, a larger than optimal computer to play with, purchase of production inputs from friends, etc. The optimum mix (in the absence of taxes) of the various pecuniary and non-pecuniary benefits is achieved when the marginal utility derived from an additional dollar of expenditure (measured net of any productive effects) is equal for each non-pecuniary item and equal to the marginal utility derived from an additional dollar or after tax purchasing power (wealth).

If the owner–manager sells equity claims on the corporation which are identical to his (i.e. share proportionately in the profits of the firm and have limited liability) agency costs will be generated by the divergence between his interest and those of the outside shareholders, since he will then bear only a fraction of the costs of any non-pecuniary benefits he takes out in maximizing his own utility. If the manager owns only 95 per cent of the stock, he will expend resources to the point where the marginal utility derived from a dollar's expenditure of the firm's resources on such items equals the marginal utility of an additional 95 cents in general purchasing power (i.e. *his* share of the wealth reduction) and not one dollar. Such activities, on his part, can be limited (but probably not eliminated) by the expenditure of resources on monitoring activities by the outside stockholders. But as we show below, the owner will bear the entire wealth effects of these expected costs so long as the equity market anticipates these effects. Prospective minority shareholders will realize that the owner–manager's interests will diverge somewhat from theirs, hence the price which they will pay for shares will reflect the monitoring costs and the effect of the divergence between the manager's interest and theirs. Nevertheless, ignoring for the moment the possibility of borrowing against his wealth, the owner will find it desirable to bear these costs as long as the welfare increment he experiences from converting his claims on the firm into general purchasing power[15] is large enough to offset them.

As the owner–manager's fraction of the equity falls, his fractional claim on the outcomes falls and this will tend to encourage him to appropriate larger amounts of the corporate resources in the form of perquisites. This also makes it desirable for the minority shareholders to expend more resources in monitoring his behavior. Thus, the wealth costs to the owner of obtaining additional cash in the equity markets rise as his fractional ownership falls.

We shall continue to characterize the agency conflict between the owner–manager and outside shareholders as deriving from the manager's tendency to appropriate perquisites out of the firm's resources for his own consumption. However, we do not mean to leave the impression that this is the only or even the most important source of conflict. Indeed, it is likely that the most important conflict arises from the fact that as the manager's ownership claim falls, his incentive to devote significant effort to creative activities such as searching out new profitable ventures falls. He may in fact avoid such ventures simply because it requires too much trouble or effort on his part to manage or to learn about new technologies. Avoidance of these personal costs and the anxieties that go with them also represent a source of on the job utility to him and it can result in the value of the firm being substantially lower than it otherwise could be.

2.2. A Simple Formal Analysis of the Sources of Agency Costs of Equity and Who Bears them

In order to develop some structure for the analysis to follow we make two sets of assumptions. The first set (permanent assumptions) are those which shall carry through almost all of the analysis in Sections 2–5. The effects of relaxing some of these are discussed in Section 6. The second set (temporary assumptions) are made only for expositional purposes and are relaxed as soon as the basic points have been clarified.

Permanent Assumptions

(P.1) All taxes are zero.
(P.2) No trade credit is available.
(P.3) All outside equity shares are non-voting.
(P.4) No complex financial claims such as convertible bonds or preferred stock or warrants can be issued.

(P.5) No outside owner gains utility from ownership in a firm in any way other than through its effect on his wealth or cash flows.

(P.6) All dynamic aspects of the multiperiod nature of the problem are ignored by assuming there is only one production–financing decision to be made by the entrepreneur.

(P.7) The entrepreneur–manager's money wages are held constant throughout the analysis.

(P.8) There exists a single manager (the peak coordinator) with ownership interest in the firm.

Temporary Assumptions

(T.1) The size of the firm is fixed.

(T.2) No monitoring or bonding activities are possible.

(T.3) No debt financing through bonds, preferred stock, or personal borrowing (secured or unsecured) is possible.

(T.4) All elements of the owner–manager's decision problem involving portfolio considerations induced by the presence of uncertainty and the existence of diversifiable risk are ignored.

Define:

$X = \{x_1, x_2, \ldots, x_n\}$ = vector of quantities of all factors and activities within the firm from which the manager derives non-pecuniary benefits;[16] the x_i are defined such that his marginal utility is positive for each of them;

$C(X)$ = total dollar cost of providing any given amount of these items;

$P(X)$ = total dollar value to the firm of the productive benefits of X;

$B(X) = P(X) - C(X)$ = net dollar benefit to the firm of X ignoring any effects of X on the equilibrium wage of the manager.

Ignoring the effects of X on the manager's utility and therefore on his equilibrium wage rate, the optimum levels of the factors and activities X are defined by $X^\star$ such that

$$\frac{\partial B(X^\star)}{\partial X^\star} = \frac{\partial P(X^\star)}{\partial X^\star} - \frac{\partial C(X^\star)}{\partial X^\star} = 0$$

Thus for any vector $X \geqq X^\star$ (i.e. where at least one element of X is greater than its corresponding element of $X^\star$), $F = B(X^\star) - B(X) > 0$ measures the dollar cost to the firm (net of any productive effects) of providing the increment $X - X^\star$ of the factors and activities which generate utility to the manager. We assume henceforth that for any given level of cost to the firm, F, the vector of factors and activities on which F is spent are those, $\hat{X}$, which yield the manager maximum utility. Thus $F = B(X^\star) - B(\hat{X})$.

We have thus far ignored in our discussion the fact that these expenditures on X occur through time and therefore there are tradeoffs to be made across time as well as between alternative elements of X. Furthermore, we have ignored the fact that the future expenditures are likely to involve uncertainty (i.e. they are subject to probability distributions) and therefore some allowance must be made for their riskiness. We resolve both of these issues by defining C, P, B, and F to be the *current market values* of the sequence of probability distributions on the period by period cash flows involved.[17]

Given the definition of F as the current market value of the stream of manager's expenditures on non-pecuniary benefits we represent the constraint which a single owner-manager faces in deciding how much non-pecuniary income he will extract from the firm by the line $\overline{V}F$ in Fig. 1. This is analogous to a budget constraint. The market value of the firm is measured along the vertical axis and the market value of the manager's stream of expenditures on non-pecuniary benefits, F, are measured along the horizontal axis. $0\overline{V}$ is the value of the firm when the amount of non-

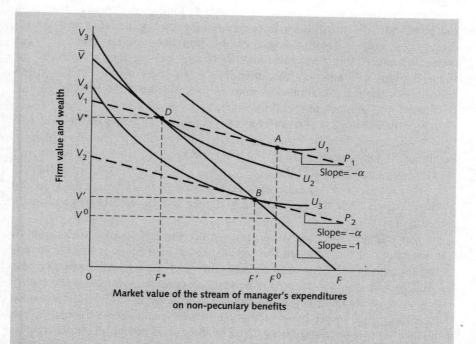

Fig. 1. The value of the firm (V) and the level of non-pecuniary benefits consumed (F) when the fraction of outside equity is $(1 - \alpha)V$, and $U_j(j = 1, 2, 3)$ represents owner's indifference curves between wealth and non-pecuniary benefits.

pecuniary income consumed is zero. By definition $\overline{V}$ is the maximum market value of the cash flows generated by the firm for a given money wage for the manager when the manager's consumption of non-pecuniary benefits are zero. At this point all the factors and activities within the firm which generate utility for the manager are at the level X^* defined above. There is a different budget constraint $\overline{V}F$ for each possible scale of the firm (i.e. level of investment, I) and for alternative levels of money wage, W, for the manager. For the moment we pick an arbitrary level of investment (which we assume has already been made) and hold the scale of the firm constant at this level. We also assume that the manager's money wage is fixed at the level W^* which represents the current market value of his wage contract[18] in the optimal compensation package which consists of both wages, W^*, and non-pecuniary benefits, F^*. Since one dollar of current value of non-pecuniary benefits withdrawn from the firm by the manager reduces the market value of the firm by \$1, by definition, the slope of $\overline{V}F$ is -1.

The owner–manager's tastes for wealth and non-pecuniary benefits is represented in Fig. 1 by a system of indifference curves, U_1, U_2, etc.[19] The indifference curves will be convex as drawn as long as the owner–manager's marginal rate of substitution between non-pecuniary benefits and wealth diminishes with increasing levels of the benefits. For the 100 per cent owner–manager, this presumes that there are not perfect substitutes for these benefits available on the outside, i.e. to some extent they are job specific. For the fractional owner–manager this presumes the benefits cannot be turned into general purchasing power at a constant price.[20]

When the owner has 100 per cent of the equity, the value of the firm will be V^* where indifference curve U_2 is tangent to VF, and the level of non-pecuniary benefits consumed is F^*. If the owner sells the entire equity but remains as manager, and if the equity buyer can, at zero cost, force the old owner (as manager) to take the same level of non-pecuniary benefits as he did as owner, then V^* is the price the new owner will be willing to pay for the entire equity.[21]

In general, however, we would not expect the new owner to be able to enforce identical behavior on the old owner at zero costs. If the old owner sells a fraction of the firm to an outsider, he, as manager, will no longer bear the full cost of any non-pecuniary benefits he consumes. Suppose the owner sells a share of the firm, $1 - \alpha$, $(0 < \alpha < 1)$ and retains for himself a share, α. If the prospective buyer believes that the owner–manager will consume the same level of non-pecuniary benefits as he did as full owner, the buyer will be willing to pay $(1 - \alpha)V^*$ for a fraction $(1 - \alpha)$ of the equity. Given that an outsider now holds a claim to $(1 - \alpha)$ of the equity, however, the *cost* to the owner–manager of consuming \$1 of non-pecuniary benefits in the firm will no longer be \$1. Instead, it will be $\alpha \times \$1$. If the prospective buyer actually paid $(1 - \alpha)V^\star$ for his share of the equity, and if thereafter the manager could choose whatever level of non-pecuniary benefits he liked, his budget constraint would be V_1P_1 in Fig. 1 and has a slope equal to $-\alpha$. Including the payment the owner receives from the buyer as part of the owner's post-sale wealth, his budget constraint, V_1P_1, must pass through D, since he can if he wishes have the same wealth and level of non-pecuniary consumption he consumed as full owner.

But if the owner–manager is free to choose the level of perquisites, F, subject only to the loss in wealth he incurs as a part owner, his welfare will be maximized by increasing his consumption of non-pecuniary benefits. He will move to point A where V_1P_1 is tangent to U_1 representing a higher level of utility. The value of the firm falls from $V^\star$, to V^0, i.e. by the amount of the cost to the firm of the increased non-pecuniary expenditures, and the owner–manager's consumption of non-pecuniary benefits rise from $F^\star$ to F^0.

If the equity market is characterized by rational expectations the buyers will be aware that the owner will increase his non-pecuniary consumption when his ownership share is reduced. If the owner's response function is known or if the equity market makes unbiased estimates of the owner's response to the changed incentives, the buyer will not pay $(1 - \alpha)V^\star$ for $(1 - \alpha)$ of the equity.

Theorem. For a claim on the firm of $(1 - \alpha)$ the outsider will pay only $(1 - \alpha)$ times the value he expects the firm to have given the induced change in the behavior of the owner–manager.

Proof. For simplicity we ignore any element of uncertainty introduced by the lack of perfect knowledge of the owner–manager's response function. Such uncertainty will not affect the final solution if the equity market is large as long as the estimates are rational (i.e. unbiased) and the errors are independent across firms. The latter condition assures that this risk is diversifiable and therefore equilibrium prices will equal the expected values.

Let W represent the owner's total wealth after he has sold a chain equal to $1 - \alpha$ of the equity to an outsider. W has two components. One is the payment, S_o, made by the outsider for $1 - \alpha$ of the equity; the rest, S_i, is the value of the owner's (i.e. the insider's) share of the firm, so that W, the owner's wealth, is given by

$$W = S_o + S_i = S_o + \alpha V(F,\alpha),$$

where $V(F,\alpha)$ represents the value of the firm given that the manager's fractional ownership share is α and that he consumes perquisites with current market value of F. Let V_2P_2, with a slope of $-\alpha$ represent the tradeoff the owner–manager faces between non-pecuniary benefits and his wealth after the sale. Given that the owner has decided to sell a claim $1 - \alpha$ of the firm, his welfare will be maximized when V_2P_2 is tangent to some indifference curve such as U_3 in Fig. 1. A price for a claim of $(1 - \alpha)$ on the firm that is satisfactory to both the buyer and the seller will require that this tangency occur along $\overline{VF}$, i.e. that the value of the firm must be V'. To show this, assume that such is not the case—that the tangency occurs to the left of the point B on the line $\overline{VF}$. Then, since the slope of V_2P_2 is negative, the value of the firm will be larger than V'. The owner–manager's choice of this lower level of consumption of non-pecuniary benefits will imply a higher value both to the firm as a whole and to the fraction of the firm $(1 - \alpha)$ which the outsider has acquired; that is, $(1 - \alpha)V' > S_0$. From the owner's viewpoint, he has sold $1 - \alpha$ of the firm for less than he could have, given the (assumed) lower level of non-pecuniary benefits he enjoys. On the other hand, if the tangency point B is to the right of the line $\overline{VF}$, the owner–manager's higher consumption of non-pecuniary benefits means the value of the firm is less than V', and hence $(1 - \alpha) V(F, \alpha) < S_0 = (1 - \alpha)V'$. The outside owner then has paid more for his share of the equity than it is worth. S_0 will be a mutually satisfactory price if and only if $(1 - \alpha)V' = S_0$. But this means that the owner's post-sale wealth is equal to the (reduced) value of the firm V', since

$$W = S_0 + \alpha V' = (1 - \alpha)V' + \alpha V' = V'.$$

Q.E.D.

The requirement that V' and F' fall on $\overline{VF}$ is thus equivalent to requiring that the value of the claim acquired by the outside buyer be equal to the amount he pays for it and conversely for the owner. *This means that the decline in the total value of the firm* $(V^\star - V')$ *is entirely imposed on the owner–manager.* His total wealth after the sale of $(1 - \alpha)$ of the equity is V' and the decline in his wealth is $V^\star - V'$.

The distance $V^\star - V'$ is the reduction in the market value of the firm engendered by the agency relationship and is a measure of the 'residual loss' defined earlier. In this simple example the residual loss represents the total agency costs engendered by the sale of outside equity because monitoring and bonding activities have not been allowed. The welfare loss the owner incurs is less than the residual loss by the value to him of the increase in non-pecuniary benefits $(F' - F^\star)$. In Fig. 1 the difference between the intercepts on the Y axis of the two indifference curves U_2 and U_3 is a measure of the owner–manager's welfare loss due to the incurrence of agency costs,[22] and he would sell such a claim only if the increment in welfare he achieves by using the cash amounting to $(1 - \alpha)V'$ for other things was worth more to him than this amount of wealth.

2.3. Determination of the Optimal Scale of the Firm

The Case of All Equity Financing. Consider the problem faced by an entrepreneur with initial pecuniary wealth, W, and monopoly access to a project requiring investment outlay, I, subject to diminishing returns to scale in I. Fig. 2 portrays the solution to the optimal scale of the firm taking into account the agency costs associated with the existence of outside equity. The axes are as defined in Fig. 1 except we now plot on the vertical axis the total wealth of the owner, i.e. his initial wealth, W, plus $V(I) - I$, the net increment in wealth he obtains from exploitation of his investment opportunities. The market value of the firm, $V = V(I, F)$, is now a function of the level of investment, I, and the current market value of the manager's expenditures of

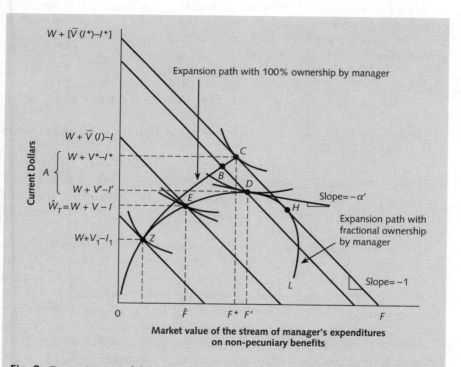

Fig. 2. Determination of the optimal scale of the firm in the case where no monitoring takes place. Point C denotes optimum investment, I^*, and non-pecuniary benefits, F^*, when investment is 100 per cent financed by entrepreneur. Point D denotes optimum investment, I', and non-pecuniary benefits, F, when outside equity financing is used to help finance the investment and the entrepreneur owns a fraction α' of the firm. The distance A measures the gross agency costs.

the firm's resources on non-pecuniary benefits, F. Let $\overline{V}(I)$ represent the value of the firm as a function of the level of investment when the manager's expenditures on non-pecuniary benefits, F, are zero. The schedule with intercept labeled $W + [\overline{V}(I^\star) - I^\star)]$ and slope equal to -1 in Fig. 2 represents the locus of combinations of post-investment wealth and dollar cost to the firm of non-pecuniary benefits which are available to the manager when investment is carried to the value maximizing point, $I^\star$. At this point $\Delta\overline{V}(I) - \Delta I = 0$. If the manager's wealth were large enough to cover the investment required to reach this scale of operation, $I^\star$, he would consume $F^\star$ in non-pecuniary benefits and have pecuniary wealth with value $W + V^\star - I^\star$. However, if outside financing is required to cover the investment he will not reach this point if monitoring costs are non-zero.[23]

The expansion path $OZBC$ represents the equilibrium combinations of wealth and non-pecuniary benefits, F, which the manager could obtain if he had enough personal wealth to finance all levels of investment up to $I^\star$. It is the locus of points such as Z and C which represent the equilibrium position for the 100 per cent owner–manager at each possible level of investment, I. As I increases we move up the expansion path to the point C where $V(I) - I$ is at a maximum. Additional investment beyond this point reduces the net value of the firm, and as it does the equilibrium path of the manager's wealth and non-pecuniary benefits retraces (in the reverse direction) the curve $OZBC$. We draw the path as a smooth concave function only as a matter of convenience.

If the manager obtained outside financing and if there were zero costs to the agency relationship (perhaps because monitoring costs were zero) the expansion path would also be represented by $OZBC$. Therefore, this path represents what we might call the 'idealized' solutions, i.e. those which would occur in the absence of agency costs.

Assume the manager has sufficient personal wealth to completely finance the firm only up to investment level I_1 which puts him at point Z. At this point $W = I_1$. To increase the size of the firm beyond this point he must obtain outside financing to cover the additional investment required, and this means reducing his fractional ownership. When he does this he incurs agency costs, and the lower is his ownership fraction the larger are the agency costs he incurs. However, if the investments requiring outside financing are sufficiently profitable his welfare will continue to increase.

The expansion path $ZEDHL$ in Fig. 2 portrays one possible path of the equilibrium levels of the owner's non-pecuniary benefits and wealth at each possible level of investment higher than I_1. This path is the locus of points such as E or D where (1) the manager's indifference curve is tangent to a line with slope equal to $-\alpha$ (his fractional claim on the firm at that level of investment), and (2) the tangency occurs on the 'budget constraint' with slope $= -1$ for the firm value and non-pecuniary benefit tradeoff at the same level of investment.[24] As we move along *ZEDHL* his fractional claim on the firm continues to fall as he raises larger amounts of outside capital. This expansion path represents his complete opportunity set for combinations of wealth and non-pecuniary benefits given the existence of the costs of the agency relationship with the outside equity holders. Point *D*, where this opportunity set is tangent to an indifference curve, represents the solution which maximizes his welfare. At this point, the level of investment is I', his fractional ownership share in the firm is α', his wealth is $W + V' - I'$, and he consumes a stream of non-pecuniary benefits with current market value of F'. The gross agency costs (denoted by A) are equal to $(V^\star - I^\star) - (V' - I')$. Given that no monitoring is possible, I' is the socially optimal level of investment as well as the privately optimal level.

We can characterize the optimal level of investment as that point, I', which satisfies the following condition for small changes:

$$\Delta V - \Delta I + \alpha' \Delta F = 0. \tag{1}$$

$\Delta V - \Delta I$ is the change in the net market value of the firm, and $\alpha' \Delta F$ is the dollar value to the manager of the incremental fringe benefits he consumes (which cost the firm ΔF dollars).[25] Furthermore, recognizing that $V = \overline{V} - F$, where $\overline{V}$ is the value of the firm at any level of investment when $F = 0$, we can substitute into the optimum condition to get

$$(\Delta V - \Delta I) - (1 - \alpha') \Delta F = 0 \tag{3}$$

as an alternative expression for determining the optimum level of investment.

The idealized or zero agency cost solution, $I^\star$, is given by the condition $(\Delta \overline{V} - \Delta I) = 0$, and since ΔF is positive the actual welfare maximizing level of investment I' will be less than $I^\star$, because $(\Delta \overline{V} - \Delta I)$ must be positive at I' if (3) is to be satisfied. Since $-\alpha'$ is the slope of the indifference curve at the optimum and therefore represents the manager's demand price for incremental non-pecuniary benefits, ΔF, we know that $\alpha' \Delta F$ is the dollar value to him of an increment of fringe benefits costing the firm ΔF dollars. The term $(1 - \alpha') \Delta F$ thus measures the dollar 'loss' to the firm (and himself) of an additional ΔF dollars spent on non-pecuniary benefits. The term $\Delta \overline{V} - \Delta I$ is the gross increment in the value of the firm ignoring any changes in the consumption of non-pecuniary benefits. Thus, the manager stops increasing the size of the firm when the gross increment in value is just offset by the incremental 'loss' involved in the consumption of additional fringe benefits due to his declining fractional interest in the firm.[26]

Michael C. Jensen and William H. Meckling

2.4. The Role of Monitoring and Bonding Activities in Reducing Agency Costs

In the above analysis we have ignored the potential for controlling the behavior of the owner–manager through monitoring and other control activities. In practice, it is usually possible by expending resources to alter the opportunity the owner–manager has for capturing non-pecuniary benefits. These methods include auditing, formal control systems, budget restrictions, and the establishment of incentive compensation systems which serve to more closely identify the manager's interests with those of the outside equity holders, etc. Fig. 3 portrays the effects of monitoring and other control activities in the simple situation portrayed in Fig. 1. Figs. 1 and 3 are identical except for the curve BCE in Fig. 3 which depicts a 'budget constraint' derived when monitoring possibilities are taken into account. Without monitoring, and with outside equity of $(1 - \alpha)$, the value of the firm will be V' and non-pecuniary expenditures F'. By incurring monitoring costs, M, the equity

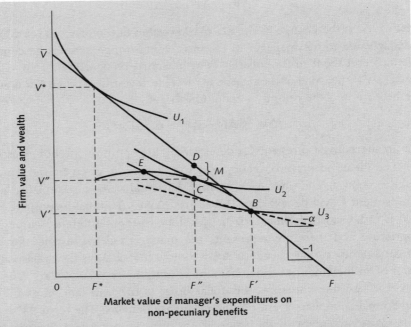

Fig. 3. The value of the firm (V) and level of non-pecuniary benefits (F) when outside equity is $(1 - \alpha)$, U_1, U_2, U_3 represent owner's indifference curves between wealth and non-pecuniary benefits, and monitoring (or bonding) activities impose opportunity set BCE as the tradeoff constraint facing the owner.

holders can restrict the manager's consumption of perquisites to amounts less than F'. Let $F(M, \alpha)$ denote the maximum perquisites the manager can consume for alternative levels of monitoring expenditures, M, given his ownership share α. We assume that increases in monitoring reduce F, and reduce it at a decreasing rate, i.e. $\partial F/\partial M < 0$ and $\partial^2 F/\partial M^2 > 0$.

Since the current value of expected future monitoring expenditures by the outside equity holders reduce the value of any given claim on the firm to them dollar for dollar, the outside equity holders will take this into account in determining the maximum price they will pay for any given fraction of the firm's equity. Therefore, given positive monitoring activity the value of the firm is given by $V = \bar{V} - F(M, \alpha) - M$ and the locus of these points for various levels of M and for a given level of α lie on the line BCE in Fig. 3. The vertical difference between the $\bar{V}F$ and BCE curves is M, the current market value of the future monitoring expenditures.

If it is possible for the outside equity holders to make these monitoring expenditures and thereby to impose the reductions in the owner–manager's consumption of F, he will voluntarily enter into a contract with the outside equity holders which gives them the rights to restrict his consumption of non-pecuniary items to F''. He finds this desirable because it will cause the value of the firm to rise to V''. Given the contract, the optimal monitoring expenditure on the part of outsiders, M, is the amount $D - C$. The entire increase in the value of the firm that accrues will be reflected in the owner's wealth, but his welfare will be increased by less than this because he forgoes some non-pecuniary benefits he previously enjoyed.

If the equity market is competitive and makes unbiased estimates of the effects of the monitoring expenditures on F and V, potential buyers will be indifferent between the following two contracts:

(i) Purchase of a share $(1 - \alpha)$ of the firm at a total price of $(1 - \alpha)V'$ and no rights to monitor or control the manager's consumption of perquisites.

(ii) Purchase of a share $(1 - \alpha)$ of the firm at a total price of $(1 - \alpha)V''$ and the right to expend resources up to an amount equal to $D - C$ which will limit the owner–manager's consumption of perquisites to F.

Given contract (ii) the outside shareholders would find it desirable to monitor to the full rights of their contract because it will pay them to do so. However, if the equity market is competitive the total benefits (net of the monitoring costs) will be capitalized into the price of the claims. Thus, not surprisingly, the owner–manager reaps all the benefits of the opportunity to write and sell the monitoring contract.[27]

An analysis of bonding expenditures. We can also see from the analysis of Fig. 3 that it makes no difference who actually makes the monitoring expenditures— the owner bears the full amount of these costs as a wealth reduction in all cases. Suppose that the owner–manager could expend resources to guarantee to the outside equity holders that he would limit his activities which cost the firm F. We call these expenditures 'bonding costs', and they would take such forms as contractual guarantees to have the financial accounts audited by a public account, explicit bonding against malfeasance on the part of the manager, and contractual limitations on the manager's decision making power (which impose costs on the firm because they limit his ability to take full advantage of some profitable opportunities as well as limiting his ability to harm the stockholders while making himself better off.)

If the incurrence of the bonding costs were entirely under the control of the manager and if they yielded the same opportunity set BCE for him in Fig. 3, he would incur them in amount $D - C$. This would limit his consumption of perquisites to F'' from F', and the solution is exactly the same as if the outside equity holders had performed the monitoring. The manager finds it in his interest to incur these costs as long as the net increments in his wealth which they generate (by reading the agency costs and therefore increasing the value of the firm) are more valuable than the perquisites given up. This optimum occurs at point C in both cases under our assumption that the bonding expenditures yield the same opportunity set as the monitoring expenditures. In general, of course, it will pay the owner–manager to engage in bonding activities and to write contracts which allow monitoring as long as the marginal benefits of each are greater than their marginal cost.

Optimal scale of the firm in the presence of monitoring and bonding activities. If we allow the outside owners to engage in (costly) monitoring activities to limit the manager's expenditures on non-pecuniary benefits and allow the manager to engage in bonding activities to guarantee to the outside owners that he will limit his consumption of F we get an expansion path such as that illustrated in Fig. 4 on which Z and G lie. We have assumed in drawing Fig. 4 that the cost functions involved in monitoring and bonding are such that some positive levels of the activities are desirable, i.e., yield benefits greater than their cost. If this is not true the expansion path generated by the expenditure of resources on these activities would lie below ZD and no such activity would take place at any level of investment. Points Z, C, and D and the two expansion paths they lie on are identical to those portrayed in Fig. 2. Points Z and C lie on the 100 per cent ownership expansion path, and points Z and D lie on the fractional ownership, zero monitoring and bonding activity expansion path.

The path on which points Z and G lie is the one given by the locus of equilibrium points for alternative levels of investment characterized by the point labeled C in Fig. 3 which denotes the optimal level of monitoring and bonding activity and resulting values of the firm and non-pecuniary benefits

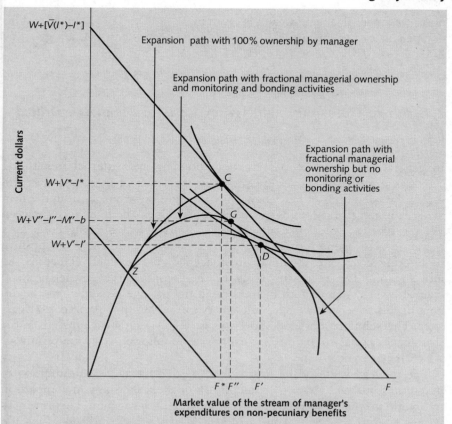

$W+[\overline{V}(I^*)-I^*]$

Expansion path with 100% ownership by manager

Expansion path with fractional managerial ownership and monitoring and bonding activities

Expansion path with fractional managerial ownership but no monitoring or bonding activities

Current dollars

$W+V^*-I^*$

$W+V''-I''-M'-b$

$W+V'-I'$

C

G

Z

D

$F^* F''$ F' F

Market value of the stream of manager's expenditures on non-pecuniary benefits

Fig. 4. Determination of optimal scale of the firm allowing for monitoring and bonding activities. Optimal monitoring costs are M'' and bonding costs are b'' and the equilibrium scale of firm, manager's wealth and consumption of non-pecuniary benefits are at point G.

to the manager given a fixed level of investment. If any monitoring or bonding is cost effective the expansion path on which Z and G lie must be above the non-monitoring expansion path over some range. Furthermore, if it lies anywhere to the right of the indifference curve passing through point D (the zero monitoring–bonding solution) the final solution to the problem will involve positive amounts of monitoring and/or bonding activities. Based on the discussion above we know that as long as the contracts between the manager and outsiders are unambiguous regarding the rights of the respective parties the final solution will be at that point where the new expansion path is just tangent to the highest indifference curve. At this point the optimal level of monitoring and bonding expenditures are M'' and b''; the manager's post-investment-financing wealth is given by $W + V'' - I'' - M'' - b''$ and his non-pecuniary benefits are F''. The total gross agency costs, A, are given by $A(M'', b'', \alpha'', I'') = (V^\star - I^\star) - (V'' - I'' - M'' - b'')$.

2.5. Pareto Optimality and Agency Costs in Manager-operated Firms

In general we expect to observe both bonding and external monitoring activities, and the incentives are such that the levels of these activities will satisfy the conditions of efficiency. They will not, however, result in the firm being run in a manner so as to maximize its value. The difference between $V^\star$, the efficient solution under zero monitoring and bonding costs (and therefore zero agency costs), and V'', the value of the firm given positive monitoring costs, are the total gross agency costs defined earlier in the introduction. These are the costs of the 'separation of ownership and control' which Adam Smith focused on in the passage quoted at the beginning of this paper and which Berle and Means (1932) popularized 157 years later. The solutions outlined above to our highly simplified problem imply that agency costs will be positive as long as monitoring costs are positive— which they certainly are.

The reduced value of the firm caused by the manager's consumption of perquisites outlined above is 'non-optimal' or inefficient only in comparison to a world in which we could obtain compliance of the agent to the principal's wishes at zero cost or in comparison to a *hypothetical* world in which the agency costs were lower. But these costs (monitoring and bonding costs and 'residual loss') are an unavoidable result of the agency relationship. Further-more, since they are borne entirely by the decision maker (in this case the original owner) responsible for creating the relationship he has the incentives to see that they are minimized (because he captures the benefits from their reduction). Furthermore, these agency costs will be incurred only if the benefits to the owner–manager from their creation are great enough to outweigh them. In our current example these benefits arise from the availability of profitable investments requiring capital investment in excess of the original owner's personal wealth.

In conclusion, finding that agency costs are non-zero (i.e. that there are costs associated with the separation of ownership and control in the corpora-tion) and concluding therefrom that the agency relationship is non-optimal, wasteful or inefficient is equivalent in every sense to comparing a world in which iron ore is a scarce commodity (and therefore costly) to a world in which it is freely available at zero resource cost, and concluding that the first world is 'non-optimal'—a perfect example of the fallacy criticized by Coase (1964) and what Demsetz (1969) characterizes as the 'Nirvana' form of analysis.[28]

2.6. *Factors Affecting the Size of the Divergence from Ideal Maximization*

The magnitude of the agency costs discussed above will vary from firm to firm. It will depend on the tastes of managers, the ease with which they can exercise their own preferences as opposed to value maximization in decision making, and the costs of monitoring and bonding activities.[29] The agency costs will also depend upon the cost of measuring the manager's (agent's) performance and evaluating it, the cost of devising and applying an index for compensating the manager which correlates with the owner's (principal's) welfare, and the cost of devising and enforcing specific behavioral rules or policies. Where the manager has less than a controlling interest in the firm, it will also depend upon the market for managers. Competition from other potential managers limits the costs of obtaining managerial services (including the extent to which a given manager can diverge from the idealized solution which would obtain if all monitoring and bonding costs were zero). The size of the divergence (the agency costs) will be directly related to the cost of replacing the manager. If his responsibilities require very little knowledge specialized to the firm, if it is easy to evaluate his performance, and if replacement search costs are modest, the divergence from the ideal will be relatively small and vice versa.

The divergence will also be constrained by the market for the firm itself, i.e. by capital markets. Owners always have the option of selling their firm, either as a unit or piecemeal. Owners of manager-operated firms can and do sample the capital market from time to time. If they discover that the value of the future earnings stream to others is higher than the value of the firm to them given that it is to be manager-operated, they can exercise their right to sell. It is conceivable that other owners could be more efficient at monitoring or even that a single individual with appropriate managerial talents and with sufficiently large personal wealth would elect to buy the firm. In this latter case the purchase by such a single individual would completely eliminate the agency costs. If there were a number of such potential owner–manager purchasers (all with talents and tastes identical to the current manager) the owners would receive in the sale price of the firm the full value of the residual claimant rights including the capital value of the eliminated agency costs plus the value of the managerial rights.

Monopoly, competition and managerial behavior. It is frequently argued that the existence of competition in product (and factor) markets will constrain the behavior of managers to idealized value maximization, i.e. that monopoly in product (or monopsony in factor) markets will permit larger divergences from value maximisation.[30] Our analysis does not support this hypothesis. The owners of a firm with monopoly power have the same incentives to limit divergences of the manager from value maximization (i.e. the ability to increase their wealth) as do the owners of competitive firms. Furthermore, competition in the market for managers will generally make it unnecessary for the owners to share rents with the manager. The owners of a monopoly firm need only pay the supply price for a manager.

Since the owner of a monopoly has the same wealth incentives to minimize managerial costs as would the owner of a competitive firm, both will undertake that level of monitoring which equates the marginal cost of monitoring to the marginal wealth increment from reduced consumption of perquisites by the manager. Thus, the existence of monopoly will not increase agency costs.

Furthermore the existence of competition in product and factor markets will not eliminate the agency costs due to managerial control problems as has often been asserted [cf. Friedman (1970)]. If my competitors all incur agency costs equal to or greater than mine I will not be eliminated from the market by their competition.

The existence and size of the agency costs depends on the nature of the monitoring costs, the tastes of managers for non-pecuniary benefits and the supply of potential managers who are capable of financing the entire venture out of their personal wealth. If monitoring costs are zero, agency costs will be zero or if there are enough 100 per cent owner–managers available to own and run all the firms in an industry (competitive or not) then agency costs in that industry will also be zero.[31]

....

3. Some Unanswered Questions Regarding the Existence of the Corporate Form

3.1. The Question

The analysis to this point has left us with a basic puzzle: Why, given the existence of positive costs of the agency relationship, do we find the usual corporate form of organization with widely diffuse ownership so widely prevalent? If one takes seriously much of the literature regarding the 'discretionary' power held by managers of large corporations, it is difficult to understand the historical fact of enormous growth in equity in such organizations, not only in the United States, but throughout the world. Paraphrasing Alchian (1968): How does it happen that millions of individuals are willing to turn over a significant fraction of their wealth to organizations run by managers who have so little interest in their welfare? What is even more remarkable, why are they willing to make these commitments purely as residual claimants, i.e. on the anticipation that managers will operate the firm so that there will be earnings which accrue to the stockholders?

There is certainly no lack of alternative ways that individuals might invest, including entirely different forms of organizations. Even if consideration is limited to corporate organizations, there are clearly alternative ways capital might be raised, i.e. through fixed claims of various sorts, bonds, notes, mortgages, etc. Moreover, the corporate income tax seems to favor the use of fixed claims since interest is treated as a tax deductible expense. Those who assert that managers do not behave in the interest of stockholders have generally not addressed a very important question: Why, if non-manager-owned shares have such a serious deficiency, have they not long since been driven out by fixed claims?[32]

3.2. Some Alternative Explanations of the Ownership Structure of the Firm

The role of limited liability. Manne (1967) and Alchian and Demsetz (1972) argue that one of the attractive features of the corporate form vis-a-vis individual proprietorships or partnerships is the limited liability feature of equity claims in corporations. Without this provision each and every investor purchasing one or more shares of a corporation would be potentially liable to the full extent of his personal wealth for the debts of the corporation. Few individuals would find this a desirable risk to accept and the major benefits to be obtained from risk reduction through diversification would be to a large extent unobtainable. This argument, however, is incomplete since limited liability does not eliminate the basic risk, it merely shifts it. The argument must rest ultimately on transactions costs. If all stockholders of GM were liable for GM's debts, the maximum liability for an individual shareholder would be greater than it would be if his shares had limited liability. However, given that many other stockholders also existed and that each was liable for the unpaid claims in proportion to his ownership it is highly unlikely that the maximum payment each would have to make would be large in the event of GM's bankruptcy since the total wealth of those stockholders would also be large. However, the existence of unlimited liability would impose incentives for each shareholder to keep track of both the liabilities of GM and the wealth of the other GM owners. It is easily conceivable that the costs of so doing would, in the aggregate, be much higher than simply paying a premium in the form of higher interest rates to the creditors of GM in return for their acceptance of a contract which grants limited liability to the shareholders. The creditors would then bear the risk of any non-payment of debts in the event of GM's bankruptcy.

It is also not generally recognized that limited liability is merely a necessary condition for explaining the magnitude of the reliance on equities, not a sufficient condition. Ordinary debt also carries limited liability.[33] If limited liability is all that is required, why don't we observe large corporations, individually owned, with a tiny fraction of the capital supplied by the entrepreneur, and the rest simply borrowed?[34] At first this question seems silly to many people (as does the question regarding why firms would ever issue debt or preferred stock under conditions where there are no tax benefits obtained from the treatment of interest or preferred dividend payments[35]). We have found that oftentimes this question is misinterpreted to be one regarding why firms obtain capital. The issue is not why they obtain capital, but why they obtain it through the particular forms we have observed for such long periods of time. The fact is that no well articulated answer to this question currently exists in the literature of either finance or economics.

The 'irrelevance' of capital structure. In their pathbreaking article on the cost of capital, Modigliani and Miller (1958) demonstrated that in the absence of bankruptcy costs and tax subsidies on the payment of interest the value of the firm is independent of the financial structure. They later (1963) demonstrated that the existence of tax subsidies on interest payments would cause the value of the firm to rise with the amount of debt financing by the amount of the capitalized value of the tax subsidy. But this line of argument implies that the firm should be financed almost entirely with debt. Realizing the inconsistence with observed behavior Modigliani and Miller (1963, 442) comment:

[I]t may be useful to remind readers once again that the existence of a tax advantage for debt financing . . . does not necessarily mean that corporations should at all times seek to use the maximum amount of debt in their capital structures . . . there are as we pointed out, limitations imposed by lenders . . . as well as many other dimensions (and kinds of costs) in real-world problems of financial strategy which are not fully comprehended within the framework of static equilibrium models, either our own or those of the traditional variety. These additional considerations, which are typically grouped under the rubric of 'the need for preserving flexibility', will normally imply the maintenance by the corporation of a substantial reserve of untapped borrowing power.

Modigliani and Miller are essentially left without a theory of the determination of the optimal capital structure, and Fama and Miller (1972, 173) commenting on the same issue reiterate this conclusion: 'And we must admit that at this point there is little in the way of convincing research, either theoretical or empirical, that explains the amounts of debt that firms do decide to have in their capital structure.'

The Modigliani–Miller theorem is based on the assumption that the probability distribution of the cash flows to the firm is independent of the capital structure. It is now recognized that the existence of positive costs associated with bankruptcy and the presence of tax subsidies on corporate interest payments will invalidate this irrelevance theorem precisely because the probability distribution of future cash flows changes as the probability of the incurrence of the bankruptcy costs changes, i.e. as the ratio of debt to equity rises. We believe the existence of agency costs provide stronger reasons for arguing that the probability distribution of future cash flows is *not* independent of the capital of ownership structure.

While the introduction of bankruptcy costs in the presence of tax subsidies leads to a theory which defines an optimal capital structure,[36] we argue that this theory is seriously incomplete since it implies that no debt should ever be used in the absence of tax subsidies if bankruptcy costs are positive. Since we know debt was commonly used prior to the existence of the current tax subsidies on interest payments this theory does not capture what must be some important determinants of the corporate capital structure.

In addition, neither bankruptcy costs nor the existence of tax subsidies can explain the use of preferred stock or warrants which have no tax advantages, and there is no theory which tells us anything about what determines the fraction of equity claims held by insiders as opposed to outsiders which our analysis in Section 2 indicates is so important. We return to these issues later after analyzing in detail the factors affecting the agency costs associated with debt.

4. The Agency Costs of Debt

In general if the agency costs engendered by the existence of outside owners are positive it will pay the absentee owner (i.e. shareholders) to sell out to an owner–manager who can avoid these costs.[37] This could be accomplished in principle by having the manager become the sole equity holder by repurchasing all of the outside equity claims with funds obtained through the issuance of limited liability debt claims and the use of his own personal wealth. This single-owner corporation would not suffer the agency costs associated with outside equity. Therefore there must be some compelling reasons why we find the diffuse-owner corporate firm financed by equity claims so prevalent as an organizational form.

An ingenious entrepreneur eager to expand, has open to him the opportunity to design a whole hierarchy of fixed claims on assets and earnings, with premiums paid for different levels of risk.[38] Why don't we observe large corporations individually owned with a tiny fraction of the capital supplied by the entrepreneur in return for 100 per cent of the equity and the rest simply borrowed? We believe there are a number of reasons: (1) the incentive effects associated with highly leveraged firms, (2) the monitoring costs these incentive effects engender, and (3) bankruptcy costs. Furthermore, all of these costs are simply particular aspects of the agency costs associated with the existence of debt claims on the firm.

4.1. The Incentive Effects Associated with Debt

We don't find many large firms financed almost entirely with debt type claims (i.e. non-residual claims) because of the effect such a financial structure would have on the owner–manager's behavior. Potential creditors will not loan $100,000,000 to a firm in which the entrepreneur has an investment of $10,000. With that financial structure the owner–manager will have a strong incentive to engage in activities (investments) which promise very high payoffs if successful even if they have a very low probability of success. If they turn out well, he captures most of the gains, if they turn out badly, the creditors bear most of the costs.[39]

To illustrate the incentive effects associated with the existence of debt and to provide a framework within which we can discuss the effects of monitoring and bonding costs, wealth transfers, and the incidence of agency costs, we again consider a simple situation. Assume we have a manager-owned firm with no debt outstanding in a world in which there are no taxes. The firm has the opportunity to take one of two mutually exclusive equal cost investment opportunities, each of which yields a random payoff, $\tilde{X}_j$, T periods in the future ($j = 1, 2$). Production and monitoring activities take place continuously between time 0 and time T, and markets in which the claims on the firm can be traded are open continuously over this period. After time T the firm has no productive activities so the payoff $\tilde{X}_j$ includes the distribution of all remaining assets. For simplicity, we assume that the two distributions are log-normally distributed and have the same expected total payoff, $E(\tilde{X})$, where $\tilde{X}$ is defined as the logarithm of the final payoff. The distributions differ only by their variances with $\sigma_1^2 < \sigma_2^2$. The systematic or covariance risk of each of the distributions, β_j, in the Sharpe (1964)–Lintner (1965) capital asset pricing model, is assumed to be identical. Assuming that asset prices are determined according to the capital asset pricing model, the preceding assumptions imply that the total market value of each of these distributions is identical, and we represent this value by V.

If the owner–manager has the right to decide which investment program to take, and if after he decides this he has the opportunity to sell part or all of his claims on the outcomes in the form of either debt or equity, he will be indifferent between the two investments.[40]

However, if the owner has the opportunity to *first* issue debt, then to decide which of the investments to take, and then to sell all or part of his remaining equity claim on the market, he will not be indifferent between the two investments. The reason is that by promising to take the low variance project, selling bonds and then taking the high variance project he can transfer wealth from the (naive) bondholders to himself as equity holder.

Let $X^\star$ be the amount of the 'fixed' claim in the form of a non-coupon bearing bond sold to the bondholders such that the total payoff to them, R_j (j = 1, 2, denotes the distribution the manager chooses), is

$$R_j = X^\star, \text{ if } \tilde{X}_j \geqq X^\star,$$
$$= X_j, \text{ if } \tilde{X}_j \leqq X^\star.$$

Let B_1 be the current market value of bondholder claims if investment 1 is taken, and let B_2 be the current market value of bondholders claims if investment 2 is taken. Since in this example the total value of the firm, V, is independent of the investment choice and also of the financing decision we can use the Black–Scholes (1973) option pricing model to determine the values of the debt, B_j, and equity, S_j, under each of the choices.[41]

Black–Scholes derive the solution for the value of a European call option (one which can be exercised only at the maturity date) and argue that the resulting option pricing equation can be used to determine the value of the equity claim on a levered firm. That is the stockholders in such a firm can be viewed as holding a European call option on the total value of the firm with exercise price equal to $X^\star$ (the face value of the debt), exercisable at the maturity date of the debt issue. More simply, the stockholders have the right to buy the firm back from the bondholders for a price of $X^\star$ at time T. Merton (1973, 1974) shows that as the variance of the outcome distribution rises the value of the stock (i.e. call option) rises, and since our two distributions differ only in their variances, $\sigma_2^2 < \sigma_1^2$, the equity value S_1 is less than S_2. This implies $B_1 > B_2$, since $B_1 = V - S_1$ and $B_2 = V - S_2$.

Now if the owner–manager could sell bonds with face value $X^\star$ under the conditions that the potential bondholders believed this to be a claim on distribution 1, he would receive a price of B_1. After selling the bonds, his equity interest in distribution 1 would have value S_1. But we know S_2 is greater than S_1 and thus the manager can make himself better off by changing the investment to take the higher variance distribution 2, thereby redistributing wealth from the bondholders to himself. All this assumes of course that the bondholders could not prevent him from changing the investment program. *If the bondholders cannot do so, and if they perceive that the manager has the opportunity to take distribution 2 they will pay the manager only B_2 for the claim $X^\star$, realizing that his maximizing behavior will lead him to choose distribution 2.* In this event there is no redistribution of wealth between bondholders and stockholders (and in general with rational expectations there never will be) and no welfare loss. It is easy to construct a case, however, in which these incentive effects do generate real costs.

Let cash flow distribution 2 in the previous example have an expected value, $E(X_2)$, which is lower than that of distribution 1. Then we know that $V_1 > V_2$ and if ΔV, which is given by

$$\Delta V = V_1 - V_2 = (S_1 - S_2) + (B_1 - B_2),$$

is sufficiently small relative to the reduction in the value of the bonds the value of the stock will increase.[42] Rearranging the expression for ΔV we see that the difference between the equity values for the two investments is given by

$$S_2 - S_1 = (B_1 - B_2) - (V_1 - V_2),$$

and the first term on the RHS, $B_1 - B_2$ is the amount of wealth 'transferred' from the bondholders and $V_1 - V_2$ is the reduction in overall firm value. Since we know $B_1 > B_2$, $S_2 - S_1$ can be positive even though the reduction in the value of the firm, $V_1 - V_2$, is positive.[43] Again, the bondholders will not actually lose as long as they accurately perceive the motivation of the equity owning manager and his opportunity to take project 2. They will presume he will take investment 2, and hence will pay no more than B_2 for the bonds when they are issued.

In this simple example the reduced value of the firm, $V_1 - V_2$, is the agency cost engendered by the issuance of debt[44] and it is borne by the owner–manager. If he could finance the project out of his personal wealth, he would clearly choose project 1 since its investment outlay was assumed equal to that of project 2 and its market value, V_1, was greater. This wealth loss, $V_1 - V_2$, is the 'residual loss' portion of what we have defined as agency costs and it is generated by the cooperation required to raise the funds to make the investment. Another important part of the agency costs are monitoring and bonding costs and we now consider their role.

4.2. The Role of Monitoring and Bonding Costs

In principle it would be possible for the bondholders, by the inclusion of various covenants in the indenture provisions, to limit the managerial behavior which results in reductions in the value of the bonds. Provisions which impose constraints on management's decisions regarding such things as dividends, future debt issues,[45] and maintenance of working capital are not uncommon in bond issues.[46] To completely protect the bondholders from the incentive effects, these provisions would have to be incredibly detailed and cover most operating aspects of the enterprise including limitations on the riskiness of the projects undertaken. The costs involved in writing such provisions, the costs of enforcing them and the reduced profitability of the firm (induced because the covenants occasionally limit management's ability to take optimal actions on certain issues) would likely be non-trivial. In fact, since management is a continuous decision making process it will be almost impossible to completely specify such conditions without having the bond-holders actually perform the management function. All costs associated with such covenants are what we mean by monitoring costs.

The bondholders will have incentives to engage in the writing of such covenants and in monitoring the actions of the manager to the point where the 'nominal' marginal cost to them of such activities is just equal to the marginal benefits they perceive from engaging in them. We use the word nominal here because debtholders will not in fact bear these costs. As long as they recognize their existence, they will take them into account in deciding the price they will pay for any given debt claim,[47] and therefore the seller of the claim (the owner) will bear the costs just as in the equity case discussed in Section 2.

In addition the manager has incentives to take into account the costs imposed on the firm by covenants in the debt agreement which directly affect the future cash flows of the firm since they reduce the market value of his claims. Because both the external and internal monitoring costs are imposed on the owner–manager it is in his interest to see that the monitoring is performed in the lowest cost way. Suppose, for example, that the bond-holders (or outside equity holders) would find it worthwhile to produce detailed financial statements such as those contained in the usual published accounting reports as a means of monitoring the manager. If the manager himself can produce such information at lower costs than they (perhaps because he is already collecting much of the data they desire for his own internal decision making purposes), it would pay him to agree in advance to incur the cost of providing such reports and to have their accuracy testified to by an independent outside auditor. This is an example of what we refer to as bonding costs.[48, 49]

4.3. Bankruptcy and Reorganization Costs

We argue in Section 5 that as the debt in the capital structure increases beyond some point the marginal agency costs of debt begin to dominate the marginal agency costs of outside equity and the result of this is the generally observed phenomenon of the simultaneous use of both debt and outside equity. Before considering these issues, however, we consider here the third major component of the agency costs of debt which helps to explain why debt doesn't completely dominate capital structures—the existence of bankruptcy and reorganization costs.

It is important to emphasize that bankruptcy and liquidation are very different events. The legal definition of bankruptcy is difficult to specify precisely. In general, it occurs when the firm cannot meet a current payment on a debt obligation,[50] or one or more of the other indenture provisions providing for bankruptcy is violated by the firm. In this event the stockholders have lost all claims on the firm,[51] and the remaining loss, the difference between the face value of the fixed claims and the market value of the firm, is borne by the debtholders. Liquidation of the firm's assets will occur only if the market value of the future cash flows generated by the firm is less than the opportunity cost of the assets, i.e. the sum of the values which could be realized if the assets were sold piecemeal.

If there were no costs associated with the event called bankruptcy the total market value of the firm would not be affected by increasing the probability of its incurrence. However, it is costly, if not impossible, to write contracts representing claims on a firm which clearly delineate the rights of holders for all possible contingencies. Thus even if there were no adverse incentive effects in expanding fixed claims relative to equity in a firm, the use of such fixed claims would be constrained by the costs inherent in defining and enforcing those claims. Firms incur obligations daily to suppliers, to employees, to different classes of investors, etc. So long as the firm is prospering, the adjudication of claims is seldom a problem. When the firm has difficulty meeting some of its obligations, however, the issue of the priority of those claims can pose serious problems. This is most obvious in the extreme case where the firm is forced into bankruptcy. If bankruptcy were costless, the reorganization would be accompanied by an adjustment of the claims of various parties and the business, could, if that proved to be in the interest of the claimants, simply go on (although perhaps under new management).[52]

In practice, bankruptcy is not costless, but generally involves an adjudication process which itself consumes a fraction of the remaining value of the assets of the firm. Thus the cost of bankruptcy will be of concern to potential buyers of fixed claims in the firm since their existence will reduce the payoffs to them in the event of bankruptcy. These are examples of the agency costs of cooperative efforts among individuals (although in this case perhaps 'non-cooperative' would be a better term). The price buyers will be willing to pay for fixed claims will thus be inversely related to the probability of the incurrence of these costs, i.e. to the probability of bankruptcy. Using a variant of the argument employed above for monitoring costs, it can be shown that the total value of the firm will fall, and the owner–manager equity holder will bear the entire wealth effect of the bankruptcy costs as long as potential bondholders make unbiased estimates of their magnitude at the time they initially purchase bonds.[53]

Empirical studies of the magnitude of bankruptcy costs are almost non-existent. Warner (1975) in a study of 11 railroad bankruptcies between 1930 and 1955 estimates the average costs of bankruptcy[54] as a fraction of the value of the firm three years prior to bankruptcy to be 2.5% (with a range of 0.4% to 5.9%). The average dollar costs were $1.88 million. Both of these measures seem remarkably small and are consistent with our belief that bankruptcy costs themselves are unlikely to be the major determinant of corporate capital structures. It is also interesting to note that the annual amount of defaulted funds has fallen significantly since 1940. [See Atkinson (1967).] One possible explanation for this phenomenon is that firms are using mergers to avoid the costs of bankruptcy. This hypothesis seems even more reasonable, if, as is frequently the case, reorganization costs represent only a fraction of the costs associated with bankruptcy.

In general the revenues or the operating costs of the firm are not independent of the probability of bankruptcy and thus the capital structure of the firm. As the probability of bankruptcy increases, both the operating costs and the revenues of the firm are adversely affected, and some of these costs can be avoided by merger. For example, a firm with a high probability of bankruptcy will also find that it must pay higher salaries to induce executives to accept the higher risk of unemployment. Furthermore, in certain kinds of durable goods industries the demand function for the firm's product will not be independent of the probability of bankruptcy. The computer industry is a good example. There, the buyer's welfare is dependent to a significant extent on the ability to maintain the equipment, and on continuous hardware and software development. Furthermore, the owner of a large computer often receives benefits from the software developments of other users. Thus if the manufacturer leaves the business or loses his software support and development experts because of financial difficulties, the value of the equipment to his users will decline. The buyers of such services have a continuing interest in the manufacturer's viability not unlike that of a bondholder, except that their benefits come in the form of continuing services at lower cost rather than principal and interest payments. Service facilities and spare parts for automobiles and machinery are other examples.

In summary then the agency costs associated with debt[55] consist of:

(1) the opportunity wealth loss caused by the impact of debt on the investment decisions of the firm,

(2) the monitoring and bonding expenditures by the bondholders and the owner–manager (i.e. the firm),

(3) the bankruptcy and reorganization costs.

4.4. Why Are the Agency Costs of Debt Incurred?

We have argued that the owner–manager bears the entire wealth effects of the agency costs of debt and he captures the gains from reducing them. Thus, the agency costs associated with debt discussed above will tend, in the absence of other mitigating factors, to discourage the use of corporate debt. What are the factors that encourage its use?

One factor is the tax subsidy on interest payments. (This will not explain preferred stock where dividends are not tax deductible.)[56] Modigliani and Miller (1963) originally demonstrated that the use of riskless perpetual debt will increase the total value of the firm (ignoring the agency costs) by an amount equal to τB, where τ is the marginal and average corporate tax rate and B is the market value of the debt. Fama and Miller (1972, chapter 4) demonstrate that for the case of risky debt the value of the firm will increase by the market value of the (uncertain) tax subsidy on the interest payments. Again, these gains will accrue entirely to the equity and will provide an incentive to utilize debt to the point where the marginal wealth benefits of the tax subsidy are just equal to the marginal wealth effects of the agency costs discussed above.

However, even in the absence of these tax benefits, debt would be utilized if the ability to exploit potentially profitable investment opportunities is limited by the resources of the owner. If the owner of a project cannot raise capital he will suffer an opportunity loss represented by the increment in value offered to him by the additional investment opportunities. Thus even though he will bear the agency costs from selling debt, he will find it desirable to incur them to obtain additional capital as long as the marginal wealth increments from the new investments projects are greater than the marginal agency costs of debt, and these agency costs are in turn less than those caused by the sale of additional equity discussed in Section 2. Furthermore, this solution is optimal from the social viewpoint. However, in the absence of tax subsidies on debt these projects must be unique to this firm[57] or they would be taken by other competitive entrepreneurs (perhaps new ones) who possessed the requisite personal wealth to fully finance the projects[58] and therefore able to avoid the existence of debt or outside equity.

....

5. A Theory of the Corporate Ownership Structure

In the previous sections we discussed the nature of agency costs associated with outside claims on the firm—both debt and equity. Our purpose here is to integrate these concepts into the beginnings of a theory of the corporate ownership structure. We use the term 'ownership structure' rather than 'capital structure' to highlight the fact that the crucial variables to be determined are not just the relative amounts of debt and equity but also the fraction of the equity held by the manager. Thus, for a given size firm we want a theory to determine three variables:[59]

S_i: inside equity (held by the manager),
S_o: outside equity (held by anyone outside the firm),
B: debt (held by anyone outside of the firm).

The total market value of the equity is $S = S_i + S_o$, and the total market value of the firm is $V = S + B$. In addition, we also wish to have a theory which determines the optimal size of the firm, i.e. its level of investment.

5.1. Determination of the Optimal Ratio of Outside Equity to Debt

Consider first the determination of the optimal ratio of outside equity to debt, S_o/B. To do this let us hold the size of the firm constant. V, the actual value of the firm for a given size, will depend on the agency costs incurred, hence we use as our index of size $V^\star$, the value of the firm at a given scale when agency costs are zero. For the moment we also hold the amount of outside financing $(B + S_o)$, constant. Given that a specified amount of financing $(B + S_o)$ is to be obtained externally our problem is to determine the optimal fraction $E^\star \equiv S_o^\star/(B + S_o)$ to be financed with equity.

We argued above that: (1) as long as capital markets are efficient (i.e. characterized by rational expectations) the price of assets such as debt and outside equity will reflect unbiased estimates of the monitoring costs and redistributions which the agency relationship will engender, and (2) the selling owner–manager will bear these agency costs. Thus from the owner–manager's standpoint the optimal proportion of outside funds to be obtained from equity (versus debt) *for a given level of internal equity* is that E which results in minimum total agency costs.

Fig. 5 presents a breakdown of the agency costs into two separate components: Define $A_{S_o}(E)$ as the total agency costs (a function of E) associated with the 'exploitation' of the outside equity holders by the

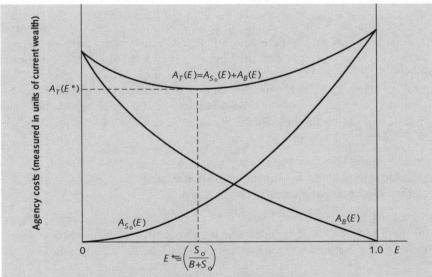

Fraction of outside financing obtained from equity

Fig. 5. Total agency costs, $A_\tau(E)$, as a function of the ratio of outside equity, to total outside financing, $E \equiv S_o(B + S_o)$, for a given firm size $V^\star$ and given total amounts of outside financing $(B + S_o)$. $A_{S_o}(E) \equiv$ agency costs associated with outside equity, $A_B(E) \equiv$ agency costs associated with debt, B. $A_\tau(E^\star) =$ minimum total agency costs at optimal fraction of outside financing $E^\star$.

owner–manager, and $A_B(E)$ as the total agency costs associated with the presence of debt in the ownership structure. $A_T(E) = A_{So}(E) + A_B(E)$ is the total agency cost.

Consider the function $A_{So}(E)$. When $E \equiv S_o/(B + S_o)$ is zero, i.e. when there is no outside equity, the manager's incentives to exploit the outside equity is at a minimum (zero) since the changes in the value of the *total* equity are equal to the changes in *his* equity.[60] As E increases to 100 per cent his incentives to exploit the outside equity holders increase and hence the agency costs $A_{So}(E)$ increase.

The agency costs associated with the existence of debt, $A_B(E)$ are composed mainly of the value reductions in the firm and monitoring costs caused by the manager's incentive to reallocate wealth from the bondholders to himself by increasing the value of his equity claim. They are at a maximum where all outside funds are obtained from debt, i.e. where $S_o = E = 0$. As the amount of debt declines to zero these costs also go to zero because as E goes to 1, his incentive to reallocate wealth from the bondholders to himself falls. These incentives fall for two reasons: (1) the total amount of debt falls, and therefore it is more difficult to reallocate any given amount away from the debtholders, and (2) his share of any reallocation which is accomplished is falling since S_o is rising and therefore $S_i/(S_o + S_i)$, his share of the total equity, is falling.

The curve $A_T(E)$ represents the sum of the agency costs from various combinations of outside equity and debt financing, and as long as $A_{So}(E)$ and $A_B(E)$ are as we have drawn them the minimum total agency cost for given size firm and outside financing will occur at some point such as $A_T(E^\star)$ with a mixture of both debt and equity.[61]

A caveat. Before proceeding further we point out that the issue regarding the exact shapes of the functions drawn in Fig. 5 and several others discussed below is essentially an open question at this time. In the end the shape of these functions is a question of fact and can only be settled by empirical evidence. We outline some a priori arguments which we believe can lead to some plausible hypotheses about the behavior of the system, but confess that we are far from understanding the many conceptual subtleties of the problem. We are fairly confident of our arguments regarding the signs of the first derivatives of the functions, but the second derivatives are also important to the final solution and much more work (both theoretical and empirical) is required before we can have much confidence regarding these parameters. We anticipate the work of others as well as our own to cast more light on these issues. Moreover, we suspect the results of such efforts will generate revisions to the details of what follows. We believe it is worthwhile to delineate the overall framework in order to demonstrate, if only in a simplified fashion, how the major pieces of the puzzle fit together into a cohesive structure.

Michael C. Jensen and William H. Meckling

5.2. Effects of the Scale of Outside Financing

In order to investigate the effects of increasing the amount of outside financing, $B + S_o$, and therefore reducing the amount of equity held by the manager, S_i, we continue to hold the scale of the firm, $V^\star$, constant. Fig. 6 presents a plot of the agency cost functions, $A_{S_o}(E)$, $A_B(E)$ and $A_T(E) = A_{S_o}(E) + A_B(E)$, for two different levels of outside financing. Define an index of the amount of outside financing to be

$$K = (B + S_o)/V^\star,$$

and consider two different possible levels of outside financing K_o and K_1 for a given scale of the firm such that $K_o < K_1$.

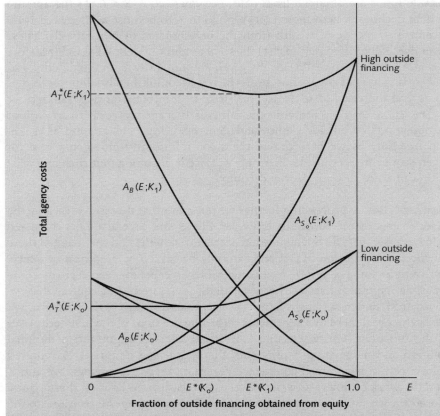

Fig. 6. Agency cost functions and optimal outside equity as a fraction of total outside financing, $E^\star(K)$, for two different levels of outside financing, K, for a given size firm, $V^\star$: $K_1 > K_o$.

As the amount of outside equity increases, the owner's fractional claim on the firm, α, falls. He will be induced thereby to take additional non-pecuniary benefits out of the firm because his share of the cost falls. This also increases the marginal benefits from monitoring activities and therefore will tend to increase the optimal level of monitoring. Both of these factors will cause the locus of agency costs $A_{So}(E; K)$ to shift upward as the fraction of outside financing, K, increases. This is depicted in Fig. 6 by the two curves representing the agency costs of equity, one for the low level of outside financing, $A_{So}(E; K_o)$, the other for the high level of outside financing, $A_{So}(E; K_1)$. The locus of the latter lies above the former everywhere except at the origin where both are 0.

The agency costs of debt will similarly rise as the amount of outside financing increases. This means that the locus of $A_B(E; K_1)$ for high outside financing, K_1, will lie above the locus of $A_B(E; K_o)$ for low outside financing, K_o because the total amount of resources which can be reallocated from bondholders increases as the total amount of debt increases. However, since these costs are zero when the debt is zero for both K_o and K_1 the intercepts of the $A_B(E; K)$ curves coincide at the right axis.

The net effect of the increased use of outside financing given the cost functions assumed in Fig. 6 is to: (1) increase the total agency costs from $A_T(E; K_o)$ to $A_T(E^\star; K_1)$, and (2) to increase the optimal fraction of outside funds obtained from the sale of outside equity. We draw these functions for illustration only and are unwilling to speculate at this time on the exact form of $E^\star(K)$ which gives the general effects of increasing outside financing on the relative quantities of debt and equity.

The locus of points $A_T(E^\star; K)$ where agency costs are minimized (not drawn in Fig. 6), determines $E^\star(K)$, the optimal proportions of equity and debt to be used in obtaining outside funds as the fraction of outside funds, K, ranges from 0 to 100 per cent. The solid line in Fig. 7 is a plot of the minimum total agency costs as a function of the amount of outside financing for a firm with scale $V^\star_o$. The dotted line shows the total agency costs for a larger firm with scale $V^\star_1 > V^\star_o$. That is, we hypothesize that the larger the firm becomes the larger are the total agency costs because it is likely that the monitoring function is inherently more difficult and expensive in a larger organization.

5.3. Risk and the Demand for Outside Financing

The model we have used to explain the existence of minority shareholders and debt in the capital structure of corporations implies that the owner–manager, if he resorts to any outside funding, will have his entire wealth

141

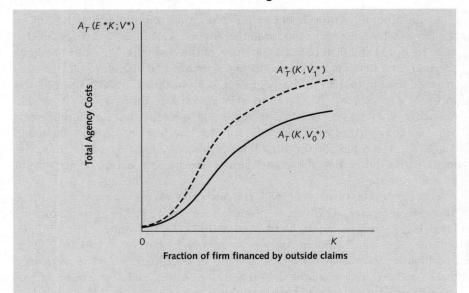

Fig. 7. Total agency costs as a function of the fraction of the firm financed by outside claims for two firm sizes, $V_1^* > V_0^*$.

invested in the firm. The reason is that he can thereby avoid the agency costs which additional outside funding impose. This suggests he would not resort to outside funding until he had invested 100 per cent of his personal wealth in the firm—an implication which is not consistent with what we generally observe. Most owner–managers hold personal wealth in a variety of forms, and some have only a relatively small fraction of their wealth invested in the corporation they manage.[62] Diversification on the part of owner–managers can be explained by risk aversion and optimal portfolio selection.

If the returns from assets are not perfectly correlated an individual can reduce the riskiness of the returns on his portfolio by dividing his wealth among many different assets, i.e. by diversifying.[63] Thus a manager who invests all of his wealth in a single firm (his own) will generally bear a welfare loss (if he is risk averse) because he is bearing more risk than necessary. He will, of course, be willing to pay something to avoid this risk, and the costs he must bear to accomplish this diversification will be the agency costs outlined above. He will suffer a wealth loss as he reduces his fractional ownership because prospective shareholders and bondholders will take into account the agency costs. Nevertheless, the manager's desire to avoid risk will contribute to his becoming a minority stockholder.

5.4. *Determination of the Optimal Amount of Outside Financing, K**

Assume for the moment that the owner of a project (i.e. the owner of a prospective firm) has enough wealth to finance the entire project himself. The optimal scale of the corporation is then determined by the condition that, $\Delta V - \Delta I = 0$. In general if the returns to the firm are uncertain the owner–manager can increase his welfare by selling off part of the firm either as debt or equity and reinvesting the proceeds in other assets. If he does this with the optimal combination of debt and equity (as in Fig. 6) the total wealth reduction he will incur is given by the agency cost function, $A_T(E^\star, K; V^\star)$ in Fig. 7. The functions $A_T(E^\star, K; V^\star)$ will be S shaped (as drawn) if total agency costs for a given scale of firm increase at an increasing rate at low levels of outside financing, and at a decreasing rate for high levels of outside financing as monitoring imposes more and more constraints on the manager's actions.

Fig. 8 shows marginal agency costs as a function of K, the fraction of the

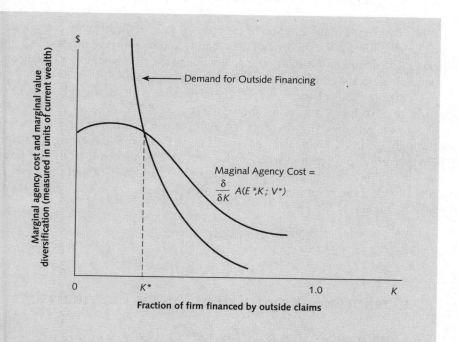

Fig. 8. Determination of the optimal amount of outside financing, K^*, for a given scale of firm.

firm financed with outside funds assuming the total agency cost function is as plotted in Fig. 7, and assuming the scale of the firm is fixed. The demand by the owner–manager for outside financing is shown by the remaining curve in Fig. 8. This curve represents the marginal value of the increased diversification which the manager can obtain by reducing his ownership claims and optimally constructing a diversified portfolio. It is measured by the amount he would pay to be allowed to reduce his ownership claims by a dollar in order to increase his diversification. If the liquidation of some of his holdings also influences the owner–manager's consumption set, the demand function plotted in Fig. 8 also incorporates the marginal value of these effects. The intersection of these two schedules determines the optimal fraction of the firm to be held by outsiders and this in turn determines the total agency costs borne by the owner. This solution is Pareto optimal; there is no way to reduce the agency costs without making someone worse off.

5.5. Determination of the Optimal Scale of the Firm

While the details of the solution of the optimal scale of the firm are complicated when we allow for the issuance of debt, equity and monitoring and bonding, the general structure of the solution is analogous to the case where monitoring and bonding are allowed for the outside equity example (see Fig. 4).

If it is optimal to issue any debt, the expansion path taking full account of such opportunities must lie above the curve ZG in Fig. 4. If this new expansion path lies anywhere to the right of the indifference curve passing through point G debt will be used in the optimal financing package. Furthermore, the optimal scale of the firm will be determined by the point at which this new expansion path touches the highest indifference curve. In this situation the resulting level of the owner–manager's welfare must therefore be higher.

6. Qualifications and Extensions of the Analysis

6.1. Multiperiod Aspects of the Agency Problem

We have assumed throughout our analysis that we are dealing only with a single investment-financing decision by the entrepreneur and have ignored the issues associated with the incentives affecting future financing-investment decisions which might arise after the initial set of contracts are consumated between the entrepreneur–manager, outside stockholders and bondholders. These are important issues which are left for future analysis.[64] Their solution will undoubtedly introduce some changes in the conclusions of the single decision analysis. It seems clear for instance that the expectation of future sales of outside equity and debt will change the costs and benefits facing the manager in making decisions which benefit himself at the (short-run) expense of the current bondholders and stockholders. If he develops a reputation for such dealings he can expect this to unfavorably influence the terms at which he can obtain future capital from outside sources. This will tend to increase the benefits associated with 'sainthood' and will tend to reduce the size of the agency costs. Given the finite life of any individual, however, such an effect cannot reduce these costs to zero, because at some point these future costs will begin to weigh more heavily on his successors and therefore the relative benefits to him of acting in his own best interests will rise.[65] Furthermore, it will generally be impossible for him to fully guarantee the outside interests that his successor will continue to follow his policies.

6.2. The Control Problem and Outside Owner's Agency Costs

The careful reader will notice that nowhere in the analysis thus far have we taken into account many of the details of the relationship between the part owner–manager and the outside stockholders and bondholders. In particular we have assumed that all outside equity is non-voting. If such equity does have voting rights then the manager will be concerned about the effects on his long-run welfare of reducing his fractional ownership below the point where he loses effective control of the corporation. That is, below the point where it becomes possible for the outside equity holders to fire him. A complete analysis of this issue will require a careful specification of the contractual rights involved on both sides, the role of the board of directors, and the coordination (agency) costs borne by the stockholders in implementing policy changes. This latter point involves consideration of the distribution of the outside ownership claims. Simply put, forces exist to determine an equilibrium distribution of outside ownership. If the costs of reducing the dispersion of ownership are lower than the benefits to be obtained from reducing the agency costs, it will pay some individual or group of individuals to buy shares in the market to reduce the dispersion of ownership. We occasionally witness these conflicts for control which involve outright market purchases, tender offers and proxy fights. Further analysis of these issues is left to the future.

6.3. A Note on the Existence of Inside Debt and Some Conjectures on the Use of Convertible Financial Instruments

We have been asked[66] why debt held by the manager (i.e. 'inside debt') plays no role in our analysis. We have as yet been unable to incorporate this dimension formally into our analysis in a satisfactory way. The question is a good one and suggests some potentially important extensions of the analysis. For instance, it suggests an inexpensive way for the owner–manager with both equity and debt outstanding to eliminate a large part (perhaps all) of the agency costs of debt. If he binds himself contractually to hold a fraction of the total debt equal to his fractional ownership of the total equity he would have no incentive whatsoever to reallocate wealth from the debt holders to the stockholders. Consider the case where

$$B_i / S_i = B_o / S_o,$$

where S_i and S_o are as defined earlier, B_i is the dollar value of the inside debt held by the owner–manager, and B_o is the debt held by outsiders. In this case if the manager changes the investment policy of the firm to reallocate wealth between the debt and equity holders, the net effect on the total value of his holdings in the firm will be zero. Therefore, his incentives to perform such reallocations are zero.[67]

Why then don't we observe practices or formal contracts which accomplish this elimination or reduction of the agency costs of debt? Maybe we do for smaller privately held firms (we haven't attempted to obtain this data), but for large diffuse owner corporations the practice does not seem to be common. One reason for this we believe is that in some respects the claim that the manager holds on the firm in the form of his wage contract has some of the characteristics of debt.[68] If true, this implies that even with zero holdings of formal debt claims he still has positive holdings of a quasi-debt claim and this may accomplish the satisfaction of condition (4). The problem here is that any formal analysis of this issue requires a much deeper understanding of the relationship between formal debt holdings and the wage contract; i.e. how much debt is it equivalent to?

This line of thought also suggests some other interesting issues. Suppose the implicit debt characteristics of the manager's wage contract result in a situation equivalent to

$$B_i / S_i > B_o / S_o.$$

Then he would have incentives to change the operating characteristics of the firm (i.e. reduce the variance of the outcome distribution) to transfer wealth from the stockholders to the debt holders which is the reverse of the situation we examined in Section 4. Furthermore, this seems to capture some of the concern often expressed regarding the fact that managers of large publicly held corporations seem to behave in a risk averse way to the detriment of the equity holders. One solution to this would be to establish incentive compensation systems for the manager or to give him stock options which in effect give him a claim on the upper tail of the outcome distribution. This also seems to be a commonly observed phenomenon.

This analysis also suggests some additional issues regarding the costs and benefits associated with the use of more complicated financial claims such as warrants, convertible bonds and convertible preferred stock which we have not formally analyzed as yet. Warrants, convertible bonds and convertible preferred stock have some of the characteristics of non-voting shares although they can be converted into voting shares under some terms. Alchian–Demsetz (1972) provide an interesting analysis regarding the use of non-voting shares. They argue that some shareholders with strong beliefs in the talents and judgements of the manager will want to be protected against the possibility that some other shareholders will take over and limit the actions of the manager (or fire him). Given that the securities exchanges prohibit the use of non-voting shares by listed firms the use of option type securities might be a substitute for these claims.

In addition warrants represent a claim on the upper tail of the distribution of outcomes, and convertible securities can be thought of as securities with non-detachable warrants. It seems that the incentive effects of warrants would tend to offset to some extent the incentive effects of the existence of risky debt because the owner–manager would be sharing part of the proceeds associated with a shift in the distribution of returns with the warrant holders. Thus, we conjecture that potential bondholders will find it attractive to have warrants attached to the risky debt of firms in which it is relatively easy to shift the distribution of outcomes to expand the upper tail of the distribution to transfer wealth from bondholders. It would also then be attractive to the owner–manager because of the reduction in the agency costs which he would bear. This argument also implies that it would make little difference if the warrants were detachable (and therefore saleable separately from the bonds) since their mere existence would reduce the incentives of the manager (or stockholders) to increase the riskiness of the firm (and therefore increase the probability of bankruptcy). Furthermore, the addition of a conversion privilege to fixed claims such as debt or preferred stock would also tend to reduce the incentive effects of the existence of such fixed claims and therefore lower the agency costs associated with them. The theory predicts that these phenomena should be more frequently observed in cases where the incentive effects of such fixed claims are high than when they are low.

6.4. *Monitoring and the Social Product of Security Analysis*

One of the areas in which further analysis is likely to lead to high payoffs is that of monitoring. We currently have little which could be glorified by the title of a 'Theory of Monitoring' and yet this is a crucial building block of the analysis. We would expect monitoring activities to become specialized to those institutions and individuals who possess comparative advantages in these activities. One of the groups who seem to play a large role in these activities is composed of the security analysts employed by institutional investors, brokers and investment advisory services as well as the analysis performed by individual investors in the normal course of investment decision making.

A large body of evidence exists which indicates that security prices incorporate in an unbiased manner all publicly available information and much of what might be called 'private information'.[69] There is also a large body of evidence which indicates that the security analysis activities of mutual funds and other institutional investors are not reflected in portfolio returns, i.e. they do not increase risk adjusted portfolio returns over a naive random selection buy and hold strategy.[70] Therefore some have been tempted to conclude that the resources expended on such research activities to find under- or over-valued securities is a social loss. Jensen (1974) argues that this conclusion cannot be unambiguously drawn because there is a large consumption element in the demand for these services.

Furthermore, the analysis of this paper would seem to indicate that to the extent that security analysis activities reduce the agency costs associated with the separation of ownership and control they are indeed socially productive. Moreover, if this is true we expect the major benefits of the security analysis activity to be reflected in the higher capitalized value of the ownership claims to corporations and *not* in the period to period portfolio returns of the analyst. Equilibrium in the security analysis industry requires that the private returns to analysis (i.e. portfolio returns) must be just equal to the private costs of such activity,[71] and this will not reflect the social product of this activity which will consist of larger output and higher *levels* of the capital value of ownership claims. Therefore, the argument implies that if there is a non-optimal amount of security analysis being performed it is too much[72] not too little (since the shareholders would be willing to pay directly to have the 'optimal' monitoring performed), and we don't seem to observe such payments.

6.5. Specialization in the Use of Debt and Equity

Our previous analysis of agency costs suggests at least one other testable hypothesis: i.e. that in those industries where the incentive effects of outside equity or debt are widely different, we would expect to see specialization in the use of the low agency cost financing arrangement. In industries where it is relatively easy for managers to lower the mean value of the outcomes of the enterprise by outright theft, special treatment of favored customers, ease of consumption of leisure on the job, etc. (for example, the bar and restaurant industry) we would expect to see the ownership structure of firms characterized by relatively little outside equity (i.e. 100 per cent ownership of the equity by the manager) with almost all outside capital obtained through the use of debt.

The theory predicts the opposite would be true where the incentive effects of debt are large relative to the incentive effects of equity. Firms like conglomerates, in which it would be easy to shift outcome distributions adversely for bondholders (by changing the acquisition or divestiture policy) should be characterized by relatively lower utilization of debt. Conversely in industries where the freedom of management to take riskier projects is severely constrained (for example, regulated industries such as public utilities) we should find more intensive use of debt financing.

The analysis suggests that in addition to the fairly well understood role of uncertainty in the determination of the quality of collateral there is at least one other element of great importance—the ability of the owner of the collateral to change the distribution of outcomes by shifting either the mean outcome or the variance of the outcomes. A study of bank lending policies should reveal these to be important aspects of the contractual practices observed there.

6.6. Application of the Analysis to the Large Diffuse Ownership Corporation

While we believe the structure outlined in the preceeding pages is applicable to a wide range of corporations it is still in an incomplete state. One of the most serious limitations of the analysis is that as it stands we have not worked out in this paper its application to the very large modern corporation whose managers own little or no equity. We believe our approach can be applied to this case but space limitations preclude discussion of these issues here. They remain to be worked out in detail and will be included in a future paper.

6.7. *The Supply Side of the Incomplete Market Question*

The analysis of this paper is also relevant to the incomplete market issue considered by Arrow (1964), Diamond (1967), Hakansson (1974a, b), Rubinstein (1974), Ross (1974) and others. The problems addressed in this literature derive from the fact that whenever the available set of financial claims on outcomes in a market fails to span the underlying state space [see Arrow (1964) and Debreu (1959)] the resulting allocation is Pareto inefficient. A disturbing element in this literature surrounds the fact that the inefficiency conclusion is generally drawn without explicit attention in the analysis to the costs of creating new claims or of maintaining the expanded set of markets called for to bring about the welfare improvement.

The demonstration of a possible welfare improvement from the expansion of the set of claims by the introduction of new basic contingent claims or options can be thought of as an analysis of the demand conditions of new markets. Viewed from this perspective, what is missing in the literature on this problem is the formulation of a positive analysis of the supply of markets (or the supply of contingent claims). That is, what is it in the maximizing behavior of individuals in the economy that causes them to create and sell contingent claims of various sorts?

The analysis in this paper can be viewed as a small first step in the direction of formulating an analysis of the supply of markets issue which is founded in the self-interested maximizing behavior of individuals. We have shown why it is in the interest of a wealth maximizing entrepreneur to create and sell claims such as debt and equity. Furthermore, as we have indicated above, it appears that extensions of these arguments will lead to a theory of the supply of warrants, convertible bonds and convertible preferred stock. We are not suggesting that the specific analysis offered above is likely to be sufficient to lead to a theory of the supply of the wide range of contracts (both existing and merely potential) in the world at large. However, we do believe that framing the question of the completeness of markets in terms of the joining of both the demand and supply conditions will be very fruitful instead of implicitly assuming that new claims spring forth from some (costless) well-head of creativity unaided or unsupported by human effort.

7. Conclusions

The publicly held business corporation is an awesome social invention. Millions of individuals voluntarily entrust billions of dollars, francs, pesos, etc., of personal wealth to the care of managers on the basis of a complex set of contracting relationships which delineate the rights of the parties involved. The growth in the use of the corporate form as well as the growth in market value of established corporations suggests that at least, up to the present, creditors and investors have by and large not been disappointed with the results, despite the agency costs inherent in the corporate form.

Agency costs are as real as any other costs. The level of agency cost depends among other things on statutory and common law and human ingenuity in devising contracts. Both the law and the sophistication of contracts relevant to the modern corporation are the products of a historical process in which there were strong incentives for individuals to minimize agency costs. Moreover, there were alternative organizational forms available, and opportunities to invent new ones. Whatever its short-comings, the corporation has thus far survived the market test against potential alternatives.

Notes

1. We do not use the term 'capital structure' because that term usually denotes the relative quantities of bonds, equity, warrants, trade credit, etc., which represent the liabilities of a firm. Our theory implies there is another important dimension to this problem—namely the relative amounts of ownership claims held by insiders (management) and outsiders (investors with no direct role in the management of the firm).

2. Reviews of this literature are given by Peterson (1965), Alchian (1965, 1968), Machlup (1967), Shubik (1970), Cyert and Hedrick (1972), Branch (1973), Preston (1975).

3. See Williamson (1964, 1970, 1975), Marris (1964), Baumol (1959), Penrose (1958), and Cyert and March (1963). Thorough reviews of these and other contributions are given by Machlup (1961) and Alchian (1965).

    Simon (1955) developed a model of human choice incorporating information (search) and computational costs which also has important implications for the behavior of managers. Unfortunately, Simon's work has often been misinterpreted as a denial of maximizing behavior, and misused, especially in the marketing and behavioral science literature. His later use of the term 'satisficing' [Simon (1959)] has undoubtedly contributed to this confusion because it suggests rejection of maximizing behavior rather than maximization subject to costs of information and of decision making.

4. See Meckling (1976) for a discussion of the fundamental importance of the assumption of resourceful, evaluative, maximizing behavior on the part of individuals in the development of theory. Klein (1976) takes an approach similar to the one we embark on in this paper in his review of the theory of the firm and the law.

5. See Coase (1937, 1959, 1960), Alchian (1965, 1968), Alchian and Kessel (1962), Demsetz (1967), Alchian and Demsetz (1972), Monsen and Downs (1965), Silver and Auster (1969), and McManus (1975).

6. Property rights are of course human rights, i.e. rights which are possessed by human beings. The introduction of the wholly false distinction between property rights and human rights in many policy discussions is surely one of the all time great semantic flimflams.

7. Cf. Berhold (1971), Ross (1973, 1974a), Wilson (1968, 1969), and Heckerman (1975).

8. Given the optimal monitoring and bonding activities by the principal and agent.

9. As it is used in this paper the term monitoring includes more than just measuring or observing the behavior of the agent. It includes efforts on the part of the principal to 'control' the behavior of the agent through budget restrictions, compensation policies, operating rules, etc.

10. As we show below the existence of positive monitoring and bonding costs will result in the manager of a corporation possessing control over some resources which he can allocate (within certain constraints) to satisfy his own preferences. However, to the extent that he must obtain the cooperation of others in order to carry out his tasks (such as divisional vice presidents) and to the extent that he cannot control their behavior perfectly and costlessly they will be able to appropriate some of these resources for their own ends. In short, there are agency costs generated at every level of the organization. Unfortunately, the analysis of these more general organizational issues is even more difficult than that of the 'ownership and control' issue because the nature of the contractual obligations and rights of the parties are much more varied and generally not as well specified in explicit contractual arrangements. Nevertheless, they exist and we believe that extensions of our analysis in these directions show promise of producing insights into a viable theory of organization.

11. They define the classical capitalist firm as a contractual organization of inputs in which there is '(a) joint input production, (b) several input owners, (c) one party who is common to all the contracts of the joint inputs, (d) who has rights to renegotiate any input's contract independently of contracts with other input owners, (e) who holds the residual claim, and (f) who has the right to sell his contractual residual status.'

12. By legal fiction we mean the artificial construct under the law which allows certain organizations to be treated as individuals.

13. For example, we ordinarily think of a product as leaving the firm at the time it is sold, but implicitly or explicitly such sales generally carry with them continuing contracts between the firm and the buyer. If the product does not perform as expected the buyer often can and does have a right to satisfaction. Explicit evidence that such implicit contracts do exist is the practice we occasionally observe of specific provision that 'all sales are final'.

14. This view of the firm points up the important role which the legal system and the law play in social organizations, especially, the organization of economic activity. Statutory laws sets bounds on the kinds of contracts into which individuals and organizations may enter without risking criminal prosecution. The police powers of the state are available and used to enforce performance of contracts or to enforce the collection of damages for non-performance. The courts adjudicate conflicts between contracting parties and establish precedent which form the body of common law. All of these government activities affect both the kinds of contracts executed and the extent to which contracting is relied upon. This in turn determines the usefulness, productivity, profitability and viability of various forms of organization. Moreover, new laws as well as court decisions often can and do change the rights of contracting parties ex post, and they can and do serve as a vehicle for redistribution of wealth. An analysis of some of the implications of these facts is contained in Jensen and Meckling (1976) and we shall not pursue them here.

15. For use in consumption, for the diversification of his wealth, or more importantly, for the financing of 'profitable' projects which he could not otherwise finance out of his personal wealth. We deal with these issues below after having developed some of the elementary analytical tools necessary to their solution.

16. Such as office space, air conditioning, thickness of the carpets, friendliness of employee relations, etc.

17. And again we assume that for any given market value of these costs, F, to the firm the allocation across time and across alternative probability distributions is such that the manager's current expected utility is at a maximum.

18. At this stage when we are considering a 100% owner-managed firm the notion of a 'wage contract' with himself has no content. However, the 100% owner-managed case is only an expositional device used in passing to illustrate a number of points in the analysis, and we ask the reader to bear with us briefly while we lay out the structure for the more interesting partial ownership case where such a contract does have substance.

19. The manager's utility function is actually defined over wealth and the future time sequence of vectors of quantities of non-pecuniary benefits, X_t. Although the setting of his problem is somewhat different, Fama (1970b, 1972) analyzes the conditions under which these preferences can be represented as a derived utility function defined as a function of the money value of the expenditures (in our notation F) on these goods conditional on the prices of goods. Such a utility function incorporates the optimization going on in the background which define $\hat{X}$ discussed above for a given F. In the more general case where we allow a time

series of consumption, $\hat{X}_t$, the optimization is being carried out across both time and the components of X_t for fixed F.

20. This excludes, for instance, (a) the case where the manager is allowed to expend corporate resources on anything he pleases in which case F would be a perfect substitute for wealth, or (b) the case where he can 'steal' cash (or other marketable assets) with constant returns to scale—if he could the indifference curves would be straight lines with slope determined by the fence commission.

21. Point D defines the fringe benefits in the optimal pay package since the value to the manager of the fringe benefits F^* is greater than the cost of providing them as is evidenced by the fact that U_2 is steeper to the left of D than the budget constraint with slope equal to -1.

    That D is indeed the optimal pay package can easily be seen in this situation since if the conditions of the sale to a new owner specified that the manager would receive no fringe benefits after the sale he would require a payment equal to V_3 to compensate him for the sacrifice of his claims to V^* and fringe benefits amounting to F^* (the latter with total value to him of $V_3 - V^*$). But if $F = 0$, the value of the firm is only $\overline{V}$. Therefore, if monitoring costs were zero the sale would take place at V^* with provision for a pay package which included fringe benefits of F^* for the manager.

    This discussion seems to indicate there are two values for the 'firm', V_3 and V^*. This is not the case if we realize that V^* is the value of the right to be the residual claimant on the cash flows of the firm and $V_3 - V^*$ is the value of the managerial rights, i.e. the right to make the operating decisions which include access to F^*. There is at least one other right which has value which plays no formal role in the analysis as yet — the value of the control right. By control right we mean the right to hire and fire the manager and we leave this issue to a future paper.

22. The distance $V^* - V'$ is a measure of what we will define as the gross agency costs. The distance $V_3 - V_4$ is a measure of what we call net agency costs, and it is this measure of agency costs which will be minimized by the manager in the general case where we allow investment to change.

23. I^* is the value maximizing and Pareto Optimum investment level which results from the traditional analysis of the corporate investment decision if the firm operates in perfectly competitive capital and product markets and the agency cost problems discussed here are ignored. See Debreu (1959, ch. 7), Jensen and Long (1972), Long (1972), Merton and Subrahmanyam (1974), Hirshleifer (1958, 1970), and Fama and Miller (1972).

24. Each equilibrium point such as that at E is characterized by $(\hat{a}, \hat{F}, \hat{W}_T)$ where $\hat{W}_T$ is the entrepreneur's post-investment financing wealth. Such an equilibrium must satisfy each of the following four conditions:

    (1) $$\hat{W}_T + F = \overline{V}(I) + W - I = \overline{V}(I) - K,$$

    where $K \equiv I - W$ is the amount of outside financing required to make the investment I. If this condition is not satisfied there is an uncompensated wealth transfer (in one direction or the other) between the entrepreneur and outside equity buyers.

(2) $$U_F(\hat{W}_T, \hat{F})/U_{wT}(\hat{W}_T, \hat{F}) = \hat{a},$$

where U is the entrepreneur's utility function on wealth and perquisites, U_F and U_{wT} are marginal utilities and $\hat{a}$ is the manager's share of the firm.

(3) $$(1 - \hat{a})V(I) = (1-\hat{a})[\bar{V}(I)-\hat{F}] \geqq K,$$

which says the funds received from outsiders are at least equal to K, the minimum required outside financing.

(4) Among all points $(\hat{a}, \hat{F}, \hat{W}_T)$ satisfying conditions (1)–(3), (α, F, W_T) gives the manager highest utility. This implies that $(\hat{a}, \hat{F}, \hat{W}_T)$ satisfy condition (3) as an equality.

25. *Proof.* Note that the slope of the expansion path (or locus of equilibrium points) at any point is $(\Delta V - \Delta I)/\Delta F$ and at the optimum level of investment this must be equal to the slope of the manager's indifference curve between wealth and market value of fringe benefits, F. Furthermore, in the absence of monitoring, the slope of the indifference curve, $\Delta W/\Delta F$, at the equilibrium point, D, must be equal to $-\alpha'$. Thus,

$$(\Delta V - \Delta I)/\Delta F = -\alpha' \qquad (2)$$

is the condition for the optimal scale of investment and this implies condition (1) holds for small changes at the optimum level of investment, I'.

26. Since the manager's indifference curves are negatively sloped we know that the optimum scale of the firm, point D, will occur in the region where the expansion path has negative slope, i.e. the market value of the firm will be declining and the *gross* agency costs, A, will be increasing and thus, the manager will not minimize them in making the investment decision (even though he will minimize them for any *given* level of investment). However, we define the *net* agency cost as the dollar equivalent of the welfare loss the manager experiences because of the agency relationship evaluated at $F = 0$ (the vertical distance between the intercepts on the Y axis of the two indifference curves on which points C and D lie). The optimum solution, I', does satisfy the condition that net agency costs are minimized. But this simply amounts to a restatement of the assumption that the manager maximizes his welfare.

Finally, it is possible for the solution point D to be a corner solution and in this case the value of the firm will not be declining. Such a corner solution can occur, for instance, if the manager's marginal rate of substitution between F and wealth falls to zero fast enough as we move up the expansion path, or if the investment projects are 'sufficiently' profitable. In these cases the expansion path will have a corner which lies on the maximum value budget constraint with intercept $\bar{V}(I^*)$ − I^*, and the level of investment will be equal to the idealized optimum, I^*. However, the market value of the residual claims will be less than V^* because the manager's consumption of perquisites will be larger than F^*, the zero agency cost level.

27. The careful reader will note that point C will be the equilibrium point only if the contract between the manager and outside equity holders specifies with no ambiguity that they have the right to monitor to limit his consumption of perquisites to an amount no less than F''. If any ambiguity regarding these rights exists in this contract then another source of agency costs arises which is symmetrical to our original problem. If they could do so the outside equity holders would monitor to the point where the net value of *their* holdings, $(1 - \alpha) V - M$, was maximized, and this would occur when $(\partial V/\partial M)(1 - \alpha) - 1 = 0$ which would be at some point between points C and E in Fig. 3. Point E denotes the point where the value of the firm net of the monitoring costs is at a maximum, i.e. where $\partial V/\partial M - 1 = 0$. But the manager would be worse off than in the zero monitoring solution if the point where $(1 - \alpha) V - M$ was at a maximum were to the left of the intersection between BCE and the indifference curve U_3 passing through point B (which denotes the zero monitoring level of welfare). Thus if the manager could not eliminate enough of the ambiguity in the contract to push the equilibrium to the right of the intersection of the curve BCE with indifference curve U_3 he would not engage in any contract which allowed monitoring.

28. If we could establish the existence of a feasible set of alternative institutional arrangements which would yield net benefits from the reduction of these costs we could legitimately conclude the agency relationship engendered by the corporation was not Pareto optimal. However, we would then be left with the problem of explaining why these alternative institutional arrangements have not replaced the corporate form of organization.

29. The monitoring and bonding costs will differ from firm to firm depending on such things as the inherent complexity and geographical dispersion of operations, the attractiveness of perquisites available in the firm (consider the mint), etc.

30. 'Where competitors are numerous and entry is easy, persistent departures from profit maximizing behavior inexorably leads to extinction. Economic natural selection holds the stage. In these circumstances, the behavior of the individual units that constitute the supply side of the product market is essentially routine and uninteresting and economists can confidently predict industry behavior without being explicitly concerned with the behavior of these individual units.

    When the conditions of competition are relaxed, however, the opportunity set of the firm is expanded. In this case, the behavior of the firm as a distinct operating unit is of separate interest. Both for purposes of interpreting particular behavior within the firm as well as for predicting responses of the industry aggregate, it may be necessary to identify the factors that influence the firm's choices within this expanded opportunity set and embed these in a formal model.' [Williamson (1964, p. 2)].

31. Assuming there are no special tax benefits to ownership nor utility of ownership other than that derived from the direct wealth effects of ownership such as might be true for professional sports teams, race horse stables, firms which carry the family name, etc.

32. Marris (1964, pp. 7–9) is the exception, although he argues that there exists some 'maximum leverage point' beyond which the chances of 'insolvency' are in some undefined sense too high.

33. By limited liability we mean the same conditions that apply to common stock. Subordinated debt or preferred stock could be constructed which carried with it liability provisions; i.e. if the corporation's assets were insufficient at some point to pay off all prior claims (such as trade credit, accrued wages, senior debt, etc.) and if the personal resources of the 'equity' holders were also insufficient to cover these claims the holders of this 'debt' would be subject to assessments beyond the face value of their claim (assessments which might be limited or unlimited in amount).

34. Alchian–Demsetz (1972, p. 709) argue that one can explain the existence of both bonds and stock in the ownership structure of firms as the result of differing expectations regarding the outcomes to the firm. They argue that bonds are created and sold to 'pessimists' and stocks with a residual claim with no upper bound are sold to 'optimists'.

    As long as capital markets are perfect with no taxes or transactions costs and individual investors can issue claims on distributions of outcomes on the same terms as firms, such actions on the part of firms cannot affect their values. The reason is simple. Suppose such 'pessimists' did exist and yet the firm issues only equity claims. The demand for those equity claims would reflect the fact that the individual purchaser could on his own account issue 'bonds' with a limited and prior claim on the distribution of outcomes on the equity which is exactly the same as that which the firm could issue. Similarly, investors could easily unlever any position by simply buying a proportional claim on both the bonds and stocks of a levered firm. Therefore, a levered firm could not sell at a different price than an unlevered firm solely because of the existence of such differential expectations. See Fama and Miller (1972, ch. 4) for an excellent exposition of these issues.

35. Corporations did use both prior to the institution of the corporate income tax in the US and preferred dividends have, with minor exceptions, never been tax deductible.

36. See Kraus and Litzenberger (1972) and Lloyd-Davies (1975).

37. And if there is competitive bidding for the firm from potential owner–managers the absentee owner will capture the capitalized value of these agency costs.

38. The spectrum of claims which firms can issue is far more diverse than is suggested by our two-way classification—fixed vs. residual. There are convertible bonds, equipment trust certificates, debentures, revenue bonds, warrants, etc. Different bond issues can contain different subordination provisions with respect to assets and interest. They can be callable or non-callable. Preferred stocks can be 'preferred' in a variety of dimensions and contain a variety of subordination stipulations. In the abstract, we can imagine firms issuing claims contingent on a literally infinite variety of states of the world such as those considered in the literature on the time-state-preference models of Arrow (1964), Debreu (1959) and Hirshleifer (1970).

39. An apt analogy is the way one would play poker on money borrowed at a fixed interest rate, with one's own liability limited to some very small take. Fama and Miller (1972, pp. 179–80) also discuss and provide a numerical example of an investment decision which illustrates very nicely the potential inconsistency between the interests of bondholders and stockholders.

40. The portfolio diversification issues facing the owner–manager are brought into the analysis in Section 5 below.

41. See Smith (1976) for a review of this option pricing literature and its applications and Galai and Masulis (1976) who apply the option pricing model to mergers, and corporate investment decisions.

42. While we used the option pricing model above to motivate the discussion and provide some intuitive understanding of the incentives facing the equity holders, the option pricing solutions of Black and Scholes (1973) do not apply when incentive effects cause V to be a function of the debt/equity ratio as it is in general and in this example. Long (1974) points out this difficulty with respect to the usefulness of the model in the context of tax subsidies on interest and bankruptcy cost. The results of Merton (1974) and Galai and Masulis (1976) must be interpreted with care since the solutions are strictly incorrect in the context of tax subsidies and/or agency costs.

43. The numerical example of Fama and Miller (1972, 172–80) is a close representation of this case in a two-period state model. However, they go on to make the following statement on p. 180: 'From a practical viewpoint, however, situations of potential conflict between bondholders and shareholders in the application of the market value rule are probably unimportant. In general, investment opportunities that increase a firm's market value by more than their cost both increase the value of the firm's shares and strengthen the firm's future ability to meet its current bond commitments.' This first issue regarding the importance of the conflict of interest between bondholders and stockholders is an empirical one, and the last statement is incomplete—in some circumstances the equity holders could benefit from projects whose net effect was to reduce the total value of the firm as they and we have illustrated. The issue cannot be brushed aside so easily.

44. Myers (1975) points out another serious incentive effect on managerial decisions of the existence of debt which does not occur in our simple single decision world. He shows that if the firm has the option to take future investment opportunities the existence of debt which matures after the options must be taken will cause the firm (using an equity value maximizing investment rule) to refuse to take some otherwise profitable projects because they would benefit only the bondholders and not the equity holders. This will (in the absence of tax subsidies to debt) cause the value of the firm to fall. Thus (although he doesn't use the term) these incentive effects also contribute to the agency costs of debt in a manner perfectly consistent with the examples discussed in the text.

45. Black–Scholes (1973) discuss ways in which dividend and future financing policy can redistribute wealth between classes of claimants on the firm.

46. Black, Miller and Posner (1974) discuss many of these issues with particular reference to the government regulation of bank holding companies.

47. In other words, these costs will be taken into account in determining the yield to maturity on the issue. For an examination of the effects of such enforcement costs on the nominal interest rates in the consumer small loan market, see Benston (1977).

48. To illustrate the fact that it will sometimes pay the manager to incur 'bonding' costs to guarantee the bondholders that he will not deviate from his promised behavior let us suppose that for an expenditure of b of the firm's resources he can guarantee that project 1 will be chosen. If he spends these resources and takes project 1 the value of the firm will be $V_1 - b$ and clearly as long as $(V_1 - b) > V_2$, or alternatively $(V_1 - V_2) > b$ he will be better off, since his wealth will be equal to the value of the firm minus the required investment, I (which we assumed for simplicity to be identical for the two projects).

On the other hand, to prove that the owner–manager prefers the lowest cost solution to the conflict let us assume he can write a covenant into the bond issue which will allow the bondholders to prevent him from taking project 2, if they incur monitoring costs of m, where $m < b$. If he does this his wealth will be higher by the amount $b - m$. To see this note that if the bond market is competitive and makes unbiased estimates, potential bondholders will be indifferent between:

(i)   a claim X^* with no covenant (and no guarantees from management) at a price of B_2,
(ii) a claim X^* with no covenant (and no guarantees from management, through bonding expenditures by the firm of b, that project 1 will be taken) at a price of B_1, and
(iii) a claim X^* with a covenant and the opportunity to spend m on monitoring (to guarantee project 1 will be taken) at a price of $B_1 - m$.

The bondholders will realize that (i) represents in fact a claim on project 2 and that (ii) and (iii) represent a claim on project 1 and are thus indifferent between the three options at the specified prices. The owner–manager, however, will not be indifferent between incurring the bonding costs, b, directly, or including the covenant in the bond indenture and letting the bondholders spend m to guarantee that he take project 1. His wealth in the two cases will be given by the value of his equity plus the proceeds of the bond issue less the required investment, and if $m < b < V_1 - V_2$, then his post-investment-financing wealth, W, for the three options will be such that $W_i < W_{ii} < W_{iii}$. Therefore, since it would increase his wealth, he would voluntarily include the covenant in the bond issue and let the bondholders monitor.

49. We mention, without going into the problem in detail, that similar to the case in which the outside equity holders are allowed to monitor the owner–manager, the agency relationship between the bondholders and stockholders has a symmetry if the rights of the bondholders to limit actions of the manager are not perfectly spelled out. Suppose the bondholders, by spending sufficiently large amounts of resources, could force management to take actions which would transfer wealth from the equity holder to the bondholders (by taking

Michael C. Jensen and William H. Meckling

sufficiently less risky projects). One can easily construct situations where such actions could make the bondholders better off, hurt the equity holders and actually lower the total value of the firm. Given the nature of the debt contract the original owner–manager might maximize his wealth in such a situation by selling off the equity and keeping the bonds as his 'owner's' interest. If the nature of the bond contract is given, this may well be an inefficient solution since the total agency costs (i.e. the sum of monitoring and value loss) could easily be higher than the alternative solution. However, if the owner–manager could strictly limit the rights of the bondholders (perhaps by inclusion of a provision which expressly reserves all rights not specifically granted to the bondholder for the equity holder), he would find it in his interest to establish the efficient contractual arrangement since by minimizing the agency costs he would be maximizing his wealth. These issues involve the fundamental nature of contracts and for now we simply assume that the 'bondholders' rights are strictly limited and unambiguous and all rights not specifically granted them are reserved for the 'stockholders'; a situation descriptive of actual institutional arrangements. This allows us to avoid the incentive effects associated with 'bondholders' potentially exploiting 'stockholders'.

50. If the firm were allowed to sell assets to meet a current debt obligation, bankruptcy would occur when the total market value of the future cash flows expected to be generated by the firm is less than the value of a current payment on a debt obligation. Many bond indentures do not, however, allow for the sale of assets to meet debt obligations.

51. We have been told that while this is true in principle, the actual behavior of the courts appears to frequently involve the provision of some settlement to the common stockholders even when the assets of the company are not sufficient to cover the claims of the creditors.

52. If under bankruptcy the bondholders have the right to fire the management, the management will have some incentives to avoid taking actions which increase the probability of this event (even if it is in the best interest of the equity holders) if they (the management) are earning rents or if they have human capital specialized to this firm or if they face large adjustment costs in finding new employment. A detailed examination of this issue involves the value of the control rights (the rights to hire and fire the manager) and we leave it to a subsequent paper.

53. Kraus and Litzenberger (1972) and Lloyd-Davies (1975) demonstrate that the total value of the firm will be reduced by these costs.

54. These include only payments to all parties for legal fees, professional services, trustees' fees and filing fees. They do not include the costs of management time or changes in cash flows due to shifts in the firm's demand or cost functions discussed below.

55. Which, incidentally, exist only when the debt has some probability of default.

56. Our theory is capable of explaining why in the absence of the tax subsidy on interest payments, we would expect to find firms using both debts and preferred stocks—a problem which has long puzzled at least one of the authors. If preferred

160

stock has all the characteristics of debt except for the fact that its holders cannot put the firm into bankruptcy in the event of nonpayment of the preferred dividends, then the agency costs associated with the issuance of preferred stock will be lower than those associated with debt by the present value of the bankruptcy costs.

However, these lower agency costs of preferred stock exist only over some range if as the amount of such stock rises the incentive effects caused by their existence impose value reductions which are larger than that caused by debt (including the bankruptcy costs of debt). There are two reasons for this. First, the equity holder's claims can be eliminated by the debtholders in the event of bankruptcy, and second, the debtholders have the right to fire the management in the event of bankruptcy. Both of these will tend to become more important as an advantage to the issuance of debt as we compare situations with large amounts of preferred stock to equivalent situations with large amounts of debt because they will tend to reduce the incentive effects of large amounts of preferred stock.

57. One other condition also has to hold to justify the incurrence of the costs associated with the use of debt or outside equity in our firm. If there are other individuals in the economy who have sufficiently large amounts of personal capital to finance the entire firm, our capital constrained owner can realize the full capital value of his current and prospective projects and avoid the agency costs by simply selling the firm (i.e. the right to take these projects) to one of these individuals. He will then avoid the wealth losses associated with the agency costs caused by the sale of debt or outside equity. If no such individuals exist, it will pay him (and society) to obtain the additional capital in the debt market. This implies, incidentally, that it is somewhat misleading to speak of the owner–manager as the individual who bears the agency costs. One could argue that it is the project which bears the costs since, if it is not sufficiently profitable to cover all the costs (including the agency costs), it will not be taken. We continue to speak of the owner–manager bearing these costs to emphasize the more correct and important point that he has the incentive to reduce them because, if he does, his wealth will be increased.

58. We continue to ignore for the moment the additional complicating factor involved with the portfolio decisions of the owner, and the implied acceptance of potentially diversifiable risk by such 100% owners in this example.

59. We continue to ignore such instruments as convertible bonds and warrants.

60. Note, however, that even when outsiders own none of the equity the stock-holder–manager still has some incentives to engage in activities which yield him non-pecuniary benefits but reduce the value of the firm by more than he personally values the benefits if there is any risky debt outstanding. Any such actions he takes which reduce the value of the firm, V, tend to reduce the value of the bonds as well as the value of the equity. Although the option pricing model does not in general apply exactly to the problem of valuing the debt and equity of the firm, it can be useful in obtaining some qualitative insights into matters such as this. In the option pricing model $\partial S / \partial V$ indicates the rate at

which the stock value changes per dollar change in the value of the firm (and similarly for $\partial B/\partial V$). Both of these terms are less than unity [cf. Black and Scholes (1973)]. Therefore, any action of the manager which reduces the value of the firm, V, tends to reduce the value of both the stock and the bonds, and the larger is the total debt/equity ratio the smaller is the impact of any given change in V on the value of the equity, and therefore, the lower is the cost to him of consuming non-pecuniary benefits.

61. This occurs, of course, not at the intersection of $A_{so}(E)$ and $A_B(E)$, but at the point where the absolute value of the slopes of the functions are equal, i.e. where $A'_{so}(E) + A'_B(E) = 0$.

62. On the average, however, top managers seem to have substantial holdings in absolute dollars. A recent survey by Wytmar (*Wall Street Journal*, Aug. 13, 1974, p. 1) reported that the median value of 826 chief executive officers' stock holdings in their companies at year end 1973 was $557,000 and $1.3 million at year end 1972.

63. These diversification effects can be substantial. Evans and Archer (1968) show that on the average for New York Stock Exchange securities approximately 55% of the total risk (as measured by standard deviation of portfolio returns) can be eliminated by following a naive strategy of dividing one's assets equally among 40 randomly selected securities.

64. The recent work of Myers (1975) which views future investment opportunities as options and investigates the incentive effects of the existence of debt in such a world where a sequence of investment decisions is made is another important step in the investigation of the multi-period aspects of the agency problem and the theory of the firm.

65. Becker and Stigler (1972) analyze a special case of this problem involving the use of non-invested pension rights to help correct for this end game play in the law enforcement area.

66. By our colleague David Henderson.

67. This also suggests that *some* outside debt holders can protect themselves from 'exploitation' by the manager by purchasing a fraction of the total equity equal to their fractional ownership of the debt. All debt holders, of course, cannot do this unless the manager does so also. In addition, such an investment rule restricts the portfolio choices of investors and therefore would impose costs if followed rigidly. Thus the agency costs will not be eliminated this way either.

68. Consider the situation in which the bondholders have the right in the event of bankruptcy to terminate his employment and therefore to terminate the future returns to any specific human capital or rents he may be receiving.

69. See Fama (1970) for a survey of this 'efficient markets' literature.

70. See Jensen (1969) for an example of this evidence and references.

71. Ignoring any pure consumption elements in the demand for security analysis.

72. Again ignoring the value of the pure consumption elements in the demand for security analysis.

References

Alchian, A. A., 1965, The Basis of some recent advances in the theory of management of the firm, Journal of Industrial Economics, Nov., 30–44.

Alchian, A. A., 1968, Corporate management and property rights, in: Economic policy and the regulation of securities (American Enterprise Institute, Washington, DC).

Alchian, A. A., 1974, Some implications of recognition of property right transactions costs, unpublished paper presented at the First Interlaken Conference on Analysis and Ideology, June.

Alchian, A. A. and W. R. Allen, 1969, Exchange and production: Theory in use (Wadsworth, Belmont, CA).

Alchian, A. A. and H. Demsetz, 1972, Production, information costs, and economic organization, American Economic Review LXII, no. 5, 777–795.

Alchian, A. A. and R. A. Kessel, 1962, Competition, monopoly and the pursuit of pecuniary gain, in: Aspects of labor economics (National Bureau of Economic Research, Princeton, NJ).

Arrow, K. J., 1963/4, Control in large organizations, Management Science 10, 397–408.

Arrow, K. J., 1964, The role of securities in the optimal allocation of risk bearing, Review of Economic studies 31, no. 86, 91–96.

Atkinson, T. R. 1967, Trends in corporate bond quality, in: Studies in corporate bond finance 4 (National Bureau of Economic Research, New York).

Baumol, W. J., 1959, Business behavior, value and growth (Macmillan, New York).

Becker, G., 1957, The economics of discrimination (University of Chicago Press, Chicago, IL).

Becker, G. S. and G. J. Stigler, 1972, Law enforcement, corruption and compensation of enforcers, unpublished paper presented at the Conference on Capitalism and Freedom, Oct.

Benston, G., 1977, The impact of maturity regulation on high interest rate lenders and borrowers, Journal of Financial Economics 4, no. 1.

Berhold, M., 1971, A theory of linear profit sharing incentives, Quarterly Journal of Economics LXXXV, Aug., 460–482.

Berle, A. A., Jr. and G. C. Means, 1932, The modern corporation and private property (Macmillan, New York).

Black, F. and M. Scholes, 1973, The pricing of options and corporate liabilities, Journal of Political Economy 81, no. 3, 637–654.

Black, F., M. H. Miller and R. A. Posner, 1974, An approach to the regulation of bank holding companies, unpublished manuscript (University of Chicago, Chicago, IL).

Branch, B., 1973, Corporate objectives and market performance, Financial Management, Summer, 24–29.

Coase, R. H., 1937, The nature of the firm, Economica, New Series, IV, 386–405. Reprinted in: Readings in price theory (Irwin, Homewood, IL) 331–351.

Coase, R. H., 1959, The Federal Communications Commission, Journal of Law and Economics II, Oct., 1–40.

Coase, R. H., 1960, The problem of social cost, Journal of Law and Economics III, Oct., 1–44.

Coase, R. H., 1964, Discussion, American Economic Review LIV, no. 3, 194–197.

Cyert, R. M. and C. L. Hedrick, 1972, Theory of the firm: Past, present and future; An interpretation, Journal of Economic Literature X, June, 398–412.

Cyert, R. M. and J. G. March, 1963, A behavioral theory of the firm (Prentice Hall, Englewood Cliffs, NJ).

De Alessi, L., 1973, Private property and dispersion of ownership in large corporations, Journal of Finance, Sept., 839–851.

Debreu, G., 1959, Theory of value (Wiley, New York).

Demsetz, H., 1967, Toward a theory of property rights, American Economic Review LVII, May, 347–359.

Demsetz, H., 1969, Information and efficiency: Another viewpoint, Journal of Law and Economics XII, April, 1–22.

Diamond, P. A., 1967, The role of a stock market in a general equilibrium model with technological uncertainty, American Economic Review LVII, Sept., 759–776.

Evans, J. L. and S. H. Archer, 1968, Diversification and the reduction of dispersion: An empirical analysis, Journal of Finance, Dec.

Fama, E. F., 1970a, Efficient capital markets: A review of theory and empirical work, Journal of Finance XXV, no. 2.

Fama, E. F., 1970b, Multiperiod consumption–investment decisions, American Economic Review LX, March.

Fama, E. F., 1972, Ordinal and measurable utility, in: M. C. Jensen, ed., Studies in the theory of capital markets (Praeger, New York).

Fama, E. F. and M. Miller, 1972, The theory of finance (Holt, Rinehart and Winston, New York).

Friedman, M., 1970, The social responsibility of business is to increase its profits, New York Times Magazine, 13 Sept, 32ff.

Furubotn, E. G. and S. Pejovich, 1972, Property rights and economic theory: A survey of recent literature, Journal of Economic Literature X, Dec., 1137–1162.

Galai, D. and R. W. Masulis, 1976, The option pricing model and the risk factor of stock, Journal of Financial Economics 3, no. 1/2, 53–82.

Hakansson, N. H., 1974a, The superfund: Efficient paths toward a complete financial market, unpublished manuscript.

Hakansson, N. H., 1974b, Ordering markets and the capital structures of firms with illustrations, Institute of Business and Economic Research Working Paper no. 24 (University of California, Berkeley, CA).

Heckerman, D. G., 1975, Motivating managers to make investment decisions, Journal of Financial Economics 2, no. 3, 273–292.

Hirshleifer, J., 1958, On the theory of optimal investment decisions, Journal of Political Economy, Aug., 329–352.

Hirshleifer, J., 1970, Investment, interest, and capital (Prentice-Hall, Englewood Cliffs, NJ).

Jensen, M. C., 1969, Risk, the pricing of capital assets, and the evaluation of investment portfolios, Journal of Business 42, no. 2, 167–247.

Jensen, M. C., 1974, Tests of capital market theory and implications of the evidence. Graduate School of Management Working Paper Series no. 7414 (University of Rochester, Rochester, NY).

Jensen, M. C. and J. B. Long, 1972, Corporate investment under uncertainty and Pareto optimality in the capital markets, Bell Journal of Economics, Spring, 151–174.

Jensen, M. C. and W. H. Meckling, 1976, Can the corporation survive? Center for Research in Government Policy and Business Working Paper no. PPS 76–4 (University of Rochester, Rochester, NY).

Klein, W. A., 1976, Legal and economic perspectives on the firm, unpublished manuscript (University of California, Los Angeles, CA).

Kraus, A. and R. Litzenberger, 1973, A state preference model of optimal financial leverage, Journal of Finance, Sept.

Larner, R. J., 1970, Management control and the large corporation (Dunellen, New York).

Lintner, J., 1965, Security prices, risk, and maximal gains from diversification, Journal of Finance XX, Dec., 587–616.

Lloyd-Davies, P., 1975, Risk and optimal leverage, unpublished manuscript (University of Rochester, Rochester, NY).

Long, J. B., 1972, Wealth, welfare, and the price of risk, Journal of Finance, May, 419–433.

Long, J. B., Jr., 1974, Discussion, Journal of Finance XXXIX, no. 12, 485–488.

Machlup, F., 1967, Theories of the firm: Marginalist, behavioral, managerial, American Economic Review, March, 1–33.

Manne, H. G., 1962, The 'higher criticism' of the modern corporation, Columbia Law Review 62, March, 399–432.

Manne, H. G., 1965, Mergers and the market for corporate control, Journal of Political Economy, April, 110–120.

Manne, H. G., 1967, Our two corporate systems: Law and economics, Virginia Law Review 53, March, 259–284.

Manne, H. G., 1972, The social responsibility of regulated utilities, Wisconsin Law Review V, no. 4, 995–1009.

Marris, R., 1964, The economic theory of managerial capitalism (Free Press of Glencoe, Glencoe, IL).

Mason, E. S., 1959, The corporation in modern society (Harvard University Press, Cambridge, MA).

McManus, J. C., 1975, The costs of alternative economic organizations, Canadian Journal of Economics VIII, Aug., 334–350.

Meckling, W. H., 1976, Values and the choice of the model of the individual in the social sciences, Schweizerische Zeitschrift für Volkswirtchaft und Statistik, Dec.

Merton, R. C., 1973, The theory of rational option pricing, Bell Journal of Economics and Management Science 4, no. 1, 141–183.

Merton, R. C., 1974, On the pricing of corporate debt: The risk structure of interest rates, Journal of Finance XXIX, no. 2, 449–470.

Merton, R. C., and M. G. Subrahmanyam, 1974, The optimality of a competitive stock market, Bell Journal of Economics and Management Science, Spring, 145–170.

Miller, M. H. and F. Modigliani, 1966, Some estimates of the cost of capital to the electric utility industry, 1954–57, American Economic Review, June, 333–391.

Modigliani, F. and M. H. Miller, 1958, The costs of capital, corporation finance, and the theory of investment, American Economic Review 48, June, 261–297.

Modigliani, F. and M .H. Miller, 1963, Corporate income taxes and the cost of capital: A correction, American Economic Review June, 433–443.

Monsen, R. J. and A. Downs, 1965, A theory of large managerial firms, Journal of Political Economy, June, 221–236.

Myers, S. C., 1975, A note on the determinants of corporate debt capacity, unpublished manuscript (London Graduate School of Business Studies, London).

Penrose, E., 1958, The theory of the growth of the firm (Wiley, New York).

Preston, L E., 1975, Corporation and society: The search for a paradigm, Journal of Economic Literature XIII, June, 434–453.

Ross, S. A., 1973, The economic theory of agency: The principals problems, American Economic Review LXII, May, 134–139.

Ross, S. A., 1974a, The economic theory of agency and the principle of similarity, in: M. D. Balch et al., eds., Essays on economic behavior under uncertainty (North-Holland, Amsterdam).

Ross, S. A., 1974b, Options and efficiency, Rodney L. White Center for Financial Research Working Paper no. 3–74 (University of Pennsylvania, Philadelphia, PA).

Rubenstein, M., 1974, A discrete-time synthesis of financial theory, Parts I and II, Institute of Business and Economic Research Working Papers nos. 20 and 21 (University of California, Berkeley, CA).

Scitovsky, T., 1943, A note on profit maximisation and its implications, Review of Economic Studies XI, 57–60.

Sharpe, W. F., 1964, Capital asset prices: A theory of market equilibrium under conditions of risk, Journal of Finance XIX, Sept., 425–442.

Shubik, M., 1970, A curmudgeon's guide to microeconomics, Journal of Economic Literature VIII, June, 405–434.

Silver, M. and R. Auster, 1969, Entrepreneurship, profit and limits on firm size, Journal of Business 42, July, 277–281.

Simon, H. A., 1955, A behavioral model of rational choice, Quarterly Journal of Economics 69, 99–118.

Simon, H. A., 1959, Theories of decision making in economics and behavioral science, American Economic Review, June, 253–283.

Smith, A., 1937, The wealth of nations, Cannan edition (Modern Library, New York).

Smith, C., 1976, Option pricing: A review, Journal of Financial Economics 3, nos. 1/2, 3–52.

Warner, J. B., 1975, Bankruptcy costs, absolute priority, and the pricing of risky debt claims, unpublished manuscript (University of Chicago, Chicago, IL).

Williamson, O. E., 1964, The economics of discretionary behavior: Managerial objectives in a theory of the firm (Prentice-Hall, Englewood Cliffs, NJ).

Williamson, O. E., 1970, Corporate control and business behavior (Prentice-Hall, Englewood Cliffs, NJ).

Williamson, O. E., 1975, Markets and hierarchies: Analysis and antitrust implications (The Free Press, New York).

Wilson, R., 1968, On the theory of syndicates, Econometrica 36, Jan., 119–132.

Wilson, R., 1969, La décision: Agrégation et dynamique des ordres de preferénce, Extrait (Editions du Centre National de la Recherche Scientifique, Paris) 288–307.

6

Transaction-Cost Economics: The Governance of Contractual Relations

Oliver E. Williamson

The new institutional economics is preoccupied with the origins, incidence, and ramifications of transaction costs. Indeed, if transaction costs are negligible, the organization of economic activity is irrelevant, since any advantages one mode of organization appears to hold over another will simply be eliminated by costless contracting. But despite the growing realization that transaction costs are central to the study of economics,[1] skeptics remain. Stanley Fischer's complaint is typical: 'Transaction costs have a well-deserved bad name as a theoretical device . . . [partly] because there is a suspicion that almost anything can be rationalized by invoking suitably specified transaction costs.'[2] Put differently, there are too many degrees of freedom; the concept wants for definition.

Among the factors on which there appears to be developing a general consensus are: (1) opportunism is a central concept in the study of transaction costs;[3] (2) opportunism is especially important for economic activity that involves transaction-specific investments in human and physical capital;[4] (3) the efficient processing of information is an important and related concept;[5] and (4) the assessment of transaction costs is a comparative institutional undertaking.[6] Beyond these general propositions, a consensus on transaction costs is lacking.

This paper has benefited from support from the Center for Advanced Study in the Behavioral Sciences, the Guggenheim Foundation, and the National Science Foundation. Helpful comments by Yoram Ben-Porath, Richard Nelson, Douglass North, Thomas Palay, Joseph Sax, David Teece, and Peter Temin and from the participants at seminars at the Yale Law School and the Institute for Advanced Study at Princeton are gratefully acknowledged. The paper was rewritten to advantage after reading Ben-Porath's discussion paper, the F-Connection: Family, Friends, and Firms and the Organization of Exchange, and Temin's discussion paper, Modes of Economic Behavior: Variations on Themes of J. R. Hicks and Herbert Simon.

Further progress in the study of transaction costs awaits the identification of the critical dimensions with respect to which transaction costs differ and an examination of the economizing properties of alternative institutional modes for organizing transactions. Only then can the matching of transactions with modes be accomplished with confidence. This paper affirms the proposition that transaction costs are central to the study of economics, identifies the critical dimensions for characterizing transactions, describes the main govern-ance structures of transactions, and indicates how and why transactions can be matched with institutions in a discriminating way.

I am mainly concerned with intermediate-product market transactions. Whereas previously I have emphasized the incentives to remove transactions from the market and organize them internally (vertical integration),[7] the analysis here is symmetrical and deals with market, hierarchical, and inter-mediate modes of organization alike. The question of why there is so much vertical integration remains interesting, but no more so than the question of why there are so many market- (and quasi-market) mediated transactions. A discriminating analysis will explain which transactions are located where and give the reasons why. The overall object of the exercise essentially comes down to this: for each abstract description of a transaction, identify the most economical governance structure—where by governance structure I refer to the institutional framework within which the integrity of a transaction is decided. Markets and hierarchies are two of the main alternatives.

Some legal background to the study of transactions is briefly reviewed in Section 1. Of the three dimensions for describing transactions that I propose, investment attributes are the least well understood and probably the most important. The special relevance of investments is developed in the context of the economics of idiosyncrasy in Section 2. A general contracting schema is developed and applied to commercial contracting in Section 3. Applications to labor, regulation, family transactions, and capital markets are sketched in Section 4. Major implications are summarized in Section 5. Concluding remarks follow.

1. Some Contracting Background

Although there is widespread agreement that the discrete-transaction para-digm—'sharp in by clear agreement; sharp out by clear performance'[8]—has served both law and economics well, there is increasing awareness that many contractual relations are not of this well-defined kind.[9] A deeper understanding of the nature of contract has emerged as the legal-rule emphasis associated with the study of discrete contracting has given way to a more general concern with the contractual purposes to be served.[10]

Ian Macneil, in a series of thoughtful and wide-ranging essays on contract, usefully distinguishes between discrete and relational transactions.[11] He further supplies twelve different 'concepts' with respect to which these differ.[12] Serious problems of recognition and application are posed by such a rich classificatory apparatus. More useful for my purposes is the three-way classification of contracts that Macneil offers in his most recent article, where classical, neoclassical, and relational categories of contract law are recognized.

1.1. Classical Contract Law

As Macneil observes, any system of contract law has the purpose of facilitating exchange. What is distinctive about classical contract law is that it attempts to do this by enhancing discreteness and intensifying 'presentiation,'[13] where presentiation has reference to efforts to 'make or render present in place or time; to cause to be perceived or realized at present.'[14] The economic counterpart to complete presentiation is contingent-claims contracting—which entails comprehensive contracting whereby all relevant future contingencies pertaining to the supply of a good or service are described and discounted with respect to both likelihood and futurity.[15]

Classical contract law endeavors to implement discreteness and presentiation in several ways. For one thing, the identity of the parties to a transaction is treated as irrelevant. In this respect it corresponds exactly with the 'ideal' market transaction in economics.[16] Second, the nature of the agreement is carefully delimited, and the more formal features govern when formal (for example, written) and informal (for example, oral) terms are contested. Third, remedies are narrowly prescribed such that, 'should the initial presentiation fail to materialize because of nonperformance, the consequences are relatively predictable from the beginning and are not open-ended.'[17] Additionally, third-party participation is discouraged.[18] The emphasis, thus, is on legal rules, formal documents, and self-liquidating transactions.

1.2. Neoclassical Contract Law

Not every transaction fits comfortably into the classical-contracting scheme. In particular, long-term contracts executed under conditions of uncertainty are ones for which complete presentiation is apt to be prohibitively costly if not impossible. Problems of several kinds arise. First, not all future contingencies for which adaptations are required can be anticipated at the outset. Second, the appropriate adaptations will not be evident for many contingencies until the circumstances materialize. Third, except as changes in states of the world are unambiguous, hard contracting between autonomous parties may well give rise to veridical disputes when state-contingent claims are made. In a world where (at least some) parties are inclined to be opportunistic, whose representations are to be believed?

Faced with the prospective breakdown of classical contracting in these circumstances, three alternatives are available. One would be to forgo such transactions altogether. A second would be to remove these transactions from the market and organize them internally instead. Adaptive, sequential decision making would then be implemented under common ownership and with the assistance of hierarchical incentive and control systems. Third, a different contracting relation which preserves trading but provides for additional governance structure might be devised. This last brings us to what Macneil refers to as neoclassical contracting.

As Macneil observes, 'Two common characteristics of long-term contracts are the existence of gaps in their planning and the presence of a range of processes and techniques used by contract planners to create flexibility in lieu of either leaving gaps or trying to plan rigidly.'[19] Third-party assistance in resolving disputes and evaluating performance often has advantages over litigation in serving these functions of flexibility and gap filling. Lon Fuller's remarks on procedural differences between arbitration and litigation are instructive:

. . . there are open to the arbitrator . . . quick methods of education not open to the courts. An arbitrator will frequently interrupt the examination of witnesses with a request that the parties educate him to the point where he can understand the testimony being received. This education can proceed informally, with frequent interruptions by the arbitrator, and by informed persons on either side, when a point needs clarification. Sometimes there will be arguments across the table, occasionally even within each of the separate camps. The end result will usually be a clarification that will enable everyone to proceed more intelligently with the case. There is in this informal procedure no infringement whatever of arbitrational due process.[20]

A recognition that the world is complex, that agreements are incomplete, and that some contracts will never be reached unless both parties have confidence in the settlement machinery thus characterizes neoclassical contract law. One important purposive difference in arbitration and litigation that contributes to the procedural differences described by Fuller is that, whereas continuity (at least completion of the contract) is presumed under the arbitration machinery, this presumption is much weaker when litigation is employed.[21]

1.3. *Relational Contracting*

The pressures to sustain ongoing relations 'have led to the spin-off of many subject areas from the classical, and later the neoclassical, contract law system, e.g., much of corporate law and collective bargaining.'[22] Thus, progressively increasing the 'duration and complexity' of contract has resulted in the displacement of even neoclassical adjustment processes by adjustment processes of a more thoroughly transaction-specific, ongoing-administrative kind.[23] The fiction of discreteness is fully displaced as the relation takes on the properties of 'a minisociety with a vast array of norms beyond those centered on the exchange and its immediate processes.'[24] By contrast with the neoclassical system, where the reference point for effecting adaptations remains the original agreement, the reference point under a truly relational approach is the 'entire relation as it has developed . . . [through] time. This may or may not include an 'original agreement', and if it does, may or may not result in great deference being given it.'[25]

2. The Economics of Idiosyncrasy

Macneil's three-way discussion of contracts discloses that contracts are a good deal more varied and complex than is commonly realized.[26] It furthermore suggests that governance structures—the institutional matrix within which transactions are negotiated and executed—vary with the nature of the transaction. But the critical dimensions of contract are not expressly identified, and the purposes of government are not stated. Harmonizing interests that would otherwise give way to antagonistic subgoal pursuits appears to be an important governance function, but this is not explicit in his discussion.

That simple governance structures should be used in conjunction with simple contractual relations and complex governance structures reserved for complex relations seems generally sensible. Use of a complex structure to govern a simple relation is apt to incur unneeded costs, and use of a simple structure for a complex transaction invites strain. But what is simple and complex in contractual respects? Specific attention to the defining attributes of transactions is evidently needed.

As developed in Section 3, the three critical dimensions for characterizing transactions are (1) uncertainty, (2) the frequency with which transactions recur, and (3) the degree to which durable transaction-specific investments are incurred. Of these three, uncertainty is widely conceded to be a critical attribute;[27] and that frequency matters is at least plausible.[28] The governance ramifications of neither, however, have been fully developed—nor can they be until joined with the third critical dimension: transaction-specific investments. Inasmuch as a considerable amount of the 'action' in the study of governance is attributable to investment differences, some explication is needed.

2.1. General

The crucial investment distinction is this: to what degree are transaction-specific (nonmarketable) expenses incurred. Items that are unspecialized among users pose few hazards, since buyers in these circumstances can easily turn to alternative sources, and suppliers can sell output intended for one order to other buyers without difficulty.[29] Nonmarketability problems arise when the *specific identity* of the parties has important cost-bearing consequences. Transactions of this kind will be referred to as idiosyncratic.

Occasionally the identity of the parties is important from the outset, as when a buyer induces a supplier to invest in specialized physical capital of a transaction-specific kind. Inasmuch as the value of this capital in other uses is, by definition, much smaller than the specialized use for which it has been intended, the supplier is effectively 'locked into' the transaction to a significant degree. This is symmetrical, moreover, in that the buyer cannot turn to alternative sources of supply and obtain the item on favorable terms, since the cost of supply from unspecialized capital is presumably great.[30] The buyer is thus committed to the transaction as well.

Ordinarily, however, there is more to idiosyncratic exchange that specialized physical capital. Human-capital investments that are transaction-specific commonly occur as well. Specialized training and learning-by-doing economies in production operations are illustrations. Except when these investments are transferable to alternative suppliers at low cost, which is rare, the benefits of the set-up costs can be realized only so long as the relationship between the buyer and seller of the intermediate product is maintained.

Additional transaction-specific savings can accrue at the interface between supplier and buyer as contracts are successively adapted to unfolding events, and as periodic contract-renewal agreements are reached. Familiarity here permits communication economies to be realized: specialized language develops as experience accumulates and nuances are signaled and received in a sensitive way. Both institutional and personal trust relations evolve. Thus the individuals who are responsible for adapting the interfaces have a personal as well as an organizational stake in what transpires. Where personal integrity is believed to be operative, individuals located at the interfaces may refuse to be a part of opportunistic efforts to take advantage of (rely on) the letter of the contract when the spirit of the exchange is emasculated. Such refusals can serve as a check upon organizational proclivities to behave opportunistically.[31] Other things being equal, idiosyncratic exchange relations which feature personal trust will survive greater stress and display greater adaptability.

Idiosyncratic goods and services are thus ones where investments of transaction-specific human and physical capital are made and, contingent upon successful execution, benefits are realized. Such investments can and do occur in conjunction with occasional trades where delivery for a specialized design is stretched out over a long period (for example, certain construction contracts). The transactions that I wish to emphasize here, however, are exchanges of the recurring kind. Although large-numbers competition is frequently feasible at the initial award stage for recurring contracts of all kinds, idiosyncratic transactions are ones for which the relationship between buyer and supplier is quickly thereafter *transformed* into one of bilateral monopoly—on account of the transaction-specific costs referred to above. This transformation has profound contracting consequences.

Thus, whereas recurrent spot contracting is feasible for standardized transactions (because large-numbers competition is continuously self-policing in these circumstances), such contracting has seriously defective investment incentives where idiosyncratic activities are involved. By assumption, cost economies in production will be realized for idiosyncratic activities only if the supplier invests in a special-purpose plant and equipment or if his labor force develops transaction-specific skills in the course of contract execution (or both). The assurance of a continuing relation is needed to encourage investments of both kinds. Although the requisite incentives might be provided if long-term contracts were negotiated, such contracts are necessarily incomplete (by reason of bounded rationality). Appropriate state-contingent adaptations thus go unspecified. Intertemporal efficiency nevertheless requires that adaptations to changing market circumstances be made.

How to effect these adaptations poses a serious contracting dilemma, though it bears repeating that, absent the hazards of opportunities, the difficulties would vanish—since then the gaps in long-term, incomplete contracts could be faultlessly filled in an adaptive, sequential way. A general clause, to which both parties would agree, to the effect that 'I will behave responsibly rather than seek individual advantage when an occasion to adapt arises,' would, in the absence of opportunism, suffice. Given, however, the unenforceability of general clauses and the proclivity of human agents to make false and misleading (self-disbelieved) statements, the following hazard must be confronted: joined as they are in an idiosyncratic condition of bilateral monopoly, both buyer and seller are strategically situated to bargain over the disposition of any incremental gain whenever a proposal to adapt is made by the other party. Although both have a long-term interest in effecting adaptations of a joint profit-maximizing kind, each also has an interest in appropriating as much of the gain as he can on each occasion to adapt. Efficient adaptations which would otherwise be made thus result in costly haggling or even go unmentioned, lest the gains be dissipated by costly subgoal pursuit. Governance structures which attenuate opportunism and otherwise infuse confidence are evidently needed.

2.2. Examples

Some illustrations may help to motivate what is involved in idiosyncratic transactions. Specialized physical capital is relatively straightforward. Examples are (1) the purchase of a specialized component from an outside supplier or (2) the location of a specialized plant in a unique, proximate relation to a downstream processing stage to which it supplies vital input.

Thus assume (a) that special-purpose equipment is needed to produce the component in question (which is to say that the value of the equipment in its next-best alternative use is much lower), (b) that scale economies require that a significant, discrete investment be made, and (c) that alternative buyers for such components are few (possibly because of the organization of the industry, possibly because of special-design features). The interests of buyer and seller in a continuing exchange relation are plainly strong under these circumstances.

Plant-proximity benefits are attributable to transportation and related flow-process (inventory, thermal economy, and so on) economies. A specialized plant need not be implied, but long life and a unique location are. Once made, the investment preempts the unique location and is not thereafter moveable (except at prohibitive cost). Buyer and supplier again need to satisfy themselves that they have a workable, adaptable exchange agreement.[32]

Idiosyncratic investments in human capital are in many ways more interesting and less obvious than are those in physical capital. Polanyi's discussion of 'personal knowledge' is illuminating:

The attempt to analyse scientifically the established industrial arts has everywhere led to similar results. Indeed even in the modern industries the indefinable knowledge is still an essential part of technology. I have myself watched in Hungary a new, imported machine for blowing electric lamp bulbs, the exact counterpart of which was operating successfully in Germany, failing for a whole year to produce a single flawless bulb.[33]

And he goes on to observe with respect to craftsmanship that:

. . . an art which has fallen into disuse for the period of a generation is altogether lost . . . It is pathetic to watch the endless efforts—equipped with microscopy and chemistry, with mathematics and electronics—to reproduce a single violin of the kind the half-literate Stradivarius turned out as a matter of routine more than 200 years ago.[34]

Polanyi's discussion of language also has a bearing on the argument advanced above that specialized code words or expressions can and do arise in the context of recurring transactions and that these yield economies. As he puts it, 'Different vocabularies for the interpretation of things divide men into groups which cannot understand each other's way of seeing things and acting upon them.'[35] And subsequently he remarks that:

To know a language is an art, carried on by tacit judgments and the practice of unspecified skills. . . . Spoken communication is the successful application by two persons of the linguistic knowledge and skill acquired by such apprenticeship, one person wishing to transmit, the other to receive, information. Relying on what each has learnt, the speaker confidently utters words and the listener confidently interprets them, while they mutually rely on each other's correct use and understanding of these words. A true communications will take place if, and only if, these combined assumptions of authority and trust are in fact justified.[36]

Babbage reports a remarkable example of transaction-specific value in exchange that occurred in the early 1800s. Although he attributes the continuing exchange in the face of adversity to values of 'established character' (trust), I believe there were other specialized human and physical investments involved as well. In any event, the circumstance which he describes is the following:

The influence of established character in producing confidence operated in a very remarkable manner at the time of the exclusion of British manufactures from the Continent during the last war. One of our largest establishments had been in the habit of doing extensive business with a house in the centre of Germany; but, on the closing of the continental ports against our manufacturers, heavy penalties were inflicted on all those who contravened the Berlin and Milan decrees. The English manufacturer continued, nevertheless, to receive orders, with directions how to consign them, and appointments for the time and mode of payment, in letters, the handwriting of which was known to him, but which were never signed, except by the Christian name of one of the firm, and even in some instances they were without any signature at all. These orders were executed; and in no instance was there the least irregularity in the payments.[37]

While most of these illustrations refer to technical and commercial transactions, other types of transactions also have an idiosyncratic quality. Justice Rhenquist refers to some of these when speaking of the general class of cases where 'the litigation of an individual's claim of deprivation of a right would bring parties *who must remain in a continuing relationship* into the adversarial atmosphere of a courtroom'[38]—which atmosphere he plainly regards as detrimental to the quality of the relationship. Examples that he offers include reluctance to have the courts mediate collective bargaining disputes[39] and to allow children to bring suit against parents.[40]

But surely we must ask what is distinctive about these transactions. I submit that transaction-specific human capital is central to each. Why else would it take the Hungarians so long to operate the German light-bulb machine? And what else explains the loss of Stradivarius's craftsmanship? Likewise the understanding and trust which evolve between Babbage's transmitter and receiver are valued human assets which, once developed, will be sacrificed with reluctance. And the disruption of continuing relationships to which Justice Rhenquist refers occasions concern precisely because there are no adequate substitutes for these idiosyncratic relations.[41]

The general argument of this paper is that special governance structures supplant standard market-cum-classical contract exchange when transaction-specific values are great. Idiosyncratic commercial, labor, and family relationships are specific examples.

3. Commercial Contracting

The discussion of commercial contracting begins with a brief statement on economizing. The proposed schema for characterizing transactions and their governance is then developed, including the relation of the schema with Macneil's three-way classification of contract.

3.1. Economizing

The criterion for organizing commercial transactions is assumed to be the strictly instrumental one of cost economizing. Essentially this takes two parts: economizing on production expense and economizing on transaction costs.[42] To the degree that transaction costs are negligible, buying rather than making will normally be the most cost-effective means of procurement.[43]

Not only can static scale economies be more fully exhausted by buying rather than making, but the supplier who aggregates uncorrelated demands can realize collective pooling benefits as well. Since external procurement avoids many of the bureaucratic hazards of internal procurement (which hazards, however, are themselves of a transaction-cost kind),[44] external procurement is evidently warranted.[45]

As indicated, however, the object is to economize on the *sum* of production and transaction costs. To the degree production-cost economies of external procurement are small and/or the transaction costs associated with external procurement are great, alternative supply arrangements deserve serious consideration. Economizing on transaction costs essentially reduces to economizing on bounded rationality while simultaneously safeguarding the transactions in question against the hazards of opportunism. Holding the governance structure constant, these two objectives are in tension, since a reduction in one commonly results in an increase in the other.[46]

Governance structures, however, are properly regarded as part of the optimization problem. For some transactions, a shift from one structure to another may permit a simultaneous reduction in both the expense of writing a complex contract (which economizes on bounded rationality) and the expense of executing it effectively in an adaptive, sequential way (by attenuating opportunism). Indeed, this is precisely the attraction of internal procurement for transactions of a recurrent, idiosyncratic kind. Not only are market-aggregation economies negligible for such transactions—since the requisite investments are transaction-specific—but market trading in these circumstances is shot through with appropriate quasi-rent hazards. The issues here have been developed elsewhere.[47] The object of this paper is to integrate them into a larger contractual framework.

Note in this connection that the prospect of recovering the set-up costs associated with specialized governance structures varies with the frequency with which transactions recur. Specialized governance structures are much easier to justify for recurrent transactions than for identical transactions that occur only occasionally.

3.2. Characterizing Transactions

I asserted earlier that the critical dimensions for describing contractual relations are uncertainty, the frequency with which transactions recur, and the degree to which investments are idiosyncratic. To simplify the exposition, I will assume uncertainty exists in some intermediate degree and focus initially on frequency and the degree to which the expenses incurred are

Table 1. Illustrative Commercial Transactions

		Investment Characteristics		
		Nonspecific	Mixed	Idiosyncratic
Frequency	Occasional	Purchasing Standard Equipment	Purchasing Customized Equipment	Constructing a Plant
	Recurrent	Purchasing Standard Material	Purchasing Customized Material	Site-Specific Transfer of Intermediate Product Across Successive Stages

transaction-specific. The separate importance of uncertainty will then be developed in Section 3.4. Three frequency and three investment categories will be recognized. Frequency can be characterized as one-time, occasional, and recurrent; and investments are classed as nonspecific, mixed, and idiosyncratic. To further simplify the argument, the following assumptions are made: (1) Suppliers intend to be in business on a continuing basis; thus the special hazards posed by fly-by-night firms can be disregarded. (2) Potential suppliers for any given requirement are numerous—which is to say that *ex ante* monopoly in ownership of specialized resources is assumed away. (3) The frequency dimension refers strictly to buyer activity in the market.[48] (4) The investment dimension refers to the characteristics of investments made by suppliers.[49]

Although discrete transactions are intriguing—for example, purchasing local spirits from a shopkeeper in a remote area of a foreign country which one never again expects to visit nor to refer his friends—few transactions have this totally isolated character. For those that do not, the difference between one-time and occasional transactions is not apparent. Accordingly, only occasional and recurrent frequency distinctions will be maintained. Table 1 thus describes the six types of transactions to which governance structures need to be matched. Illustrative transactions appear in the cells.

3.3. Governance Structures

Three broad types of governance structures will be considered: non-transaction-specific, semi-specific, and highly specific. The market is the classic nonspecific governance structure within which 'faceless buyers and sellers . . . meet . . . for an instant to exchange standardized goods at equilibrium prices.'[50] By contrast, highly specific structures are tailored to the special needs of the transaction. Identity here clearly matters. Semi-specific structures, naturally, fall in between. Several propositions are suggested immediately. (1) Highly standardized transactions are not apt to require specialized governance structure. (2) Only recurrent transactions will support a highly specialized governance structure.[51] (3) Although occasional transactions of a nonstandardized kind will not support a transaction-specific governance structure, they require special attention nonetheless. In terms of Macneil's three-way classification of contract, classical contracting presumably applies to all standardized transactions (whatever the frequency), relational contracting develops for transactions of a recurring and nonstandardized kind, and neoclassical contracting is needed for occasional, nonstandardized transactions.

1. *Market Governance: Classical Contracting*. Market governance is the main governance structure for nonspecific transactions of both occasional and recurrent contracting. Markets are especially efficacious when recurrent transactions are contemplated, since both parties need only consult their own experience in deciding to continue a trading relationship or, at little transitional expense, turn elsewhere. Being standardized, alternative purchase and supply arrangements are presumably easy to work out.

Nonspecific but occasional transactions are ones for which buyers (and sellers) are less able to rely on direct experience to safeguard transactions against opportunism. Often, however, rating services or the experience of other buyers of the same good can be consulted. Given that the good or service if of a standardized kind, such experience rating, by formal and informal means, will provide incentives for parties to behave responsibly.

To be sure, such transactions take place within and benefit from a legal framework. But such dependence is not great. As S. Todd Lowry puts it, 'the traditional economic analysis of exchange in a market setting properly corresponds to the legal concept of *sale* (rather than contract), since sale presumes arrangements in a market context and requires legal support primarily in enforcing transfers of title.'[52] He would thus reserve the concept of contract for exchanges where, in the absence of standardized market alternatives, the parties have designed 'patterns of future relations on which they could rely.'[53]

The assumptions of the discrete-contracting paradigm are rather well satisfied for transactions where markets serve as a main governance mode. Thus the specific identity of the parties is of negligible importance; substantive content is determined by reference to formal terms of the contract; and legal rules apply. Market alternatives are mainly what protect each party against opportunism by his opposite.[54] Litigation is strictly for settling claims; concentrated efforts to sustain the relation are not made because the relation is not independently valued.[55]

2. *Trilateral Governance: Neoclassical Contracting.* The two types of transactions for which trilateral governance is needed are occasional transactions of the mixed and highly idiosyncratic kinds. Once the principals to such transactions have entered into a contract, there are strong incentives to see the contract through to completion. Not only have specialized investments been put in place, the opportunity cost of which is much lower in alternative uses, but the transfer of these assets to a successor supplier would pose inordinate difficulties in asset valuation.[56] The interests of the principals in sustaining the relation are especially great for highly idiosyncratic transactions.

Market relief is thus unsatisfactory. Often the setup costs of a transaction-specific governance structure cannot be recovered for occasional transactions. Given the limits of classical contract law for sustaining these transactions, on the one hand, and the prohibitive cost of transaction-specific (bilateral) governance, on the other, an intermediate institutional form is evidently needed.

Neoclassical contract law has many of the sought-after qualities. Thus rather than resorting immediately to strict reliance on litigation—with its transaction-rupturing features—*third-party assistance* (arbitration) in resolving disputes and evaluating performance is employed instead. (The use of the architect as a relatively independent expert to determine the content of form construction contracts is an example.)[57] Also, the expansion of the specific-performance remedy in past decades is consistent with continuity purposes—though Macneil declines to characterize specific performance as the 'primary neoclassical contract remedy.'[58] The section of the Uniform Commercial Code which permits the 'seller aggrieved by a buyer's breach . . . unilaterally to maintain the relation'[59] is yet another example.

3. *Transaction-specific Governance: Relational Contracting.* The two types of transactions for which specialized governance structures are commonly devised are recurring transactions of the mixed and highly idiosyncratic kinds. The nonstandardized nature of these transactions makes primary reliance on market governance hazardous, while their recurrent nature permits the cost of the specialized governance structure to be recovered.

Two types of transaction-specific governance structures for intermediate-production market transactions can be distinguished: bilateral structures, where the autonomy of the parties is maintained, and unified structures, where the transaction is removed from the market and organized within the firm subject to an authority relation (vertical integration). Bilateral structures have only recently received the attention they deserve and their operation is least well understood.

(a) *Bilateral Governance: Obligational Contracting.* Highly idiosyncratic transactions are ones where the human and physical assets required for production are extensively specialized, so there are no obvious scale economies to be realized through interfirm trading that the buyer (or seller) is unable to realize himself (through vertical integration). In the case, however, of mixed transactions, the degree of asset specialization is less complete. Accordingly, outside procurement for these components may be favored by scale-economy considerations.

As compared with vertical integration, outside procurement also is good in eliciting cost control for steady-state supply. Problems, however, arise when adaptability and contractual expense are considered. Whereas internal adaptations can be effected by fiat, outside procurement involves effecting adaptations across a market interface. Unless the need for adaptations has been contemplated from the outset and expressly provided for by the contract, which often is impossible or prohibitively expensive, adaptations across a market interface can be accomplished only by mutual, follow-on agreements. Inasmuch as the interests of the parties will commonly be at variance when adaptation proposals (originated by either party) are made, a dilemma is evidently posed.

On the one hand, both parties have an incentive to sustain the relationship rather than to permit it to unravel, the object being to avoid the sacrifice of valued transaction-specific economies. On the other hand, each party appropriates a separate profit stream and cannot be expected to accede readily to any proposal to adapt the contract. What is needed, evidently, is some way for declaring admissible dimensions for adjustment such that flexibility is provided under terms in which both parties have confidence. This can be accomplished partly by (1) recognizing that the hazards of opportunism vary with the type of adaptation proposed and (2) restricting adjustments to those where the hazards are least. But the spirit within which adaptations are effected is equally important.[60]

Quantity adjustments have much better incentive-compatibility properties than do price adjustments. For one thing, price adjustments have an unfortunate zero-sum quality, whereas proposals to increase, decrease, or delay delivery do not. Also, except as discussed below, price-adjustment proposals involve the risk that one's opposite is contriving to alter the terms within the bilateral monopoly trading gap to his advantage. By contrast, a presumption that exogenous events, rather than strategic purposes, are responsible for quantity adjustments is ordinarily warranted. Given the mixed nature of the exchange, a seller (or buyer) simply has little reason to doubt the representations of his opposite when a quantity change is proposed.

Thus buyers will neither seek supply from other sources nor divert products obtained (at favorable prices) to other uses (or users)—because other sources will incur high setup costs and an idiosyncratic product is nonfungible across uses and users. Likewise, sellers will not withhold supply because better opportunities have arisen, since the assets in question have a specialized character. The result is that quantity representations for idiosyncratic products can ordinarily be taken at face value. Since inability to adapt both quantity and price would render most idiosyncratic exchanges non-viable, quantity adjustments occur routinely.

Of course, not all price adjustments pose the same degree of hazard. Those which pose few hazards will predictably be implemented. Crude escalator clauses which reflect changes in general economic conditions are one possibility. But since such escalators are not transaction-specific, imperfect adjustments often result when these escalators are applied to local conditions. We should therefore consider whether price adjustments that are more closely related to local circumstances are feasible. The issue here is whether interim price adjustments can be devised for some subset of conditions such that the strategic hazards described above do not arise. What are the preconditions?

Crises facing either of the parties to an idiosyncratic exchange constitute one class of exceptions. Faced with a viability crisis which jeopardizes the relationship, ad hoc price relief may be permitted. More relevant and interesting, however, is whether there are circumstances whereby interim price adjustments are made routinely. The preconditions here are two: first, proposals to adjust prices must relate to exogenous, germane, and easily verifiable events; and second, quantifiable cost consequences must be confidently related thereto. An example may help to illustrate. Consider a component for which a significant share of the cost is accounted for by a basic material (copper, steel). Assume, moreover, that the fractional cost of the component in terms of this basic material is well specified. An exogenous change in prices of materials would under these circumstances pose few hazards if partial but interim price relief were permitted by allowing pass-through according to formula. A more refined adjustment than aggregate escalators would afford thereby obtains.

It bears emphasis, however, that not all costs so qualify. Changes in overhead or other expenses for which validation is difficult and which, even if verified, bear an uncertain relation to the cost of the component

Table 2. Matching governance structures with commercial transactions

			Investment Characteristics		
			Nonspecific	Mixed	Idiosyncratic
Frequency	Occasional	Market Governance (Classical Contracting)		Trilateral Governance (Neoclassical Contracting)	
	Recurrent			Bilateral Governance (Relational Contracting)	Unified Governance

will not be passed through in a similar way. Recognizing the hazards, the parties will simply forgo relief of this kind.

(b) *Unified Governance: Internal Organization.* Incentives for trading weaken as transactions become progressively more idiosyncratic. The reason is that, as the specialized human and physical assets become more specialized to a single use, and hence less transferable to other uses, economies of scale can be as fully realized by the buyer as by an outside supplier.[61] The choice of organizing mode then turns on which mode has superior adaptive properties. As discussed elsewhere, vertical integration will invariably appear in these circumstances.[62]

The advantage of vertical integration is that adaptations can be made in a sequential way without the need to consult, complete, or revise interfirm agreements. Where a single ownership entity spans both sides of the transactions, a presumption of joint profit maximization is warranted. Thus price adjustments in vertically integrated enterprises will be more complete than in interfirm trading. And quantity adjustments, of course, will be implemented at whatever frequency serves to maximize the joint gain to the transaction.

Unchanging identity at the interface coupled with extensive adaptability in both price and quantity is thus characteristic of highly idiosyncratic transactions which are vertically integrated. Obligational contracting is supplanted by the more comprehensive adaptive capability afforded by administration.

The match of governance structures with transactions that results from these economizing efforts is shown in Table 2.

3.4. Uncertainty

Transactions conducted under certainty are relatively uninteresting. Except as they differ in the time required to reach an equilibrium-exchange configuration, any governance structure will do. More relevant are transactions where uncertainty is present to an intermediate or high degree. The foregoing has dealt with the first of these. The question here is how the governance of transactions is affected by increasing the degree of uncertainty.

Recall that nonspecific transactions are ones for which continuity has little value, since new trading relations are easily arranged. Increasing the degree of uncertainty does not alter this. Accordingly, market exchange continues and the discrete-contracting paradigm (classical contract law) holds across standardized transactions of all kinds, whatever the degree of uncertainty.

Matters are different with transaction-specific investments. Whenever investments are idiosyncratic in nontrivial degree, increasing the degree of uncertainty makes it more imperative that the parties devise a machinery to 'work things out'— since contractual gaps will be larger and the occasions for sequential adaptations will increase in number and importance as the degree of uncertainty increases. This has special relevance for the organization of transactions with mixed investment attributes. Two possibilities exist. One would be to sacrifice valued design features in favor of a more standardized good or service. Market governance would then apply. The second would be to preserve the design but surround the transaction with an elaborated governance apparatus, thereby facilitating more effective adaptive, sequential decision making. Specifically, a more elaborate arbitration apparatus is apt to be devised for occasional, nonstandard transactions. And bilateral governance structures will often give way to unified ones as uncertainty is increased for recurrent transactions.

Reductions in uncertainty, of course, warrant shifting transactions in the opposite direction. To the extent that uncertainty decreases as an industry matures, which is the usual case, the benefits that accrue to integration presumably decline. Accordingly, greater reliance on obligational market contracting is commonly feasible for transactions of recurrent trading in mature industries.

4. Other Applications

The three dimensions for describing transactions—frequency, investment idiosyncrasy, and uncertainty—apply to transactions of all kinds. The same general considerations that apply to governance structures for commercial transactions carry over as well. The specific governance structures for organizing commercial transactions do not, however, apply without modification to the governance of other types of transactions. Applications of the framework to the study of labor markets, regulation, family law, and capital markets are briefly sketched here.

4.1. Labor

Occasional labor-market transactions typically take the form of repair or replacement services—the plumber, electrician, and so forth. Especially in older homes or structures, these transactions can take on an idiosyncratic quality. Although such transactions can be interesting, the transactions on which I want to focus are recurrent labor-market transactions of the non-specific, mixed, and idiosyncratic kinds.

Clyde Summers's examination of collective agreements in relation to the law of contracts disclosed that, while the collective bargain differed greatly from the ordinary bargain of commerce, collective agreements are none-theless a part of the 'mainstream of contract.'[63] He suggested that the study of contract proceed on two levels: the search for an underlying framework and, within that framework, an examination of the distinctive institutional attributes that distinguish each type of transaction. With respect to the first of these he conjectured that 'the principles common to the whole range of contractual transactions are relatively few and of such generality and competing character that they should not be stated as legal rules at all.'[64]

I am persuaded that Summers's two-part strategy for studying contract leads to a deeper understanding of the issues. And I believe that the framework set out in the preceding sections of this paper provides much of the underlying unity called for by Summers. What differs as one moves across various contracting activities is the institutional infrastructure.

1. *Nonspecific Transactions.* Nonspecific labor-market transactions are one where employer and employee are largely indifferent to the identity of each. Migrant farm labor is an example. Although an unchanging employment association between firm and worker may be observed to continue over long intervals for some of these employees, each party is essentially meeting bids

in the spot market. A valuable ongoing relationship, in which specific training and on-the-job learning yield idiosyncratic benefits, is thus not implied. Both wages and employment are variable and market governance applies to transactions of this kind. Consider, therefore, mixed and idiosyncratic labor-market transactions.

2. *Mixed Transactions.* Probably the most interesting labor-market transactions are those where large numbers of workers acquire an intermediate degree of firm-specific skill. Note that, inasmuch as the degree of idiosyncrasy is a design variable, firms would presumably redesign jobs to favor more standardized operations if it were impossible to devise governance structures which prevented antagonistic bargaining relations from developing between firms and idiosyncratically skilled employees. Although least-cost production technologies would be sacrificed in the process, net gains might nevertheless be realized since incumbent workers would realize little strategic advantage over otherwise qualified but inexperienced outsiders.

Justice Rhenquist has observed that 'Adjudicatory review of the decisions of certain institutions, while perhaps insuring a "better" decision in some objective sense, can only disrupt on-going relationships within the institution and thereby hamper the institution's ability to serve its designated societal function.'[65] Examples of adjudicatory review with respect to which he counsels caution include collective bargaining agreements.

The reasons for this are that adjudicatory review is not easily apprised of the special needs of the transaction and the prospect of such review impairs the incentive of the parties to devise bilateral governance structure. The *Vaca v. Stipes* holding, which Justice Rhenquist cites, is fully consistent with this interpretation. There the Court held that an individual could not compel his union to take his grievance to arbitration, since if the law were otherwise 'the settlement machinery provided by the contract would be substantially undermined, thus . . . [introducing] the vagaries of independent and unsystematic negotiations.'[66] Archibald Cox elaborates as follows:[67]

. . . giving the union control over all claims arising under the collective agreement comports so much better with the functional nature of a collective bargaining agreement. . . . Allowing an individual to carry a claim to arbitration whenever he is dissatisfied with the adjustment worked out by the company and the union . . . discourages the kind of day-to-day cooperation between company and union which is normally the mark of sound industrial relations—a relationship in which grievances are treated as problems to be solved and contracts are only guideposts in a dynamic human relationship. When . . . the individual's claim endangers group interests, the union's function is to resolve the competition by reaching an accommodation or striking a balance.

The practice described by Cox of giving the union control over arbitration claims plainly permits group interests—whence the concern for system viability—to supersede individual interests, thereby curbing small-numbers opportunism.

General escalator or predetermined wage adjustments aside, wages are unchanging under collective bargaining agreements.[68] Interim adaptations are nonetheless essential. These take three forms: (1) quantity adjustments, (2) assignment changes, and (3) refinement of working rules as a result of grievances.

Quantity adjustments are made in response to changing market opportunities. Either the level or the mix of employment is adjusted as economic events unfold. Given that valuable firm-specific training and learning reside in the workers, layoffs with a presumption of reemployment when conditions improve are common. Conformably, the degree to which the machinery governing access to jobs is elaborated ought to vary directly with the degree to which jobs in a firm are idiosyncratic. Thus promotion ladders in firms where a succession of interdependent jobs are highly idiosyncratic should be long and thin, with access mainly restricted to the bottom, whereas promotion ladders in nonidiosyncratic activities should be broadly structured.[69] Likewise, promotion on merit ought to be favored over promotion strictly by seniority in firms where jobs are more idiosyncratic.[70]

3. *Highly Idiosyncratic Transactions*. Recall that idiosyncratic transactions involve not merely uniqueness but uniqueness of a transaction-specific kind. Also recall that our concern in this section is with recurring transactions. Thus, although there are many uniquely skilled individuals (artists, athletes, researchers, administrators), unique skills are rarely of a transaction-specific kind. On the contrary, most of these individuals could move to another organization without significant productivity losses.

The exceptions are those where the benefits which accrue to experience (inside knowledge) and/or team interaction effects are great. Whereas commercial transactions of a highly idiosyncratic nature are unified under a common ownership, limits on indenture foreclose this option for labor-market transactions. Instead of 'merger,' complex contracts designed to tie the interests of the individual to the organization on a long-term basis are negotiated. Severe penalties are provided should either party seek unilateral termination. Nonvested, long-term, contingent reward schemes are devised. More generally, transaction-specific infrastructure will be highly individuated for such transactions.

4.2. *Regulation of Natural Monopoly*

Again the argument is that specialized governance structure is needed to the degree efficient supply necessarily joins buyers and sellers in a bilateral trading relation of a continuing nature. And again, the object of governance is to (1) protect the interests of the respective parties and (2) adapt the relationship to changing circumstances.

Although differing in details, both Victor Goldberg[71] and I[72] have argued that specialized governance structure is needed for services for which natural monopoly features are great. Such structure presumably has the purpose of providing sellers (investors) and buyers with security of expectations, which is a protective function, while at the same time facilitating adaptive, sequential decision making. Rate-of-return regulation with periodic review has these features. To the extent, however, that such regulation is observed in conjunction with activities where transaction-specific investments are insubstantial (as, for example, in the trucking industry), the case for regulation is not at all apparent—or, if it is to be made, must appeal to arguments very different from those set out here.

4.3. Family Law

The issue here is whether the role of adjudication should be *expanded* to help govern family relationships. Granting that adjudication as ultimate relief can and often does serve a useful role for sustaining family relations, such relations are plainly idiosyncratic to an unusual degree and a specialized governance structure is surely the main mode of governance. As the role of adjudication is expanded, reliance upon internal structure is apt to be reduced. Therefore, except when individual rights are seriously threatened, withholding access to adjudication may be indicated.

Justice Rhenquist's remarks concerning the corrosive effects of adversary hearings on the family are apposite: 'Any sort of adversary hearing which pits parent against child is bound to be disruptive, placing stresses and tensions on the intra-familial relationships which in turn weaken the family as an institution.'[73] Whether, as this suggests, parent–child family relations are optimized where adjudication is zero or negligible is beyond the scope of this paper. It suffices for my purposes merely to note that valued family relations are recurrent and idiosyncratic and that a specialized, transaction-specific governance structure must be encouraged lest the parties withhold investing heavily in the institution.[74]

4.4. Capital Market Transactions

The ease of verification is critical to the operation of capital markets.[75] Where verification is easy, markets work well and additional governance is unnecessary. Where verification is difficult or very difficult, however, additional governance may be indicated. Occasional transactions are apt to benefit from third-party assistance, while recurring transactions are ones for which bilateral or unified governance will presumably be observed. Assessing capital-market transactions within the proposed framework is thus accomplished by substituting 'ease of verification' for 'degree of transaction-specific investment.' Once this is done, the governance structures appropriate to capital markets are broadly similar to those within which commercial transactions are organized.

5. Implications

Dimensionalizing transactions and examining the costs of executing different transactions in different ways generate a large number of institutional implications. Some of these are summarized here.

5.1. General

1. Nonspecific transactions, either occasional or recurrent, are efficiently organized by markets.
2. Occasional transactions that are nonstandardized stand most to benefit from adjudication.
3. A transaction-specific governance structure is more fully developed where transactions are (1) recurrent, (2) entail idiosyncratic investment, and (3) are executed under greater uncertainty.

5.2. Commercial Transactions

1. Optimization of commercial transactions requires simultaneous attention to (1) production economies, (2) transaction-cost economies, and (3) component design.
2. The reason why Macaulay observes so few litigated cases in business[76] is because markets work well for nonspecific transactions, while recurrent, nonstandard transactions are governed by bilateral or unified structures.
3. As uncertainty increases, the obligational market-contracting mode will

not be used for recurrent transactions with mixed investment features. Such transactions will either be standardized, and shifted to the market, or organized internally.

4. As generic demand grows and the number of supply sources increases, exchange that was once transaction-specific loses this characteristic and greater reliance on market-mediated governance is feasible. Thus vertical integration may give way to obligational market contracting, which in turn may give way to markets.

5. Where inventory and related flow-process economies are great, site-specific supply and transaction-specific governance (commonly vertical integration) will be observed. Generic demand here has little bearing.

6. The organization of the interface between manufacturing and distribution reflects similar investment considerations: goods and services that can be sold without incurring transaction-specific investment will be distributed through conventional marketing channels while those where such investments are great will be supported by specialized—mainly bilateral (for example, franchising) or unified (forward integration)—governance structures.

7. The governance of technical change poses special difficulties. The frequently noted limits of markets[77] often give way to more complex governance relations, again for the same general reasons and along the same general lines as are set out here.[78]

5.3. Other Transactions

1. The efficiency benefits of collective organization are negligible for nonspecific labor. Accordingly, such labor will be organized late, often only with the assistance of the political process.

2. Internal labor markets become more highly individuated as jobs become more varied and idiosyncratic.

3. Regulation can be interpreted in part as a response to the transactional dilemma posed by natural monopoly.

4. A transaction-cost justification for regulating activities for which transaction-specific investments are lacking (for example, trucking) is not apparent. The possibility that politics is the driving consideration in such industries warrants consideration.

5. Adjudication should proceed with caution in the area of family law lest valued transaction-specific investments be discouraged.

6. Ease of verification is the capital-market counterpart of transaction-

Oliver E. Williamson

specific investments. Upon making this substitution, the organization of capital markets and intermediate-product markets is broadly similar.

6. Concluding Remarks

Transaction-cost economics is an interdisciplinary undertaking that joins economics with aspects of organization theory and overlaps extensively with contract law. It is the modern counterpart of institutional economics and relies heavily on comparative analysis.[79] Frictionless ideals are useful mainly for reference purposes.

Although mathematical economics captures only a fraction of the transaction-cost phenomena of interest,[80] this has not been the only obstacle. Headway with the study of transaction-cost issues has been impeded by lack of verbal definitions. Identifying the critical dimensions with respect to which transactions differ has been a significant omission.

This paper attempts to rectify this deficiency and identifies uncertainty, frequency of exchange, and the degree to which investments are transaction-specific as the principal dimensions for describing transactions. The efficient organization of economic activity entails matching governance structures with these transactional attributes in a discriminating way.

Although the main applications in this paper are to commercial contracting, the proposed approach generalizes easily to the study of labor contracts. It also has ramifications for understanding both public utility regulation and family relations. A unified approach to contract thus emerges.

The fact that the broad features of so many varied transactions fit within the framework is encouraging. The importance of transaction costs to the organization of economic activity is thus confirmed. But the world of contract is enormously complex,[81] and the simple economizing framework proposed here cannot be expected to capture more than main features. Elaborating the framework to deal with microanalytic phenomena, however, should be feasible. And extending it to include additional or substitute dimensions (of which the ease of verification, in the case of capital-market transactions, is an example) may sometimes be necessary.

Notes

1. Ronald Coase has forcefully argued the importance of transaction costs at twenty-year intervals. See R. H. Coase, The Nature of the Firm, 4 Economica 386 (n.s. 1937), reprinted in Readings in Price Theory 331 (George J. Stigler & Kenneth E. Boulding eds. 1952) and R. H. Coase, The Problem of Social Cost, 3 J. Law & Econ. 1 (1960). Much of my own work has been 'preoccupied' with transaction costs during the past decade. See especially Oliver E. Williamson, Markets and Hierarchies: Analysis and Antitrust Implications (1975). Other works in which transaction costs are featured include: Guido Calabresi, Transaction Costs, Resource Allocation, and Liability Rules: A Comment, 11 J. Law & Econ. 67 (1968); Victor P. Goldberg, Regulation and Administered Contracts, 7 Bell J. Econ. 426 (1976); Benjamin Klein, Robert G. Crawford, and Armen A. Alchian, Vertical Integration, Appropriable Rents, and the Competitive Contracting Process, 21 J. Law & Econ. 297 (1978); and Carl J. Dahlman, The Problem of Externality, 22 J. Law & Econ. 141 (1979). For an examination of Pigou in which transaction costs are featured, see Victor P. Goldberg, Pigou on Complex Contracts and Welfare Economics (1979) (unpublished manuscript).

2. S. Fischer, Long-Term Contracting, Sticky Prices, and Monetary Policy: Comment, 3 J. Monetary Econ. 317, 322 n. 5 (1977).

3. Opportunism is a variety of self-interest seeking but extends simple self-interest seeking to include self-interest seeking with guile. It is not necessary that all agents be regarded as opportunistic in identical degree. If suffices that those who are less opportunistic than others are difficult to ascertain *ex ante* and that, even among the less opportunistic, most have their price. For a more complete discussion of opportunism, see Oliver E. Williamson, *supra* note 1, at 7–10, 26–30. For a recent application see Benjamin Klein, Robert G. Crawford, & Armen A. Alchian, *supra* note 1.

4. The joining of opportunitism with transaction-specific investments (or what Klein, Crawford, and Alchian refer to as 'appropriable quasi rents') is a leading factor in explaining decisions to vertically integrate. See Oliver E. Williamson, The Vertical Integration of Production: Market Failure Considerations, 61 Am. Econ. Rev. 112 (Papers & Proceedings, May 1971); Oliver E. Williamson, *supra* note 1, at 16–19, 91–101; and Benjamin Klein, Robert G. Crawford, & Armen A. Alchian, *supra* note 1.

5. But for the limited ability of human agents to receive, store, retrieve, and process data, interesting economic problems vanish.

6. See Carl J. Dahlman, *supra* note 1.

7. See note 4 *supra*

8. I. R. Macneil, The Many Futures of Contract, 47 S. Cal. L. Rev. 691, 738 (1974) [hereinafter cited without cross-reference as Macneil, Many Futures of Contract].

9. With respect to commercial contracts, see Karl N. Llewellyn, What Price Contract?—An Essay in Perspective, 40 Yale L. J. 704 (1931); Harold C. Havighurst, The Nature of Private Contract (1961); Lon L. Fuller, Collective Bargaining

and the Arbitrator, 1963 Wis. L. Rev. 3; *id.*, The Morality of Law (1964); Stewart Macaulay, Non-Contractual Relations in Business, 28 Am. Soc. Rev. 55 (1963); Lawrence M. Friedman, Contract Law in America (1965); Arthur Allen Leff, Contract as a Thing, 19 Am. U. L. Rev. 131 (1970); I. R. Macneil, Many Futures of Contracts; *id.*, Contracts: Adjustment of Long-Term Economic Relations under Classical, Neoclassical, and Relational Contract Law, 72 Nw. U. L. Rev. 854 (1978) [hereinafter cited without cross-reference as Macneil, Contracts]; and Victor P. Goldberg, Toward and Expanded Economic Theory of Contract, 10 J. Econ. Issues 45 (1976). Labor lawyers have made similar observations regarding contracts governing the employment relationship. See Archibald Cox, The Legal Nature of Collective Bargaining Agreements, 57 Mich. L. Rev. 1 (1958); Clyde W. Summers, Collective Agreements and the Law of Contracts, 78 Yale L. J. 525 (1969); and David E. Feller, A General Theory of the Collective Bargaining Agreement, 61 Cal. L. Rev. 663 (1973).

10. The technical versus purposive distinction is made by Clyde Summers, *supra* note 9. He distinguishes between 'black letter law,' on the one hand (539, 543, 548, 566) and a more circumstantial approach to law, on the other (549–51, 561, 566). 'The epitome of abstraction is the *Restatement*, which illustrates its black letter rules by transactions suspended in mid-air, creating the illusion that contract rules can be stated without reference to surrounding circumstances and are therefore generally applicable to all contractual transactions' (566). He observes that such a conception does not and cannot provide a 'framework for integrating rules and principles applicable to all contractual transactions' (566) but that this must be sought in a more affirmative view of the law in which effective governance relations are emphasized. Contract interpretation and completing contracts are among these affirmative functions.

11. See especially Macneil, Many Futures of Contract: Macneil, Contracts; and references to related work of his cited therein.

12. Macneil, Many Futures of Contracts 738–40; Macneil, Contracts 902–05.

13. Macneil, Contracts 862.

14. *Id.* at 863 n. 25.

15. For a discussion of complex contingent-claims contracting and its mechanics, see Kenneth J. Arrow, Essays in the Theory of Risk Bearing 121–34 (1971); J. E. Meade, The Controlled Economy 147–88 (1971); and Oliver E. Williamson, *supra* note 1, at 20–40.

16. As Lester G. Telser & Harlow N. Higinbotham put it: 'In an organized market the participants trade a standardized contract such that each unit of the contract is a perfect substitute for any other unit. The identities of the parties in any mutually agreeable transaction do not affect the terms of exchange. The organized market itself or some other institution deliberately creates a homogeneous good that can be traded anonymously by the participants or their agents.' Organized Futures Markets: Costs and Benefits 85 J. Pol. Econ. 969, 997 (1977).

17. Macneil, Contracts 864.

18. *Id.*

19. *Id.* at 865.

20. Lon L. Fuller, *supra* note 9, at 11–12.

21. As Lawrence Friedman observes, relationships are effectively fractured if a dispute reaches litigation. *Supra* note 9, at 205.

22. Macneil, Contracts 885.

23. *Id.* at 901.

24. *Id.*

25. *Id.* at 890.

26. To be sure, some legal specialists insist that all of this was known all along. There is a difference, however, between awareness of a condition and an understanding. Macneil's treatment heightens awareness and deepens the understanding.

27. For a recent study of contractual relations in which uncertainty is featured, see Peter Temin, Modes of Economic Behavior: Variations on Themes of J. R. Hicks and Herbert Simon (March 1979) (Working Paper No. 235, MIT Dep't of Econ.).

28. Gordon Whinston emphasizes frequency in his 'A Note on Perspective Time: Goldberg's Relational Exchange, Repetitiveness, and Free Riders in Time and Space' (October 1978) (unpublished paper).

29. See Lester A. Telser & Harold N. Higinbotham, *supra* note 16; also Yoram Ben-Porath, The F-Connection: Families, Friends, and Firms and the Organization of Exchange (December 1978) (Report No. 29/78, The Hebrew University of Jerusalem) and Yoram Barzel, Measurement Cost and the Organization of Markets (April 1979) (unpublished paper). Note that Barzel's concern with standardization is mainly in connection with final-product markets, whereas I am more interested in nonstandard investments. The two are not unrelated, but identical quality can often be realized with a variety of inputs. I am concerned with specialized (transaction-specific) inputs.

30. This assumes that it is costly for the incumbent supplier to transfer specialized physical assets to new suppliers. On this, see Oliver E. Williamson, Franchise Bidding for Natural Monopolies—in General and with Respect to CATV, 7 Bell J. Econ. 73 (1976). Klein, Crawford, & Alchian use the term 'appropriable quasi rent' to refer to this condition. Use versus user distinctions are relevant in this connection: 'The quasi-rent value of the asset is the excess of its value over its salvage value, that is, its value in its next best *use* to another renter. The potentially appropriable specialized portion of the quasi rent is the portion, if any, in excess of its value to the second highest-valuing *user*.' Benjamin Klein, Robert G. Crawford, & Armen A. Alchian, *supra* note 1, at 298.

31. Thorstein Veblen's remarks on the distant relation of the head of a large enterprise to transactions are apposite. He observes that under these impersonal circumstances 'The mitigating effect which personal conduct may have in dealings between man and man is . . . in great measured eliminated . . . Business management [then] has a chance to proceed . . . untroubled by sentimental considerations of human kindness or irritation or of honesty.' The Theory of Business Enterprise 53 (1927). Veblen evidently assigns slight weight

to the possibility that those to whom negotiation responsibilities are assigned will themselves invest the transactions with integrity.

32. The *Great Lakes Carbon* case is an example of the latter, 1970–1973 Trade Reg. Rep. Transfer Binder ¶ 19,848 (FTC Dkt No. 8805).

33. Michael Polanyi, Personal Knowledge: Towards a Post-Critical Philosophy 52 (2d ed. 1962).

34. *Id*. at 53.

35. *Id*. at 112.

36. *Id*. at 206.

37. Charles Babbage, On the Economy of Machinery and Manufacturers 220–21 (1832). More recent examples of contracts wherein private parties can and evidently do 'ignore' the law, even at some peril, when the law and the interests of the parties are at variance are offered by Stewart Macaulay, The Use and Nonuse of Contracts in the Manufacturing Industry, 9 Practical Lawyer 13, 16 (1963): 'Requirements contracts probably are not legally enforceable in Wisconsin and a few other States. Yet, chemicals, containers, and a number of other things are still bought and sold there on the basis of requirements contracts.

   'Decisions of the United States Court of Appeals for the Seventh Circuit indicate that a clause calling for a 'seller's price in effect at time and place of delivery' makes a contract unenforceable. The Wisconsin cases are not clear. Yet steel and steel products usually are sold in this way.'

38. Remarks of Mr. Justice Rhenquist, The Adversary Society, Baron di Hirsch Meyer Lecture, University of Miami School of Law, February 2, 1978, at 19 (emphasis added).

39. *Id*. at 11–13.

40. *Id*. at 16–19.

41. As Ben-Porath puts it, 'The most important characteristic of the family contract is that it is embedded in the identity of the partners without which it loses its meaning. It is thus specific and non-negotiable or nontransferable.' Yoram Ben-Porath, *supra* note 29, at 6.

42. More generally, the economizing problem includes choice between a special-purpose and a general-purpose good or service. A general-purpose item affords all of the advantages of market procurement, but possibly at the sacrifice of valued design or performance characteristics. A special-purpose item has the opposite features: valued differences are realized but market procurement here may pose hazards. For the purposes of this paper, intermediate-product characteristics are mainly taken as given and I focus principally on production and transaction-cost economies. A more general formulation would include product characteristics in the optimization.

43. This ignores transient conditions, such as temporary excess capacity. (In a zero-transaction-cost world, such excesses vanish as assets can be deployed as effectively by others as they can be by the owner.)

44. On these hazards and their transaction-cost origins, see Oliver E. Williamson, *supra* note 1, at 117–31.

45. Dennis Carlton shows that economies of 'vertical integration' can frequently be

realized in a market where, absent integration, buyers and suppliers are randomly paired. As he defines vertical integration, however, this can be accomplished as effectively by long-term contract as it can by in-house production. Dennis W. Carlton, Vertical Integration in Competitive Markets under Uncertainty, 27 J. Indus. Econ. 189 (1979).

46. Thus a reduction in monitoring commonly gives rise to an increase in opportunism. Monitoring the employment relation, however, needs to be done with special care. Progressively increasing the intensity of surveillance can elicit resentment and have counterproductive (for example, work-to-rule) results. Such perversities are less likely for interfirm trading.

47. See note 30 *supra*.

48. This seems reasonable for most intermediate-product market transactions.

49. Production aspects are thus emphasized. Investments in governance structure are treated separately.

50. Yoram Ben-Porath, *supra* note 29, at 7.

51. Defense contracting may appear to be a counterexample, since an elaborate governance structure is devised for many of these. This reflects in part, however, the special disabilities of the government as a production instrument. But for this, many of these contracts would be organized in-house. Also, contracts that are very large and of long duration, as many defense contracts are, do have a recurring character.

52. S. Todd Lowry, Bargain and Contract Theory in Law and Economics, 10 J. Econ. Issues 1, 12 (1976).

53. Id. at 13.

54. Although recurrent, standard transactions are ones for which an active spot market commonly exists, term contracting may also be employed—especially as planning economies are thereby realized by the parties. See Dennis W. Carlton, Price Rigidity, Forward Contracts, and Market Equilibrium, J. Pol. Econ. (forthcoming). The duration of these contracts will not be long, however, since the assets in question can be employed in other uses and/or in the service of other customers. The result is that changing market circumstances will be reflected relatively quickly in both price and quantity and relatively stringent contracting attitudes may be said to prevail.

55. 'Generally speaking, a serious conflict, even quite a minor one such as an objection to a harmlessly late tender of the delivery of goods, terminates the discrete contract as a live one and leaves nothing but a conflict over money damages to be settled by a lawsuit. Such a result fits neatly the norms of enhancing discreteness and intensifying . . . presentation.' Macneil, Contracts, 877.

56. See the articles cited in note 30 *supra*.

57. Macneil, Contracts 866.

58. *Id*. at 879.

59. *Id*. at 880. The rationale for this section of the Code is that 'identification of the goods to the contract will, within limits, permit the seller to recover the price of the goods rather than merely damages for the breach . . . ([where the] latter may be far less in amount and more difficult to prove).' *Id*.

60. As Stewart Macaulay observes, 'Disputes are frequently settled without reference to the contract or to potential or actual legal sanctions. There is a hesitancy to speak of legal right or to threaten to sue in . . . negotiations' where continuing business is valued. Stewart Macaulay, *supra* note 9, at 61.

 The material which follows in this subsection was originally developed in connection with the study of inflation. See Michael L. Wachter & Oliver E. Williamson, Obligational Markets and the Mechanics of Inflation, 9 Bell J. Econ. 549 (1978).

61. This assumes that factor prices paid by buyer and outside supplier are identical. Where this is not true, as in some unionized firms, buyers may choose to procure outside because of a differential wage rate. This is a common problem in the automobile industry, which has a very flat and relatively high wage scale.

62. See the references cited in note 4 *supra*.

63. Clyde W. Summers, *supra* note 9, at 527.

64. *Id*. at 568.

65. Remarks of Mr. Justice Rhenquist, *supra* note 38, at 4.

66. 386 U.S. 171, 191 (1967).

67. Archibald Cox, *supra* note 9, at 24.

68. The reason, of course, is that it is very costly and apt to be unproductive to reopen wage bargaining during the period covered by a contract. Since to reopen negotiations for one type of job is to invite it for all, and as objective differences among jobs may be difficult to demonstrate, wage bargaining is foreclosed except at contract-renewal intervals.

69. Michael L. Wachter & Oliver E. Williamson, *supra* note 60, at 567.

70. Thus although both nonidiosyncratic jobs may be organized collectively, the way in which the internal labor markets associated with each are organized should reflect objective differences between them. Additionally, the incentive to provide an orderly governance structure varies directly with the degree to which efficiencies are attributable thereto. *Ceteris paribus*, nonidiosyncratic jobs ought to be organized later and the governance structure less fully elaborated than for idiosyncratic jobs. Both propositions are borne out by the evidence.

71. Victor P. Goldberg, *supra* note 1.

72. Oliver E. Williamson, *supra* note 30.

73. Remarks of Mr. Justice Rhenquist, *supra* note 38, at 19.

74. For a more extensive discussion of family transactions, see Yoram Ben-Porath, *supra* note 29, at 4–7.

75. This feature was called to my attention by Sanford Grossman.

76. Stewart Macaulay, *supra* note 9.

77. Kenneth J. Arrow, Economic Welfare and the Allocation of Resources for Invention, in The Rate and Direction of Economic Activity 609 (1962).

78. Aspects are discussed in Oliver E. Williamson, *supra* note 1, at 203–05.

79. Reliance on comparative analysis has been repeatedly emphasized by R. H. Coase, *supra* note 1.

80. See Carl J. Dahlman, *supra* note 1, at 144–47.

81. Benjamin Klein, Robert C. Crawford, & Armen A. Alchian, *supra* note 1, at 325.

7

An Economist's Perspective on the Theory of the Firm

Oliver Hart

An outsider to the field of economics would probably take it for granted that economists have a highly developed theory of the firm. After all firms are the engines of growth of modern capitalistic economies, and so economists must surely have fairly sophisticated views of how they behave. In fact, little could be further from the truth. Most formal models of the firm are extremely rudimentary, capable only of portraying hypothetical firms that bear little relation to the complex organizations we see in the world. Furthermore, theories that attempt to incorporate real world features of corporations, partnerships and the like often lack precision and rigour, and have therefore failed, by and large, to be accepted by the theoretical mainstream.

This article attempts to give lawyers a sense of how economists think about firms. It does not pretend to offer a systematic survey of the area; rather, it highlights several ideas of particular importance, and then explores an alternative theoretical perspective from which to view the firm.[1] Part 1 introduces various established economic theories of the firm. Part 2 turns to a newer theory of the firm, based not upon human capital structures, but rather upon property rights. Part 3 synthesizes this property rights-based theory of the firm with more established theories.

Helpful comments from Jeffrey Gordon, Bengt Holmstrom and Jean Tirole are gratefully acknowledged. This article is based in part on the author's Fisher-Schultze lecture delivered to the Econometric Society in Bologna, Italy in August 1988. Some of the work was done while the author was visiting the Harvard Business School as a Marvin Bower Fellow. He would like to thank that institution for its hospitality and financial support. The author would also like to acknowledge financial assistance from the Guggenheim and Olin Foundations, the Center for Energy and Policy Research at MIT and the National Science Foundation.

1. Established Theories

1.1. Neoclassical Theory

Any discussion of theories of the firm must start with the neoclassical approach, the staple diet of modern economists. Developed over the last one hundred years or so, this approach can be found in any modern-day textbook; in fact, in most textbooks, it is the *only* theory of the firm presented.[2]

Neoclassical theory views the firm as a set of feasible production plans.[3] A manager presides over this production set, buying and selling inputs and outputs in a spot market and choosing the plan that maximizes owners' welfare. Welfare is usually represented by profit, or, if profit is uncertain so that profit-maximization is not well defined, by expected net present value of future profit (possibly discounted for risk) or by market value.

To many lawyers and economists, this is a caricature of the modern firm; it is rigorous but rudimentary. At least three reasons help explain its prolonged survival. First, the theory lends itself to an elegant and general mathematical formalization. Second, it is very useful for analyzing how a firm's production choices respond to exogenous change in the environment, such as an increase in wages or a sales tax.[4] Finally, the theory is also very useful for analyzing the consequences of strategic interaction between firms under conditions of imperfect competition;[5] for example, it can help us understand the relationship between the degree of concentration in an industry and that industry's output and price level.

Granted these strengths, neoclassical theory has some very clear weaknesses. It does not explain how production is organized within a firm, how conflicts of interest between the firm's various constituencies—its owners, managers, workers, and consumers—are resolved, or, more generally, how the goal of profit-maximization is achieved. More subtly, neoclassical theory begs the question of what defines a given firm or what determines its boundaries. Since the theory does not address the issue of each firm's size or extent, it does not explain the consequences of two firms choosing to merge, or of one firm splitting itself into two or more smaller firms. Neoclassical theory describes in rudimentary terms how firms function, but contributes little to any meaningful picture of their structure.

1.2. Principal-Agent Theory

Principal-agent theory, an important development of the last fifteen years, addresses some of the weaknesses of the neoclassical approach.[6] Principal-agent theory recognizes conflicts of interest between different economic actors, formalizing these conflicts through the inclusion of observability problems and asymmetries of information. The theory still views the firm as a production set, but now a professional manager makes production choices, such as investment or effort allocations, that the firm's owners do not observe. Because the manager deals with the day-to-day operations of the firm, she also is presumed to have information about the firm's profitability that the owners lack. In addition, the manager has other goals in mind beyond the owners' welfare, such as on-the-job perks, an easy life, empire building, and so on. Under these conditions, principal-agent theory argues that it will be impossible for the owners to implement their own profit-maximizing plan directly, through a contract with the manager—in general, the owners will not even be able to tell ex post whether the manager has chosen the right plan. Instead, the owners will try to align the manager's objectives with their own by putting the manager on an incentive scheme. Even under an optimal incentive scheme, however, the manager will put some weight on her own objectives at the expense of those of the owners, and conflicting interests remain. Hence, we have the beginnings of a managerial theory of the firm.[7]

Principal-agent theory enriches neoclassical theory significantly, but still fails to answer the vital questions of what defines a firm and where the boundaries of its structure are located. To see why, consider the example of Fisher Body, which for many years has supplied car bodies to General Motors.[8] Principal-agent theory can explain why it might make sense for GM and Fisher to write a profit-sharing agreement, whereby part of Fisher Body's reward is based on GM's profit from car sales: this encourages Fisher to supply high-quality inputs. The theory does not tell us, however, whether it matters if this profit-sharing agreement is accomplished through the merger of Fisher and GM into a single firm, with GM having authority over Fisher management; or whether GM and Fisher should remain as separate firms; or whether GM and Fisher should merge, with Fisher management having authority over GM management.[9] In other words, principal-agent theory tells us about optimal incentive schemes, but not (at least directly) about organizational form. Hence, in the absence of a parallel between the two, which turns out to be difficult to draw, principal-agent theory provides no predictions about the nature and extent of the firm.[10]

2.3. Transaction Cost Economics

While the neoclassical paradigm, modified by principal-agent theory, progressed along the above lines, a very different approach to the theory of the firm developed under the heading of transaction cost economics. Introduced in Coase's famous 1937 article,[11] transaction cost economics traces the existence of firms to the thinking, planning and contracting costs that accompany any transaction, costs usually ignored by the neoclassical paradigm. The idea is that in some situations these costs will be lower if a transaction is carried out within a firm rather than in the market. According to Coase, the main cost of transacting in the market is the cost of learning about and haggling over the terms of trade; this cost can be particularly large if the transaction is a long-term one in which learning and haggling must be performed repeatedly.[12] Transaction costs can be reduced by giving one party authority over the terms of trade, at least within limits. But, according to Coase, this authority is precisely what defines a firm: within a firm, transactions occur as a result of instructions or orders issued by a boss, and the price mechanism is suppressed.[13]

Such an arrangement, however, brings costs of its own. Concentrating authority in one person's hands is likely to increase the cost of errors and lead to greater administrative rigidity. In Coase's view, the boundaries of the firm occur at the point where the marginal cost savings from transacting within the firm equal these additional error and rigidity costs.[14]

Coase's ideas, although recognized as highly original, took a long time to catch on.[15] There are probably two reasons for this. First, they remain to this day very hard to formalize. Second, there is a conceptual weakness, pointed out by Alchian and Demsetz,[16] in the theory's dichotomy between the role of authority within the firm and the role of consensual trade within the market. Consider, for example, Coase's notion that an employer has authority over an employee—an employer can tell an employee what to do.[17] Alchian and Demsetz questioned this, asking what ensures that the employee obeys the employer's instructions. To put it another way, what happens to the employee if he disobeys these instructions? Will he be sued for breach of contract? Unlikely. Probably the worst that can happen is the employee will be fired. But firing is typically the sanction that one independent contractor will impose on another whose performance he does not like. To paraphrase Alchian and Demsetz's criticism, it is not clear that an employer can tell an employee what to do, any more than a consumer can tell her grocer what to do (what vegetables to sell at what prices); in either case, a refusal will likely lead to a termination of the relationship, a firing. In the case of the grocer, this means that the consumer shops at another grocer.[18] Thus, according to

Alchian and Demsetz's argument, Coase's view that firms are characterized by authority relations does not really stand up.[19]

Finding Coase's characterization of the firm wanting, Alchian and Demsetz developed their own theory, based on joint production and monitoring. Transactions involving joint or team production require careful monitoring so that each actor's contribution can be assessed. According to Alchian and Demsetz, the best way to provide the monitor with appropriate incentives is to give him the following bundle of rights, which effectively define ownership of the capitalist firm: 1) to be a residual claimant; 2) to observe input behavior; 3) to be the central party common to all contracts with inputs; 4) to alter membership of the team; and, 5) to sell rights 1–4.[20] We will return to some of these ideas below, but at this stage it suffices to note that the theory suffers from the same criticism leveled at Coase: it is unclear why the problems of joint production and monitoring must be solved through the firm and cannot be solved through the market. In fact, one does not need to look far to see examples of market solutions to these problems, such as auditing between independent contractors.

At the same time that doubts were being expressed about the specifics of Coase's theory, Coase's major idea—that firms arise to economize on transaction costs—was increasingly accepted. The exact nature of these transaction costs, however, remained unclear. What lay beyond the learning and haggling costs that, according to Coase, are a major component of market transactions? Professor Oliver Williamson has offered the deepest and most far-reaching analysis of these costs.[21] Williamson recognized that transaction costs may assume particular importance in situations where economic actors make relationship-specific investments—investments to some extent specific to a particular set of individuals or assets.[22] Examples of such investments include locating an electricity generating plant adjacent to a coal mine that is going to supply it; a firm's expanding capacity to satisfy a particular customer's demands; training a worker to operate a particular set of machines or to work with a particular group of individuals; or a worker's relocating to a town where he has a new job.[23]

In situations like these, there may be plenty of competition before the investments are made—there may be many coal mines next to which an electricity generating plant could locate or many towns to which a worker could move. But once the parties sink their investments, they are to some extent locked into each other. As a result, external markets will not provide a guide to the parties' opportunity costs once the relationship is underway. This lack of information takes on great significance, since, in view of the size and degree of the specific investment, one would expect relationships like these to be long lasting.[24]

In an ideal world, the lack of ex post market signals would pose no problem, since the parties could always write a long-term contract in advance of the investment, spelling out each agent's obligations and the terms of the trade in every conceivable situation. In practice, however, thinking, negotiation and enforcement costs will usually make such a contract prohibitively expensive. As a result, parties must negotiate many of the terms of the relationship as they go along. Williamson argues that this leads to two sorts of costs. First, there will be costs associated with the ex post negotiation itself—the parties may engage in collectively wasteful activities to try to increase their own share of the ex post surplus; also, asymmetries of information may make some gains from trade difficult to realize.[25] Second, and perhaps more fundamental, since a party's bargaining power and resulting share of the ex post surplus may bear little relation to his ex ante investment, parties will have the wrong investment incentives at the ex ante stage.[26] In particular, a far-sighted agent will choose her investment inefficiently from the point of view of her contracting partners, given that she realizes that these partners could expropriate part of her investment at the ex post stage.[27]

In Williamson's view, bringing a transaction from the market into the firm—the phenomenon of integration—mitigates this opportunistic behavior and improves investment incentives. Agent A is less likely to hold up agent B if A is an employee of B than if A is an independent contractor. However, Williamson does not spell out in precise terms the mechanism by which this reduction in opportunism occurs. Moreover, certain costs presumably accompany integration. Otherwise, all transactions would be carried out in firms, and the market would not be used at all. Williamson, however, leaves the precise nature of these costs unclear.[28]

1.4. The Firm as a Nexus of Contracts

All the theories discussed so far suffer from the same weakness: while they throw light on the nature of contractual failure, none explains in a convincing or rigorous manner how bringing a transaction into the firm mitigates this failure.

One reaction to this weakness is to argue that it is not really a weakness at all. According to this point of view, the firm is simply a nexus of contracts,[29] and there is therefore little point in trying to distinguish between transactions within a firm and those between firms. Rather, both categories of transactions are part of a continuum of types of contractual relations, with different firms or organizations representing different points on this continuum.[30] In other words, each type of business organization represents nothing more than a particular 'standard form' contract. One such 'standard form' contract is a public corporation, characterized by limited liability, indefinite life, and freely transferable shares and votes. In principle it would be possible to create a contract with these characteristics each time it is needed, but, given that these characteristics are likely to be useful in many different contexts, it is much more convenient to be able to appeal to a 'standard form'. Closely held corporations or partnerships are other examples of useful 'standard forms'.

Viewing the firm as a nexus of contracts is helpful in drawing attention to the fact that contractual relations with employees, suppliers, customers, creditors and others are an essential aspect of the firm. Also, it

serves to make it clear that the personalization of the firm implied by asking questions such as 'what should be the objective function of the firm . . . is seriously misleading. *The firm is not an individual* . . . The 'behavior' of the firm is like the behavior of a market, i.e., the outcome of a complex equilibrium process.[31]

At the same time, the nexus of contracts approach does less to resolve the questions of what a firm is than to shift the terms of the debate. In particular, it leaves open the question of why particular 'standard forms' are chosen. Perhaps more fundamentally, it begs the question of what limits the set of activities covered by a 'standard form'. For example, corporations are characterized by limited liability, free transferability of shares, and indefinite life. But what limits the size of a corporation—what are the economic consequences of two corporations merging or of one corporation splitting itself into two? Given that mergers and breakups occur all the time, and at considerable transaction cost, it seems unlikely that such changes are cosmetic. Presumably they have some real effects on incentives and opportunistic behavior, but these effects remain unexplained.

......

2. A Property Rights Approach to the Firm

One way to resolve the question of how integration changes incentives is spelled out in recent literature that views the firm as a set of property rights.[32] This approach is very much in the spirit of the transaction cost literature of Coase and Williamson, but differs by focusing attention on the role of physical, that is, nonhuman, assets in a contractual relationship.

Consider an economic relationship of the type analysed by Williamson, where relationship-specific investments are important and transaction costs make it impossible to write a comprehensive long-term contract to govern the terms of the relationship. Consider also the nonhuman assets that, in the postinvestment stage, make up this relationship. Given that the initial contract has gaps, missing provisions, or ambiguities, situations will typically occur in which some aspects of the use of these assets are not specified. For example, a contract between GM and Fisher might leave open certain aspects of maintenance policy for Fisher machines, or might not specify the speed of the production line or the number of shifts per day.

Take the position that the right to choose these missing aspects of usage resides with the *owner* of the asset. That is, ownership of an asset goes together with the possession of residual rights of control over that asset; the owner has the right to use the asset in any way not inconsistent with a prior contract, custom, or any law. Thus, the owner of Fisher assets would have the right to choose maintenance policy and production line speed to the extent that the initial contract was silent about these.[33]

Finally, identify a firm with all the nonhuman assets that belong to it, assets that the firm's owners possess by virtue of being owners of the firm. Included in this category are machines, inventories, buildings or locations, cash, client lists, patents, copyrights, and the rights and obligations embodied in outstanding contracts to the extent that these are also transferred with ownership. Human assets, however, are not included. Since human assets cannot be bought or sold, management and workers presumably own their human capital both before and after any merger.

We now have the basic ingredients of a theory of the firm. In a world of transaction costs and incomplete contracts, ex post residual rights of control will be important because, through their influence on asset usage, they will affect ex post bargaining power and the division of ex post surplus in a relationship. This division in turn will affect the incentives of actors to invest in that relationship. Hence, when contracts are incomplete, the boundaries of firms matter in that these boundaries determine who owns and controls which assets.[34] In particular, a merger of two firms does not yield unambiguous benefits: to the extent that the (owner-)manager of the acquired firm loses control rights, his incentive to invest in the relationship will decrease. In addition, the shift in control may lower the investment incentives of workers in the acquired firm. In some cases these reductions in investment will be sufficiently great that nonintegration is preferable to integration.[35]

Note that, according to this theory, when assessing the effects of integration, one must know not only the characteristics of the merging firms, but also who will own the merged company. If firms *A* and *B* integrate and *A* becomes the owner of the merged company, then *A* will presumably control the residual rights in the new firm. *A* can then use those rights to hold up the managers and workers of firm *B*. Should the situation be reversed, a different set of control relations would result in B exercising control over A, and A's workers and managers would be liable to holdups by B.

It will be helpful to illustrate these ideas in the context of the Fisher Body–General Motors relationship.[36] Suppose these companies have an initial contract that requires Fisher to supply GM with a certain number of car bodies each week. Imagine that demand for GM cars now rises and GM wants Fisher to increase the quantity it supplies. Suppose also that the initial contract is silent about this possibility, perhaps because of a difficulty in predicting Fisher's costs of increasing supply. If Fisher is a separate company, GM presumably must secure Fisher's permission to increase supply. That is, the status quo point in any contract renegotiation is where Fisher does *not* provide the extra bodies. In particular, GM does not have the right to go into Fisher's factory and set the production line to supply the extra bodies; Fisher, as owner, has this residual right of control. The situation is very different if Fisher is a subdivision or subsidiary of GM, so that GM owns Fisher's factory. In this case, if Fisher management refuses to supply the extra bodies, GM always has the option to fire management and hire someone else to supervise the factory and supply extra bodies (they could even run Fisher themselves on a temporary basis). The status quo point in the contract renegotiation is therefore quite different.

To put it very simply, if Fisher is a separate firm, Fisher management can threaten to make both Fisher assets and their own labor unavailable for the uncontracted-for supply increase. In contrast, if Fisher belongs to GM, Fisher management can only threaten to make their own labor unavailable. The latter threat will generally be much weaker than the former.[37]

Although the status quo point in the contract renegotiation may depend on whether GM and Fisher are one firm rather than two, it does not follow that the outcomes after renegotiation will differ. In fact, if the benefits to GM of the extra car bodies exceed the costs to Fisher of supplying them, we might expect the parties to agree that the bodies should be supplied, regardless of the status quo point. However, the divisions of surplus in the two cases will be very different. If GM and Fisher are separate, GM may have to pay Fisher a large sum to persuade it to supply the extra bodies. In contrast, if GM owns Fisher's plant, it may be able to enforce the extra supply at much lower cost since, as we have seen in this case, Fisher management has much reduced bargaining and threat power.

Anticipating the way surplus is divided, GM will typically be much more prepared to invest in machinery that is specifically geared to Fisher bodies if it owns Fisher than if Fisher is independent, since the threat of expropriation is reduced.[38] The incentives for Fisher, however, may be quite the opposite. Fisher management will generally be much more willing to come up with cost-saving or quality-enhancing innovations if Fisher is an independent firm than if it is part of GM, because Fisher management is more likely to see a return on its activities. If Fisher is independent, it can extract some of GM's surplus by threatening to deny GM access to the assets embodying these innovations. In contrast, if GM owns the assets, Fisher management faces total expropriation of the value of the innovation to the extent that the innovation is asset-specific rather than management-specific, and GM can threaten to hire a new management team to incorporate the innovation.[39]

So far, we have discussed the effects of control changes on the incentives of top management. But workers' incentives will also be affected. Consider, for example, the incentive of someone who works with Fisher assets to improve the quality of Fisher's output by better learning some aspect of the production process. Suppose further that GM has a specific interest in this improvement in car body quality, and that none of Fisher's other customers cares about it. There are many ways in which the worker might be rewarded for this, but one important reward is likely to come from the fact that the worker's value to the Fisher-GM venture will rise in the future and, due to his additional skills, the worker will be able to extract some of these benefits through a higher wage or promotion. Note, however, that the worker's ability to do this is greater if GM controls the assets than if Fisher does. In the former case, the worker will bargain directly with GM, the party that benefits from the worker's increased skill.[40] In the latter case, the worker will bargain with Fisher, who only receives a fraction of these benefits, since it must in turn bargain with GM to parlay these benefits into dollars. In consequence, the worker will typically capture a lower share of the surplus, and his incentive to make the improvement in the first place will fall.

In other words, given that the worker may be held up no matter who owns the Fisher assets—assuming that he, himself, does not—his incentives are greater if the number of possible hold-ups is smaller rather than larger. With Fisher management in control of the assets, there are two potential hold-ups: Fisher can deny the worker access to the assets, and GM can decline to pay more for the improved product.[41] As a result, we might expect the worker to get, say, a third of his increased marginal product (supposing equal division with Fisher and GM). With GM management in control of the Fisher assets, there is only one potential hold-up, since the power to deny the worker his increased marginal product is concentrated in one agent's hands. As a result, the worker in this case might be able to capture half of his increased marginal product (supposing equal division with GM).[42]

The above reasoning applies to the case in which the improvement is specific to GM. Exactly the opposite conclusion would be reached, however, if the improvement were specific to Fisher, such as the worker learning how to reduce Fisher management's costs of making car bodies, regardless of Fisher's final customer (a cost reduction, furthermore, which could not be enjoyed by any substitute for Fisher management). In that event, the number of hold-ups is reduced by giving control of Fisher assets to Fisher management rather than GM. The reason is that with Fisher management in control, the worker bargains with the party who benefits directly from his increased productivity, whereas with GM management in control, he must bargain with an indirect recipient; GM must in turn bargain with Fisher management to benefit from the reduction in costs.

Up to this point we have assumed that GM management will control GM assets. This, however, need not be the case; in some situations it might make more sense for Fisher management to control these assets—for Fisher to buy up GM. One thing we can be sure of is that if GM and Fisher assets are sufficiently complementary, and initial contracts sufficiently incomplete, then the two sets of assets should be under common control. With extreme complementarity, no agent—whether manager or worker—can benefit from any increase in his marginal productivity unless he has access to both sets of assets (by the definition of extreme complementarity, each asset, by itself, is useless). Giving control of these assets to two different management teams is therefore bound to be detrimental to actors' incentives, since it increases the number of parties with hold-up power.[43] This result confirms the notion that when lock-in effects[44] are extreme, integration will dominate nonintegration.[45]

These ideas can be used to construct a theory of the firm's boundaries. First, as we have seen, highly complementary assets should be owned in common, which may provide a minimum size for the firm. Second, as the firm grows beyond a certain point, the manager at the centre will become less and less important with regard to operations at the periphery in the sense that increases in marginal product at the periphery are unlikely to be specific either to this manager or to the assets at the center. At this stage, a new firm should be created since giving the central manager control of the periphery will increase hold-up problems without any compensating gains. It should also be clear from this line of argument that, in the absence of significant lock-in effects, nonintegration is always better than integration—it is optimal to do things through the market, for integration only increases the number of potential hold-ups without any compensating gains.[46]

Finally, it is worth noting that the property rights approach can explain how the purchase of physical assets leads to control over human assets. To see this, consider again the GM-Fisher hypothetical. We showed that someone working with Fisher assets is more likely to improve Fisher's output in a way that is specifically of value to GM if GM owns these assets than if Fisher does. This result can be expressed more informally as follows: a worker will put more weight on an actor's objectives if that actor is the worker's boss, that is, if that actor controls the assets the worker works with, than otherwise. The conclusion is quite Coasian in spirit, but the logic underlying it is very different. Coase reaches this conclusion by assuming that a boss can tell a worker what to do; in contrast, the property rights approach reaches it by showing that it is in a worker's self-interest to behave in this way, since it puts him in a stronger bargaining position with his boss later on.

To put it slightly differently, the reason an employee is likely to be more responsive to what his employer wants than a grocer is to what his customer wants is that the employer has much more leverage over his employee than the customer has over his grocer. In particular, the employer can deprive the employee of the assets he works with and hire another employee to work with these assets, while the customer can only deprive the grocer of his custom and as long as the customer is small, it is presumably not very difficult for the grocer to find another customer.

....

3. Property Rights and the Established Theories of the Firm

The property rights approach has features in common with each of the approaches described previously.[47] It is based on maximizing behavior (like the neoclassical approach); it emphasizes incentive issues (like the principal-agent approach); it emphasizes contracting costs (like the transaction cost approach); it treats the firm as a 'standard form' contract (like the nexus of contracts approach);[48] and, it relies on the idea that a firm's owner has the right to alter membership of the firm: the owner has the right to decide who uses the firm's assets and who doesn't.[49] Its advantage over these other approaches, however, is its ability to explain both the costs and the benefits of integration; in particular, it shows how incentives change when one firm buys up another one.

Some react skeptically to the notion that a firm can be characterized completely by the nonhuman assets under its control.[50] That is, there is a feeling that one should be able to make sense of a firm as a mode of organization, even if there are no definable assets on the scene. In his analysis of GM's decision to acquire Fisher Body in 1926, Professor Klein argues that getting control over Fisher's organizational assets rather than their physical capital was the crucial motivating factor:

By integrating with Fisher, General Motors acquired the Fisher Body organizational capital. This organization is embedded in the human capital of the employees at Fisher but is in some sense greater than the sum of its parts. The employees come and go but the organization maintains the memory of past trials and the knowledge of how to best do something (that is, how to make automobile bodies).[51]

Klein's conclusion is in no way inconsistent with the property rights approach. The control of physical capital can lead to control of human assets in the form of organizational capital.[52] However, Klein appears to argue that his conclusion would hold true even if physical assets were irrelevant.[53] The problem with this point of view is that, in the absence of physical assets, it is unclear how GM can get control over an intangible asset like organizational capital by purchasing Fisher. For example, what is to stop Fisher management from trying to reassert control of the organizational capital after the merger? Klein writes:

A threat that all the individuals will simultaneously shirk or leave if their wages were not increased to reflect the quasirents on the organizational capital generally will not be credible. After vertical integration the Fisher brothers will not be able to hold up General Motors by telling all the employees to leave General Motors and show up on Monday morning at a new address.[54]

This conclusion is reasonable when physical capital is important since it would be difficult at best for Fisher employees to find a substitute for this capital, particularly by Monday morning. However, it is not reasonable in the absence of physical assets. In this case, to paraphrase Alchian and Demsetz, the Fisher brothers have no more ability to hold up GM by telling all the employees to leave GM or, more generally, by countermanding GM's instructions, when Fisher is separate than when Fisher belongs to GM. Their ability to do so will be determined by factors such as the motivation, talent, knowledge and charisma of the Fisher brothers; the quality of worker information;[55] and the degree of worker inertia—factors that do not seem to have anything to do with ownership structure. To put it another way, GM's response to a hold-up attempt by the Fisher brothers will be the same whether GM owns Fisher or Fisher is independent: to try to persuade Fisher workers to desert the Fisher brothers and join GM.[56]

As noted previously, one of the weaknesses of the property rights approach as described here is that it does not take account of the separation of ownership and control present in large, publicly held corporations.[57] In principle, it should be possible to extend the existing analysis to such situations. A public corporation can still be usefully considered a collection of assets, with ownership providing control rights over these assets. Now, however, the picture is more complicated. Although owners (shareholders) typically retain some control rights, such as the rights to replace the board of directors, in practice they delegate many others to management, at least on a day-to-day basis.[58] In addition, some of the shareholders' rights shift to creditors during periods of financial distress. Developing a formal model of the firm that contains all these features, and that includes also an explanation of the firm's financial structure, is an important and challenging task for future research. Fortunately, recent work suggests that the task is not an impossible one.[59]

4. Conclusion

This article began with the observation that the portrayal of the firm in neoclassical economics is a caricature of the modern firm. It then went on to discuss some other approaches that attempt to develop a more realistic picture. The end product to date is still, in many ways, a caricature, but perhaps not such an unreasonable one. One promising sign is that the different approaches economists have used to address this issue—neoclassical, principal-agent, transaction cost, nexus of contracts, property rights— appear to be converging. It is to be hoped that in the next few years the best aspects of each of these approaches can be drawn on to develop a more comprehensive and realistic theory of the firm. Such a theory would capture the salient features both of modern corporations and of owner-managed firms, and would illuminate the issues for economists and lawyers alike.

Notes

1. Several recent surveys provide other perspectives on this material. See, e.g., Holmstrom & Tirole, 'The Theory of the Firm' in 1 *Handbook of Industrial Organization* (R. Schmalensee & R. Willig eds., forthcoming 1989); Milgrom & Roberts, 'Economic Theories of the Firm: Past, Present and Future', 21 *Can. J. Econ.* 444 (1988); Williamson, 'The Logic of Economic Organization', 4 *J. L. Econ. & Organization* 65 (1988).
2. See, e.g. J. Henderson & R. Quandt, *Microeconomic Theory: A Mathematical Approach* 64–134 (1980); H. Varian, *Microeconomic Analysis* 6–78 (1984).
3. For example, one feasible plan might be to use 10 person-hours and one acre of land to produce one hundred pounds of wheat, while another feasible plan might be to use 12 person-hours and one and one-half acres to produce fifty pounds of corn.

4. See H. Varian, *supra* n. 2, at 47; Bishop, 'The Effects of Specific and Ad Valorem Taxes, 82 *Q. J. Econ.* 198 (1968).

5. See J. Tirole, *The Theory of Industrial Organization* 205–301 (1988).

6. See, e.g., Holmstrom, 'Moral Hazard and Observability', 10 *Bell J. Econ.* 74 (1979); Shavell, 'Risk Sharing and Incentives in the Principal and Agent Relationship', 10 *Bell J. Econ.* 55 (1979). For a recent survey, see Hart & Holmstrom, 'The Theory of Contracts', in *Advances in Economic Theory: Fifth World Congress* 71, 75–106 (T. Bewley ed. 1987).

7. It is also possible to extend the principal-agent view of the firm to analyze conflicts of interests between managers and workers, and those between managers and consumers. See Calvo & Wellisz, 'Supervision, Loss of Control and the Optimum Size of the Firm', 86 *J. Pol. Econ.* 943 (1978).

8. I will discuss the GM-Fisher Body relationship at several points in the text. In doing so, I draw on material from Klein, Crawford & Alchian, 'Vertical Integration, Appropriable Rents, and the Competitive Contracting Process', 21 *J. L. & Econ.* 297, 308–10 (1978); Klein, 'Vertical Integration as Organizational Ownership: The Fisher Body-General Motors Relationship Revisited', 4 *J. L. Econ. & Organization* 199 (1988).

9. As a matter of history, GM and Fisher started off as separate firms linked by a long-term contract, but after a dispute GM bought Fisher in 1926. Klein, Crawford & Alchian, *supra* n. 8, at 310.

10. Drawing a parallel might be possible if, say, profit- or cost-sharing arrangements were only found within a single firm. This is not the case, however. For example, consider cost-plus contracts between the United States Government and private defense contractors. See generally F. Scherer, *The Weapons Acquisition Process: Economic Incentives* 131–309 (1964) for a discussion of defense contracts.

11. Coase, 'The Nature of the Firm', 4 *Economica* 386 (1937).

12. One can distinguish between learning and haggling costs incurred at the beginning of the relationship when the parties reach an initial agreement and those incurred as the relationship proceeds and the parties revise their agreement. For present purposes, the latter costs are more important.

13. A related idea can be found in Simon, 'A Formal Theory of the Employment Relationship', 19 *Econometrica* 293 (1951) (arguing that it is efficient for employee to accept employer's authority if employee is approximately indifferent about tasks he performs, but employer has a strict preference). It is also worth noting that the superior adaptive properties of the employment relation were emphasized by Chester Barnard at around the same time that Coase was writing. See C. Barnard, *The Functions of the Executive* 139–60 (1938) (discussing incentives necessary to induce individuals to contribute to organizations).

14. Coase, 'Nature of the Firm', 395.

15. In Coase's words, they were 'much cited and little used' (until the 1970s). Coase, 'The Nature of the Firm: Influence', 4 *J. L. Econ. & Organization* 33, 33 (1988).

16. Alchian & Demsetz, 'Production, Information Costs, and Economic Organization', 62 *Am. Econ. Rev.* 777 (1972).

17. Coase, 'Nature of the Firm', 404.

18. Alchian & Demsetz, 'Production, Information Costs, and Economic Organization', 777–8, 783–4. But cf. Masten, 'A Legal Basis for the Firm', 4 *J. L. Econ. & Organization* 181, 186–7 (1988) (law makes a distinction between an employer-employee relationship and one between independent contractors, in that an employee owes her employer duties of loyalty and obedience that do not exist between independent contractors).

19. It bears noting that the second part of Coase's thesis, maintaining that firms suppress the price mechanism, is also flawed. The use of prices to allocate resources within a multidivisional firm—the phenomenon of transfer pricing, probably more common now than it was when Coase wrote—seems a fairly immediate counterexample. For a recent discussion of the use of transfer pricing, see Eccles & White, 'Price and Authority in Inter-Profit Center Transactions', 94 *Am. J. Soc.* S17 (Supp. 1988).

20. See Alchian & Demsetz, 'Production, Information Costs . . .', 783.

21. See generally O. Williamson, *The Economic Institutions of Capitalism* (1985) [hereinafter *Economic Institutions*]; O. Williamson, *Markets and Hierarchies: Analysis and Antitrust Implications* (1975). For another significant analysis of these costs, see generally Klein, Crawford & Alchian, 'Vertical Integration'.

22. See *Economic Institutions*, 30.

23. Ibid. 95–6.

24. Ibid. 61. For empirical evidence on the importance of relationship-specific investments and lock-in effects, see Joskow, 'Asset Specificity and the Structure of Vertical Relationships: Empirical Evidence, 4 *J. L. Econ. & Organization* 95 (1988).

25. *Economic Institutions*, 21.

26. Ibid. 88–9.

27. Ibid. 30–2.

28. Williamson argues that a major benefit of integration comes from the fact that the party with authority can resolve disputes by fiat (as opposed to litigation), while a major cost comes from the fact that the party with authority cannot commit himself to intervene selectively in the affairs of other parties. See ibid. 76, 133–5. Williamson, however, is not very clear about what mechanisms are at work here. For example, a boss may try to resolve a dispute, but what guarantee is there that the parties will follow his edicts? To paraphrase Alchian and Demsetz, what disciplinary power does a boss have that an independent contractor does not? A similar issue arises with regard to selective intervention. In what activities will the boss intervene, and how will this intervention be enforced? What power to intervene does a boss have that an independent contractor does not have? See *supra* notes 16–18 and accompanying text.

    The greater powers of a boss relative to an independent contractor can be understood if one takes a property rights-based view of the firm—in particular, if one recognizes that a firm consists of nonhuman assets as well as human assets and that a boss typically has control over these nonhuman assets. See *infra* notes 33–46 and accompanying text.

29. The nexus of contract theory is often associated with Jensen and Meckling. See

Jensen & Meckling. 'Theory of the Firm: Managerial Behavior, Agency Costs and Ownership Structure'. 3 *J. Fin. Econ.* 305, 310 (1976).

30. Note that lawyers' and economists' ideas of what constitutes a contract may differ. Economists tend to view contracts as relationships characterized by reciprocal expectations and behavior: lawyers consider the enforceable legal duties implicit in such relationships and look for formalization through the standard indicia of contract formation, such as offer and acceptance. See Gordon, 'The Mandatory Structure of Corporate Law', 89 *Colum. L. Rev.* 1549, 1549–50 (1989).

31. Jensen & Meckling, 'Theory of the Firm', 311.

32. See generally Grossman & Hart, 'The Costs and Benefits of Ownership: A Theory of Vertical and Lateral Integration', 94 *J. Pol. Econ.* 691 (1986); Holmstream & Tirole, 'The Theory of the Firm'; O. Hart & J. Moore, 'Property Rights and the Nature of the Firm' (Massachusetts Institute of Technology, Dept. of Economics Working Paper No. 495, 1988). This literature owes much to the earlier property rights literature on the efficiency of private property in an externality-free world. See, e.g., Demsetz, 'Toward a Theory of Property Rights', *Am Econ. Rev.*, May 1967, 347.

33. This view of ownership seems consistent with the standard one adopted by lawyers: 'But what are the rights of ownership? They are substantially the same as those incident to possession. Within the limits prescribed by policy, the owner is allowed to exercise his natural powers over the subject-matter uninterfered with, and is more or less protected in excluding other people from such interference. The owner is allowed to exclude all, and is accountable to no one.' O. Holmes, *The Common Law* 193 (1963 ed.).

34. This consolidation of ownership and control points to an important lacuna in the property rights approach. The approach makes no distinction between ownership and control, assuming that both rest with the same entity. In most of the formal models that have been developed, such an arrangement turns out to be optimal since agents are assumed to be risk-neutral and to have sufficient wealth to buy any asset. If managers were risk-averse and had limited wealth, however, this conclusion would no longer be valid. Moreover, from a descriptive point of view, the assumption that owners manage is seriously inadequate; while it may apply to small firms such as partnerships or closed corporations, it certainly does not apply to large, publicly held corporations. For how the ownership/control dichotomy might affect the property rights approach. see *infra* notes 58–9 and accompanying text.

35. It is important to emphasize that the property rights approach distinguishes between ownership in the sense of possession of residual control rights over assets and ownership in the sense of entitlement to a firm's (verifiable) profit stream. In practice, these rights will often go together, but they do not have to. The property rights approach takes the point of view that the possession of control rights is crucial for the integration decision. That is, if firm *A* wants to acquire part of firm *B*'s (verifiable) profit stream, it can always do this by

contract. It is only if firm A wants to acquire control over firm B's assets that it needs to integrate.

36. See *supra* note. 8.

37. If current Fisher management is indispensable for the operation of Fisher assets, there is, of course, no difference between the two threats. It is rare, however, that current management is completely irreplaceable.

38. It should be emphasized that there is no inconsistency in assuming that an initial contract is incomplete and at the same time that the parties anticipate how the ex post surplus will be divided up as a result of this incompleteness. For example, suppose there are many individually unlikely states with similar characteristics to an uncontracted-for increase in demand. It may be prohibitively expensive for the parties to contract for each of these states, and yet they may be well aware of the average degree to which their investments will be expropriated as a result of not contracting for these states.

39. Under some conditions expropriation problems can be avoided regardless of organizational form. One possibility is for the parties to write an ex ante profit-sharing agreement. However, a profit-sharing agreement may be insufficient to encourage ex ante investments to the extent that some returns from an asset's use are unverifiable. Examples of unverifiable returns are effort costs, nonmonetary rewards such as perks, and monetary returns that can be diverted so that they do not show up in the firm's accounts.

    Another way the parties might overcome expropriation problems is to share investment expenditure. For example, if Fisher and GM are independent, Fisher could compensate GM for its later hold-up power by contributing towards GM's initial Fisher-specific investment. Note, however, that this strategy will work only to the extent that either GM contractually agrees to make the investment or Fisher can make part of the investment on GM's behalf. Otherwise, GM could use an up-front payment from Fisher to make a *non*relationship-specific investment.

40. This is not quite correct since the worker will actually bargain with GM management rather than with GM shareholders, who are arguably the ultimate beneficiaries. However, it is approximately correct to the extent that, perhaps because GM management is on an incentive scheme, GM management benefits from an increase in GM's profit or market value. For the remainder of the discussion, we will, at a cost both in precision and realism, ignore the distinction between management and shareholders, and also treat management as a monolithic group. But see *supra* note 34; *infra* note. 46 (explaining how this analysis can be generalized to include more complicated forms of group ownership); *infra* notes 58–9 and accompanying text.

41. We assume that no payment was specified for the improved product in the initial contract.

42. For a formal treatment of the division of surplus, see O. Hart & J. Moore, 'Property Rights', 11. The numbers one-half and one-third should not be taken too seriously. The important point is that, in the context described, the worker is

likely to get a larger share of his increased marginal product when GM controls the assets than when Fisher does.

43. See ibid. 11, 19.

44. For examples of lock-in effects, see *supra* notes 22–4 and accompanying text.

45. Klein, Crawford & Alchian, 'Vertical Integration' 300. However, Klein, Crawford and Alchian fail to provide a formal justification for this notion.

46. In the above we have concentrated on ownership by an individual or by a homogeneous and monolithic group ('management'). However, the analysis can be generalized to include more complicated forms of group ownership, such as partnerships, or worker-, manager-, or consumer-cooperatives. It turns out that these will be efficient when increases in agents' marginal products are specific to a group of individuals of variable composition, rather than to a fixed group. For example, if the increase in an agent's marginal product can be realized only if the agent has access to a majority of the members of a management team, as well as to a particular asset, then it will be optimal to give each of the managers an equal ownership share in the asset and equal voting rights, and adopt majority rule. See O. Hart & J. Moore, 'Property Rights', 19.

47. See *supra* notes 2–31 and accompanying text.

48. In the language of the property rights approach, 'firm' is shorthand for a collection of assets; 'ownership' is shorthand fo the possession of residual rights of control over these assets.

49. See Alchian & Demsetz, 'Production, Information Costs, and Economic Organization', 783 (manager should have right to alter membership of production team).

50. See, e.g., Klein 'Vertical Integration as Organizational Ownership, 205–8.

51. Ibid. 208.

52. See *supra* notes 32–46 and accompanying text. Note that the observation that the whole of organizational capital is typically greater than the sum of its parts is equivalent to the observation that the total output of a group of workers typically exceeds the sum of the workers' individual outputs, to the extent that there are complementarities.

53. Klein, 'Vertical Integration', 208 n. 11.

54. Ibid. 208.

55. See G. Mailath & A. Postlewaite, 'Workers Versus Firms: Bargaining Over a Firm's Value' 14 (University of Pennsylvania, Center for Analytic Research in Economics and the Social Sciences Working Paper No. 88–11, 1988).

56. This is not without qualification. It can be argued that if GM acquires Fisher, Fisher workers become liable for damages if they try to organize a new firm since, as employees, they owe GM a duty of loyalty. See Masten, 'Legal Basis for the Firm', 189. But, in practice, employees *do* leave to form new firms. Moreover, the courts facilitate this process by sometimes hesitating to enforce covenants not to compete even when such covenants are explicit. See, e.g., E. Farnsworth, *Contracts* § 5.3 at 337–8 (1982) (courts enforce non-compete covenants 'only if . . . employee acquired confidential information' in course of

employment). Thus, it is unclear how important this factor could have been in the GM-Fisher acquisition.

57. See *supra* note 34.

58. See, e.g., Clark, 'Agency Costs Versus Fiduciary Duties', in *Principals and Agents: The Structure of Business* 55 (J. Pratt & R. Zeckhauser eds., 1985); Easterbrook & Fischel, 'Voting in Corporate Law', 26 *J. L. & Econ.* 395 (1983); Fama & Jensen, 'Separation of Ownership and Control', 26 *J. L. & Econ.* 301 (1983).

59. See e.g., Grossman & Hart, 'One Share-One Vote and the Market for Corporate Control', 20 *J. Fin. Econ.* 175 (1988); Harris & Raviv, 'Corporate Governance: Voting Rights and Majority Rules', 20 *J. Fin. Econ.* 203 (1988); P. Aghion & P. Bolton, 'An "Integrated complete Contract', Approach to Bankruptcy and the Financial Structure of the Firm, (Stanford University, Institute for Mathematical Studies in the Social Sciences Technical Report No. 536, 1988); C. Kahn & G. Huberman, 'Default, Foreclosure, and Strategic Renegotiation' (paper presented at Conference on Economics of Contract Law, Duke University, March 1988).

II. MARKETS AND INDUSTRIAL ORGANIZATION

Just as the readings in Section I demonstrate that the concept of the 'firm' is not a simple one, so the readings in Section II demonstrate that the same is true for the concept of the 'market'. Supposedly market processes are repeatedly found to be highly organized events with, in the words of the title of the piece from Imai and Itami, a degree of 'interpenetration of firm and market'. The question of 'what is a firm?' was presented above with the alternative to the firm being the individual undertaking productive activities alone (contracting via the market). The distinction in this section is not between the firm and the individual but rather between the firm and the market. The question then arises whether a clear dichotomy really exists between a production process organized consciously by a firm, on the one hand, and a market process guided by an invisible hand on the other? Once again, there is found to be no clear dichotomy; rather, the organization of industry is characterized by a range of cooperative arrangements and agreements between firms, in the market (as analysed in the paper by Mariti and Smiley). No clear dichotomy exists between the integrated firm and the disintegrated market, but rather a range of quasi-integration is found, with many activities being neither contracted for simply through the market nor organized internally by firms, but rather as a result of agreements across firms (as analysed in the context of vertical quasi-integration in the paper by Blois).

Thus, the idea that the 'market' is something necessarily quite distinct and separate from productive activities which result from conscious, human organizational efforts, needs to be discarded. So too should the idea of an

Section II

invisible hand uninfluenced by corporate culture (as discussed in the article by Kreps) or goodwill (as expounded on in the paper from Dore). The hand is often visible and its nature certainly differs from market to market, across cultures, states and over time. How the resulting 'market' relations between businesses actually operate, and in particular to what extent legal contracts are entered into and how these are used, is discussed in the paper by Macaulay.

8 Corporate Culture and Economic Theory

David M. Kreps

1. Introduction

In this chapter, I explore how an economic theorist might explain or model a concept such as corporate culture. While the theoretical construction that is given is far from inclusive (which is to say that many aspects of corporate culture are not covered), I conclude that economic theory is moving in the direction of what seems a reasonable story. But before that story can be considered told, we must employ tools that are currently missing from the economist's tool kit. In particular, we require a framework for dealing with the unforeseen.

I can give two explanations for why I present this topic. The first concerns

This work was prepared in 1984 for presentation to the Second Mitsubishi Bank Foundation Conference on Technology and Business Strategy. It subsequently appeared in Japanese in *Technological Innovation and Business Strategy*, M. Tsuchiya (ed.), Nippon Keizai Shimbunsha Press, Tokyo, 1986, and appears here in English with the kind permission of the previous publishers. The chapter surveys the current state of research and is, of course, quite dated now. But, with the kind permission of the current editors, it appears now much as it was written in 1984, except that references have been updated where appropriate and punctuation and English have been made more correct. In a very brief postscript, following the appendix, I engage in a bit of updating and revisionist thinking. And, in one place in the text, where it is too painful to reread what I wrote, I alert the reader that something more on this issue will be said in the postscript.

I have benefited from discussion with too many colleagues to give a comprehensive list, but two individuals must be cited for particularly helpful ideas: Jose Scheinkman, concerning the overlapping generations model, and Bengt Holmstrom for stressing to me the important distinction between observability and verifiability. The financial assistance of the National Science Foundation (Grants SES–8006407 and SES–8408468), the Sloan Foundation, and the Mitsubishi Bank Foundation are all gratefully acknowledged.

how economists (and those weaned on the economic paradigm) deal with the topic of business strategy. If we take Porter (or Caves or Spence) as the prototype, business strategy could roughly be called applied industrial organization. The firm and its capabilities are more or less taken as givens, and one looks at the tangible characteristics of an industry to explain profitability. It sometimes seems, in this approach, that there are good industries (or segments of industries) and bad: find yourself in a bad industry (low entry barriers, many substitutes, powerful customers and suppliers, many and surly competitors), and you can do nothing except get out at the first opportunity. Now, this is assuredly a caricature of the Porter approach. The size of entry barriers, relations with suppliers / customers, and, especially, competitive discipline within an industry are all at least partially endogenous. Bad industries can sometimes be made good, and (perhaps a more accurate rendering of Porter) good niches can be found or formed even in bad industries.

This approach carries with it a powerful legacy from textbook micro-economics: The firm is an exogenously specified cost function or production possibilities set, and market structures (also exogenous) determine how it will fare. The actual purpose of the firm qua organization is not considered. This is rather strange, for if one has an economic mind-set, one must believe that the firm itself performs some economic (efficiency-promoting) function. From there it is a short step to consider as part, perhaps the largest part, of successful strategy those actions designed to increase the firm's organizational efficiency.[1] But since textbook economics doesn't explain firms qua organizations, it comes up empty as a discipline for analyzing this part of strategy.

Of course, disciplines other than economics deal with organizational efficiency or effectiveness. One could simply assert that Porter's approach is incomplete, to be supplemented or, better, taken concurrently with other disciplines and approaches. The dangers here are that prescriptions from the economic approach may interact negatively with organizational efficiency in specific cases and that individuals trained in one approach may ignore the other. In order to reduce these dangers, it seems a good idea to develop a theory that addresses issues of organizational efficiency in the language of economics and then to integrate it with Porter-style analysis.

When I say that economics has not come to grips with issues of implementation, I mean standard textbook economics. I believe that the foundations for such analysis have been and are being laid. There are the obvious and very visible contributors: Williamson and his colleagues. But I believe that 'higher' theorists (which, in economics, means more mathematical) dealing in such topics as agency theory, the theory of repeated games and reputation, and (less formally) the theory of focal points in noncooperative games should also be counted.

This, then, gives rise to my second and primary reason for writing this chapter. I think economists are moving in a profitable direction, and I want to present the outlines of the theory that is developing. I hope in so doing to interest readers in further developments.

With my objectives stated, I can describe the nature of this chapter. With significant exceptions, no new theory is being presented here. What little is new is undeveloped—it constitutes conjecture and little else. This chapter is meant to be expositional and exploratory and, perhaps, just a bit synthetic: I want to sketch out the pieces of the theory that have been developed, to connect them (as they are connected in my mind), and to conjecture as to what is missing. (Needless to say, what is missing largely coincides with my current research agenda.) I have tried as much as possible to stay away from technical details; sometimes, however, this has been impossible to avoid, and I apologize.

This chapter sprawls somewhat, but I have in mind a very definite plot that ties things together. At the risk of completely losing the reader, let me give here an outline of the plot. It has three fundamental building blocks. The first is that in many transactions, in particular ongoing ones, contingencies typically arise that were unforeseen at the time of the transaction itself. Many transactions will potentially be too costly to undertake if the participants cannot rely on efficient and equitable adaptation to those unforeseen contingencies. Note that such reliance will necessarily involve blind faith; if we cannot foresee a contingency, we cannot know in advance that we can efficiently and equitably meet it. (For those who find the notion of an unforeseen contingency unpalatable, we could equally well imagine how costly it is to specify how every contingency will be met.)

Transactions can be characterized by the adjudication processes that meet unforeseen contingencies. In particular, some transactions will be hierarchical in that one party will have much more authority in saying what adaptation will take place. The firm (or other organization) is meant in this theory to play the canonical role of the authorative party: When I am employed by a firm, I accept within broad limits the firm's right, as expressed by my superior, to specify how my time will be spent as contingencies arise. Or, to take another example, when students attend a university, they accept the university's right, through its administrators, to spell out the terms of the commodity students have bought.[2]

If employees or students are to grant such authority to a firm or university, they must believe that it will be used fairly. What is the source of this faith? It is that the firm and university are characterized by their reputations. The way an organization adapts to an unforeseen contingency can add to or detract from that reputation, with consequences for the amount of faith future employees or students will have. This faith is the glue that permits mutually beneficial transactions to take place, transactions that would otherwise not be made because of their costs. The organization, or, more precisely, those in the organization who have decision-making authority, will have an interest in preserving or even promoting a good reputation to allow for future beneficial transactions. Thus, workers or students can trust the organization to act equitably in its own interest to protect its valuable reputation. Note that the organization must be an ongoing entity here: if ever it loses its incentive to protect its reputation, an incentive derived from the incentive to undertake future beneficial transactions, then it can no longer be trusted, and the hierarchical transaction will fall apart.[3]

With these three blocks in place, we come to corporate culture. In order for a reputation to have an effect, both sides involved in a transaction must *ex ante* have some idea of the meaning of appropriate or equitable fulfillment of the contract. Potential future trading partners must be able to observe fulfillment (or lack of) by the hierarchically superior party. These things are necessary; otherwise the hierarchically superior party's reputation turns on nothing. When we speak of adaptation to unforeseen contingencies, however, we cannot specify *ex ante* how those contingencies will be met. We can at best give some sort of principle or rule that has wide (preferably universal) applicability and that is simple enough to be interpreted by all concerned. In the language of game theory, unforeseen contingencies are best met by the sort of principle that underlies what Schelling (1960) calls a focal point. The organization will be characterized by the principle it selects. It will (optimally) try to promote understanding of that principle in the minds of its hierarchical inferiors. In order to protect its reputation for applying the principle in all cases, it will apply the principle even when its application might not be optimal in the short run. It will apply the principle even in areas where it serves no direct organizational objective, if doing so helps preserve or clarify the principle. Because decision-making authority in a firm is diffuse, those who make decisions in the firm's name will be judged by their diligence in applying and embracing the principle. In this light, I interpret corporate culture as partly the principle itself (or, more realistically, the interrelated principles that the organization employs) and partly the means by which the principle is communicated to hierarchical inferiors (so they can monitor its application) and hierarchical superiors (so they can apply it faithfully). It says how things are done, and how they are meant to be done in the organization. Because it will be designed through time to meet unforeseen contingencies as they arise, it will be the product of evolution inside the organization and will be influenced by the organization's history.

This, very roughly, is the economic theory of corporate culture that I wish to lay out. As noted earlier, this theory captures at most one face of corporate culture. The economic paradigm also contains explanations that rely on the screening function of internal cultures. Outside of the economic paradigm, at least so far as I can see, are explanations that rely on concepts such as need for affiliation and other things that I know nothing about. I don't mean to advance the theory as all inclusive; rather, it fits in well with recent advances in the economic theory.

Rather than proceeding with the theory as already outlined, I will first exposit those pieces of the story that are in the extant literature and then go on to pieces that are missing or underdeveloped. This will make the basic plot harder to understand, but if readers can keep this plot in mind it will make it easier to see how several strands in economic theory interrelate. Since underlying this plot is the basic need to render efficient otherwise inefficient transactions, I begin with a section on the basic transactions theory of Coase and Williamson. I give here as well the standard criticism of Williamson: he analyzes why (and when) market-based transactions are costly but insufficiently justifies his assumption that when market-based transactions are costly, hierarchy-based transactions are not equally (or more) costly.

Next, in the section on Grossman and Hart, I discuss a recent paper by those authors (1986) that gives an example of an adjudication process for dealing with unforeseen (or, more precisely, uncontracted-for contingencies. In their model the authority to decide to employ capital rests with the legal owners of the capital. The authors use this, together with an inability to contract for certain contingencies, to explain particular patterns of ownership for particular transactions. This is not quite the theory I will later employ— authority in hierarchical transactions is typically much less tangibly based than in something like ownership—but it provides a reference point for the type of theory I am suggesting.

In the next section, the parts of game theory that are needed to discuss reputation are put in place and are used to make a first pass at theory of the firm. The section begins by reviewing repeated games, in folk theorem, and implicit contracts, and then recasts the folk theorem into a story of reputation.

Finally, I give a simple parable that shows how something as intangible as a reputation could become an economic good—one that economic actors would invest in and, when the time comes, sell. This gives us a rather pat explanation for what a firm is: an intangible asset carrying a reputation that is beneficial for efficient transactions, conferring that reputation upon whoever currently owns the asset.

The theory developed in the section on reputation will seem rather disconnected from notions such as corporated culture, or even from the concept of a hierarchical transaction. But in later sections, I will use the reputation construction to move in the direction of these ideas. The first step is to make the basic reputation construction encompass transactions that are hierarchical in the sense already given. This is the subject of the section titled 'Hierarchical Transactions'. Also in this section, we refine a point made in the previous section: Reputations for behaving in a particular way work more efficiently the more deviations from that behavior are observable.

Through the section on hierarchical transactions, we will work within the standard framework of neoclassical microeconomics. The theory developed in the sections on reputation and hierarchical transactions plays entirely within the usual rules of economic theory. As a consequence of this, however, it does not provide a very good case for its own importance. A stronger case emerges if one considers the possibility of contingencies arising that parties to a particular transaction have not *ex ante* thought through, either because they were *ex ante* unimaginable or because it is simply too costly to think through all possible contingencies. The section on unforeseen contingencies that follows also speculates as to how a (useful) formal theory of this sort of unforeseen contingencies might develop. Then, the section on focal points takes a brief excursion into Schelling's (1960) very underdeveloped area of game theory. This concept of focal points will play an important role in the theory finally constructed in the section titled 'Corporate Culture'.

In this last-mentioned section, the various pieces are assembled into an economic theory of the role of corporate culture. More precisely, the outlines of such a theory, together with some conjectures as to where that theory might lead, are given. It is my hope that the theory will be in line with the well-developed theories reported in earlier sections and that readers will see that the final steps, while not yet accomplished, are not excessively difficult to traverse. Concluding remarks and questions are given in the final section.

2. Williamson, Transaction Costs, and the Theory of the Firm

Following in the footsteps of Coase (1937), Simon (1965), and Arrow (1974), among others, Williamson and his students have been developing a theory of what hierarchical organizations such as firms accomplish. Williamson states this theory most fully in his 1975 book—his more recent work and a very good summary statement can be found in his 1981 article.

The heart of the theory is the concept of transaction costs. For parties to consummate a transaction or an exchange they must expend resources other than those contained in the terms of the transaction. Among these transaction costs are resources expended to spell-out in advance the terms of the transaction, so that each side knows what it is getting, and resources expended to enforce the terms of the transaction. Textbook economic theory, which calls for the images of the exchange of one physical good for a second or of one physical good for money, tends to treat transaction costs as being near enough to zero to be ignored. Costs can, however, be substantial in more complex transactions, such as those in which one party sells labor to the other, in which the good sold has hidden qualities or in which one side must sink resources in preparing for the transaction before the other side fulfills its part of the bargain. In deciding whether to undertake a transaction, both parties must weigh the benefits they will accrue, net of the cost of transacting. Transactions that give the parties positive benefits gross of transaction costs (which, according to textbook economics, would therefore take place) may not give benefits sufficient to cover the transaction costs and so will not take place.

The organizational structure the transaction takes place within can affect transaction costs. An exchange in the marketplace may be more or less costly than the same exchange in a hierarchical organization. Holding benefits constant, a transaction will tend to occur within whatever infrastructure minimizes its cost. When transactions take place in firms, the presumption (and direction for analysis) should be that the transactions are less costly within the firm than they would be in the marketplace.

That, very briefly, is the basic theory that Coase advanced (1937) and that Williamson extended and elaborated on. The study of markets and other organizations that transactions take place in becomes a study of the relative transaction costs within those organizations. Note well the type of firm in this analysis: the firm is like individual agents in textbook economics, which finds its highest expression in general equilibrium theory (see Debreu 1959, Arrow and Hahn 1971). The firm transacts with other firms and with individuals in the market. Agents have utility functions, firms have a profit motive; agents have consumption sets, firms have production possibility sets. But in transaction-cost economics, firms are more like markets—both are arenas within which individuals can transact. Indeed, we might think of firms as market places, contrasting them with other marketplaces, such as the stock exchanges, within all of which transactions take place.

Williamson goes on to study five factors that make transactions relatively more costly. He divides these factors into two categories—those that pertain to the transaction itself and those that pertain to the parties to the transaction. The transaction itself can be described according to its complexity, which includes the amount of uncertainty that the transaction bears, especially uncertainty about future contingencies; according to the thinness of the transaction, or the number of alternative trading partners involved in it; and according to the extent of impacted information in it, information some but not all parties to the transaction possess. Their transacting parties may be more or less opportunistic, in that they pursue selfish interests in a guileful manner. They may also be limitedly rational, in that it is costly and sometimes impossible for them to carry out all the computations required to find a truly optimal course of action or to elaborate and think through all contingencies that might bear on the transaction. Relatively greater complexity and/or thinness and/or impacted information, joined with relatively greater guile and/or relative more limited rationality, will raise transaction costs.

Williamson goes on to analyze particular scenarios in which transaction costs are high, suggesting that in these cases there is a clear case for organizing the transaction in a hierarchy rather than in a traditional marketplace. Examples drawn from Williamson (1981) include vertical integration, when costs need to be sunk in transaction-specific capital before the transaction is actually executed, and franchising, when the quality of the good sold depends in part on services a sales-person delivers.

Williamson builds quite a substantial case in these and other instances for large transaction costs in market-mediated transactions. He is less convincing in arguing that transacting through a hierarchical organization lessens transaction costs. This is a frequent criticism of his work: He explicitly recognizes that transacting through a hierarchical framework incurs costs (what he sometimes refers to as the costs of bureaucracy), but he doesn't say enough about how they would differ from market-mediated transaction costs. Increasing the five factors cited will mainly increase market-mediated transaction costs. There is little reason, though, to think that these factors will not simultaneously increase (and perhaps by more) hierarchy-mediated transaction costs. Therefore we cannot, without a leap of faith, expect to see more hierarchical mediation and less market mediation in transactions with large levels of Williamson's five factors. This is not to say that we do not see this; casual empiricism suggests that we do, and overwhelmingly so. But the argument why this is so has not been completely made (please see the postscript).

3. Grossman and Hart and the Residual Rights Conferred by Ownership

One hinge on which the argument could turn is the legally mandated default clauses in contracts. Grossman and Hart make such an argument in a recent article (1986). They give a story for Williamson's vertical integration due to transaction-specific capital. Roughly put, they argue that contracts that would be optimal under vertical disintegration and a market transaction cannot be written, while contracts that would be more efficient in an integrated setting can be. The key to their argument is the notion of residual rights; owners of capital equipment own the right to use that capital as they see fit, subject to the specific contractual arrangements that have been made. If certain contingent contracts cannot be made (because they are costly to make or enforce), then the second-best arrangement between an upstream and a downstream entity might well be one where the residual rights associated with capital ownership are concentrated in one hand. Grossman and Hart suppose that detailed contingent contracts cannot be made and thus that ownership (and the residual rights thereby entailed) changes the space of feasible contracts (a 'contract' here means all clauses, including unwritable ones that are nonetheless created by a pattern of ownership). In such a case, they show that certain ownership patterns for physical capital might be more efficient that others.

Besides providing an interesting analysis, Grossman and Hart point us in what I believe is the right direction to pursue. Williamson, following Coase, wishes to make the transaction the unit of analysis; Grossman and Hart do so with a vengeance. Indeed, taking Grossman and Hart at their word, one might expect a much more active market in physical capital: As the particular transaction for which that capital is employed changes, ownership of the capital (optimally) changes as well. That is, the authors explain ownership patterns for a particular transaction but not the permanence or stability of that pattern, which marks the modern corporation. (Of course, Grossman and Hart can easily defend themselves on two grounds: Insofar as other identical or even similar transactions follow the one being analyzed, the optimal ownership arrangement might be quite stable. And markets for physical capital will have severe moral hazard and adverse-selection problems.)

My point is that Grossman and Hart study the requirements for a particular (ideal) transaction and the way various institutional arrangements approximate those requirements. Theirs is not a theory of the firm per se;

rather, they entitle their work 'The Cost and Benefits of Ownership'. At the level of their analysis, capital ownership by single entrepreneurs is as likely a consequence as is ownership by an entity with a firm's legal status. One can begin with their analysis and, using other pieces, build a theory of why firms exist.[4] But their specific concern is with transaction efficiency. The tie to the theory of the firm comes from the observation that conditions conducive for efficiency in the sorts of transactions the authors examine (concentrated ownership of capital) correlate with conditions in which one finds 'firms' (efficient sharing of risk).

This leads to a second (niggling) criticism of Williamson: he tries too hard to dichotomize directly the market and the firm. It will prove more fruitful, I think, to characterize particular sorts of transactions and to then correlate the characteristics that lead to efficient transacting with firms/markets. Drawing a clean line between firms and markets will not prove possible; cleaner lines can be drawn if the transaction is the unit of analysis.

As outlined in the introduction, I develop in this chapter a dichotomy in transactions that correlates well with the distinction between firms and markets. I will also attempt to explain the source of the correlation. The dichotomy is between hierarchical transactions and, for lack of a better name, specified transactions. Roughly, in a specified transaction all terms are spelled out in advance. In a hierarchical transaction, certain terms are left unspecified; what is specified is that one of the two parties has, within broad limits, the contractual right to specify how the contract will be fulfilled. There is, to be sure, less than a perfect dichotomy here, for one can think of many other variations—for example, transactions with *ex ante* unspecified clauses, with *ex post* fulfillment determined by negotiation and requiring unanimous consent; or where the authority to determine *ex post* fulfillment is split among the parties. Here I will concentrate on arrangements where one party has the authority to determine *ex post* fulfillment, comparing this with cases where there is no need for such authority. (This notion is far from original to me; see, for example, Simon 1951.)

Note that Grossman and Hart's residual rights from ownership are very much of this flavor. They assume that the contract cannot provide for the use of the capital in certain contingencies and that the owner of the capital has the right to decide on how those contingencies will be met. The difference between their analysis and the one developed here is that they assume that ownership confers this authority and that thus the efficient placement of this authority determines the pattern of ownership. In what follows, ownership will not determine who retains hierarchical authority. Instead, we will attempt to use the notion of reputation to endogenize the determination of (efficient) authority. (This particular endogenization will provide the raison d'être for the firm—the source of correlation between firms and hierarchical

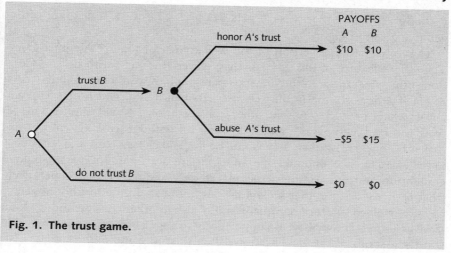

PAYOFFS

honor A's trust

$$A \quad B$$

$10 \quad $10

trust B

B

abuse A's trust

-$5 \quad $15

A

do not trust B

$0 \quad $0

Fig. 1. The trust game.

transactions, and, eventually, the role of corporate culture.) But still, the similarity is more important than the difference; they, as we, concentrate on explicit contracts that are incomplete descriptions of the transactional relationship and on how those contracts might be completed as circumstances arise.

4. Reputation and the Role of Firms

We leave for the time being transaction costs and hierarchical transactions in order to supply another of the three pieces from which the theory will be constructed—the theory of reputations that emerges from noncooperative game theory.

4.1. Repeated Games, the Folk Theorem, and Implicit Contracts

Consider an individual, A, who is playing the following game against some second party, B. First A must choose whether or not to trust B. If A elects not to trust B, then both A and B get nothing. If A elects to trust B, B is made aware of this and has the option either to honor that trust or to abuse it. If A trusts B, and B chooses to honor that trust, both get $10. But if A trusts B and

231

B chooses to abuse that trust, B gets \$15 and A loses \$5. a diagram of this game is given in Figure 1.

This is a one-sided version of the well-known prisoners' dilemma game. The salient feature of this game is that, played once and with no considerations other than those in the previous paragraph, A would not willingly trust B. For if A does so, the B must choose between honor, which nets \$10, and abuse which nets \$15. Absent other considerations, B will choose \$15. So trust will lead A to pay \$5, and A is better off without trust. Of course, this makes both worse off than they would be if A had chosen trust and B honor— in the language of economics, it is an inefficient outcome. But it is the unique equilibrium outcome of this game, played once and played noncooperatively (that is, if we assume that individuals are motivated only by the monetary payoffs involved—part of our qualification 'absent other considerations'—and if we assume that they have no opportunity to sign a binding and enforceable contract—more of the qualification—then this outcome is the unique self-enforcing outcome of this game).

This is meant to represent the archetypal transaction with some element of moral hazard. A, say, must sink some resources into preparing for a transaction with B, who can (at personal gain) take advantage of A's position to an extent that makes the entire thing unworthwhile for A.

'Absent other considerations' can now be examined. One thing that the two transacting parties might do is to sign at the outset a contract that binds B to honor. Note that *ex ante* each will willingly sign such a contract as long as it is enforceable, because without it each will net nothing. But such a contract's execution may be costly. B will have an incentive to violate the contract once A has sunk resources. So some enforcement mechanism must be provided; this could also be costly. These are typical examples of Coase/Williamsonian transaction costs. If they are sufficiently great—if, for example, enforcement costs are greater then \$20, or if the contract cannot be enforced because courts cannot distinguish between honor and abuse—then this otherwise mutually beneficial transaction will be foregone, the victim of transaction costs that are too high.

Now suppose that A and B are involved in this situation not once but repeatedly. Specifically, suppose that after each round of play, there is a 90 per cent chance that they will play at least once more and a 10 per cent chance that this (current) round will be the last. Suppose, for simplicity, that both want to maximize their winnings (less losses) from the sequence of plays. (If you wish, you can discount those winnings, but then the product of this continuation probability times the discount factor plays the role of the 90 per cent in what follows.) Now the analysis changes dramatically. A could, for example, say to B, 'I will begin by trusting you, hoping that you will honor that trust. Indeed, I will continue to trust you as long as you do not abuse that trust. But if ever you abuse that trust, I will never again trust you.' If B hears and believes this statement, B will indeed honor the trust. The following becomes the relevant calculation: abuse in any round will increase the payoff in that round by $5. But weighed against that is the fact that the payoff will be nothing in all subsequent rounds (if any). There is a 90 per cent chance of at least one more round, and if honor is chosen in that round, then in the next round at least $10 will be obtained, so the expected profits in the future from honor in this round outweigh the immediate gain of $5 from abuse.

Note that B must always have some substantial stake in the future if this is to work. If, say, there is only a 10 per cent chance of a continuation of the game or if, say, A only chooses to trust B 10 per cent of the time, then the calculation will come out the other way: B should (optimally) take the money and run.

This sort of result is the subject of the so-called folk theorem of non-cooperative game theory. It is called the folk theorem because it has been well-known for so long, and no one has the presumption to claim to have originated it. (Actually, there are many versions of the folk theorem. The earlier ones concern games that are infinitely repeated with probability one and for which an average-payoff-per-round objective function is used. For a version appropriate to the discounted game we have posed, see Fudenberg and Maskin 1986.) Roughly, the folk theorem states that we can sustain feasible expected payoffs as noncooperative equilibrium payoffs for players that are sufficiently above the worst that others can inflict on them. The term 'feasible' means that there must be some way to play the game and get those expected payoffs; for example, since the most in present value either player can get is $150 ($15/.1), we can't sustain an equilibrium for the game in which each side nets an expected $10,000. The term 'sufficiently' has to do with the discount factor and with the most players can get in the short run by defecting from the arrangement. The bigger the discount factor (the smaller the probability of continuing for another round at least), the greater must be the payoffs to be sustained as an equilibrium; and the greater the possible short-run gains, the greater must be the payoffs to be sustained. One mechanism for sustaining such payoffs as equilibria is in our example. Each player says to the other, 'As long as you stick to the arrangement that gets us the payoffs we are aiming for, we will continue to cooperate. But if you try to take short-run advantage, you will be punished.' As long as the punishment (including at least the loss of subsequent cooperation) looms large enough relative to the gains from cooperation (the source of the qualifier 'sufficiently'), neither will want to defect from the arrangement, which will become self-enforcing.

Note well what has been accomplished here. We began with a transaction that, on the face of it, looked beneficial to both sides. To assure that one side does not take advantage of the other, we argued that transaction costs would need to be expended on writing and enforcing a contract. Should that contract prove too expensive or even impossible to write or to enforce, then the transaction might not take place at all (it must be beneficial net of transaction costs). But by repeating the situation (with sufficiently high probability), we are able to avoid transaction costs entirely; the trust-honor arrangement is self-enforcing.

There are three problems with this result:

1. It says how trust-honor might emerge as an equilibrium outcome, but it allows for many other equilibria as well and doesn't offer any guidance as to which we will see. For example, in the game we began with, B might say to A, 'I intend to honor your trust two out of three times and to abuse it once every three, as long as you continue to trust me. But if ever you choose not to trust me, then I will abuse your trust every time I get the opportunity.' If A accepts such a declaration, A's best response is to trust B and take lumps every third round. The two $10 prizes outweigh (even with the 10 per cent chance of the game ending at any moment) the $5 loss A sustains every third time. The point is that each player has many feasible expected payoffs sufficiently above the maximum point of zero that can sustain an equilibrium. The theory doesn't say which will emerge; it just says that the repeated character of the situation makes them possible outcomes.

Indeed, the folk theorem requires that a person repeat this encounter over and over against the same opponent. Williamson might argue that this transaction thinness actually increases transaction costs; he certainly lists thinness as one of the cost-increasing qualities of a transaction. We see something of this arising from the richness of the equilibrium set: We can get many efficient arrangements once we repeat the encounter, but the two participants might then expend time and resources bargaining over which arrangement they will in fact follow. Having arrived at an agreement, they might expend further resources to guarantee somehow that neither side subsequently tries to renegotiate. Perhaps the cleanest way to think of the power of repetitions is to imagine that many parties of each type fall into two-party arrangements; a market-determined agreement is reached through supply and demand for partners. That is, the equilibrium reached between A and B is determined by their opportunities with other trading partners. We have the thickness needed to avoid Williamson's problems with thin markets. At the same time, repetition allows partners to trade efficiently without fixing on paper (or needing to enforce) the market-determined terms of trade. (The astute reader will see a problem in this argument: if B has many alternative trading partners, why not abuse a current trading partner and then find another? Somehow, abuse must have deleterious future consequences or the entire construction falls apart. This anticipates what will happen in the next subsection, so we leave the reader to guess the answer that will be supplied.)

2. Suppose that we modify things ever so slightly as follows: We will play the game over and over, just as before, with a 90 per cent chance each time of proceeding with another round. But should it ever be reached, the game will definitely terminate on round one hundred million. It seems unlikely that this will have much effect on the way the game is played (in experimental situations, it doesn't), but the theory suggests otherwise: If we do reach round one hundred million, then trust, if given, will surely be abused. There is at this point no future to be traded off against the current benefit from abusing trust. Thus, in round one hundred million, if reached, A should offer no trust. But then if A offers trust in round 99,999,999, it is sure to be abused: There is no point in B honoring it, because it will not be offered in the last round. Thus, trust will not be offered in round 99,999,999. And so on—the whole thing unravels from the back.

This problem, noted first by Selten (1978) and called (in a slightly different context) the chain-store paradox, can be resolved theoretically, at the cost of complicating the analysis. This is not an appropriate forum to discuss what ensues, but the basic idea runs as follows: Suppose that, at the outset, there is a small (say, one in a thousand) chance that B is the type of person who on moral grounds would never abuse trust. B knows, of course, whether he or she is of this type, but A is unsure. This small change is enough to restore for most of the game the trust-honor outcome.[5] Indeed, we get the same result if, say, A is sure that an opponent is not this sort of person and B knows that A knows this and A knows that B knows this. But B is a little unsure that A knows that B knows that A knows that B is not of this type. This can be modeled formally, and it is enough to get us back to the trust-honor outcome, as long as a large but finite number of rounds are left to go. (For the basics of the approach, see Kreps, Milgrom, Roberts, and Wilson 1982 and Kreps and Wilson 1982. This approach can help with the problem (1) of too many equilibrium outcomes, but it does not solve the problem entirely; see Fudenberg and Maskin 1986.)

3. Suppose that A cannot observe directly whether B chooses to honor or abuse A's trust. Instead, what A sees is simply a payoff from this round. Suppose that A's payoffs are not quite what we have discussed: If A trusts B and B honors that trust, then A's payoff is normally distributed with mean $10 and variance $1, whereas trust followed by abuse nets A a payoff that is normally distributed with mean $-5 and variance $1. Suppose A makes the speech that we began this section with: A will trust B as long as that trust is met with honor. A trusts B in the first round, and then A receives a payoff of $-4. If A complains that this trust has been abused, B could reply (indignantly) that this is not the case; that A was simply unlucky. And,

after all, this is a possible (but unlikely) outcome. What does A do? Carry out the threat and close off all possibilities of future cooperation? Or modify the threat to punish B (by choosing not to trust) for a long but finite length of time? And, if the second, for how long? And what should trigger this punishment?

The point is that when one player cannot observe directly that the agreement is being carried out, and when this player can only rely on noisy, indirect observations, the problem of finding self-enforcing arrangements is vastly more complicated. Some loss will necessarily result from the efficient arrangements, because some punishment will be required in any arrangements: If A never punishes, B, then B will optimally respond by always abusing A's trust. To be a viable mechanism when there is noise, punishment must be used at least occasionally. In deciding when and how much to punish B, A must consider that the quicker or more severe the punishment, the more will be lost during punishment. But the slower and less severe the punishment, the more incentive B will have to take advantage of A by abusing trust. (For a formal analysis of this type of situation, see Green and Porter 1984.)

Repetition allows for the possibility of self-enforcing implicit contracts. We needn't write down the terms of the contract, nor need we provide an enforcement mechanism for it. But because enforcement is by punishment when the contract is broken, we must be able to observe compliance. As we become less and less able to observe compliance, we become less and less able to use this device at all.

Let me throw in a remark at this point that foreshadows later developments: when we say that compliance must be observable, we naturally suppose that we understand what 'compliance' means. In simple toy problems like the one under discussion, this is not a very strong supposition, except for the problem of knowing which of the many equilibria constitutes the implicit contract. But when we turn to the real world, in which circumstances arise that no one initially foresaw or in which so many circumstances arise that it would be too costly to think through what compliance would mean to all of them, knowing what the contract calls for is problematic at best. The contract may be implicit, but that doesn't mean it is vague; the clearer it is, the better for monitoring compliance. Correspondingly, such contracts will be written in ways that give the best chance for observing compliance. Absolute clarity will not be possible in real settings, limiting the ability of participants to monitor compliance and, hence, the ability of this sort of arrangement to get us to efficient outcomes.

4.2. *Reputation*

In the game in the preceding section two participants engaged in a transaction repeatedly. This would seem to limit the game's applicability, because many transactions between individuals do not recur much or even occur only once. So it seems sensible to ask, to what extent must the participants to the transaction endure as trading partners?

Suppose that, instead of having one individual offer trust and a second honor or abuse that trust, we had a sequence of individuals A who must choose whether or not to trust a single trading partner B. For the sake of exposition, let us call the sequence of individuals $A_1, A_2, \ldots$ Let us make the following formal assumptions: A_1, must decide whether or not to trust B, and then (if trusted) B must choose to honor or abuse that trust, with payoffs to the two as before. Then, with 90 per cent probability, B faces the same situation with A_2. And so on.

A moment's reflection should convince you that the following arrangement is self-enforcing. Party B carries a reputation from past behavior. For simplicity, we will suppose that B begins with an unsullied reputation, and B's reputation is irrevocably sullied if ever B abuses trust. Any A will trust B if B has an unsullied reputation, and A will refuse to trust B if B's reputation is sullied. Then B will always honor trust, and all As will (in sequence) put their trust in B. This is just like the self-enforcing agreement of the previous section, except here we see that only B must be enduring, *as long as B's opportunities in later rounds can be tied to behavior in earlier rounds.*

There are two parts to this statement. First, B's behavior, not A's posed the original problem in getting to the efficient transaction, so in this case only B must endure. Compare this with the situation in which A and B are both at risk in the transaction. For example, suppose A and B were engaged in the well-known prisoners' dilemma. In this game, A and B must simultaneously and without binding contracts each choose whether to cooperate or take advantage of the other. If they both cooperate, both get, say, $5. If one cooperates and the other takes advantage, the one cooperating loses $1 and the one taking advantage makes $7. If both take advantage, neither wins nor loses anything. Played noncooperatively and only once, both sides will choose to take advantage: each does better doing so, regardless of what the other does. This leads to an inefficient outcome where neither makes any money, compared with the $5 that each can make if each cooperates. If we repeat this, however, with there always being a, say, 90 per cent chance of playing at least one more time, then cooperation can emerge as an equilibrium outcome. (Each side will cooperate as long as the other does and threatens, say, never to again cooperate if the opponent takes advantage.) The point is that in this case both sides must endure. If one side played a sequence of opponents, each of whom played only once, then the opponents would always take advantage, and the one enduring side would have no reason to do otherwise. Whether it is enough to have only one side enduring (as it is in our model transaction) depends on the nature of the specific transaction.

Second, there must be a mechanism that ties B's opportunities in future rounds to past behavior. It is critical to our story that the A's are able to observe B's past actions and that they condition their behavior on B's actions. If either condition is not met, then B's incentive to honor trust in any particular round disappears and, therefore, so does the incentive of the As to give trust.

Note our use of 'reputation' to describe what transpires in this situation. B has a reputation built up from past encounters, and the As consider that reputation when deciding whether to trust B. The nature of the reputation is quite circular—it works because it works: B guards a reputation because it influences future trading opportunities; it has this influence because B guards it.

In this game, some caveats must be observed.

1. Just as before, many reputations would work. B, for example, might have the reputation of abusing trust randomly, with, say, a probability of one-third each time. If any particular A feels there is a one-third chance that trust will be abused, that A is still willing to trust B. Of course, such a reputation will allow B to make greater profits. In general, we would expect that, in a situation where there are many long-lived Bs, competition among them would limit the extent to which they can take advantage of the As they deal with. This fleshes out the point made earlier concerning competition between Bs. Whether or not the As are long- or short-lived, we can imagine that they can, in any round, select from among a number of alternative B trading partners, selecting the B that has the best general reputation for trust. The Bs will then compete for As through their reputation. When a single B is the only possible trading partner for the As, then the economics of the situation suggests that this B will take maximal advantage of his or her power, just as any monopolist would.

2. This story about reputations depends critically on there being no last round. As before, more complex models can get around this problem.

3. Reputations must be based on observables in order to work. Ambiguity and uncertainty cause problems. This point is best made by considering the reputation previously described above in point 1: B abuses trust with probability one-third in any particular round. Before, with only one A and one B, B could abuse trust every third round, threatening to abuse trust every time if A didn't trust every time (suffering every third). It would be easy for A to monitor compliance with this arrangement, because there is no uncertainty

about what B will do in any single round. But this won't work at all if one B faces a sequence of As. Threatening to abuse trust every third round would only result in every third A deciding not to trust. Each A must have a sufficiently large probability that trust will be honored. Hence, B can only do something like abuse trust each round with probability one-third.

But if B tries to build such a reputation, how do the As know whether B is living up to the deal? Suppose that, as is possible but unlikely, B abuses trust ten times in a row. Should the As conclude that B is no longer living up to a reputation? At some point the As must punish B for too much abuse, otherwise B will (optimally) abuse trust every time. But how severe should that punishment be? When should it be triggered, and how long should it last? These are difficult questions, and when real-world ambiguity is added to the game, they become questions that might never get sorted out. This is getting us closer to a theory of the type of reputation that might be expected—better to use a reputation that is easier to monitor. (Note that B could abuse trust based on some *ex post* observable random number. For example, B could abuse trust if the closing stock price of AT&T, on a day after trust is offered or not but before B must choose to honor or abuse trust, is an even multiple of one dollar, or a dollar plus one-eighth, or a dollar plus two-eighs. Because it is *ex post* observable whether B follows this rule, we have perfect ability to monitor, and no loss in efficiency from punishment periods is required.)

4.3. Firms

In the previous section we made the As short-lived, as long as B endured. But what if the Bs were also short-lived? For concreteness, suppose that at discrete dates $t = 1, 2, \ldots$ we have an A_t and a B_t who might engage in the transaction described. Absent binding contracts or some other costly contrivance, the transaction seems unlikely to take place. A_t, cannot trust B_t *because B_t* has no incentive to do other than abuse trust. We are almost out of business, but with one change we can resurrect our constructions. We suppose that B_t lives for two dates, at t and at $t + 1$. At date t, B_t engages in the potential transaction with A_t; at date $t + 1$, B_t retires to Florida and lives off savings. Also, we suppose that B_t comes endowed in period t with some resources, perhaps the fruits of labor early in period t.

Now consider the following arrangement: In this society there is a partnership called B Associates. At date t (prior to the transaction between A_t and B_t), B Associates is owned by B_{t-1}, who is about to move to Florida. For a price,

David M. Kreps

B_{t-1} will sell a position in B Associates to B_t, who would purchase it out of preexisiting resources.

Why would B_t pay anything for this place? Suppose that B Associates has a reputation for never abusing trust. A_t claims to be ready and willing to trust B_t, if B_t is a member of B Associates but not otherwise. The B_t will certainly be willing to pay something to B_{t-1}, in order to have the opportunity to undertake the transaction with A_t.

Why should A_t trust B_t if B_t purchases a place in B Associates and not otherwise? Suppose that the As have a somewhat more complex decision rule: They will trust a member of B Associates as long as no previous member has ever abused the trust of some previous A. In other words, a member of B Associates will be trusted as long as the company's reputation is unsullied. Then B_t, having purchased a place in B Associates and having received the trust of A_t, must make the following calculations: The trust of A_t can be abused, which will net $15 today. But then the reputation of B Associates will be sullied, and B_{t+1} will pay nothing tomorrow for a place in it. On the other hand, honoring the trust of A_t will net only $10 today, but it will preserve the association's reputation, an asset that can be sold to B_{t+1}. The proceeds from that sale can be used to finance retirement in Florida. As long as the value of that asset is enough greater than five dollars so that its discounted value to B_t at date t exceeds $5, B_t will, having purchased a place in the association, optimally honor the trust of A_t. And A_t, realizing this, will happily trust B_t if B Associates is unsullied.

There is perhaps less to this argument than meets the eye initially. Suppose, for example, that the market price of a place in B Associates is $9. (We'll justify this as the approximate value in a second.) Then buying a place and protecting its reputation will probably be a good deal for the Bs. Not to buy will net nothing, because the corresponding A will not grant trust. To buy and then abuse trust nets $6 today ($15 from dealings with A, less the $9 purchase price) and nothing tomorrow. To buy and then honor trust nets $1 today and $9 tomorrow. Assuming a discount rate of 0.9 between the two dates, the last course is optimal, with net present value $9.10. (Hence the $9 price for a place; assuming competition for places, we would have an equilibrium with a slightly higher price or a slightly greater discount rate.)

Now suppose that instead of this elaborate construction we allowed Bs to make the following contract with As: B_t posts a bond of nine dollars at date t if A_t gives trust, a bond that is forfeit if B_t abuses that trust. But if B_t honors the trust given, then B_t gets back the posted bond (perhaps with interest?) in period $t + 1$. It is hardly surprising that such contracts, if they can be written and enforced, will lead to the trust-honor outcome. From a mathematical point of view, this is all that the invention of B Associates has done for us. Although they are mathematically similar, the two arrangements work differently. With the bonding arrangement, even in this simple setting, we must have some agency that enforces the forfeiture of the bond. Courts would be natural candidates. That is, the two parties could write up a contract with the bonding provision, giving them recourse to the courts if the contract provisions are not fulfilled. But the drafting and (if necessary) subsequent enforcement of the contract might be costly. Such costs need to be weighed against the benefits accrued from the transaction. Indeed, because enforcement must occur after the transaction is completed, it may not be in the interests of A_t ex post to go to court if B_t fails to fulfill the contract. A_t certainly would want B_t to believe that he or she will in fact go to the courts, but it isn't clear that this is altogether believable. What does A_t gain ex post for expending time and money? If the threat to go to court is not credible, then the bonding arrangement won't work at all. (A simple cure, it would seem, is to stipulate in the contract that the bond is forfeited to B.)

Another problem, more nettlesome and more fundamental to what will follow, arises if honor is observable but nor verifiable. This distinction here is important. A and B and others as well may be able to observe whether B honors A's trust, but to substantiate this in a court of law is quite another thing. Verification of substantiation will be required if we are to have the courts as an enforcement agency, and this verification may be very costly or even impossible. If the costs of verification rise above the value to either party of any effective bond that can be posted, or if verification is simply impossible, a bonding scheme would not work.

With B Associates, however, the arrangement is self-enforcing as long as the As can observe whether trust has been abused or not. It needn't be verified in court; no third party need be employed at all to enforce the agreement. If future As simply refuse to transact with a sullied B Associates, then any B's honoring of trust is enforced by self-interest—namely interest in recovering the full value of the asset originally purchased.

This very simple example gives our first cut at a theory of the firm. The firm is a wholly intangible object in this theory—a reputation bearer. It exists so that short-term transactors can be made sufficiently enduring to permit efficiencies borne of reputation or enduring relationships. Two things are necessary in this simple story: reputation or enduring relationships must have some role to play, and the entity or entities that make decisions in the firm's name must have some vested interest in the firm's continuing to have a good reputation. It is crucial to our story that B_t lives beyond the association with B Associates and that the good name of B Associates represents to B_t a valuable asset to be (self-interestedly) preserved in order to sell later. But given these two requirements, we can see a potential role for an entirely intangible name.

Of course, in building a case for the use of B Associates, we have looked at a setting that ignores some of the major disadvantages of this sort of arrangement. The reputation construction is decidedly fragile: If reputation works only because it works, then it could fall apart without much difficulty. In real life, these risks will appear as substantial costs of undertaking transactions in this way. We don't see such costs here because our model is insufficiently rich to capture them. Still, these costs do exist; and it would not be unreasonable to conclude that the case for firms and other organizations we have made so far is hardly convincing.

5. Hierarchical Transactions

Consider the following elaboration on the simple game between A and B. For concreteness, we will adopt a version of the game with a sequence of As (labeled, where necessary, A_1, A_2, . . .), and a single, enduring B. But what follows can be adapted to the other two scenarios as well.

In this elaboration, A_t may hire B to perform some task that requires B's expertise. It is unclear at the outset how hard B will have to work to accomplish this task. We suppose that the task is either *easy* or *difficult*, each with probability one-half. The difficulty of the task is irrelevant to A_t in determining his or her value for it. A_t simply values it at $9 if it is adequately accomplished and A_t can tell whether or not it has been adequately accomplished *ex post*. The difficulty is relevant to B: if it is easy, a $3 compensation is adequate to B; if it is hard, a $13 compensation is required. A bargaining problem between the two parties must be solved here, but that bargaining problem is not germane to my point. So I will assume that for some reason the equilibrium arrangement gives B a $3 compensation if the job is easy and $13 if it is hard, as long as this arrangement can be enforced. Also, I assume that this equilibrium generates positive surplus for B, for reasons that will become apparent later.

We assume that *ex ante A* doesn't know how hard the job is. Imagine that the two could sign and enforce the following contract: A pays B $3 if the job is easy and $13 if it is hard, with no payment paid to B if the job is inadequately done. Then, assuming that the no-payment clause gives B the incentive to do an adequate job, A nets $9 in benefit against an *expected* payment of $8, making this a worthwhile transaction for A.

Now suppose that this contract cannot be enforced. Specifically, we assume that its provisions are observable but not verifiable. The distinction here is just as before: *ex post* both sides can observe the difficulty of the task and whether the task was adequately performed. But offering adequate proof of either thing in the courts is impossible.

If both A and B deal once only, this will kill the precise transaction already described. Indeed, the transaction will be killed even if we can enforce adequacy of performance. This is so because we cannot enforce payment— A will always want to pay the lesser amount, and B will want to collect the greater amount. How is the payment amount to be determined and enforced if we cannot enforce clauses contingent on the job's difficulty? (If it is possible to enforce such a contingent contract, we would still need to reckon in the cost of enforcement.) Seemingly, we must have a payment that is not contingent on the job's difficulty. Now if B is risk-neutral this might allow another transaction to take place: The two agree that B will be paid $8 regardless of the difficulty of the task, which is the same to B as the contingent payment. But the entire transaction may be rendered infeasible if B is risk-averse. The certain payment required to get B to undertake the task may then exceed the $9 value that A places on it. (We could, by elaborating the situation still further, get other reasons that lack of contingent fees would make the transaction impossible. For example, we could suppose that A ascribes a higher value to a more difficult task, give A the ability at some cost to ascertain the difficulty of the task *ex ante*, and then put the usual adverse selection argument to work.)

But we are concerned here not with one A and one B but rather with a B who might perform this service for a sequence of As. Then we can get the contingent fee arrangement, even supposing that adequacy of performance is observable but not verifiable. That observability is sufficient to ensure adequate performance is our old story: future As may refuse to deal with B if ever B fails to perform adequately. (Of course, B must derive enough positive surplus from this transaction so that benefits from future transactions outweigh any present benefits from inadequate performance.) But a similar construction will yield the contingent fee structure. Imagine that A_t and B sign a contract that leaves payment unspecified and at the discretion of B, subject to a limit of $13. That is, A_t agrees *ex ante* to pay any bill B submits up to that limit. As adopt the following rule in deciding whether to transact with B: They will enter into transactions only if B has never gouged a former client; that is, if B has always charged $3 when the task was easy and $13 when it was hard. Because we are assuming that difficulty is observable, the As have sufficient data to adopt such a rule. If the value to B of future transactions exceeds the immediate $10 extra to be had by gouging a customer, this arrangement is self-enforcing.

In a mathematical sense, there is absolutely nothing new here. If we simply reinterpret *honor* to mean *to perform adequately and to bill appropriately* and *abuse* (now multifaceted) to mean to *do anything else*, then we are noting that sufficient potential gains from future trade, combined with As who observe and react to what B does in the right way, suffice to get the trust-honor outcome. The new twist is that we see how, in certain circumstances, trust could involve agreeing *ex ante* to obey dictates from the other party that are *ex ante* unspecified, awaiting the resolution of some uncertainty. In this sense, trust can encompass transactions that are hierarchical, where one party grants to the other the right to specify *ex post* just what the contract in fact calls for (always within limitations).

Even though mathematically there is nothing novel here, the reinterpretation in terms of hierarchical transactions and the connection between such transactions and reputation is key. We often see contracts that are *ex ante* quite vague about what will happen as contingencies arise. These contracts often include adjudication procedures. There may be specified recourse to independent arbitration of some form or another. Further negotiation may be called for (without specification as to what will happen if those negotiations fail to come to an agreement). In a large number of cases, discretion is left to one party or the other (always within broad limits). I contend that such transactions are characteristic of hierarchies; at some point, the hierarchically superior party, either explicitly or implicitly, has the right to direct the inferior party. Why would anyone ever willingly enter into such a contract in the inferior position? It might be because the worst that could happen is good enough so that the transaction, even on those terms, is worthwhile. But when the superior party has a reputation to protect or enhance, a reputation that turns on how that party exercises authority, then the inferior party need not presume the worst. That party can count on the superior party to live up to an implicit contract in his or her own interests.

The notion of a hierarchical transaction and the connection with reputation goes back to Simon (1951). He makes clear the distinction between this sort of transaction and the usual exchange of goods for money that is the basis of standard economic theory. He argues that hierarchical transactions are particularly prevalent in employment relationships. Beginning with a transaction in which A presumes the worst (or, rather, that B will act solely for short-run interests), Simon shows that in such cases the authority that A willingly grants to B can be quite small. Then he argues, just as we have done, that this authority can be enlarged (or the compensation demanded by A decreased) in cases where A and B may wish to repeat the transaction over time, with B implicitly threatened by suspension of the transaction for abuses of hierarchical authority.

Of course, in this particular explanation for hierarchical transaction, authority *must* rest with a long-lived party. Suppose that A is long-lived, participating in this transaction with a sequence of Bs. If there is no problem in enforcing adequate performance, then the proper hierarchical form could have *A* paying whatever is appropriate, with each *B* agreeing *ex ante* to let *A* determine what is appropriate (no less than $3). (What if adequate performance is not enforceable? With a small enough discount rate, we could even have *A*'s payment of whatever is appropriate be zero in cases involving inadequate performance.)

In the story just told, it seems crucial that the task's difficulty be observable. What would happen if we changed the story so that this is not so? Note well that this unobservability need only be on the part of future *As*; they and not the current *A* must be able to monitor compliance with the implicit contract. Again, we know the answer from the previous section: Some inefficiencies will enter, but all is not necessarily lost. If, say, the difficulty of the task cannot be observed, then *B* could claim to follow the billing rule already explained but will have to be watched carefully and punished (by withholding transactions) occasionally. The *As* can ascertain whether *B* is indeed charging $3 around half the time, according to the billing rule described. If there is a history of too many $13 charges, then the *As* can (for a while) refuse to transact with *B*. Note that it is crucial that *B* be punished occasionally. We cannot arrange things so that punishment is avoided altogether, for that would mean accepting without question any bill *B* submits. *B* would then charge $13 every time. There is no way to avoid some loss of efficiency when the *As* are unable to observe the task's difficulty. But lack of observability needn't completely prevent a transaction.

Considerations of observability will play a large role in what is to follow, so let me make this point one more time in a different way. Imagine that the task's difficulty is indeed unobservable, but concrete signs are observable that imperfectly indicate whether the job was difficult. To be precise, suppose that each job either does or does not require calculus. Of the difficult jobs, 97.5 per cent require calculus, and 2.5 per cent don't. Of the easy jobs, 20 per cent require calculus, while the other 80 per cent don't. If it is observable whether calculus is required for the job but not whether the job is difficult, then it might well be better to base payment on whether the job required calculus than on whether the job was really difficult. That is, we can, using the reputation construction, have a self-enforcing arrangement in which the bill is $13 if the job requires calculus and $3 otherwise, even if the requirement to use calculus is observable but not verifiable. This may not be the first-best arrangement; that will be the one for which payment is based directly on the job's difficulty. But to try to base the bill directly on difficulty runs us into inefficiencies that exist because the job's difficulty is unobservable. It may be better to contract implicitly on some contingency that is clearly observable but that is not the ideal contingency to base the arrangement on, because what is lost in moving away from the ideal contingent contract may be regained from the greater efficiency of the reputation arrangement. (In the spirit of results by Holmstrom [1979], it is natural to conjecture that the most efficient implicit contract will not be based solely on the observable contingency. In the simple example we have described, one can show that this is so. But I am unaware of any general result in this direction.)

A concrete example of this phenomenon may be helpful in understanding it. In the United States, it is a commonplace observation that doctors run too many tests on patients in order to protect themselves from malpractice suits. The phrase 'too many' presumably means that more tests are given than are necessary, given the doctor's information. But it is hard to observe (*ex post*) whether a doctor's subjective *ex ante* judgments were professional. It is far easier to observe whether the doctor followed some pattern of generally accepted practice that allows for few subjective options. That such a clearly laid-out pattern of practice is suboptimal relative to the (first-best) application of subjective judgment is obvious. But it is also irrelevant to any reasonable analysis of the problem: We have to consider the full equilibrium implications of having doctors rely more on subjective judgments. (So that no one gets upset, I am not suggesting that what we see in the United States is the most efficient feasible arrangement; I haven't thought about it nearly enough to have an informed opinion. But the simplistic argument that one often hears is incomplete, ignoring as it does the costs of monitoring, enforcement, and so on.) Another, quite similar example, comes from the accounting profession, where accounts are kept according to Generally Accepted Accounting Principles, even when those practices might not be the most informative for the particular accounts being kept.[6]

6. Unforeseen Contingencies

We have now reached the point where orthodox economic theory will be abandoned because it lacks the two final ingredients of the stew being concocted. Before we head off into less orthodox waters, let me offer the following summary of where we've been.

In transactions where one side must trust the other, the reputation of the trusted party can be a powerful tool for avoiding the transaction costs of specifying and enforcing the terms of the transaction. Indeed, when the contingencies upon which the terms are based are observable but not verifiable, reputation may be the only way to effect the transaction. Reputation works as follows: the trusted party will honor that trust because to abuse it would preclude or substantially limit opportunities to engage in future valuable transactions. Such a reputation arrangement can work even when the reputation rests in a wholly intangible entity (the firm), as long as those who make decisions or take actions in the entity's name have a stake in preserving its reputation. Among the types of contracts to which this pertains are those that are hierarchical, where the contract calls *ex ante* for one party to decide *ex post* how the contract will be fulfilled, with the second party agreeing *ex ante* to abide by the first party's dictates, within broad limitations. Finally, this arrangement works best when the actions of the trusted party are based on contingencies observable to all concerned; reputation based on unobservable contingencies is not impossible, but it will always involve some degree of inefficiency. Put another way, the best reputation, from the point of view of effecting the type of arrangement we are talking about, is one that is clear-cut and easy to monitor.

All of these conclusions have been derived from orthodox economic theory. But the examples so far discussed present a fairly weak case for the importance of this theory. Too much seems to rest on the distinction between observable and verifiable contingencies. How many of those are there, and how important are they in real-life transactions?

I contend that there are many such contingencies and that they are very important, if we stretch this theory to include unforeseen contingencies. An unforeseen contingency is a set of circumstances that *ex ante* the parties to the transaction had not considered. Unforeseen contingencies need not be unimaginable: individuals may simply be unwilling *ex ante* to spend time thinking through all possibilities, on the grounds that it is too time-consuming and expensive to do so. Or it could be that the circumstances really are *ex ante* unimaginable. From the point of view of our development, either interpretation is fine.

Before adding unforeseen contingencies to our analysis of transactions, consider briefly how individuals act when faced with unforeseen contingencies. Introspection suggests that while a particular contingency may be unforeseen, provision for it is not completely impossible. While the exact circumstances of future contingencies may be unimaginable (or too costly to think through), aspects of those contingencies can be anticipated. I contend that unforeseen contingencies follow patterns. At least, I, and, I suspect, others, act as if this is so. Accordingly, my provisions for the unforeseen are somewhat evolutionary. I examine what has happened that was surprising in the recent and sometimes distant past, and I provide for roughly similar contingencies.

Formal models of behavior such as this are easy to produce. Imagine, for example, that I have at my disposal several possible remedies in varying amounts, remedies that may or may not be applicable to a wide range of circumstances. Simple examples are cash and fire extinguishers. Holding these remedies at the ready is expensive: cash on hand doesn't earn interest, and fire extinguishers are costly. The amount of each remedy that I keep on hand is related to how useful I suspect it will be. In so far as I can anticipate relatively greater need for a remedy in a particular circumstance, I will adjust my holdings upward. (For example, having just bought a house, I am holding relatively more cash in my checking account to meet the numerous small expenses that I discover.) But I will also be guided by the relative usefulness of the various remedies in the recent past. (In the month that has elapsed since I bought the house, I have discovered that I need to keep more cash in my checking account than I had originally anticipated was necessary.) If there is indeed a stationary pattern to unforeseen contingencies, then in the long run I will wind up holding correct levels of the remedies. If, as seems more likely, there is a pattern that is not stationary but that has secular trends, then although I may not achieve the best levels of remedy holdings, I will still be better off by paying attention to recent events than not.

I meander concerning how individuals (or at least how I) act in the face of the unforeseen because economic theory does not provide an accepted model of behavior. One knows the appropriate model for, say, decision making under uncertainty, from the axiomatic development by von Neumann and Morgenstern, Savage, and others. But there is no corresponding standard model of decision making through time when there are unforeseen contingencies.

Although there is nothing to my knowledge written on the subject, it might be instructive to speculate on what a standard model of choice with unforeseen contingencies might look like. The usual models of choice under uncertainty, of which Savage's theory (1954) is the exemplar, presume that individuals can foresee all conceivable future contingencies; they are uncertain only over which contingencies will develop. Or rather, the standard model posits that individuals act as if that were so at any point in time. This could continue to be so for choice at any single point in time, but with one major change: one of the fundamental pieces of the standard model is the state space—the set of all conceivable future contingencies. This is a given in the model; in the usual interpretation this piece of the model is objectively fixed, not a part of an individual's behavior. But if there are unforeseen contingencies and if individuals attempt at any point to make provision for them, then one might better regard the state space in an individual's model as part of the subjective inputs the individual provides. That is, just as in the standard model the individual's choice behavior reveals probability assessments and utility function, so in a model with unforeseen contingencies might subjective choice behavior reveal the individual's conception of what the future might hold. In such a model, it would then become important to speak of how the individual's state space (and probability assessments and utility function) evolves through time: I have a strong bias toward models in which past surprises are taken as guides to what the future might hold. More precisely, such a model would generate behavior in which provision for future contingencies is positively influenced by what would have been useful in the past; this evolutionary behavior will be modelled by corresponding evolution in the individual's state space and probability assessments. These are no more than speculations, but I do wish to indicate the importance that will be attached to the evolution of behavior: the past, and especially past surprises, will guide how individuals prepare for future surprises.

A model of dynamic choice behavior when there are unforeseen contingencies is an essential precursor to a solid theory of transactions in the face of unforeseen contingencies. As I do not have and do not know of the former, it is somewhat dangerous to speculate on the latter. But I will try, nonetheless. Unforeseen contingencies make explicit and complete contracting impossible. How can we provide *ex ante* for contingencies that *ex ante* we cannot anticipate? Yet many transactions live so long that unforeseen contingencies must be met. An especially good example is that of individuals seeking employment. In many cases, individuals commit themselves to more than a day's or a week's work. Individuals will develop human capital peculiar to a particular firm, and the employment relationship will be relatively more efficient if it continues for many years in the future. In so far as this is so, it is impossible for workers and the firm to specify everything the workers will do during their employment. Future contingencies are extraordinarily complex, involved, and even unimaginable. Consider also the contract between students and a university. *Ex ante*, students have little idea what courses they will want to take, when they will want to take them, and so forth. There is no possibility of enumerating and providing for the myriad contingencies that could arise.

In such transactions, the workers and the firm, and students and the university, agree *ex ante* not so much on what will be done in each particular contingency as they do on the procedure by which future contingencies will be met. The workers and students have certain rights that cannot be violated by the firm and the university. They have the right to terminate the relationship at will, but workers and students usually agree at the outset that, in the face of unforeseen contingencies, adaptation to those contingencies will be at the discretion of a boss or dean. That is, the adaptation process is hierarchical, in just the sense of the last section. (This can be qualified in important ways when workers or students have a body representing their interests—a labor union or student union, for example.)

Why will workers and students enter into such arrangements? What protection do they get? It is that the firm or university develops and maintains a reputation for how it meets unforeseen contingencies by the way in which it actually meets those contingencies. How the contingencies will be met is not verifiable, at least not in the sense that workers or students could take a firm or university to court and enforce a violated implicit contract. But the meeting of the contingencies is observable *ex post*; others can see what the firm or university did and decide whether to enter into similar transactions with either.

Of course, our previous qualifications to the reputation construction continue to hold. The firm or university does not make decisions: Boss *B* or Dean *B* does so in the organization's name. These people must have some real stake in maintaining their organization's good reputation. Most crucially, the meeting of unforeseen contingencies must conform to some pattern or rule that is observable—that is, the organization's reputation must be for something. This is especially problematic in the case of unforeseen contingencies. Once they arise, we may know what they are, but how do we know that they have been met as they are supposed to be met? Because the contingencies are unforeseen, we cannot specify in advance how to meet all possible contingencies and then observe that advance specifications have been fulfilled. We are in a situation somewhat more analogous to that where the meeting of future contingencies is not perfectly observable, with an attendant loss in efficiency. At best, participants will have a rough sense as to general principles with which unforeseen contingencies will be met, and they will have to gauge the extent to which those principles have been honestly applied. To discuss further such principles, we need to return one final time to the tool box of economic theory.

7. Focal Points

Consider the following relatively simple game. Here are eleven letters, *A*, *B*, *C*, *D*, *H*, *K*, *L*, *M*, *N*, *P*, *S*. Assigned to each letter is a number of points, between 1 and 100. I won't tell you what assignments the letters have, except to tell you that *N* is assigned the highest number of points (100) and *K* the least (1). I ask you and another person, unknown to you, to pick simultaneously and independently a subset of these letters. Your list must have the letter *S* on it, and your opponent's must have the letter *B*. Each of you is aware of the requirement imposed on the other. Otherwise, you are free to pick as many or as few letters as you want. We will compare lists and make payments to each of you as follows: for any letter on one list and not on the other, the person listing that letter wins as many dollars as that letter has points. For any letter appearing on both lists, both players must forfeit twice the number of dollars as that letter has points. If the two lists precisely partition the set of letters so that each letter appears in only one list, prices will be tripled.

Before going further, what list of letters would you submit? If you were assigned the letter B instead of S, what list would you submit?

Notice that this game has a vast number of equilibria—two lists of letters, one for each player, such that neither player would wish to change his or her list unless the other person did so. Namely *any* of the 512 partitions of the nine other letters constitutes an equilibrium. Yet I am fairly confident that many readers came up with the list L, M, N, P, S. And, putting yourselves in the role of the player assigned letter B, you thought of the list A, B, C, D, H, and perhaps K. The rule is simple: alphabetical order. One player takes the first five letters, the other player takes the last five. The letter K is problematic, because there are eleven letters. But many of you may have replicated the following argument: the player with the end of the alphabet is getting N, which is the best letter to have, and K is worth only one dollar, so why not let the other person have it?

Note that the rule applied here is wholly dependent on context. I have played a very similar game with Stanford MBA students and Harvard undergraduates that comes to a very different solution. I tell them I have a list of eleven US cities, namely Atlanta, Boston, Chicago, Dallas, Houston, Kansas City, Los Angeles, Miami, New York, Philadelphia, and San Francisco. Each city has been assigned a number of points reflecting its relative importance to commerce, trade, and the arts in the United States, with New York the highest at 100 points and Kansas City the lowest at 1. Two students unknown to each other, one from Harvard and the other from Stanford, are to list simultaneously and independently some subset of the cities, with the Harvard participant required to list Boston and the Stanford participant required to list San Francisco. The game continues as before.

Before reading on, how would you proceed if you had the Stanford role? If you had the Harvard role?

In a surprisingly large number of cases (my rough estimate is 75 per cent), Harvard people select Atlanta, Boston, Chicago, Miami, New York, and Philadelphia, while Stanford people take the complement Dallas, Houston, Kansas City, Los Angeles, and San Francisco. When asked why, the usual response referred to which side of the Mississippi River the city is on— Harvard gets everything east of the Mississippi, Stanford everything west. (Kansas City causes problems for individuals unschooled in geography. Miami also sometimes causes problems, when people use Sunbelt/Snowbelt division as the principle for their selections, although the joint presence of Atlanta, which belongs to the Sunbelt, and Miami, usually causes students to reject

David M. Kreps

this principle because of the unequal numbers of Snowbelt and Sunbelt cities. Substituting Detroit for either Atlanta or Miami is a good way to make the Sunbelt principle live in at least some minds, and substituting Detroit for Dallas definitely favors it. Putting either Minneapolis/St. Paul or New Orleans into the list causes great confusion. Foreign students resent this game *ex ante*—they seem to know what the nature of the principle applied will be without knowing just what the principle will be or how to apply it, and they are quick to point out how unfair this is to them.)

These are examples of focal points. This concept, derived from Schelling (1960), refers (roughly) to some principle or rule individuals use naturally to select a mode of behavior in a situation with many possible equilibrium behaviors. (More precisely, the focal point is the equilibrium suggested by some focal principle.) Schelling's discussion is informal but persuasive; he is able to cite many games like these two in which, somehow, most participants know what to do. He finds that most focal points can be characterized by simple qualitative principles. Symmetry is a powerful focal principle, when it can be applied. When one principle singles out a unique equilibrium and other principles do not give a clear-cut answer, the first tends to be applied; uniqueness is a fairly powerful principle. Often the focal point seems a product of culture. For example, the use of the Mississippi River to divide the eleven cities occurs with astonishing frequency to Americans; non-Americans rarely if ever come up with that means of division.

The notion of a focal point is well outside orthodox economic theory. No formal work I am aware of addresses the concept. (I suspect that psychologists have something quite substantial to tell economists on this score, and I am looking forward to getting references from readers of this book.) So, again, reliance on casual introspection seems in order.

One point the game examples just described make is that in any particular situation many focal points may be applied. The individual, trying to decide between them, will look for which one fits best. Which is most suggested by context? (A geographical rule seems more appropriate to cities than does an alphabetical rule. One wonders if an American student who knows that his opponent is from overseas and is relatively unschooled in US geography then focuses on the alphabetical rule?) Which does least violence to other principles? (For example, the presence of both Atlanta and Miami in the list of cities makes application of the Sunbelt principle problematic, since it violates badly the equal division principle. But if I took away Dallas and added Detroit, then the Mississippi River principle would give a seven-to-four division, and, I expect, the Sunbelt principle would get somewhat more play, especially because it lumps New York into a group of five and Kansas City into a group of six.) A choice of a principle to apply must be made, and the choice is usually far from capricious.

Second, it seems to me that focal points arise in part because of evolutionary fitness. A good, useful focal principle in a particular situation will tend to have had successful wide applicability in similar past situations for the individual using it. This will tend to favor principles that are more universal or broader and, of course, that are clearer in a particular context.

A related point, supported by experimental evidence, is that focal points can be learned—and quite quickly. Roth and Schoumaker (1983) have conducted the following experiment. Two individuals play a game in which they bargain over 100 chips. The bargaining procedure is simple: each simultaneously and independently proposes a number of chips that he or she would like to have. Let the two initial bids be x_A and x_B. If these bids are compatible in the sense that $x_A + x_B \leq 100$, then each gets the number of chips asked for. If the sum of the bids exceeds 100, then each is asked to concede or stick to the initial bid. Those who concede get 100 less the number of chips originally requested by their opponents. If one sticks and the other concedes, the one who sticks gets his or her original bid. If both stick, then both get no chips. These chips are then redeemed: if a player has won n chips, that player is given an $n/100$ chance at winning a monetary prize. The first player's prize is $10, while the second's is $40. Both players are told all this, and both are told that the other is being told. In so far as is practical, all the above is made common knowledge between the players. Bidding and conceding/sticking are done via computer; communication between the two players is strictly limited. Players participate in this game not once but repeatedly; they are told before each round how well their opponent has done (in terms of chips) in previous rounds.

As a formal game, the bidding situation described has many equilibria. For any number between 0 and 100, if one player is going to ask for and then stick to that number of chips, the second's best response is to ask for and stick to 100 minus that number. That is, there are 101 pure strategy equilibria here. Moreover, there are two somewhat natural focal points: split the chips 50–50, or split the chips so that each player has the same expected value, that is, 80 chips to the first player and 20 chips to the second. (Another focal point, perhaps to economists only, is the efficient outcome where one player gets all the chips.) In previous experiments, Roth found that the second (80–20) focal point seems to predominate in the population he tested (students at the University of Illinois).

Roth and Schoumaker add a new wrinkle. Unbeknownst to the participants, in their first ten or so rounds of play, they are matched against a computer. In some cases the computer is programmed to insist on the 50–50 split of chips (or, when the computer is the $10 player, to accede to this split); in other cases the computer is programmed to insist on or accede to the 80–20 split. After this training period, players are matched against each other with predictable results: those whose training has equipped them to come to exact agreement stay at that agreement. Those whose training leads to inconsistent demands (one demanding 50 and the other 80) tend not to come to any agreement. Those whose training leads them to leave chips on the table (one asks for 20 and the other for 50) tend to head for one of the two focal points after a while. (Interested readers should consult the paper, which I am abridging with abandon here.)

The point is clear: focal points are in part the product of experience. They can be taught through repeated application. It is a heroic leap from this experiment to the evolutionary process we have already conjectured, but, having made the conjecture, I can now finally throw it into the stew and emerge with corporate culture.

8. Corporate Culture

Recall where we were in the main development before detouring into the subject of focal points: unforeseen contingencies provide both a golden opportunity for the reputation/hierarchical transaction construction to take life and provide a problem for that construction. The problem is that the reputation argument turned on the ability of future potential trading partners to observe and monitor their degree of compliance with the implicit contract they have with current trading partners. Current trading partners could enter into a hierarchical transaction in the inferior position with equanimity because each could trust the other to carry out the implicit contract in her or his own interests, to protect their reputations and safeguard future beneficial transactions. But the implicit contract is more than implicit in the face of unforeseen contingencies. Practically by definition, it cannot be clear *ex ante* precisely what is called for in a contingency that *ex ante* has not been foreseen. So on what might a reputation turn?

It is not logically impossible for the reputation construction to work without flaw. What is needed is (i) the ability, after observing a particular contingency, to know what should be done, and (ii) a belief *ex ante* by the hierarchical inferiors that application of what should be done will be good enough to warrant undertaking the transaction. Truly unambiguous and universal rules could be imagined that could be applied *ex post* to any contingency that arises, and as long as test (ii) above is passed we meet all of the requirements for the reputation construction with such rules. (More elaborate, real-life adjudication procedures have this flavor. For example, the (legal) hierarchical superior may seek third-party mediation in the case of any disputes and have a reputation for always abiding by the recommendations of the mediator.)

But it seems unlikely that unambiguous and universal rules exist, at least in most situations. Or rather, it is unclear that such rules will exist that at the same time will pass test (ii). (An unambiguous and universal rule is: 'I decide according to my whims'. But this will probably inspire trust insufficient to pass test [ii].) Because every contingency that arises must be dealt with somehow (which is to say that the rule actually applied must be universal), one should expect ambiguity. The hierarchical inferiors, and, more importantly, the population of potential future hierarchical inferiors, will sometimes be uncertain that the rule is being followed. By analogy with formal work on reputation based on unobservable or partially observable behavior, we expect some loss of efficiency.

Yet, as in the formal literature, some loss need not mean complete loss. One might doubt whether, in the face of unforeseen contingencies, there can ever be a rule the application of which is sufficiently unambiguous and sufficiently advantageous to the hierarchical inferior to permit the reputation construction to live at all. But, again arguing by analogy, I contend that the literature on focal points indicates that such rules or principles can in fact exist. Faced with a competitive situation that one has never imagined before, a situation with many equilibrium actions that could be taken, one is often able to see how to proceed, applying a general principle. Indeed, this is so even if one is aware of only the slightest details of one's fellow players and if one must identify on one's own what principle is appropriate. It would seem that this is more likely to be true in cases where the fellow player has a long track record of applying a particular principle in similar but not quite identical situations.

Moreover, features that make for a good focal principle ought to make for a good rule to base the implicit contract/reputation on. *Ex post* unambiguity, as long as test (ii) is passed, is the *sine qua non*.[7] Note in this regard that a quite effective scheme might be to exclude purposely some contingencies from the rule. That is, the rule is to act in some specified manner (or according to some principle) in most cases, but it is not meant to be applied in a few others. Here it will only be necessary that we can agree, *ex post*, that a particular contingency was one in which the rule was meant to be applied. 'We do XYZ as long as it makes sense' can be quite effective as long as it makes sense most of the time and everyone can agree on cases where it doesn't.

Enter corporate culture. Let us consider first the organization as a single decision-making entity or as a sequence of decision-making entities who, when they have decision-making authority, have that authority all to

David M. Kreps

themselves. This entity's problem is to identify a rule that permits relatively efficient transactions to take place and on which a viable reputation can be based and then to communicate that rule to current and potential future trading partners. In the preceding formal analysis, we supposed a particular equilibrium, giving passing mention of the problem of multiplicity. In real life, communication becomes much more of a problem, especially where the rule is to some extent abstract. The communication of this principle is crucial: potential trading partners are judging our decision-making entity on its faithful application of the principle; it is clearly important that the entity let others know just what is the principle. Especially in a world with private information, the entity will want to have a principle tailored to it. Perhaps more importantly, the principle, if communicated well, can be used effectively as a screening device, warning off potential trading partners for whom the arrangement will not be good.

As in most communication problems of this kind, the simpler the message being sent and the more internally consistent it is, the easier it will be to communicate. By analogy with focal principles, simplicity and consistency will be virtues in application. As readers no doubt guessed long ago, I wish to identify corporate culture with the principle and with the means by which the principle is communicated. My (limited) understanding of corporate culture is that it accomplishes just what the principle should—it gives hierarchical inferiors an idea *ex ante* how the organization will react to circumstances as they arise; in a strong sense, it gives identity to the organization.

More than this, corporate culture communicates an organization's identity to hierarchical superiors. Firms and other large organizations do not have a single decision maker but instead have many individuals who make decisions in the organization's name. Even if we suppose that these individuals all have internalized as their objective functions the common good of the organization, it will be hard for them, in the face of circumstances they hadn't foreseen, to know how to proceed. Costly communication will render infeasible completely centralized decision making, yet it will be advantageous to have some consistency and coordination in the decentralized decisions of the many Bs in the organization. Corporate culture plays a role here by establishing general principles that should be applied (in the hope that application of that principle will lead to relatively high levels of coordination). But it is more than merely a coordinating device: it is especially useful in coordinating the exercise of the organization's hierarchical authority. If the organization is to have a reputation in its hierarchical transactions, it must be consistent in exercising hierarchical authority. Thus, the organization has a crucial task: to communicate the general decision rule it applies to all those who undertake the actual application. The culture inside

256

the organization will do this as well—it will communicate the principle to all concerned.

Corporate culture also provides a means of measuring the performance of hierarchical superiors. In many organizations, individuals have not fully internalized the common good—they are concerned with their own welfare. Thus, an organization must monitor and control individual performance. If individuals within an organization who exercise hierarchical authority are supposed to exercise that authority according to some clear principle, then it becomes easier *ex post* to monitor their performance. (This is simply another variation on our *ex post* observability story.) Hence, in the usual fashion, efficiency can be increased by monitoring adherence to the principle (culture). Violation of the culture generates direct negative externalities in so far as it weakens the organization's overall reputation. Rewarding good outcomes that involve violations of the culture generates negative externalities indirectly through the chain: this weakens individual incentives to follow the principle and thus increases (potentially) the costs of monitoring and control.[8]

This, then, is how economic theory (or rather an economic theorist) might try to explain the phenomenon of corporate culture. It clearly gives corporate culture an economic role to play; indeed, the role is part and parcel of the organization's role. As such, design and maintenance of the culture is crucial to efficient organization. If strategy consists of finding economic opportunities and then maintaining and protecting them, this puts corporate culture in the centre of strategy.

The theory (if something so incomplete and bare-boned can be dignified with that title) given here may indicate that corporate culture can be tendered in economic terms, but it would be a good deal nicer if that rendering suggested some consequences. I close by giving a few suggested consequences, although readers will quickly discern that I pay more attention to intuition than to any theoretical constructs. (Perhaps it would be more honest to call what follows my wish list for this theory, things I would like to derive from a fully developed theory.) I will also point out conclusions that are not borne out by any of the formal constructs that I have reported here, but that I think ought to be obtainable.

1. Consistency and simplicity being virtues, the culture/principle will reign even when it is not first best. There are three parts to this hypothesis. First, as part of the communication process, the culture will be taken into areas where it serves no direct purpose except to communicate or reinforce itself. This seems outside the realm of economic theory, which does not have good models of the difficulties encountered in real-life communication. One possibility suggested by Roth and Schoumaker, which can be modelled formally, would be to regard application in irrelevant areas as training for

others—that is, to communicate the principle, we administer it repeatedly so that others learn it. This does, however, raise the question, why not engage in direct communication instead? (Or we could spin an allied economics story by discussing the use of culture as a screen, a device to select from among potential transaction partners those individuals who are most appropriate to the transaction desired.)

Second, contingencies will arise in which the principle will not be in the best interests of the two immediate parties involved, yet it will still be applied for the benefit of third parties in order to ensure a general reputation for applying the principle. This follows directly from the formal constructions discussed in the chapter.

Third, cases may arise in which everyone concerned understands that the principle is inefficient, yet still it will be applied. This will come about in cases where the basis of a reputation is a belief that faithful application of the principle per se is valuable to a hierarchical superior. To provide formal justification for this, we would have to use the reputation arguments that turn on incomplete information, such as in Kreps, Milgrom, Roberts, and Wilson (1982). We have refrained from giving details on this literature, and this is no time to begin, so simply note that a key to this argument is that something may be in everyone's best interests and everyone may know that this is so, but still it may not be done if, say, not everyone is aware that everyone knows that it is in everyone's best interests. In formal terms, it may not be common knowledge.

2. In general, it will be crucially important to align culture with the sorts of contingencies that are likely to arise. There are planted axioms here: unforeseen contingencies in a particular enterprise do follow patterns. Even though one cannot think through the contingencies, one might be able to predict what principle will be good at meeting them. Principles are better or worse depending on how they adapt to the contingencies that do arise. At this level, this observation has little substance. But there is something potentially substantial here: one can expect difficulties when an organization's mission changes, because reputations grow and die hard (that is, reputations are assets fairly specialized and immutable once created). The theory presented earlier is completely inadequate to provide a reason that this would be so. There is nothing to prevent reputation from having secular trends or discontinuities, as long as everyone understands what is expected of B in every situation and B fulfills those expectations. In order to derive formally the desired rigidity in reputations, it again seems necessary to access the incomplete information construction of reputation, with an appeal to simplicity in the initial conjectures of the As concerning what motivates B. (This last remark is likely to be incomprehensible to readers unfamiliar with the reputation and incomplete information literature.)

(As long as I am putting in remarks incomprehensible to all but the cognoscenti, let me add another: note that a story based on personal quirks of the Bs is not going to fly in the context of the story of B Associates unless we believe that becoming a member of B Associates changes B_t's preferences or if we make the characteristics of the various B_t's exchangeable or something similar or if we embellish the story by supposing that B Associates, as part of its economic function, screens potential partners. Any of these would get us the probability of a persistent quirk that is necessary to make the incomplete information construction fly. And the last, which is my favorite, also gets us another screening role for corporate culture.)

3. What will corporate culture (or the principle) be based on, and how can we expect it to evolve? I have stressed the evolutionary character of beliefs about unforeseen contingencies and focal principles. In so far as the principle is meant to provide an adaptation to unforeseen contingencies and is to be based on something like a focal principle, I would expect the similar evolutionary adaptation. Of course, I have no theoretical models to back this up with, and it is a conclusion to which I would like to add caveats. Suppose one could argue convincingly that reputation is somewhat rigid and immutable once in place. Then, one would conclude that the early history of an organization is likely to play a decisive role in the formation of that organization's culture/principle. It is then that the organizational reputation is largely formed, for better or worse. Because the culture will form at least in part in response to unforeseen contingencies that do arise, the nature of an organization will be strongly influenced by early happenstance.

Suppose moreover that interrelated parts of a particular reputation/principle all live or die together. That is, trust of an organization (and its adherence to its various implicit contracts) is not perfectly divisible—violation of one implicit contract raises doubts about the commitment to others. (This could be derived theoretically using the reputations and incomplete information technology by controlling the probability assessments held *ex ante* about managers. The details, though, seem complex, for the same reasons that make the incomplete information story harder to tell. Then the evolution of the organizational culture/principle will be episodic and discontinuous. Events that cause some portion of the contracts to be violated (or that give greater opportunity to break those contracts) will tend to be accompanied by redefinition of the entire culture/set of principles.

4. Since I suggested as subtitle for this paper 'The Economics of the Focus Strategy', let me now make that connection. The theory sketched in this chapter has a natural extension into considerations of the optimal size of an organization, when we recast that as the optimal span of the implicit contract. Of course, in so far as an implicit contract permits greater transactional efficiency, an expansion in the span of the contract will be beneficial. But

weighed against this is the problem that as the span of the contract is increased, the range of contingencies that the contract must cover also must increase. Either it will then be harder for participants to determine *ex post* whether the contract was applied faithfully or the contract will be applied to contingencies for which it is not suited. Let me take an analogy. If your opponent in the eleven cities game is an individual, *B*, who plays games like this often, and *B* has a reputation for using rivers or mountain ranges to divide the cities, then *following* play of the eleven cities game, you would have no problem in checking whether *B* is living up to this reputation by using the Mississippi River to divide the cities. But suppose *B* also plays other games using the alphabet as the focal principle and still others using other principles. In playing the eleven cities game, *B* uses the principle, among the many applicable ones, that gives the best advantage. Since *B* did have a number of choices, it would be hard to say that *B* did not live up to his or her end of the deal, which is quite ambiguous. But it is equally true that, in playing with *B*, you might get the feeling that his or her selection of rule is not entirely random. Or imagine that *B* faces a vast array of games where sets must be divided and always uses a geographical rule to divide the set. When dividing sets of fruits, *B* divides according to where they grow; for books, according to where their authors reside; and so on. The problem with such an opponent is that geographical division will be hard to apply to a wide range of division games. *B*'s principle is not ambiguous, but it is appropriate only to some of the possible games.

The point is simple: wider scope, in the sense of more types of contingencies that must be dealt with, can be dealt with in one of two ways. One could employ a wider range of principles/contracts, but then one may increase ambiguity about how any single contingency should be handled. Increased ambiguity is bad for maintaining reputations. Alternatively, one can keep (in a larger and larger span) the same quite clear focal principle/implicit contract/corporate culture. But then as the span or type of contingencies encountered increases, that principle/contract/culture is being applied in contingencies to which it will be less and less appropriate. At some point, the benefits from widening the scope of the organization are outweighed by the inefficiencies engendered, and we will have a natural place to break between organizations.

Of course, transactions will need to take place across the break points. But these can be transactions undertaken under a different implicit contract—the contract of the impersonal marketplace, for example where *caveat emptor* rules. Where we have formal, recognized breaks, it will be easiest to have a change in the contract. Included here are formal breaks inside a legal entity— different divisions in a single corporation (cf. Williamson and the M-form hypothesis), or 'plants within a plant' (see Skinner 1974), and so on.

From this perspective, the focus strategy becomes a strategy of reducing the range of contingencies with which the implicit contract must deal, in order to deal better–less ambiguously—with those that are met.

5. In this chapter we have kept to cases in which one party A is short-lived and a second B is either long-lived or has vested interests in the reputation of a long-lived entity. Accordingly, any hierarchical transacting places hierarchical authority in B. This is but one arrangement that could be found. A second, quite prevalent arrangement is where As as well have vested interests in a second long-lived entity, and A_t deals with B_t through their two (respective) organizations. Examples are two corporations with an enduring relationship, and a labor union and a corporation. In such cases, transactions would not need to be hierarchical—rather, it would seem that the two parties could deal on equal terms. We would expect to see more transactions in which neither dictates what is done in the face of an unforeseen contingency, but where the two deal with these contingencies as they arise. (More hierarchical authority would rest with one of the parties, *ceteris paribus*, the easier it was to observe that the decisions of that party live up to an implicit contract.)

Since the range of possible implicit contracts is thus increased, one expects an increase in efficiency with such bilateral long lived relationships. It would also seem likely that, when compared with the situation in which only the Bs are organized, the case of bilateral organization would increase the share of surplus garnered by the As, at least in cases where Bs in the transaction are not perfectly competitive. In the case of labor unions as the A organization and firms as the B, these conclusions are borne out empirically (see Brown and Medoff 1978).

....

8. Concluding Remarks and Questions

I hope that this chapter has been able to communicate to a wide range of social scientists answers to the questions: How might an economist explain the role of corporate culture? How does that explanation tie in to extant economic theory? What pieces of theory are missing, and what might they look like when put in place? As I imagine is the case with most disciplines, economists tend to be intellectual imperialists, trying to render everything into their own terms of reference. This, then, has been an exercise in imperialism.

I have little doubt that this is a useful exercise for economic theorists. Until recently, we have had very little to say of any substance concerning the role of organizations. The theory outlined here is full of lacunae, and it is far from all-encompassing. But, following from a number of quite active areas of research, it does give a definite role to organization and culture within the organization. In so doing it helps to think (in terms of economics) about the role of organization/culture in strategy. (To readers who are economists: is this so?)

The questions I wish to leave noneconomists with (and have your answers to) are: Does this 'theory' hold together? From your perspectives, what is missing, and what is wrong? Is this imperialism of any value to social scientists other than economic theorists? Are the economic terms of discourse helpful in thinking about these questions?

....

Appendix

I provide here a simple formal model of some of the ideas discussed in the chapter. Consider the situation where A must decide whether to contract with B to perform a task that is either *easy* or *difficult*, each with probability $\frac{1}{2}$ A values performance of this task at \$9 and is risk neutral. B is risk-averse, and the utility B derives from performing the task and being paid for it depends on the task's difficulty and the amount paid. We give B's von Neumann-Morgenstern utility as a function of the amount paid and the task's difficulty (for several values of the amount paid) in tabular form. (You can check that these numbers are consistent with utility functions that are concave in dollar amounts.)

We will assume that B can obtain utility equal to zero in any period when not allowed to perform this task for A. Moreover, we assume that B's marginal utility for money when the task is difficult and payment is \$13 equals the marginal utility for money when the task is easy and payment is \$3. (This is consistent with the numbers given in the table.)

We will not be explicit for a while as to which version of the story we are

Table 4.1 Utilities for B for certain payment and task difficulty combinations

| | Payment to B | | | | | |
	\$3	\$3.40	\$8	\$9	\$12.50	\$13
Easy Task	2	2.32	4	4.3	4.9125	5
Difficult	−16	−15	−6	−4.4	1.2	2

telling—a story with one A and one B or one B and a sequence of As or a sequence of each type and B Associates—for any of these the calculations to follow will work. (For the sake of definiteness, we will speak in terms of the first of these three stories.) Also, we will speak in terms of an infinite horizon version of the story, with a per-period discount rate, rather than in terms of a probability of continuing. Of course, the mathematics works precisely the same for the continuation probability version of the story.

Note first that if we cannot make a contract contingent on the task's difficulty at all, then A and B cannot strike a deal. (This would pertain if, say, they played only once, there was nothing like B Associates, and the task's difficulty was not verifiable.) For then B's payment would have to be certain. A is willing to pay no more than $9 and B's expected utility with a sure payment of $9 is less than zero, which is B's reservation utility level. (We assume B must accept or reject the task prior to learning how difficult it is. If the difficulty is observable *ex ante*, then B can always take the task when it is easy.)

A.1. The Base Case: Observable Difficulty in a Repeated Setting

If the task difficulty is observable and we have a long-lived B concerned with reputation, then the reputation construction works. Suppose the pair agree that B will submit a bill of no more than $13 after the task is done (and they know how difficult it was), with the implicit understanding that the bill will be $3 if the task is easy and $13 if hard. This gives B a per-period expected utility of 2. Moreover, if B will be forestalled from any further work of this type by gouging A in any period (that is, if A will never deal with B again if B does gouge A once), then by gouging (charging $13 for an easy task) nets B utility of 5 this period and zero ever after. This is as opposed to (at least) utility of 2 stretching out into the future, which, with a discount factor of 0.9, has a present utility value of 20. Thus B does better not gouging, and A can trust B not to do so, giving A an expected gain of $1.

One further point on this case: our statement earlier on the equality of B's marginal utilities, combined with A's risk neutrality, makes this particular contingent (implicit) contract efficient. There is no way to make B better off without making A worse off, and vice versa. This is not to say that this is the only efficient arrangement. By lowering payments, keeping the marginal utilities equal, we will decrease the expected utility of B and increase the expected payoff to A. Raising both payoffs will do the reverse. These increases can continue until A's expected value from this arrangement hits zero—at the

David M. Kreps

point where the expected payment is $9. On the other side, the decreases in the two payments must stop *before* we reach an expected utility level of zero per period for B, because at zero utility, B will not keep to the equilibrium. The constraint for decreases in B's payments comes at the point where, faced with an easy job, B would prefer to charge the higher amount and have no further dealings of this sort to continuing with the implicit contract.

A.2. Unobservable Difficulty

Now imagine that only B can discern the difficulty of the task. A cannot determine how hard the task was either *ex post* or *ex ante*. A certainly would never *always* agree to pay any bill that B submits; for then B would *always* submit a bill of $13, which leaves A with an expected loss of $4 per period. A *must* 'punish' B if A thinks B is engaged in gouging. A could employ many complex strategies to do this, choosing behavior based on past bills submitted by B. But, to keep matters simple, we will look at a strategy with a particularly simple form. *Whenever B submits a bill of $13, A will refuse to trust B for the subsequent n periods.* (To make this part of a perfect Nash equilibrium, we will suppose as well that B will gouge A if ever A fails to carry out on this threat, and A will refuse to deal with B ever again in the same instance.)

How will B react to A's strategy? Let v denote B's expected utility from following an optimal strategy in response to A's strategy. Then when the task is easy, B has a choice of either submitting a bill of $3, which will net expected utility $2 + .9v$, or submitting a bill of $13, which will net expected utility $5 + .9^{n+1}v$. Note the difference in the discount factors. We assumed that B nets zero in the n periods it will take to get A to trust once again. Similarly, when the task is hard, B has a choice of submitting the bill of $13 which nets $2 + .9^{n+1}v$, and submitting a bill of $3, which nets utility $-16 + .9v$.

Let us suppose that B submits the correct bill, namely $3 when the task is easy and $13 when it is hard. Then the functional equation that defines v is

$$v = .5(2 + .9v) + .5(2 + .9^{n+1}v),$$

where the first term on the right-hand side is the utility derived if the task is easy, and the second is the utility derived if the task is hard. Solving for v, this gives

$$v = \frac{2}{1 - (.45 + .5 \times .9^{n+1})}.$$

264

For this v, in order to verify that submitting the correct bill is a best response by B, we must verify that

$$2 + .9v > 5 + .9^{n+1}v \text{ and } 2 + .9^{n+1}b > -16 + .9v,$$
$$\text{or } 18 > .9(1 - .9^n)v > 3.$$

As n increases, v decreases (because punishment which follows every \$13 bill—that is, after every hard task—lasts longer). But for low values of n, the inequality $2 + .9v > 5 + .9^{n+1}v$ is violated, which simply means that if punishment is not substantial enough, B will always submit a \$13 bill. Both A and B have it in their interests to make n as low as possible, consistent with inducing B to submit the correct bill, because both lose during a punishment period. We look, then, for the least n such that the needed inequality holds. This turns out to be $n = 11$, with $v = 4.89$. (It should be noted that for all $n > 11$ we also have equilibria, but the equilibria for larger n are Pareto-inferior to the equilibrium with $n = 11$.)

How well does A do in this equilibrium? The functional equation for u, the expected (discounted) monetary value to A (when we are not in a punishment period), is

$$u = 1 + .5 \times .9u + .5 \times .9^{12}u,$$

this being the expected monetary value from the immediate period (\$1) plus the discounted average continuation expected monetary value—if the task is easy, u discounted one period; if the task is difficult, u discounted by twelve periods. This is $u = 2.45$, as compared to the \$10 expected discounted present value that A receives without the observability problem. That is, both A and B get approximately 25 per cent of their best-expected discounted monetary value/utility when there are problems of observability and we use this equilibrium.

By giving A the ability to use a slightly more complex strategy, we can push up these values a bit. If A punishes B for eleven periods, then B has a strict incentive to send the correct bill. That is, the punishment above is more strict than need be. We could lessen the punishment by having A, say, punish B for eleven periods with probability .99 each time that B submits a bill of \$13. Let me be quite precise about this. I mean to assume that A randomizes, and this randomization is observable to B. Suppose, for instance, that there is a month between B's submission of a bill and the next time A must decide whether to contract with B, and in this interim period the government issues, say, a monthly report on the level of M1. A then announces the following strategy: following the submission of a bill of \$13, A will look up the next report on the level of M1; specifically, A will look at the third and fourth significant digits of that report. If the third and fourth digits are, respectively, 1 and 7, A will continue to deal with B; if the two digits are anything else, A

will refrain for eleven periods. Note well that B can monitor A's compliance with this randomization procedure (and, for those technically minded, we will work out strategies following any defection so this becomes a perfect Nash equilibrium).

Does this weaker punishment give B appropriate incentives? Let me generalize slightly and consider the following strategy by A. Following submission of a \$13 bill, A will (publicly) randomize so there is a probability p that A will withhold business from B for n periods and a probability $1-p$ that A will go on trusting B (until the next time A gets a bill of \$13). Then to ensure that submission of the correct bill is B's best response, we must check that

$$2 + .9v \geq 5 + .9(1 - p)v + .9^{n+1}pv,$$

where v, as before, is the value of following the correct bill strategy. This inequality simply ensures that, when the task is easy, submitting the correct bill does at least as well as submitting the incorrect, inflated bill. (There is a second inequality to check—that punishment is not so severe that B will submit a bill of \$3 even when the task is difficult. We'll refrain from explicitly doing this calculation in what follows.) And v will be given by the functional equation

$$v = 2 + (.5 + .5(1 - p)).9v + .5p(.9^{n+1})v.$$

If we call $\delta = .9(1 - .9^n)p$, the functional equation and the inequality become

$$v = \frac{2}{.1 + .5\delta} \quad \text{and} \quad 3 \leq \delta v,$$

respectively. Solving for the largest v that satisfies the inequality yields $v = 5$ and $\delta = .6$. (Readers should not be misled by the fact that both v and the utility of \$13 when the task is easy are 5; this is a coincidence. Indeed, as we lower the utility of \$13 when the task is easy, we will raise the value of the game to B, since lesser punishment is necessary.)

Similar calculations will yield that the expected discounted monetary value to A of using a strategy with a p and n as above is a simple function of δ, namely $1/(.1 + .5\delta)$, so for any p and n combination that yields $\delta = .6$ (just large enough to keep B honest), the value to A is \$2.50.

All this was based on the hypothesis that A could play an observable randomized strategy (in determining whether to start a punishment period). Suppose that A cannot do this. A always has the ability to randomize, but we suppose now that B cannot be given proof that A has carried out an intended randomization. This will raise problems for the equilibria above. If we tried to implement the *precise* $\delta = .6$ equilibrium above, then p cannot be zero or one. And then, once a bill of \$13 is submitted, as long as B is submitting correct bills, it is in the interests of A to go on trusting B. If the randomization cannot be observed (and penalties cannot be enforced if A fails to follow through), then A will have an incentive to *pretend* that the randomization came out in favor of further trust. This then destroys the equilibrium.

We can get an equilibrium with a p different from one, but it has an unfortunate property. We do this by (i) supposing that δ is set so that, given an easy task, B is indifferent between submitting bills of $3 and of $13, and by (ii) having B randomize between these two bills in a way that makes A indifferent between triggering punishment (in the face of a $13 bill) and continuing to trust B. Assuming that u is the game's value to A, requirement (ii) is $.9u = .9^{n+1}u$. Of course, this has a single solution (for $n \neq 1$, which must be so to induce correct billing by B)—namely, $u = 0$. This simple set of strategies yields an equilibrium only when the value to A is driven to zero. This does not raise the value of the game to B, who must be indifferent between gouging and not, and so the same functional equation defines v (as a function of δ).

This scenario pertains only to the simple strategies given here. Since B is having problems with observability, we might consider an A-like strategy for B—say, gouge with high probability for a while if A accepts a $13 bill. To compute such an equilibrium gets quite tedious, however, so we'll leave this notion here.

Observability of randomization is not, of course, a problem when A is not randomizing. We always have at our disposal the $n = 11$, $p = 1$ equilibrium originally given. (A comment is irresistible here, but readers who are getting a bit lost should skip to the next paragraph: note the sense in which this *pure strategy* equilibrium is really the limit of the sort of equilibrium suggested in the preceding paragraph. A is not supposed to accept a bill of $13 and proceed blithely on. What keeps A to this is the supposed out-of-equilibrium behavior by B: should A accept a bill of $13 and not begin a punishment period, B responds by gouging perpetually. This is clearly the limit of a strategy of A accepting a $13 bill, then, with positive probability, gouging for some length of time.)

We have assumed that A follows a simple type of strategy, and we've derived from that equilibria that give B up to an expected utility of 5 and A an expected (overall) payment of $2.50. Are there equilibria, involving more complex sorts of strategies, in which B can do better than this, without having A do worse? (Of course, we can make B better off in equilibrium at the expense of A by raising the levels of each payment.) In other words, is this an efficient equilibrium?

We will not attempt here to answer this question. But it is worthwhile to note that, in principle, the question is answerable. The techniques that are necessary (more or less) are given by Abreu, Pearce, and Stachetti (1987).

A.3 Using Imperfect Signals

This analysis presumes that the A's could not observe the task's difficulty and that payment can be based on nothing else of relevance. Now consider the possibility of there being an imperfect signal that payment could be based on. Namely, suppose that each task either did or didn't require calculus. Easy tasks require calculus with probability 0.2, and hard tasks require calculus with probability 0.975. It is observable (*ex post*) whether the task really did require calculus. Even though this is observable, we assume it is not verifiable. With the usual construction we can have a scheme in which B is given the authority to submit any bill up to $13; B bills A_t that amount if the task required calculus and $3 if it didn't. Or, rather, we can make this an equilibrium as long as both sides have an incentive to participate in this scheme and as long as B hasn't the incentive to submit a higher bill when the task didn't require calculus.

To check that this is an equilibrium, note first that it results in the following round by round: with probability 0.1, the task is easy and the task required calculus, giving B utility 5. With probability 0.4, the task is easy and no calculus is required; B's utility is 2. With probability 0.4875, the task is difficult and calculus is required; the bill is $13 and utility 2. With probability .0125 the task is difficult and calculus wasn't required—a bill of $3 and utility—16. In each round, then, the expected bill is $8.875—enough to keep A interested in the arrangement. And B's expected utility in each round is 2.075. This gives B a present value of 20.75 in keeping to the scheme. And so B will be willing to submit the correct bids: the crucial computation is what happens if the task is difficult and calculus is not required. If B tries to gouge A by submitting a bill of $13, B gets utility 2 today and (assuming punishment forever) zero thereafter. Submitting the correct bill nets—16 today and a (discounted) $.9 \times 20.75 = 18.675$ in the future. Hence B slightly prefers to stick to the arrangement.

Is this an efficient equilibrium among all those that base payments solely on whether calculus is or isn't needed? No. Recall the assumption about marginal utilities of money to B; this told us that bills of $3 and $13 gave an efficient arrangement when the task's difficulty was observable. But now, when the task's difficulty is unobservable, unless the marginal utilities to B of money at $13 when the task is easy and at $3 when it is hard are equal (and equal to the other two marginal utilities), we will not have a second-best scheme. Assuming concavity of B's utility function, these margins will not equate given the values in Table 1. So we do better for B, holding A's expected value constant, if we simultaneously increase the smaller payment and decrease the larger payment in such a way that the expected value of the payment stays fixed, up until the point where the conditional expected marginal utilities (conditional on the task requiring calculus or not) are equated. This, note, will not upset the equilibrium, because B will be *more* inclined to follow the equilibrium in the one case where it matters—where calculus is not required but the job is hard. (The other constraint, that B will not wish to upset the arrangement by charging the greater amount when the job is easy and calculus is not required, is not binding.)

How does this compare with the equilibria we computed without the use of calculus? B is certainly better off: an expected utility of 20.75, versus 5 before. But the A's are worse off; they make a bare $0.125 per round in expectation, versus $0.25 on average that they got before. Happily, we can make both sides better off as follows.

Lower the payment that B receives when calculus is required to $12.50 and raise the payment when it is not to $3.40. This gives an expected payment of $8.74625 per period—just better than before. It gives B an expected utility of 18.1675 per period, certainly better than before. And it is an equilibrium: the constraint to check is that B doesn't want to break up the deal when a hard job comes along that doesn't require calculus. By breaking up the deal, B charges $12.50, for utility level 1.2 this round and zero thereafter. By sticking to the deal, B must swallow a utility of—15 this round, plus a continuation value of 18.1675. Discounting the continuation value appropriately, B's net for keeping to the arrangement is 1.35, and B will keep on.

In the construction just made, we barely made A better off than if we had ignored the imperfect calculus signal. Note that B is much better off than in the equilibrium where we ignored calculus and depended on punishments—a utility of 18 or so versus one of 5. It would have seemed that we could borrow more of that surplus from B in order to make A better off. But this is an illusion. B's utility *must* be kept fairly high in the calculus—dependent equilibrium so that, faced with a hard job that does not require calculus, B will swallow that large dose of negative utility. It is a very severe constraint to keep B happy enough to swallow that dose.

The constraint gets no easier as the odds of a hard job that doesn't need calculus fall to zero. As long as this has positive probability of happening and we wish to keep B honest in these circumstances, B must be getting a large continuation level of utility. Note the discontinuity here: when the probability of this is zero, we don't need to worry about this constraint; then the binding constraint is that B must be willing to settle for the lower payment when there is an easy job that doesn't require calculus.

David M. Kreps

This suggests that, given this imperfect signal, we might well do better to stop trying to satisfy this constraint. Instead of breaking cooperation forever if B charges the high amount when calculus is not required, A will stop dealing with B for a few periods. This punishment will be enough to keep B from charging the higher amount for an easy job that doesn't require calculus, but it will be insufficient to keep B from charging that amount for a hard job that doesn't require calculus. That is, in the equilibrium, B will be expected to charge the higher amount for hard jobs that don't require calculus, paying for this privilege with a loss of work for a few periods. And even though this payment will be worthwhile when the job is hard, it will be too much to pay when the job is easy (and calculus is not needed).

Specifically, suppose that the two enter into the following arrangement. The bills will be B's choice of $12.50 or $3.00. A bill of $12.50 will be considered warranted if calculus was indeed required, and A will enter into the agreement again in the next period. A bill of $3.00 is always happily accepted by A—and the agreement will again ensue in the next period. But a bill of $12.50 when calculus is not required will be considered unwarranted, and A will refuse to deal with B for three periods thereafter.

In the equilibrium, B will set the bill at $12.50 whenever calculus is required *or* the job is hard. B will bill $3.00 only for easy jobs that don't require calculus. In this case, one can work out the expected utility for B in any period when the two deal. It is the solution to

$$v = .1 \times (4.9125 + .9v) + .4 \times (2 + .9v) + .4875 \times (1.2 + .9v) \\ + .0125 \times (1.2 + .9^4 v),$$

which is $v = 18.35296$. To ensure that this is an equilibrium, we must ensure that B is willing to charge the lesser amount for an easy job that doesn't require calculus: charging the lesser amount nets utility $2 + .9v = 17.718$, while charging the greater amount nets utility $4.9125 + .9^4 v = 16.95$, and we see that B will go along. Note that B is doing better here than in the equilibrium we computed just earlier.

A does better, on average, as well. In any round in which there is a contract, A expects to pay $8.70 for a net of $.30. Now in approximately .0375 of the rounds, A will get zero, since A is punishing B. But, if you work out the exact expected present value to A of this scheme, you come up with $2.91, which is more than before.

This, of course, doesn't demonstrate that an efficient contract that can be obtained through strict adherence to the calculus signal is worse than some equilibrium that allows B to put in some unwarranted charge some of the time, at the cost of punishment. In the case of this problem, I am fairly well convinced, however, that this will be so, at least as long as B is not risk-neutral. (My conjectured proof requires that two randomizations be publicly observable *ex post*—*A*'s randomization to determine whether to enforce punishment and *B*'s randomization to determine whether to defect from strict adherence.) I conjecture as well that a very general proposition of this sort can be derived, but this will have to await another essay.

....

Postscript—1988

In the four or so years that have passed since I wrote 'Corporate Culture', there has been a fair amount of energy devoted to some of the themes surveyed there. Even given the normal publication lag, it would be unfortunate not to pay some attention to those themes. At the same time, it is amusing to reread the last line of the introduction: 'readers will see that the final steps, while not accomplished, are not excessively difficult to traverse.' As some of those final steps are barely closer to fulfillment now than then, either I misestimated their difficulty or their inherent interest. I think the former is more likely to be true.

The one point at which, in rereading the chapter, I winced so hard that I felt compelled to signal that I would say something more is where I criticized Williamson for having little to say about the relative advantages and disadvantages of internal organization. (Hereafter, I will use his term and call it unified governance.) I would have profited enormously in writing this chapter from a close reading of Williamson (1985) and, especially in this instance, in reading chapter 6, on the inefficiencies of unified governance. To recast slightly what Williamson has to say there, when one moves from market governance to unified governance, one trades one set of inefficiencies for another, as the nature of what is exchanged changes. In market governance, a decision maker deals with others only to purchase the outputs derived from their labors. When we move to unified governance, the single decision maker can command the use of all the capital, but now that person must employ the labor services of those he or she earlier dealt with only for the output of their labor. The high-powered market-based incentives for labor are replaced by lower-powered internal incentives. Why are market-based incentives more high-powered? Williamson gives a number of specific reasons, many of which come down to the fact that it is hard in some cases to preserve *ex post* in internal organization the *ex ante* incentives that one has. To say more will take us too deeply into a whole new subject, except to say that Williamson (1985) answers my initial criticism rather substantially. Moreover, Williamson's more verbal theorizing on this point has been met by a number of more mathematical contributions, most notably by Holmstrom (1982) on the general issues of career concerns and by Milgrom (1986) and Milgrom and Roberts (1987) on quasi-rents and influence activities within organizations. Note well that these papers all speak to the diseconomies of unified governance, whereas I was criticizing transaction-cost economics for not being explicit about unified governance's relative economies. But this is a case where analysis of one side makes clear the other.

Another point on which I would have benefited from a close reading of Williamson concerns the dichotomy I draw between traditional and hierarchical transactions. There is hardly a dichotomy here. Williamson (chapter 3) adds to this stark picture bilateral and trilateral relational transactions and, of course, unified governance. Having concentrated my own attention on hierarchical transactions, I might accuse him of not paying enough attention to that form of governance. But it is clear that the picture is much richer than the naive reader of this chapter might come to believe.

This chapter is also severely unbalanced in the role it gives to reputation as the sole *raison d'être* for the firm. I did wish to stress that role, because I think it connects the firm and its culture, but I don't mean to dismiss other reasons for having firmlike organizations. Beyond the one paper in the chapter that I do cite (i.e. Grossman and Hart 1986), there has been a substantial amount of work recently on those other reasons and especially work on reasons related to the inability to write complete contingent contracts. The very excellent survey by Holmstrom and Tirole (1987) should be consulted for a more balanced view of the subject than one gets here.

There have been some substantial advances on the technical fronts associated with the ideas of the section on reputation. In particular, the technology appropriate for dealing with noisy observables in the folk theorem (and in related agency problems) has been substantially advanced by Abreu, Pearce, and Stachetti (1987), by Fudenberg, Holmstrom, and Milgrom (1987), by Fudenberg and Maskin (1986), and by Holmstrom and Milgrom (1987), among others. Also, the variation on the folk theorem appropriate for the case where there is one long-lived party and several short-lived ones is worked out in Fudenberg, Kreps, and Maskin (1987).

There has been relatively little (or no) formal development of the ideas associated with focal points and with unforeseen contingencies. Regarding focal points, only Crawford and Haller (1987) comes to mind as a really innovative approach to the subject, although Fudenberg and Kreps (1988) will have a bit to say about the evolution of something that will share some of the characteristics of a focal point.

By comparison, bounded rationality has been rather a growth area in economic theory recently; there has been, for example, a great deal of work concerning modelling players as machines (finite state automata or

Turing machines), and somewhat more on measures of complexity of strategies for supporting supergame equilibria. But these approaches have not, I think, led us in directions that will help with the problems encountered in this chapter, and I will not, in consequence, bother with references. Unforeseen contingencies have not otherwise arisen in the formal literature to my knowledge, and so on that subject, four years after it was originally promised, I can do nothing more than at long last offer for the reader's enjoyment Kreps (1988).

....

Notes

1. In writing this chapter, I had tremendous difficulties coming up with a term for what it is that textbook economics and the Porter approach to strategy does not analyze. I will use organizational efficiency and effectiveness and words of that ilk, but I confess much unhappiness with them.

2. The notion of a hierarchical transaction and its particular relevance to employment relationships is quite old—going back at least to Simon (1951).

3. The role of reputation in hierarchical transactions also appears in Simon (1951).

4. It might run thus: concentrated ownership of capital can be, as they show, efficient. Capital ownership by an individual might subject the individual to too much risk. Hence, for purposes of risk sharing we invent the limited stock corporation.

5. The argument's flavor is easiest to suggest if we assume that the game will run precisely one hundred million rounds. In this case, roughly, the argument runs as follows: A, with many rounds to go, will want to test B to see if B will honor trust. At worst A loses $5 by doing so, and there is a one-in-one-thousand chance that A will make at least $10 in each of the many rounds left to go. But then what will B do when A tries him or her out? Even if B is not a moral person, B will honor that trust: to abuse it would reveal B's true character to A and would mean obtaining nothing in all subsequent rounds; honoring trust will cause A to take another chance for a long time to come worth $10 each time.

6. The reader desiring a more exact analysis of the issues discussed here may wish to refer at this point to the Appendix near the end of the chapter, where a simple example is presented.

7. Well, that is a bit of an overstatement. One must trade off unambiguity and the overall efficiency of the arrangement. In our earlier example of easy and hard problems and problems that do or do not require calculus, applying the calculus rule might be completely unambiguous, but as we make the necessity of calculus less and less predicative on the difficulty of the job, we lower the surplus derived from basing payment on the necessity of calculus. We could lower the predicative power of calculus to just the point where the arrangement still lives (test (ii) is just

passed with enough surplus left for B so that the maintained reputation is worthwhile, and then we could not wish to apply the unambiguous and not very productive calculus based scheme. Some measure of ambiguity is worth tolerating if there is a corresponding gain in the arrangement's efficiency. The Appendix near the end of the chapter contains an explicit illustration of this point.

8. Seemingly outside the scope of economic theory are notions such as the following: a strong corporate culture increases the degree to which individuals internalize the common good of the organization. But one can approach this notion within an economic framework on the supposition that control in the organization will be based on adherence to the culture. An easy approach is to view this form of control as a simple screen. Somewhat less direct would be a story in which individuals are happier in situations in which they will be evaluated by criteria that leave little to chance—where they have relatively greater control of their own destinies. This could be a primitive taste, or one induced from risk aversion to capricious evaluation. In either case, if adherence to the culture provides an evaluation criterion that is predictable in application, it can provide an economic bond to the organization.

References

Abreu, D., Pearce, D., and Stachetti, E. (1987), 'Towards a Theory of Discounted Repeat Games with Imperfect Monitoring', mimeo, Harvard University.

Arrow, K. (1974), *The Limits of Organization* (New York: Norton).

—— and Hahn, F. (1971), *General Competitive Analysis* (San Francisco: Holden-Day).

Brown, C. and Medoff, J. (1978), 'Trade Unions in the Production Process', *Journal of Political Economy*, 86: 355–78.

Coase, R. (1937), 'The Nature of the Firm', *Economica*, 4: 386–405.

Crawford, V. and Haller, H. (1987), 'Learning How to Cooperate: Optimal Play in Repeated Coordination Games', Mimeo, University of California, San Diego.

Fudenberg, D., Holstrom, B., and Milgrom, P., 'Short-Term Contracts and Long-Term Agency Relationships', *Journal of Economic Theory*, forthcoming.

—— and Kreps, D., (1988), *A Theory of Learning, Experimentation and Equilibrium in Games*, mimeo, Stanford University.

—— and Maskin, E. (1986), 'The Folk Theorem with Discounting and with Incomplete — Information', *Econometrica*, 54: 533–54.

Grossman, S. and Hart, O. (1986), 'The Costs and Benefits of Ownership: A Theory of Vertical and Lateral Integration', *Journal of Political Economy*, 94: 691–719.

Holstrom, B. (1979), 'Moral Hazard and Observability', *Bell Journal of Economics*, 10: 74–91.

—————— and Milgrom, P. (1987), 'Aggregation and Linearity in the Provision of Intertemporal Incentives', *Econometrica*, 55: 303–28.

—————— and Tirole, J., 'The Theory of the Firm', in R. Schmalensee and R. Willig (eds.), *Handbook of Industrial Organization* (forthcoming).

Kreps, D. (1988), 'On Modelling Unforeseen Contingencies', mimeo, Stanford University.

—————— Milgrom, P., Roberts, J., and Wilson, R. (1982), 'Rational Cooperation in the Finitely Repeated Prisoners' Dilemma', *Journal of Economic Theory*, 16: 310–34.

—————— and Wilson, R. (1982), 'Reputation and Imperfect Information', *Journal of Economic Theory*, 27: 253–79.

Milgrom, P. (1986), 'Quasi-Rents, Influence and Organization Form', mimeo, Yale University.

—————— and Roberts, J. (1986), 'Relying on the Information of Interested Parties', *Rand Journal of Economics*, 17: 18–32.

Porter, M. E. (1987), 'From Competitive Advantage to Corporate Strategy', *Harvard Business Review*, 65: 43–59.

Roth, A. and Schoumaker. F. (1983), 'Expectations and Reputations in Bargaining: An Experimental Study', *American Economic Review*, 73: 362–72.

Savage, L. (1954), *The Foundations of Statistics* (New York: Wiley).

Schelling, T. (1960), *The Strategy of Conflict* (Cambridge, Mass.: Harvard University Press).

Simon, H. (1951), 'A Formal Theory of the Employment Relationship', 19: 293–305.

—————— (1965), *Administrative Behavior (New York: Free Press)*.

Skinner, W. (1974), 'The Focused Factory', *Harvard Business Review*, 5: 113–21.

Spence, A. M. (1975), 'Monopoly, Quality, and Regulation', *Bell Journal of Economics*, Autumn: 417: 417–29.

von Neumann, J. and Morgenstern, O. (1945), *The Theory of Games and Economic Behavior*, (Princeton, NJ: Princeton University Press).

Williamson, O. (1975), *Markets and Hierarchies: Analysis and Antitrust Implications* (New York: Free Press).

—————— (1981), 'The Modern Corporation: Origins, Evolution and Attributes', *Journal of Economic Literature*, 19: 1537–70.

—————— (1985), *The Economic Institutions of Capitalism* (New York, Free Press).

9

Co-operative Agreements and the Organization of Industry

P. Mariti and R. H. Smiley

1. Introduction

The field of industrial organization involves, in major part, the study of how industry is organized and why. The organization of industry, including for example the size distribution of firms, depends in turn on how firms interact. In *Markets and Hierarchies*, Williamson (1975) has identified two major types of interaction: the marketplace (either competition between firms or single transactions between buyers and sellers), and mergers. Earlier, Coase (1937) identified the two methods for organizing economic activity as internal to the firm or external to the firm. This paper investigates an intermediate form of interrelationship between firms, which provides yet another way of organizing economic activity, the co-operative agreement.

It is important to state just what we mean by co-operative agreements, and to differentiate these type of agreements from other transactions. For our purposes, a co-operative agreement is any long term, explicit agreement amongst two or more firms. This agreement may or may not involve financial remuneration. There can be payment for some good or service: alternatively, the firms may agree to exchange information or other commodity or service: both are co-operative agreements. To meet our definition, the agreement must be long term: a one time purchase of goods and services

A preliminary draft of this paper was presented at the 8th Conference of the European Association for Research in Industrial Economics, September 16 & 18, 1981, in Basel, Switzerland. The Consiglio Nazionale delle Ricerche (CNR) provided funding for Professor Smiley while he was a visiting professor at the University of Pisa.

is not a co-operative agreement, but an agreement to purchase all inputs from one supplier over the next ten years is a co-operative agreement. The agreement must be explicit: just because a majority of all purchases happen *ex-post* to have been from one supplier does not imply that a co-operative agreement was in force unless there was an explicit understanding before the fact that this would be so. Although the agreement must be explicit, there need not be a written contract for a co-operative agreement to exist. Co-operative agreements can be made verbally, although most agreements are indeed based on a written contract. Finally, a co-operative agreement can take various legal forms: two legal forms that are investigated in this paper are the joint venture and the bidding consortium (which itself may or may not be a joint venture). Since the objective of this paper is to study that transactional middle ground between single transactions in the marketplace and internal organization which often occurs through merger, acquisitions and mergers are not treated as co-operative agreements.

As the reader can see from the above definition, this paper undertakes a rather broad field of study. Since there have been virtually no previous attempts to study this field, most of this paper is purposely rather descriptive. Our objective is to draw the attention of the academic community to a broad range of interfirm transactions which have been previously ignored.

The organization of the paper is as follows. Section 2 discusses some earlier research in the field, and offers some preliminary comments on the study. Section 3 discusses data sources and concepts used to classify the information gathered, while Section 4 presents some overall findings. Section 5 deals with the analysis of and factors affecting the various motivations for co-operative agreements; in Section 6 there is a preliminary discussion of trends in the use of co-operative agreements and Section 7 discusses public policy towards co-operative agreements. The paper ends with some final comments.

2. The Field of Study

The firm is most commonly viewed as an entity purchasing inputs from which it obtains marketable products according to its underlying production function. What the firm does—its range of activities—is treated as a datum of the problem. However as Stigler (1951) points out, to reach the stage of marketable products or services, firms engage in a whole series of distinct activities or functions which may or may not be technologically related:

buying inputs; transforming them into semifinished products; designing products and doing research for product innovation; searching for financing; extending credit to buyers; searching for suppliers and new markets; etc.

For each such activity a firm has at least three alternatives:

1. organizing it internally;
2. making recourse to individual market transactions;
3. developing a co-operative agreement with one or more firms (intermediate forms of organization).

Alternatives (1) and (2) can be illustrated by reference to the technological approach—based on economies and diseconomies of scale and Adam Smith's principle of division of labor—refined by Stigler integrated with the transaction approach originally advocated by Coase, and elaborated on by Williamson (1975, 1979), amongst others (Mariti, 1980).

Several authors have mentioned the existence of intermediate forms of organization of economic activity. As early as 1952, P. W. S. Andrews wrote:

. . . Industrial Economics has a lively interest in the relationship between individual businesses . . . One thinks at once of competitive relationships—of the ways in which many prices, for example, emerge out of the competitive struggle between businesses. But in fact, even in very competitive industries it is important not to overlook the complementary relationships which exist as well. (77)

K. Arrow has written:

'The price system, for all its virtues, is only one conceivable form of arranging trade, even in a system of private property. Bargaining can assume extremely general forms'. (50)

Aside from these and several other papers (e.g. Richardson 1972), co-operative agreements have received almost no attention in the academic literature. This is a serious deficiency which this paper is intended to correct.

There are several reasons for studying co-operative agreements. Casual perusal of the financial press indicates that they are indeed an important component of interfirm relations. In addition, ignoring the existence of co-operative agreements can lead on to incorrect theoretical results and policy descriptions. For example, Baumol and Fischer (1978) argue that one can deduce the optimal number of firms in an industry from the size of the market and knowledge of economies of scale in the production process. However, they ignore the possibility that is investigated in this paper: namely that through co-operative agreements, firms can take advantage of economies of scale in one or more of their production processes while remaining separate entities. The realization that the achievement of economics of scale is available (through co-operative agreements) to firms that are otherwise unrelated leads one to predict a greater number of firms than would be predicted by the Baumol and Fischer results.

3. Data Sources and Co-operative Agreement Classification

This study develops and makes use of two sources of data. First, we examined published reports of all co-operative agreements that were initiated in 1980 in the European financial press. Second, we interviewed a number of senior executives in European firms. These firms were chosen for interview because they had engaged in a large number of co-operative agreements. The firms interviewed were in the automobile, basic metals, computer, and electronic systems industries.

Due to the nature of the data gathering process, the sample is not a random one. The firms whose activities are reported in the financial press are generally quite large, and only important co-operative agreements between these firms are reported. Also, while the in depth interviews span a broad range of economic activity, the industries were not selected at random.

Seventy agreements were identified for the year 1980 in the financial press. Through a careful reading of the text of the article, each of the agreements was classified as to the major motivation of the partners. The motivations, which are discussed in detail below, are: technology transfer, technological complementarity, marketing agreement, risk sharing, and economies of scale (in production or other fields). We also noted whether the agreement took the legal form of a joint venture and/or a bidding consortium.

Two of the motivations are knowledge or technology related. The first, *technology transfer*, refers to the transfer of technology from one firm to another, in exchange for some consideration such as money or the right to market certain products. A patent license is the most common form of technology transfer, although the examples cited in this study were of a more permanent or ongoing type of technology transfer than a single patent license would provide.

Technology transfer implies a one way flow of information, while the category *technological complementarity* is for long term transactions where technology is exchanged or shared between two parties. Each of the firms will possess some unique knowledge or patent, and the co-operative agreement provides for a sharing of the knowledge of the two firms, usually in developing new products or services.

Marketing agreements can vary from something as simple as a single product marketing and distribution contract to a long term multi-product agreement, usually between a manufacturer and a firm with wholesale or retail outlets (often in different parts of the world than its partner currently covers). The marketing agreements included in this study are of the latter type, where a long term relationship is initiated by the agreement. Several agreements are between retailing chains with strengths in different parts of the world, rather than an agreement between a manufacturer and a distributor.

Economies of scale agreements refer to both production and distribution efficiencies which come with larger size. These agreements often involve production rationalization where one firm will manufacture all of several components while the other will manufacture all of remainder of the components. Such an arrangement allows longer production runs for each of the firms and the achievement of economies of scale and learning by doing.

The final motivation for co-operative agreements identified in this study is *risk sharing*. Agreements of this type generally provide for the management of operation by one of the partners, while the others merely contribute capital and absorb some of the risk of failure. In order for an agreement to be classified as a risk sharing agreement in this study, it must possess none of the attributes of agreements listed above; i.e. it must not be an agreement to achieve economies of scale, it must not be a marketing agreement, etc. If we did not use this classification rule, all co-operative agreements would be classified as risk sharing since in every case risk is shared between the parties. However, we wanted to identify those agreements where risk sharing was the only motivation.

One motivation for co-operative agreements which is omitted from this study is *reduction in transactions costs*. Reading Coase and Williamson, one would expect to find the avoidance of the cost of repeated transactions to be a primary motivation for undertaking co-operative agreements. It was because of this sort of expectation that we asked each of the senior executives we interviewed whether transactions cost were important in their decision making regarding co-operative agreements. We defined transactions costs as all costs of negotiating contracts including management's time, legal fees, and other identifiable costs. In all cases, they replied that avoiding transactions costs was not an issue in deciding to undertake co-operative agreements. The amount of money involved in the cost of making transactions was in all cases overwhelmed by other benefits and costs from co-operative agreements. For this reason, we have eliminated the transactions costs motivation from this paper. However, we should recognize that some would argue that we defined transactions costs too narrowly in discussing only the costs of normal transactions. If that is the case, then perhaps some of the motivations listed above could also be taken to read transactions costs motivations.

The co-operative agreements identified in this study take several legal forms. Two of the forms that are expressly identified are the *joint venture* and the *bidding consortium*. The joint venture is defined as an agreement in which two independent legal partners establish a third independent legal firm. A bidding consortium is a co-operative agreement that exists for a single project. The partners will each contribute some skill or portion of the task, and the project usually involves some sort of construction. A bidding consortium project can be a joint venture. Also, many of the technological complementarity or economies of scale co-operative agreements are joint ventures.

Firms taking part in the agreements were classified into industries at the two digit level according to the Italian standard industrial classification system, which is comparable to the classification schemes of the European Economic Community. Many agreements identified had more than one motivation, so there is some double counting in the tables below. Also, a motivation (such as economies of scale) was reported for every joint venture and bidding consortium.

....

4. Overall Findings

Table 1 presents the overall picture which emerges after classification of the seventy co-operative agreements identified. The most frequent motivation for co-operative agreements is technological complementarity, with forty-one per cent of the total agreements. Since technology transfer is an additional twenty-nine per cent of the total number of agreements, we see that seventy per cent of the total number of agreements in 1980 involved a transfer or sharing of knowledge. (Note that unlike the other categories, technological transfer and technological complementarity are mutually exclusive. A knowledge related agreement is either one or the other.) Economies of scale, risk sharing, and marketing agreements make up much smaller proportions of the total number of co-operative agreements.

Fifty-five per cent of the co-operative agreements take the legal form of a joint venture. This does not imply that in forty-five per cent of the cases there is no contract between the parties; in some cases an explicit contract is

Table 1. Motivations in the Sample of 70
Co-operative Agreements

Motivation and Legal Form	Percentage
Technology Transfer	29
Technological Complementarity	41
Marketing Agreement	21
Economies of Scale	16
Risk Sharing	14
Joint Ventures	55
Bidding Consortium	29

negotiated although no new firm is established, and therefore the agreement is not a joint venture. There are, however, some occasions in which a co-operative agreement is established with *no* legal contract.

The two-digit industry was identified for each of the parties to the seventy co-operative agreements, and this identification provides the basis for Table 2. The figure 1 is indicated in the appropriate category in Table 2 for each case in which the firms are in the same two-digit industry; a zero is entered if the firms are in different two-digit industries. There will therefore be twice as many zeros entered in the table as there were co-operative agreements between firms.

Before turning to a discussion of motivation for co-operative agreements on the part of different industries, we can state some general findings from an inspection of Table 2:

(a) The two-digit industries most active in establishing co-operative agreements are electrical and electronic appliances, chemicals, electronics (including equipment for data processing), automobiles, and oil refining.

(b) The legal form—joint venture—is chosen by these industries with roughly the same frequency.

(c) Bidding consortia predominate in the oil refining industry.

(d) For the industries which have a large number of co-operative agreements both inter- and intra-industry agreements are chosen, with the exception of oil refining where firms make agreements predominantly with firms in other industries.

Table 2. Motivation of Agreements by Industry

Two-digit Industry	Technology Transfer	Technological Complementarity	Marketing Agreement	Economies of Scale	Risk Sharing	Joint Venture	Bidding Consortium
Electrical and Electronic Appliances, Telecommunications Equipment	1110	1111111000	11100	10	0	111111000	1
Electronics, Equipment for Data Processing	10	00					
Chemicals	11	11000	110	0	0	100	0
Automobiles	111	10	1			11110	11
Means of Transportation other than Automobiles			0	111110		11100	
Mechanical Engineering	1	111		111			111
Retailing of Food, Textiles, Pharmaceuticals	11	1000	0			100	0
Precision Machinery and Appliances		10	10			110	
Services to Firms		00	00			00	
Oil refining	0	000			1	1	0
Metal Production and Transformation	00	00		0	100000	0000	1000000
Food and Beverages	0	00			0	10	00
Food Raw Materials	1		1			00	
Pulp and Paper	10		1		0	1	0
Metal Mining	1					1	1
Banking			10		0	1	1
Coal Mining					00	00	00
Utilities			0		0	0	0
Travel Agency, Transportation Intermediates							
Oil and Natural Gas Drilling	0				0	0	0
Non Ferrous Mining (Diamonds)	0						0
Agriculture	0						0
Air Transportation						0	
Wholesaling						0	
Retailing (Vehicles, Books, Gas)						0	
Building		1				1	

1. Indicates intra-industry agreement and 0 inter-industry agreement

283

5. The Motivation for Co-operative Agreements

In this section we analyze firms' motivations for entering into co-operative agreements, utilizing both the sample of seventy co-operative agreements reached in 1980 and our personal interviews with senior executives in a number of European firms.

The most common type of co-operative agreement involves the exchange of information. Co-operative agreements of this type can take two forms: technology transfer and technological complementarity representing twenty-nine and forty-one percent respectively of the total number of co-operative agreements in our sample of seventy. From the point of view of the firm acquiring the information, a reason for entering into a technology transfer agreement is that it is often cheaper and less risky to purchase information than it is to produce it. Technology transfer agreements involve, in most cases, purchase of the information by a large firm with the necessary manufacturing scale and distribution outlets, and sale of the information by a smaller firm which does not have the necessary manufacturing and/or marketing scale.

One of the more interesting types of technology transfer co-operative agreements to emerge in recent years is between the automobile industry and the electronics instrumentation industry. Both Renault and Peugeot have recently signed long term research and development contracts for automobile instrumentation and control technology. The benefits of a longer term agreement for the purchase of technology include a reduction in search costs, a better working relationship, and a better understanding by the research group of the needs of the automobile company. Both firms feel that these benefits exceed the benefits of a shorter term contracting strategy (such as the opportunity to choose the best product available from a number of different producers).

Technological complementarity agreements, in which each firm contributes some basic technological expertise to a joint project, are even more frequent than technology transfer agreements. One would expect to find such co-operative agreements where markets are expanding rapidly and/or technology is changing quickly. These conditions are both met in the electrical and the electronics' industries, which make up sixteen out of thirty-nine of the cases. They are also common in the mechanical engineering and means of transportation industries.

The introduction of new products is often accompanied by a different type of co-operative agreement, the marketing or distribution agreement. We would expect to find more marketing co-operative agreements in those industries with more rapidly changing technology, since more new products will be introduced in those industries. Fifteen of the seventy agreements studied indicated marketing as a major motivation, and eight of these fifteen were in the electronics industries (including electronic data processing, telecommunications equipment, and electrical and electronic appliances).

If production is characterized by economies of scale and learning by doing, firms may attempt to decrease costs by expanding output to achieve these benefits. Low product demand and the costs of firm growth may, however, limit this strategy. Horizontal mergers are another possible way to achieve the cost reducing benefits of larger output. But mergers involve the combination of whole firms with numerous uncertainties about the ability of the parts to function smoothly together, and the resulting difficulties of the merger may overwhelm the cost reducing benefits of larger volume in one or several individual products. Co-operative agreements, on the other hand, allow firms in the same industry to rationalize production, thus reducing costs through economies of scale and learning by doing, without the uncertainties and difficulties of full scale mergers.

Co-operative agreements for economies of scale or production rationalization are important in the automobile industry. Eleven of the seventy co-operative agreements studied indicated production economies of scale as a major motivation. Six of these eleven were in the automobile industry, and three others were in the non-automobile transportation industry (motor-cycles and aircraft). As an example of one of these production rationalization co-operative agreements, Alfa Romeo and Nissan have just concluded an agreement whereby Alfa Romeo will produce the engine and Nissan will produce the body for a new automobile to be marketed throughout Europe. The benefits to each firm include the introduction of a new automobile at a substantially reduced investment cost, and the savings due to learning which will accompany a larger production run than either firm could have achieved separately.

Investment rationalization also appears to be important in the metals industry. For example, an Italian firm and the Italian subsidiary of a French non-ferrous metals company reached an agreement in the mid 1970s to avoid duplicating irreversible capacity investments in Italy, thereby rationalizing production capacity between them. Production economies of scale and learning can also be reached by such simple co-operative agreements as long term purchase contracts. The longer the term of the contract, the more extensive will be the learning induced cost reductions for the supplier. One of the automobile companies interviewed was making a special attempt to reduce its purchased parts cost through concentrating contracts on fewer suppliers, with longer production runs resulting.

Another motive for entering a co-operative agreement is *risk sharing*. In this type of agreement one of the partners is responsible for the project, while the others contribute only capital. Ten of the seventy agreements studied were risk sharing: six of these risk sharing projects were in the oil refining industry.

In our interviews with senior executives of European firms, a number of important points were made that do not lend themselves to the classification in Table 2. These are essentially strategic aspects that managers consider when deciding whether or not to engage in a co-operative agreement, and in deciding on the form of the agreement. For example, large defense firms may not prefer to develop weapons systems through technological complementarity co-operative agreements with foreign firms, but strategic considerations dictate they do so since the purchaser (e.g. NATO) prefers it. One acknowledged side benefit is that there are then fewer competitors (they are part of the co-operative agreement) when the weapons system is marketed in other countries.

Strategic considerations also modify the speed or pace with which firms enter into agreements. If the industry is highly concentrated, there will be a limited number of potential partners for production rationalization agreements, and firms will reach agreements earlier than otherwise would be the case for fear of being left out in the future. Firms interviewed in the automobile industry indicated that this was an important factor. If, however, there are a large number of firms, such as in small computers or basic metals, this factor is much less important.

Firms are also careful in reaching agreements that the product of the agreement doesn't harm their own position: two examples will illustrate the point. When metals companies build plants in less developed countries, the new firm (even if partly owned by the original metals company) may export its low cost product back into the country that originated the plant, thereby harming its parents. Also when Renault agreed to allow Talbot (a Citroen-Peugeot subsidiary) to use its superior engine, the overall acceptance of the Talbot was considerably enhanced, thereby harming Renault. As might be expected, firms attempt to reduce these types of risks through restrictive clauses in the agreements and careful preagreement planning.

Other factors can also cause firms to seek out partners for co-operative agreements. For example, Nissan Motors agreed to co-operate with Alfa Romeo only after being thwarted by prohibitive quotas in its attempts to import automobiles into Italy. The only way that non-EEC firms can enter the Italian automobile market is through such agreements. Another factor is at work causing an increased use of co-operative agreements in the consumer electronics market, in that market worldwide competition is putting intense pressure on firms to reduce costs. These firms are attempting to reduce costs through the economies of scale benefits of large output and the learning by doing benefits of longer production runs. In order to sell the large volume of products required to reap these benefits, consumer electronics firms are making numerous marketing co-operative agreements.

6. Trends in the Use of Co-operative Agreements

It is difficult to establish for certain whether there is a trend in the use of co-operative agreements among firms because no institution has collected data for a sufficient period of time. The discussion in this section should therefore be viewed as somewhat tentative, since it is not based on hard data but rather on interviews with senior managers in European firms.

Most managers felt that competition had increased markedly in their industry in the last ten years. In autos and basic metals this increase in competition is due to a drop in the annual real growth rate of demand in the industry from 5.6 per cent to 2.3 per cent. This decrease in the real growth rate makes substantial individual firm growth more difficult without an increase in the firm's market share. Managers in these industries felt that the pace of battles for market share had increased. In the automobile industry the form of competition has shifted (probably as a result of the Japanese influence) from styling and the number of different models toward price (and thus cost) competition. Finally, the improvement in worldwide communications has increased international competition. All these factors together have increased pressures on firms to minimize costs. In the past, cost minimization was necessary for profit maximization (as always), but not for survival. Now cost minimization is necessary for survival. Since co-operative agreements appear to allow a reduction in costs without the disadvantageous side effects of mergers, it is not surprising that the managers interviewed reported that their use has increased markedly in the last 15 years. As can be seen from Table 2, the auto industry engages heavily in agreements motivated by economies of scale.

But if co-operative agreements do allow reductions in costs, why were they not in use as much 15 years ago as they are today? Is it possible that firms were indeed not minimizing costs in the past? (It does not appear that much in the technology of auto production has changed, so these agreements would probably have reduced costs 15 years ago just as they do now.) At least two hypotheses are possible: firms were not minimizing costs in the past. It has taken the increased competition resulting from decreases in demand growth (and fears for survival) to push firms into a full cost minimization mode. Alternatively, when demand was growing rapidly, the best (most profitable) use of management's scarce time was in serving the growing market and expanding output, not in minimizing costs through co-operative agreements. Indeed, one auto industry manager said that reaching an agreement like those in effect now would have been impossible 15 years ago: there were no interested partners. Every firm was too busy building up its own capacity.

The reasons for the increasing trend in basic metals and computers are similar to autos, but have some aspects of their own. In metals, there were major investments made in the late 1940s which were due for replacement in the mid 1970s. As the firms considered replacing entire plants with essentially irreversible costly facilities, it occurred to them to limit industry excess capacity through co-operative agreements.

In computers the reasons for the increased use of co-operative agreements include the speed of technological development and the fact that many innovations come from firms with no marketing experience. It is marketing agreements to solve these problems that are providing the trend in computers and other high technology industries. (See Table 3).

Finally, managers in the defense industry felt that there is no trend in that industry. Co-operative agreements have been used extensively for the past 15–20 years.

7. Public Policy Towards Co-operative Agreements

Public policy can affect the rate at which co-operative agreements are reached in several ways. Specific agreements can be prevented through anti-trust policy, while a general atmosphere toward agreements of all types can be provided by government through various means discussed below. While policy toward any particular agreement should only be developed through an analysis of the details of that agreement, some things can be said at a general level about all co-operative agreements, and some comments can be made about the desirability of different types of agreements.

By their nature as a relatively long term accord between firms, co-operative agreements usually exclude other firms from doing business with the parties to the agreement. If firm A agrees to work with firm B to develop new products in a particular industry, co-operation or individual transactions between other firms and firms A and B is precluded. If firm C agrees to purchase all future electronic instrumentation for its automobiles from firm *D*, other makers of instrumentation are precluded from supplying parts to firm *C*. As a result, competition is lessened. On the other hand, competition can be enhanced by co-operative agreements. Competition for partners for co-operative agreements is usually much more intense than is the usual competition in shorter term or individual transactions. So the effect of co-operative agreements on competition is mixed.

The one thing that is clear is that the increased use of co-operative agreements will change the process of competition. Competition for partners to a long term co-operative agreement involves more negotiation, more search, and more consideration of the internal versus external production (make vs. buy) type of decision than will individual transactions of the more traditional type.

Some comments can be made only about certain types of agreements: consider first horizontal production rationalization or economies of scale and learning agreements. If successful, these agreements will generally increase minimum efficient scale and will always reduce unit costs. Both factors will make future entry less likely since the new entrant will then be forced to enter at a larger scale (with higher capital costs) or enter only after reaching a co-operative agreement of its own. (Concluding co-operative agreements *before* entering an industry will be difficult, if not impossible.) It is difficult, however, seriously to challenge co-operative agreements because they reduce costs and increase minimum efficient scale: to do so and to be consistent we would need also to oppose nearly all technological progress.

Horizontal agreements to exploit scale economies may decrease the number of competitors if both firms cease production of their independently produced products. As a result, competition may be less intense. Again, however, the picture is not so simple. Co-operative agreements may be the only way that a firm can enter the market: e.g. Nissan was denied entry into the Italian auto market and could enter only through an agreement with Alfa Romeo. Or one or both firms may have failed if the co-operative agreement had not taken place, opening the possibility that an agreement may actually increase the number of firms and thus competition. Finally, two firms may cooperate to enter a new industry when, without the advantages yielded by this co-operation, they would not have entered for economic reasons. Again, competition can be enhanced by this type of co-operation.

All co-operative agreements require the establishment of interorganizational linkages; e.g. between the production departments. These linkages, as well as the cordial atmosphere that prevails between partners may preclude vigorous competition between the partners on other products or after the agreement has ended. Mead (1967) found that oil firms which enter into joint venture bids for oil leases are less likely to compete for future leases.

Collusion and cartellization are also facilitated by the communication taking place as a result of horizontal co-operative agreements.

Horizontal co-operative agreements should be especially suspect in concentrated industries for two reasons. The removal of competition through a horizontal agreement will be more damaging the fewer the number of competitors that remain. Also, firms in a more concentrated industry are more likely to be large, and thus able internally to take advantage of the benefits of economies of scale and learning that horizontal co-operative agreements offer.

Turning to co-operative agreements for the purpose of utilizing established marketing distribution networks for small firms which develop new products, we must be careful to specify the alternative to such an agreement. When a small firm makes a technological breakthrough, it faces three alternatives in bringing the new product to market. It can develop a distribution network itself, which can be costly or infeasible in well-developed markets characterized by intense rivalry. Alternatively, it can sell the patent (or the entire firm) to a larger firm which does possess the required distribution network. Finally, the firm with the new product can reach a co-operative agreement with a firm which has a well-developed marketing/distribution network. Although an analysis of the effect of each mode on competition is difficult without details of the specific situation, we would expect a priori that a co-operative agreement would be more pro competitive than the sale of the firm, at least to the extent that the smaller innovative firm continues to exist as a potential competitor.

Public policy recommendations for co-operative agreements which involve technological exchange are very complex: again, a major consideration is what institutional or competitive arrangement would exist in the absence of the co-operative agreement. One can always say that the existence of a co-operative agreement will reduce duplicative research and development expenditures which would otherwise be made by the partners. Technological transfer agreements increase the market for innovations, and thus increase the reward to the provision of information. Since information is a public good, increasing the rewards to the production of information through co-operative agreements has a beneficial social impact. When each of two or more firms contributes some knowledge or innovation as in a technological complementarity agreement, the resulting final product will generally be produced at lower cost and more quickly than in the absence of an agreement.

But the reduction in duplication of research and development expenditures may have negative side effects. One of the main benefits of a market system for producing innovation is that many different approaches are taken to the solution of important research and development problems: co-operative agreements for the exchange of information necessarily reduce the number of such duplicate approaches. Also, co-operative agreements for the purpose of knowledge exchange obviously foreclose firms who are not members of the agreement from some segment of the market for the period of the agreement. If the agreement is only for the purpose of a single project, such as the bidding consortiums reported in Table 2, this foreclosure will almost never be a problem. However, several French automobile electronics producers do have reason to complain over the fact that they are now foreclosed from selling to the two leading French automobile manufacturers for a period of many years.

Finally, managers of small firms in the computer industry complain of a sort of predatory behavior on the part of large computer firms. They stated that some time after they had signed long term licensing agreements, and ceased a portion of their own research and development activities as a result, the larger licensing firm (usually American) would bring out a superior product, and refuse to license this product to the smaller firm. In some cases the smaller firm can be forced out of business as a result of being denied access to the improved technology while at the same time being limited to inferior technology by the long term co-operative agreement.

8. Some Final Remarks

The field of study of co-operative agreements between firms seems a very promising one. It has been neglected in the literature of industrial organization in the past, with the possible exceptions of research on joint ventures (see Berg and Friedman (1978) and vertical integration (see Blois (1972). One reason for such lack of attention may be traced to a tendency to look at industrial organization in terms of a sharp dichotomy between markets and individual transactions on one side, and conscious planning within the firm on the other; the great variety of forms co-operative agreements can take may also have discouraged research.

Co-operative agreements appear as an intermediate form for both resource allocation and firms' activities organization. As an alternative to the firm as a managed (co-ordinated) system, they seem to require an extension of the boundary of firms and a reconsideration of the firm as an integrating device. As an alternative to the market, they seem to serve to compensate for failure or limitation of markets, though each agreement is likely to involve transaction costs of its own.

P. Mariti and R. H. Smiley

The final impact of co-operative agreements on competition is somewhat mixed, especially if one thinks of competition as a short run, deterministic principal of social organization and not as a long run process. One could also argue that co-operative agreements reduce the importance of price in the bargaining mix, thereby changing the mode of competition. Many co-operative agreements resemble barter in that no funds change hands between the partners.

References

Andrews, P. W., 'Industrial Economics as a Specialist Subject', *Journal of Industrial Economics*, Vol. 1, No. 1, (November 1952), 72–9.

Arrow, K. J., 'The Organization of Economic Activity: Issues Pertinent to the Choice of Market versus Nonmarket Allocation', in *The Analysis and Evaluation of Public Expenditures: The PPB System*, Vol. 1, No. 1, 47–64 (Joint Economic Committee, Washington, D. C., 1969).

Baumol, W. J. and Fischer, D., 'The Cost Minimizing Number of Firms and the Determination of Industry Structure', *Quarterly Journal of Economics*, Vol. XC11, No. 3, (Aug. 1978), 439–68.

Berg, S. V. and Friedman, P., 'Technological Complementarities and Industrial Patterns of Joint Venture Activity, 1964–1975', *Industrial Organization Review*, Vol. 6, 1978, 110–16.

Blois, K. J., 'Vertical Quasi Integration', *Journal of Industrial Economics*, Vol. XX, No. 3 (July 1972), 253–72.

Coase, R., 'The Nature of the Firm', *Economica*, Vol. IV, No. 16, (November 1937), 386–405.

Mariti, P., 'Sui Rapporti tra Imprese in una Economia Industriale Moderna', *Franco Angeli*, (Milano, 1980).

Mead, W. J., 'The Competitive Significance of Joint Ventures', Antitrust Bulletin, Vol. XII, (Fall, 1967), 819–49.

Richardson, G. B., 'The Organization of Industry', *Economic Journal*, Vol. 82, No. 327, (September 1972), 883–96.

Stigler, G. J., 'The Division of Labor is Limited by the Extent of the Market', *Journal of Political Economy*, Vol. LIX, No. 3, (June 1951), 185–93.

Williamson, O. E., *Market and Hierarchies: Analysis and Antitrust Implications* (The Free Press, London, 1975).

——— 'Transaction–Cost Economics: the Governance of Contractual Relations', *Journal of Law and Economics*, Vol. XXII, No. 2, (October 1979), 233–61.

10

Interpenetration of Organization and Market: Japan's Firm and Market in Comparison with the US

Ken-ichi Imai and Hiroyuki Itami

1. Introduction

We have two purposes in this paper. One is to present a general conceptual framework of resource allocation mechanisms which will enable us to analyse resource allocation both in the market and in the organization (i.e., the firm here) from a common vantage point. Our emphasis is on the mixture of market principles and organization principles in allocating resources either in the market or in the organization. Market principles penetrate resource allocation in the organization and organization principles creep into resource allocation in the market. This mixing phenomenon which we call interpenetration is essential to understanding various resource allocation patterns in the real world.

The second purpose of this paper is to apply this conceptual framework to the analysis of the differences of resource allocation patterns between Japan and the US. Our major conclusion is that the patterns of interpenetration are different between the two countries and we will try to explain why such differences emerge. We will also analyse the effects of these different interpenetration patterns on corporate behavior.

Section 2 below presents the basic conceptual framework and section 3

We are indebted to many executives of Japanese corporations whom we interviewed in our project on 'Empirical Study and International Comparison of Firm's Behavior and Organization', at the Department of Commerce. Hitotsubashi University. The project was founded by grants from the Ministry of Education.

describes the US-Japan differences in resource allocation. In section 4 we will ask 'why are there differences in interpenetration?'. Section 5 considers the implications of differences of interpenetration on corporate behavior in the two countries.

2. Market Principle and Organization Principle

It is often said that resources are allocated by either the market mechanism or the organization mechanism. Examples of resource allocation by the organization mechanism are allocation performed by the state in a planned economy and that by the firm within its organization. Resource allocation by the market mechanism is exemplified by the market in a free economy. Take, for example, Japan. Many observers say that resources are allocated by the market mechanism in the national economy, while they are allocated by the organization mechanism within the firm. Is this really an accurate description of reality?

In any discussion of the role of 'market' and 'organization' in resource allocation, these concepts bear two connotations. One is in the sense of the 'arena' in which the resource allocation takes place, or the 'arena' where transactions that lead to resource allocation occur. In the case of the market the arena refers to inter-firm transactions and transactions between the firm and the consumer. Resources move around between organizations or between the firm and the household. In the case of the organization, the arena is restricted to the inside of the firm.

The two concepts, 'market' and 'organization', also connote the typical 'principle' of transaction or 'mechanism' by which resources are allocated. The term 'market principle' clearly epitomizes its usage in this sense.

Thus, when one speaks of 'resource allocation in the market' or 'resource allocation in the firm', it is essential to explicitly indicate whether one is referring to the 'arena' of resource allocation or to the 'principle' concerned. Of course, if all resource allocations in the market as the 'arena' are performed by the market mechanism as its 'principle', then there would be no need to differentiate between the 'arena' and 'principle'. The same is true in the case of the 'firm'.

The basic hypothesis of this paper is that resource allocation in the market as the arena is done not *only* by the market principle but also, to a great extent, by the organization principle. On the other hand, the market principle is used to a certain extent in the resource allocation within the firm as the arena alongside the organization principle. Thus, both in the market and within the firm, two principles coexist. By analyzing the patterns of mixtures of these two principles, a new perspective for industry analysis and business behavior can be obtained.

Since the market is the 'arena' in which resource allocation within the economy takes place, the market principle naturally plays a major role in resource allocation in the economy. Also, in resource allocation within the firm, the organization principle plays a central role. These patterns are normal. But, we think that the analysis of the way 'the less normal' of these two principles of resource allocation is used in the two arenas of resource allocation sheds an interesting light on the problem.

But, what do we really mean by 'market principle' and 'organization principle'? The allocation of resources results from transactions. Transaction is the transfer of the right to use goods. Even a simple looking allocation of resources may frequently consist of a complicated series of transactions, if we try to resolve it into basic units of transactions. In each transaction, two parties (decision makers), are invariably involved—the offerer of goods and the acquirer of those goods. In a complicated series of transactions, inevitably a large number of decision makers are involved. In this allocation of resources through a series of transactions, the aggregate decisions of many decision makers produce the resultant resource allocation.

Any resource allocation principle can be characterized by two variables related to the transactions:

1. decision-making principle of each participant in transactions leading to resource allocation,

2. membership of these participants and their mutual relationships.

The purest case of market transaction is characterized by the individual's decision-making principle,

$$M_1 = \text{free private interest maximization in which price, or some other equivalent signal, is used as the major medium of information.}$$

(Here 'M' stands for market, and the subscripts to the variables concerned.)

The individual is free to participate or not in market transactions: hence, membership in the transaction participating group is characterized by

$$M_2 = \text{free entry and exit.}$$

The right to freely enter and exit transactions implies that participants are provided with opportunities for freely revealing information on the resources, capabilities and tastes they possess or prefer.

On the other hand, pure organizational transaction is characterized by the fact that decision is made, in the final analysis, following the authority hierarchy for common interest maximization. Thus, the decision principle is

O_1 = direction based on authority, for common interest maximization.

('O' stands for organization.)

The participants to a transaction are limited to the members of the organization. Unless an individual becomes a member, he cannot participate in the organization's transactions. Also, if an individual wants to exit from the organization's transactions, it means his exit from the organization itself, if the transaction is ordered by the ruling authority of the organization. Moreover, in view of the fact that the organization is created for continual activities, its membership characteristics of participation in intra-organizational transactions is

O_2 = fixed and continual relationship.

Thus we can describe the pure market principle and the pure organizational principle by two vectors (M_1, M_2) and (O_1, O_2). But many types of transactions should fall under categories intermediate between these two pure types. For instance, the following two cases are examples of M_1+O_1.

One is the case where the final decision on transactions is made by the fiat of authority but where the process leading up to that final decision involves the exchange of information of M_1 type and employment of the free competition type mechanism. For instance, when a decentralized planning system which employs accounting price as an information medium is used for resource allocation of a planned economy or firm, it represents an example of M_1+O_1.

The second is the case where the final decision on transactions is ultimately determined by free exchange as in the case of M_1, but where the process leading to the decision is influenced by an O_1 type intervention process. The case where free transaction is affected by the administrative guidance of a government agency is such an example. For this kind of case to actually function, the existence of an agent is necessary who is empowered with some regulatory power over certain transactions of participants (e.g., Japanese MITI), is necessary.

Likewise, there can be intermediate cases of membership in the types of groups of participants, which can be expressed as M_2+O_2. There are two such cases:

One is the case where, in principle, O_2 prevails but there exists the latent fear of M_2, where entry and exit of participants are possible. This is exemplified by the case of the auto maker who has organized a network of parts subcontractors but reserves the right to freely drop any arbitrarily and does sometimes exercise this right. Under this circumstance, the resource allocation process involving the assembler and subcontractors is characterized by $M_2 + O_2$.

The other is the reverse of the first, where the model is M_2, where participants can freely enter or exit, but cannot actually do so because of a fixed and continual relationship in which locked-in common interest develops. Such would be the kind of relationship prevailing between major Japanese banks and their clientele, the big corporations.[1]

When these intermediate types are included, we find (1) three categories (M_1, $M_1 + O_1$, O_1) of the decision principle, and (2) three categories (M_2, $M_2 + O_2$, O_2) of the membership principle. When (1) and (2) are laid out on intersecting axis, as shown in Fig. 1, then the intersections of the categories of (1) and (2), respectively, will produce nine combinations of principles (or mechanisms) of resource allocation.

The upper left-hand corner represents the pure market principle and the lower right-hand corner is the pure organization principle. Neither the upper right-hand corner nor the lower left-hand corner seems likely since the decision principle and the membership principle are mutually contractory in either cell. Two neighboring cells of the pure market [i.e., (M_1, $M_2 + O_2$), ($M_1 + O_1$, M_2)] are 'market' principles with some 'organization-like' elements. We call these three cells 'market mechanism', which is used in resource allocation in the market as the arena. Likewise, the two neighboring cells of the pure organization cell, (O_1, $M_2 + O_2$) and ($M_1 + O_1$, O_2), represent organizational resource allocation mechanisms with market-like elements

(1) \ (2)	M_2	M_2+O_2	O_2
M_1	Pure market	Organization-like market	
M_1+O_1	Organization-like market	Intermediate organization	Market-like organization
O_1		Market-like organization	Pure organization

Fig. 1. 7-cell framework of resource allocation mechanisms.

which are used within the firm. These three will be called 'organization mechanism'.

The remaining center cell, $(M_1 + O_1, M_2 + O_2)$, is interesting. Here, both decision principle and membership are a mixture of the market principle and the organization principle. It is neither 'market' nor 'organization' but, at the same time, equally both. We call this mechanism the 'intermediate organization principle'. This mechanism can be used both 'in the market' resource allocation and 'within the firm' resource allocation. We will argue later that prolonged usage of this mechanism will tend to create an important new arena of resource allocation other than market or firm, which will be 'intermediate organization'.

3. Japan–US Comparison of Resource Allocation Mechanism

As we emphasized earlier, the pattern of mixture of M and O for resource allocation is quite revealing in both describing and understanding the resource allocation mechanisms of two (or more) different allocation entities (e.g., between countries, between industries and between firms). In this section we will make a brief comparison of resource allocation (labor, capital, intermediate goods) in Japan and the United States using the 7-cell framework alone. In either country, the organization-like elements creep into market resource allocation to remedy market failure and the market-like elements are used in the firm's resource allocation process to offset organizational failure. But the patterns of mixture are different in the two countries. In Section 4, we will offer our tentative explanation of why this is so and why a mixture (or interpenetration) of the two principles emerges in the first place.

3.1. Labor Allocation

We take up labor allocation as a start. In the market as an arena, Japanese labor allocation has at least three distinctive characteristics compared with the US. They are (1) low labor mobility, (2) limited port of entry for new employees, and (3) low profile of labor unions, which are mostly enterprise unions rather than industry or trade unions. The third point may need clarification. Unlike American labor unions which conduct industry-wide bargaining and are sometimes union shops, Japanese labor unions play a less active role in market-wide labor allocation. Japanese enterprise unions certainly play a major role in wage determination and job determination 'within the firm', but not on an industry-wide or market-wide scale.

Ports of entry to a Japanese firm from the external labor market are more limited than in the US along two dimensions. One is the mid-career entry, especially among college graduates, since most hiring is done at the time of graduation from the school. The second dimension is the central control of hiring by the firm's personnel department. In a sense, there is only one port of entry through the personnel department in Japan, whereas in the US each division or even each manager, in some extreme cases, possesses hiring authority. In other words, the port of entry is singular and centralized in Japan and multiple and decentralized (or Balkanized) in the US.

Low labor mobility and limited port of entry in Japan implies that internal labor allocation and reallocation has to be more active to cope with changing demand conditions and changing technology. Labor adjustment through external labor markets is less prevalent in Japan, which has led to a more extensive development of internal labor markets than in the US.[2]

Workers often move from one job category to another in the firm without too much resistance from the union. This is sometimes done regularly as a part of their career development programme and at other times irregularly as part of the internal labor adjustment to changing demand and technology. Divisions often bid for more or less internal allocation of labor to the central personnel department as their business conditions change.

As a buffer for business fluctuation, many Japanese firms rely on subcontractors more than the US firms either for the supply of parts and other intermediate goods or for supply of various services (i.e., labor).[3] This is Japanese firms, quasi-internal labor adjustment mechanism. When the recession comes, the firms can first cut back on subcontracted works instead of laying off their own core workers.

The personnel department of the Japanese firm functions as the operator of this extensive internal labor market as well as the central port of entry from the external labor market. As can be expected, the power and relative status of Japanese personnel managers is much higher than that of their American counterparts.[4]

In summary, the US relies more on the market as an arena in the total labor allocation (i.e., allocation through market plus internal allocation) than Japan. On the other hand, the organization as an arena plays more of a major role in Japan than in the US. To cope with various inefficiencies and inequities of the market and the organization as arena for labor allocation, the American external labor market has seen the penetration of organization-like principles of allocation into their market-based resource allocation mechanism. One example of this are the strong industry-wide trade unions, which function to protect collective interests of workers in one trade. Through this device, the decision principle of American external labor allocation has become $M_1 + O_1$, rather than the pure O_1. Another example is the union shop. This certainly limits the freedom of entry into labor transactions by each individual worker. Thus, the membership principle of labor transaction is now changed from M_2 to $M_2 + O_2$, i.e., some element of fixed membership now creeps in.

In contrast, we can see the penetration of more market-like principles into Japanese internal labor allocation. Flexible movement of workers across job boundaries, often at their own initiative, is an example of $M_1 + O_1$. Bidding—like requests for labor by divisions is another example of $M_1 + O_1$. Widespread use of subcontracting can be seen as a way to make the membership pool of internal labor transaction less fixed and open to a group of specified outside subcontractors, i.e., transition from O_2 to $O_2 + M_2$.

We can summarize the net effect as follows: the total labor allocation and reallocation in the US is conducted by workers crossing the firm-market boundary but staying within the job boundary (category) more often than in Japan. Japan accomplishes its allocation by workers staying within the firm-market boundary but crossing the job boundary more often than in the US.

3.2. Capital Allocation

As has been well-documented (e.g., Wallich and Wallich (1976) and Flaherty and Itami (1984)), the three major characteristics of Japanese corporate financing in comparison with the US are: (1) heavier reliance on bank loans, (2) less internal financing, and (3) less dependence on the equity market.

Heavy reliance on bank loans naturally leads to extensive and deep involvement by the banks in market capital allocation. Moreover, the number of significant banks is much smaller than in the US. There are only 13 city banks who control 52% of Japan's total bank lending to corporations.[5] The capital they control originates from investors who historically have not had too many alternatives other than bank deposits for their financial investment. A very rough sketch of Japanese market capital allocation is: the banks gather most of the capital from individual investors and then allocate it to the borrowing firms. Perhaps as a natural outgrowth, highly intimate and long-term relationships emerge between the banks and the firms. A firm commonly has one lead bank which acts as the de facto leader among the banks lending money to the firm. The lead bank monitors the firm's operation and performance with much greater care than other lenders and often shoulders a major responsibility when the firm gets into a crisis situation.

The Japanese equity and corporate bond markets have been much less developed than in the US.[6] And in these smaller markets, the Japanese banks have also been major players. Unlike the US, the Japanese banks can (and do) hold equity of the borrowing firms. This makes the bank-firm relationship even tighter.

All of this suggests that capital transactions between a Japanese bank and a borrowing firm are not typical arm's length market transactions. The intimate and long-term relationship between the lender and the borrower and the frequent information flows associated with it make their transactions 'quasi-organizational' or 'quasi-internal'. Clearly, some organizational elements creep into what was originally a free market transaction. The institutional framework of the Japanese capital market suggests that this has occurred on a relatively large scale.

Financing within the business group (or group finance) is perhaps a very good example. There are six major business groups in Japan, each of them having a major city bank as one of their leaders. Although a business group is not a conglomerate with central authority, it is a loosely connected group of firms who often act together for their collective interest (see Caves and Uekusa (1976)). The member firms get their major share of financing from the lead bank of the same business group. Clearly, this capital transaction is not a pure arm's length market transaction.

The fact that internal financing plays a much larger role in the US seems to indicate that the internal capital market is much better developed in the US, employing more market-like principles. This is perhaps a necessity for the American firms as they try to cope with the (potential) failures of organizational-only mechanisms to manage such a large pool of internal capital, a capital pool in a sense separated from the external capital market.

There is much supporting evidence for the greater development of internal capital markets in the US. For example, American firms place more emphasis on ROI in internal capital allocation than Japanese firms. ROI-based systems of allocation look somewhat like price mechanisms. The techniques for internal capital allocation such as PPM (product portfolio management), which are much more widespread in the US, assume the headquarter's centralized power to collect capital from various divisions and reallocate it according to a given criteria (quite often financial, like ROI). The chief financial officer acts like an auctioneer of this internal capital market and thus has a prestigious status within the management hierarchy of the firm.

In Japan, partly because financing for capital projects is often done through the banks (i.e., external market), central coordination of internal capital flows is less important than in the US. On a project-by-project basis, capital flows quite often between the divisions and the banks (even though transactions have to go through the headquarter's finance department). In general, the role of Japanese chief financial officers has been equivalent to that of a chief borrowing strategist, rather than a chief auctioneer of internal capital flow. Thus, their internal status has not been as high as compared to the US.

The fact that conglomerates do not exist in Japan is another evidence of a less developed internal capital market. One of the major reasons for their existence in the US is to form a large internal capital market.

In summary, the organization as an arena has much greater weight in total capital allocation in the US, whereas the market's weight is greater in Japan than in the US. As a consequence, we can see in the Japanese external capital market more organization-like principles. The fixed long-term relationship with one or a few major banks is an example of semi-fixed membership of capital transaction (an example of $M_2 + O_2$). In the case of group finance, the decision principle also becomes more organization-like (i.e., $M_1 + O_1$) in order to pursue collective interests.

American internal capital markets are penetrated with more market-like principles, like pseudo-price mechanisms of ROI capital allocation (an example of $M_1 + O_1$), although the operation of these market-like mechanisms is under central control of the firm's headquarter.

In a sense, the US conducts total capital allocation by letting capital cross the firm-market boundary less than Japan but the divisional boundary more. Japanese capital crosses the firm–market boundary more than the US but the divisional boundary less. Since the divisional boundary for capital is somewhat similar to the job boundary for labor, the US–Japanese difference in total capital allocation is a complete reverse of the differences in labor allocation. Even the arena weights are reversed. For labor, the market's weight is greater in the US. It is greater in Japan for capital. The American organization's weight for capital allocation is greater than Japan, whereas it is the opposite for labor.

3.3. Goods Allocation

Most observers of the Japanese economic scene would agree on the two major characteristics that differentiate Japanese industrial organization from the US. The first is more organized activities among the producers of the same goods, be it legalized cartel, joint R&D efforts, or coordinated behavior through governmental administrative guidance. The second is more co-operative vertical relationships between the selling firm and the buying firm. Related to the second characteristic is the fact that the degree of vertical integration of many Japanese firms is generally much less both forward and backward than that of their American counterparts in the same industry.[7] That is, the Japanese use market transactions more than the US for many intermediate goods, but these transactions are done not as pure arm's length transactions but in a framework of cooperative vertical (and sometimes horizontal) relationships among the firms. Keiretsu, a group of cooperating (and often subcontracting) firms headed by a parent firm (a major manufacturing firm like Toyota), is such an example. The parent firms do not have majority ownership and very often do not hold even any equity of these cooperating suppliers and distributors.

On the first characteristic, more organized activities among the producers, it is well known that anti-trust laws are much less strict in Japan than in the US. For example, the Japanese law allows many anti-recession cartels an example of $(M_1 + O_1, M_2)$].[8] The idea behind the cartels is to create a common cushion to absorb the shocks of a recession which each individual firm may find difficult to cope with independently. Figuratively speaking, when the market size shrinks by 15%, these Japanese anti-recession cartels let all the firms in the industry go bankrupt 15% each, saving all the firms from disappearing completely from the industry. On the other hand, a typical American way in a similar situation would be to let 15% of the firms go bankrupt and disappear, with the remaining firms sharing the smaller pie. Bankruptcy would eliminate the least efficient firms and market forces would determine who those least efficient firms are.

In a sense, the Japanese anti-recession cartel presumes that all the firms would become viable in the long run unless they are drained too much by cutthroat short-run competition during recessions. The Japanese solution is like a slow therapeutic method for curing an infection and the American way like a drastic surgical excision to save the rest of the body. The Japanese solution always has a danger of degenerating into a collusion for monopoly.

The same is true in a government-guided joint R&D programme among otherwise competing firms. If left to the market principle alone, there is a danger of under-investment in R&D. Some kind of organized R&D activities among the firms is needed to avoid this danger. There is, however, always a danger that this cooperation would not stop in R&D but extend into collusion in production and marketing of the products resulting from the developed technology.

Because of this danger, a typical American way has been to restrict such joint R&D. The Japanese often legally allow it or the government would be instrumental in making such a joint activity possible. A good example is the VLSI (Very Large Scale Integration) Research Cooperative, formed by major

Japanese computer manufacturers and IC producers under the guidance of MITI. Partly to avoid the danger of collusion in the product market, the cooperative's life was set from the beginning at 5 years. This cooperative has been generally regarded as a success.[9]

These examples of the organized activities by the Japanese firms are examples of the decision principle of market transactions changing from pure M_1 to $M_1 + O_1$.

The second characteristic of Japanese industrial organization, co-operative vertical relationships, leads to the emergence of what we call 'intermediate organization' in Japan. An intermediate organization is comprised of closely connected but still independent firms, making transactions among themselves on a continual and long-term basis. The participating firms, however, reserve the freedom to exit if they wish. So, the typical membership of this 'organization' is neither O_2 (fixed) nor M_2 (free entry and exit). The decision principle of the participating firms is not pure M_1 (private interest maximization) but includes a consideration for common interests. At the same time, no one really has total authoritative control over the members' behavior, thus making the decision principle of the members not O_1, but $M_1 + O_1$.

Thus, transactions among the member firms of this intermediate organization are neither pure market transactions nor pure organizational transactions. Both in decision principle and in membership, they are $M_1 + O_1$ and $M_2 + O_2$. We may call them quasi-organizational or intermediate transactions. These intermediate organizations sometimes become so important that we can call them 'the third arena of resource allocation', alongside with markets and organizations. The relationship between the banks and the borrowing firms we saw earlier, in which capital transactions are performed as 'quasi-organizational', can also be classified as intermediate organization. Both in capital transactions and in goods transactions, the prevalence of intermediate organizations seems to be a major Japanese characteristic. Of course this is not to say a similar relationship does not exist in the US. Our claim is that it is much more widespread in Japan.

Concerning the transactions of goods within the firm, the American internal resource allocation mechanism has more elements of market-like principles than in Japan. Examples of this include the well-developed transfer pricing system and the pervasive use of profit center control in the US [examples of $(M_1 + O_1, O_2)$]. Behind these lies the more widespread usage of divisionalized organizational structure among the American firms than in Japan.[10]

Again, the US–Japanese contrast is similar to the capital allocation case. American internal allocation has more market-like elements, while Japanese market allocation has more organization-like elements. Furthermore, the relative weight of markets as an arena (including intermediate organizations) in total goods allocation is greater in Japan than in the US. This means that internal allocation plays a greater role in the US than in Japan as can be seen in the difference in the degrees of vertical integration of firms in the two countries and the difference in general concentration. The greater role of market transactions in Japan has led to the emergence of the third area of transactions, namely intermediate organization.

In a sense, the American industrial organization is bipolarized. One pole is organizational allocation in large firms in which mass production and mass marketing are combined internally and O principles dominate (although market-like principles are used more than in Japan). The other pole is market allocation where purer M principles dominate.[11] Bipolarization is much less pronounced in Japan where intermediate organizations play a more significant role.

4. Patterns and Reasons of Interpenetration of the Two Principles

When we talk about penetration of non-standard principles into resource allocation (i.e., organization-like principles into market allocation and market-like principles into organizational allocation), it is useful to specify 'among whom' this penetration takes place. Take, for example, the case of market allocation of intermediate goods. Assuming non-monopoly and non-monopsony, organization-like elements can penetrate into the relationship: (1) between a producer and a buyer, (2) among producers, and (3) among buyers. A vertical relationship (V) is formed among the players in the first case and a horizontal relationships (H) in the second and the third cases. An example of penetration of organizational elements in V is the Japanese intermediate organization. When this penetration becomes complete, it becomes vertical integration. Cartels, on the other hand, are an example of penetration of organizational elements into H.

It is obvious that a similar distinction is possible in capital allocation and labor allocation in the market as well as in organizational allocation. Organizational allocation is composed of internal transaction of resources. Any transaction has two parties, one who gives the resource and the other who takes it. It is easy to think of vertical and horizontal relationships among transaction participants within the firm. For example, different divisions of the firm are in horizontal relationship in internal labor and capital allocation, although some of them may be in vertical relationship with each other concerning intermediate goods. The reasons behind interpenetration do not seem to differ substantially between V and H as long as we keep our discussion to the fundamentals. Thus, we will develop fundamental reasons in the next section mainly in terms of penetration of non-standard principles into V both in the market and in the firm. We will later show that these reasons apply to the H case as well.

4.1. Why Interpenetration?

To put it simply, interpenetration occurs to remedy the 'failures' of the pure mechanism of allocation in each arena. Thus, organizational elements emerge in the market to offset market failures and market-like principles will be employed in the firm to remedy 'organizational failures'.[12] Let us examine this in a little more detail.

There are two major reasons why the pure market principle (M_1, O_1) may fail.[13] One is chiefly related to its decision principle, M_1. In the pure market, the transaction participants often adopt basically short-term-oriented behavior with a rather narrow decision scope. They often behave very opportunistically. Market failures occur, unless the price signals contain so much information to make these short-run, narrow-scoped and opportunistic behaviors based on prices quite efficient in the long-run and for the total economy. But, as is well known, the price mechanism has a lot of difficulties in accommodating uncertainty (which is invariably involved in the long-run decisions) and externalities.

One remedy is to introduce O_1 into M_1. For example, the parent firm in keiretsu may exercise authority to decide on each member firm's behavior for the long-run and overall interests of the group as a whole. Or the government may influence private lending decisions by the banks as part of its industrial policy. Thus, $M_1 + O_1$ emerges. Another remedy might be for the transaction participants to enter into a long term, semi-fixed relationship with each other, i.e., to introduce O_2 into M_2 as a remedy for M_1. Thus, even though each participant continues to behave in its self-interest, its optimal behavior will change because M_2 has now changed to $M_2 + O_2$. It may not be optimal any more for the participants to become so short-term oriented, so narrow-scoped, or so opportunistic. Thus, $M_2 + O_2$ may attenuate some of the market failures.[14]

The second major reason why the pure market principle may fail rests on its membership principle, M_2. There is little scope for accumulation of *common* information among transaction participants, under free entry and exit into transactions (assuming entry and exit occurs frequently). Presumably, from each transaction its participants can learn about other participants (which will lead to reputation and trust), about the nature of technology and the product involved, about the necessary resources and capabilities, and so on. If transaction participants change so often, the opportunity for common information accumulation on those things becomes small.

Lack of such accumulation can create several difficulties. For example, lack of common information will make transaction negotiation tenuous, if not impossible. Negotiation is, after all, a process of finding the middle ground through common understanding. This difficulty seems to be becoming more and more significant as the goods and services transacted in the market become more complex and more packed with information and software. Take, for instance, automated machine tools or sophisticated computer-controlled equipment. Since they are complex and require know-hows and softwares to operate them, the buyer needs continued support in the forms of after-sales information feeding and after-sale services. The buyer needs a lot of information to evaluate these 'invisible things' in the negotiation process. If we can create separate markets for these know-hows, softwares and services, separate from the machine market itself, there may be much less need for continual relationships between the buyer and the seller ($M_2 + O_2$). But there is little possibility for the separate market because these things are often inseparable from the machine and there is little chance for a market for information, even if this information is separable. Thus, $M_2 + O_2$ emerges.

Another example of difficulties created by lack of shared information is externality in production of new information. If each transaction participant has some valuable pieces of information—which can create new information (e.g., new technology) if combined but are much less useful if they remain separate—making these pieces of information common leads to efficient usage. Since many innovations are the result of a combination of several existing pieces of information, the lack of common information accumulation is undesirable. Here again, lack of market for information is a key limitation.

One of the remedies for this second market failure is penetration of organizational principles into the market. We have already seen an example of direct remedies (i.e., $M_2 + O_2$) above. An example of indirect remedies (i.e., emergence of $M_1 + O_1$) is joint research efforts by the buyer and the seller, often based on government incentives or administrative guidance.

We now turn our discussion to organizational failures and penetration of market principles into the firm. Here again, there are two major reasons for the failures, one principally due to the organizational decision principle (O_1) and the other mainly due to the membership principle (O_2).

First, common interest maximization based on authority (O_1) has two dangers. One is a lack of sufficient private incentives for each individual and the other is the potentially high cost of information processing to manage the hierarchical organization. The organization has a risk of X-inefficiency and lax management because of these two dangers. Market principles are sometimes employed to cope with this risk. Pseudo-price mechanisms, like transfer pricing and decentralized planning, are such examples. O_1 is now penetrated by M_1, to some extent.

There are also indirect remedies through the membership principle for the difficulty created by O_1. Internal transactions can be supplemented by market transactions, like in the case of double sourcing the supply of parts from both the internal supplier and outside vendors. The membership principle for the transaction changes from O_2 to $M_2 + O_2$.

The second major reason for the organizational failures is again related to information accumulation. The fixed and continual membership of O_2 leads to the danger of rigidity of accumulated information. This can mean maladaptation of the firm to changing environments because accumulated information (i.e., accumulated capabilities of the firm, like technology) is the basis of the firm's ability to adapt.

Information accumulation may become rigid because (1) membership of the transactions would be slow to change (due to severance cost of these members), and (2) potential variety of accumulated information could be limited (or at least not widely available as in the outside market) because of limited membership.

Various remedies for this danger using some market-like principles are available. For example, parallel research within the firm or competitive bidding of in-house research teams and outside laboratories will widen potential variety of information available to the firm. This is an example of O_2 changing into $M_2 + O_2$. Or, using profit center control (i.e., $M_1 + O_1$), the firm may try to create internal pressure for better information accumulation. Poor profit signals the necessity for better adaptation (and thus information accumulation for adaptation).

Although we have been discussing interpenetration of principles into vertical relationship, penetration into the horizontal relationships can be similarly explained to a large extent. For example, some effort toward common interest maximization (i.e., M_1 changing into $M_1 + O_1$) by some joint activities, like cartels, may arise when the short-run, narrow-scoped and opportunistic behavior of the producers of goods become too detrimental. When the producers think that separate information accumulation activity is too costly and anticipate externality in information production, they may form a joint R&D cooperative (both $M_1 + O_1$ and $M_2 + O_2$). When the workers in the same trade realize that their best interest is not served by each worker pursuing his self-interest alone, a labor union would be formed in the labor market. These examples show that we do not have to treat horizontal penetration any differently from vertical penetration.

As we said in the beginning, interpenetration occurs to remedy the failures of the pure principles in each arena of resource allocation. But, it also means that market transactions remain in the market even after organizational elements penetrate. Likewise, organizational transactions remain within the firm after penetration of market-like principles. The point is: transactions do not change their arena in the interpenetration cases we have been discussing.

However, if the failures are great, transactions will change their arena. The arena can change from market to organization or vice versa. This is actually the main issue Williamson (1975) discusses. When the failures are in the medium range, interpenetration occurs. When the failures are insignificant, the market will remain (M_1, M_2) and the firm (O_1, O_2). Our implicit hypothesis has been that medium range failures are so common that interpenetration becomes widespread.

4.2. Why the Japan–US Difference?

The most salient difference between Japan and the US with respect to patterns of interpenetration is summarized in Fig. 2. This figure indicates resources for whose allocation non-standard principles penetrate significantly and shows where penetration occurs (either into market allocation or into organizational allocation). For example, in Japan, market allocation of capital and goods is more penetrated by non-standard principles than in the US, whereas for market labor allocation, the US has more organization-like elements. For organization allocation, Japanese firms use market principles for labor and American firms for capital and goods. Thus, the Japanese have developed internal labor markets and the Americans internal capital markets and internal goods markets. It is immediately clear from this figure that Japan and the US have diametrically opposite patterns. Why is this so?

The first, and perhaps the most significant, reason that comes to our mind is the relative weight of each arena in total resource allocation. For labor, the relative weight of Japanese organizational allocation in total Japanese labor allocation is greater than the weight of American organizational allocation of labor in total labor allocation. Thus, Japanese firms play a more significant role than US firms in labor allocation. When the organization weighs more heavily, its organizational failures are likely to become more pronounced, leading to the penetration of market principles into the firm.

Similarly, the American labor market weighs more heavily in total labor allocation than its Japanese counterpart. A greater danger of market failures

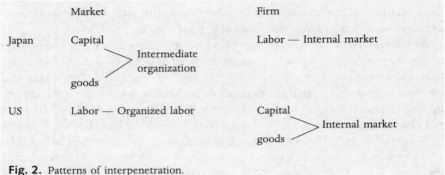

Fig. 2. Patterns of interpenetration.

in the American labor market arises and hence penetration of organizational principles into the market occurs.

For both capital and goods, the relative weights of market and firms as arenas of resource allocation are as follows:

$$\text{Japanese market} > \text{American market}$$
$$\text{Japanese firms} < \text{American firms}$$

This is just the opposite of labor allocation. But the same logic applies here as well: greater weight as arena→greater danger of failures-→more penetration of non-standard principles.

The second reason relates to the legal differences between the two countries as far as market allocations of capital and goods are concerned. Both in anti-trust regulations and in banking regulations, the American system tends to be more strict in prohibiting joint behaviors and close relationships between buyers/sellers or between lenders/borrowers than the Japanese system.[15] Thus, the American legal system is much less conducive to the large scale emergence of intermediate organizations even if the firms and the banks so desire.

Usually, systems like intermediate organizations tend to be unstable and transient. Consider how they resolve conflict among the members. There is no apparent last authority, nor is exit so free. They seem to be just stuck in the middle. They could be just a midway station on the road from the market to the organization, but nothing more. But against this interpretation stands the fact that the Japanese intermediate organizations are quite widespread and have been in steady existence for many years. The Japanese social fabric, which is the third reason for Japan–US difference, can shed some light here.

Generally speaking, the Japanese society is more homogeneous and close-knit and more tolerant of ambiguity than the American society. This social fabric has two implications for intermediate organizations. First, it makes consensus formation among the members of an intermediate organization easier. Ultimate leadership in the group may emerge more easily and the leader can resolve conflict among members as 'the first among equals', not as a dictator. Second, the Japanese social fabric seems to imply relatively heavy social monitoring of how its members behave. This reduces the private cost that the intermediate organization has to pay to monitor 'moral hazard' phenomena. In other words, agency cost is less in Japan, and this makes an intermediate organization in which no one has clear sanctioning power easier to maintain.

The fourth reason behind the Japan–US difference is purely economic: the steady high growth of the Japanese economy during the last three decades. Without growth, the chances of conflict among the members escalate, thus making intermediate organizations harder to maintain. Without growth, the firm's heavy reliance on internal labor markets would also be hard to maintain. Layoff may become inevitable. Internal reallocation among different jobs is difficult if the firm cannot find enough growth areas to reallocate workers to. Economic growth in the past has been in a sense a cure-all to some extent for many potential troubles of Japanese resource allocation mechanisms.

5. Effects on Corporate Behavior

The differences in the resource allocation mechanisms of the two countries are bound to affect the behavior of firms who operate in and with these mechanisms. We shall discuss in this section how the differences in patterns of interpenetration of market and organization create different corporate behavior in two countries. Three aspects of corporate behavior we treat here are: diversification, financing, and innovation and venture business.

5.1. Diversification

Perhaps the most important benefit of a well-developed internal labor market is the opportunity of enlarging each employee's firm-specific skills and know-how. Employees in a typical Japanese firm, both white-collar and blue-collar, tend to be periodically transferred among various jobs within the firm to expand the range of their skills, experience and intrafirm interpersonal relationships. Internal development of such capabilities is the norm (and the benefit) in the Japanese internal labor market.

Given this norm, Japanese diversification strategy tends to become 'related' strategy, i.e., diversification into areas related to the firm's existing core skills, capabilities, market connections and interfirm relationships. They will try to utilize internally developed capabilities as much as possible. If somewhat new capability is required in a diversified area, they will try to develop it internally by transferring people from other related areas. Hence, the diversified area cannot be too far away from the existing lines of business.

Two other factors reinforce this tendency. One is the Japanese internal decision-making process and the other is the relationship with the external capital market. Two noteworthy aspects of the Japanese internal decision making process are the bottom-up process of plan generation and the consensus-orientated approval process of the generated plan. A diversification plan would typically be prepared at the middle management level and channeled upward through the firm's organizational hierarchy, as informal communications are exchanged between the different hierarchical levels to arrive at a consensus and necessary modifications. No drastic diversification plan is likely to come out from this process. People will propose things they know well and consensus is easy to obtain for things many in the hierarchy know well.

The second reinforcing factor is the bankers' close involvement in the firm's external financing. A very drastic diversification plan to the areas unrelated to the firm's existing capabilities is usually hard to sell to the outside bankers, even if they may be better informed about the firm than their American counterpart.

Thus, Japanese diversification strategy is much more 'related' than the American strategy.[16] Of course, there are some cases of unrelated diversification by top management's independent decision that bypasses the traditional bottom-up procedure. Even then, the common American practice of entrusting an outside consultant to plan a new project and recruiting new employees to run the business is much less common in the Japanese firms.

In contrast, what is the likely pattern of diversification taken by the US firm? In contrast to Japan, internal mobility of labor among jobs and various divisions is restricted, and capital allocation within the firm's internal capital market occupies the central place of concern. Remember also that capital, unlike labor, does not embody or accumulate technological skills and know-how. Capital is firm-specific only in the sense it is at its management's total disposal and invested in accordance with corporate strategy. Under this circumstance, one avenue for the firm's development would be geographical expansion as a multinational corporation. This option is attractive because it involves an extension of its accumulated resources, only on a geographical basis. If labor is necessary at overseas localities, the firm can employ workers there. Much of the risk of multinationalization, e.g., unforeseen political upheavals in host countries, can be absorbed by its internal capital market.

At the same time, the American firm tends to diversify into businesses that are very much unrelated to its main product lines, as typified by conglomerates. This type of diversification is in sharp contrast to multi nationalization involving only geographical extension of a firm's existing resources. The conglomerate transforms its resources by adding those quite unrelated to its existing resources portfolio. But both the conglomerate and the multinational have a common strategic logic in that they are highly demand-driven, not resources- or capabilities-driven. Even if a firm's resources (or capabilities) are highly specialized in a particular set of domain, it may try to enter the markets solely based on the prospects for future demand.

In fact, in the now-famous product portfolio management model (PPM), strategy is mainly based on prospects of future demand and dynamic balancing of internal cash flows. The new field of diversification is selected as if it were creating an investment portfolio of stocks. Capital required for the selected diversification plan, sometimes for corporate take-overs, is supplied by the firm's internal capital market. Competent personnel to run the new businesses is recruited from the external labor market. In short, the resources needed for implementing the diversification plan are often procured from outside, except for capital.

Hence, the success of this kind of diversification plan depends, to a large extent, on the quality of the designed strategy. If the corporate strategy foresees the future accurately, the corporate sales will grow and the firm's resources and capabilities may undergo qualitative transformation, as a result of the injection of new blood. Nonetheless, if the original strategic projection proves wrong little margin is left for fine tuning or the possibility to integrate with the firm's other businesses. The result could be traumatic. In contrast, a typical Japanese firm can better adapt or fine tune to environmental changes because its diversification strategy tends to be 'related' to the existing businesses. To put it differently, medium performance can be expected from the Japanese strategy and a very high or very low performance for the American strategy.

In sum, an oversimplified generalization would be: the Japanese strategy is human resources-driven, the American strategy capital-driven: the Japanese strategy is capabilities-driven, the American strategy demand-driven.

5.2. Financing

As we already saw in Section 3, the Japanese firms rely more on debt financing, while the American firms generally rely more on equity financing when external financing becomes necessary. In addition, the Japanese firms have on their balance sheets much more accounts receivables and accounts payables than the American firms. This difference in corporate behavior can be explained by the different interpenetration patterns.

First, let us take the case of debt financing vs. equity financing in external financing. Since the Japanese banks lend 'too much' money to already 'risky' firms (risky meaning a high debt/equity ratio), at least according to American standards, some observers have claimed that a Japanese government's loan guarantee (either explicit or implicit) must have existed. But, given the penetration of organizational elements into the Japanese capital (especially debt) market, seemingly 'high-risk' lending practices of the banks and 'high-risk' borrowing practices of the firms can be quite rational without any government guarantee.

Within the intermediate organization among the bank and the firms, information flows more freely and accumulates more over time. Thus, 'risky' lending may not be so risky, given these information sources. From the firm's viewpoint, it can expect its lead bank to come to its rescue at the time of financial adversity. High debt/equity ratios do not automatically mean high chance of bankruptcy. Thus, the bank can lend more and the firms can borrow more in Japan. Without these intermediate organizations in place (at least not to the extent of the Japanese case), the American firms naturally try not to borrow so much and the banks do not lend as much as the Japanese banks.

On the contrary, when the American firms need external capital for risky projects, they go to the equity market, a market designed for risky, long-term capital. This is quite natural in a pure capital market with mostly arms' length transactions. Since the Japanese equity market has not developed quite as well as in the US and the Japanese debt market is penetrated with organizational elements, the Japanese firms have relied less on equity financing and more on debt financing.

Second, high interfirm credit in Japan is partly related to the widespread existence of intermediate organizations in the Japanese goods market. When the relationship among the member firms becomes long-term and semi-fixed, it spills over into areas other than mere transactions of goods. One example is credit relationship. The lack of intermediate organizations in the US makes interfirm credit much less.

5.3. Innovation and Venture Business

Different patterns of interpenetration affects innovation and venture business in the two countries along three dimensions: (1) cooperative R&D effort among otherwise competing producers or between the buyer and the seller, (2) radical innovation and incremental innovation, and (3) venture business activity. For these three aspects, the stylized facts are: (1) there is more cooperative R&D in Japan, (2) the US leads in radical innovation whereas Japanese firms are good at incremental innovation, and (3) there are a lot more venture business activities in the US.

First, the basic reason why more cooperative R&D efforts exist in Japan is similar to that in the case of interfirm credit. Penetration of organizational elements into the Japanese goods market paves the way to cooperation in R&D. Furthermore, intermediate organizations created in the Japanese capital market can become the seedbed of cooperation in innovative activities. For example, the lead bank in the intermediate organization (or the business group) may provide the initial leadership (or may act as a go between) to form a joint research team among the member firms, who may or may not have transactions among themselves.

The benefit of cooperation would be hard to discover without someone with a wide range of information (like the lead bank in this case), or without the close contact over time to get to know each other well. Without some orientation for joint interests maximization, the initiative for cooperation would be difficult to come by and moral hazard problems would be hard to control. All these problems are even more severe than cooperation in pricing or production of goods because in R&D we are dealing with production of *information*, which is a much more difficult good to deal with.

The well-developed internal labor market and the low mobility of researchers in Japan will also make the benefit of cooperative R&D greater and more easily realisable by each member firm. Because of low mobility, the firms are not so concerned with the risk of losing the fruits of cooperation to either cooperating firms or competitors. The well-developed internal labor market implies that the results and experiences of the firm's researchers in cooperative R&D activities will be utilized widely in the firm.

Second is the pattern of American radical innovation and Japanese incremental innovation. One of the explanations of this difference is the same as in the case of diversification strategy, i.e., drastic American strategy vs. incremental (or related) Japanese strategy. So, we will not repeat it here.

Another reason is related to the way internal labor markets are organized within the firm and the way these internal markets are related to the external markets. As we saw in Section 3, internal labor allocation in the US is localized but has an easy access to the external market. As a result, the American manager of a research lab or a project team can move quickly and assemble the best talents available from outside, if money is available. Creating a high caliber team and infusing new ideas from outside would be conducive to radical innovation, other things being equal.

On the other hand, incremental innovation comes from knowing the details of existing technology and its relationship with other related technologies as well. The Japanese internal labor market for researchers, in which they tend to move from the lab to the shop floor ever so often and from one division to the other once in a while under central personnel management, may not be so appropriate in accumulating deep knowledge in one narrow area (which is often necessary for radical innovation) but may fit better to the requisites of incremental innovation.

Finally, we touch on the difference in venture business activities in the two countries. From the point of view of interpenetration the difference seems to lie in the ways external markets work in Japan in contrast to the US. In essence, the supply of core people in ventures is smaller because of the Japanese external labor market. The supply of venture capital has been much less because of the Japanese capital market. The demand for products of venture business, if ever formed, would be more limited because of the Japanese goods markets.

Low labor mobility in the Japanese labor market (for top-flight engineers) and limited port of entry into the Japanese firms means that an entrepreneur has a very small chance of re-entry into established firms if he fails in a spinoff attempt. Thus, the cost of failure for entrepreneurs is considerably higher in Japan, which, in turn, reduces the supply of potential entrepreneurs.

The supply of capital for potential entrepreneurs is also limited in Japan because of the intermediate organization in the bank loan market and the underdeveloped equity market. If an entrepreneur tries to raise capital through bank loans, he will have great difficulty becoming a member of a bank-centered intermediate organization. He probably still lacks reputation and lacks a record of past earnings to persuade the bankers. If he tries to raise capital in equity, he will again face a major difficulty because the public offering of his stocks, out of which venture capitalists reap capital gains, has been very restricted in the Japanese market. Given a small chance for capital gains, very few capitalists would be willing to provide seed money for risky ventures.

Venture businesses would be difficult to garner enough sales in their formative stage unless they can provide very novel products at irresistibly low prices. Although this would be true anywhere, the pressure is higher in Japan, where intermediate organizations are more developed in the goods market than in the US. The basic logic is the same as in the capital case. An entrepreneur has to become a member of an intermediate organization first. The buying firms (or distributors) would prefer the products of long-time partners if similar products are available or if prices are not so different.

In all three markets, the American situation is a reverse of what we discussed thus far. It is no wonder that there is a large difference in venture activities in the two countries. To some extent these reasons also explain why many venture activities in Japan are either part of or under the control of large established firms.

··

6. Conclusion

We hope that the foregoing analysis has been able to convince the readers that our basic framework (especially that of interpenetration) is a worthwhile vehicle to enhance our conceptual understanding of how real-life resource allocations are conducted both in the markets and in the organizations. By having a single common framework to view resource allocation in these two arenas, the hope is to understand two allocation mechanisms and their interpenetration in a better perspective.

Commonality of the conceptual framework is also evident in our discussions of American and Japanese resource allocation. We have analysed several examples using the same framework presented in Section 2. Any meaningful international comparison has to analyse the different behavior patterns from the same, common perspective. We hope that we can now understand corporate behavior in the two countries better and that seemingly 'mystical or irrational' behavior of Japanese firms and other economic agents is no longer so mystical nor irrational.

This paper is only a beginning. There is a lot more to be done. On the conceptual level, for example, the question of 'optimal mixture' or 'optimal penetration' of various resource allocation principles is intriguing. For example, a firm can choose which mechanism to use for its internal resource allocation and can also select among various alternative transaction modes with the external markets. The firm should make these internal and external transaction decisions simultaneously. This is a decision on the design of the total transaction system of the firm. What would the optimal transaction system design be? What kind of variables will effect the choice of system design? These are but a few examples of questions we can begin to ask using our interpenetration framework.

....

Notes

1. They often form business groups of loosely tied firms. See Section 3.
2. Koike (1978) gives detailed evidence on this. In this paper we will try to give data or show the references (preferably English-language ones) for the major factual statements like this one. For many well-known empirical phenomena related to Japan, we will omit references.
3. See Caves and Uekusa (1976. 112).
4. Kagono et al. (1983) have done an extensive survey on Japanese and US corporations and their management. On a 5-point scale of organizational influence, the power of Japanese personnel managers is rated 2.74 against American 2.34. The difference is statistically significant.
5. Data is for 1981. Source: *Money Flow Accounts Statistics*, Bank of Japan.
6. In 1980, the total market value of all the listed stocks in the US was about 4 times larger than that of Japan, whereas total new corporate bond issues in the US were about 10 times as large as in Japan. GNP difference is only 2.5. Source: Japan Securities Industry Association (1981).
7. See Caves and Uekusa 1976) or Imai (1980).
8. The shipment of legally-cartelized products was 30.7% of total Japanese manufacturing shipment in 1970, for example. Source: Imai (1976).
9. See Sakakibara (1983) for details of this cooperative and the reasons for its success.
10. Among the major manufacturing firms in the US and Japan of comparable size (US top 500 and Japan top 100), 77% had divisional organizations in the US in 1969, and 42% in Japan in 1973. Source: Yoshihara et al (1981).
11. See Chandler (1977).
12. When these failures become too great, the transaction concerned will change its arena, i.e., the former market transaction will become an internal transaction or the firm will break up into two units transacting in the market.
13. For a similar but somewhat different analysis of market failure and choice among governance structures of transactions, see Williamson (1975, 1979), and Ouchi and Barney (1981).
14. Note that the second remedy is indirect in the sense that an organizational element creeps into the membership principle as a remedy to the failure arising chiefly because of the market decision principle. In a similar vein, the first remedy is direct.
15. For some discussion of legal differences between the two capital markets, see Flaherty and Itami (1984).
16. See Imai et al. (1975), and Yoshihara et al. (1981). For example, among the major manufacturing firms in the US and Japan (the US top 500 and the Japan top 100), the percentages of the firms with a single business, with a dominant business, with related businesses and with unrelated businesses are 6.2, 29.2, 45.2, 19.4 for the US in 1969 and 16.2, 40.6, 36.4, 6.8 for Japan in 1973.

....

References

Caves, Richard and Masu Uekusa (1976), *Industrial Organization in Japan* (Brookings Institution, Washington, DC).

Chandler, Alfred D., Jr., (1977), *The Visible Hand* (Belknap Press of Harvard University Press, Cambridge, MA).

Flaherty, M.-Thérèse and Hiroyuki Itami (1984). 'Finance', ch 5 in: D. Okimoto *et al.* (eds.), *Competitive edge: The semiconductor industry in the US and Japan* (Stanford University Press, Stanford, CA).

Hirschman, Albert O. (1970), *Exit, voice and loyalty* (Harvard University Press, Cambridge, MA).

Imai, Ken-ichi, (1976), *Modern industrial organization* (in Japanese) (Iwanami. Tokyo).

——— (1980), 'Japan's industrial organization', in: K. Sato (ed.) *Industry and business in Japan* (Sharpe, White Plains, NY).

——— Akira Goto and Kei Ishiguro (1975), 'Empirical analysis of corporate diversification', Working paper (in Japanese) (Japan Economic Data Development Centre).

Japan Securities Industry Association (1981), *Report of the Mission on American Securities Market* (Japan Securities Industry Association).

Kagono, Tadao, Ikujiro Nonaka, Kiyonori Sakakibara and Akihiro Okumura (1983), 'Japan-US comparison of corporate management' (in Japanese), *Japan Economic Journal*.

Koike, Kazuo (1976), 'Labor union and participation on the shop floor' (in Japanese) *Oriental Economist*.

——— (1978), 'Japan's industrial relations: Characteristics and problems', *Japanese Economic Studies*, Fall.

Ouchi, William G. and Jay B. Barney (1981), 'Efficient boundaries', Working paper (Graduate School of Management, UCLA, CA) Nov.

Rumelt, Richard P. (1974), *Strategy, structure, and economic performance*, Harvard Business School, Harvard University, Cambridge, MA.

Sakakibara, Kiyonori (1983), 'From imitation to innovation: The very large scale integrated (VSLI) semiconductor project in Japan', Working paper (Sloan School, MIT, Cambridge, MA) Oct.

Wallich, Henry C. and Mable I. Wallich (1976), 'Banking and Finance', in: H. Patrick and H. Rosovsky (eds.) *Asia's new giant* (Brookings Institution, Washington, DC).

Williamson, Oliver E. (1975), *Markets and hierarchies*, (Free Press, New York).

——— (1979), 'Transaction-cost economics: The governance of contractual relations', *The Journal of Law and Economics*, Oct.

Yoshihara, Hideki, Akimitsu Sakuma, Hiroyuki Itami and Tadao Kagono (1981), 'Diversification strategies of Japanese firms' (in Japanese), *Japan Economic Journal*.

11 Vertical Quasi-Integration

K. J. Blois

1. Introduction

The recent financial problems of Rolls-Royce Ltd., have acted as an effective reminder of the extensive interdependence of business organizations within the British economy. The fact that, if Rolls-Royce had ceased to trade, then a large number of supplying organizations would have found themselves in severe financial difficulties is a reminder that, although these suppliers are legal entities separate from Rolls-Royce, such organizations are extensively dependent on and inter-related with Rolls-Royce. This situation is not peculiar to Rolls-Royce or even to the aero-engine industry, for there are many firms whose financial collapse would seem likely to result in the failure, or at least severe disruption, of a large number of supplying firms and the financial difficulties of Upper Clyde Shipbuilders Ltd. provide another illustration of this. Indeed the repercussions of such a failure would extend far beyond the legal entity of the firm which originally failed.

The relationship between firms and their suppliers is obviously complex and this paper seeks to describe certain aspects of this relationship. It will discuss under what conditions a supplier can become dependent upon a particular customer and will also discuss the ways in which a large customer is able to assert its influence over a supplier and the types of influence brought to bear. Finally it will consider whether or not a situation is developing in certain cases where some firms are gaining the advantages of vertical integration (i.e. the organization of production under which a single business unit carries on successive stages in the processing or distribution of a

The author wishes to acknowledge the support of a Houblon–Norman Grant for research into this topic.

product which is sold by other firms without further processing) without assuming the risks or rigidity of ownership—a situation which might be described as 'vertical quasi-integration'.

....

2. The Advantages and Disadvantages of Vertical Integration

The benefits which a firm might obtain through vertical integration clearly vary from industry to industry but the following are among those most frequently cited:

1. decreased marketing expenses
2. stability of operations
3. certainty of supplies of materials and services
4. better control over product distribution
5. tighter quality control
6. prompt revision of production and distribution policies
7. better inventory control
8. additional profit margins or the ability to charge lower prices on final products.

The importance and validity of such advantages will depend upon the specific situation considered, but in each case the benefits must be weighed against disadvantages which are bound to arise and typically will include some of the following:

1. disparities between productive capacities at various stages of production
2. public opinion and governmental pressure
3. lack of specialization
4. inflexibility of operations
5. extension of the management team
6. lack of direct competitive pressures on the costs of intermediate products.

When a firm considers a merger or take-over which would result in its being more integrated in the vertical sense, it must seek to evaluate the relevant costs and benefits of a financial and non-financial nature. However, if it is possible for a firm to develop a relationship with some of its suppliers such that the advantages of vertical integration can be obtained without the normally associated disadvantages then it must be expected to do so.

3. Large Customers

In this section consideration will be given to the circumstances which might enable a firm to establish a relationship with one or more of its suppliers which might be described as vertical quasi-integration. One factor which would seem to be necessary is that the firm should be a 'large customer' of a particular supplier. Throughout this paper a 'large customer' will be taken to mean a customer which takes a significant proportion of a supplier's output and not necessarily a firm which is large in the sense of its number of employees, capital employed or even large relative to the supplier. What is considered 'significant' will vary between firms and in one firm through time but the following indicates the type of situation envisaged.

Consider first a firm which has only one product line and let that firm be operating in an industry which currently has excess capacity. In such circumstances any customer whose purchases are so large that the supplier would operate at a loss if that business were removed would be considered a large customer. If the supplying industry now finds itself working at full capacity and has an excess demand for its products then clearly some firms previously considered as large in the earlier situation would no longer be so considered because if they removed their business then it could be replaced. However, there would be some customers who would, even under these conditions, be considered as large, especially if the supplier did not consider only the short-term but take account of the possibility of a future decrease in demand when customers might remember treatment received in times of shortage of supply.

In cases where a firm is a supplier of a range of products, there is a need to consider each customer both with regard to each individual product line, and also the range of products as a whole. Thus, a situation might arise whereby a customer's purchases from any one product line might be relatively unimportant, no matter what the state of the supplying industry's capacity, but if the customer's purchases from all product lines are considered, then it becomes a large customer.

Now if a customer is large in this sense, it would seem likely that a supplier would be especially sensitive to that customer's needs. Moreover, observation of business practice indicates that many large customers are equally sensitive to their ability to bring influence to bear upon their suppliers and thus to obtain from them special terms and conditions. The type of special requirement such customers might make will be discussed below, in Section 4, but at this stage the basis for such ability to bring influence upon a supplier needs further consideration.

A large customer was described above in such a way as to imply that if such a customer removed its business from a particular supplier, this would be a very serious blow to that supplier. Now the customer's ability to bring pressure upon the supplier revolves around the question of how likely it is that a customer would be able to remove its business. It would appear that a large customer has a limited number of alternatives open to it if it needs a particular product or service but wishes to change its source of supply. It may:

1. offer its business to another supplier within the country,
2. offer its business to a foreign supplier,
3. encourage a new supplier to enter the industry,
4. set up its own production unit, or
5. take over an existing supplier.

The problem which a supplier, faced with a threat from a large customer of withdrawal of its business, has to consider is the likelihood of the customer being in a position to carry out one or other of these alternatives.

As far as the first alternative is concerned, the capacity situation in the supplying industry will be of crucial importance, for if there is a severe shortage of capacity, then a customer might have to accept very disadvantageous terms if it is to persuade another supplier to take its business. However, as was indicated above, capacity situations can vary very quickly and only a short-sighted supplier would disregard the possibility that current demand might fall or that the customer might encourage, say by guaranteeing orders, a competitor to expand its capacity.

The second alternative is out of the question in the case of certain products whose nature makes transportation extremely costly. However, modern developments in transport make this less of a problem, but the combined costs of transport and, in some cases, tariffs often make an otherwise attractive foreign source uneconomic. For example, it was reported that it would cost £1.25 a car extra to import wheels from Spain.[1]

The feasibility of the third alternative depends very much upon the nature of the technology of the supplying industry. In many cases there will be basic difficulties with regard to patents and licences, but frequently the technical expertise necessary to manufacture the product is not easily obtained. In addition, the production economics may be such that a new supplier can only compete if it is able to obtain a large share of the market very quickly and the economies of scale may mean that even the guarantee of a large customer's business may not be sufficient to encourage a new entrant to the industry. A firm already in the supplying industry should be sufficiently aware of such technological factors and thus be in a position to judge the likelihood of a customer being able to encourage a new entrant to the industry. The encouragement given by some car manufacturers to GKN (BRD) to enter into competition with Hardy Spicer is a good illustration of this third alternative in practice. Ford, in particular, guaranteed GKN (BRD) minimum shares of its orders for propeller shafts over a period of time when GKN (BRD) was starting production, but in this case the product was not considered particularly complex to manufacture.[2]

Similar comments can be made about the fourth alternative. In addition, in this case, there is a clear understanding in many firms of where their expertise lies and the manufacture of components, purchased items or raw materials may be considered to lie outside of this area of activities.

The fifth alternative also presents some obvious difficulties for a customer considering it, and not the least of these is to find a suitable company which is willing to be taken over or to merge in some way with a customer. Even if such a supplier can be found the operation has to be financed and this may be difficult. In addition a firm would be extremely lucky to find a supplier to take over whose capacity matched its own requirements. If the supplier's capacity is too small then the customer must, in the short-term while it builds up the capacity, purchase from other suppliers; or if the capacity is greater than its requirements then the excess production must be sold. Neither of these situations is very satisfactory to the customer.

The supplier must, of course, consider both the short-term and the long-term likelihood of a large customer being able to pursue one of these five alternatives. It does appear that the first two alternatives are open to most large customers in the long-term but that the last three are only open to those large customers whose total demand for the product under consideration is sufficient to represent a very considerable proportion of the output required to achieve the same sort of economies of scale as existing suppliers. Therefore, unless a supplier is in a position to produce some other product with the spare capacity which would become available through the loss of a large customer, it will feel, for its own security, that it must treat the requirements of its large customers in a sympathetic manner—particularly those customers which are in a position to take up either the third, fourth or fifth alternative.

Underlying the above argument is the question of the flexibility or lack of flexibility of the supplying firm—a problem which seems to have two dimensions. Firstly, there are many firms who make products, a very large proportion of which are sold to one industry because the product is specific to the requirements of that industry. Such firms might be described as market specific with regard to that product and unless the firm produces other products sold to a different industry, it can be considered as totally market specific. The Rolls-Royce case has brought to light several firms who were in this situation and also divisions of large companies which were apparently dependent upon Rolls-Royce for a large part of their sales. The second dimension is with regard to product specificity, by which is meant the type of situation where the firm's plant and machinery is only capable of manufacturing the current product range. It should also be noted that it is not infrequent to meet firms where employees at all levels in the firm only have experience in that firm or industry and it is far from apparent that they could work so effectively in an organization making anything but their current product range. Again the Rolls-Royce crisis illustrates several such cases—the *Financial Times* reporting, for example, that 'Smith Clayton Forge . . . developed a forging technique for the production of titanium fan-blades'.[3]

If a firm is both market and product specific then the influence of a large customer over that firm can be very considerable as the removal of its business would cause the supplier very considerable difficulties.

To sum up this section, it is suggested that if a firm is a large customer of a particular supplier it may be in a position to use as a bargaining weapon the threat of obtaining supplies elsewhere. If the supplier is market and/or product specific this threat is of very great importance and will greatly influence the responsiveness of the suppliers to any requests such a customer may make.

4. Large Customers' Special Requirements

In this section some of the special terms which large customers may seek to obtain from their suppliers will be described. Many of these terms impose extra costs upon the supplier but, as will be indicated, some of them also bring benefits to the supplier. However, many of these requirements are of the type that vertically integrated organizations are able to obtain within their organizations by virtue of their legal powers as distinct from the situation described in this paper where large customers obtain these terms only because of the size of their purchases. Though from the supplier's point of view such large orders are often attractive because of the possibility they bring of achieving economies of scale. It should be noted that these require-ments can only be considered as 'special' in the sense that they differ from the terms and conditions usually available from the supplying industry. In other words they might be terms and conditions which other customers would equally well like to obtain if possible. On the other hand, they might be special in the sense that they are only required by a particular customer.

Stocks and delivery. Some large customers, for a variety of reasons, carry only very small stocks of items that they purchase either for resale or for use in production. Those which do this rely upon their suppliers to hold enough stocks and to have a sufficiently flexible delivery system to meet unexpected increases in demand. If, on the other hand, the customer's requirements suddenly decrease, say as a result of a strike in its factory, then the supplier will be expected to hold back deliveries of even so-called 'firm orders' until such time as demand rises once again. The car industry is particularly well-known for following this policy with regard to stocks of components, as is illustrated by the effect of the strike at Fords in the first quarter of 1971 on Armstrong Equipment Ltd., which reported laying off workers and holding £250,000 worth of front suspension struts and shock absorbers for Ford after five weeks of the Ford strike.[4] In some cases large customers require more than one delivery of goods a day as, for example, some multiple food outlets require two deliveries of bread a day even though each delivery may be less than a lorry load, thus enabling them to allocate less store space to a high-volume, low-value item.[5] When customers expect such a stocking and delivery service from suppliers this adds considerably to the suppliers' costs.

Another aspect of special delivery requirements is found in cases where a large customer has several factories or stores spread over a wide area. In such cases suppliers may be asked to switch deliveries between various locations at very short notice. If such changes are requested they can impose significantly increased delivery charges upon a supplier.

Special products. Large customers frequently ask a supplier to provide an amendment to an existing standard design or specification, or for a product specifically for their purposes. There can be many reasons for such a request, such as the fact that the customer may not think that the standard product is of high enough quality for its own purposes or that it requires some distinctive feature to help distinguish its products from that of its competitors. In some cases the volume of the order for a special product will make the order worth accepting, but in others where there is just one item out of a range of products purchased, this will not be so but the supplier may still feel obliged to produce this item. Lucas, for example, found that in one period of three years the percentage of direct labour employed on standard products fell from 70 to 60 per cent in spite of the declared intention to raise the figure to 82 per cent.[6]

Technical service. The provision of technical service and advice is becoming an increasingly important element in industrial marketing, especially as, with increasing technical complexity of many products, even the biggest firms find that they cannot employ an expert in all areas. In some industries the supplying firms' technical experts will become actively involved in the design of relevant parts of their customers' products. This often occurs well in advance of the time when a supplier knows whether or not it will receive an order for this item from the customer and this means that this technical advice, if provided free (as it typically is), is very much an investment with a definite possibility of a zero return in the immediate future. The problems of controlling expenditure in this area were discussed in the Monopolies Commission Report on the Man-made Cellulosic Fibre Industry, where it was recognized that suppliers can find that provision of technical advice is not always an economic proposition.[7]

Access to plant and records. Some large customers make it a condition of business that they should have access to the supplier's plant at any time. This might be so that they can make spot quality checks on their product or check general standards, such as hygiene in the case of food manufacturers. In certain cases customers also request that the suppliers should disclose the costs which it meets in manufacturing the products it intends purchasing. The refusal of Hardy Spicer to allow car manufacturers access in this way was raised by the car manufacturers as a significant criticism of that company in a case before the Monopolies Commission.[8] It is also recorded in another Monopolies Commission case that the British Electrical Authority demanded cost breakdowns from suppliers of insulated electric cables and wires.[9]

Marketing policies. Once a customer becomes a large customer it may seek to interfere with the supplier's relations with other customers. This may take some forms including, for example, stating that the supplier must not also act as a supplier to certain of the customer's immediate competitors, or inform-ing the supplier that a proposed advertising campaign in conjunction with a competitor is not to be carried out. Such an action was reported in *The Sunday Times* when the Spar Organization attempted to put on a promotional campaign with the co-operation of a number of large food manufacturers.[10] It was reported that the Multiple Grocers Association 'warned' these manufac-turers from co-operating with Spar in this way. In another case before the Monopolies Commission it was stated that Triplex[11] had bound certain furnace manufacturers, which had supplied Triplex, not to undertake work of a similar nature for anybody engaged in the manufacture of safety glass. A third illustration of this type of request was the withdrawal of certain advertisements put out by the British Steel Corporation. Pressure was brought to bear by a large customer—in this case the British Leyland Corporation—which decided that the advertisement might mislead the public.[12]

Labour relations. If a supplier has poor labour relations, then this is rightly a matter of concern to any customer, for these poor relationships may cause poor quality, irregular delivery, low productivity and finally may result in strikes. In such situations, cases have been recorded of large customers offering the services of their own labour relations staff to their suppliers and in many cases these services have been readily accepted, especially by suppliers who are not big enough to employ such experts themselves. A more difficult situation for the supplier is when a strike occurs which results in the disruption of a large customer's production through lack of supplies. The cost of such disruption is so great to some firms that their prime concern is to get their production on the move again and to achieve this aim they may directly or indirectly encourage a supplier to end a strike as quickly as possible—which may mean on terms which the supplier would not have otherwise agreed upon. As the *Economist* pointed out at the time of the GKN-Sankey strike in 1970, 'GKN must have been under great pressure from customers to buy the strikers off. There were, after all, only 5,000 of them but they had put another 20,000 men in the motor industry out of work. . . . '[13] Also the removal, by Fords, of a $1\frac{1}{2}$-ton die from Sage and Company after that company's work-force had been on strike for only 5 days must have been noted by other suppliers with its implied threat of permanent loss of business if a strike affected this important customer.[14]

Management. The ability to appoint senior managers and particularly executive directors is to some extent an indication of a firm's independence from outsiders—either individuals or organizations. However, the calibre of a supplier's management is of such importance to a customer that some big firms, when considering whether or not to accept a firm as a new source of supply, will not only insist on inspecting the firm's premises but expect to meet and vet all the firm's senior managers as well. If the management is not considered competent, then either the firm will not be accepted as a supplier or suggestions will be made as to how the management team might be strengthened. In the latter case the suggestion might not just be that, say, a new Marketing Director is needed, but an individual, sometimes from the customer's own organization, might be suggested as a suitable candidate.

Materials. The right of a customer to specify the use of certain materials, even by name of manufacturer, in the products which it is purchasing is undisputed. However, in some cases a customer may decide that it will provide the supplier with some or all of the raw materials needed to produce the item it purchases. The argument used to support this action is that if the customer is purchasing this item from several suppliers it can achieve economies by buying the raw materials in bulk and distributing them to its suppliers. From the suppliers' point of view, apart from the general intrusion into its activities, such action by a customer may affect its profits especially if it uses cost-plus pricing methods.

Credit. Suppliers of all types expect to supply items on credit by agreement or in fact accept some delay in being paid by customers, as a normal part of business. Nevertheless, in times when there is a general shortage of funds, some customers will delay payment for goods received for longer periods and the cost of this, often involuntary, provision of credit to a supplier can be considerable. A small customer if threatened with a withdrawal of supplies is more likely to pay within a reasonable period than a large customer to whom the supplier may feel unable to make such a threat. The amount of credit reportedly extended to Rolls-Royce by some of its suppliers immediately prior to the appointment of the Official Receiver seemed unusually large in terms of these suppliers' annual sales to the company and is perhaps an illustration of this type of situation.

Price. This is the most important area in which a customer can seek special terms not least because several of the items considered above impose extra costs upon the supplier which, unless they can be incorporated into the price, will reduce its profitability. Indeed, as was stated above, the forms of special requirement considered above might only be special in the sense that they are different from the terms and conditions currently available in the supplying industry. In other words, they might be terms which the small customers would desire to obtain as much as the large customers but they may include terms which are special in the sense that they are only required by a few customers. The fact that they are considered as special in a particular industry will of course be reflected in the fact that the cost of providing for them will not be included in the standard prices offered in that industry. Thus, when considering 'price' under the heading of 'special requirements' it is necessary to consider whether or not special price concessions are requested by larger customers and to separately consider whether or not customers demanding other special terms and conditions, such as those discussed above, are prepared to pay for them.

A large customer may be in a position to argue for a special low price per unit on a particular product it is purchasing purely on the basis of the size of the order and the economies of scale that such an order should enable the supplier to achieve. Most suppliers, of course, operate discount schemes which they believe take adequate account for such economies, but many customers appear to believe either that the supplier's average cost curve falls more rapidly than the supplier accepts, or that the supplier's profit per unit is too high. Lucas, for example, indicated that its volume rebates took account not only of the size of a customer's total purchases but also in certain cases 'the inherent threat . . . to use or create an alternative source of supply' and that this threat 'has to be weighed in the light of the size of the business at stake'.[15] The customer's attitude is of course understandable to the extent that it wishes to keep its costs as low as possible within the bounds of ensuring a continuing supply of the items it purchases, but England (a leading American authority on Purchasing) defines a 'fair price' as 'the lowest price that ensures a continuous supply of the proper quality to him who needs it, where and when he needs it . . . '.[16] However, as one Purchasing Director has stated, 'it is easier to be a good buyer than to be a good supply manager . . . ',[17] by which he meant it is easier to consider only today's price than to consider the impact of that price upon the continuance of supply and it does seem that quite often large customers, for a variety of reasons, do press for specially low prices without due consideration of the effect of such prices upon their suppliers' future.

With regard to the question of whether or not customers are prepared to meet the costs of the provision of special requirements, it must be first considered if the supplier was aware of these special requirements when calculating the price to quote to its customer. In fact it is not uncommon for the agreement under which the business is transacted to be quite vague on items other than price, and for special delivery requirements, for example, to be stipulated later. Similarly, other items are also not always made explicit and so, unless the supplier has previous experience of dealing with this customer, it is impossible to include a cost allowance in the price for these items.

A second question to be considered is whether or not the supplier is capable of making adequate cost estimates for the provision of any special services requested in advance. In theory, there should be little difficulty in accurately estimating the costs, say, of providing an amendment to a standard design, but in fact the standard of cost estimating in many firms, both big and small, is very poor. Even if the costs could be accurately estimated, it seems that often the large customer is not prepared to meet them.

A growing number of large customers now attempt, before negotiating with suppliers, to estimate how much it should cost to supply the items it wishes to purchase, and to this estimated cost is added an allowance for profit. The accuracy of these customers' estimates is a matter of some debate, with the customers maintaining that they achieve a high level of accuracy but most suppliers maintaining that large errors are frequently made. While it would seem that an experienced engineer together with a competent cost estimator should be able to make a good estimate of the material and direct labour costs of manufacturing an item, it does seem that the problem of estimating a supplier's other costs is an extremely complex one, involving in many cases the difficult problem of allocating overheads between several separate production lines. Also when it comes to adding a profit margin to these cost estimates, it is difficult to see how a customer is able to determine the size of the margin to be allowed, for this would often involve apportioning the capital employed by the supplier to its different product classes.

In some cases where a customer buys a range of products from one supplier it is common to find that the customer will maintain that it wishes the supplier to make a profit on each individual line. The reason being given for this is that the customer wishes to feel free to drop or add products from its range of purchases without causing the supplier difficulties. It is important from the supplier's point of view that this should indeed be the case, but even suppliers making what they consider to be an adequate profit on their total business from a particular customer indicate that they make a loss on individual product lines supplied to that customer, even though the prices received are those calculated by the customer concerned.

To sum up this section, a list of special requirements which might be required by any customer has been presented but, as was indicated in Section 3, it seems likely that a large customer will be in a position to force a supplier to provide these services, quite possibly below total cost in cases where a cost is applicable. The fact that many of these requirements are of the type that would be found in a vertically integrated concern is noted. In comparison some of the disadvantages of vertical integration listed in Section 2 are avoided.

5. The Supplier's Point of View

It is necessary to consider this situation from the point of view of the supplier with considerable care, for the picture painted above is of a situation in which the supplier is very much at a disadvantage with regard to large customers. However, consideration of typical situations does indicate that dominance by a large customer does sometimes offer advantages to a supplier but also that the supplier does not need to be entirely passive in response to a large customer's demands.

One benefit which some large customers give to their suppliers is the opportunity to obtain technical expertise and advice of an up-to-date nature. Thus a large customer may find that its development of a new product is held back by its supplier's inability to handle the latest techniques and in such cases the customer may offer its technical expertise, free of charge, to a supplier. Other cases of a similar nature have arisen when a supplier has quoted a price far higher than the customer expected and in the resulting discussion between the two parties it becomes apparent that the supplier is inefficient in some way. The fact that this is pointed out by a customer may be sufficient, in that once aware of the problem, the supplier may be capable of overcoming the difficulty by itself, but alternatively the supplier may appeal to the customer for advice and assistance. Marks and Spencer Ltd. is the firm which is perhaps best known for this positive approach to its suppliers of offering a variety of assistance to their suppliers, but many other large customers do follow this type of policy including, for example, Fords.[18]

Another advantage which a supplier sometimes gains through dealing with a large customer is that economies of scale can be obtained as a result of the volume of orders achieved. These economies might arise from savings in production costs, distribution costs or selling costs and, if they are not 'sucked off' by the large customers, are obviously beneficial to a supplier.

As to the forms of resistance to large customers' demands, there seem to be several possibilities. The most obvious is, of course, for a supplier not to commit more than a certain proportion of its output to any one customer so that, if that customer should withdraw its business, the blow to the firm would not be critical. However, in some cases such a policy is not a possibility because the number of potential customers for a particular product may be small, for example in the case of a supplier to the aircraft industry, and therefore if the product is to be sold at all it becomes inevitable that a large proportion of the output of that product must go to large customers.

An alternative policy is to diversify into other product ranges that sell to different markets. Such a policy, though appearing superficially attractive, is very complex to implement both from the point of view of finding a suitable product range into which to diversify and, once having chosen, to set up the necessary organization to carry out the diversification programme. On the former aspect of this problem the firm has to carry out a search for areas where it can make use of some aspect of its current expertise and experience, unless it is prepared effectively to start a new organization to deal with the new product. On the latter point, there are many obvious problems but, if a company can manage to diversify into an entirely new field, it will be able to lessen its dependence upon any one customer in terms of its total business. Even so it takes a big company to be able to manage itself successfully through a period when it loses a large customer.

In some fields one form of resistance can take the form of making the customer at least as dependent upon the supplier as the supplier is upon the customer. This is possible especially in a field where high level technology is involved or where very special services have been developed. It is apparent that, with increasing technological complexity, in many fields, firms are no longer able to maintain a technical expert in each area of their interests and in consequence it is becoming more common for firms to rely upon their suppliers for advice on a range of topics connected with the products they purchase. In many cases this advice may even include assistance with the design of a particular component, and in such situations it is often impossible to determine who was responsible for the final product because the co-operation between customer and potential supplier is so close.[19] In fact, the offer of such technical advice is very influential in determining which potential suppliers finally become the suppliers and it is a well-recognized marketing strategy to offer such a service.[20] There is evidence that a firm will think very carefully before it decides to dispense with the services of a supplier which has provided extensive and useful technical advice.[21] On the other hand, from the point of view of the supplier, the cost of building up a team with such knowledge is very considerable and represents a great investment of cash, and the concern must be as to how specific to the current range of products this technical expertise is. If the knowledge is not of use outside of the current customer industry, then the supplier is again tying itself into a position of dependence by virtue of its need to gain a return on its investment. Finding other fields of use for technical expertise is not easy, but there are some examples, such as the Dowty Group's exploitation of its research into hydraulics.[22]

Another way of gaining some power of resistance is by achieving such a volume of output that none of the customers can compete with the economies of scale achieved. For example, when Automotive Products Ltd. appeared before the Monopolies Commission it made the following statement: 'in the popular sizes of clutch used in motor cars . . . a manufacturer, in order to achieve competitive costs, must have an output of some 300,000 a year of a particular size, which is equivalent to something like one-fifth or less of the present total requirements for such clutches for initial equipment'.[23] This will mean of course that in many cases the supplier must become a monopolist itself although, as was pointed out above, these circumstances can occur in cases where there are perhaps two or three suppliers, and slightly more customers.

However, this situation is currently becoming less easy to maintain in some industries because in certain customer industries, as a result of takeovers and mergers and also the integration of some firms' activities throughout Europe, bigger customers are being created and thus making it possible for a customer to compete with its suppliers' economies.

Another form of defence lies in the specificity of the supplier's activities. This may seem to be in contradiction to the point made earlier—namely, that specificity makes a supplier vulnerable to its customers. However, it follows from the fact that skills, machinery, etc., are highly specific and not immediately—certainly in the short term—as effectively applicable elsewhere that it would take time for a customer to collect together the necessary skills and machinery to produce the product itself. Thus it appears to have taken GKN (BRD) about three years from starting production of propeller shafts to make a profit even with active support of certain car manufacturers.[24] The existence of this time period and the additional gap between the creation of a productive facility and its reaching an economic level of production costs give the supplier time to seek out diversification opportunities itself. This situation is not truly a defence but means that the supplier knows that it has time in which to adapt if a customer removes its business from it.

Another form of defence is to diversify but not away from existing markets, but into them—thus offering a range of products and marketing them as an entity or in such a manner as to stress the group of products. For example, the so-called 'package deal', where, if a customer indicates its intention of removing some part of its business, through the use of price adjustments it is possible for the supplier to make the removal of this business a relatively expensive procedure. Thus, if a customer is currently purchasing a range of twenty different products, in equal volume and each of equal price, from a particular supplier then the supplier might arrange its prices, possibly through a discount structure, so that if the customer tries to buy one of these products elsewhere, then the reduction in cost to the customer is marginal and certainly less than one-twentieth. Clearly, such an action would discourage a customer from removing one item from the range purchased and it might be that it is impossible to remove all purchases from such a supplier at one time. However, it is not easy for a supplier to establish itself in this sort of position, though Lucas have admitted doing so,[25] as customers with alert and effective purchasing departments usually are able to foresee this sort of situation arising.

6. Does Vertical Quasi-Integration Really Exist?

The preceding sections have sought to show that some suppliers and customers develop a very close relationship which is based primarily upon the supplier's dependence for a significant proportion of its total business upon a particular customer. As was indicated this type of situation gives a customer considerable bargaining power over such a supplier and some customers use this power to call for special conditions and terms of trade some of which, e.g. special products, may actually increase the supplier's dependence upon that customer. It was suggested that this type of relationship is the type often found within vertically integrated organizations and this section considers whether or not such a relationship between customer and supplier can be considered as a type of vertical integration without legal form.

In seeking to answer this question it is first necessary to consider what is meant by 'a firm'. Penrose states that:

The concept of the firm . . . does not depend on the ramifications of stock ownership or the mere existence of the power to control, although extensive stock ownership may, and probably should, be one important consideration in any attempt to apply it.

On the other hand, long-term contracts, leases, and patent license agreements may give an equally effective control.[26]

and later she states

It [a firm which is a subsidiary because of stock ownership] should not be classed as part of the larger firm [the parent company] if it appears to operate independently of the managerial plans and administrative arrangements of the larger firm, for in this case any influence the larger firm exerts should be viewed as an extension of economic power and not as an extension of the co-ordinated planning of the productive activity.[27]

Similarly other definitions of 'a firm' emphasize not the legal concept but the integration of planning.[28]

If, as these definitions suggest, the essence of a firm is the co-ordination of managerial planning it becomes necessary to consider if the forms of behaviour described in Section 4 represent an interdependence of managerial plans between customer and supplier. As was argued in Section 3 these forms of behaviour are based upon economic dependence.

In some cases large customers are prepared to indicate that they regard their suppliers as being extensions of themselves. Statements such as 'we impose our patterns of discipline on our vendors' and 'vendors are an integrated part of a manufacturer' have been made to the author by senior purchasing personnel in the automobile industry, and would seem to be fairly representative of their attitude to their suppliers. On the other hand it must be admitted that there seem to be few suppliers who would wholeheartedly agree with this statement: ' . . . in the case of a major car component the customer and the supplier virtually function as a single unit, and we are, in effect, merely an extension of their production facilities',[29] which was made by the Managing Director of a car component firm. Nevertheless, although not many other manufacturers would seem to agree completely with this statement neither are there many who would seem prepared to disagree totally with its theme. However, the ability of Rootes and Vauxhall to force Triplex Glass Company to distribute spares through them rather than through its own distributors[30] seems to indicate considerable co-ordination of managerial plans with the initiative clearly being with the customers. Similarly the car manufacturers' ability to obtain single-tier prices (i.e. a single price for components regardless of whether or not they are for the replacement trade or for manufacturing) very much against the wishes of many suppliers[31] seems to show a lack of managerial independence on the part of the suppliers. Thus it would seem that there is some evidence in the automobile industry's case in particular of this form of quasi-integration, on the admission of the parties concerned.

In other industries evidence is less easy to obtain but if Section 4 is considered it would seem that many of the special requirements listed there do carry with them some implication of managerial control by the customer, over certain aspects of the supplier's activities. For example the influence of multiple retail food stores on the allocation of even the largest food manufacturers' promotional expenditure between 'below-the-line activity' (including such items as premium selling, game promotions, incentive schemes, etc.) and media advertising through the introduction of Private Brands is a case in point.[32] The food manufacturers would very much prefer not to have to increase below-the-line expenditure but have been forced into this position by the economic power of the large multiple stores, and by their direct demands for increased contributions for such items as 'key money' which the manufacturers seem unable to resist.

To conclude this section, it would seem that there is some evidence that many suppliers in a variety of industries are finding it very difficult to maintain their managerial independence from large customers.

7. Conclusions

There does seem to be some evidence that what this paper has described as 'vertical quasi-integration' does exist. The importance of understanding the extent of such relationships lies not only in the need to understand more fully the effect of a single firm's collapse—as in the Rolls-Royce case—but also because it may represent a considerable extension of large firms' influence in the economy which needs to be considered on policy grounds. As Barnes has pointed out:

Some of the important consequences of bigness depend, not upon the power of certain large enterprises, but upon the relative place of large-scale business organization in the economy as a whole. The farther we move toward an economy of a few large business units, the less we can count upon the automatic competitive adjustments to harmonize production demand, prices, and costs.[33]

Perhaps what is required is some measure of a firm's influence in the vertical plane so that as well as having indicators of a firm's influence within its own industry, some measure of a firm's influence in the economy as a whole is obtained. Perhaps some measure along the lines of Hirschman's linkage concept would provide an indication of the extent of a firm's relationship with supplying industries.[34] Finally it should be noted that, in considering the power of one organization over another in the vertical plane, examples have been drawn from cases when organizations are adjacent to one another in the sense that there is a direct flow of goods between them. However, the influence of some organizations spreads much further and affects supplier's suppliers, e.g. by specification of particular raw materials or sub-components, and also, through franchise agreements, customer's customers.

......

Notes

1. James Ensor, 'The car makers hunt for suppliers', *Financial Times*, September 17th, 1970, 18.
2. *Guest, Keen & Nettlefolds Ltd., and Birfield Ltd.*, The Monopolies Commission, January 1967, 33.
3. Michael Donne, 'How the ripples will spread', *Financial Times*, February 5th, 1971, 17.
4. 'Ford supplier to lay off 250 workers', *Daily Telegraph*, March 6th, 1971, 13.
5. P. Maunder, *The Bread Industry in the United Kingdom*, Department of Agricultural Economics, University of Nottingham, and Department of Social Sciences and Economics, University of Technology, Loughborough, 94.
6. *Report on the Supply of Electrical Equipment for Mechanically Propelled Land Vehicles*, The Monopolies Commission, December 1963, 48.
7. *Man-made cellulosic fibres*, The Monopolies Commission, March 1968, 49.
8. *Guest, Keen & Nettlefolds Ltd.*, 26.
9. Report on the Supply of Insulated Electric Wires and Cables, Monopolies and Restrictive Practices Commission, June 1952, 12.
10. 'Give-away battle', *The Sunday Times*, October 4th, 1970.
11. *Flat Glass*, The Monopolies Commission, February 1968, 112.
12. 'Rust', *Drive*, Autumn 1970, 28–9.
13. 'Wages: industry has little stomach for the fight', *The Economist*, October 5th, 1970, 74.
14. 'Ford sends die to Germany to maintain production', *Financial Times*, October 1st, 1970, 36.
15. *Report on the Supply of Electrical Equipment*, 215.
16. Wilbur B. England, 'Modern Procurement Management', 5th edition, Richard D. Irwin, 1970, 589.
17. Private communication with author.
18. Anthony Harris, 'Ford's formula for living with suppliers', *Financial Times*, October 5th, 1968.
19. *Clutch Mechanisms for Road Vehicles*, The Monopolies Commission, December 1968, 36.
20. E. Raymond Corey, *Industrial Marketing* (Prentice-Hall Inc., 1962), 453.

21. Patrick J. Robinson, Charles W. Faris and Yoram Wind, *Industrial Buying and Creative Marketing*, (Allyn & Bacon Inc., 1967), 198.
22. Ronald S. Edwards and Henry Townsend, *Studies in Business Organization* (Macmillan & Co. Ltd., 1961), 31–2.
23. *Clutch Mechanisms for Road Vehicles*, 45.
24. *Guest, Keen & Nettlefolds* Ltd., 23.
25. *Report on the Supply of Electrical Equipment*, 286.
26. E. T. Penrose, *The Theory of the Growth of the Firm* (Basil Blackwell, 1959), 20–1.
27. Ibid. 21.
28. For example: Ronald S. Edwards and Harry Townsend, *Business Enterprise* (Macmillan & Co. Ltd., 1962), 64; Arthur Seldon and F. G. Pennance, *Everyman's Dictionary of Economics* (J. M. Dent & Sons Ltd.), 173.
29. Ronald S. Edwards and Harry Townsend, *Business Growth* (Macmillan & Co. Ltd., 1966), 267.
30. *Flat Glass*, 35–6, 65.
31. *Clutch Mechanisms for Road Vehicles*, 34–6.
32. *A study of the long term consequences of below-the-line activity*, Audits of Great Britain Ltd., November 1970, 5.
33. National Bureau Committee for Economic Research, *Business Concentration and Price Policy* (Princeton University Press, 1955). Article by R. Barnes, 'Conglomerate Bigness', 349–50.
34. Albert O. Hirschman, *The Strategy of Economic Development* (Yale University Press, 1958), 98–104.

12 Non-Contractual Relations In Business: A Preliminary Study

Stewart Macaulay

What good is contract law? who uses it? when and how? Complete answers would require an investigation of almost every type of transaction between individuals and organizations. In this report, research has been confined to exchanges between businesses, and primarily to manufacturers.[1] Furthermore, this report will be limited to a presentation of the findings concerning when contract is and is not used and to a tentative explanation of these findings.[2]

This research is only the first phase in a scientific study.[3] The primary research technique involved interviewing 68 businessmen and lawyers representing 43 companies and six law firms. The interviews ranged from a 30-minute brush-off where not all questions could be asked of a busy and uninterested sales manager to a six-hour discussion with the general counsel of a large corporation. Detailed notes of the interviews were taken and a complete report of each interview was dictated, usually no later than the evening after the interview. All but two of the companies had plants in Wisconsin; 17 were manufacturers of machinery but none made such items as food products, scientific instruments, textiles or petroleum products. Thus the likelihood of error because of sampling bias may be considerable.[4] However, to a great extent, existing knowledge has been inadequate to permit more rigorous procedures—as yet one cannot formulate many precise questions to be asked a systematically selected sample of 'right

Revision of a paper read at the annual meeting of the Americal Sociological Association, August, 1962. An earlier version of the paper was read at the annual meeting of the Midwest Sociological Society, April, 1962. The research has been supported by a Law and Policy Research Grant to the University of Wisconsin Law School from the Ford Foundation. I am grateful for the help generously given by a number of sociologists including Robert K. Merton, Harry V. Ball, Jerome Carlin and William Evan.

people'. Much time has been spent fishing for relevant questions or answers, or both.

Reciprocity, exchange or contract has long been of interest to sociologists, economists and lawyers. Yet each discipline has an incomplete view of this kind of conduct. This study represents the effort of a law teacher to draw on sociological ideas and empirical investigation. It stresses, among other things, the functions and dysfunctions of using contract to solve exchange problems and the influence of occupational roles on how one assesses whether the benefits of using contract outweigh the costs.

To discuss when contract is and is not used, the term 'contract' must be specified. This term will be used here to refer to devices for conducting exchanges. Contract is not treated as synonymous with an exchange itself, which may or may not be characterized as contractual. Nor is contract used to refer to a writing recording an agreement. Contract, as I use the term here, involves two distinct elements: (a) Rational planning of the transaction with careful provision for as many future contingencies as can be foreseen, and (b) the existence or use of actual or potential legal sanctions to induce performance of the exchange or to compensate for non-performance.

These devices for conducting exchanges may be used or may exist in greater or lesser degree, so that transactions can be described relatively as involving a more contractual or a less contractual manner (a) of creating an exchange relationship or (b) of solving problems arising during the course of such a relationship. For example, General Motors might agree to buy all of the Buick Division's requirements of aluminum for ten years from Reynolds Aluminum. Here the two large corporations probably would plan their relationship carefully. The plan probably would include a complex pricing formula designed to meet market fluctuations, an agreement on what would happen if either party suffered a strike or a fire, a definition of Reynolds' responsibility for quality control and for losses caused by defective quality, and many other provisions. As the term contract is used here, this is a more contractual method of creating an exchange relationship than is a home-owner's casual agreement with a real estate broker giving the broker the exclusive right to sell the owner's house which fails to include provisions for the consequences of many easily foreseeable (and perhaps even highly probable contingencies. In both instances, legally enforceable contracts may or may not have been created, but it must be recognized that the existence of a legal sanction has no necessary relationship to the degree of rational planning by the parties, beyond certain minimal legal requirements of certainty of obligation. General Motors and Reynolds might never sue or even refer to the written record of their agreement to answer questions which come up during their ten-year relationship, while the real estate broker might sue, or at least threaten to sue, the owner of the house. The broker's method of *dispute settlement* then would be more contractual than that of General Motors and Reynolds, thus reversing the relationship that existed in regard to the 'contractualness' of the *creation* of the exchange relationships.

1. Tentative Findings

It is difficult to generalize about the use and nonuse of contract by manufacturing industry. However, a number of observations can be made with reasonable accuracy at this time. The use and nonuse of contract in creating exchange relations and in dispute settling will be taken up in turn.

1.1. *The Creation of Exchange Relationships*

In creating exchange relationships, businessmen may plan to a greater or lesser degree in relation to several types of issues. Before reporting the findings as to practices in creating such relationships, it is necessary to describe what one can plan about in a bargain and the degrees of planning which are possible.

People negotiating a contract can make plans concerning several types of issues: (1) They can plan what each is to do or refrain from doing; e.g., S might agree to deliver ten 1963 Studebaker four-door sedan automobiles to B on a certain date in exchange for a specified amount of money. (2) They can plan what effect certain contingencies are to have on their duties; e.g., what is to happen to S and B's obligations if S cannot deliver the cars because of a strike at the Studebaker factory? (3) They can plan what is to happen if either of them fails to perform; e.g., what is to happen if S delivers nine of the cars two weeks late? (4) They can plan their agreement so that it is a legally enforceable contract—that is, so that a legal sanction would be available to provide compensation for injury suffered by B as a result of S's failure to deliver the cars on time.

As to each of these issues, there may be a different degree of planning by the parties. (1) They may carefully and explicitly plan; e.g., S may agree to deliver ten 1963 Studebaker four-door sedans which have six cylinder engines, automatic transmissions and other specified items of optional equipment and which will perform to a specified standard for a certain time. (2) They may have a mutual but tacit understanding about an issue; e.g., although the subject was never mentioned in their negotiations, both S and B may assume that B may cancel his order for the cars before they are delivered if B's taxi-cab business is so curtailed that B can no longer use ten additional cabs. (3) They may have two inconsistent unexpressed assumptions about an issue; e.g., S may assume that if any of the cabs fails to perform to the specified standard for a certain time, all S must do is repair or replace it. B may assume S must also compensate B for the profits B would have made if the cab had been in operation. (4) They may never have thought of the issue; e.g., neither S nor B planned their agreement so that it would be a legally enforceable contract. Of course, the first and fourth degrees of planning listed are the extreme cases and the second and third are intermediate points. Clearly other intermediate points are possible; e.g., S and B neglect to specify whether the cabs should have automatic or conventional transmissions. Their planning is not as careful and explicit as that in the example previously given.

The following table represents the dimensions of creating an exchange relationship just discussed with 'X's' representing the example of S and B's contract for ten taxi-cabs.

Most larger companies, and many smaller ones, attempt to plan carefully and completely. Important transactions not in the ordinary course of business are handled by a detailed contract. For example, recently the Empire State Building was sold for $65 million. More than 100 attorneys, representing 34 parties, produced a 400 page contract. Another example is found in the agreement of a major rubber company in the United States to give technical assistance to a Japanese firm. Several million dollars were involved and the contract consisted of 88 provisions on 17 pages. The 12 house counsel—lawyers who work for one corporation rather than many clients—interviewed said that all but the smallest businesses carefully planned most transactions of any significance. Corporations have procedures so that particular types of exchanges will be reviewed by their legal and financial departments.

More routine transactions commonly are handled by what can be called standardized planning. A firm will have a set of terms and conditions for purchases, sales, or both printed on the business documents used in these

Table 1.

	Definition of Performances	Effect of Contingencies	Effect of Defective Performances	Legal Sanctions
Explicit and careful	x			
Tacit agreement		x		
Unilateral assumptions			x	
Unawareness of the issue				x

exchanges. Thus the things to be sold and the price may be planned particularly for each transaction, but standard provisions will further elaborate the performances and cover the other subjects of planning. Typically, these terms and conditions are lengthy and printed in small type on the back of the forms. For example, 24 paragraphs in eight point type are printed on the back of the purchase order form used by the Allis Chalmers Manufacturing Company. The provisions: (1) describe, in part, the performance required, e.g., 'DO NOT WELD CASTINGS WITHOUT OUR CONSENT'; (2) plan for the effect of contingencies, e.g., '. . . in the event the Seller suffers delay in performance due to an act of God, war, act of the Government, priorities or allocations, act of the Buyer, fire, flood, strike, sabotage, or other causes beyond Seller's control, the time of completion shall be extended a period of time equal to the period of such delay if the Seller gives the Buyer notice in writing of the cause of any such delay within a reasonable time after the beginning thereof'; (3) plan for the effect of defective performances, e.g., 'The buyer, without waiving any other legal rights, reserves the right to cancel without charge or to postpone deliveries of any of the articles covered by this order which are not shipped in time reasonably to meet said agreed dates'; (4) plan for a legal sanction, e.g., the clause 'without waiving any other legal rights', in the example just given.

In larger firms such 'boiler plate' provisions are drafted by the house counsel or the firm's outside lawyer. In smaller firms such provisions may be drafted by the industry trade association, may be copied from a competitor, or may be found on forms purchased from a printer. In any event, salesmen and purchasing agents, the operating personnel, typically are unaware of what is said in the fine print on the back of the forms they use. Yet often the normal business patterns will give effect to this standardized planning. For example, purchasing agents may have to use a purchase order form so that all transactions receive a number under the firm's accounting system. Thus, the required accounting record will carry the necessary planning of the exchange relationship printed on its reverse side. If the seller does not object to this planning and accepts the order, the buyer's 'fine print' will control. If the seller does object, differences can be settled by negotiation.

This type of standardized planning is very common. Requests for copies of the business documents used in buying and selling were sent to approximately 6,000 manufacturing firms which do business in Wisconsin. Approximately 1,200 replies were received and 850 companies used some type of standardized planning. With only a few exceptions, the firms that did not reply and the 350 that indicated they did not use standardized planning were very small manufacturers such as local bakeries, soft drink bottlers and sausage makers.

Stewart Macaulay

While businessmen can and often do carefully and completely plan, it is clear that not all exchanges are neatly rationalized. Although most businessmen think that a clear description of both the seller's and buyer's performances is obvious common sense, they do not always live up to this ideal. The house counsel and the purchasing agent of a medium size manufacturer of automobile parts reported that several times their engineers had committed the company to buy expensive machines without adequate specifications. The engineers had drawn careful specifications as to the type of machine and how it was to be made but had neglected to require that the machine produce specified results. An attorney and an auditor both stated that most contract disputes arise because of ambiguity in the specifications.

Businessmen often prefer to rely on 'a man's word' in a brief letter, a handshake, or 'common honesty and decency'—even when the transaction involves exposure to serious risks. Seven lawyers from law firms with business practices were interviewed. Five thought that businessmen often entered contracts with only a minimal degree of advance planning. They complained that businessmen desire to 'keep it simple and avoid red tape' even where large amounts of money and significant risks are involved. One stated that he was 'sick of being told, 'We can trust old Max', when the problem is not one of honesty but one of reaching an agreement that both sides understand.' Another said that businessmen when bargaining often talk only in pleasant generalities, think they have a contract, but fail to reach agreement on any of the hard, unpleasant questions until forced to do so by a lawyer. Two outside lawyers had different views. One thought that large firms usually planned important exchanges, although he conceded that occasionally matters might be left in a fairly vague state. The other dissenter represents a large utility that commonly buys heavy equipment and buildings. The supplier's employees come on the utility's property to install the equipment or construct the buildings, and they may be injured while there. The utility has been sued by such employees so often that it carefully plans purchases with the assistance of a lawyer so that suppliers take this burden.

Moreover, standardized planning can break down. In the example of such planning previously given, it was assumed that the purchasing agent would use his company's form with its 24 paragraphs printed on the back and that the seller would accept this or object to any provisions he did not like. However, the seller may fail to read the buyer's 24 paragraphs of fine print and may accept the buyer's order on the seller's own acknowledgment-of-order form. Typically this form will have ten to 50 paragraphs favoring the seller, and these provisions are likely to be different from or inconsistent with the buyer's provisions. The seller's acknowledgment form may be received by the buyer and checked by a clerk. She will read the *face* of the acknowledgment but not the fine print on the back of it because she has neither the time nor ability to analyse the small print on the 100 to 500 forms she must review each day. The face of the acknowledgment—where the goods and the price are specified—is likely to correspond with the face of the purchase order. If it does, the two forms are filed away. At this point, both buyer and seller are likely to assume they have planned an exchange and made a contract. Yet they have done neither, as they are in disagreement about all that appears on the back of their forms. This practice is common enough to have a name. Law teachers call it 'the battle of the forms'.

Ten of the 12 purchasing agents interviewed said that frequently the provisions on the back of their purchase order and those on the back of a supplier's acknowledgment would differ or be inconsistent. Yet they would assume that the purchase was complete without further action unless one of the supplier's provisions was really objectionable. Moreover, only occasionally would they bother to read the fine print on the back of suppliers' forms. On the other hand, one purchasing agent insists that agreement be reached on the fine print provisions, but he represents the utility whose lawyer reported that it exercises great care in planning. The other purchasing agent who said that his company did not face a battle of the forms problem, works for a division of one of the largest manufacturing corporations in the United States. Yet the company may have such a problem without recognizing it. The purchasing agent regularly sends a supplier both a purchase order and another form which the supplier is asked to sign and return. The second form states that the supplier accepts the buyer's terms and conditions. The company has sufficient bargaining power to force suppliers to sign and return the form, and the purchasing agent must show one of his firm's auditors such a signed form for every purchase order issued. Yet suppliers frequently return this buyer's form *plus* their own acknowledgment form which has conflicting provisions. The purchasing agent throws away the supplier's form and files his own. Of course, in such a case the supplier has not acquiesced to the buyer's provisions. There is no agreement and no contract.

Sixteen sales managers were asked about the battle of the forms. Nine said that frequently no agreement was reached on which set of fine print was to govern, while seven said that there was no problem. Four of the seven worked for companies whose major customers are the large automobile companies or the large manufacturers of paper products. These customers demand that their terms and conditions govern any purchase, are careful generally to see that suppliers acquiesce, and have the bargaining power to have their way. The other three of the seven sales managers who have no battle of the forms problem, work for manufacturers of special industrial machines. Their firms are careful to reach complete agreement with their customers. Two of these men stressed that they could take no chances because such a large part of their firm's capital is tied up in making any one machine. The other sales manager had been influenced by a law suit against one of his competitors for over a half million dollars. The suit was brought by a customer when the competitor had been unable to deliver a machine and put it in operation on time. The sales manager interviewed said his firm could not guarantee that its machines would work perfectly by a specified time because they are designed to fit the customer's requirements, which may present difficult engineering problems. As a result, contracts are carefully negotiated.

A large manufacturer of packing materials audited its records to determine how often it had failed to agree on terms and conditions with its customers or had failed to create legally binding contracts. Such failures cause a risk of loss to this firm since the packaging is printed with the customer's design and cannot be salvaged once this is done. The orders for five days in four different years were reviewed. The percentages of orders where no agreement on terms and conditions was reached or no contract was formed were as follows:

1953	.... 75.0%
1954	.... 69.4%
1955	.... 71.5%
1956	.... 59.5%

It is likely that businessmen pay more attention to describing the performances in an exchange than to planning for contingencies or defective performances or to obtaining legal enforceability of their contracts. Even when a purchase order and acknowledgment have conflicting provisions printed on the back, almost always the buyer and seller will be in agreement on what is to be sold and how much is to be paid for it. The lawyers who said businessmen often commit their firms to significant exchanges too casually, stated that the performances would be defined in the brief letter or telephone call; the lawyers objected that nothing else would be covered. Moreover, it is likely that businessmen are least concerned about planning their transactions so that they are legally enforceable contracts.[5] For example, in Wisconsin requirements contracts—contracts to supply a firm's requirements of an item rather than a definite quantity—probably are not legally enforceable. Seven people interviewed reported that their firms regularly used requirements contracts in dealings in Wisconsin. None thought that the lack of legal sanction made any difference. Three of these people were house counsel who knew the Wisconsin law before being interviewed. Another example of a lack of desire for legal sanctions is found in the relationship between automobile manufacturers and their suppliers of parts. The manufacturers draft a carefully planned agreement, but one which is so designed that the supplier will have only minimal, if any, legal rights against the manufacturers.

The standard contract used by manufacturers of paper to sell to magazine publishers has a pricing clause which is probably sufficiently vague to make the contract legally unenforceable. The house counsel of one of the largest paper producers said that everyone in the industry is aware of this because of a leading New York case concerning the contract, but that no one cares. Finally, it seems likely that planning for contingencies and defective performances are in-between cases—more likely to occur than planning for a legal sanction, but less likely than a description of performance.

Thus one can conclude that (1) many business exchanges reflect a high degree of planning about the four categories—description, contingencies, defective performances and legal sanction—but (2) many, if not most, exchanges reflect no planning, or only a minimal amount of it, especially concerning legal sanctions and the effect of defective performances. As a result, the opportunity for good faith disputes during the life of the exchange relationship often is present.

1.2. *The Adjustment of Exchange Relationships and the Settling of Disputes.*

While a significant amount of creating business exchanges is done on a fairly noncontractual basis, the creation of exchanges usually is far more contractual than the adjustment of such relationships and the settlement of disputes. Exchanges are adjusted when the obligations of one or both parties are modified by agreement during the life of the relationship. For example, the buyer may be allowed to cancel all or part of the goods he has ordered because he no longer needs them; the seller may be paid more than the contract price by the buyer because of unusual changed circumstances. Dispute settlement involves determining whether or not a party has performed as agreed and, if he has not, doing something about it. For example, a court may have to interpret the meaning of a contract, determine what the alleged defaulting party has done and determine what, if any, remedy the aggrieved party is entitled to. Or one party may assert that the other is in default, refuse to proceed with performing the contract and refuse to deal ever again with the alleged defaulter. If the alleged defaulter, who in fact may not be in default, takes no action, the dispute is then 'settled'.

Business exchanges in non-speculative areas are usually adjusted without dispute. Under the law of contracts, if B orders 1,000 widgets from S at $1.00 each, B must take all 1,000 widgets or be in breach of contract and liable to pay S his expenses up to the time of the breach plus his lost anticipated profit. Yet all ten of the purchasing agents asked about cancellation of orders once placed indicated that they expected to be able to cancel orders freely subject to only an obligation to pay for the seller's major expenses such as scrapped steel.[6] All 17 sales personnel asked reported that they often had to accept cancellation. One said, 'You can't ask a man to eat paper (the firm's product) when he has no use for it.' A lawyer with many large industrial clients said,

Often businessmen do not feel they have 'a contract'—rather they have 'an order'. They speak of 'canceling the order' rather than 'breaching our contract'. When I began practice I referred to order cancellations as breaches of contract, but my clients objected since they do not think of cancellation as wrong. Most clients, in heavy industry at least, believe that there is a right to cancel as part of the buyer-seller relationship. There is a widespread attitude that one can back out of any deal within some very vague limits. Lawyers are often surprised by this attitude.

Disputes are frequently settled without reference to the contract or potential or actual legal sanctions. There is a hesitancy to speak of legal rights or to threaten to sue in these negotiations. Even where the parties have a detailed and carefully planned agreement which indicates what is to happen if, say, the seller fails to deliver on time, often they will never refer to the agreement but will negotiate a solution when the problem arises apparently as if there had never been any original contract. One purchasing agent expressed a common business attitude when he said,

if something comes up, you get the other man on the telephone and deal with the problem. You don't read legalistic contract clauses at each other if you ever want to do business again. One doesn't run to lawyers if he wants to stay in business because one must behave decently.

Or as one businessman put it, 'You can settle any dispute if you keep the lawyers and accountants out of it. They just do not understand the give-and-take needed in business.' All of the house counsel interviewed indicated that they are called into the dispute settlement process only after the businessmen have failed to settle matters in their own way. Two indicated that after being called in house counsel at first will only advise the purchasing agent, sales manager or other official involved; not even the house counsel's letterhead is used on communications with the other side until all hope for a peaceful resolution is gone.

Law suits for breach of contract appear to be rare. Only five of the 12 purchasing agents had ever been involved in even a negotiation concerning a contract dispute where both sides were represented by lawyers; only two of ten sales managers had ever gone this far. None had been involved in a case that went through trial. A law firm with more than 40 lawyers and a large commercial practice handles in a year only about six trials concerned with contract problems. Less than 10 per cent of the time of this office is devoted to any type of work related to contracts disputes. Corporations big enough to do business in more than one state tend to sue and be sued in the federal courts. Yet only 2,779 out of 58,293 civil actions filed in the United States District Courts in fiscal year 1961 involved private contracts.[7] During the same period only 3,447 of the 61,138 civil cases filed in the principal trial courts of New York State involved private contracts.[8] The same picture emerges from a review of appellate cases.[9] Mentschikoff has suggested that commercial cases are not brought to the courts either in periods of business prosperity (because buyers unjustifiably reject goods only when prices drop and they can get similar goods elsewhere at less than the contract price) or in periods of deep depression (because people are unable to come to court or have insufficient assets to satisfy any judgement that might be obtained). Apparently, she adds, it is necessary to have 'a kind of middle-sized depression' to bring large numbers of commercial cases to the courts. However, there is little evidence that in even 'a kind of middle-sized depression' today's businessmen would use the courts to settle disputes.[10]

At times relatively contractual methods are used to make adjustments in ongoing transactions and to settle disputes. Demands of one side which are deemed unreasonable by the other occasionally are blocked by reference to the terms of the agreement between the parties. The legal position of the parties can influence negotiations even though legal rights or litigation are never mentioned in their discussions; it makes a difference if one is demanding what both concede to be a right or begging for a favor. Now and then a firm may threaten to turn matters over to its attorneys, threaten to sue, commence a suit or even litigate and carry an appeal to the highest court which will hear the matter. Thus, legal sanctions, while not an everyday affair, are not unknown in business.

One can conclude that while detailed planning and legal sanctions play a significant role in some exchanges between businesses, in many business exchanges their role is small.

2. Tentative Explanations

Two questions need to be answered: (A) How can business successfully operate exchange relationships with relatively so little attention to detailed planning or to legal sanctions, and (B) Why does business ever use contract in light of its success without it?

2.1 Why are Relatively Non-contractual Practices so Common?

In most situations contract is not needed.[11] Often its functions are served by other devices. Most problems are avoided without resort to detailed planning or legal sanctions because usually there is little room for honest misunderstandings or good faith differences of opinion about the nature and quality of a seller's performance. Although the parties fail to cover all foreseeable contingencies, they will exercise care to see that both understand the primary obligation on each side. Either products are standardized with an accepted description or specifications are written calling for production to certain tolerances or results. Those who write and read specifications are experienced professionals who will know the customs of their industry and those of the industries with which they deal. Consequently, these customs can fill gaps in the express agreements of the parties. Finally, most products can be tested to see if they are what was ordered; typically in manufacturing industry we are not dealing with questions of taste or judgment where people can differ in good faith.

When defaults occur they are not likely to be disastrous because of techniques of risk avoidance or risk spreading. One can deal with firms of good reputation or he may be able to get some form of security to guarantee performance. One can insure against many breaches of contract where the risks justify the costs. Sellers set up reserves for bad debts on their books and can sell some of their accounts receivable. Buyers can place orders with two or more suppliers of the same item so that a default by one will not stop the buyer's assembly lines.

Moreover, contract and contract law are often thought unnecessary because there are many effective non-legal sanctions. Two norms are widely accepted. (1) Commitments are to be honored in almost all situations; one does not welsh on a deal. (2) One ought to produce a good product and stand behind it. Then, too, business units are organized to perform commitments, and internal sanctions will induce performance. For example, sales personnel must face angry customers when there has been a late or defective performance. The salesmen do not enjoy this and will put pressure on the production personnel responsible for the default. If the production personnel default too often, they will be fired. At all levels of the two business units personal relationships across the boundaries of the two organizations exert pressures for conformity to expectations. Salesmen often know purchasing agents well. The same two individuals occupying these roles may have dealt with each other from five to 25 years. Each has something to give the other. Salesmen have gossip about competitors, shortages and price increases to give purchasing agents who treat them well. Salesmen take purchasing agents to dinner, and they give purchasing agents Christmas gifts hoping to improve the chances of making sale. The buyer's engineering staff may work with the seller's engineering staff to solve problems jointly. The seller's engineers may render great assistance, and the buyer's engineers may desire to return the favor by drafting specifications which only the seller can meet. The top executives of the two firms may know each other. They may sit together on government or trade committees. They may know each other socially and even belong to the same country club. The inter-relationships may be more formal. Sellers may hold stock in corporations which are important customers; buyers may hold stock in important suppliers. Both buyer and seller may share common directors on their boards. They may share a common financial institution which has financed both units.

The final type of non-legal sanction is the most obvious. Both business units involved in the exchange desire to continue successfully in business and will avoid conduct which might interfere with attaining this goal. One is concerned with both the reaction of the other party in the particular exchange and with his own general business reputation. Obviously, the buyer gains sanctions insofar as the seller wants the particular exchange to be completed. Buyers can withhold part or all of their payments until sellers have performed to their satisfaction. If a seller has a great deal of money tied up in his performance which he must recover quickly, he will go a long way to please the buyer in order to be paid. Moreover, buyers who are dissatisfied may cancel and cause sellers to lose the cost of what they have done up to cancellation. Furthermore, sellers hope for repeat for orders, and one gets few of these from unhappy customers. Some industrial buyers go so far as to formalize this sanction by issuing 'report cards' rating the performance of each supplier. The supplier rating goes to the top management of the seller organization, and these men can apply internal sanctions to salesmen, production supervisors or product designers if there are too many 'D's or 'F's' on the report card.

While it is generally assumed that the customer is always right, the seller may have some counterbalancing sanctions against the buyer. The seller may have obtained a large downpayment from the buyer which he will want to protect. The seller may have an exclusive process which the buyer needs. The seller may be one of the few firms which has the skill to make the item to the tolerances set by the buyer's engineers and within the time available. There are costs and delays involved in turning from a supplier one has dealt with in the past to a new supplier. Then, too, market conditions can change so that a buyer is faced with shortages of critical items. The most extreme example is the post World War II grey market conditions when sellers were rationing goods rather than selling them. Buyers must build up some reserve of good will with suppliers if they face the risk of such shortage and desire good treatment when they occur. Finally, there is reciprocity in buying and selling. A buyer cannot push a supplier too far if that supplier also buys significant quantities of the product made by the buyer.

Not only do the particular business units in a given exchange want to deal with each other again, they also want to deal with other business units in the future. And the way one behaves in a particular transaction, or a series of transactions, will color his general business reputation. Blacklisting can be formal or informal. Buyers who fail to pay their bills on time risk a bad report in credit rating services such as Dun and Bradstreet. Sellers who do not satisfy their customers become the subject of discussion in the gossip exchanged by purchasing agents and salesmen, at meetings of purchasing agents' associations and trade associations, or even at country clubs or social gatherings where members of top management meet. The American male's habit of debating the merits of new cars carries over to industrial items. Obviously, a poor reputation does not help a firm make sales and may force it to offer great price discounts or added services to remain in business. Furthermore, the habits of unusually demanding buyers become known, and they tend to get no more than they can coerce out of suppliers who choose to deal with them. Thus often contract is not needed as there are alternatives.

Not only are contract and contract law not needed in many situations, their use may have, or may be thought to have, undesirable consequences. Detailed negotiated contracts can get in the way of creating good exchange relationships between business units. If one side insists on a detailed plan, there will be delay while letters are exchanged as the parties try to agree on what should happen if a remote and unlikely contingency occurs. In some cases they may not be able to agree at all on such matters and as a result a sale may be lost to the seller and the buyer may have to search elsewhere for an acceptable supplier. Many businessmen would react by thinking that had no one raised the series of remote and unlikely contingencies all this wasted effort could have been avoided.

Even where agreement can be reached at the negotiation stage, carefully planned arrangements may create undesirable exchange relationships between business units. Some businessmen object that in such a carefully worked out relationship one gets performance only to the letter of the contract. Such planning indicates a lack of trust and blunts the demands of friendship, turning a co-operative venture into an antagonistic horse trade. Yet the greater danger perceived by some businessmen is that one would have to perform his side of the bargain to its letter and thus lose what is called 'flexibility'. Businessmen may welcome a measure of vagueness in the obligations they assume so that they may negotiate matters in light of the actual circumstances.

Adjustment of exchange relationships and dispute settlement by litigation or the threat of it also has many costs. The gain anticipated from using this form of coercion often fails to outweigh these costs, which are both monetary and non-monetary. Threatening to turn matters over to an attorney may cost no more money than postage or a telephone call; yet few are so skilled in making such a threat that it will not cost some deterioration of the relationship between the firms. One businessman said that customers had better not rely on legal rights or threaten to bring a breach of contract law suit against him since he 'would not be treated like a criminal' and would fight back with every means available. Clearly actual litigation is even more costly than making threats. Lawyers demand substantial fees from larger business units. A firm's executives often will have to be transported and maintained in another city during the proceedings if, as often is the case, the trial must be held away from the home office. Top management does not travel by Greyhound and stay at the YMCA. Moreover, there will be the cost of diverting top management, engineers, and others in the organization from their normal activities. The firm may lose many days work from several key people. The non-monetary costs may be large too. A breach of contract law suit may settle a particular dispute, but such an action often results in a 'divorce' ending the 'marriage' between the two businesses, since a contract action is likely to carry charges with at least overtones of bad faith. Many executives, moreover, dislike the prospect of being cross-examined in public. Some executives may dislike losing control of a situation by turning the decision-making power over to lawyers. Finally, the law of contract damages may not provide an adequate remedy even if the firm wins the suit; one may get vindication but not much money.

2.2. Why do Relatively Contractual Practices ever Exist?

Although contract is not needed and actually may have negative consequences, businessmen do make some carefully planned contracts, negotiate settlements influenced by their legal rights and commence and defend some breach of contract law suits or arbitration proceedings. In view of the findings and explanation presented to this point, one may ask why. Exchanges are carefully planned when it is thought that planning and a potential legal sanction will have more advantages than disadvantages. Such a judgment may be reached when contract planning serves the internal needs of an organization involved in a business exchange. For example, a fairly detailed contract can serve as a communication device within a large corporation. While the corporation's sales manager and house counsel may work out all the provisions with the customer, its production manager will have to make the product. He must be told what to do and how to handle at least the most obvious contingencies. Moreover, the sales manager may want to remove certain issues from future negotiation by his subordinates. If he puts the matter in the written contract, he may be able to keep his salesmen from making concessions to the customer without first consulting the sales manager. Then the sales manager may be aided in his battles with his firm's financial or engineering departments if the contract calls for certain practices which the sales manager advocates but which the other departments resist. Now the corporation is obligated to a customer to do what the sales manager wants to do; how can the financial or engineering departments insist on anything else?

Also one tends to find a judgement that the gains of contract outweigh the costs where there is a likelihood that significant problems will arise.[12] One factor leading to this conclusion is complexity of the agreed performance over a long period. Another factor is whether or not the degree of injury in case of default is thought to be potentially great. This factor cuts two ways. First, a buyer may want to commit a seller to a detailed and legally binding contract, where the consequences of a default by the seller would seriously injure the buyer. For example, the airlines are subject to law suits from the survivors of passengers and to great adverse publicity as a result of crashes. One would expect the airlines to bargain for carefully defined and legally enforceable obligations on the part of the airframe manufacturers when they purchase aircraft. Second, a seller may want to limit his liability for a buyer's damages by a provision in their contract. For example, a manufacturer of air conditioning may deal with motels in the South and Southwest. If this equipment fails in the hot summer months, a motel may lose a great deal of business. The manufacturer may wish to avoid any liability for this type of injury to his customers and may want a contract with a clear disclaimer clause.

Similarly, one uses or threatens to use legal sanctions to settle disputes when other devices will not work and when the gains are thought to outweigh the costs. For example, perhaps the most common type of business contracts case fought all the way through to the appellate courts today is an action for an alleged wrongful termination of a dealer's franchise by a manufacturer. Since the franchise has been terminated, factors such as personal relationships and the desire for future business will have little effect; the cancellation of the franchise indicates they have already failed to maintain the relationship. Nor will a complaining dealer worry about creating a hostile relationship between himself and the manufacturer. Often the dealer has suffered a great financial loss both as to his investment in building and equipment and as to his anticipated future profits. A cancelled automobile dealer's lease on his showroom and shop will continue to run, and his tools for servicing, say, Plymouths cannot be used to service other makes of cars. Moreover, he will have no more new Plymouths to sell. Today there is some chance of winning a law suit for terminating a franchise in bad faith in many states and in the federal courts. Thus, often the dealer chooses to risk the cost of a lawyer's fee because of the chance that he may recover some compensation for his losses.

An 'irrational' factor may exert some influence on the decision to use legal sanctions. The man who controls a firm may feel that he or his organization has been made to appear foolish or has been the victim of fraud or bad faith. The law suit may be seen as a vehicle 'to get even' although the potential gains, as viewed by an objective observer, are outweighed by the potential costs.

The decision whether or not to use contract—whether the gain exceeds the costs—will be made by the person within the business unit with the power to make it, and it tends to make a difference who he is. People in a sales department oppose contract. Contractual negotiations are just one more hurdle in the way of a sale. Holding a customer to the letter of a contract is bad for 'customer relations'. Suing a customer who is not bankrupt and might order again is poor strategy. Purchasing agents and their buyers are less hostile to contracts but regard attention devoted to such matters as a waste of time. In contrast, the financial control department— the treasurer, controller or auditor—leans toward more contractual dealings. Contract is viewed by these people as an organizing tool to control operations in a large organization. It tends to define precisely and to minimize the risks to which the firm is exposed. Outside lawyers—those with many clients—may share this enthusiasm for a more contractual method of dealing. These lawyers are concerned with preventive law—avoiding any possible legal difficulty. They see many unstable and unsuccessful exchange transactions, and so they are aware of, and perhaps overly concerned with, all of the things which can go wrong. Moreover, their job of settling disputes with legal sanctions is much easier if their client has not been overly casual about transaction planning. The inside lawyer, or house counsel, is harder to classify. He is likely to have some sympathy with a more contractual method of dealing. He shares the outside lawyer's 'craft urge' to see exchange transactions neat and tidy from a legal standpoint. Since he is more concerned with avoiding and settling disputes than selling goods, he is likely to be less willing to rely on a man's word as the sole sanction than is a salesman. Yet the house counsel is more a part of the organization and more aware of its goals and subject to its internal sanctions. If the potential risks are not too great, he may hesitate to suggest a more contractual procedure to the sales department. He must sell his services to the operating departments, and he must hoard what power he has, expending it on only what he sees as significant issues.

The power to decide that a more contractual method of creating relationships and settling disputes shall be used will be held by different people at different times in different organizations. In most firms the sales department and the purchasing department have a great deal of power to resist contractual procedures or to ignore them if they are formally adopted and to handle disputes their own way. Yet in larger organizations the treasurer and the controller have increasing power to demand both systems and compliance. Occasionally, the house counsel must arbitrate the conflicting positions of these departments; in giving 'legal advice' he may make the business judgement necessary regarding the use of contract. At times he may ask for an opinion from an outside law firm to reinforce his own position with the outside firm's prestige.

Obviously, there are other significant variables which influence the degree that contract is used. One is the relative bargaining power or skill of the two business units. Even if the controller of a small supplier succeeds within the firm and creates a contractual system of dealing, there will be no contract if the firm's large customer prefers not to be bound to anything. Firms that supply General Motors deal as General Motors wants to do business, for the most part. Yet bargaining power is not size or share of the market alone. Even a General Motors may need a particular supplier, at least temporarily. Furthermore, bargaining power may shift as an exchange relationship is first created and then continues. Even a giant firm can find itself bound to a small supplier once production of an essential item begins for there may not be time to turn to another supplier. Also, all of the factors discussed in this paper can be viewed as *components* of bargaining power—for example, the personal relationship between the presidents of the buyer and the seller firms may give a sales manager great power over a purchasing agent who has been instructed to give the seller 'every consideration'. Another variable relevant to the use of contract is the influence of third parties. The federal government, or a lender of money, may insist that a contract be made in a particular transaction or may influence the decision to assert one's legal rights under a contract.

Contract, then, often plays an important role in business, but other factors are significant. To understand the functions of contract the whole system of conducting exchanges must be explored fully. More types of business communities must be studied, contract litigation must be analysed to see why the nonlegal sanctions fail to prevent the use of legal sanctions and all of the variables suggested in this paper must be classified more systematically.

Notes

1. The reasons for this limitation are that (a) these transactions are important from an economic standpoint, (b) they are frequently said in theoretical discussions to represent a high degree of rational planning, and (c) manufacturing personnel are sufficiently public-relations-minded to cooperate with a law professor who wants to ask a seemingly endless number of questions. Future research will deal with the building construction industry and other areas.

2. For the present purposes, the what-difference-does-it-make issue is important primarily as it makes a case for an empirical study by a law teacher of the use and nonuse of contract by businessmen. First, law teachers have a professional concern with what the law ought to be. This involves evaluation of the consequences of the existing situation and of the possible alternatives. Thus, it is most relevant to examine business practices concerning contract if one is interested in what commercial law ought to be. Second, law teachers are supposed to teach law students something relevant to becoming lawyers. These business practices are facts that are relevant to the skills which law students will need when, as lawyers, they are called upon to create exchange relationships and to solve problems arising out of these relationships.

3. The following things have been done. The literature in law, business, economics, psychology, and sociology has been surveyed. The formal systems related to exchange transactions have been examined. Standard form contracts and the standard terms and conditions that are found on such business documents as catalogues, quotation forms, purchase orders, and acknowledgment-of-order forms from 850 firms that are based in or do business in Wisconsin have been collected. The citations of all reported court cases during a period of 15 years involving the largest 500 manufacturing corporations in the United States have been obtained and are being analysed to determine why the use of contract legal sanctions was thought necessary and whether or not any patterns of 'problem situations' can be delineated. In addition, the informal systems related to exchange transactions have been examined. Letters of inquiry concerning practices in certain situations have been answered by approximately 125 businessmen. Interviews, as described in the text, have been conducted. Moreover, six of my students have interviewed 21 other businessmen, bankers and lawyers. Their findings are consistent with those reported in the text.

4. However, the cases have not been selected because they *did* use contract. There is as much interest in, and effort to obtain, cases of nonuse as of use of contract. Thus, one variety of bias has been minimized.

5. Compare the findings of an empirical study of Connecticut business practices in Comment, 'The Statute of Frauds and the Business Community: A Re-Appraisal in Light of Prevailing Practices', *Yale Law Journal*, 66 (1957), 1038–71.

6. See the case studies on cancellation of contracts in *Harvard Business Review*, 2 (1923–24), 238–40, 367–70, 496–502.

7. *Annual Report of the Director of the Administrative Office of the United States Courts*, 1961, 238.

8. State of New York, The Judicial Conference, Sixth Annual Report, 1961, 209–11.

9. My colleague Lawrence M. Friedman has studied the work of the Supreme Court of Wisconsin in contracts cases. He has found that contracts cases reaching that court tend to involve economically-marginal-business and family-economic disputes rather than important commercial transactions. This has been the situation since about the turn of the century. Only during the Civil War period did the court deal with significant numbers of important contracts cases, but this happened against the background of a much simpler and different economic system.

10. New York Law Revision Commission, *Hearings on the Uniform Code Commercial Code*, 2 (1954), 1391.

11. The explanation that follows emphasizes a *considered* choice not to plan in detail for all contingencies. However, at times it is clear that businessmen fail to plan because of a lack of sophistication; they simply do not appreciate the risk they are running or they merely follow patterns established in their firm years ago without reexamining these practices in light of current conditions.

12. Even where there is little chance that problems will arise, some businessmen insist that their lawyer review or draft an agreement as a delaying tactic. This gives the businessman time to think about making a commitment if he has doubts about the matter or to look elsewhere for a better deal while still keeping the particular negotiations alive.

13 Goodwill and the Spirit of Market Capitalism

Ronald Dore

HOBHOUSE MEMORIAL LECTURE

Why have large factories given way to the co-ordinated production of specialized family units in segments of the Japanese textile industry? One reason is the predominance of 'obligated relational contracting' in Japanese business. Consumer goods markets are highly competitive in Japan, but trade in intermediates, by contrast, is for the most part conducted within long-term trading relations in which goodwill 'give-and-take' is expected to temper the pursuit of self-interest.

Cultural preferences explain the *unusual* predominance of these relations in Japan, but they are in fact more common in Western economies than textbooks usually recognize. The recent growth of relational contracting (in labour markets especially) is, indeed, at the root of the 'rigidities' supposedly responsible for contemporary stagflation. Japan shows that to sweep away these rigidities and give markets back their pristine vigour is not the only prescription for a cure of stagflation. The Japanese economy more than adequately compensates for the loss of allocative efficiency by achieving high levels of other kinds of efficiency—in many respects thanks to, rather than in spite of, relational contracting. We would do well to be more concerned about those kinds of efficiency too.

One of economists' favourite Adam Smith quotations is the passage in the *Wealth of Nations* in which he sets out one of his basic premises.

It is not from the benevolence of the butcher, the brewer and the baker, that we expect our dinner, but from their regard to their own interest. We address ourselves, not to their humanity, but to their self-love, and never talk to them of our necessities but of their advantages.[1]

I wish to question that sharp opposition between benevolence and self-interest. Perhaps, so that he should be alert for signs of possible bias, the reader should be warned that a prolonged soaking in the writings of Japanese eighteenth- and nineteenth-century Confucianists at an early age has left me with a soft spot for the virtue of benevolence, even a tendency to bristle when anyone too much disparages it. At any rate I wish to argue, apropos of benevolence, or goodwill, that there is rather more of it about than we sometimes allow, further that to recognize the fact might help in the impossible task of trying to run an efficient economy and a decent society—an endeavour which animated Hobhouse's life, and about which, as Ginsburg makes clear in his 1950s preface to *Morals in Evolution*, even the pains of old age and the rise of fascism in the 1920s did not destroy his eventual optimism.

My title refers to goodwill rather than benevolence because benevolence, in my Confucian book, though not I think in Adam Smith's, is something shown in relations between unequals, by superior to inferior, the reciprocal of which is usually called loyalty. Goodwill is more status-neutral, more an expression of Hobhouse's 'principle of mutuality'. And it is that broader meaning which I intend. A formal definition of my subject might be: the sentiments of friendship and the sense of diffuse personal obligation which accrue between individuals engaged in recurring contractual economic exchange. (By 'economic', I mean only that the goods and services exchanged should be commonly subject to market valuation.)

Goodwill, of course, is a term of art in the commercial world. In the world of petty proprietorships, familiar to most of us, if you are selling a corner store you set a price on the premises, a price on the stock and a price on the goodwill. Back in the old Marshallian days when economists took their concepts from everyday life rather than trying to take everyday life from their concepts, goodwill meant the same things to economists too. Palgrave's 1923 dictionary of economics defines goodwill as:

The expectancy of a continuance, to the advantage of a successor in an established business, of the personal confidence, or of the habit of recurring to the place or premises or to the known business house or firm, on the part of a circle or connection of clients or customers.[2]

The next economics dictionary I find, McGraw-Hill's exactly half a century later, has a very different definition of goodwill:

An accounting term used to explain the difference between what a company pays when it buys another company and what it gets in the form of tangible assets.[3]

Samuelson, to his credit one of the very few textbook writers in whose index one will find the word goodwill, illustrates the concept with J. P.

Morgan taking over Carnegie's steel interests, making it clear that Morgan paid a premium well over the market value of the fixed assets primarily because he thereby advanced significantly towards a monopoly position.[4] In other words the goodwill concept is extended to cover not just the benefits accruing to the purchaser of a business from the affectionate or inertial habits of its customers, but also those accruing out of his consequent shift from the position of price-taker to that of price-maker—his enhanced ability to hold those customers up to ransom. To be fair to the economists who have adopted this use of the term, and partially to retract my earlier gibe, one could say that the standard definition of the term has changed because everyday life has changed. A world in which the terms appropriate to the small owner-managed business formed the dominant norm, has given way to a world dominated by the large corporations and their accountants' terms. Certainly, if anyone wanted to write an Old Testament Prophet-style denunciation of modern capitalism *à la* Marx, he could hardly ask for a better illustration than the corruption of the concept of 'goodwill', that primordial embodiment of basic social bonds, into a term for some of the more ugly anti-social forms of profit-seeking.

1. The Disaggregation of Factory Production

I have been caused to ponder the role of goodwill in economic life by the recent experience of studying the organization of the textile industry, or to be more precise, the weaving segment of it, in Britain and Japan. One place I visited in the course of that research was the small town of Nishiwaki in western Japan whose industry is almost wholly devoted to the weaving of ginghams chiefly for export to Hong Kong to be made up into garments for Americans to wear when square-dancing in the Middle West. This is an area where hand-loom weaving goes back some centuries. Power-looms came in in the late nineteenth century and they brought with them the factory system as they did everywhere else. And 25 years ago, although many small weaving establishments had survived, the bulk of the output was accounted for by larger mills, many of which were part of vertically integrated enterprises with their own cotton-importing, spinning and finishing establishments.

By 1980, however, the picture had changed. The larger mills had closed. The integrated firms had retreated, as far as direct production was concerned, to their original base in spinning. Most of them were still, either alone or in collaboration with a trading company, producing their own brand cloth, dyed and finished. But they were doing so through the co-ordination of the activities of a large number of family enterprises. The key family business was that of the merchant-converter who contracted with the spinning company to turn its yarn into a certain type of cloth at a given contract price. The converter would send the yarn to another small family concern specializing in yarn dyeing, then it would go on to a specialist beamer who would wind it on to the warp beams in the desired pattern and also put the warp through the sizing process. Then it would be delivered to the weaver who might do his own weft preparation and the drawing-in (putting the harness on the beams ready for the looms) or might use other family businesses—contract winders or drawers in—for the process. And so on to the finishers who did the bleaching or texturizing or over-printing.

What is the reason for this fragmentation? What changes in Japanese society and the Japanese economy account for what most orthodox notions of the direction of the evolution of modern economies would count as a regression—the replacement of a system of production co-ordination within a vertically integrated firm by a system of production co-ordination between a large number of fragmented small firms; the replacement, to use Williamson's terms, of co-ordination through hierarchy by co-ordination through the market?[5]

I can think of four possible long-term secular trends which might help to explain the change.

1. The first is the rise in wages and the shorter working week of employees in union-organized firms. Wages are commonly lower in small firms—especially in Japan where the privileged position of the large enterprise elite has become firmly conventionalized, and inter-scale wage differentials are very great. But that is not all. Family enterprisers themselves are often willing to work much longer than 40 hours a week for what may or may not be a larger *total* income than wage workers get, but for an *average* return per hour of labour—hence wage cost per metre of cloth—which is below the employee's wage. If you like, family enterprisers are now willing to exploit themselves more than the unions or the law permit employees to be exploited—a condition which did not hold when *employees* were already working close to the human maximum—a 70 hour week for a subsistence level wage. The clear superiority of the factory system at that time may have been lost since.

2. Second, the secular trend to high taxation and higher levels of taxation-allergy make the family enterpriser's advantage in both tax avoidance and tax evasion more attractive—*vide* the growth of the secondary 'black' and quasi-black economy in many other countries.

3. Third, there is a technical factor: the capital lumpiness of some of the new technology. For example expensive, large and fast sizing machines can

362

hardly get the through-put necessary to make them profitable within a single firm. Inter-firm specialization becomes the best way of realizing economies of scale.

4. Fourth, much higher levels of numeracy and literacy mean a much wider diffusion of the accounting and managerial skills necessary to run a small business, the prudent ability to calculate the rentability of investments, etc.

These are all features common to societies other than Japan and may well be part of the explanation why the woollen industry of Prato has also moved to a fragmented structure in recent years. But there is another factor which applies especially in Japan. The reason why the dominant trend in the west seems to be in the reverse direction—away from co-ordination through the market towards co-ordination through the hierarchy of a vertically integrated firm—is, as Oliver Williamson is never tired of telling us, because of the transaction costs entailed, the costs arising from the imperfections of markets with small numbers of buyers and sellers in which the bargaining transactions are made difficult by what the jargon calls 'impacted information'. These features so enhance the bargaining power of each party that, when there are no significant economies of scale to be gained by their mutual independence one party (usually the stronger one) buys out the other to put a stop to his 'opportunism' (rapid response not only to price signals—which of course is always admirable—but also to information about vulnerable weaknesses of the other party).

2. Relational Contracting

Here is another of those timeless generalizations about 'capitalist economies' about which Japan gives pause. Transaction costs for large Japanese firms may well be lower than elsewhere. 'Opportunism' may be a lesser danger in Japan because of the explicit encouragement, and actual prevalence, in the Japanese economy of what one might call moralized trading relationships of mutual goodwill.

The stability of the relationship is the key. Both sides recognize an obligation to try to maintain it. If a finisher re-equips with a new and more efficient dyeing process which gives him a cost advantage and the opportunity of offering discounts on the going contract price he does not immediately get all the business. He may win business from one or two converters if they had some *other* reason for being dissatisfied with their own

Ronald Dore

finisher. But the more common consequence is that the other merchant-converters go to their finishers and say: 'Look how X has got his price down. We hope you can do the same because we really would have to reconsider our position if the price difference goes on for months. If you need bank finance to get the new type of vat we can probably help by guaranteeing the loan.'

It is a system, to use a distinction common in the Williamson school, of relational contracting rather than spot-contracting[6]—or to use Williamson's more recent phrase[7] 'obligational contracting'. More like a marriage than a one-night stand as Robert Solow has said about the modern employment relation.[8] The rules of chastity vary. As is commonly the case, for those at the lower end of the scale, monogamy is the rule. A weaver with a couple of dozen automatic looms in a back garden shed will usually weave for only one converter, so that there should be no dispute about prior rights to the fruits of his looms—no clash of loyalties. Specialists with faster, larger volume, through-puts, like beamers—scarcer, more attractive, more in demand, therefore—may have a relation à trois or à quatre. For the converters themselves, at the top of the local hierarchy, there have grown up curious conventions rather like polyandrous concubinage. The Japan Spinners Association is dominated by the so-called Big Nine firms. None of the Big Nine will tolerate one of its converters taking cotton yarn from *another* of the Big Nine. However, one rank below the Big Nine are the so called New Spinners, and below them the post-war upstarts, the New New Spinners. A Big Nine spinner will tolerate its converters having relations with them, though, of course a New Spinner will not tolerate a relation with another New Spinner. So the converter can end up with one of each—a first husband and a number two and a number three husband as it were.

As in nearly all systems of marriage, divorce also happens. That is why I said that a finisher with a cost advantage could attract other converters who happen for other reasons to be dissatisfied with their finisher. When I use the analogy of divorce, I mean traditional divorce in obligation-conscious societies, rather than the 'sorry I like someone else better: let's be friends' divorce of modern California. That is to say, the break usually involves recrimination and some bitterness, because it usually has to be justified by accusing the partner of some failure of goodwill, some lack of benevolence—or, as the Japanese phrase is more often translated, 'lack of sincerity'. It is not enough that some external circumstances keep his prices high.

I have made these relations sound like the kinship system of a Himalayan village, but of course the specific patterns of who may trade with whom are of very recent origin. What are entirely traditional, however, are, first, the basic pattern of treating trading relations as particularistic personal relations; second, the values and sentiments which sustain the obligations involved, and third, such things as the pattern of mid-summer and year-end gift exchange which symbolizes recognition of those obligations.

But how on earth, the economist will want to know, do the prices and ordered quantities get fixed? The answer seems to be that, once established, prices can be re-negotiated at the initiative of either party on the grounds either of cost changes affecting either party, or else of changes in the competitive conditions in the final market in which the brand cloth is sold. There are also fringe spot-markets for cotton yarn and grey cloth, and the prices ruling in these markets and reported in the daily textile press provide guides. To further complicate the issue there is some collective bargaining. Both the weavers and the converters in Nishiwaki have their own co-operative union and guide prices may be agreed between them; alternatively, in some other textile areas, the weavers co-op sets a minimum contract price which its members are not supposed to undercut, though there is general scepticism about the effectiveness of such an agreement.

3. Relational Contracting Between Unequals

The basic principles on which these price and quantity negotiations rest appear to be three-fold. First that the losses of the bad times and the gains of the good times should be shared. Second, that in recognition of the hierarchical nature of the relationship—of the fact that weavers are more dependent on converters than converters are on weavers—a fair sharing of a fall in the market may well involve the weaker weaver suffering more than the converter—having his profits squeezed harder. But, third, the stronger converter should not use his bargaining superiority in recession times, and the competition between his weavers to have their orders cut as little as possible, to drive them over, or even to, the edge of bankruptcy.

It is in the interpretation of these principles, of course, that ambiguity enters. Benevolence all too easily shades into exploitation when the divorce option—the option of breaking off the relationship—is more costlessly available to one party than to the other. There is, even, an officially-sponsored Association for the Promotion of the Modernization of Trading Relations in the Textile Industry in Japan which urges the use of written rather than verbal contracts in these relationships and is devoted to strengthening moral constraints on what it calls the abuse—but our economic textbooks would presumably call the legitimate full use—of market power. As for the nature of such abuse, surveys conducted by the Association show that suppliers with verbal contracts are more likely to have goods returned for quality deficiencies than those with proper written contracts.[9] Weavers will wryly remark that returns become strangely more common when the price is falling (and a rejected lot contracted at a higher price can be replaced by a newly contracted cheaper lot).

The work of the Association is an interesting illustration of the formal institutionalization of the ethics of relational contracting—doing, perhaps, for contracting what the post-war labour reform did to transform the employment system of large firms from manipulative paternalism into something less exploitative and better described as welfare corporatism.[10] All one can say about the contemporary trading reality is that those ethics appear to be sufficiently institutionalized, to be sufficiently constraining on a sufficient number of the firms and families in Nishiwaki textiles, for the pattern of trading I have described to be a stable and viable one.

That pattern is repeated in many other areas of the Japanese economy—between, for example, an automobile firm like Toyota and its sub-contractors. Here again, the obligations of the relationship are unequal; the sub-contractor has to show more earnest goodwill, more 'sincerity', to keep its orders than the parent company to keep its supplies. But equally the obligatedness is not entirely one-sided, and it does limit the extent to which the parent company can, for example, end its contracts with a sub-contractor in a recession in order to bring the work into its own factory and keep its own workforce employed.

I have been taken to task by Okumura, the Japanese economist who has written most interestingly about these relationships, for speaking of the 'obligatedness' of a firm like Toyota as if a corporation was, or behaved like, a natural person.[11] But I still think the term is apt. The mechanisms are easy to intuit, if ponderous to spell out. First of all, there are *real* personal relations between the purchasing manager of Toyota and the manager or owner-manager of a sub-contracting firm. But, of course, managers change frequently, particularly in firms with a bureaucratic career-promotion structure like Toyota. It is part of the commitment of such managers, however, that they identify with their firm and their department. If it were said, therefore, in the world outside, that Toyota, or its purchasing department in particular, had behaved badly by playing fast and loose with its sub-contractors, the manager responsible would feel that he had let his firm down. If the accountants in the costing department urge a tough line with sub-contractors, he may well tell them that they are short-sighted and even disloyal to the firm in under-estimating the importance of its reputation. These seem to me readily understandable mechanisms by which the patterns of obligation between individual owner-managing converters and weavers in Nishiwaki can be duplicated between corporations.

I have discussed two cases of obligated trading relationships which are explicitly hierarchical. If there is any doubt as to who pecks whom in the pecking order look at the mid-summer and year-end gifts. Although it may vary depending on the precise nature of the concessions sought or granted in the previous six months or anticipated in the next, the weaver's gift to the converter will usually cost more than vice versa—unless, that is, either of them miscalculates the gift inflation rate, the point of transition, say, from Black Label against Suntory Old to Napoleon brandy against Dimple Haig.

4. Relational Contracting Between Equals

But these relations are not confined to the hierarchical case. Even between firms of relatively equal strength the same forms of obligated relational contracting exist. Competition between Japanese firms is intense, but only in markets which are (a) consumer markets and (b) expanding. In consumer markets which are not expanding cartelization sets in rather rapidly, but that is a rather different story which does not concern us here. What does concern us here are markets in producers' goods, in intermediates. And for many such commodities markets can hardly be said to exist. Take steel, for instance, and one of its major uses for automobiles. The seven car firms buy their steel through trading companies, each from two or three of the major steel companies, in proportions which vary little from year to year. Prices, in this market, are set by the annual contract between the champions—Toyota on the one side, New Japan Steel on the other.

It is the concentration of such relationships which is the dominant characteristic of the famous large enterprise groups, known to Japanese as *grūpu*, and to foreigners, usually, as *zaibatsu* or *keiretsu*. There are six main ones of which the two best known are Mitsui and Mitsubishi. These groups are quite distinct from the hierarchical groupings of affiliates and subsidiaries around some of the giant individual firms like Hitachi or Matsushita or MHI. The Mitsubishi group, for example, has no clear hierarchical structure. In its core membership of 28 firms, there is a certain amount of intra-group share ownership—on average about 26 per cent of total equity widely dispersed throughout the group in three or four per cent shares. There is a tiny amount of interlocking directorships—about three per cent of all directors' seats. And most of the firms have the group bank as their lead bank, and bank of last pleading resort, but that bank provides on average less than 20 per cent of all loan finance to group firms. The only thing which formally defines the identity of the group is the lunch on the last Friday of the month when the Presidents of every company in the group get together, often to listen to a lecture on, say, the oil market in the 1990s, to discuss matters like political party contributions, sometimes to hear news of, or give blessings to, some new joint venture started up by two or more member firms, or a rescue operation for a member firm in trouble.[12]

But the main *raison d'etre* of these groups is as networks of preferential, stable, obligated *bilateral* trading relationships, networks of relational contracting. They are not conglomerates because they have no central board or holding company. They are not cartels because they are all in diverse lines of business. Each group has a bank and a trading company, a steel firm, an automobile firm, a major chemical firm, a shipbuilding and plant engineering firm and so on—and, except by awkward accident, not more than one of each. (The 'one set' principle as the Japanese say.) Hence, trade in producer goods within the group can be brisk. To extend earlier analogies; it is a bit like an extended family grouping, where business is kept as much as possible within the family, and a certain degree of give and take is expected to modify the adversarial pursuit of market advantage—a willingness, say, to pay above the market price for a while to help one's trading partner out of deep trouble.

5. The Preference for Relational Contracting: Cultural Sources?

The starting point of this discussion of relational contracting was the search for reasons to explain why it made sense for the spinning firms producing brand cloth to co-ordinate production neither through hierarchy in the usual Williamson sense of full vertical integration, nor through the market in the normal sense of continuously pursuing the best buy, but through 'relational contracting'. It was, I said, because such arrangements could be *relied on* in Japan more than in most other economies. There is one striking statistic which illustrates the extent to which it is in fact relied on. The volume of wholesale transactions in Japan is no less than four times as great as the volume of retail transactions. For France the multiple is not four but 1.2; for Britain, West Germany and the USA the figure is between 1.6 and 1.9.[13]

How does one explain the difference between Japan and other capitalist economies? Williamson has 'theorized' these 'obligational relationships' and explained the circumstances in which they will occur—when the extent to which the commodities traded are idiosyncratically specific (such that the economies of scale can be as easily appropriated by buyer or by seller), and the extent to which either party has invested in equipment or specialized knowledge for the trading relationship, are not quite such that vertical integration makes sense, but almost so. He also asserts that in such relationships quantity adjustments will be preferred to price adjustments and price adjustments will be pegged to objective exogenous indicators (though he allows, in passing, for the not very 'relevant' or 'interesting' possibility that 'ad hoc price relief' might be given as an act of kindness by one party to the other).[14]

Perhaps Williamson has evidence that that is the way it is in America and the fact that his argument is couched in the terms of a timeless generalization merely reflects the tendency of American economists to write as if all the world were America. (Just as British economists write micro-economics as if all the world were America, and macro-economics as if all the world were Britain.) Or perhaps he does not have much evidence about America either, and just assumes that 'Man' is a hard-nosed short-run profit-maximizer suspicious of everyone he deals with, and allows everything else to follow from that. At any rate Williamson's account does not provide the tools for explaining the difference between the Japanese and the British or American economies. There is nothing particularly idiosyncratic about the steel or cloth traded in many of the obligated relationships, little specialized assets involved (though there are in automobile sub-contracting). Nor is there clear avoidance of price adjustments—weaving contract prices, in fact, look like graphs of nineteenth century business cycles.

Clearly we have to look elsewhere for an explanation. Try as one might to avoid terms like 'national character' which came naturally to Hobhouse, in favour of the scientific pretensions of, say, 'modal behavioural dispositions', it is clearly national differences in value preferences, or dispositions to action, with which we are concerned. And, as Macfarlane showed when he looked into the origins of English individualism,[15] to attempt to explain *those* takes one on a long speculative journey—at least into distant ill-recorded history, even if, for ideological reasons, one wishes to rule out genes. But it is legitimate and useful to ask: what are the concomitants of these dispositions? What do they correlate with? Are they an expression of more general traits?

One candidate explanation is that the Japanese are generally very long-term-future-oriented. At this moment, for example, the Japanese Industry Ministry's Industrial Structure Council is already composing what it calls a 'vision' of the shape of the world economy in the mid-1990s. The economist is likely to seize on this explanation with relief, because it will allow him to ignore all dangerous thoughts about benevolence, and accommodate the

Ronald Dore

relational contracting phenomenon in the conventional micro-economics of risk aversion and low time-discounts. Any sacrifice of short-run market advantage is just an insurance premium for more long-term gains.

And he would find some good evidence. Nakatani has recently done an interesting calculation comparing 42 large firms inside one of the large kinship groupings like Mitsui and Mitsubishi which I have just described and a matched sample of 42 loners. The loners had higher average profit levels and higher growth rates in the 1970s. *But* they also had a considerably higher dispersal around the means. The group firms were much more homogeneous in growth and profit levels. What went on in the groups, he concluded, was an overall sacrifice of efficiency in the interests of risk-sharing and greater equality.[16]

Relational contracts, in this interpretation, are just a way of trading off the short term loss involved in sacrificing a price advantage, against the insurance that one day you can 'call off' the same type of help from your trading partner if you are in trouble yourself. It is a calculation, perhaps, which comes naturally to a population which until recently was predominantly living in tightly nucleated hamlet communities in a land ravished by earthquake and typhoon. Traditionally, you set to, to help your neighbour rebuild his house after a fire, even though it might be two or three generations before yours was burnt down and your grandson needed the help returned.

But you could be *sure* that the help *would* be returned. And this is where we come back to Adam Smith. The Japanese, in spite of what their political leaders say at summit conferences about the glories of free enterprise in the Free World, and in spite of the fact that a British publisher with a new book about Adam Smith can expect to sell half the edition in Japan, have never really caught up with Adam Smith. They have never managed actually to bring themselves to *believe* in the invisible hand. They have always insisted—and teach in their schools and their 'how to get on' books of popular morality—that the butcher and the baker and the brewer *need* to be benevolent as well as self-interested. They need to be able to take some personal pleasure in the satisfaction of the diners quite over and above any expectation of future orders. It is not just that benevolence is the best policy—much as we say, rather more minimally, that honesty is the best policy. They do not doubt that it is—that it is not a matter of being played for a sucker, but actually the best way to material success. But that is not what they most commonly say. They most commonly say: benevolence is a duty. Full stop. It is that sense of duty—a duty over and above the terms of written contract—which gives the assurance of the pay-off which makes relational contracting viable.

Note that this is a little different from what Durkheim had in mind when he was talking about the non-contractual elements in contract and refuting Spencer's claim that modern societies were held together solely by an organic

370

web of individualistic contracts.[17] Durkheim was talking about the intervention of *society* both in enforcing the basic principles of honesty and the keeping of promises, and in regulating the content of contracts, deciding what was admissible and what offended social decency or basic human rights. And in Durkheim's book it is the consciousness of an obligation imposed by society as a whole—or, on its members, by an occupational group of professional practitioners—which enforces those rules. Hobhouse, likewise, in his brisker and more historically rooted discussion of the way freedom of contract and the rights of private property come to be curtailed by, for example, redistributive welfare measures, stressed the benefits the individual receives from society and the corresponding obligations to society.[18] In Japanese relational contracting, by contrast, it is a particular sense of diffuse obligation to the individual trading partner, not to society, which is at issue. To put the matter in Parson's terms, relational contracting is to be understood in the universalism/particularism dimension, whereas the Durkheim point relates to the fifth dichotomy that Parsons later lost from sight: collective-orientation versus individual-orientation. To put it another way, the Japanese share with Durkheim the perception that contract, far from being fundamentally integrative, is basically a marker for conflict. Every harmonization of interest in a contract simply conceals a conflict either latent or adjourned, as Durkheim said.[19] The Durkheim solution is to have universalistic social institutions contain the conflict—an engine cooling system to take away the heat. The Japanese prefer particularistically to reduce the friction in all the moving parts with the emollient lubrication of mutual consideration.

Perhaps one should not overdraw the contrast, however, in view of the empirical fact that the Japanese, who stand out among other capitalist societies for their addiction to relational contracts, also stand out as the nation whose businessmen and trade unionists seem to have a more lively sense of their obligated membership in the national community than those of other nations. Japan has fewer free-rider problems in the management of the national economy; patriotism seems to supplement profit-seeking more substantially in, say, the search for export markets, and so on. Perhaps the common syndrome is a generalized dutifulness, or to put it in negative form, a relatively low level of individualistic self-assertion. I am reminded of the Japanese scholar and publicist, Nitobe. In his lectures in the USA in the 1930s he used to tell the national character story about the international prize competition for an essay about the elephant. In his version the Japanese entry was entitled 'The duties and domestication of the elephant'.

But there is, it seems to me, a third element in the Japanese preference for relational contracting besides risk sharing and long-term advantage on the one hand and dutifulness on the other. That is the element, to go back to

Ronald Dore

Parsons' variables again, best analysed in his affectivity/affective-neutrality dimension. People born and brought up in Japanese society do not much *like* openly adversarial bargaining relationships—which are inevitably low-trust relationships because information is hoarded for bargaining advantage and each tries to manipulate the responses of the other in his own interest. Poker is not a favourite Japanese game. Most Japanese feel more comfortable in high-trust relations of friendly give-and-take in which each side recognizes that he also has some stake in the satisfaction of the other.

All of which, of course, is not necessarily to say that the affect is genuine. Pecksniffs can do rather well in exploiting these relationships when they are in a stronger bargaining position—the point made earlier about the ambiguities of these relationships.

6. Employment Practices and Relational Contracts

The discussion so far has centred on markets in intermediates and capital goods, and about relational contracting between enterprises. I have not so far mentioned labour markets, though the predominance of relational contracting in Japanese labour markets is, of course, much more widely known than its predominance in inter-firm trading. By now every television viewer has heard of the life-time commitment pattern—the transformation of the employment contract from a short-term spot contract agreement to provide specific services for a specific wage (termination by one week or one month's notice on either side), into a long-term commitment to serve as needs may from time-to-time dictate, with wages negotiated according to criteria of fairness which have precious little to do with any notion of a market rate-for-the-job. The contract is seen, in fact, less as any kind of bilateral bargain, than as an act of admission to an enterprise community wherein benevolence, goodwill and sincerity are explicitly expected to temper the pursuit of self-interest. The parallel between relational contracting in the intermediates market and in the labour market is obvious. There can be little doubt that the same cultural values explain the preferred patterns in both fields.

7. Relational Contracting and Efficiency

But anyone looking at the competitive strength of the Japanese economy today must also wonder whether this institutionalization of relational contracting, as well as serving the values of risk-sharing security, dutifulness and friendliness *also* conduces to a fourth valued end—namely economic efficiency. Any economist, at least any economist worth his neo-classical salt, would be likely to scoff at the idea. Just think, he would say, of the market imperfections, of the misallocation and loss of efficiency involved. Think how many inefficient producers are kept out of the bankruptcy courts by all this give-and-take at the expense of the consuming public. Think of the additional barriers to entry against new, more efficient, producers. Gary Becker, in a lecture at the LSE a couple of years ago, claimed that give-and-take trading was even an inefficient way of being altruistic. In the end, he said, through greater survival power, you get more dollars-worth of altruism by playing the market game and then using the profits to endow a charitable foundation like Rockefeller—which I suppose is true and would even be significant if 'altruism' were a homogeneous commodity indifferently produced either by being friendly to your suppliers or by posthumously endowing scholarship.[20]

But that apart, the main point about sub-optimality is well-taken. The Japanese economy is riddled with misallocation. A lot of the international dispute about non-tariff barriers, for example, has its origin in relational contracting. Take the market for steel which I mentioned earlier. Brazil and Korea can now land some kinds of steel in Japan more cheaply than Japanese producers can supply it. But very little of it is sold. Japan can remain as pure as the driven snow in GATT terms—no trigger prices, minimal tariffs, no quotas—and still have a kind of natural immunity to steel imports which Mr. MacGregor would envy. None of the major companies would touch Brazilian or Korean steel, especially now that things are going so badly for their customers, the Japanese steel companies. Small importers are willing to handle modest lots. But they will insist on their being landed at backwater warehouses away from where any domestic steel is going out, so that the incoming steel is not seen by a steel company employee. If that happens, the lorries taking the steel out might be followed to their destination. And the purchaser, if he turned out to be a disloyal customer, would be marked down for less than friendly treatment next time a boom brings a seller's market. What distortions, an economist would say. What a conspiracy against the consumer! What a welfare loss involved in sacrificing the benefits of comparative advantage! If the Japanese economy has a good growth record, that

Ronald Dore

can only be *in spite of* relational contracting and the consequent loss of efficiency.

And yet there are some good reasons for thinking that it might be *because of*, and not *in spite of* relational contracting that Japan has a better growth performance than the rest of us. There is undoubtedly a loss of allocative efficiency. But the countervailing forces which more than outweigh that loss can *also* be traced to relational contracting. Those countervailing forces are those which conduce to, not allocative efficiency, but what Harvey Leibenstein calls X-efficiency—those abilities to plan and programme, to co-operate without bitchiness in production, to avoid waste of time or of materials, capacities which Leibenstein tries systematically to resolve into the constituent elements of selective degrees of rationality and of effort.[21] We have recently been told by a solemn defender of the neo-classical paradigm that we need not bother about Leibenstein and X-efficiency because he is only reformulating the utility-maximizing paradigm of the generalized equilibrium theory as developed by the Williamson school (i.e. that which incorporates transaction costs, property-right constraints, etc.).[22] To argue thus is not only to destroy the usefulness of 'utility-maximization' for any precise calculations, it is also to ignore the achievement of Leibenstein in actually noticing (a) that individuals, firms and nations differ greatly in degrees of generalized *sloppiness*, and (b) that other kinds of sloppiness are far more important for output growth and welfare than that involved in failing to fine-tune economic behaviour in response to changes in price signals—or *even* in failing to calculate the relative transaction costs of internal and external procurement.

In his book Leibenstein tries a rough comparison between the estimated welfare loss from tariffs and price distortions in a number of empirical cases, and that implied by the 'inefficiency' of business firms inferrable from the range in outputs with similar inputs as between 'best practice' and 'worst practice' firms. His evidence that for most economies for most of the time the latter vastly exceeds the former is of crucial policy importance, and any theory which succeeds in assimilating both phenomena within the same umbrella framework is, like unisex fashions, less an achievement than a distraction. The distinction between allocative efficiency which has to do with rational responses to price signals and all those other kinds of efficiency which raise the productivity of inputs in a business organization is an extremely useful one, and X-efficiency is as good a catch-all term for the second bundle of qualities as any other.

It is in the second dimension, in its effect in making 'best practice' better and more widely diffused, that the Japanese system of relational contracting has merits which, I suggest, more than compensate for its price-distorting consequences. To take the case of employment and the life-time commitment

374

first, the compensatory advantages which go with the disadvantage of inflexible wage costs, are reasonably well known. In a career employment system people accept that they have continually to be learning new jobs; there can be great flexibility, it makes more sense for firms to invest in training, the organization generally is more likely to be a learning environment open to new ideas. If a firm's market is declining, it is less likely to respond simply by cutting costs to keep profits up, more likely to search desperately for new product lines to keep busy the workers it is committed to employing anyway. Hence a strong growth dynamism. And so on.

As for relational contracting between enterprises, there are three things to be said. First, the relative security of such relations encourages investment in supplying firms. The spread of robots has been especially rapid in Japan's engineering sub-contracting firms in recent years, for example. Second, the relationships of trust and mutual dependency make for a more rapid flow of information. In the textile industry, for example, news of impending changes in final consumer markets is passed more rapidly upstream to weavers and yarn dyers; technical information about the appropriate sizing or finishing for new-chemical fibres is passed down more systematically from the fibre firms to the beamers and dyers. Third, a by-product of the system is a general emphasis on quality. What holds the relation together is the sense of mutual obligation. The butcher shows his benevolence by never taking advantage of the fact that the customer doesn't know rump from sirloin. If one side fails to live up to his obligations, the other side is released from his. According to the relational contract ethic, it may be difficult to ditch a supplier because, for circumstances for the moment beyond his control, he is not giving you the best buy. It is perfectly proper to ditch him if he is not giving the best buy and not *even trying* to match the best buy. The single most obvious indicator of effort is product quality. A supplier who consistently fails to meet quality requirements is in danger of losing even an established relational contract. I know that even sociologists should beware of anecodotal evidence, but single incidents can often illustrate national norms and I make no apology for offering two.

1. The manager of an automobile parts supplier said that it was not uncommon for him to be rung up at home in the middle of the night by the night-shift supervisor of the car factory 60 miles away. He might be told that they had already found two defective parts in the latest batch, and unless he could get someone over by dawn they were sorry, but they'd have to send the whole lot back. And he would then have to find a foreman whom he could knock up and send off into the night.

2. The manager of a pump firm walking me round his factory explains that it is difficult to diagnose defects in the pump-castings before machining though the founders are often aware when things might have gone wrong.

'I suspect', he said cheerfully, 'our supplier keeps a little pile of defective castings in the corner of his workshop, and when he's got a good batch that he thinks could stand a bit of rubbish he throws one or two in.'

I leave the reader to guess which is the Japanese and which the British story.

8. How *Uniquely* Japanese?

So if it is the case that relational contracting has some X-efficiency advantages which compensate for allocative inefficiencies, what lessons should we draw from all this about how to run an efficient economy and build a decent society? The first thing to do is to look around at our economies and take stock of the ways in which benevolence/goodwill actually modify the workings of the profit motive in daily practice. So far I have referred to relational contracting as something the Japanese have an *unusual* preference for. But that is far from saying that they are *uniquely* susceptible to it. If we look around us we will find far more evidence of relational contracting than we think. This is so even in America where capitalism seems generally to be more hard-nosed than in Europe. In an interesting article written 20 years ago, Stewart Macaulay examined the relative importance of personal trust and enforceable legal obligation in business contracts in the USA. He found many businessmen talking of the need for give-and-take, for keeping accountants and lawyers, with their determination to press every advantage, out of direct dealings with other firms.[23] Among those with experience of large projects in the civil construction industry it is a truism that successful work requires a bond of trust between client and contractor. Engineers, as fellow-professionals, sharing a commitment to the project's success, can create that trust. Their firms' lawyers can endanger it by the confrontational stance with which they approach all potential conflicts of interest. Recently I got a simple questionnaire answered by seven managers or owner-managers of weaving mills in Blackburn asking them about their trading practices, and found a strong preference for stable long-term relationships with give-and-take on the price, and a claim that, on average, two-thirds of their business already was that way. In the British textile trade, of course, Marks and Spencers is well known for its relational contracting, squeezing suppliers a bit in times of trouble but not ditching them as long as they are maintaining quality standards, and accepting some responsibility for helping them technically. In the supermarket world, Sainsbury's have the same reputation, supposedly very different from that of Tesco's which believes that frequent switching of suppliers encourages the others to keep the price down.

9. Quality, Affluence and Relational Contracting

There may be something very significant in the nature of these examples. Try adding together the following thoughts.

1. Marks and Spencers is well known for one thing besides relational contracting, namely that it bases its appeal on product quality more than on price.

2. There is also an apparent relation between a quality emphasis and relational contracting in Japan.

3. Sainsburys is up-market compared with Tesco which is for keen pricers.

4. Japan's consumer markets are *generally* reckoned to be more middle-class, more quality sensitive and less price sensitive than Britain's. (Textile people, for instance, have given me rough estimates that if one divides the clothing market crudely into the AB groups, fastidious about quality and not too conscious of price, and the rest who look at price and superficial smartness rather than the neatness of the stitching, in Britain the proportions are: 25:75; in Japan 60:40.)

5. Japan of the 1920s, and again in the post-war period, was much more of a cut-throat jungle than it is today. Not the ethics of relational contracting nor the emphasis on product quality nor the life-time employment system, seem to have been at all characteristic of earlier periods of Japanese industrialization.

Add all these fragments together and an obvious hypothesis emerges that relational contracting is a phenomenon of affluence, a product, Hobhouse would say, of moral evolution. It is when people become better off and the market-stall haggle gives way to the world of *Which*, where best buys are defined more by quality than by price criteria, that relational contracting comes into its own.

It does so for two reasons: first because quality assurance has to depend more on trust. You always *know* whether the butcher is charging you sixpence or sevenpence. But if you don't know the difference between sirloin and rump, and you think your guests might, then you *have* to trust your butcher: you have to depend on his benevolence. Also, I suspect, when affluence reduces price pressures, any tendencies to prefer a relationship of friendly stability to the poker-game pleasures of adversarial bargaining—tendencies which might have been formerly suppressed by the anxious concern not to lose a precious penny—are able to assert themselves. Japan's difference from Britain, then, is explained both by the fact that the cultural preferences, the suppressed tendencies, are stronger *and* by the fact that the price pressures have been more reduced by a much more rapid arrival at affluence, and consequently a greater subjective sense of affluence.

The fragmentary evidence about relational contracting in inter-firm trading relations in Britain, is much more easily complemented by evidence of its growth in the labour market. Not only Britain, but Europe in general—even the USA to a lesser extent—are no longer countries where employers hire and fire without compunction. Statutory periods of notice gradually lengthen. National redundancy payment schemes recognize the expectation of continuance of an employment contract as a property right. In industries like steel, job tenures are valued at well over a year's wages. More generally, labour mobility has been falling for 15 years. Factory flexibility agreements take the employment contract further away from the original rate-for-the-specific-job basis. More attention to career promotion systems within the firm, managerial doctrines about 'worker involvement' in the affairs of the enterprise and, intermittently, talk of, and even occasional moves towards, enterprise-based industrial democracy all exemplify the transformation of the employment contract into a more long-term, more diffuse commitment.

10. Relational Contracting, Rigidities and Economic Policy

Economists have occasionally noted these trends, but have generally treated them as market imperfections, basically lag problems of the long and the short run—for in the end, habit always succumbs to the pursuit of profit. And among imperfection problems they have found them less interesting to analyse than other kinds like monopoly. And those bold souls among them who *have* taken aboard the new phenomenon of stagflation, and tried to explain the tendency for contraction in demand to lead to a contraction in output not a fall in price, to increased unemployment but only slow, delayed and hesitant deceleration in the rate of wage increase, have rarely recognized the importance of a general growth in relational contracting—of the effects on the effectiveness of fiscal and monetary regulators of the fact that more and more deals are being set by criteria of fairness not by market power. More commonly, they speak of the growth of oligopoly on the one hand and on the other of trade union monopoly consequent on statutory job protection and higher welfare benefits. They have explained stagflation, in other words, not as the result of creeping benevolence—the diffusion of goodwill and mutual consideration through the economy—but as the result of creeping malevolence, increasing abuse of monopoly power. And the cure which our modern believers in the supreme virtues of the market have for these 'rigidities', is a deflation stiff enough to restore the discipline of market forces, to make firms competitive again and force the inefficient out of business, to weaken trade union monopolies and get firms hiring and firing according to their real needs.

A few people have given relational contracting and its growth the importance it is due. Albert Hirschman, first in this as in so many things, described the general syndrome of voice and loyalty taking over from exit and entry as the characteristic disciplining force of advanced capitalism.[24] More recently Arthur Okun developed before his untimely death a similarly comprehensive view of relational contracting and, moreover, explained in his *Prices and Quantities* its connection to worsening stagflation.[25] He wrote of the tendency in capital goods and intermediate markets, and to some extent in consumer markets, for what he called 'customer markets', to grow at the expense of 'auction markets', and of the corresponding growth of 'career labour markets'—employment characterized by an implicit contract of quasi-permanence—the invisible handshake is one of his phrases—all adding up to what he called a 'price-tag economy' as opposed to the 'auction economy' of orthodox text books. What I do not think he fully took aboard is the way in which social relations in customer markets and career-labour markets take on a moral quality and become regulated by criteria of fairness. Consequently, his remedies, apart from being far more imaginatively interventionist, are not so very different in kind from the more common marketist prescriptions for dealing with the rigidities of stagflation. That is to say, he also concentrates on devices to change (a) incentives and (b) expectations under the unchanged assumption that economic behaviour will continue to be guided solely by short-run income-maximizing considerations.

There is no mention of Japan in his index, and none that I have discovered in his book. But if we do think of Japan, a society which has far more developed forms of relational contracting than ours and glories in it, *and* achieves high growth and technical progress, we might think of a different prescription.

It would run something like this. First, recognize that the growth of relational contracting can provide a very real enhancement of the quality of life. Not many of us who work in a tenured job in the academic career market, for example, would relish a switch to freelance status. I hear few academics offering to surrender their basic salary for the freedom to negotiate their own price for every lecture, or even demanding personally negotiated annual salaries in exchange for tenure and incremental scales. And if you overhear a weaving mill manager on the telephone, in a relaxed friendly joking negotiation with one of his long-standing customers, you may well wonder how much more than the modest profits he expects would be required to tempt him into the more impersonal cut-and-thrust of keen auction-market-type competition.

But the second point is this, Having recognized that relational contracting is something that we cannot expect to go away, and that inevitably a lot of allocative efficiency is going to be lost, try to achieve the advantages of X-efficiency which can compensate for the loss.

This prescription has a macro-part and a micro-part. The macro-part includes, first of all, maintaining the conditions for free competition in the one set of markets which remain impersonally competitive—the markets for final consumer goods. This is necessary to provide the external stimulus for the competing chains or pyramids of relational-contract-bound producers to improve their own internal efficiency. It means on the one hand an active competition policy, and on the other, where monopoly is inevitable, the organization of countervailing consumer watchdog groups. Also included in the macro-part are first, an incomes policy, since if it *is* now criteria of fairness rather than the forces of supply and demand which determine wages in career labour markets, those fairness criteria had better be institutionalized. Second it means an attempt, if you like, to tip the ideology towards benevolence; in Fred Hirsch's terms, to try to revive an 'ethos of social obligation' to replenish the 'depleting moral legacy' which capitalism inherited from an earlier more solidary age[26], not least by stressing the importance of quality and honest thoughtful service, the personal satisfactions of doing a good job well as a source of price and self-respect—letting profits be their own reward, not treated as if they were a proxy measure of social worth. The Department of Industry's recent announcement of an £8 million programme of subsidies for improvements in quality assurance systems in British factories is at least a recognition of the enhanced importance of quality in the modern world, even if there are no signs of a recognition that this might entail new attitudes and values (or a new affirmation of old ones now lost), a move away from the spirit of *caveat emptor*.

The micro-part of the prescription involves a better specification of the ethics of relational contracting; perhaps, as the French have been contemplating, criteria for deciding what constitutes unfair dismissal of a sub-contractor, parallel to those for employees, with protection depending on performance, including quality criteria and conscientious timing of deliveries. Second, at the enterprise level, it means taking the growth of job tenure rights not just as an unfortunate rigidity, but as an opportunity for developing a sense of community in business enterprises. It means, that is to say, reaping the production advantages which can come from a shared interest in the firm's success, from co-operation and free flow of information and a flexible willingness not to insist on narrow occupational roles. What those advantages can be we can see in Japan, but in Britain, where attitudes to authority are very different from those of Japan, the prescription probably means not manipulative policies of worker 'involvement' in existing hierarchies, but some real moves towards constitutional management, industrial democracy or what you will—anything *except* the extension of traditional forms of collective bargaining made for, and growing out of, the era of auction markets for labour.

I think Hobhouse would not have objected to a lecture in his honour being used as an occasion for preaching, though I am not sure that he would have approved of the contents. I am enough of an old-fashioned liberal, however, to hope that he might.

Notes

1. A. Smith, *The Wealth of Nations* (London: J. M. Dent, 1910), 13.
2. R. H. I. Palgrave, *Dictionary of Political Economy*, ed. H. Higgs (London: Macmillan, 1923–6).
3. D. Greenwald, *McGraw-Hill Dictionary of Modern Economics* (New York: McGraw-Hill, 1973).
4. P. A. Samuelson, *Economics*, Eleventh Edition (New York; London: McGraw-Hill, 1980), 121–2.
5. O. E. Williamson, 'The modern corporation: Origins, evolution, attributes', *Journal of Economic Literature*, vol. 19, no. iv, December 1981.
6. V. P. Goldberg, 'A relational exchange perspective on the employment relationship', Paper for SSRC Conference, York, 1981.
7. O. E. Williamson, 'Transaction-cost economics: the governance of contractual relations', *Journal of Law and Economics*, vol. 22, no. ii, 1979, 233–61.
8. R. M. Solow, 'On theories of unemployment', *American Economic Review*, vol. 70, i, 1980.
9. Seni Torihiki Kindaika Suishin Kyogikai (Association for the Promotion of the Modernization of Trading Relations in the Textile Industry), *Nenji Hōkoku* (Annual Report), 1980.
10. R. Dore, *British factory: Japanese Factory: The Origins of National Diversity in Industrial Relations* (Berkeley: University of California Press, 1973), 269 ff.
11. H. Okumura, 'Masatsu o umu Nihonteki keiei no heisa-sei' (The closed nature of Japanese corporate management as a source of international friction),

Ekonomisuto, 6 July 1982; 'The closed nature of Japanese intercorporate relations', *Japan Echo*, vol. 9, no. iii, 1982.

12. H. Okumura, 'Interfirm relations in an enterprise group: The case of Mitsubishi', *Japanese Economic Studies*, Summer 1982; *Shin Nihon no Rokudaikigyō-
shūdan. (A new view of Japan's six great enterprise groups)* (Tokyo: Diamond, 1983).

13. Okumura in *Japan Echo*, 1982.

14. O. E. Williamson, 'Transaction-cost economics: the governance of contractual
relations', *Journal of Law and Economics*; vol. 22. no. ii, 1979, 233–61.

15. A. Macfarlane, *The Origins of English Individualism* (Oxford: Basil Blackwell,
1978).

16. I. Nakatani, *The Role of Inter-market keiretsu Business Groups in Japan*, Australia-
Japan Research Centre, Research Paper, no. 97 (Canberra: ANU); Risuku-
shearingu kara mita Nihon Keizai, ('Risk-sharing in the Japanese economy'),
'Osaka-daigaku Keizaigaku', col. 32, nos. ii–iii, December 1982.

17. E. Durkheim, *De la Division du travail social* (Paris: Felix Alcan, 1893), tr. G.
Simpson, *The Division of Labour in Society* (1960).

18. L. T. Hobhouse, *Morals in Evolution* (London: Chapman & Hall, 1908, 7th ed.,
1951).

19. Durkheim, *Division du travail social*, 222.

20. G. Becker, *Altruism in the Family and Selfishness in the Market Place*, Centre for
Labour Economics, LSE, Discussion Paper No. 73, 1980.

21. H. Leibenstein, *Beyond Economic Man: A New Foundation for Micro Economics*
(Cambridge, Mass.: Harvard University Press, 1976).

22. L. De Alessi, 'Property rights transaction costs and X-efficiency: An essay in
economic theory', *American Economic Review*, vol. 73, no. i, March 1983.

23. S. Macaulay, 'Non-contractual relations in business: a preliminary study', *American Sociological Review*, vol. 28, no. i. February, 1963.

24. A. O. Hirschman, *Exit, Voice and Loyalty: Responses to Decline in Firms, Organizations and States* (Cambridge, Mass.: Harvard University Press, 1970).

25. A. Okun, *Prices and Quantities* (Oxford: Basil Blackwell, 1981).

26. F. Hirsch, *Social Limits to Growth* (London: Routledge & Kegan Paul, 1977).

III. JOINT VENTURES, NETWORKS, AND CLANS

Having considered the literature on why individuals are to be found in many cases working together in firms rather than operating individually (Section I), and on why the 'market' cannot be seen as existing in isolation from firms and their actual operation (Section II), the readings in Section III explore in more depth an issue referred to in the introductory comments to Section I, namely that production takes place largely within firms and other organizations. It is this latter distinction—between firms on the one hand and other organizations on the other—which is explored in more detail in the various articles reproduced in this Section.

The fact that firms form joint ventures—doing more than simply contracting with each other through market processes, yet not necessarily actually merging or even holding shares in each other—is discussed in the first article, by Pfeffer and Nowack. The most striking development of this phenomena in recent times has been its increased spread across national borders, with a range of cooperative patterns emerging internationally, and it is the theory of this cooperation in international business which is analysed in the reading reproduced from Buckley and Casson. The article by Miles and Snow discusses a range of organizational forms, and in particular various forms of networking across firms, and examines the implications of this for management practice, organizational redesign, and government policy in trade and industry issues.

The starting point for the literature highlighted in this volume, on the economics of contracts and industrial organization, was said in the introduction to Section I to be the recognition that an analysis of economies had to go beyond the individual as the building block from which all else is thought to follow. What is required instead includes a recognition of the importance of firms (Section I) and other organizations—including inter-firm linkages (Section II). This does not just replace an assumption of individuals contracting in a market with one of firms and other organizations contracting in a market. It forces a recognition that the very concept of a 'market' is not a simple one. What is being described when reference is made to the 'market' is not some 'natural' creation, with which people and organizations are faced. Instead, the market is largely a creation of those individuals and organizations. Similarly, when the 'black box' which is the firm in economic theory is opened up it can be seen that the concept of the firm/organization itself describes a multitude of arrangements. Some of these are analysed in the paper by Ouchi who considers in what circumstances bureaucracies and clans may be preferable routes for the organization of economic activity, as opposed to mediation through the market.

Finally, Milgrom and Roberts survey the implications of much of the above literature—including pieces from Sections I and II of this volume—for the understanding of firms and markets. They stress the importance of accepting that rationality is bounded, and call for more attention to be paid to changing technology.

14 Joint Ventures and Interorganizational Interdependence

Jeffrey Pfeffer and Phillip Nowak

There are many varieties of interorganizational linkage. Corporations inter-lock their boards of directors (Dooley, 1969; Levine, 1972; Pfeffer, 1972a); there is movement of personnel from one organization to another (Baty, Evan, and Rothermel, 1971; Pfeffer and Leblebici, 1973); forms of contractual and noncontractual relations develop (Macaulay, 1963); and, at times, orga-nizations absorb other organizations through merger (Pfeffer, 1972b). The varieties of linkage have been discussed by Thompson and McEwen (1958), who noted that goals and actions of organizations inevitably are constrained by their environments. Interorganizational linkages enable the organization to manage some of its environmental constraints and control some of the contingencies it confronts. Thompson and McEwen wrote that organizations face a dilemma in dealing with their environments. To the extent that the organization becomes more interlocked with another organization, it can rely more on the other organization's performance; but, also, it loses some of its own independence and discretion. Guetzkow (1966), discussing interorganizational relations, has hypothesized that less formal varieties of interorganizational linkage precede more formal arrangements.

There are several conceptual frameworks available for use in under-standing interorganizational phenomena. Levine and White (1961) have argued for the utility of an exchange framework, and Evan (1966) has proposed the organization-set as a useful analytical concept. Pfeffer (1972b) has argued that interorganizational activity is undertaken to manage the

The authors gratefully acknowledge the support of the Institute of Industrial Relations at the University of California at Berkeley. The Federal Trade Commission, particularly Mr David Penn, was most helpful in furnishing the data used in this study. The conclusions and inferences are those of the authors alone. The comments of Howard Aldrich and Hans Pennings on an earlier version of the article are appreciated.

385

organization's interdependence, and that a focus on the resource interdependence of organizations provides a useful analytical perspective. Litwak (Litwak and Hylton, 1962; Litwak and Rothman, 1970) has hypothesized that co-ordination between organizations is a function of (1) the degree and type of organizational interdependence, (2) the organizational awareness of the interdependence, (3) the number of organizations involved, (4) the extent to which linkages deal with uniform or nonuniform events, (5) the resources an organization has to commit to interorganizational linkages, and (6) the type of organization (Litwak and Rothman, 1970: 145).

This article analyzes one type of interorganizational linkage, joint ventures among domestic corporations. The dependent variable in the analysis is the pattern of interorganizational linkage activity accomplished through joint ventures. In analyzing linkages among organizations, several variables could be analyzed: (1) the number of linkages a given organization has with its environment; (2) the intensity, formalization, standardization, duration, and reciprocity characterizing the relationship between two organizations; and (3) the presence of a link between organizations and the pattern of that linkage. The focus of this article is on the latter variable—the pattern of interorganizational linkage that is observed focusing on joint ventures as the mechanism for accomplishing the integration of two or more organizations.

Joint ventures, like mergers and interlocking boards, are common to both economic and nonprofit organizations. Allen (1974) has taken organizational sociology to task for not frequently analyzing activities of corporations, one of the dominant forms of organization in our society. The requirements needed to manage resource interdependence, establish negotiated environments, and transact with the environment are common to all forms of organizations. It is an empirical question whether propositions developed for one form of organization will explain equally well the behavior of organizations of a different type. But the variables and discussion of Benson (1974), for example, who analyzed interorganizational activity from a political economy perspective, are generally applicable. The implication is that while certain propositions may be applicable to a given organizational context, the general theoretical framework for analyzing interorganizational activity should be more generally relevant.

The theoretical position taken here is that interorganizational linkages are undertaken to manage interorganizational interdependence. If joint ventures are undertaken to manage the organizations' interdependence with the environment, patterns of joint venture activity should be systematically related to the patterns of competitive and symbiotic interdependence confronted by the organizations. The data reported suggest that this is the case, and that variance in the pattern of joint venture activity of corporations can be analyzed by viewing joint ventures as responses to organizational interdependence.

1. Background

The term *joint venture*, used interchangeably with the term *joint subsidiary*, means the creation of a new organizational entity by two or more partner organizations (Boyle, 1968). The creating organizations are referred to as the parents, and the created joint venture as the progeny. Joint ventures may be created by either profit-making or nonprofit organizations. The term *joint venture* is not quite equivalent to Aiken and Hage's (1968) discussion of joint activities. The joint venture concept involves the creation of a new, separate, organizational entity, jointly owned and controlled by the parent organizations. This new entity can incur debt, sign contracts, or undertake other activities in its own name, and without consequence to the financial or legal position of the parents, except to the extent of their investment in the joint venture. Other types of joint activities, on the other hand, may not necessarily involve the creation of a separate organizational entity.

Bernstein (1965: 25) distinguished joint ventures from mergers as follows: 'In a merger, two or more companies (organizations) combine *all* of their assets to create a new entity. In a joint venture, two or more companies *combine less than all* of their assets to create a new entity.' Mead (1967) suggested, however, that the difference between mergers and joint ventures may not be great, though for economic organizations, merger activity is more readily prosecuted under the existing antitrust regulations.

There has been very little research on joint ventures, and virtually all of the research that has been undertaken has dealt with business organizations. In one exception, Aiken and Hage (1968) examined general joint activities—which are not the same as joint ventures—among health and welfare organizations. These authors argued that organizations are pushed into joint activities because of the need for resources, including money, skill, and manpower (1968: 914–15). In their study, Aiken and Hage took the creation of the joint program as creating interdependence among the organizations, and attempted to assess the consequences of this interdependence for internal organizational functioning. Specifically, Aiken and Hage argued that a large number of joint programs lead to less formalization, less centralization, and a higher rate of internal communication.

It is argued here that the need for resources is only one possible cause of joint ventures or joint programs, and that this position is better stated as a hypothesis rather than as an assumption. Second, this study differs from Aiken and Hage in that it is argued that interdependence causes the creation of joint ventures to manage the interdependence, rather than the joint ventures themselves creating the interorganizational interdpendence.

Clark (1965) has maintained that alliances of private colleges have arisen in a search for competitive advantage. He noted that by banding together, expensive facilities could be shared and stronger fund raising efforts could be developed. Clark also described the Physical Science Study Committee as a link between federal agencies and the local schools, and argued that the private committee was an important linking device in the movement for curriculum reform.

Within the literature that has examined joint ventures undertaken by business organizations, the prevailing concern has been with whether such linkages among organizations operated to restrict competition. The evidence indicates that joint ventures do have some possible anticompetitive effect. Fusfeld (1958) examined joint subsidiaries in the iron and steel industry, identifying 70 joint subsidiaries. Of these 70 joint ventures, 53 were controlled solely by firms within the industry, and the remaining 17 involved at least one firm that was outside of the iron and steel industry. Of the 53 joint ventures that were started solely by firms within the iron and steel industry, all 53 involved backward integration, or the production of material that itself was used in the production of iron and steel (1958: 581). Of the 17 interindustry joint ventures, 4 involved backward integration, such as iron ore mining or coal mining, and 13 involved diversification and forward integration—such as metal fabricating and titanium production. These companies have not used joint ventures primarily to diversify. Of even greater interest, Fusfeld indicated that the pattern of joint venture activities is seen to provide some community of interests. Two groupings of large producers emerge, with each of these groupings bound together by yet additional joint ventures. While not employing sociometric analysis, the picture presented by Fusfeld is striking: joint ventures have been used to organize the steel industry, leaving the industry with (1) United States Steel, (2) two groups of large producers linked closely within each group, with a few links between the two groups, and (3) the remaining smaller producers. Much as with boards of directors (Levine, 1972), Fusfeld indicated that joint ventures may be used to create interorganizational organizations.

Pate (1969: 18), examining domestic joint ventures, concluded that 'it appears that a majority of new manufacturing progenies were formed to produce conventional products for well-established markets rather than truly new products.' Examining the relationship among the parents, Pate (1969: 19) noted that 'nearly one-half of all participating firms were horizontally related on the basis of this (two digit SIC) classification, with more than 80 per cent having some horizontal or vertical relationship.' Pate thus argued that joint ventures were not undertaken to reduce the uncommonly high risk of a new venture, but, rather, to overcome some of the effects of competition. Pate (1969: 23) summarized his findings by writing that 'during the period 1960–1968, it appears many firms achieved through joint ventures some of the benefits normally associated with horizontal or vertical expansion—benefits that, for a variety of reasons (such as antitrust), were not available under prevailing conditions.'

Boyle (1968: 85), studying 276 joint subsidiaries, found that, rather than being used primarily by smaller firms that might have more need for outside resources, joint subsidiary participation increased as the size of the parent firm increased. Examining the relationship between the industry of the parent company and the industry of the joint subsidiary, Boyle (1968: 88–9) discovered that in less than 10 per cent of the cases were the joint subsidiaries not related either horizontally or vertically to the parent, and that in many cases, the parent organizations were also closely related in terms of the products they produced and sold. Finally, for those few joint subsidiaries where financial data on the subsidiary itself were available, Boyle found that, in 75 per cent of the instances, the joint venture involved $5 million or less in assets.

While the data developed by Pate and Boyle are suggestive, Mead (1967) attempted to obtain more direct evidence on the effect of joint ventures on competition. Mead (1967: 840) examined joint bidding for oil and gas leases, and found that in cases of joint bidding, the same firms were not likely to be bidding competitively on other leases in the same sale. 'In Alaska, where 885 bids were examined, only 16 cases were found where two partner firms had submitted opposing bids for any tract included in the same sale in which they participated as joint bidders. As one should expect, simultaneous joint bidding and competitive bidding is a rare event.' Mead (1967: 844) further demonstrated that the restriction on competitive bidding lasted for two years after the joint action. Since the amount of the highest bid was significantly related to the number of bids received, this apparent restriction on bidding behavior was an important effect.

The few empirical investigations of joint venture activity are consistent with the argument that joint ventures are used to organize groups of organizations, and tend to occur among either competitors or organizations which are in a buyer-seller relationship. The extent to which patterns of joint venture activity can be predicted by considerations of interdependence, however, remains to be quantitatively examined.

2. Hypotheses

There are two types of organizational interdependence. First, there is competitive interdependence. While business organizations, the object of this study, compete for markets and for financial and human resources, such competition also occurs among other organizations, as Thompson and McEwen (1958) have argued. Competition tends to arise in organizations that are functionally equivalent, in that they are attempting to produce similar products and services for similar markets. Elesh (1973) noted that universities compete for students, and certainly all organizations are in a generalized competition for scarce resources (Yuchtman and Seashore, 1967). Organizations, particularly business organizations, do not like to face unrestrained competition and the uncertainty that results from such competition. The numerous cases of collusive action by organizations, such as the electrical generating equipment cases of the early 1960s, attest to this. Cyert and March (1963) have argued that organizations seek to establish negotiated environments, and one dimension of this concept is negotiating a stable position in the environment vis-à-vis one's competitors.

Organizations also face symbiotic interdependencies with other organizations. Hawley (1950: 36) defined symbiosis as 'a mutual dependence between unlike organizations'. Steel producers require iron and coal, paper companies require wood, gasoline stations require gasoline, and organizations also must be able to successfully dispose of their outputs. In economics terminology, competitive interdependence exists on a horizontal level among like organizations, while symbiotic interdependence exists between organizations vertically related in the production process.

While it is argued here that joint ventures are primarily organizational responses taken to cope with these two forms of interdependence, there are other possible explanations for joint venture activities.

The most frequently cited purposes of joint participation are: 1) to spread the risks of new industrial developments; 2) to establish joint or combined facilities for greater economy; 3) to accumulate large amounts of needed capital, and 4) to undertake programmes that are too extensive for individual companies to handle (Pate, 1969: 16).

Joint ventures, then, are undertaken when there are economies of scale in operation, when capital requirements are too high for a single organization to handle, and when there is a great deal of technological risk from the venture. The latter reason is commonly cited in justifying joint ventures among oil exploration organizations. Another reason for possibly undertaking a joint venture is to use the complementary strengths of the two organizations in developing a new product or service or entering a new market. Thus, a firm with expertise in the production of some product may engage in a joint venture with a firm that has an outstanding marketing capability that can be used for the product. This hypothesis of joint ventures being undertaken to develop new activities presents a direct alternative to the resource inter-dependence argument, as it posits an essentially independent relationship between the organizations participating in the joint venture activities. These are the most frequently mentioned alternative hypotheses to the argument that joint ventures are undertaken to manage interorganizational interdependence.

2.1. Joint Ventures as a Response to Symbiotic Interdependence

Symbiotic interdependence of the organization and sources of supply and customer organizations may cause problems because there are critical inter-dependencies outside the control of the focal organization. To manage relationships with sources of purchase or sales interdependence, the organi-zation may seek to engage in joint ventures with others that can facilitate coping with the interdependence. Patterns of joint venture activity should, therefore, correspond to patterns of transactions interdependence between the organization and its environment. The first hypothesis is:

Hypothesis 1. Patterns of joint venture activity will correspond to patterns of transactions interdependence; to the extent an organization in industry A is more interdependent with organizations in industry B, a higher proportion of its joint venture activities should be with firms in that industry.

This hypothesis does not mean that a given firm necessarily will engage in a joint venture with a given other firm with which it has a major proportion of its transactions, but, rather, it is more likely to engage in a joint venture with any firm in that industry. For example, if a steel firm requires coal and has been buying it from firm A, a joint venture with a different coal firm is still consistent with the hypothesis, as the firm is still pursuing an interorganizational linkage to solve a critical resource dependency.

A correlation between resource interdependence and merger activity was observed by Pfeffer (1972b). Similar reasoning would apply in the case of joint ventures. This interorganizational linkage creates a bond between the focal organization and others with which it transacts. Such a bond, accom-plished through the pooling of resources, increases the interdependence present in the relationship, and can help to assure the focal organization of the performance of its transaction partners.

The organization faces both interdependence when acquiring inputs—purchase interdependence—and when disposing of finished products or services—sales interdependence. It is possible to specify some conditions that may affect the extent to which the focal organization will attend to one or the other area of interdependence.

To the extent that the organization is operating in a more highly concentrated environment, its interdependence with suppliers of input, it is argued, will be relatively more important that its interdependence with customers. As a result, the following prediction is made:

Hypothesis 2. There will be a higher correlation between joint venture activities and purchase interdependence the higher the concentration of the organization's economic environment.

The concept of concentration means that the given organization has few competitors for sales. In turn, this presumably gives it market power (Caves, 1970). But this market power is power based on its relation to those organizations to whom it sells. Because they have few alternative sources of supply, these customers are more dependent on the focal organization. Since the organization in a more concentrated environment has relatively more power than those organizations to whom it sells, it would be expected that it would focus its attention on managing its purchase interdependence, or the interdependence with those organizations from which it purchases input.

A second factor affecting the organization's relative concern with sales or purchase interdependence is the extent to which it is operating in a high technology industry. Industries with a high component of research and development costs tend to be more highly concentrated, but technological intensity again would serve to provide the organization with some degree of market power over those organizations to whom it sells. Therefore, it is hypothesized:

Hypothesis 3. The more technologically intense the industry, the more joint venture activity will be related to purchase rather than sales interdependence.

To the extent that concentration is in an intermediate range, organizations should be relatively more concerned with managing their sales interdependence. At very high levels of concentration, they have market power resulting from their relation to those organizations to whom they sell. At very low levels of concentration, there is not much chance for interorganizational linkages to sufficiently organize the industry to produce a meaningful reduction in competition. Thus, it is further hypothesized:

Hypothesis 4. There will be a positive relationship between the extent to which joint venture activity is explained by sales rather than purchase interdependence and the extent to which the organization is in an industry of intermediate concentration.

Finally, a condition that will make both sales and purchase interdependence relatively more important in explaining patterns of joint venture activity can be specified. This factor is whether the industry is capital or labor intensive. To the extent that industry is not labor intensive and uses a great deal of capital equipment per unit of output produced, the organization operating in that industry faces high fixed costs. If the organization cannot obtain necessary inputs, or if it cannot successfully sell its product, it is in a worse position if it is capital rather than labor intensive. Workers can be laid off, but machines, once purchased, cannot easily be abandoned. Therefore, it is predicted:

Hypothesis 5. Sales and purchase interdependence as predictors of joint venture activity will be less important to the extent the organization operates in a labor intensive industry, and more important to the extent it operates in an industry that is capital intensive.

It has been argued that one use of joint ventures is to link more closely organizations that are in a symbiotic relationship to the focal organization. This general proposition posits a correlation between patterns of resource interdependence and patterns of joint venture activity. The argument can be refined to consider the conditions under which either purchase or sales interdependence is likely to be most problematic. To the extent the organization operates in a highly concentrated industry and has market power due to its position vis-à-vis customer organizations, the concern will be with managing those relationships in which it does not have power, involving purchase interdependence or interdependence with suppliers of input. When the organization is not in a highly concentrated industry, but does not face a large number of customers either, sales interdependence will be most problematic. Joint ventures will be related to this form of interdependence when concentration is intermediate. To the extent that the organization has high fixed costs, both sales and purchase interdependence will be critical. The organization's joint venture activities will be more highly related to both forms of interdependence. The argument is that interorganizational linkages, in this case, joint ventures, are used to manage relationships in which the organization has relatively less power.

2.2. *Joint Ventures as a Response to Competitive Interdependence*

While symbiotic relationships can exist between organizations in the same industry or with organizations in different industries, competitive interdependence occurs only in organizations operating in the same industry. Consequently, in this case, only those joint ventures which occur among organizations in the same industry are considered. In the case of mergers within the same industry, Pfeffer (1972b: 389) found that the extent of within-industry merger activity was significantly correlated with the extent to which there existed high transactions—buyer-seller—interdependence within the industry and to the extent concentration of the industry was intermediate. In other words, merger apparently was being undertaken for both competitive and symbiotic interdependence. In the case of joint ventures, Pate (1969), Mead (1967) and others have suggested that joint ventures may be undertaken when mergers are more difficult to accomplish without strong antitrust opposition. If this is the case, it can be hypothesized:

Hypothesis 6. There will be little or no association between joint ventures within the same industry and the amount of within industry transactions—symbiotic interdependence; there will be a greater association between joint ventures within the same industry and the possibility of reducing competitive interdependence. The comparison of greater and less association is with the correlates of merger activity (Pfeffer, 1972b).

It has been argued (Pfeffer, 1972b; Pfeffer and Leblebici, 1973) that inter-organizational linkages to reduce competitive interdependence are most likely to be undertaken when industrial concentration, or the number of firms, is at an intermediate range. At very low levels of industrial concentration, when there are many firms active in the market, interorganizational linkages through joint ventures or other devices will accomplish little because there are so many organizations that must be linked. On the other hand, with only a few firms, formal interorganizational linkage, such as through joint ventures, merger, or the movement of executive personnel among firms, is not necessary. In these highly concentrated market situations, tacit interfirm coordination will be sufficient as only a few other firms must be monitored. Therefore, it is hypothesized:

Hypothesis 7. The proportion of joint venture activities undertaken with firms within the same industry will be highest at an intermediate level of concentration. Stated differently, the proportion will be negatively related to the difference in industry concentration from a median value.

It has been argued that patterns of joint venture activity can be explained by considerations of symbiotic and competitive interdependence. It is also contended that technological intensity, the proportion of labor used in producing output, and industrial concentration can be used to predict when sales or purchase interdependence will be more highly related to joint venture activity. Thus, the model proposed to account for joint venture activity predicts differences in the consequences of different types of inter-dependence, as well as making the general argument that joint ventures are attempts on the part of organizations to manage their interorganizational interdependence.

It is useful to specify how joint ventures, as a form of interorganizational linkage, stabilize and manage relationships among organizations. To co-ordinate activity among organizations, there must be at a minimum some exchange of information. To the extent that personnel and resources are also involved in the relationship, one can argue that the organizations are more committed to the linkage and are more closely linked. Allen (1974), Dooley (1969), and Pfeffer (1972a) have written of interfirm linkages accomplished through interlocking directorates. The linkage is even greater when there is an actual pooling of resources involved, as in the case of a joint venture. Associations among firms may lead to sharing of information, the develop-ment of norms of behavior, and the opportunity reduces competition and increases collaboration among the firms. This possibility was recognized by the court in the case of Minnesota Mining when it wrote:

. . . the intimate association of the . . . producers in day-to-day manufacturing operations, their exchange of patent licenses and industrial knowhow, and their common experience in marketing and fixing prices (for the joint venture) may inevitably reduce their zeal for competition (United States vs. Minnesota Mining and Manufacturing Company, 92 F. Supp. 947, 961–2).

The data of Mead (1967) on the lack of competitive bidding among joint bidding partners presents another illustration.

3. Data

The hypotheses were tested using Federal Trade Commission data collected on joint venture activities during the period of 1960 to 1971. Unlike the case with mergers, the Federal Trade Commission has, until recently, had only a limited interest in joint venture activity. The commission collects the joint venture data from perusal of trade association magazines, the business press, and the *Wall Street Journal*. No claim can be made for either the comprehensiveness or the accuracy of the coverage of the data. If there are biases, one is probably that the larger firms are overrepresented in the series. These data are, however, the only ones available for examining joint ventures, and since they were not collected by the authors, are not contaminated by a collection or recording process that intentionally favored the hypotheses.

Joint ventures among domestic firms were studied. The majority of all joint ventures are between domestic partners and foreign business firms. These joint ventures are undertaken as means of entry into foreign markets, when local ownership is frequently required or advisable. The rationale for these joint ventures is fundamentally different than that motivating linkages among domestic organizations, and moreover, data on the foreign partners is almost impossible to obtain. Further, only joint ventures among manufacturing organizations and with the oil and gas extraction industry were studied. Attention was restricted to manufacturing joint ventures because of the general unavailability of industry data outside of manufacturing. Oil and gas extraction was included because of the many joint ventures between firms in that industry and firms in the petroleum refining industry. A further constraint on the sample was that financial data—sales, assets, and net income—had to be available for all participating partners in the joint venture. Because the study was limited to joint ventures among domestic corporations, in manufacturing or in oil or gas extraction, and only to joint ventures for which data were available on all parent organizations, the number of joint ventures studied is somewhat smaller than the sample employed by Pate (1969) or Boyle (1968). There were 166 joint ventures included in the final sample.

Because resource interdependence measures are available only on an aggregated basis, the analysis is based on a classification of joint ventures by the 21 two-digit Standard Industrial Code classifications for the 20 manufacturing industries and oil and gas extraction. Firms are circumspect regarding their transactions with other organizations; recent Federal Trade Commission efforts to have firms report sales on a disaggregated basis have met with resistance. This necessitates the use of available statistics on transactions flows, which are consistently available only on this more aggregated level. Transactions flows have been proposed as measures of integration among political subunits (Savage and Deutsch, 1960), and particularly as measures of economic integration. Three measures of resource interdependence were computed: (1) purchase interdependence (p_{ij}) is the proportion of industry i's purchases within the set of 21 industries made from industry j; (2) sales interdependence (s_{ij}) is the proportion of industry i's sales made to industry j; and (3) total transactions interdependence (t_{ij}), which is the proportion of industry i's total transactions made with industry j, including both sales and purchases. The purchase and sales transactions measures are conceptually, if not empirically, independent. The transactions data were obtained from analyzing input-output tables showing resource flows among sectors of the American economy (Leontief, 1966).

While the Federal Trade Commission data tended to list the larger parent organization first, there is no basis for distinguishing among the partners in terms of which one initiated contact or, in many cases, which had the major ownership position in the joint subsidiary. Therefore, the matrix of joint venture activity was created in the following fashion. The 21 possible industries from which each partner could come were listed both vertically and horizontally, creating a matrix with 441 (21×21) cells. Each joint venture, except those that occurred between firms in the same industry, entered the matrix twice, once above the diagonal, and once below. Thus, for example, a joint venture between a firm in the chemicals industry (SIC 28) and one in petroleum refining (SEC 29) is listed once in the row headed by SEC 29 and in the column headed by SIC 28. Having constructed this matrix, the number of joint ventures in each cell were transformed into proportions by dividing the row totals. The dependent variable, then, is the proportion of the industry i's total joint venture activity that was with industry j (jv_{ij}). Using the example above, there were nine joint ventures between firms in the chemical industry and firms in petroleum refining. These nine joint ventures were 14.1 per cent of the total joint ventures of firms in industry 28, and 37.5 per cent of the joint ventures of those firms in industry 29.

Classification of firms into two-digit SIC industries was accomplished using the Federal Trade Commission data where available, and were based on the description of the company's activities in the few remaining instances. The sales, assets, and net income for each parent organization involved in a joint venture were obtained from *Moody's Industrial Manual* for the year in which the joint venture was founded. Data on industry concentration were obtained from Weiss (1963), whose measures are adjusted for geographic market areas and for aggregation effects. Data on the proportion of labor input and the capital intensity of the industry were obtained from the *Internal Revenue Service Statistics of Income, Corporation Tax Returns* for the years 1963 to 1967. A five-year average was taken to provide reliable estimates for the variables. The measure of the technological intensity of the industry was the proportion of scientists and engineers in research and development to total industry employment in 1969. The number of scientists and engineers was obtained from the Bureau of Labor Statistics (1969), and total industry employment from the Bureau of Labor Statistics *Handbook of Labor Statistics* (1972). Resource interdependence data were computed on a proportional basis consistent with the method used for computing the dependent variable.

4. Results

Several alternative explanations for the pattern of joint venture activities were discussed, including the need to achieve economies of scale in operation, overcome resource limitations and share risk among the joint venture participants. The size of the firms involved in these joint ventures makes these explanations implausible. The mean level of sales of the parent organizations was \$945.26 million, with a median sales level of \$567.60 million. The mean assets of the parent organizations at the time of the joint venture were \$999.53 million, and the median value was \$549.47 million. As Boyle (1968) found, there is every indication that joint ventures are under-taken by some of the largest domestic corporations. While the unavailability of data on the size of the joint ventures themselves makes rejection of the resource scarcity argument impossible, since large organizations may still face resource scarcity, the initial indications suggest other reasons for joint venture creation.

Examining the number of joint ventures that occurred between parent organizations in the same two-digit industry, out of 166 joint ventures, 92 were between parents in the same industry. This means that 55.5 per cent of the joint venture activity was undertaken with a partner in the same industry, a result consistent with those reported by Pate (1969). While the two-digit classification of firms is quite broad, if joint ventures are being undertaken for purposes of diversification, the diversification is limited to somewhat similar activities. There is little evidence that there are many conglomerate joint ventures, or joint activities undertaken by firms operating in very different industries.

Considering the relationship between the proportion of joint ventures with a given other industry and the proportion of resource exchanges with that industry, the data support the hypothesis that joint ventures tend to follow patterns of resource interdependence (Hypothesis 1). In Table 1 correlations between the proportion of industry i's joint ventures with partners in industry j, transactions between industry i and industry j, and various other characteristics of the jth industry are displayed for the entire data set. Since the variables measuring resource interdependence are independent of the variable assessing the technological intensity of the industry—the correlations between the variables are all less than .05, the data in Table 1 indicate that there are two complementary explanations for joint venture activity. As hypothesized, joint ventures are partially explained by resource interdependence among the organizations. Joint ventures are also undertaken more, however, with industries that have more advanced technology, which is

Table 1. Correlations of the Proportion of Industry i's Joint Ventures with Industry j with Other Variables

Variable	Correlation	Level of Significance
Proportion of industry i's sales to industry j	.28	$p < .001$
Proportion of industry i's purchases from industry j	.25	$p < .001$
Proportion of industry i's total transactions with industry j	.28	$p < .001$
Concentration ratio in industry j	.16	$p < .05$
Proportion of total employment engaged in research and development in industry	.25	$p < .001$

consistent with the explanation that joint ventures are used to reduce the technological risk associated with a project.

In a multiple regression, both the transactions interdependence and technology variables are statistically significant at less than the .001 level of probability. The concentration of the partner industry, however, is not significant. This indicates that joint ventures are not used primarily to enter industries that are highly concentrated, but, rather, joint ventures are undertaken to manage transactions interdependence and deal with technological risk or complexity. Recalling that jv_{ij} is the proportion of joint ventures of industry i that were with industry j, t_{ij} is the proportion of total transactions of industry i that are with industry j, c_j is the concentration ratio of industry j, and sci_j is the proportion of total employment in research and development in industry j, the estimated equation for all industries is:

$$jv_{ij} = -.526 + .271\ t_{ij} + 1.887\ sci_j + .028c \quad r^2 = .14.$$
$$\phantom{jv_{ij} = -.526 + } (.046) \qquad (.456) \qquad (.038)$$

where the numbers in parentheses are the standard errors of the respective regression coefficients.

While the results are statistically significant, only a small amount of variance has been explained. This may occur for several reasons. First, there are 166 joint ventures to be distributed over 441 cells in the matrix, which means the expected value of observing a joint venture in any given cell, assuming uniform distribution, is less than .5. Since joint ventures either occur or do not, zero is the modal expectation for observing a joint venture. Thus, zeroes in the matrix may be error or the result of a decision not to engage in joint ventures with certain industries. If those industries which have engaged in two or fewer joint ventures are eliminated, the results improve substantially. Second, it was hypothesized that resource interdependence will have differential effects on joint venture activity depending upon other characteristics of the industry. To test these hypotheses and examine the predictive power of the explanatory variables on an individual industry basis

Table 2. Correlations between Patterns of Joint Venture Activity among Parent Organizations and Independent Variables for Individual Industries

Industry	s_{ij}	p_{ij}	t_{ij}	sci_j	c_j	Number of Joint Ventures
Oil and natural gas extraction	.61•	.40••	.62•	.57•	.32•••	28
Food	.93•	.91•	.92•	−.08	.04	7
Lumber and wood products	−.07	−.06	−.07	.27	.36•••	6
Paper	−.14	−.02	−.09	−.24	−.48•	4
Printing and publishing	.76•	.36••	.56•	.30•••	.04	8
Chemicals	.93•	.97•	.96•	.56•	.21	64
Petroleum refining	.90•	.82•	.88•	.45••	.22	24
Rubber and miscellaneous products	.18	−.11	−.01	.37•••	.25	3
Stone, clay, and glass products	.86•	.69•	.84•	−.07	.21	7
Primary metals	.68•	.92•	.83•	.13	.34•••	23
Fabricated metals	.42••	−.01	.17	.73•	.26	5
Machinery, except electrical	.83•	.67•	.78•	.48••	.13	16
Electrical machinery	.89•	.90•	.95•	.58•	.31•••	28
Transportation equipment	−.09	.48••	.07	.40••	.29	8
Instruments	.61•	.47••	.62•	.60•	.20	5

Note: sij=proportion of industry i's sales to j;
  pij=proportion of industry i's purchases from j;
  tij=proportion of i's total transactions with j;
  scij=proportion of total employment in R and D for industry j; and
  cj=concentration ratio of industry j.
Since a joint venture involving industry i and industry j counts for both i and j when i ≠ j, the numbers of joint ventures in the table add up to more than 166.
  • $p < .01$ •• $p < .05$ ••• $p < .10$

for those industries that have more than two joint ventures, individual industry results are presented in Table 2.

An examination of Table 2 leads one to conclude that the hypotheses are confirmed when there are more than six joint ventures in the industry. Further, after examining patterns of joint venture activity on an industry-by-industry basis, it is evident that measures of transactions interdependence have the best explanatory utility, and the concentration ratio of the industry being linked have virtually no explanatory power. These results confirm the hypothesis that joint ventures are undertaken to manage resource interdependence and also to overcome technological risks or constraints.

The sales interdependence and transactions interdependence columns show that there is variation in the extent to which either or both measures of interdependence are related to the observed pattern of joint venture activity. It was hypothesized that purchase interdependence would be a better predictor of joint venture activity the higher the concentration of the industry (Hypothesis 2) and the more technologically intense the industry was (Hypothesis 3). Conversely, sales interdependence would be a better predictor of joint venture activity when concentration was in an intermediate range (Hypothesis 4), and both sales and purchase interdependence would be more highly correlated with observed patterns of joint venture activity to the extent that industry was capital intensive and had a relatively small ratio of labor used in its production process (Hypothesis 5).

Data relevant to these hypotheses are presented in Table 3. In this table, the variables being explained are the correlations between sales interdependence and joint venture activity, the correlation between purchase interdependence and joint venture activity, and the difference between the correlations between sales and purchase interdependence with joint venture activity. Even with the very small sample size, the hypotheses are supported. The more highly concentrated the industry, the more is purchase interdependence related to joint venture activity; the same holds for the variable measuring the technological intensity of the industry. On the other hand, sales interdependence is more highly related to joint venture activity in those industries in which concentration differs little from the median values, and both sales and purchase interdependence are less related to joint venture activity to the extent that labor forms a larger part of the input in the production process.

The results in Table 3 are important because they indicate that not only can a framework focusing on resource interdependence explain variations in

Table 3. Predicting the Relative Strength of the Relationship between Sales and Purchase Interdependence and Joint Venture Activity ($N = 15$ industries)

	Concentration Ratio	Proportion of employment in R and D	Difference in Concentration from Median Value	Labour Output Ratio	Capital Output Ratio
Correlation between sales interdependence and joint venture activity	.26	.18	−.34	−.43•	.24
Correlation between purchase interdependence and joint venture activity	.50•	.44•	−.08	−.46•	.27
Correlation between sales interdependence and joint ventures minus the correlation between purchase interdependence and joint venture activity	−.37	−.39	−.41•	.02	−.04

• $p < .10$

patterns of joint venture activity among corporations, but that considerations of the criticality and nature of the interdependence can be used to predict the conditions under which each measure of interdependence will have more or less explanatory power. In other words, the model of joint ventures as a response to interorganizational interdependence permits one to explain when the model itself will work differentially well.

Hypothesis 7 explaining variations in the extent to which parent organizations choose partners within the same industry is also confirmed by the data. The proportion of joint venture activity carried out with firms in the same two-digit industry is correlated $.39 (p < .05)$ with the concentration ratio, and is correlated $-.55$ $(p < .01)$ with the difference in industry concentration from the median value for all industries. These results indicate that to the extent that industries are more concentrated, and to the extent that they fall in an intermediate range of concentration, joint venture activity can be expected to occur more frequently with firms in the same industry.[1] And, as expected (Hypothesis 6), joint venture activity within the same industry shows little relationship to intra-industry transactions interdependence, with the correlations with sales, purchase, and total transactions interdependence all less than .07. These results indicate that joint ventures with firms in the same industry are undertaken for purposes of reducing competitive interdependence, and are unrelated to the symbiotic interdependence that exists among the organizations.

These results are particularly interesting when contrasted with the analysis of merger activity within the same industry reported by Pfeffer (1972b: 289). Merger activity within the same industry was significantly related to transactions interdependence, was not related to concentration of the industry, and was about equally as strongly related to the difference in concentration from a median value as it was to transactions interdependence. The results for merger and joint ventures taken together suggest that, as Pate (1969) has argued, joint ventures may be undertaken when mergers are proscribed, and are used relatively more than merger to cope with competitive interdependence.

....

5. Relationship between Joint Venture Parents and Progeny

It is argued that the joint venture is a form of interorganizational linkage, and that it is used to cope with environmental interdependence among the organizations. This premise can be further supported or refuted by considering the relationship between the parents and the joint ventures they are associated with.

The following data transformations were performed. First, only those joint subsidiaries that were in either manufacturing or oil and gas extraction were considered. It is possible for both the parent organizations to be in manufacturing and the joint subsidiary to be in a nonmanufacturing industry. These instances were not considered. Each of the 145 joint subsidiaries in manufacturing has two or more parent organizations. Thus, each joint subsidiary leads to two data points in a matrix of industry of parent by industry of joint subsidiary, one point for the first partner, and one point for the second. Having filled in a matrix in which the industry of the joint subsidiary is the column, and the industry of the parent organization is the row, the numbers are transformed into proportions by dividing by the row totals. The new dependent variable is the proportion of industry i's joint subsidiaries that were in industry j.

The argument is that if joint ventures are being used to deal with interdependence, the joint ventures themselves should bear some predictable relationship to the patterns of interdependence of the parent organizations. On the other hand, if joint ventures are being undertaken to diversify the organization's activities, the industry of the joint subsidiary would bear no predictable relationship to the pattern of interdependence of the parent organization.

In Table 4, correlations between (a) the proportion of parents from one industry with joint subsidiaries in another industry with (b) transactions between the two industries and other variables are presented. Considering the relationship between the industry of the parent and the industry of the joint subsidiary, even more of the variance in joint venture activity in Table 4

Table 4. Correlations of the Proportion of Industry i's Joint Subsidiaries in Industry with Other Variables

Variable	Correlation	Level of Significance
Proportion of industry i's sales to industry j	.37	$p < .001$
Proportion of industry i's purchases from industry j	.42	$p < .001$
Proportion of industry i's total transactions with industry j	.39	$p < .001$
Proportion of total employment engaged in research and development in industry j	.16	$p < .05$
Concentration ratio in industry j	.10	$p < .10$

Table 5. Correlations between Patterns of Joint Venture Activities between Parent Organizations and Progeny and Independent Variables for Individual Industries

Industry	s_{ij}	p_{ij}	t_{ij}	sci_j	c_j
Oil and natural gas extraction	.42•	.51•	.43•	.49•	.18
Food	.22	.37•	.29	−.04	−.03
Lumber and wood products	.31••	.40•	.36••	.29	.09
Paper	.81•••	.99•••	.94•••	−.10	−.12
Printing and publishing	.99•••	.55•••	.79•••	−.18	−.14
Chemicals	.98•••	.99•••	.99•••	.52•	.17
Petroleum refining	.87•••	.79•••	.85•••	.48•	.23
Stone, clay, and glass products	.81•••	.87•••	.91•••	−.12	.19
Primary metals	.61•••	.94•••	.80•••	−.07	.40•
Fabricated metals	.08	−.08	−.04	.67•••	.28
Machinery, except electrical	.93•••	.77•••	.89•••	.15	.02
Electrical machinery	.85•••	.80•••	.87•••	.65•••	.26
Transportation equipment	.60•••	.37•	.57•••	.71•••	.38•
Instruments	.66•••	.64•••	.75•••	.46•	.21

Note: s_{ij} is the proportion of industry i's sales to industry j;
  p_{ij} is the proportion of industry i's purchases from industry j;
  t_{ij} is the proportion of industry i's total transactions with j;
  sci_j is the proportion of total employment in industry j that is engaged in research and development; and
  c_j is the concentration ratio of industry j.
  • $p < .05$ •• $p < .10$ ••• $p < .01$

is accounted for by transactions interdependence, with the concentration of the industry and the proportion of research and development personnel less important. If parent jv_{ij} is defined the proportion of joint ventures from parents in industry i that are in industry j, estimating a regression equation shows:

$$\text{parent } jv_{ij} = -.568 + .464\ t_{ij} + 1.42\ sci_j + .012\ c_j \quad r^2 = .18,$$
$$(.053) \quad (.525) \quad\quad (.045)$$

where the other variables are defined as before. The coefficient of the transactions variable is statistically significant at less than the .001 level of probability, and the coefficient on the technological intensity variable is statistically significant at less than the .01 level.

In Table 5, the analyses for individual industries are displayed. Consistent with the overall regression results, an examination of the relationship between the parents and the progeny they founded indicates that transactions interdependence accounts for even more of the variance than it did in examining the relationship among the parents.

Considering the proportion of parent organizations that had joint subsidiaries in the same two-digit industry, it was observed that there was virtually no correlation with any of the transactions interdependence measures ($r=-.09$ with sales interdependence, $r=.16$ with purchase interdependence, and $r=.04$ with total transactions interdependence). The proportion of organizations having joint subsidiaries in the same industry was positively related to the concentration ratio ($r=.29$, $p < .15$), positively related to the proportion of technical personnel in the industry ($r=.43$, $p < .05$), and negatively related to the extent to which industry concentration deviated from the median value ($r=-.43$, $p < .05$). These results indicate that, considering joint subsidiaries in the same industry, transactions interdependence is not important, but the reduction of competitive interdependence is important in accounting for observed variations in patterns of joint venture activity.

The fact that the relationship among the parent organizations and the relationship between the parent organizations and the joint subsidiaries were related to resource interdependence measures as well as concentration—which is an indicator of the competitive relationship—leaves the argument that joint ventures are undertaken to take advantage of complementary strengths in doubt. The relationships follow too clearly a consistent pattern predicted by considerations of interdependence management to accept without further investigation the alternative which posits no competitive or symbiotic relationship between the parent organizations. The only other plausible hypothesis is that of technology sharing or the sharing of technological risk. This alternative is a complementary explanation for the observed pattern of joint venture activity, adding to the predictive power of the resource interdependence arguments.

6. Discussion

Two tasks confront researchers examining interorganizational behavior. The first is to develop, for a specific interorganizational behavior, a theoretical model that can account for observed variance in the behavior being examined. The second is to explain the conditions under which organizations choose some rather than other interorganizational behaviours.

This study, of joint venture activities among American corporations, addresses the first task of developing a theoretical model that can account for variance in the patterns of interorganizational behavior. It was found that considerations of managing interdependence with the environment could

Jeffrey Pfeffer and Phillip Nowak

account for some of the variance in the observed pattern of joint ventures and for variations across industries in the extent to which sales or purchase interdependence could explain these patterns. The basic findings of this study are consistent, with those authors who have argued that organizations attempt to establish stable, predictable patterns of interaction with other organizations in their environment (Cyert and March, 1963; Caves, 1970; Pfeffer, 1972b; Pfeffer and Leblebici, 1973; Phillips, 1960; Allen, 974). The evidence is accumulating that organizations do attempt to reduce uncertainty, and one source of this uncertainty is the competitive and symbiotic interdependence between the organization and other organizations and its environment.

Although the hypotheses were not disconfirmed by the available data on the pattern of joint venture activities, a large amount of unexplained variance remains. It is possible that factors unique to the organization, such as the strategy pursued by its particular management, mitigate the effect of context on the use of joint ventures. As joint ventures require pooling of resources, resource availability may affect the observed pattern of joint ventures. The development of refined measures and theories of organizational context and the relationship to organizational strategies for coping with the environment remains an important task.

While various forms of interorganizational linkage can be explained in part by considerations of resource interdependence, such explanations have said little about the use of one type of linkage rather than another. For this question, several possible explanations are available. Guetzkow (1966) argued that interorganizational relations, if mutually satisfactory, tend to become more formalized over time. Thompson and McEwen (1958) viewed the problem as one involving a trade-off between the loss of autonomy and obtaining increased certainty about the performance of other organizations. In addition to considerations of loss of autonomy, there may be legal restrictions that constrain the choice of interorganizational behaviours, as well as financial limitations that may make merger, for instance, impossible. It is also likely that firms, or even industries, develop experience with one pattern of interorganizational linkage, which then seems more comfortable. If a firm has engaged in many joint ventures in the past, this form of behavior is more familiar and less risky than if the proposed joint venture will be its first.

The present study has been concerned with joint ventures among corporations, but the extension of the propositions to nonprofit organizations is fairly straightforward, and empirical testing of the generalizability of this conceptual framework across types of organizations is important and necessary in developing an understanding of interorganizational behavior. The relative size of the joint venture compared to the size of the parent organization can be examined as one way of exploring the hypothesis that joint ventures are undertaken to overcome resource limitations. Measures of the proportion of scientific or technical personnel, or the amount of research activity undertaken may be relevant for exploring the hypothesis that nonprofit organizations undertake joint ventures for sharing technology or reducing technological risk. There are clear analogues to the concepts of purchase and sales interdependence in nonprofit organizations; since these organizations are frequently publicly funded, tracing transactions flows and resource exchanges should be substantially easier on a disaggregated basis. The structure of competition among organizations may be assessed by noting the dependence on common resources, markets, or sources of input (Elesh, 1973). Nonprofit organizations, too, have varying degrees of fixed and variable costs, which should make interdependence management more or less problematic.

The concepts of resource interdependence, relative power resulting from various sources of interdependence, and strategic actions taken to manage interdependence are all also found in Benson's (1974) political economy analysis of interorganizational behavior. The emphases on power, strategic actions, and a contest for resources and resource control add a dimension to the perspectives on interorganizational activity that have stressed cooperation and planning. The testing of propositions from this framework in a variety of contexts is required, however, before it will be possible to determine how useful these ideas are for understanding interorganizational behavior.

Note

1 Empirically, the concentration ratio of the industry and the difference in concentration from the median value are virtually independent, with $r = -.11$.

References

Aiken, Michael, and Jerald Hage (1968), 'Organizational interdependence and intra-organizational structure', *American Sociological Review*, 33: 912–30.

Allen, Michael Patrick (1974), The structure of interorganization elite cooptation: interlocking corporate directorates', *American Sociological Review*, 39: 393–406.

Baty, Gordon B., William M. Evan and Terry W. Rothermel (1971), 'Personnel flows as interorganizational relations', *Administrative Science Quarterly*, 16: 430–43.

Benson, J. Kenneth (1974), 'The Interorganizational Network as a Political Economy', paper presented at the Eighth World Congress of Sociology, International Sociological Association, Toronto, Canada, August 18–24, 1974.

Bernstein, Lewis (1965), 'Joint ventures in the light of recent antitrust developments: anti-competitive joint ventures', *The Antitrust Bulletin*, 10: 25–9.

Boyle, Stanley E. (1968), 'An estimate of the number and size distribution of domestic joint subsidiaries', *Antitrust Law and Economics Review*, 1: 81–92.

Bureau of Labor Statistics (1969), *Scientific and Technical Personnel in Industry*, Bulletin No. 1723 (Washington: GPO).

———(1972), *Handbook of Labor Statistics* (Washington: GPO).

Caves, Richard E. (1970), 'Uncertainty, market structure and performance: Galbraith as conventional wisdom' in J. W. Markham and G. F. Papanek (eds.), *Industrial Organization and Economic Development* (Boston: Houghton Mifflin) 283–302.

Clark, Burton R. (1965), 'Interorganizational patterns in education', *Administrative Science Quarterly*, 10: 224–37.

Cyert, Richard M., and James G. March (1963), *A Behavioral Theory of the Firm* (Englewood Cliffs, N.J.: Prentice-Hall).

Dooley, Peter C. (1969), 'The interlocking directorate' *American Economic Review*, 59: 314–23.

Elesh, David (1973), 'Organization sets and the structure of competition for new members', *Sociology of Education*, 46: 371–95.

Evan, William M. (1966), 'The organization-set: toward a theory of interorganizational relations', in James D. Thompson (ed.), *Approaches to Organizational Design* (Pittsburgh: University of Pittsburgh Press) 173–91.

Fusfeld, Daniel R. (1958), 'Joint subsidiaries in the iron and steel industry', *American Economic Review*, 48: 578–87.

Guetzkow, Harold (1966), 'Relations among organizations', in R. V. Bowers (ed.), *Studies on Behavior in Organizations* (Athens: University of Georgia Press) 13–44.

Hawley, Amos (1950), *Human Ecology* (New York: Ronald Press).

Internal Revenue Service (1963–7), *Statistics of Income, Corporation Income Tax Returns* (Washington: GPO).

Leontief, Wassily (1966), *Input-Output Economics* (New York: Oxford University Press).

Levine, Joel H. (1972), 'The sphere of influence', *American Sociological Review*, 37: 14–27.

Levine, Sol, and Paul E. White (1961), 'Exchange as a conceptual framework for the study of interorganizational relationships', *Administrative Science Quarterly*, 5: 583–601.

Litwak, Eugene, and Lydia F. Hylton (1962), 'Interorganizational analysis: a hypothesis on coordinating agencies', *Administrative Science Quarterly*, 6: 395–420.

Litwak, Eugene, and Jack Rothman (1970), 'Towards the theory and practice of coordination between formal organizations', in William R. Rosengren and Mark Lefton (eds.), *Organizations and Clients* (Columbus, Ohio: Merrill) 137–186.

Macaulay, Stewart (1963), 'Non-contractual relations in business: a preliminary study', *American Sociological Review*, 28: 55–67.

Mead, Walter J. (1967), 'The competitive significance of joint ventures', *Antitrust Bulletin*, 12: 819–49.

Moody's Investors Service (1960ff), *Moody's Industrial Manual* (New York: Moody's Investors Service).

Pate, James L. (1969), 'Joint venture activity, 1960–1968', *Economic Review*, Federal Reserve Bank of Cleveland, 16–23.

Pfeffer, Jeffrey (1972a), 'Size and composition of corporate boards of directors: the organization and its environment', *Administrative Science Quarterly*, 17: 218–28.

————(1972b), 'Merger as a response to organizational interdependence', *Administrative Science Quarterly*, 17: 382–94.

Pfeffer, Jeffrey, and Huseyin Leblebici (1973), 'Executive recruitment and the development of interfirm organizations', *Administrative Science Quarterly*, 18: 449–61.

Phillips, Almarin (1960), 'A theory of interfirm organization', *Quarterly Journal of Economics*, 74: 602–13.

Savage, I. Richard, and Karl W. Deutsch (1960), 'A statistical model of the gross analysis of transaction flows', *Econometrica*, 28: 551–72.

Thompson, James D., and W. J. McEwen (1958), 'Organizational goals and environment', *American Sociological Review*, 23: 23–31.

Weiss, Leonard W. (1963), 'Average concentration ratios and industrial performance', *Journal of Industrial Economics*, 11: 237–54.

Yuchtman, Ephraim, and Stanley E. Seashore (1967), 'A system resource approach to organizational effectiveness', *American Sociological Review*, 32: 891–903.

Peter J. Buckley and Mark Casson

1. Introduction

Joint ventures (JVs) have always been an important aspect of business organization. The partnership, which is so common in the professions, is an example of a joint venture between individuals. Inter-firm joint ventures have played an important role in the expansion of MNEs into new markets—as when a sales affiliate is established with an indigenous distribution company as a partner. Recently joint ventures have become a popular form of alliance between established MNEs, and the high profile of these ventures means that JVs have attracted much more attention (Contractor and Lorange, 1988; Harrigan, 1985; Hladik, 1985; Killing, 1983).

As a result of this trend, JVs are playing an important role in the restructuring of the international economy. In some cases they are simply transitional arrangements, associated with the gradual spinning off of an existing plant to a new owner. The joint venture, in other words, is a form of staggered divestment or acquisition. This approach may be useful in avoiding loss of face for the divesting firm, and in minimizing the risk of unfavourable political reaction when the acquiring firm is a foreign one. It also allows the diversing firm to tutor the acquiring firm in managerial and technical skills during the transition period. Given that such JVs are specifically transitional, the fact that they last only a limited time does not necessarily mean that they have failed in their purpose (Kogut, 1988).

In other cases, however, JVs are expected to establish enduring links between the partners—as, for example, in some ventures concerning basic R&D. These ventures are often hailed as 'collaborative' agreements. This is particularly true in respect of 50:50 equity joint ventures, whose symmetry of ownership is often taken as symbolic of a new spirit in international business—a creative alternative to the competitive forces on which so many previous corporate and industrial policies have been based.

This raises the crucial question of whether 50:50 ventures can really support such an optimistic interpretation. On the face of it, the ambiguity of control implied by the symmetry of ownership suggests that there must be a high degree of trust between the two parties. On the other hand, a more detailed investigation of a venture often reveals that the right to manage is assigned to just one of the partners and that the other has an essentially sleeping role. Even if there is genuine joint participation in management, the way the venture is linked to the partner's own activities may give one partner considerably more bargaining power than the other.

It would be wrong to suggest, however, that the spirit of co-operation has no place within the JV at all. This chapter sets out to examine first how far a successful JV strategy can be explained entirely in conventional terms—that is, in terms of the internalization decisions of profit-maximizing firms who have no spirit of co-operation at all. The analysis in Sections 2–7 shows that such a 'reductionist' explanation is indeed possible, although the costs arising from ambiguity of control mean that a JV would be preferred only under rather extreme conditions.

The introduction of a spirit of co-operation in Sections 8–12 modifies this analysis in two main ways. First, it shows that a spirit of co-operation will reduce transaction costs generally, and that it will reduce them particularly significantly for JV operation. Secondly, it shows that JV operation may be a technique for creating a spirit of co-operation in the first place. Thus JV operation may be an investment in which high transaction costs are incurred in the short run in order to reduce transaction costs in the long run. The future savings in transaction costs arise from the improved climate of trust in which further ventures can be negotiated.

The chapter concludes with some reflections on the pitfalls and potentials of cross-cultural joint venturing, with special reference to Japan.

2. The Internalization Approach to Joint Ventures

The analysis focuses on a 50:50 JV involving two private firms. Although arrangements involving state-owned firms and government agencies are very important in practice (particularly in developing countries), they raise issues which lie beyond the scope of this chapter. To the extent, however, that the state sector is primarily profit-motivated, the analysis below will still apply.

It is assumed that each partner in the JV already owns other plants.

It is also assumed that the JV is pre-planned, and that the equity stakes are not readily tradable in divisible units. This means, in particular, that the joint ownership of the venture cannot be explained by a 'mutual-fund' effect—in other words, it is not the chance outcome of independent portfolio diversification decisions undertaken by the two firms.

Working under these assumptions, theory must address three key issues:

1. Why does each partner wish to own part of the JV rather than simply trade with it on an arm's-length basis? The answer is that there must be some net benefit from internalizing a market in one or more intermediate goods and services flowing between the JV and the parties' other operations. A *symmetrically motivated* JV is defined as one in which each firm has the same motive for internalizing. This is the simplest form of JV to study, and is the basis for the detailed discussion presented later.

2. Why does each firm own half of the JV rather than all of another plant? The force of this question rests on an implicit judgement that joint ownership poses managerial problems of accountability that outright ownership avoids. To the extent that this is true, there must be some compensating advantage in not splitting up the jointly owned plan into two (or possibly more) separate plants. In other words, there must be an element of economic indivisibility in the plant. The way this indivisibility manifests itself will depend upon how the JV is linked into the firms' other operations.

(a) If the JV generates a homogeneous output which is shared between the partners, or uses a homogeneous input which is sourced jointly by them, then the indivisibility is essentially an economy of scale.

(b) If the JV generates two distinct outputs, one of which is used by one partner and the other by the other, then the indivisibility is essentially an economy of scope.

(c) If the JV combines two different inputs, each of which is contributed by just one of the parties, then the indivisibility manifests itself simply as a technical complementarity between the inputs (i.e. a combination of a diminishing marginal rate of technical substitution and non-decreasing returns to scale).

3. Given that, in the light of (1) and (2), each partner wishes to internalize a linkage to the same indivisible plant, why do the partners not merge themselves, along with the JV, into a single corporate entity? The answer must be that there is some net disadvantage to such a merger. It may be managerial diseconomies arising from the scale and diversity of the resultant enterprise, legal obstacles stemming from anti-trust policy or restrictions on

foreign acquisitions, difficulties of financing because of stock market scepticism. And so on.

It is clear, therefore, that JV operation is to be explained in terms of a combination of three factors, namely internalization economies, indivisibilities, and obstacles to merger. Other factors too can be added, if other questions are asked: for example, why are there only *two* partners in the JV, and not more, and why does each partner hold an equal share of the equity? The answer to the first question lies in indivisibilities—both technological and organizational—within the partner firms themselves. The answer to the second lies in the nature of the risks to which each partner is exposed as a result of the other partner's actions, and the way that the votes of equity-owners are aggregated to determine who has effective control. For the purposes of this chapter, however, it is sufficient to work with just the three main factors noted above.

There are many contractual alternatives to JV operations (see Casson, 1987, ch. 5), but for policy purposes particular interest centres on the question of when a JV will be preferred to outright ownership of a foreign subsidiary. Given that location factors, such as resource endowments, result in two interdependent plants being located in different countries, the first of the three factors mentioned above—internalization economies—militates in favour of outright ownership. It is the extent to which it is constrained by the other two factors—indivisibilities and obstacles to merger—that governs the strength of preference for a JV. The larger indivisibilities are, the greater the obstacles to merger, and the smaller internalization economies are (relative to the other two factors), the more likely it is that the JV will be chosen.

3. The Configuration of a JV Operation

The configuration of a JV is a concept derived from the systems view of production. The configuration is determined by whether the plant stands upstream or downstream with respect to each partner's other operations, and by the nature of the intermediate products that flow between them. A JV arrangement is said to be *symmetrically positioned* if each partner stands in exactly the same (upstream or downstream) relation to the JV operation as does the other. Fig. 1a illustrates symmetric forward integration, and Fig. 1b symmetric backward integration. Sometimes an operation may be integrated both backwards and forwards into the same partner's operations. Fig. 1c illustrates a symmetric buy-back arrangement in which each partner effectively subcontracts the processing of a product to the same jointly owned plant.

Some writers suggest that 50:50 JVs are inherently symmetrical because of the pattern of ownership, but this is far from actually being the case. JVs may, for a start, be asymmetrically positioned with respect to the partners' operations. Fig. 1d illustrates a multi-stage arrangement in which one partner integrates forward into the JV and the other integrates backwards; such an arrangement is quite common in JVs formed to transfer proprietary technology to a foreign environment.

Even if a JV is symmetrically positioned, it does not follow that it is symmetrically configured, for the intermediate products flowing to and from the respective partners may be different. It is only when both the positioning is symmetrical and the products are identical that the configuration is fully symmetrical in the sense defined above.

The fact that the configuration is symmetrical does not guarantee that the motivation for internalization is symmetrical too. If each partner, for example, resells the JV output within a different market structure, then the motivation for internalization may differ in spite of the fact that the configuration is symmetric.

The symmetry properties illustrated in Figs. 1a–1c refer only to the immediate connections between the JV and the rest of the partners' operations. Each partner's operations may be differently configured from the others. This means that while the activities directly connected with the JV are symmetrically configured, the operations when considered as a whole may be asymmetric. Thus the symmetry concept used above was essentially one of local symmetry, and not of global symmetry. While global symmetry implies local symmetry, the converse does not apply.

The distinction between local and global symmetry has an important bearing on the question of the distribution of economic power between the parties. It is important to appreciate that local symmetry does not guarantee that there is a balance of economic power between the parties to the JV. It is quite possible, for example, that one of the partners may own plants which are potential substitutes for the jointly owned plant, while the other partner does not. This becomes important if the other partner could not easily gain access to an alternative plant should the first partner place some difficulty in his way. It may be, for example, that the first partner holds a monopoly of alternative plants. This means that in bargaining over the use of the jointly owned plant, the first partner is likely to have the upper hand. He can use his power either to secure priorities for himself through non-price rationing, or to insist on trading with the JV at more favourable prices. The fact that the JV is 50:50 owned implies only that the residual income is

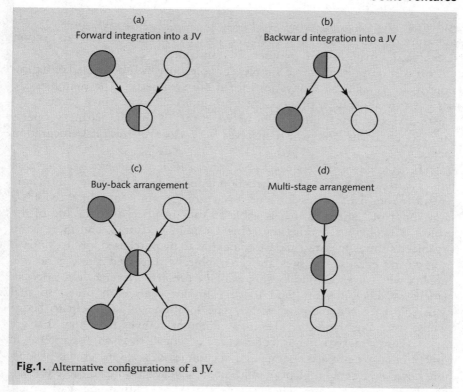

Fig.1. Alternative configurations of a JV.

divided equally between the partners; it does not guarantee that total income is divided equally. And, as argued above, a locally symmetrical configuration does not guarantee that total income will be divided equally. It is symmetry of substitution possibilities that is crucial in this respect. Symmetry of substitution is likely to occur only with global symmetry, and this is a much less common type of configuration.

4. JV Operations Motivated by Lack of Confidence in Long-Term Arm's-Length Contracts

The next four sections illustrate how different motives for internalization manifest themselves in various contexts. Some rather mundane examples are given, to emphasize that the analysis is quite general, and does not apply just to large international ventures. Readers familiar with the most recent literature on internalization theory may prefer to proceed directly to Section 8, where the main line of argument is resumed.

This section presents three simple examples in which both the configuration of the JV and the motivations for it are symmetric. The examples are designed to illustrate a progression from internalization which involves no day-to-day operational integration between the JV and the partners' operations to internalization which involves very close operational integration indeed.

1. *Hedging intermediate product price movements in the absence of a long-term futures market.* Consider the construction industry, in which main contractors have to quote fixed prices for long-term projects, some of which require a large input of cement, which is liable to vary in price over the life of the project. For obvious reasons the cement cannot be stored, and there is no organized futures market either. Cement has to be purchased locally for each project, and because the sites are geographically dispersed, there is no one supplier who can economically supply all the projects. Nevertheless, prices of cement at different sites tend to vary in line with each other, so that ownership of a cement plant at any one location will still help to hedge against price fluctuations in the many different sources of supply that are used. There are two major contractors of equal size who specialize in cement-intensive projects. Because of economies of scale in cement production, however, a cement plant of efficient scale generates much more cement that either contractor uses. There is one plant whose output price varies most closely with the average price of cement paid by the contractors, and so they each acquire half of the equity in this plant. This is the most efficient mechanism available for diversifying their risks relating to the price of cement. It involves no operation integration whatsoever between the cement plant and the site activities.

2. *Avoiding recurrent negotiation under bilateral monopoly over the price of a differentiated intermediate product.* Suppose there are two firms which are the only users of an intermediate product which is produced with economies of scale. It is difficult for either firm to switch away from the product, since it has no close substitutes. Upstream, therefore, there is a natural monopoly, while downstream there is a duopsony. Before any party incurs non-recoverable set-up costs through investment in specific capacity, it would be advantageous to negotiate once and for all long-term supply contracts for the product (Klein, Crawford and Alchian, 1978; Williamson, 1985). Because of the difficulty of enforcing such contracts, however, the duopsonists may prefer to acquire jointly the upstream facility. This insures both of them against a strategic price rise initiated by an independent natural monopolist. The fact that both share in the residual risks also helps to discourage them

from adversarial behaviour towards each other. A modest degree of operational integration is likely in this case.

3. *Operational integration between upstream and downstream plants in the absence of efficient short-term forward markets.* Extending the construction industry example, suppose that the two firms have long-term projects in hand at adjacent sites, and require various types of form-work to be supplied to mould the concrete foundations. The form-work is customized and each piece has to be in place precisely on time. Both firms are sceptical about devising enforceable incentives for prompt supply by a sub-contractor, as arm's-length forward contracts are difficult to enforce in law. Because of the small scale of local demand relative to the capacity of an efficient-size team of workers, the two contractors may decide to ensure timely deliveries through backward integration into a JV. Unlike the previous arrangements, this involves close day-to-day management of an intermediate product flow between the owners and the JV.

5. Quality Uncertainty

Quality uncertainty can manifest itself in many different contexts. Four examples are given below to demonstrate the ubiquity of this phenomenon.

1. *Insuring against defective quality in components.* This example relates to forward integration involving two distinct flows of materials. Consider two components which are assembled to make a product. The quality of the components is difficult to assess by inspection, and other methods of assessment, such as testing to destruction, are expensive—not least in terms of wasted product. Reliable performance of the final product is crucial to the customer, and failure of the final product is often difficult to diagnose and attribute to one particular component. Because of legal impediments, it is impossible to integrate the assembly with the production of both components comprehensively and an independent assembler would lack confidence in subcontracted component supplies. If two independent component producers form a JV, however, then each can enjoy a measure of confidence in the other, since each knows that the other bears half the penalty incurred by the venture if he supplies a defective product to it. This is the JV analogue of the 'buyer uncertainty' argument emphasized in the internalization literature.

2. *Adapting a product to an overseas market.* This example involves the combination of two distinct but complementary types of know-how in the

operation of an indivisible facility. The first type of know-how is technologi-cal, and is typically embodied in the design of a sophisticated product developed in an industrialized country. The other is knowledge of an over-seas market possessed by an indigenous foreign firm. The complementarity concerns their use in adapting the design and marketing strategy of the product to overseas conditions. The indivisible facility is the plant used to manufacture it overseas. Together these elements make up the classic example of the use of a JV to commence overseas production of a maturing product.

3. *Management training and the transfer of technology.* In some cases a JV may be chosen as a vehicle for training. Employees of a technologically advanced firm are seconded to a JV to train other employees who will remain with the venture when it is later spun off to the currently technolo-gically backward partner. Training involves two inputs, rather than just the one that is usually assumed. It requires not only the knowledge and teaching ability of the tutor, but also the time, attention, and willingness to learn of the tutee. The tutee may be uncertain of the quality of the tutor's knowledge and ability, and may demand that the tutor bears all the commercial risks associated with the early stages of the venture. The tutor, on the other hand, may be uncertain of the effort supplied by the tutee, which could jeopardize the performance of the venture if it were poor, and so may require the tutee to bear some of the risks as well. These conflicting requirements are partially reconciled by a JV which requires both to bear some of the risks and thereby gives each an incentive to maintain a high quality of input. Those incentives can be further strengthened, in some cases, by a buy-back arrange-ment—or production-sharing arrangement as it is sometimes called—which encourages each party to use the output that the newly trained labour has produced and thereby gives an additional incentive to each party to get the training right (Mirus and Yeung, 1986).

4. *Buy-back arrangements in collaborative R&D.* Buy-back arrangements, which combine backward and forward integration, are particularly common in collaborative research. In the research context, both the inputs to and the outputs from the JV are services derived from the heterogeneous intangible assets (i.e. they are flows of knowledge).

Consider two firms, each with a particular area of corporate expertise, who license their patents and second personnel to a joint research project (the indivisible facility). The planned output—new knowledge—is a proprie-tary public good, which is licensed back to the two firms. Each firm may be suspicious of the quality of the input supplied by the other firm, but the fact that the other firm not only holds an equity stake in the project, but also plans to use the product of the research for its own purposes serves to reassure the first firm that the quality will be good (though there still remains a risk that personnel and ideas of the very best quality will be held back). Likewise, the fact that the firm itself has partially contributed to the production of the new knowledge is a reassuring factor when it comes to implementing this knowledge in downstream production.

6. Collusion

The role of indivisibility facilities in the previous discussion can, in fact, be taken over by any arrangement which either reduces the costs of two plants by co-ordinating their input procurement, or enhances the value of their outputs by co-ordinating their marketing. The former is relevant to backward integration by firms into a JV, while the latter pertains to forward integration instead. The forward integration case, discussed below, shows the JV to be an alternative to a cartel.

Consider two firms which have identified an opportunity for colluding in their sales policy. They may have independently discovered a new technology, territory, or mineral deposit and wish to avoid competition between them in its exploitation. They may, on the other hand, be established duopolists operating behind an entry barrier, who would benefit from fixing prices or quotas to maximize their joint profits from the industry, (The nature of the entry barrier is irrelevant to the argument—it may be based on technological advantage, or brand names, statutory privilege, exclusive access to inputs, and so on).

The main problem with a sales cartel is the mutual incentive to cheat by undercutting the agreed price—for example, by selling heavily discounted items through unofficial outlets. This poses an acute monitoring problem for each party. Channelling sales through a JV reduces the incentive to cheat, since the gains from cheating are partially outweighed by the reduction in profits earned from the JV. Economies in monitoring costs may also be achieved if both parties specialize this function with the JV.

7. Hostages: Internalizing the Implementation of Counter-threats

In an atmosphere of mutual distrust, an imbalance in the vulnerability of two parties to a breakdown of the venture can further undermine confidence in it. This suggests the possibility that instead of collaborating on a single venture they should collaborate on two ventures instead. The function of the second venture is to counteract the imbalance in the first venture by giving the least vulnerable party in the first venture the greatest vulnerability in the second venture. Suppose, for example, that the two firms wished to collude in a product market where one firm has a much larger market share, coupled with much higher fixed costs, than the other. This is the firm that is most vulnerable to cheating by the other (Casson, 1987, ch. 3). To redress the balance, it may be advantageous for the two firms to agree on some other venture—say collaborative research—to run in parallel with a collusive JV to give the weaker firm an effective sanction against the stronger one. In such a case, the primary motive for the second JV concerns nothing intrinsic to the venture itself, but simply its ability to support the other venture.

It should be clear from the preceding examples that there are an enormous number of different forms that JV operation can take. Each of the three main factors—the internalization motive, the indivisibility, and the obstacle to merger—can take several different forms. The internalization motive may differ between the firms. Add to this the considerable diversity of global configurations, and it can be seen that the permutations to which these aspects lend themselves make any simple typology of JV operations out of the question. While the economic principles governing the logic of JV operation are intrinsically quite straightforward, the way that environmental influences select the dominant factors in any one case is extremely complex.

8. The Role of Co-operation

The concept of 'co-operative spirit', outlined in Section 1, will now be examined. Spontaneous co-operation can be elicited as a rational response to the gains from co-ordination available in small, stable, compact groups. Enlightened self-interest encourages people to initiate and to reciprocate friendly behaviour. They do this by forbearing from taking advantage of other people in the group. Co-ordination of activities, effected through mutual forbearance of this kind, may be regarded as the essence of co-operation. Correspondingly, an expectation that the other party will forbear is the basis of trust.

Enlightened self-interest will not motivate co-ordination under all conditions, however. For example, in a chance encounter between two parties who are never likely to meet again, the problem of the 'prisoner's dilemma' remains unresolved, and each party is likely to cheat the other. It is possible, however, that co-operation could be pursued not merely as a means to an end, but as an end in itself. It was noted earlier that there is a moral dimension to preferences, so that, within limits, what individuals want is mainly what they regard as morally legitimate. Moral arguments in favour of co-operation, if convincing, can therefore establish co-operation as an end in itself. The close contact between individuals within a compact social group means that there is an ample opportunity to promote co-operation through personal example and rhetoric. It is easy to share information within a compact group, and this 'information' includes moral values.

Although these remarks are directed principally at co-operation between individuals, they may be applied to co-operation between firms as well. For the leadership of a firm has the opportunity to develop a corporate culture in which the spirit of co-operation plays an important part. The leadership of each firm can therefore encourage the employees to adopt a co-operative attitude to the partner firm.

The degree of commitment to a venture is likely to be conditional upon certain characteristics of the venture. The commitment of the partners is likely to be higher, for example, the more socially meritorious or strategically important the output is deemed to be. Commitment will also tend to be higher if the distribution of rewards from the venture, when it is successfully completed, is deemed equitable by all parties. Envy of the share of gains appropriated by another partner can not only diminish motivation, but can encourage cheating—which may be 'justified' as a means of generating a more equitable outcome. It is one of the characteristics of the 50:50 JV that, superficially at least, the distribution of rewards seems fair.

9. Co-operation as an Output

To what extent can it be said that one contractual arrangement is more co-operative than another? To answer this question, it is necessary to distinguish between co-operation as an input to a venture, and co-operation as an output from it. An arrangement which gives all parties a strong incentive to cheat requires a great deal of mutual forbearance if it is to be successful. Loosely speaking, it requires a large input of co-operation. In one respect, this is a weakness rather than a strength of the arrangement, since it means that in practice the arrangement is quite likely to fail.

Co-operation may be regarded as an output when an arrangement leads to greater trust between the parties, which reduces the transaction costs of subsequent ventures in which they are involved. Focusing on co-operation as an output gives a perspective which is closest to the common-sense view that co-operative ventures are a 'good thing'.

There is a connection, however, between input and output. This is because an arrangement which calls for a considerable input of co-operation, and turns out successfully, enhances the reputations of the parties. First and foremost, it enhances their reputations with each other, but if there are spectators to the arrangement, then it enhances their reputations with them too.

The connection between input and output suggests that some arrangements may be more efficient than others in transforming an input of co-operation into an output. More precisely, co-operation is efficient when a given amount of mutual forbearance generates the largest possible amount of mutual trust. Efficiency is achieved by devising the arrangement of the venture so as to speed up the acquisition of reputation. The reason why the reputation-building may be slow is that cheating is often a covert practice—it is more viable if it goes undetected—and so it may be a long time before parties can be certain whether an agent has cheated or not. The importance of this factor varies from one venture to another, depending upon how easy it is for agents to make their own contribution, and monitor and supervise their partners at the same time.

To speed up reputation-building, it may be advantageous to create, with the arrangement itself, additional opportunities for agents to forbear reciprocally. Thus a venture may provide for a sequence of decisions to be taken by each party, in each of which there is a degree of conflict between their interests. Each agent (except the first-mover) has an opportunity to respond to his partner's move. The essence of this reputation-building mechanism is threefold:

1. the decisions are open and overt, rather than secret and covert;

2. behaviour in the covert decisions is related to behaviour in the overt ones; and

3. behaviour is not modified as the incentive structure changes due to the greater opportunities for cheating that present themselves as the partner becomes more trusting.

These conditions ensure that commitment cannot simply be mimicked until the greatest gains from cheating can be appropriated. They imply that the alternative to commitment is some other kind of habitual behaviour, whose dishonesty will reveal itself in small things as well as large. The willingness to enter a JV arrangement in the first place will therefore reflect the degree of optimism not only that commitment is present, but that subtle deviousness which cannot be screened out is not present either. While a committed partner can be trusted whether or not he is clever, an uncommitted partner should, for preference, be a rather stupid creature of habit.

There are certain types of venture which naturally facilitate reputation-building. In long-term ventures in a volatile environment, for example, there is very sound logic for deferring certain decisions until after the venture has begun—namely that new information may subsequently become available that is relevant to how later parts of it are carried out. It may well be appropriate to delegate these decisions to the individuals who are most likely to have this information to hand. It then becomes possible to 'fine tune' the degree of discretion to the amount of trust already present. Thus it is quite common to observe that when a number of parties work together for the first time, a tight discipline is imposed to begin with, which is then progressively relaxed as the parties begin to trust each other more.

10. The Influence of Functional Specialization on the Co-operative Content of a JV

Some ventures lend themselves naturally to an internal organizational structure which encourages reputation-building. These ventures call for widespread decentralization of decision-making, afford decisions of varying degrees of responsibility, and call for the sharing of information. They provide ample opportunity for overt behaviour, and only limited opportunity for covert behaviour. These considerations suggest that certain motives for JV operation are far more conducive to co-operation than are others. It is, in fact, the combination of the motive and the main activity performed by the JV that seems to be crucial in this respect.

In the production sector, JVs which involve very little operational integration with the partners' other activities provide little opportunity for the partners to meet and interact on a regular basis. The greater the degree of operational integration, the greater is the regularity with which forbearance may have to be exercised when short-term hold-ups occur in production, and the greater are the opportunities for sharing information in the planning of production. Quality uncertainty provides a motive for both parties to open up their wholly owned operations to their JV partner once a certain degree of trust has been established, and so provides a natural route through which co-operation could progress to a point where it embraces production, product development and basic research.

Joint R&D is naturally co-operative because it is based upon the sharing of information and, for reasons already noted, the sharing of information often leads to the emergence of shared values too. This may, perhaps, partly explain why collaborative R&D seems to enjoy a special mystique all of its own.

Of the various functional areas in which JV operations can occur, sales and procurement are the least promising so far as true co-operation is concerned. A dominant motive for JV operations in this area is collusion. Collusion affords large incentives to cheat, and therefore requires a major input of co-operation. The maintenance of a high price in a static market environment—so characteristic of many collusive arrangements—does not, however, create much need for meetings at which open forbearance and reciprocity can be displayed. Collusion emphasizes the covert rather than overt dimension of behaviour. It therefore generates little output of trust. The most promising area for co-operation in marketing arises when a proprietary product is transferred to a new country, for then both the source firm and the recipient firm need to share information. Since the demand is uncertain, but has considerable growth potential, the market environment is dynamic rather than static, and so, unlike the case of collusion, it provides opportunities for deferring key decisions and delegating in a way that allows both parties to demonstrate forbearance.

11. The International Dimension

So far nothing has been said specifically about the international aspects of JV operation. To a certain extent this is deliberate, since there are no reasons to believe that the familiar factors of international cost differentials, tariffs, transport costs and variations in the size of regional markets are any different for JVs than they are for other international operations. It can, however, be argued that the political risks of expropriation, the blocking of profit repatriation, and so on, are lower in the case of a JV than in the case of a wholly owned operation, though empirical support for this view is very limited, to say the least. Tax-minimizing transfer pricing, though not impossible with JVs, is more difficult to administer because of the need to negotiate the prices with the partner, and to find a subterfuge for paying any compensation involved.

So far as the general concept of co-operation is concerned, the international dimension is much less important than the intercultural dimension. In purely conventional analysis of transaction costs, the focus is on the legal enforcement of contracts, and so the role of the nation state is clearly paramount in respect of both its legislation and its judicial procedures. The mechanism of co-operation, however, is trust rather than legal sanction, and trust depends much more on the unifying influence of the social group than on the coercive power of the state. Trust will normally be much stronger between members of the same extended family, ethnic group, or religious group, even though it transcends national boundaries, than between members of different groups within the same country.

This means that in comparing the behaviour of large firms legally domiciled in different countries, differences in behaviour are just as likely to reflect cultural differences in the attitudes of senior management as the influence of the fiscal and regulatory environment of the home country. Cultural attitudes are certainly likely to dominate in respect of the disposition to co-operate with other firms. In this context, it may be less important to know whether a corporation is British or Italian, say, than to know whether its senior management is predominantly Quaker or Jewish, Protestant or Catholic, Anglo-Saxon or Latin, and so on. National and cultural characteristics are correlated, but not perfectly so. In some instances, such as Japanese firms, it has proved extremely problematic to disentangle them.

In the light of these remarks, it is clear that JV operations involving firms with different cultural backgrounds are of particular long-term significance. Once established, they provide a mechanism for cultural exchange, particularly as regards attitudes to co-operation. The success of this mechanism will depend upon how receptive each firm is to ideas emanating from an alien culture. Where the firm is receptive, participation in international JVs may have lasting effects on its behaviour not only in international operations, but in many other areas too.

12. Networks of Interlocking JVs

The recent proliferation of international JVs means that many firms are now involved in several JVs. Two JVs are said to interlock when the same firm is a

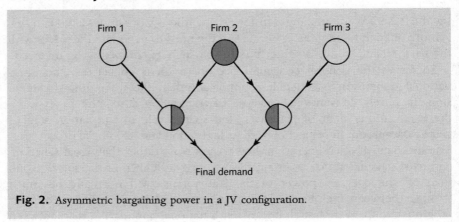

Fig. 2. Asymmetric bargaining power in a JV configuration.

partner in both. It is not always recognized as clearly as it should be that a set of interlocking JVs is an extremely effective way for a firm to develop monopoly power at minimal capital cost. By taking a part-interest in a number of parallel ventures, producing the same product with a different partner in each case, the firm can not only establish a strong market position against buyers of the product, but it can also create a strong bargaining position against each partner as well.

Once an individual partner is committed to a venture, he is vulnerable if the monopolist threatens to switch production to one of his other JVs instead. The partner has no similar option because the remaining facilities are all partly controlled by the monopolist. The vulnerable firm may be obliged to renegotiate terms under duress. Although the monopolist may stand to lose by withdrawing production from one JV, he will be able to recover most of these losses from enhanced profits arising from the JVs to which production is switched.

A situation of this kind is illustrated in Fig. 2. Firm 2 has the ability to switch production between the two downstream plants, but neither Firm 1 nor Firm 3 has this option because the only other plant is partly controlled by Firm 2. Although each JV is symmetrically configured in a local sense, the overall situation is globally asymmetric. Superficially, it may seem that Firm 2 is a 'good co-operator' because it is involved in more JVs than either of the other firms, but in reality its claim to co-operate may simply be a subterfuge. Firm 2 can, in fact, not only exercise monopoly power against the buyers of downstream output, but also play off its partners against each other. In this case it is conflict, not co-operation, and deception, not trust, that is the driving force in Firm 2's choice of JV operation.

13. Conclusion

JVs are, first and foremost, a device for mitigating the worst consequences of mistrust. In the language of internalization theory, they represent a compromise contractual arrangement which minimizes transaction costs under certain environmental constraints. But some types of JV also provide a suitable context in which the parties can demonstrate mutual forbearance, and thereby build up trust. This may open up possibilities for co-ordination which could not otherwise be entertained. The prospect of this encourages partners to take an unusually open-ended view of JV partnerships, and gives JVs their political and cultural mystique.

An important role of JVs, from the limited perspective of internalization economics, is to minimize the impact of quality uncertainty on collaborative research and training. From the more open-ended perspective of long-term co-operation, however, JVs designed to cope with quality uncertainty are also well adapted to help partners to reciprocate, and also to learn the values which inspire the other partner to unreserved commitment to a venture. Without doubt, JVs of this type offer a way forward to genuine co-operation in international economic relations in the future.

The analysis also suggests, however, that a degree of cynicism may be warranted in respect of the claims advanced for JVs of certain kinds. A JV may be merely a subterfuge, luring partners into making commitments which leave them exposed to the risk of renegotiation under duress. It may be a device for enhancing collusion—a practice that may be warranted if it is necessary to recover the costs of technological or product innovation, but not otherwise. It may represent a pragmatic response to regulatory distortion—as when a misguided national competition policy outlaws a merger between the partners that would afford considerable efficiency gains; the JV, in this case, is better than nothing at all, but is only second best to a policy of removing the distortion itself.

One of the most topical applications of the theory of the JV is to industrial co-operation and production-sharing arrangements involving Japanese firms (Hull, Slowinski, Wharton, and Azumi, 1988; Pucik, 1988). To what extent, for example, can quality uncertainty in the training process support the argument that the Japanese JV is an appropriate vehicle for tutoring partners in developing countries? Are Japanese JV networks in South East Asia merely agglomerations of independent JV operations, or are they part of a wider strategy to play off one partner against another in an effort to maintain low prices for Japanese imports and thereby assure the competitiveness of Japanese re-exports?

Peter J. Buckley and Mark Casson

Other questions may be asked, for example, of Western corporations that seem anxious to co-operate with the Japanese. Are they really interested in long-term collaboration in the development of leading edge technologies, or is it their hope that token research collaboration with the Japanese can open the door to short term cartel-like restrictions on international trade? Do Western collaborators really hope to learn something of a co-operative ethic, and perhaps even a new system of values, from the Japanese, or are they merely interested in co-operation as a mask to disguise the replacement of competition by collusion?

There do not seem to be any easy answers to these questions. More empirical evidence is required. It is hoped that the analysis presented here affords a framework within which such evidence can be interpreted. So far, it is possible only to clarify the questions, but eventually it should be possible to answer them.

References

Casson, M. C. (1987), *The Firm and the Market: Studies on Multinational Enterprise and the Scope of the Firm* (Cambridge, Mass.: MIT Press).

Contractor. F. J., and Lorange, P. (eds.) (1988), *Co-operative Strategies in International Business* (Lexington, Mass.: Lexington Books, D. C. Heath).

Harrigan, K. R. (1985), *Strategies for Joint Ventures* (Lexington, Mass.: Lexington Books, D. C. Heath).

Hladik, K. J. (1985), *International Joint Ventures: An Economic Analysis of US-Foreign Business Partnerships* (Lexington, Mass.: Lexington Books, D. C. Heath).

Hull, F., Slowinski, G., Wharton, T., and Azumi, K. (1988), 'Strategic Partnerships between Technological Entrepreneurs in the United States and Large Corporations in Japan and the United States', in Contractor and Lorange (1988), 445–56.

Killing, J. P. (1983), *Strategies for Joint Venture Success* (New York: Prager).

Klein, B., Crawford, R. G., and Alchian, A. (1978), 'Vertical Integration, Appropriable Rents and Competitive Contracting Process', *Journal of Law and Economics,* 21: 297–320.

Kogut, B. (1988), 'A Study of the Life Cycle of Joint Ventures' in Contractor and Lorange (1988), 169–86.

Mirus, R., and Yeung, B. (1986), 'Economic Incentives for Counter-trade', *Journal of International Business Studies,* 17(3): 27–39.

Pucik, V. (1988), 'White Collar Human Resource Management in Large Japanese Manufacturing Firms', *Human Resource Management,* 23(3): 257–76.

Williamson, O. E. (1975), *Markets and Hierarchies: Analysis and Anti-Trust Implications* (New York: Free Press).

Organizations: New Concepts for New Forms

Raymond E. Miles and Charles C. Snow

These are turbulent times in the world of organizations. Following a decade of declining productivity and failed organizations, many US companies in the eighties have been forced to rethink their competitive approaches. Rapid technological change, as well as shifting patterns of international trade and competition, have put intense strain on these organizations' ability to keep pace with a set of new and often unpredictable competitors. One prominent executive, describing the current business landscape, says, 'Not only is it a competitive jungle out there, new beasts are roaming around that we can't even identify'.

Two major outcomes of the search for new competitive approaches are already apparent:

1. The search is producing a new organizational form—a unique combination of strategy, structure and management processes that we refer to as the *dynamic network*. The new form is both a cause and a result of today's competitive environment: The same 'competitive beast' that some companies do not understand has been the solution to other companies' competitive difficulties.

2. As is always the case, the new organizational form is forcing the development of new concepts and language to explain its features and functions and, in the process, is providing new insights into the workings of existing strategies and structures. In the future, many organizations will be designed using concepts such as vertical disaggregation, internal and external brokering, full-disclosure information systems, and market substitutes for administrative mechanisms.

In the following sections, we describe these new concepts and the dynamic network forms. We then examine their implications for management

Raymond E. Miles and Charles C. Snow

practice, organizational redesign, and government policy in trade and industry issues.

1. Building Blocks of Current Theory: Strategic Choice and Fit

Based on research conducted during the late sixties and seventies, there is now widespread agreement that most industries can contemporaneously support several different competitive strategies. Sociologists, for example, have described 'generalist' organizations that are able to survive in a variety of environments alongside 'specialist' organizations that thrive only in narrower segments or niches.[1] Economists have shown that in a given industry some firms compete primarily on the basis of cost leadership, some differentiate their product or service in the eyes of consumers, and others simply focus on a particular market segment.[2]

The most common competitive strategies, sometimes referred to as generic strategies, have been labelled Prospectors, Defenders, and Analyzers.[3] Prospectors are 'first-to-the-market' with a new product or service and differentiate themselves from their competitors by using their ability to develop innovative technologies and products. Alternatively, Defenders offer a limited, stable product line and compete primarily on the basis of value and/or cost. Analyzers pursue a 'second-in' strategy whereby they imitate and improve upon the product offerings of their competitors. Thus, they are frequently able to sell widely because of their ability to rationalize other firms' product designs and methods of production.

The Prospector-Defender-Analyzer typology, besides indicating overall strategic orientation, also specifies the major organizational and managerial features needed to support these competitive strategies. Defenders, for example, rely heavily on the functional organization structure developed around the turn of the century and its accompanying managerial characteristics of centralized decision making and control, vertical communications and integration, and high degrees of technical specialization.[4] Prospectors, on the other hand, use more flexible structures such as autonomous workgroups or product divisions in which planning and control are highly decentralized. These structures, pioneered in the twenties and thirties and refined in the fifties, facilitate market responsiveness but at the expense of overall specialization and efficiency. Finally, Analyzers often employ a 'mixed' structure such as the matrix wherein project, program, or brand managers act as integrators between resource groups and program units. Matrix structures, which were widely adopted in the sixties, blend features of both the functional and divisional structures and thus are designed to be simultaneously efficient and flexible.[5]

Current theory in the area of strategy, structure, and process is founded largely on the twin concepts of strategic choice and fit. Managers make strategic choices based on their perceptions of the environment and of their organizations' capabilities. The success of these choices rests on how well competitive strategy matches environmental conditions and whether organization structure and management processes are properly fitted to strategy. Historically, strategy and structure have evolved together. Each advance in structural form was stimulated by the limitations of the previous form, and, because each new form built on the previous form, it helped to clarify the strengths and limitations of its predecessor. Also, each development in structure permitted new competitive strategies to be pursued. Saying all of this in different language, ways of doing business traditionally have been highly contingent on ways of organizing, and major competitive breakthroughs have been achieved by firms that invented, or were quick to apply, new forms of organization and management.[6]

2. Building Blocks of New Theory: Dynamic Networks and Industry Synergy

New organizational forms arise to cope with new environmental conditions. However, no new means of organizing or managing arrives full-blown; usually it results from a variety of experimental actions taken by innovative companies. The competitive environment of the eighties is pushing many companies into this innovative mode, and the United States is on the verge of another breakthrough in organizational form. In order to describe this emerging form, illustrate its distinctive competence, and discuss the contributions it makes to the understanding of previous organizational forms, we must broaden the current theoretical framework summarized above to include new ways of looking at individual organizations and how they interact with each other in their respective industries.

Signs of the new organizational form—such as increased use of joint ventures, subcontracting and licensing activities occurring across international borders, and new business ventures spinning off of established companies—are already evident in several industries, so the realization of this new form simply awaits articulation and understanding. As noted, we have chosen to call this form the dynamic network to suggest that its major components can be assembled and reassembled in order to meet complex and changing competitive conditions.[7] Briefly, the characteristics of the dynamic network are as follows (see Fig. 1):

Vertical Disaggregation. Business functions such as product design and development, manufacturing, marketing, and distribution, typically conducted within a single organization, are performed by independent organizations within a network. Networks may be more or less complex and dynamic depending on competitive circumstances.

Brokers. Because each function is not necessarily part of a single organization, business groups are assembled by or located through brokers. In some cases, a single broker plays a lead role and subcontracts for needed services. In other cases, linkages among equal partners are created by various brokers specializing in a particular service. In still others, one network component uses a broker to locate one or more other functions.

Market Mechanisms. The major functions are held together in the main by market mechanisms rather than plans and controls. Contracts and payment for results are used more frequently than progress reports and personal supervision.

Full-Disclosure Information Systems. Broad-access computerized information systems are used as substitutes for lengthy trust-building processes based on experience. Participants in the network agree on a general structure of payment for value added and then hook themselves together in a continuously updated information system so that contributions can be mutually and instantaneously verified.

In order to understand all of its ramifications, the dynamic network must be viewed simultaneously from the perspective of its individual components and from the network as a whole. For the individual firm (or component), the primary benefit of participation in the network is the opportunity to pursue its particular distinctive competence. A properly constructed network can display the technical specialization of the functional structure, the market responsiveness of the divisional structure, and the balanced orientation characteristic of the matrix. Therefore, each network component can be seen as complementing rather than competing with the other components. Complementarity permits the creation of elaborate networks designed to handle complex situations, such as international construction projects, which cannot be accomplished by a single organization. It also permits rapid adjustment to changing competitive conditions such as those found in many consumer goods industries (such as apparel or electronics).

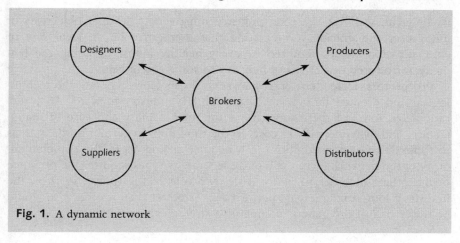

Fig. 1. A dynamic network

Viewing the network as a whole, each firm's distinctive competence is not only enhanced by participation in the network, it is held in check by its fellow network members. That is, if a particular component performs its role poorly or somehow takes unfair advantage of another component, then it can be removed from the network (due to the independence that allows the network to reshape itself whenever necessary). However, removal of a component means that the initiating component and/or the responsible broker must find a replacement part or encourage one of the remaining components to perform the missing function. In either case, the network as a whole is likely to operate temporarily at undesirable levels. Thus, there is complementarity present in every well-conceived network that encourages each participant, singly and in combination, to perform capably and responsibly.

With this grasp of the means and motivation underlying the dynamic network form, it is possible to create a theoretical analog that enhances understanding of the role played by existing organizational forms within their own industries. We refer to this phenomenon as *industry synergy*. This concept comes from our belief that there is symmetry between the characteristics and operations of the dynamic network and the features and behavior of the firms within an industry (or major industry segment).

As noted earlier, most industries are able to support companies pursuing different competitive strategies. Each strategy type both contributes to, and benefits from, the demand for goods and services in the industry, shaping its contribution around its own distinctive competence. Each firm, according to current theory, competes symbiotically with other firms in the industry for a share of the total market. However, when viewed from the industry perspective, each firm also has a synergistic role to play that might be described as *implicit interdependence* among competitors. For example, in order to maintain

433

its long-run viability, the total industry must meet the dual objectives of innovation and efficiency, suggesting that there may be an ideal mix of competitive strategies required by every healthy industry.[8] Using the language introduced earlier, every industry to some extent *requires* the presence of Prospectors, Defenders, and Analyzers. Prospectors generate the technological and product innovations that push the industry forward. Analyzers rationalize some of these innovations for marketability and ease of manufacture, and Defenders lower costs to the minimum in certain product areas to facilitate mass consumption. In a manner analogous to the complementarity of the network form, each of these strategy types requires the presence of the others in order to perform its own role to the fullest. In turn, the industry's long-run aggregate performance is better than it otherwise would be if any one of the generic competitive strategies was missing.

3. Dynamic Synergy

Although no definitive research can be cited as evidence, it appears from case studies and observation that the mix of strategic roles required for industry synergy changes as the industry evolves. Several different patterns can be ascertained. First, and perhaps most obviously, embryonic industries are heavily populated with firms pursuing the Prospector strategy. A current example is the bioengineering 'industry' in which many relatively small firms are experimenting with different technologies and product-service configurations. Less obvious is the claim that such industries are likely to remain latent until firms begin playing Analyzer and Defender roles. In the early days of the automobile industry, growth was not especially dramatic as various companies experimented with steam, electric, and internal combustion technologies, as well as various distribution methods. Rapid growth occurred only after Henry Ford played a Defender role by installing an assembly-line for manufacturing a single type of car on a standardized basis and by forming a distribution network of franchise dealers that sold cars to the mass market. Similarly, one would predict that in today's bioengineering industry, growth gains will be greatest when some large established company acquires one or more small R&D firms and begins to produce standardized products in large volume.

A second pattern of strategic mix involves mature industries. Here one would expect fewer participants than in new industries and a much greater proportion of firms using the efficiency-oriented Defender strategy. However, in order to prevent the industry from heading into decline, a few firms must behave as Prospectors (probably in limited areas). An example is the major home appliance industry. Over the last 15 years, dramatic gains in market share have been made by White Consolidated Industries, a company that relies exclusively on the Defender approach. Although much of the industry appears to have the characteristics of a commodity business, with advanced automated production systems churning out standardized products on a cost-effective basis, portions of the industry deal with innovative products and technologies (e.g., the 'smart' kitchen). In these innovative areas, the leadership role is played by companies such as General Electric. To maintain its health, a mature industry requires the successful performance of both kinds of strategic roles.

Finally, there are industries in transition, for which the desired mix of competitive strategies is more varied and changing. One example is the electronics industry (including computers and semiconductors). Neither a new nor a mature industry, electronics is in the growth stage, but its segments are growing at much different rates. Consequently, over the next several years, there is the potential for this industry to achieve great success if it develops a comprehensive mix of competitive strategies, However, there is also the possibility that this industry will not realize its potential if the strategic mix becomes too narrow.

Consider the following scenario. Hewlett-Packard, a company that has traditionally competed as a Prospector across most of the markets in which it operates recently has attempted to play an uncustomary role in its computer business. Within its Business Computers Group, Hewlett-Packard has tried to achieve the standardization, coordination, and integration most characteristic of the Analyzer, and it is having difficulty grafting this approach onto its present organization and management culture. If the approaches taken in the reorganization of its computer business are forced onto other HP businesses, then it is possible that across the entire company Hewlett-Packard will dilute its strength as *both* a Prospector and an Analyzer. Similarly, Intel, which has traditionally prided itself on its high-technology production competence, has recently begun to design, produce, and market business computer network systems. It, too, must be careful not to dilute its primary distinctive competence as it moves into new businesses requiring different technical and organizational abilities. If, as these examples suggest, certain companies do not maintain their primary distinctive competence, then the industry as a whole may not exhibit the comprehensive mix of competitive strategies needed to achieve long-term success.

In sum, a healthy industry's needs for innovation and efficiency are met through the complementary efforts of firms pursuing different strategies, each of which is based on a primary distinctive competence. By regularly being 'first-to-the-market' Prospectors sustain technological innovation and are the principal contributors to the design of new products and services. By competing primarily as efficient producers, Defenders uphold quality levels while driving down the costs of standardized goods and services. The most important role played by Analyzers is that of transferring information throughout the industry, especially as it concerns the standardization of technology and product design. By sorting through the experiments conducted by Prospectors to determine those technologies, products, and services most amenable to rationalization, Analyzers establish a new plateau from which the next round of innovation can be launched. Subsequently, by developing successful approaches to mass production and marketing of new products, the Analyzer sets broad efficiency targets that Defenders try to surpass.

4. Diffusion of the Dynamic Network Form

Returning to the dynamic network shown in Figure 1, it can be argued that Prospectors essentially play the *designer* role within an industry, Analyzers play the *marketing/distribution* role (and also contribute as information brokers) and Defenders perform the *producer* role. By relating the components of the network form to the synergistic roles played by firms within an industry, it is possible to forecast where and how rapidly the network form may emerge.

Aspects of the new form can be identified even in capital-intensive industries where large investments, relatively indivisible production functions, and other factors make it difficult for companies to move toward the network structure. Often firms in these industries have a limited range of distinctive competence even though they may perform all of the activities associated with a given business. In the petroleum industry, for example, most of the major firms have sought vertical integration as a means of assuring an uninterrupted flow of operations, ranging from the acquisition of raw materials to the sale of consumer petroleum products. Yet, these companies are not all equally skilled at performing each step of the exploration (supply), refining (production), product development (design), and marketing/distribution process. Thus, even though vertical disaggregation may be feasible in this industry, it is unlikely to occur in the short run. Presumably, if vertical disaggregation were easier to implement, some of the major firms would divest their less central functions and focus only on those value-added activities most closely associated with their abilities. Our prediction is that Defender companies would choose to perform the producer role, Prospectors would select the designer role, and so on.

In labor-intensive industries, where vertical disaggregation is less costly and easier to administer, the network form is gaining in popularity much more rapidly. In fact, one of our studies uncovered the partial use of the network structure over twenty years ago.[9] During the sixties and seventies, developments in the college textbook publishing industry caused many of the major firms to reevaluate their publishing activities and to modify their organization structures. For example, virtually every publishing company got out of the printing and binding business and simply contracted for these services as needed. Also, several companies allowed key editors to form their own publishing firms which then became subsidiaries of the parent companies. These subsidiaries usually engaged in new publishing approaches, thereby developing an expertise that the parent company could tap into whenever appropriate. Lastly, some publishers drastically cut back their in-house operations in art, graphics, and design, choosing instead to subcontract this work to smaller, specialized groups that comprised a cottage industry around the major publishers. Thus, in the space of ten years or so, several of the major college textbook publishers in effect developed networks in which portions of the producer and designer roles were moved out of the original companies into smaller speciality firms. The major companies simply retained those functions that were closest to their traditional distinctive competence (such as McGraw-Hill in product development and Prentice-Hall in sales).

As the United States continues to become more of a service economy, the case of textbook publishing (and many other examples) may well suggest the pattern by which other labor-intensive industries move toward the dynamic network model. The rationale for 'people' and service businesses to adopt this structure is clearcut. The dynamic network is a far more flexible structure than any of the previous forms, it can accommodate a vast amount of complexity while maximizing specialized competence, and it provides much more effective use of human resources that otherwise have to be accumulated, allocated, and maintained by a single organization. The practice of leasing entire workforces, already in use in construction, hotel management, and retail sales, is a network characteristic that will become even more prevalent in future. As managers gain experience and confidence in these network designs and practices, the dynamic network form will spread accordingly.

5. Implications

A new organizational form is both a cause and a result of the changing nature of competition. As organizations formulate new strategies to meet new competitive conditions, they find that their structures and management systems also require modification. Simultaneously, as new organizational forms become better understood and more widely used, new competitive strategies are easier to implement. The dynamic network form, as indicated earlier, has appeared as a means of coping with the business environment of the seventies and eighties. Its arrival now has implications for the way managers view the future directions of their companies, for the approaches used to manage existing structures, and for the way in which public policy is used to restore competitive vigor.

Strategists. Strategic planners have a growing literature to call upon as they formulate objectives and strategies for their companies. Frameworks are available to help strategists determine their companies' distinctive competence, generate strategic options, analyze competitors' behavior, and so on. However, all of these frameworks ignore or underemphasize the concept of industry synergy and the key industry roles defined by the network model. From these concepts, several recommendations for the strategic decision maker can be derived. First, the strategist must examine the industry's current mix of competitive strategies as a means of forecasting the industry's prospects for long-term viability. A healthy industry must at a minimum have firms with the ability to perform the designer and producer roles. Next, the strategist must try to anticipate how the industry's strategic mix might change over time. All firms are generally aware that as an industry matures, the mix of competitive strategies is likely to shift from a high proportion of Prospectors to a high proportion of Defenders. Therefore, the astute strategist can develop moves within this overall scenario that are not obvious at first glance. For example, it might be advantageous to become the first Defender in an embryonic industry. Or it might be desirable to be the last Prospector in a mature industry. Basically, the strategist can be prepared to offer 'nonobvious' strategies by thinking in terms of strategic roles and synergies at the industry level. Finally, the strategist must be ready to show the organization how it can change directions in order to take advantage of new opportunities or counter competitive threats. The logic of the dynamic network model indicates that this flexibility can be achieved largely through vertical disaggregation. Thus, an organization may be able to obtain competitive advantage by performing only those activities closest to its distinctive competence, contracting with other components of a network for goods or services on an ad hoc basis, and perhaps serving as a broker in yet other areas. IBM used this approach in developing its personal computer (the PC jr.). Initially lagging behind its competitors, IBM quickly assembled a network of designers, suppliers, producers, and marketers to put together its first product offering. Later, after it had established itself in the market, IBM reintegrated portions of the network into its primary operating system.

Policymakers. The concepts of industry synergy and dynamic network can be used to examine aspects of international competition and their implications for public policy. The US economy is becoming increasingly connected to world markets, so dynamic networks in many industries now operate across national boundaries. This fact complicates the recommendations made above to strategists. For example, in the case of a purely domestic industry, long-term viability rests on member firms playing a heterogeneous set of roles such as designer, producer, and marketer/distributor. In the case of an international industry, however, one or more of these roles may be best suited to foreign firms. Presently, some large US industries have the bulk of their manufacturing and assembly operations located overseas. The domestic portion of the industry is quite homogeneous, with a few firms performing the designer role and the remainder performing the marketing/distribution role. In these situations long-term industry health is an international concern, and individual firm strategists must take this into account as they try to anticipate the industry's strategic mix over time. Further, calls for a national industrial policy to revitalize declining industries will fail, according to the logic of the dynamic network model, if they implicitly rely on an improper role for American firms. The realities of international competition indicate that many American 'producers' should rethink their industry role and attempt to find a more valuable location in an international network. Apparently, this is happening in the steel industry. Several American firms have achieved recent success by reorienting their plants toward customized products and applications instead of commodity products.[10] These companies cannot compete well in most commodity steel markets, so it is to their advantage to play a designer role in the industry and leave the producer role to foreign competitors.

Managers and Organization Designers. The final set of implications applies to managers, especially those in a position to redesign their organizations. Executives who perceive the network form as a competitive advantage for their companies now have an explicit model to guide their redesign efforts. On the other hand, some companies cannot or will not vertically disaggregate and completely adopt the new form. Nevertheless, these companies desire the benefits of the network approach. Managers of these companies need ideas for, and the means of, altering their existing organizations so as to simulate desirable features of the dynamic network.

In companies whose distinctive competence is best served by traditional organization structures, there may still be pressure to demonstrate more flexible, innovative behavior. The network model suggests that these companies can be more innovative by setting up special units focused on innovation in which brokers bring resources together and later transfer results to the larger operating system. A number of mechanisms for supplementing existing structures are available, including internal venturing or 'intrapreneurship', external coventuring, idea markets, and innovator roles such as idea champions, sponsors, and orchestrators. Taken together, these structures, processes, and interpersonal roles comprise an innovating organization that operates parallel to the main system.[11] Developed and used in companies such as IBM, Texas Instruments, Minnesota Mining and Manufacturing, and others, these innovating mechanisms can be employed by more traditional firms to keep pace with developments in their industries. Some companies may choose to internally generate more ideas and innovations, while others may rely on external coventuring schemes to create needed innovations. In either case, advances made by the innovating system are integrated into the larger organization only after their utility has been clearly demonstrated.

6. Conclusions

Current 'merger mania' notwithstanding, it seems likely that the eighties and nineties will be known as decades of largescale disaggregation and redeployment of resources in the United States and of a reshaping of strategic roles across the world economy. By the turn of the century, we expect US firms to be playing producer roles primarily in high-technology goods and service industries (agriculture may be regarded as a high-tech industry). These industries are characterized by sophisticated products and delivery systems for which the United States has a worldwide competitive advantage. In more mature industries, especially those containing a large proportion of commodity products or services, we would expect US firms to play primarily designer and distributor roles, with production limited to special-needs products and prototype designs to be licensed for production abroad. Of course, the United States will play a major marketer/distributor role in most industries throughout this period.

These shifting alignments will create both competitive challenges and opportunities for managers and policymakers. The greatest barrier to success will be outmoded views of what an 'organization' must look like and how it must be managed. Future forms will all feature some of the properties of the dynamic network form, particularly heavy reliance on self-managed workgroups and a greater willingness to view organizational boundaries and membership as highly flexible. We anticipate, ultimately, that key business units—such as a design engineering group or prototype production team—will be autonomous building blocks to be assembled, reassembled, and redeployed within and across organizational and national boundaries as product or service life cycles demand.

Notes

1. Michael T. Hannan and John H. Freeman, 'The Population Ecology of Organizations', *American Journal of Sociology*, vol. 82 (March 1977): 929–64: and Howard E. Aldrich, *Organizations and Environments* (Englewood Cliffs, NJ: Prentice-Hall, 1979).
2. Michael E. Porter, *Competitive Strategy* (New York, NY: Free Press, 1980).
3. Raymond E. Miles and Charles C. Snow, *Organizational Strategy, Structure and Process*, (New York, NY: McGraw-Hill, 1978).
4. Alfred D. Chandler, Jr., *Strategy and Structure* (New York, NY: Doubleday, 1962).
5. Stanley M. Davis and Paul R. Lawrence, *Matrix* (Reading, MA: Addison-Wesley, 1977).
6. Raymond E. Miles and Charles C. Snow, 'Fit, Failure, and the Hall of Fame', *California Management Review*, vol. XXVI (Spring 1984): 10–28.
7. Ibid.
8. Economists do not agree on a single definition of industry health. Classical equilibrium theory states that firms in a competitive industry should not make profits in excess of the normal bank rate of return. Another economic theory, however, says that excess profits are required for industry innovation. Yet another theory maintains that excess profits may be rightfully earned by firms that minimize buyers' search and information-processing costs (by consistently offering high-quality products, etc.). Our criteria of long-run industry health are taken from Paul R. Lawrence and Davis Dyer, *Renewing American Industry* (New York, NY: Free Press, 1983).
9. Miles and Snow, *Organizational Strategy, Structure, and Process*, Chapter 10.
10. Joel D. Goldhar and Mariann Jelinek, 'Plan for Economies of Scope', *Harvard Business Review*, vol. 61 (November/December 1983): 141–8.
11. See Jay R. Galbraith, 'Designing and Innovating Organization', *Organizational Dynamics* (Winter 1982), 5–25; and Gifford Pinchot, III, *Intrapreneuring* (New York, NY: Harper and Row, 1985).

17 Markets, Bureaucracies, and Clans

....

William G. Ouchi

....

1. The Nature of Organizations

What is an organization, and why do organizations exist? Many of us would answer this question by referring to Barnard's (1968) technological imperative, which argues that a formal organization will arise when technological conditions demand physical power, speed, endurance, mechanical adaptation, or continuity beyond the capacity of a single individual (1968: 27–8). Yet when the stone is too large or the production facility too complex for a single person, what is called for is cooperation, and cooperation need not take the form of a formal organization. Indeed, grain farmers who need a large grain elevator do not form corporations which take over the farms and make the farmers into employees; instead, they form a cooperative to own and operate the elevator.

Others would refer to March and Simon's (1958) argument that an organization will exist so long as it can offer its members inducements which exceed the contributions it asks of them. While this position explains the conditions under which an organization may continue to exist, it does not explain how an organization can create a whole which is so much greater than the sum of its parts that it can give them more than they contribute.

Most of us, however, would refer to Blau and Scott's (1962) definition of a formal organization as a purposive aggregation of individuals who exert concerted effort toward a common and explicitly recognized goal. Yet we can hardly accept this definition whole, suspecting as Simon (1945: 257–78)

I am indebted to many colleagues for their constructive criticisms of this paper, particularly to Chris Argyris, Peter Blau, Larry Cummings, Charles Horngren, Joanne Martin, John Meyer, Jerry Porras, Edgar Schein, W. Richard Scott, Arnold Tannenbaum, Richard Walton, and Oliver Williamson.

has that individuals within organizations rarely have a common understanding of goals.

Another point of view on the question of why organizations exist began with an inquiry by Coase (1937) and has recently been developed by Williamson (1975). In this view, an organization such as a corporation exists because it can mediate economic transactions between its members at lower costs than a market mechanism can. Under certain conditions, markets are more efficient because they can mediate without paying the costs of managers, accountants, or personnel departments. Under other conditions, however, a market mechanism becomes so cumbersome that it is less efficient than a bureaucracy. This transactions cost approach explicitly regards efficiency as the fundamental element in determining the nature of organizations.

2. Markets, Bureaucracies, and Clans

Transactions costs are a solution to the problem of cooperation in the realm of economic activity. From the perspective of Mayo (1945) and Barnard (1968), the fundamental problem of cooperation stems from the fact that individuals have only partially overlapping goals. Left to their own devices, they pursue incongruent objectives and their efforts are uncoordinated. Any collectivity which has an economic goal must then find a means to control diverse individuals efficiently.

Many helpful ideas have flowed from this definition of the problem of cooperation. Some (e.g., Etzioni, 1965; Weick, 1969) have emphasized the tension between individual autonomy and collective interests which must attend cooperative action, while others (e.g., Simon, 1945) have emphasized the impossibility of achieving a completely cooperative effort. Our interests is in the efficiency with which transactions are carried out between individuals who are engaged in cooperative action.

Cooperative action necessarily involves interdependence between individuals. This interdependence calls for a transaction or exchange in which each individual gives something of value (for example, labor) and receives something of value (for example, money) in return. In a market relationship, the transaction takes place between the two parties and is mediated by a price mechanism in which the existence of a competitive market reassures both parties that the terms of exchange are equitable. In a bureaucratic relationship, each party contributes labor to a corporate body which mediates the relationship by placing a value on each contribution and then compensating it fairly. The perception of equity in this case depends upon a social agreement that the bureaucratic hierarchy has the legitimate authority to provide this mediation. In either case, individuals must regard the transaction as equitable; it must meet the standards of reciprocity which Gouldner (1961) has described as a universal requirement for collective life.

It is this demand for equity which brings on transactions costs. A transactions cost is any activity which is engaged in to satisfy each party to an exchange that the value given and received is in accord with his or her expectations.

Transactions costs arise principally when it is difficult to determine the value of the goods or service. Such difficulties can arise from the underlying nature of the goods or service or from a lack of trust between the parties. When a company is being sold by one corporation to another corporation, for example, it may not be unambiguously clear what the true value of the company is. If firms similar to the company are frequently bought and sold, and if those transactions occur under competitive conditions, then the market process will be accepted as a legitimate estimator of the true value. But if the company is unique, and there is only one potential buyer, then market forces are absent. How will the buyer and seller determine a fair price? They may call upon a third party to estimate the value of the company. Each party may in addition call upon other experts who will assist them in evaluating both the value of the company and the adequacy of the judgment of the third party. Each side may also require an extensive and complete contract which will describe exactly what is being bought and sold. Each of these activities is costly, and all of them are regarded here as transactions costs: they are necessary to create a perception of equity among all parties to the transaction.

This same argument applies to transactions in which a service, such as the labor of an individual, is the object of exchange. If one individual sells his or her services to another, it may be difficult to assess the true value of that labor. In particular, if the labor is to be used in an interdependent technology, one which requires teamwork, it may be difficult to assess the value contributed by one worker as opposed to another, since their joint efforts yield a single outcome in this case, or in a case where it is likely that task requirements will change, then the auditing and complex contracting required to create the perception of equity can become unbearably costly.

We have identified two principal mechanisms for mediating these transactions: a market and a bureaucracy. These alternatives have received the greatest attention from organization theorists (e.g., Barnard 1968; Weber, 1968) and economists (e.g., Coase, 1937; Arrow, 1974). However, the paradigm also suggests a third mechanism: If the objectives of individuals are congruent (not mutually exclusive), then the conditions of reciprocity and equity can be met quite differently.

Both Barnard and Mayo pointed out that organizations are difficult to operate because their members do not share a selfless devotion to the same objectives. Mayo (1945) argued that organizations operated more efficiently in preindustrial times, when members typically served an apprenticeship during which they were socialized into accepting the objectives of the craft or organization. Barnard (1968: 42–3) posed the problem thus:

A formal system of cooperation requires an objective, a purpose, an aim. . . . It is important to note the complete distinction between the aim of a cooperative effort and that of an individual. Even in the case where a man enlists the aid of other men to do something which he cannot do alone, such as moving a stone, the objective ceases to be personal.

While Barnard, like Arrow, views markets and bureaucracies as the basic mechanisms for achieving the continued cooperation of these individuals, he also allowed (1968: 141) for the possibility of reducing the incongruence of goals in a manner consistent with Mayo's view of the preindustrial organization:

An organization can secure the efforts necessary to its existence, then, either by the objective inducement it provides or by changing states of mind. It seems to me improbable that any organization can exist as a practical matter which does not employ both methods in combination.

If the socialization of individuals into an organization is complete, then the basis of reciprocity can be changed. For example, Japanese firms rely to a great extent upon hiring inexperienced workers, socializing them to accept the company's goals as their own, and compensating them according to length of service, number of dependents, and other nonperformance criteria (see Abegglen, 1958; Dore, 1973; Nakane, 1973). It is not necessary for these organizations to measure performance to control or direct their employees, since the employees' natural (socialized) inclination is to do what is best for the firm. It is also unnecessary to derive explicit, verifiable measures of value added, since rewards are distributed according to nonperformance-related criteria which are relatively inexpensive to determine (length of service and number of dependents can be ascertained at relatively low costs). Thus, industrial organizations can, in some instances, rely to a great extent on socialization as the principal mechanism of mediation or control, and this 'clan' form ('clan' conforms to Durkheim's meaning of an organic association which resembles a kin network but may not include blood relations, 1933: 175) can be very efficient in mediating transactions between interdependent individuals.

Markets, bureaucracies, and clans are therefore three distinct mechanisms which may be present in differing degrees, in any real organization.[1] Our next objective is to specify the conditions under which the requirements of each form are most efficiently satisfied.

....

3. The Market Failures Framework

We can approach this question most effectively by examining the markets and hierarchies approach provided by Williamson (1975), which builds upon earlier statements of the problem by Coase (1937) and others (for a more detailed description of the functioning of each mechanism, see Ouchi, 1979).

Market transactions, or exchanges, consist of contractual relationships. Each exchange is governed by one of three types of contractual relations, all of which can be specified completely. That is, because each party is bound only to deliver that which is specified, the contract must specify who must deliver what under every possible state of nature. The simplest form of contract is the 'spot' or 'sales' contract. This is what occurs when you walk up to a candy counter, ask for a candy bar, and pay the amount the sales-person asks. In such a transaction, all obligations are fulfilled on the spot. However, the spot market contract is, by definition, incapable of dealing with future transactions, and most exchange relationships involve long-term obligations.

A common device for dealing with the future is the 'contingent claims contract', a document that specifies all the obligations of each party to an exchange, contingent upon all possible future states of nature. However, given a future that is either complex or uncertain, the bounded rationality of individuals makes it impossible to specify such a contract completely. Leaving such a contract incompletely specified is an alternative, but one that will succeed only if each party can trust the other to interpret the uncertain future in a manner that is acceptable to him. Thus, given uncertainty, bounded rationality, and opportunism, contingent claims contracting will fail.

Instead of trying to anticipate the future in a giant, once-and-for-all contract, why not employ a series of contracts, each one written for a short period within which future events can confidently be foreseen? The problem with such 'sequential spot contracting' is that in many exchange relationships, the goods or services exchanged are unique, and the supplier requires specialized knowledge of how to supply the customer best and most efficiently. The supplier acquires this knowledge over time and in doing so gains a 'first mover advantage', which enables him to bid more effectively on subsequent contracts than any potential competitor can. Knowing this, potential competitors will not waste their time bidding, thus producing a situation of 'small numbers bargaining' or bilateral monopoly, in which there is only one buyer and seller. Under this condition, competitive pressures are absent, and each party will opportunistically claim higher costs or poor quality, whichever is in his or her interest. In order to maintain such an exchange, each party will have to go to considerable expense to audit the costs or performance of the other. If these transactions costs are too high, the market relationship will fail due to the confluence of opportunism with small numbers bargaining even though the limitations of uncertainty and bounded rationality have been overcome.

Thus, under some conditions no completely contractual market relationship is feasible. Table 1 summarizes the conditions which lead to market failure. According to the paradigm, no one of the four conditions can produce market failure, but almost any pairing of them will do so.

The idea of market failure is an analytical device. Economists do not agree on a specific set of conditions that constitute the failure of a market; indeed one point of view argues that even monopolistic conditions may be competitive. However, the idea of market failure as expressed by Williamson (1975) is useful as a conceptual framework within which to compare the strengths of markets as opposed to bureaucracies. The technique is to contend that all transactions can be mediated entirely by market relations, and then ask what conditions will cause some of these market mechanisms to fail and be replaced by bureaucratic mechanisms. In this sense, every bureaucratic organization constitutes an example of market failure.

The bureaucratic organization has two principal advantages over the market relationship. First, it uses the employment relation, which is an incomplete contract. In accepting an employment relation, a worker agrees to receive wages in exchange for submitting to the legitimate right of the organization to appoint superior officers who can (1) direct the work activities of the employee from day to day (within some domain or zone of indifference), thus overcoming the problem of dealing with the future all at once and (2) closely monitor the employee's performance, thus minimizing the problem of opportunism.

Second, the bureaucratic organization can create an atmosphere of trust between employees much more readily than a market can between the parties to an exchange. Because members of an organization assume some commonality of purpose, because they learn that long-term relationships will reward good performance and punish poor performance, they develop some goal congruence. This reduces their opportunistic tendencies and thus the need to monitor their performance.

Bureaucracies are also characterized by an emphasis on technical expertise

William G. Ouchi

Table 1. The Market Failures Framework

Human Factors		Environmental Factors
Bounded rationality	<---------->	Uncertainty/Complexity
Opportunism	<---------->	Small numbers

Source: Williamson (1975: 40).

which provides some skill training and some socialization into craft or professional standards. Professionals within a bureaucratic setting thus combine a primary affiliation to a professional body with a career orientation, which increases the sense of affiliation or solidarity with the employer and further reduces goal incongruence. [2]

In summary, the market failures framework argues that markets fail when the costs of completing transactions become unbearable. At that point, the inefficiencies of bureaucratic organization will be preferred to the relatively greater costs of market organization, and exchange relationships move from one domain into the other.

Consider one example. The 10,000 individuals who comprise the workforce of a steel mill could be individual entrepreneurs whose interpersonal transactions are mediated entirely through a network of market or contractual relationships. Each of them could also have a market relation with yet another combine which owned the capital equipment and facilities necessary to produce steel. Yet steel mills are typically bureaucratic in form and each worker is in an employment, not market, relation with the corporation. Market forces have failed because the determination of value contributed by one worker is highly ambiguous in the integrated steelmaking process, which makes the transactions cost attendant upon maintaining a market too high.

....

4. Extending the Market Failures Framework: Clans

Bureaucracies can fail when the ambiguity of performance evaluation becomes significantly greater than that which brings about market failure. A bureaucratic organization operates fundamentally according to a system of hierarchical surveillance, evaluation, and direction. In such a system, each superior must have a set of standards to which he can compare behavior or output in order to provide control. These standards only indicate the value of an output approximately, and are subject to idiosyncratic interpretation.

People perceive them as equitable only as long as they belive that they contain a reasonable amount of performance information. When tasks become highly unique, completely integrated, or ambiguous for other reasons, then even bureaucratic mechanisms fail. Under these conditions, it becomes impossible to evaluate externally the value added by any individual. Any standard which is applied will be by definition arbitrary and therefore inequitable.

If we adopt the view that transactions costs arise from equity considerations, then we can interpret Table 1 in a different light. Simon's work on the employment relation (1957: 183–95) shows that Table 1 contains some redundancy. He emphasized that under an employment contract, the employer pays a worker a premium over the 'spot' price for any piece of work. From the point of view of the worker, this 'risk premium' compensates him for the likelihood that he will be asked to perform duties which are significantly more distasteful to him than those which are implied in the employment contract. The uncertainty surrounding the likelihood of such tasks and the expectation that the employer will or will not ask them determines the size of the risk premium. If the employee agreed with all the employer's objectives, which is equivalent to completely trusting the employer never to request a distasteful task, then the risk premium would be zero.

The employment relation is relatively efficient when the measurement of performance is ambiguous but the employer's goals are not. In an employment relation, each employee depends on the employer to distribute rewards equitably; if employees do not trust the employer to do so, they will demand contractual protections such as union representation and the transactions cost will rise.

Thus, the critical element in the efficiency of market versus employment relations has to do with (1) the ambiguity of the measurement of individual performance, and (2) the congruence of the employees' and employer's goals. We can now reformulate the transactions cost problem as follows: in order to mediate transactions efficiently, any organizational form must reduce either the ambiguity of performance evaluation or the goal incongruence between parties. Put this way, market relations are efficient when there is little ambiguity over performance, so the parties can tolerate relatively high levels of opportunism or goal incongruence. And bureaucratic relations are efficient when both performance ambiguity and goal incongruence are moderately high.

What form of mediation succeeds by minimizing goal incongruence and tolerating high levels of ambiguity in performance evaluation? Clearly, it is one which embodies a strong form of the employment relation as defined by Simon (1945), which is a relationship in which the risk premium is minimized. The answer is what we have referred to as the clan, which is the obverse of the market relation since it achieves efficiency under the opposite conditions: high performance ambiguity and low opportunism.

Perhaps the clearest exposition of the clan form appears in what Durkheim (1933: 365) refers to as the case of organic solidarity and its contrast with contractual relations:

For organic solidarity to exist, it is not enough that there be a system of organs necessary to one another, which in a general way feel solidarity, but it is also necessary that the way in which they should come together, if not in every kind of meeting, at least in circumstances which most frequently occur, be predetermined. . . . Otherwise, at every moment new conflicts would have to be equilibrated. . . . It will be said that there are contracts. But, first of all, social relations are not capable of assuming this juridical form. . . . A contract is not self-sufficient, but supposes a regulation which is as extensive and complicated as contractual life itself. . . . A contract is only a truce, and very precarious, it suspends hostilities only for a time.

The solidarity to which Durkheim refers contemplates the union of objectives between individuals which stems from their necessary dependence upon one another. In this sense, any occupational group which has organic solidarity may be considered a clan. Thus, a profession, a labor union or a corporation may be a clan, and the professionalized bureaucracy may be understood as a response to the joint need for efficient transactions within professions (clan) and between professions (bureaucracy). Goal congruity as a central mechanism of control in organizations also appears repeatedly in Barnard:

The most intangible and subtle of incentives is that which I have called the condition of communion. . . . It is the feeling of personal comfort in social relations that is sometimes called solidarity, social integration. . . . The need for communion is a basis of informal organization that is essential to the operation of every formal organization (1968: 148; see also 89, 152, 169, 273).

Descriptions of organizations which display a high degree of goal congruence, typically through relatively complete socialization brought about through high inclusion (Etzioni, 1965), are also found in Lipset, Trow, and Coleman (1956: 79–80), Argyris (1964: 10, 175), Selznick (1966), and Clark (1970). In each case, the authors describe the organization as one in which it is difficult to determine individual performance. However, such organizations are not 'loosely coupled' nor are they 'organized anarchies' simply because they lack market and bureaucratic mechanisms. A clan, as Durkheim points out, provides great regularity of relations and may in fact be more directive than the other, more explicit mechanisms. That clans display a high degree of discipline is emphasized by Kanter (1972) in her study of utopian communities, some of which were successful businesses such as Oneida and Amana. According to Kanter, this discipline was not achieved through contractualism or surveillance but through an extreme form of the belief that individual interests are best served by a complete immersion of each individual in the interests of the whole (1972: 41).

More recently, Ouchi and Jaeger (1978) and Ouchi and Johnson (1978) have reported on modern industrial organizations which closely resemble the clan form. In these organizations, a variety of social mechanisms reduces differences between individual and organizational goals and produces a strong sense of community (see also Van Maanen, 1975; Katz, 1978). Where individual and organizational interests overlap to this extent, opportunism is unlikely and equity in rewards can be achieved at a relatively low transactions cost. Moreover, these organizations are typically in technologically advanced or closely integrated industries, where teamwork is common, technologies change often, and therefore individual performance is highly ambiguous.

When a bureaucracy fails, then due to excessively ambiguous performance evaluation, the sole form of mediation remaining is the clan, which relies upon creating goal congruence. Although clans may employ a system of legitimate authority (often the traditional rather than the rational-legal form), they differ fundamentally from bureaucracies in that they do not require explicit auditing and evaluation. Performance evaluation takes place instead through the kind of subtle reading of signals that is possible among intimate coworkers but which cannot be translated into explicit, verifiable measures. This means that there is sufficient information in a clan to promote learning and effective production, but that information cannot withstand the scrutiny of contractual relations. Thus, any tendency toward opportunism will be destructive, because the close auditing and hard contracting necessary to combat it are not possible in a clan.

If performance evaluation is so ambiguous and goals so incongruent that a clan fails, what then? We can only speculate, but it seems that this final cell may be the case discussed by Meyer and Rowan (1977) in which control is purely ceremonial and symbolic. School systems, like other organizations, do employ a variety of mechanisms. Yet if there is no effective mechanism of mediation between individuals, the perception of equity may be purely superstitious, based on a broad, community-based acceptance of the legitimacy of the institution.

....

5. Markets, Bureaucracies, and Clans: an Overview

Having distinguished three mechanisms of intermediation, we can now summarize them and attempt to set out the general conditions under which each form will mediate transactions between individuals most efficiently. Table 2 discriminates markets, bureaucracies, and clans along two dimensions: their underlying normative and informational requirements.

Normative requirements refer to the basic social agreements that all members of the transactional network must share if the network is to function efficiently, without undue costs of performance auditing or monitoring. A norm of reciprocity, according to Gouldner (1961), is one of only two social agreements that have been found to be universal among societies across time and cultures (the other is the incest taboo). If no such norm were widely shared, then a potential trader would have to consume so much energy in setting the contractual terms of exchange in advance and in auditing the performance of the other party afterwards that the potential transaction would cost too much. Under such conditions, a division of labor is unthinkable and social existence impossible. Therefore, a norm of reciprocity underlies all exchange mechanisms.

A norm of legitimate authority is critical for two reasons. As discussed above, it permits the assignment of organizational superiors who can, on an ad hoc basis, specify the work assignments of subordinates, thus obviating the need for a contingent claims employment contract which would be either so complex as to be infeasible or so simple as to be too confining or else incomplete. Legitimate authority also permits organizational superiors to audit the performance of subordinates more closely than is possible within a market relationship. In a bureaucracy, legitimate authority will commonly take the 'rational/legal' form, whereas in a clan it may take the 'traditional' form (see Blau and Scott, 1962: 27–38). Legitimate authority is not ordinarily created within the organization but is maintained by other institutions such as the church or the educational system (Weber, 1947; Blau and Scott, 1962;

Table 2. An Organizational Failures Framework

Mode of control	Normative requirements	Informational requirements
Market	Reciprocity	Prices
Bureaucracy	Reciprocity	Rules
	Legitimate authority	
Clan	Reciprocity	Traditions
	Legitimate authority	
	Common values and beliefs	

Barnard, 1968: 161–84). While the legitimacy of a particular organization may be greater or smaller as a result of its managerial practices, it is fundamentally maintained within a society generally.

Common values and beliefs provide the harmony of interest that erase the possibility of opportunistic behavior. If all members of the organization have been exposed to an apprenticeship or other socialization period, then they will share personal goals that are compatible with the goals of the organization. In this condition, auditing of performance is unnecessary except for educational purposes, since no member will attempt to depart from organizational goals.

A norm of reciprocity is universal, legitimate authority is accepted, though in varying degree, in most formal organizations, and common values and beliefs are relatively rare in formal organizations. Etzioni (1965) has described this last form of control as being common only to 'total organizations' such as the military and mental hospitals, and Light (1972) describes its role in ethnically bound exchange relationships. However, we have also noted that a partially complete form of socialization, accompanied by market or bureaucratic mechanisms, may be effective across a wider range of organizations. Mayo (1945) contended that instability of employment, which upsets the long socialization period necessary, is the chief enemy of the development of this form of control.

The informational prerequisites of each form of control are prices, rules and traditions. Prices are a highly sophisticated form of information for decision making. However, correct prices are difficult to arrive at, particularly when technological interdependence, novelty, or other forms of ambiguity obscure the boundary between tasks or individuals. Rules, by comparison, are relatively crude informational devices. A rule is specific to a problem, and therefore it takes a large number of rules to control organizational responses. A decision maker must know the structure of the rules in order to apply the correct one in any given situation. Moreover, an organization can never specify a set of rules that will cover all possible contingencies. Instead, it specifies a smaller set of rules which cover routine decisions, and refers exceptions up the hierarchy where policymakers can invent rules as needed. As Galbraith (1973) has pointed out, under conditions of uncertainty or complexity the number of exceptions becomes so great that the hierarchy becomes overloaded and the quality of decision making suffers.

Traditions are implicit rather than explicit rules that govern behavior. Because traditions are not specified, they are not easily accessible, and a new member will not be able to function effectively until he or she has spent a number of years learning them (Van Maanen and Schein, 1978). In terms of the precision of the performance evaluation they permit, traditions may be the crudest informational prerequisite, since they are ordinarily stated in a general way which must be interpreted in a particular situation. On the other hand, the set of traditions in a formal organization may produce a unified, although implicit philosophy or point of view, functionally equivalent to a theory about how that organization should work. A member who grasps such an essential theory can deduce from it an appropriate rule to govern any possible decision, thus producing a very elegant and complete form of control. Alternatively, a disruption of the socialization process will inhibit the passing on of traditions and bring about organizational inefficiency.

6. Some Concluding Thoughts

Under conditions of extreme uncertainty and opportunism, transactions cost may rise. Indeed, Denison (1978) has observed that net productivity declined in the United States between 1965 and 1975 due to changes in 'the industrial and human environment within which business must operate' (1978: 21). According to Denison, output per unit of input has declined for two reasons: 78 per cent of the decline is due to increased costs of air, water, and safety on the job, and the remaining 22 per cent is attributable to increased needs for surveillance of potentially dishonest employees, customers, contractors and thieves. The resources put into improvements in air, water, and safety are not a net loss to society although they may reduce corporate profitability. The increased need for surveillance in business, however, may represent the fact that the cost of monitoring transactions has risen. Mayo (1945) might have predicted this change as an inevitable result of the instability which accompanies industrialization. In our framework, we could advance the following explanation: exchange relationships are generally subject to so much informational amgibuity that they can never be governed completely by markets. Consequently, they have been supplemented through cultural, clan mechanisms. As instability, heterogeneity, and mobility have intensified in the United States, however, the effectiveness of these cultural mechanisms has been vitiated and bureaucratic mechanisms of surveillance and control have increased. Although bureaucratic surveillance may be the optimal strategy under present social conditions, it is nonetheless true that the United States is devoting more of its resources to transactional matters than it did ten years ago, and that represents a net decline in its welfare.

The degree of uncertainty and opportunism that characterize American society may be such that no mechanisms of control ever function very well. We have already observed that the conditions necessary for a pure market, bureaucracy, or clan are rare. Even a combination of those control mechanisms may be insufficient in many cases, however. In organizations using new technologies or in the public sector, the rate of change, instability of employment, or ambiguity of performance evaluation may simply overwhelm all rational control attempts.

In these cases, exchange becomes institutionalized. Meyer and Rowan's (1977) central thesis is that school systems, by their nature, evade any form of rational control. They have no effective price mechanism, no effective bureaucratic control, and no internally consistent cultures (see also Meyer et al., 1978). Thus school systems (as distinguished from education, which need not be done by large organizations) continue to grow and survive because the objectives which they are believed to pursue have been accepted as necessary by society. Since rational control is not feasible within the school, no one knows whether it is actually pursuing these goals, but an institutionalized organization (the church is another example) need not give evidence of performance (see also Ouchi, 1977: 97–8).

All work organizations are institutionalized in the sense that fundamental purposes of all viable organizations must mesh at least somewhat with broad social values (Parsons and Shils, 1951). This institutionalization permits organizations to survive even under conditions that severely limit their capacity for rational control. Ultimately, organizational failure occurs only when society deems the basic objectives of the organization unworthy of continued support.

What is an organization? An organization, in our sense, is any stable pattern of transactions between individuals or aggregations of individuals. Our framework can thus be applied to the analysis of relationships between individuals or between subunits within a corporation, or to transactions between firms in an economy. Why do organizations exist? In our sense, all patterned transactions are organized, and thus all stable exchanges in a society are organized. When we ask 'why do organizations exist', we usually mean to ask 'why do bureaucratic organizations exist', and the answer is clear. Bureaucratic organizations exist because, under certain specifiable conditions, they are the most efficient means for an equitable mediation of transactions between parties. In a similar manner, market and clan organizations exist because each of them, under certain conditions, offers the lowest transactions cost.

William G. Ouchi

Notes

1. In the broader language necessary to encompass both economics and organization theory, an organization may be thought of as any stable pattern of transactions. In this definition, a market is as much an organization as is a bureaucracy or a clan. The only requirement is that, for the purposes of this discussion, we maintain a clear distinction between the idea of 'bureaucracy' and the idea of 'organization'. Bureaucracy as used here refers specifically to the Weberian model, while organization refers to any stable pattern of transactions between individuals or aggregations of individuals.
2. Despite these desirable properties, the bureaucratic type has continually been under attack and revision. As Williamson points out, the move from U-form (functional) to M-form (divisional) organization among many large firms has been motivated by a desire to simulate a capital market within a bureaucratic framework because of its superior efficiency. By regrouping the parts of the organization, it is possible to create subentities that are sufficiently autonomous to permit precise measurement and the determination of an effective price mechanism. Although each division may still operate internally as a bureaucracy, the economies which accrue from this partial market solution are often large, offsetting the diseconomies of functional redundancy which often accompany the separation of the organization into divisions.

References

Abegglen, James C. (1958), *The Japanese Factory: Aspects of Its Social Organization.* (Glencoe, II: Free Press).

Argyris, Chris (1964), *Integrating the Individual and the Organization* (New York: Wiley).

Arrow, Kenneth J. (1974), *The Limits of Organization.* (New York: Norton).

Barnard, Chester I. (1968), *The Functions of the Executive,* 30th anniversary ed. (Cambridge: Harvard).

Blau, Peter M., and W. Richard Scott (1962), *Formal Organizations* (San Francisco: Scott, Foreman).

Clark, Burton R. (1970), *The Distinctive College: Antioch, Reed, and Swarthmore* (Chicago: Aldine).

Coase, R. H. (1937), 'The nature of the firm', *Economica,* new series, 4: 386–405.

Denison, Edward F. (1978), *Effects of Selected Changes in the Institutional and Human Environment upon Output Per Unit of Input* Brookings General Series Reprint #335 (Washington: Brookings).

Dore, Ronald (1973), *British Factory–Japanese Factory.* (Berkeley: University of California).

Durkheim, Emile (1933), *The Division of Labor in Society,* G. Simpson, trans. (New York: Free Press).

Etzioni, Amitai (1965), 'Organizational control structure', in James G. March (ed.), *Handbook of Organizations* (Chicago: Rand McNally), 650–77.

Galbraith, Jay (1973), *Designing Complex Organizations* (Reading, MA: Addison-Wesley).

Gouldner, Alvin W. (1961), 'The norm of reciprocity', *American Sociological Review,* 25: 161–79.

Kanter, Rosabeth Moss (1972), *Commitment and Community* (Cambridge: Harvard).

Katz, Ralph (1978), 'Job longevity as a situational factor in job satisfaction', *Administrative Science Quarterly,* 23: 204–23

Light, Ivan H. (1972), *Ethnic Enterprise in America* (Berkeley: University of California).

Lipset, Seymour M., Martin A. Trow, and James S Coleman (1956), *Union Democracy* (Glencoe, II.: Free Press).

March, James G., and Herbert A. Simon (1958), *Organizations.* (New York: Wiley).

Mayo, Elton (1945), *The Social Problems of an Industrial Civilization,* (Boston: Division of Research, Graduate School of Business Administration, Harvard University).

Meyer, John W., and Brian Rowan (1977), 'Institutionalized organizations: Formal structure as myth and ceremony', *American Journal of Sociology,* 83: 340–63

Meyer, John W., W. Richard Scott, Sally Cole and Jo-Ann K. Intili (1978), 'Instructional dissensus and institutional consensus in schools', in Marshall W. Meyer and Associates (eds.), *Environments and Organizations* (San Francisco: Jossey-Bass), 233–63.

Nakane, Chie (1973), *Japanese Society* (rev. ed.) (Middlesex, England: Penguin).

Ouchi, William G. (1977), 'The relationship between organizational structure and organizational control', *Administrative Science Quarterly,* 22: 95–113.

————(1979), 'A conceptual framework for the design of organizational control mechanisms', *Management Science,* 25: 833–48.

————and Alfred M. Jaeger (1978), 'Type Z organization: Stability in the midst of mobility', *Academy of Management Review,* 3: 305–14.

————and Jerry B. Johnson (1978), 'Types of organizational control and their relationship to emotional well-being', *Administrative Science Quarterly,* 23: 293–317.

Parsons, Talcott, and Edward A. Shils (1951), 'Values, motives, and systems of action', in Talcott Parsons and Edward A Shills (eds.), *Toward a General Theory of Action* (Cambridge: Harvard), 47–275.

Selznick, Philip (1966), *TVA and the Grass Roots* (orig. ed. 1949) (New York: Harper Torchbooks).

Simon, Herbert A. (1945), *Administrative Behavior* (New York: Free Press).

————(1957), *Models of Man* (New York: Wiley).

Van Maanen, John (1975), 'Police socialization: A longitudinal examination of job

William G. Ouchi

attitudes in an urban police department', *Administrative Science Quarterly,* 20: 207–28.

Van Maanen, John, and Edgar H. Schein (1978), 'Toward a theory of organizational socialization', Manuscript, Sloan School of Industrial Administration, Massachusetts Institute of Technology.

Weber, Max (1947), *The Theory of Social and Economic Organization* (orig. ed., 1925), A.M. Henderson and T. Parsons, trans. (New York: Free Press).

———(1968), *Economy and Society* (orig. ed., 1925), G. Roth and C. Wittich, eds. (New York: Bedminster Press)

Weick, Karl E. (1969), *The Social Psychology of Organizing* (Reading, MA: Addison-Wesley).

Williamson, O. E. (1975), *Markets and Hierarchies: Analysis and Antitrust Implications* (New York: Free Press).

Economic Theories of the Firm: Past, Present, and Future

Paul Milgrom and John Roberts

1. Markets, Firms, and Western Economic History

When economists today write about the firm, they most often proceed by comparing its characteristics with those of markets. The reason is not hard to understand: As economic historians have repeatedly argued (Innis, 1938; North and Thomas 1973; Rosenberg and Birdzell, 1985); the emergence, expansion and eventual dominance of the market system in western economies since the Middle Ages crucially contributed to economic growth and the resulting accumulation of wealth and rising standards of living for much of the population. More recently, the spectacular successes of the market-oriented economies of the rapidly industrializing nations of Asia have shown that the strengths of the market as a basis for organizing economic activity are not limited to western societies. These considerable achievements of market economies have led some to suggest that other sorts of economic organizations basically arise only to compensate for failures of the market (Arrow, 1974). Others, much taken with the past successes of market economies, challenge any proposed intervention with the question: Why not rely on a market solution?

There is another, quite opposite, view according to which markets are a primitive way of organizing activity—one that worked well enough in simpler times when agricultural products were traded for finished foreign goods or for the hand-made products of local craftsmen and that still works well enough for distributing consumer goods and for buying and selling standardized items (grains, financial assets), but one that has proved inferior as a way

Paul Milgrom and John Roberts

of organizing the transactions arising in complex, multistage production systems. In this view, the market's declining importance is evidenced by the emergence and growing importance of large, integrated firms, internal labour markets, joint research ventures, and the like. For if market-mediated transactions work so well, why don't firms hire more inputs—both products and services—from independent suppliers in the market? Why do they so often distribute and sell their own products? Mine their own raw materials? Provide their own personnel, accounting, computer and other services? The successes of firms that organize so many of their own activities without relying on markets has led some economists (Coase, 1937; Knight 1971; Williamson, 1975) to pose this question: Why can't a large firm (or a centrally planned economy) always operate at least as efficiently as a chaotic, unorganized market?

In his classic 1921 study, *Risk, Uncertainty and Profit,* Frank Knight (1971) identified a number of factors that might limit the efficient size of firms. Entrepreneurial firms, he reasoned, were constrained by the limited financial resources of the founder, while larger partnerships were limited by the 'free rider' problem arising from many partners sharing in a single pool of profits. However, with the rapidly developing financial markets of his day, the only deterrent Knight could identify to the unlimited growth of publicly traded corporations was the problem of properly motivating employees.[1] But even to view this as a problem presupposes that corporations cannot install market-like incentive-compensation packages.

Coase (1937) is commonly credited as the first economist to pose the question of which activities are most efficiently carried out within the firm, and which without. To answer this question, Coase posited that there are different costs in carrying out transactions in the firm and in the market. He identified the costs of negotiating agreements and determining appropriate prices as the principal costs of market-mediated transactions. Both of these since have received extensive attention. Coase had little to say, however, about what costs might be uniquely and necessarily associated with transactions taking place within the firm. Instead, he posited that any firm could utilize only a fixed amount of management or entrepreneurial talent, so that taking best advantage of the talent of society's entrepreneurs and managers requires an economy with many firms. This assumption obviously begs the question, but little that is more satisfactory has been proposed until recently.

2. Recent Theories

Chief among the purported virtues of the market system are that it econo-mizes on the information and communication needs of individuals and firms (Hayek, 1945) and that it provides proper incentives for self-interested individuals to economize on resource usage and to innovate with improved products and production techniques. The idea that a price system econo-mizes on information and communication has been the subject of numerous theoretical studies (e.g., Hurwicz, 1977) which show that under certain conditions the announcement by buyers and sellers of quantities supplied and demanded to a hypothetical market auctioneer and by the auctioneer of prices to the buyers and sellers is the minimal amount of communication required to sustain efficient outcomes as an equilibrium of any dynamic process. These conclusions, however, are based on a paradigm in which all goods are potentially useful to all producers and consumers and all relevant information regarding resource availability can be mirrored in prices. These two conditions mean, for example, that knowledge of the wages of barbers in Ankara, Turkey is useful to a Palo Alto semi-conductor manufacturer while knowledge of the willingness of an accomplished chip-design engineer to switch jobs is extraneous or redundant. The team-theoretic models of Marschak and Radner (1972) do begin to represent the problem of commu-nication when specialized local knowledge is necessary for effective decisions and yet some coordination of the dispersed decision-makers is vital. Research in this area is important for understanding the substitution of explicit management activity for market-guided activity: Managers spend the greater part of their time collecting informal information by telephone or in face-to-face contact for use in decision-making (Mintzberg 1973),

Just as markets can fail as the least-cost way to communicate production information, traditional markets can fail in various ways to provide correct incentives or to provide them efficiently. First, the market traditionally provides incentives to producers by requiring them to bear the full conse-quences of their decisions. But bearing full responsibility may be impossible if the producer has limited financial resources, or undesirable if the producer is risk averse (Wilson, 1969). These problems are compounded when the results of production depend on the contributions of several individuals—the case of 'team production' (Alchian and Demsetz, 1972)—or when informational asymmetrices are present, either before or after contracting. One partial solution is to substitute monitoring of inputs for standard, output-based, incentive schemes, thus moving away from tradi-tional market forms of organization and creating a role for other, more formal, sorts of organizations. Standard sources of market failure such as externalities or increasing returns give still other reasons for abandoning pure market solutions in favour of other organizational forms.

Another role for formal organizations is to resolve disputes or economize on bargaining costs that a market relationship would entail (Williamson, 1975). Bargaining costs presume that there is (or might be) some surplus to bargain over—some reason why the parties have something more to gain by working together rather than with some other partners. This can happen, for example, if one of the parties has made a specialized investment and the parties must later agree how to divide the returns it produces. In simple situations it may be possible to avoid bargaining costs by agreeing in advance how the assets are to be used and the benefits shared. But in complex long-term relationships, the desired contracts may be so detailed that it becomes impractical to specify and enforce them. Then, some form of governance arrangement, or *relational contract*,[2] in which the parties agree to *procedures* for making production-related decisions, determining how revenues are to be shared, and resolving disputes, may be more efficient than a loosely structured market relationship. Vertical integration is seen from this perspective as one extreme of relational contracting, in which the parties submit to the common authority of a chief executive (Williamson, 1985; Klein, Crawford, and Alchian, 1979).

The foregoing theories explain why there are unavoidable costs of transacting in the marketplace. But are there corresponding costs that are necessarily incurred in other methods of governing these transactions, and, if so, what are they? Our focus will be on the *inevitable* costs of non-market arrangements. If some particular tasks can be done most efficiently through the market (because, for example, prices are efficient transmitters of information), we want to allow the possibility that the organization could continue to use market arrangements for these. Still, all deviations from purely voluntary exchange involve placing some control in the hands of a central authority (e.g., the corporate head office or the state planning bureau), even if the rules prescribe that the central authority may intervene only when such intervention is efficient. The issue is why is a centralized organization using a strategy of selective intervention not able to do at least as well as the market under all circumstances, and better than the market in some circumstances?

The answer is that, for the reasons explored below, the very existence of a central authority inevitably affects how the system operates even in those situations where interventions are not helpful. First, there is the problem of opportunistic behaviour by the central authority. Its decisions might be determined not only by considerations of efficiency but also by considerations of personal interest (Williamson, 1985: Grossman and Hart, 1986) or even by bribes and favours. This problem can sometimes be alleviated by subjecting the executive authority to monitoring by an outside judicial authority, but that procedure requires (1) specifying clearly what constitutes proper behaviour by the executive, (2) expending extra resources in monitoring and extra documentation to justify the executive's decisions, and (3) properly motivating the judicial authority. If the executive authority is opportunistic, the costs associated with (1)–(3) are likely to be quite high.

Even if the executive authority is unusually competent, public spirited, and immune to bribes—and all these qualities are commonly known—it may still be desirable to limit its discretion, for two reasons. First, in order to provide correct incentives to others in the organization, the authority must be able to make commitments to act against its own interests in the future, and these commitments are not credible unless there are some effective limits on the centre's powers. For example, the government may wish to commit a policy of issuing patents to the discoverers of new drugs, even though, once a drug has been discovered, the public would benefit from withholding the patent and allowing unrestricted competition in the provision of the drug. The *policy* of providing patents is socially beneficial, even though the *act* of issuing of an individual patent does not serve the public interest. Similarly, the owner of a firm might want to commit to share the fruits of an innovation with the innovator, even though, once the innovation has been made, the owner's interests are best served by keeping the innovation for himself. A common form of commitment in both of these examples is the establishment of some kind of property right: the drug company has exclusive rights to market its discovery and the innovator has the right to receive royalties on sales of her innovation.[3]

The second reason to limit the discretion of an honest, competent decision-maker is to discourage rent-seeking behaviour by others who are affected by the centre's decisions. As we have argued elsewhere (Milgrom, 1988: Milgrom and Roberts, 1987a), the mere willingness of the centre to consider seriously a decision with large redistributional consequences will cause other economic agents to waste significant resources in attempts to influence or block it or to delay its implementation. In public decision-making, for example, enormous resources are spent in proposing legislation or regulations and in advocating or opposing these proposals, as well as in filing and manoeuvring for advantage in lawsuits. In bureaucracies—private as well as public—individuals angle for promotions and pay rises, lobby for the adoption of their programs and projects, and advocate rule changes that enhance their power or status. Selling costs in the private sector represent yet another example of costs incurred to affect decisions. As with the previous category of costs of centralized decision-making, a common and effective means of limiting the costs in this category is to establish suitable property rights, which either limit the powers of the central authority to make decisions or require full compensation for any property it seizes.

Our account so far has exaggerated somewhat the costs associated with market and centralized forms of resource allocation. Opportunistic behaviour of the kind we have described is at least partially alleviated by norms, codes of conduct, and the like. It is important to understand that these social restrictions are themselves perfectly consistent with self-interested individual behaviour. For example, suppliers may honour agreements and replace defective goods even when they aren't legally required to do so because they value their reputations for honesty, quality, or fairness (Klein and Leffler, 1981). Failure to live up to expectations may cause a seller to lose profitable business in the future. Similarly, employers may treat their employees well in order to make it easier to hire desired employees in the future.

The efficacy of the reputation mechanism depends on how much a firm gains by cheating, how quickly its cheating is likely to be detected, how widely its misbehaviour is known, how much is lost when the detected misbehaviour damages the firm's reputation, and how costly it is to rebuild a lost reputation. In particular, if cheating is detected instantly and becomes widely known throughout the relevant community, and if entry into other, more remote communities is difficult, then increasing the number and frequency of interactions within the community increases the opportunity costs of cheating and makes it possible to support rigorous codes of conduct.[4] This suggests that a society of long-lived, formal organizations may be especially effective in using reputation mechanisms. Conversely, the reputation mechanism cannot operate effectively in fluid, impersonal, anonymous market settings—such as the Middle Eastern suq—where there is no expectation of long-term, repeated dealings and no market-wide reputations. Only in more developed markets, with extensive communications among traders and repeated dealings, do market reputations matter. Thus, 'the market' is seen to be not a single form of organization but a whole category,[5] and any clear-cut distinction between markets and other organizations quickly blurs.

3. Possible Future Directions

All the theories reviewed above are incomplete in important ways, and our main prediction—and prescription—is that the development of these theories will—and should—continue. We shall examine some of the likely avenues of development below. A second prediction/prescription is founded on our view that the incentive-based transaction costs theory has been made to carry too much of the weight of explanation in the theory of organizations. We expect competing and complementary theories to emerge—theories that are founded on economizing on bounded rationality and that pay more attention to changing technology or to evolutionary considerations. We shall have more to say about some of these possibilities, too, below.

Although widespread interest among economists in the study of organizations and, more particularly, in the firm as an actual institution is a relatively recent phenomenon, this is not the case in other disciplines. Organization behaviour, business policy, and parts of sociology have been primarily concerned with these issues for several decades. Moreover, the nature of research in these fields—especially the relatively underdeveloped state of formal theorizing—means that they have generated numerous field studies, case histories, and other empirical work on the organization, design, policies, behaviour, and performance of actual firms, and on the behaviour of individuals in these contexts. This is in striking contrast to the situation in the economics of organization, where the vast bulk of the research has been primarily deductive theorizing and where too often the questions that the latest paper seeks to answer arise not from consideration of puzzling aspects of observed practice or from present trends in business organization but from the desire to extend the analysis in an earlier paper that, in turn, may have been only tenuously connected to observation.

We would be the last to denigrate the value of specialization among researchers; it is quite likely that efficiency requires that economists first focus primarily on theoretical analyses of organizations. Moreover, it is certainly true that the research done in other disciplines, having been aimed at answering questions other than those that occur naturally to economists and, even more, having been informed by very different modes of theorizing than we employ, are not always directly relevant to our work. Still, the best work in these fields can be enormously valuable to economists (see, e.g., Baron, 1987), and it seems abundantly clear that the economics of organization could be enriched by insights and observations imported from these other fields, as well as, of course, by empirical studies by economists.

Finally, the shape of future theory will and should be influenced by the important applied issues of the day. Just as the growth of the modern firm led Knight and Coase to begin theorizing about firms, and the Russian Revolution led to new theories of socialist central planning and analyses of the market as a planning mechanism, such modern phenomena as corporate take-overs and restructuring, the increasing use of subcontractors in manufacturing industries, and the move of various finance and strategy formulation functions out of the firm to be provided by investment bankers and consulting firms, ought to (and probably will) attract the attention of economic theorists.

Here are some of the areas in which we expect progress to be made most rapidly. The topics in Sections 3.1–3.5 all fall generally under the current transaction costs paradigm. The remaining topics look in other directions to explain important aspects of firm organization.

3.1. Incomplete Contracts

Governance structures or relational contracts, are now commonly seen as substitutes for detailed long-term exchange contracts (Simon, 1951; Williamson, 1986). However, relational contracts are but one alternative to detailed long-term exchange contracts. Another is a series of short-term contracts, renegotiated frequently as conditions change. Short-term contracts are often simpler and may involve far fewer contingencies than long-term contracts. Even in the presence of moral hazard, a series of 'complete' short-term contracts[6] can, in a surprisingly wide range of circumstances, perform fully as well as complete long-term contracts (Fudenberg, Holmström, and Milgrom, 1987). This suggests that—when conditions of the theorem apply[7]—it is the costs of negotiating short-term agreements, rather than any necessary limitations of the short-term contracts themselves, that are the fundamental cost of market transactions (Milgrom and Roberts, 1987a).

Several caveats should be attached to this conclusion. Most important, even when the provisions of a long-term contract can be effectively reproduced with a sequence of short-term contracts, it is by no means true that the short-term contracts are always simpler. For example, a 'whole life' insurance contract in which the insured pays a fixed premium every year and his heirs collect a fixed sum upon his death is equivalent to the combination of a series of 'one-year renewable term insurance' contracts in which a different premium is paid each year as the insured ages and a savings plan in which deposits in each year vary with age. Contracts of both these kinds are actually marketed. We could go further, however, and imagine that the premium rates for each year were not guaranteed but instead were determined in the spot market as a function of the insured's health as well as his age. Then, to duplicate a whole life contract, the short-term contracts would have to specify payments at the end of each year, contingent on the insured's health, that are just sufficient to offset the increased future premiums. The long-term ('whole life') contract requires many fewer contingent payments, fewer and easier calculations by the insurance buyer, and fewer evaluations of the insured's health: Surely it is simpler in these respects than a series of shorter-term contracts.

Even when costs of complexity are not at issue, short-term contracts cannot perform as well as long-term ones when either of two conditions hold: asymmetric information at recontracting dates prevents the parties from smoothly negotiating an efficient agreement; or monetary incentives are of limited effectiveness (due to either financial constraints or limited product markets), requiring a reliance on payments in kind over time that can be delivered only in a long-term relationship. The first condition suggests that it may be enlightening to study contracting problems when one party makes an unobserved investment that affects his productivity. The second suggests a comparative study of labour markets over time and place, to see how differences in the wealth of workers and access to capital and product markets affect the nature of labour contracts. For example, to what extent was the efficient movement of workers from the feudal manor to the town delayed by the difficulty experienced by the lord in collecting a share of the resultant gain once the move occurred and by the serfs' inability to borrow against future earnings to compensate the lord in advance? In this regard, how do such factors relate to the survival of serfdom in czarist Russia long after it had disappeared in western Europe?

3.2. Bargaining Theory

There have been several recent attempts to explain inefficiencies in bargaining—delays or total failures to agree—as resulting from asymmetric information.[8] Most of the effort to date has focused on developing appropriate equilibrium concepts and proving existence; comparatively little of this work has proved informative in understanding the relative efficiency of bargaining in differing contexts. We still do not fully understand, for example, what determines the magnitude of efficiency losses in these models. Such results should be sought.

Given the importance of bargaining inefficiencies for transaction cost theories, it should also be useful to widen our perspective about how bargaining inefficiencies may occur. For example, suppose that two parties are bargaining over an item that is certainly more valuable to the potential buyer than to the seller. The value of the item to each party is an increasing function of some unobserved characteristic, which we call 'quality'. Information about quality can be acquired privately by either party, but only at a cost. In that case, a bargain struck quickly is no evidence of efficiency, since both parties may have wastefully acquired information to protect themselves. If quality uncertainty is great and information is moderately expensive (so that the gains from trade are less than the cost of having both parties become informed, but either party could gain by becoming unilaterally informed), then the parties may be unwilling to enter negotiations without information and yet be unable to benefit if both acquire information. Thus, they may fail to reach any agreement on an appropriate price, despite the certain gains from trade and the perfect symmetry of information at equilibrium. If the parties can anticipate that circumstances like these will arise, both could benefit by agreeing to be bound to allow the price to be set by an impartial arbitrator, that is, to substitute an 'organization' for a market.

3.3. Reputations

In long-term relationships or when a firm has many customers, reputations function to alleviate opportunism in the way that we described earlier. According to the received theory, a firm may sometimes act against its own short-term or one-customer interests in order to preserve its reputation for the longer term or among other customers. How effective is this reputation mechanism compared, say, with contractual solutions like warranties?

To illustrate the problem, imagine Customer 2 is supposed (at equilibrium) to punish a supplier by refusing to purchase from it if Customer 1 is treated unfairly. The first issue is what constitutes unfair treatment? Can Customer 2 identify it when it happens? If there is some uncertainty about that point, and the supplier does treat Customer 1 unfairly, might not Customer 2 benefit by pretending not to recognize the episode? What incentive does Customer 1 have to bring its unfair treatment to Customer 2's attention, if doing so is costly? For reputations involving punishments by third parties to operate effectively, it seems that the reputation must be about some simple, easily recognized policy, like one of refunding the purchase price to any dissatisfied customer or repairing or replacing a product free for a year from the date of purchase. But these sorts of policies are also easily written into legally binding contracts. Contracts that specify damages have the advantage, compared with reputation mechanisms, that they make it worthwhile for the damaged party to inform the third party about the violation and so enhance the information flow in the system.

Even when third-party punishments are not an issue, simplicity and ease of recognizability can still be important for the efficacy of reputations. A reputation may be most quickly and effectively built by extreme actions: one US clothing retailer has built a reputation for superb service by graciously accepting 'returns' on products that could not possibly have been purchased there, including automobile tyres! The role of simple stories in teaching members of an organization the sort of behaviour expected of them and in inculcating the corporation's culture has been documented in the organization behaviour literature (Martin, 1982). Generally, the circumstances in which reputation mechanisms might work well and the means by which reputations are built, used, and lost are ripe for further study.

3.4. Influence Activities and Rent-seeking

The term 'rent-seeking' was coined by Krueger (1974) to refer to the activities of private firms and individuals seeking to capture rents created by government interventions in the economy. Rent-seeking theories suggest that government involvement in the economy causes inefficiencies, and these theories have been adapted, as indicated above (Milgrom and Roberts, 1987), to explain the diseconomies that accompany centralization of authority in firms.

This line of analysis seems likely to branch in two directions. The first is to develop the basic theory of influence in organizations more fully. As a particular example, if limiting influence activities (rent-seeking) requires that rules be established limiting the discretion of executives and managers, how are the rules to be made? Can't rent-seeking occur in the rule-making process, just as it does in legislative decisions in government? Having decisions made behind a veil of ignorance may help, at least in some matters, as may limiting opportunities for making transfers to those formulating the rules. Influence activities will in this case be practised only to the level justified by the returns to the current actors, rather than the higher level that would be generated if the benefits accruing to succeeding generations could be captured by those currently active.[9] Still, it seems likely that an optimal arrangement will entail separating operational from rule-making decisions, and employing a more cumbersome, difficult-to-manipulate process for the latter. Rules that are too easily changed are hardly rules at all.[10]

The second direction is to expand the new private sector theories of rent-seeking to include rent-seeking in markets, courtrooms, and boardrooms. Are the huge salaries of arbitrageurs and securities lawyers simply returns to inefficient private sector rent-seeking? If so, then the empirical techniques of Posner (1975) suggest that all such returns are to be regarded as being a pure social loss, since competition among businessmen to earn these rents leads to their full dissipation. What of the contingency fees of lawyers, the earnings of corporate chief executives, and the greenmail paid to corporate raiders?

3.5. Ownership: Residual Returns or Residual Rights?

In Roman law, ownership of property meant the right to use or abuse it. Knight (1971) identifies ownership of a firm as the right to control it or to pick those who will manage it. The actual concept of ownership, at least as it applies to firms, has evolved considerably, however, from these simple, clean formulations. The connection between ownership and control is quite subtle in North American corporations; with US mutual savings banks, mutual insurance companies, and most Japanese corporations, there seems to be little connection at all. Meanwhile, what relevance does the concept of ownership have to private, not-for-profit organizations, co-ops, and crown corporations? Refining our understanding of what ownership means, or whether its meaning is situation-dependent, seems essential not only for understanding a variety of phenomena from corporate take-overs in the United States to the incentives of managers in Japan, but also for formulating sensible policies, both public and private, regarding decision-making on take-overs, investments and disinvestments, compensation forms and levels, and employment practices.

Grossman and Hart (1986) have championed 'residential rights of control' as the appropriate concept of ownership of assets. These rights give the owner the power to make decisions regarding the use or disposition of an asset in all respects that are not explicitly designated or limited by a written contract. This definition is problematic in its application; for the typical large firm with many physical assets (as well as various intangible ones), it is never the case that a single party is the owner in the sense of exercising all the residual rights of control. Even if, by setting policies and monitoring adherence to them, the owners of the firm might try to control the decisions made by others, it will never be possible in a large firm to exercise total control.

A simple alternative view holds that the owner is the one who collects residual returns after all other factors have been paid. In a long-lived firm, where all the product from a single period's activities does not accrue in that period and may never be accurately measured, the way these returns are allocated may significantly affect incentives—and hence the efficiency of the organization. The full integration of residual rights with residual returns is a key problem in the newly emerging theory of ownership rights.

3.6. Adapting to Uncertainty

Galbraith (1977) has formulated the problem of organization design as one of allowing the organization to adapt to the uncertainty in its own environment.

The organization can adapt either by processing more information or by reducing the need to process information. Within the second class of adaptations are environmental management (produce a different product, serve a different market), creation of slack resources (inventories, production capacity), and creation of self-contained tasks (reduced specialization). Within the first are vertical and lateral communication systems.

What determines the optimal mix of these adaptations? Galbraith's framework offers the possibility of price theoretic explanations of changes in organization form. Some initial steps in this direction are taken in Milgrom and Roberts (1987b). For example, cheaper communications, reduced costs of expanding the product line, and fall costs of flexibility in production costs and increasing levels of demand levels favour substituting vertical communications for holding inventory. Similarly, increases in the complexity of the product and frequency of the product change can be met by using more highly trained employees performing less specialized tasks.

3.7. Planning and Budgeting

Another subject area where continued research promises new understandings is that of iterative planning. What *kinds* of information do price systems economize on in the planning process? What sorts of non-market communications are helpful in planning and controlling production? What are the incentives for correct revelation of information in iterative planning (Roberts, 1987)? How does one properly account for the bounded rationality of the people who must make the planning process work?

There is some literature touching on aspects of these issues in the context of national economic planning but little focusing on the planning within or between autonomous firms. Yet the planning and budgeting processes seem to absorb large amounts of time and effort within formal organizations and to be important aspects of the decision-making, control, and evaluation systems of these organizations. Achieving an understanding of the nature and role of these processes and of their characteristics would seem important to understanding resource allocation in the firm.

4. Changing Concepts of the Firm

In the Arrow-Debreu theory of the private ownership economy, the distinction between firm and market is absolutely clear: a firm is a production set summarizing the possibilities for transforming one bundle of time-, event-, and location-differentiated commodities into another; a market is the coming together of economic agents (firms and consumers) to exchange ownership of such commodity bundles. However, as our analysis of the firm deepens, the firm-market distinction blurs; for production itself involves exchange. The boundaries of firms are fuzzy: two legally separate firms may be more closely integrated in their planning and operations than are any pair of divisions in a conglomerate; and even though there is no commonality of ownership or explicit long-term contract linking them, they may continue their close relations over indefinitely extended periods. Moreover, decentralized firms may adopt market-like solutions to their organizational problems, using, for example, arms-length negotiations to determine transfer prices and evaluating employee and divisional performance on profit criteria.

The extreme response to such observations is to deny any difference between market contracts and those made between members of a firm (Alchian and Demsetz, 1972[11]). More reasonably, there is a multidimensional spectrum of institutional arrangements with simple, discrete markets and tightly managed hierarchies at two of the extremes. Understanding organization in its many economic dimensions—including ownership, communication, planning, and incentives—will occupy the attention of economists for many years to come.

Notes

1. Knight writes (p. 253): 'With reference to the first of our two points above mentioned, the extension of the scope of operations, the corporation may be said to have solved the organization problem. There appears to be hardly any limit to the magnitude of enterprise which it is possible to organize in this form, so far as mere ability to get the public to buy the securities is concerned. On the second score, however, the effective unification of interests, though the corporation has accomplished much in comparison with other forms of organization, there is still much to be desired'.
2. See Macneil (1981) or Goetz and Scott (1981) for account of the law and economics of relational contracting.
3. Laffont and Tirole (1985) and Baron and Besanko (1987) have explored the nature of optimal contracts when the authority is unable to commit itself.
4. This assertion is just one version of the Folk Theorem from the theory of repeated games—see Fudenberg and Maskin (1986) for a more complete account.
5. Douglass North (1987) emphasizes the historical and regional variations among markets in the way performance is assured.

6. These are one-period contracts that can be made contingent on anything that is common knowledge at the end of the period.
7. Sufficient conditions are that there is common knowledge of preferences and productive opportunities at renegotiation dates and that there is no lower bound on the utility of consumption.
8. See Sutton (1986) and Rubinstein (1987) for surveys.
9. Of course, if the interests of future generations are not represented in decisions that affect them, there is the familiar potential for an inefficiency arising from externalities.
10. See Fama and Jensen (1983) for a related view of the separation of powers and responsibilities within organizations.
11. They wrote: 'I can "punish" you only by withholding future business or by seeking redress in the courts for any failure to honor our exchange agreement. That is exactly all an employer can do. He can fire or sue, just as I can fire my grocer by stopping purchases from him or sue him for delivering faulty products'. This view overlooks substantial differences, perhaps most importantly that an employee typically works exclusively for his employer, which helps alleviate the problems of common agency.

References

Alchian, Armen and Harold Demsetz (1972), 'Production, information costs, and economic organization', *American Economic Review*, 62: 777–95.

Arrow, Kenneth (1974), *The Limits of Organization* (New York: Norton).

Baron, James N. (1987), 'The employment relation as a social relation', *Journal of Japanese and International Economics* (forthcoming).

Baron, David and David Besanko (1987), 'Commitment and fairness in a dynamic regulatory relationship', *Review of Economic Studies* (forthcoming).

Chandler, Alfred (1977), *The Visible Hand* (Cambridge, MA: Harvard University Press).

Coase, Ronald (1937), 'The nature of the firm', *Economica*, 4: 386–405.

Fama, Eugene and Michael Jensen (1983), 'The separation of ownership and control', *Journal of Law and Economics*, 26: 301–25.

Fudenberg, Drew, Bengt Holmström and Paul Milgrom (1987), 'Short-term contracts and long-term agency relationships', unpublished paper.

Fudenberg, Drew and Eric Maskin (1986), 'The folk theorem in repeated games with discounting and with incomplete information', *Econometrica*, 54: 533–54.

Galbraith, Jay R. (1977), *Organization Design* (Reading, PA: Addison-Welsey).

Goetz, Charles and Robert Scott (1981), 'Principles of relational contracts', *Virginia Law Review*, 67: 1089–150.

Paul Milgrom and John Roberts

Grossman, Sanford and Oliver Hart (1986), 'The costs and benefits of ownership: a theory of vertical and lateral integration', *Journal of Political Economy*, 94: 691–719.

Hayek, F. A. (1945), 'The use of knowledge in society', *American Economic Review*, 35: 519–30.

Holmström, Bengt (1982), 'Moral hazard in teams', *Bell Journal of Economics*, 13: 324–40.

Hurwicz, Leonid (1977), 'On the dimensional requirements of informationally decentralized pareto-satisfactory processes', in K. J. Arrow and L. Hurwicz, *Studies in Resource Allocation Processes* (Cambridge: Cambridge University Press).

Innis, Harold A. (1938), 'The penetrative powers of the price system,' *Canadian Journal of Economics and Political Science*, 4: 299–319.

Klein, Benjamin, Robert Crawford and Armen Alchian (1978), 'Vertical integration, appropriate rents, and the competitive contracting process', *Journal of Law and Economics* 21: 297–326.

Klein, Benjamin and Keith Leffler (1981), 'The role of market forces in assuring contractual performance', *Journal of Political Economy*, 89: 615–41.

Knight, Frank H. (1971), *Risk, Uncertainty and Profit* (Chicago: University of Chicago Press).

Laffont, Jean-Jacques and Jean Tirole (1985), 'The dynamics of incentive contracts', MIT Economics Working Paper No. 403.

Macneil, Ian (1981), 'Economic analysis of contractual relations: its shortfalls and the need for a "rich" classifactory apparatus', *Northwestern University Law Review*, 1018–63.

Marschak, Jacob and Roy Radner (1972), *Economic Theory of Teams* (New Haven: Yale University Press).

Martin, Joanne (1982), 'Stories and scripts in organizational settings', in A. H. Hastorf and A. M. Isen (eds.) *Cognitive Social Psychology* (New York: Elsevier/North Holland).

Milgrom, Paul (1988), 'Employment contracts, influence activities and efficient organizational design', *Journal of Political Economy*, 96: 42–60.

Milgrom, Paul and John Roberts (1987a), 'Bargaining and influence costs and the organization of economic activity', Research Paper, Graduate School of Business, Stanford University.

————(1987b) 'Communications and inventories as substitutes in organizing production', *Scandinavian Journal of Economics* (forthcoming).

————(1987c), 'An economic approach to influence activities in organizations', *American Journal of Sociology* (forthcoming).

Mintzberg, Henry (1973), *The Nature of Managerial Work* (New York: Harper & Row).

North, Douglass C. (1987), 'Institutions, transaction costs and economic growth', *Economic Inquiry*, 25: 419–28.

North, Douglass C. and Robert Paul Thomas (1973), *The Rise of the Western World: A New Economic History* (Cambridge: Cambridge University Press).

Posner, Richard (1975), 'The social costs of monopoly and regulation', *Journal of Political Economy*, 83: 807–27.

Roberts, John (1987), 'Incentives in iterative planning under incomplete information', in T. Groves, R. Radner and S. Reiter (eds.) *Information, Incentives and Economic Mechanisms* (Minneapolis: University of Minnesota Press).

Rosenberg, Nathan and L. E. Birdzell, Jr. (1986), *How the West Grew Rich* (New York: Basic Books).

Rubinstein, Ariel (1987), 'A sequential strategic theory of bargaining', in Truman Bewley (ed.) *Advances in Economic Theory Fifth World Congress*.

Simon, Herbert (1951), 'A formal theory of the employment relation', *Econometrica*, 19: 293–305.

Sutton, John (1986), 'Non-cooperative bargaining theory: an introduction', *Review of Economic Studies*, 53: 709–24.

Williamson, Oliver (1975), *Markets and Hierarchies Analysis and Antitrust Implications* (New York: Free Press).

————(1985) *The Economic Institutions of Capitalism* (New York: Free Press).

Wilson, Robert (1969), 'The structure of incentives for decentralization', in *La Decision* (Paris: Centre Nationale de la Recherche Scientifique).

DATE DUE
